Images of the Body in Architecture: Anthropology and Built Space

Images of the Body in Architecture: Anthropology and Built Space

EDITED BY KIRSTEN WAGNER AND JASPER CEPL

Wasmuth

KIRSTEN WAGNER & JASPER CEPL

Images of the Body in Architecture: Anthropology and Built Space

INTRODUCTION

The essays gathered here on images of the body in architecture are intended as a contribution to a critical anthropology of built space.[1] While earlier research on architectural anthropology has focused either on the existential relationship between man and space, or on the cultural conditions of dwelling, this volume is concerned with the *images* of the human body that have determined the practice and theory of architecture since the beginning.

The notion of 'image' comprises not only the material images of the body, its depiction in sketchbooks, treatises, or on architectural plans, but also collective mental images of the body, which precede and influence the processes of the production and reception of architecture. The sometimes explicit, sometimes implicit images of the body transferred to architecture correspond to an anthropomorphic as well as anthropocentric conception of the built environment. As such they have repeatedly drawn criticism within architectural theory.

Our approach is directed less against the notorious transfers between the human body on the one hand and the 'bodies' of buildings and cities on the other. Nor will an attempt be made here to consider or outline a non-anthropocentric architecture that goes beyond the human. In view of a body that in architecture is often thought of in essentialist terms, we turn rather to its plurality and historicity, as articulated for example in the various images of a metrological, anatomical, physiological, or cerebral body. It was this diversity of definitions of the body that called for the collaboration between architectural theory and cultural history on which the conference and research project on images of the body in architecture is based.

IN / KIRSTEN WAGNER AND JASPER CEPL (EDITORS) /
IMAGES OF THE BODY IN ARCHITECTURE: ANTHROPOLOGY AND BUILT SPACE /
TÜBINGEN · BERLIN / ERNST WASMUTH VERLAG / 2014 / PP. 7–24

Architecture's fundamental reference to man, and hence also to his body, is already suggested by the word's etymology.[2] Formed from the Greek *arche* and *tektainomai,* architecture designates a primal shaping or working with the axe in wood or stone.[3] The verb *tektainomai* is derived from the noun *tekton,* which, like the adjective *techne,* goes back to the Indo-European root *tek-*. As a practical ability carried out according to specific rules, *techne* may have initially referred only to the skills of the *tekton,* as someone who builds ships and houses. Later applied to other skills as well, it lost this immediate link to the *tekton* working in wood and stone, which only remains visible in the stem.[4] According to mythical tradition, architecture, just like the other *technai,* was given to man by the gods. It is associated with Hephaestus, the god of blacksmiths and artisans in general. From an anthropomorphic point of view, however, it might be said that the *technai* as human skills are objectified in the anthropomorphic gods.[5] In this sense, Hephaestus is a personification of the skills belonging to smithery and other crafts. Whatever perspective one takes, architecture names a *techne* carried out by human beings.

Accordingly, all other types of architecture, like those of machines, computers, and brains, as well as the structures produced by animals, are metaphorical translations based, on the one hand, on the fact that not only humans can divide and assemble — thus the narrower meaning of the verb *tektainomai*[6] — and, on the other, on the fact that an object, in its being divided and assembled, is conceptually compared to architecture. When Rudolf Löbl remarks for the ancient term *techne* that it is an "anthropological category [...], with which statements are made about man,"[7] then that includes architecture. Thus, man is revealed as a *homo faber* who constructs the world by creating buildings from wood, stone, and other materials, which in their physical and symbolic orders simultaneously define and form culture. However, the concept of architecture is not exhausted in this active positing. Among architecture's inherent properties is its capacity to direct bodies itself, to prescribe movement and perception. To speak in this context of an anthropology of architecture or an architectural anthropology would seem to be a tautology.

Nevertheless, the connection between architecture and anthropology is considerably less natural than the etymology of the word architecture suggests. Aside from some advances in the 1960s, particularly in the research of Edward T. Hall,[8] architectural anthropology has only existed as a specific field of research since the 1980s. That is not to say that there had previously been no links between anthropology and architecture. One aspect of the precarious prehistory of architectural anthropology was the attempt on the part of architecture to draw on the physical anthropology of the 19th century. If in its beginnings physical anthropology saw its task above all in classifying and hierarchizing — on the basis of anatomical features and in the context of modern racial theories — the cultures made known through expeditions, a number of architects followed it in this by associating physical features and the character traits derived from them with historical and non-European forms and styles of building. Exemplary in this respect is a natural history of architecture oriented to a human natural history, as proposed by Eugène Emmanuel Viollet-le-Duc in his *Histoire de l'habitation humaine depuis les temps préhistoriques jusqu'à nos jours* from 1875, and the *Habitation humaine*[9] of Charles Garnier with the historian Auguste Ammann from 1892.

Contemporary approaches to an architectural anthropology have notably distanced themselves from such traditions, which still await a comprehensive critical appraisal. Instead, significant impulses for the more recent architectural anthropology originated in an opening up of academic architectural training to pedagogy, sociology, ethnography, and anthropology in the 1970s. Over the last two decades this has led in France to an anthropology of space, which investigates the relation between social and spatial or architectural structures.[10] Here, the focus is less on the body (or images of the body) than on societal ways of using and appropriating architecture. Parallel to this, in the 1990s, a biological branch of architectural anthropology appeared, which, following the thesis developed in paleontology that hominization takes place dependent on the use of tools, assumes a coevolution of architecture and man; one even finds the proposition that man's upright posture can be traced back to the building of terrestrial nest constructions.[11] Although in evolutionary terms the body is subjected to change, in the framework of this approach it nonetheless remains a natural, essentialist body, to which certain forms of architecture correspond more clearly than others. Finally, a third branch of contemporary architectural anthropology has its roots in American environment-behavior studies.[12]

While in contemporary efforts toward an architectural anthropology there is no explicit mention of the body — which appears merely in the form of social acts and orders, or else is subjected to essentialist conceptions — this contribution is concerned with the images of the body in architecture, that is, the body's historical conceptions and constructions, which are, in manifold ways, at the basis of the discourses and practices of building. These images of the body are not only part of a history of the body, as investigated in historical anthropology;[13] they are also in two respects part of a history of architecture: on the one hand, images of the body enter into architecture; on the other, the spatial orders produced through architecture evoke certain images and orders of the body. As mentioned above, the notion of the image is not limited to physical images; it also comprises collective mental images of the body, which are formed in relation to visual media. The way in which these mental images, beyond analog and digital visual media, are also embodied in architecture — architecture in this sense being a (spatial) medium itself, through which ideas of the body are articulated — could be developed further along the lines of Hans Belting's anthropology of images.[14]

Belonging to the plurality and historicity of the body in architecture are particular moments of intense reference to the body. According to the standard architectural historiography, such a moment coincides with the reception of Vitruvius at the end of the 15th and the beginning of the 16th centuries, and represents the supposed high point and conclusion of anthropomorphic and anthropometric traditions in architecture. Subsequently, the rationalistic and mechanistic tendencies characterizing the modern period as a whole are assumed to have rendered the body as a measure of what is built obsolete. Underlying this understanding is the idea of a progressive reason that attempts to move away from the body's inscrutability. However, the contributions gathered in the present study show that interest in the body extends right up to the present. Indeed, the body also remains constitutive for the architecture of the modern period; what changes are the images of the body referred to. Hence, the task of an architectural anthropology is not only to study the transformations of images of the body in architecture, but also to inquire into the knowledge about the body that is articulated in such images. In the modern period this knowledge is formulated in part by anthropology as a historical discipline — whereby anthropology is itself a crucial generator of images, one to be investigated with regard to its significance for images of the body.

The separation of anthropology from philosophy, and the founding of anthropological societies in the 19th century, which established anthropology as an independent discipline, is mirrored by the modern conception of man as the subject and object of knowledge.[15] This subject that becomes an object to itself, is a bodily one. In the first half of the 19th century sensory physiology ascribed perception and knowledge to the structural features of the sensory organs, and hence of the body.[16] With sensory physiology and comparative anatomy a new experimental knowledge became available. This experimental knowledge was not only at the basis of physical anthropology; it would also find its way into the arts and architecture. This is shown by the related borrowings in the writings of empathy estheticians, art historians, and architectural theorists at the end of the 19th and the beginning of the 20th centuries.

Given little attention until now in this connection are artistic anatomies and theories of proportion, which in the modern period come increasingly under the influence of empiricism. Here, alongside the Greco-Roman canon reconstructed with the help of antique sculptures, one also finds living models, and hence bodies that differ from ideal norms.[17] At the same time, artistic anatomies are supplemented with detailed descriptions of the construction and physiological functions of the human body. For the reception of the new findings of the humanities in the arts, in their theory and practice, these manuals represent an important source.

The experimental proliferation of knowledge about the body in the 19th century was accompanied by a return of architecture to the body-subject. A body projecting itself into the building and sympathizing with it in its (the body's) movements in the case of the empathy estheticians and Heinrich Wölfflin, a tactile and optical space in the case of Alois Riegl, a space of touch, movement, and vision in the case of August Schmarsow — all these show the reception and production of architecture to be based on human anatomy and physiology. The art historian Schmarsow for instance symbolically extends a hand to the ethnologist and anthropologist in order to come, via the definition of man in his axial corporeality and perceptual organization, to a definition of architecture as a shaper of space.[18] In this way man enters once again into architecture as measure — perhaps even for the first time insofar as all anthropometric and anthropomorphic references up to the early modern period were based on a body that was merely a representation of a divine order. This development reflects an extension of the concept of anthropomorphism during the 19th century. Originally limited to religion, it was transferred to aesthetic perception and epistemology.[19]

Against this background one can no longer speak of a radical overcoming of the body and of merely isolated renaissances of apparently antiquated references to the body in the modern period, such as with Le Corbusier's *Modulor*. The fact that deconstructivism can still busy itself with anthropocentrism in architecture[20] underlines how lastingly references to the body were and are at work, references that, one might add, are still contained negatively in the deconstructivist counter-model of the *corps morcelé*. However, what the models of the fragmented body and the decentered subject formulated in psychoanalysis and poststructuralism have made clear is the idea — characteristic for architecture — of an idealized natural male body. The ensuing critique of the body in architecture,[21] which has been strongly influenced by Michel Foucault, led to a further historicizing of the images of the body in architecture. This also in view of an architectural practice in which the body, as previously, either appears as a blind spot, is at the basis of the idealized standard bodies of manuals such as Neufert's *Bauentwurfslehre,* or is the architect's own unscrutinized body at the basis of his practice.[22]

ON THE CONTRIBUTIONS IN THIS VOLUME

Both the virulence of the body in the architectural theory of the modern period, its re-centering — now in a secular form — as an inevitable reference of built space — one that cannot be reconciled with a break with anthropometric and anthropomorphic figures at the end of the early modern period — and the essentialist images of the body widespread in architecture historically and presently provided the impetus for the conference "Images of the Body in Architecture. Anthropology and Built Space." The conference had three main points of focus, which can also be found in the present volume. While not all contributions to the conference could be included here, three further contributions, by Heleni Porfyriou, Beatrix Zug-Rosenblatt, and Tobias Cheung, have been added.

The first focus is on anthropometric and anthropomorphic concepts in architecture, which are traced from antiquity up to the present. While anthropometry in architecture has its origins in a metrological practice in which the units of measurement are derived from the human body, anthropomorphism denotes a thinking of built space in concepts and images of the body, its outer form as well as its anatomy and physiological functions. The second focus is on 19th-century physiological concepts of the body, which have proven central to the theory of architecture and city planning. Thirdly, body orders evoked through architecture will be investigated in relation to the work of Michel Foucault. In this way only a small fraction of the images of the body are brought together that have determined architecture in its history. Conceptions of the body developed in other fields, whether in the sciences and humanities, or in the sociopolitical field, have repeatedly had an effect on images of the body and theoretical models of architecture.

With regard to Greco-Roman antiquity, the transfers between the human body and architecture are known to us through Vitruvius, but extend both historically and culturally far beyond this.[23] In many places in his *Ten Books on Architecture,* written in the first century BC, the anthropometric and anthropomorphic references are established on different levels: in connection with temple construction, the classical orders, caryatids, and the city planning of Dinocrates. Vitruvius himself did not provide illustrations for these references; indeed, it was not until the early modern reception of Vitruvius that a series of visualizations were made. These range from the so-called *homo ad quadratum* and *homo ad circulum,* in which intellectual and visual traditions — independent of Vitruvius — of an anthropomorphically construed world-building are inscribed,[24] to the columns representing the genders, and Mount Athos in human form designed by the Herculean architect Dinocrates as a seated man holding the polis in his left hand and a basin of water in his right. As becomes clear from these visualizations alone Vitruvius has fundamentally influenced the images of the body in architecture.

However, already Vitruvius' architectural theory raises the question of whose body is being referred to when one speaks of *the* body in relation to architecture. A question that Indra Kagis McEwen brings up to date with the example of a body installation by the American artist Spencer Tunick, and answers to the effect that this is neither a single concrete body nor a plurality of concrete bodies. In connection with her philological study on Vitruvius,[25] she shows rather that Vitruvius' references to the body presuppose less a physical than an ideal body.

They address the political body of the king, which the *Ten Books on Architecture* commends as an ideal textual *corpus,* as the embodiment of a divine *logos,* on whose basis the *natural* system of rule can be implemented in space. This implication is still present in the early modern reception of Vitruvius, and acquires new significance in relation to the power politics and building policies of the royal courts. At the same time, Vitruvius' anthropomorphic and anthropometric references to the body are formulated as visual analogies between body and building or body and city (plan).

The extent to which early modern visualizations of the Vitruvian figure are based on a misinterpretation of the corresponding textual passages in Vitruvius has been shown on a number of occasions by Frank ZÖLLNER.[26] In contrast to the standard representations, *homo ad circulum* should be understood as having vertically upstretched arms and closed legs, a posture that can be traced back to an ancient measurement obtained from the body as well. In addition, Zöllner makes a link between the anthropomorphism, typical for early modern architectural treatises, and the low level of theory especially of the early treatises, which are still clearly under the influence of building and surveying practices. In later texts references to the body are neglected in favor of other systems of reference, such as music, until at the end of the 17th century they are entirely relativized. For Claude Perrault, architectural proportions previously discussed in relation to the body proved to be dependent on cultural conventions. Zöllner traces the renewed relevance of anthropometric and anthropomorphic references in the modern period beyond Le Corbusier's *Modulor* in relation to the writings of Ernst Neufert. Here, 'classical' proportion theories are applied to a body that has been measured in the framework of industrial commodity production, and hence also standardized and normalized. It was precisely this body, however, that proved to be compatible with the political instrumentalization of the body by the National Socialists.

Measurement practices and the resulting theories of proportion also remain a central topic for the art of the modern period.[27] Neither the crisis of representation nor the avant-garde's critique of academicism, with its canonical conception of the body, would have any effect on this. For Eckhard LEUSCHNER, painting's confrontation with these practices and theories between the wars results from the prevalence of anthropometry in the 19th century. Here, too, industrial commodity production with its standardized production processes appears as a major driving force behind measurements of the body. Leuschner also points to the sciences, in which, as in comparative anatomy and physiology, not a single millimeter, right up to the subcutaneous layers, of the resting and moving body is left uncharted. In the work of Alphonse Bertillon, the inventor of an anthropometric system for the identification of delinquent subjects,[28] we find a combination of two applications of anthropometry in the modern period which had already been given prominence by Erwin Panofsky: anthropology and criminalistics. Exhibition projects such as *Der schöne Mensch in der Neuen Kunst* from 1929 do not only attest to the discussion on the ideal images of the body carried out in the arts on the basis of anthropometry, they also show connections to a popular culture in which certain ideas of the body and beauty become virulent. With these examples, it becomes especially clear that apparently objective measurement practices represent "social acts" (Leuschner) that play a fundamental role in the construction of images of the body.

With its references to the golden section, Le Corbusier's *Modulor* is also tied to the 19th century. In the context of formal and experimental aesthetics, the mathematical-geometrical law of beauty became an empirical object of investigation, and in this way gained in popularity.[29] If the *Modulor*'s image of the body is equally a mathematically constructed one, then Christoph SCHNOOR is able to show a further series of body concepts that determined Le Corbusier's theory and practice. Each of these concepts is directly linked to conceptions of space. In Le Corbusier's early works, with his reception of the literature on urban design, physiological concepts dominate — an aspect of urban design which Heleni Porfyriou explores in her contribution with the example of Camillo Sitte. As a result, the bodily perception of space comes to the fore. The references to a seeing, touching, and moving body likewise determine Le Corbusier's architecture of the 1920s, a period in which in his writings the physiological image of the body is substituted by a mechanistic one. In the machine age of the modern period, the body itself turns out to be a machine. Related ideas of a standardization of the body and its measurements anticipate the *Modulor*. These in turn are relativized by organic concepts. In its materiality and in the principle of enclosure, architecture appears as an embodiment of man, up to the exteriorization of the body's functions. In the 1930s Le Corbusier combines these different conceptualizations of architecture in the image of the city as an anthropomorphically thought biomechanism. As Schnoor points out in relation to the tensions in Le Corbusier between organic and anthropomorphic images of the body on the one hand, and mechanistic and anthropometric images of the body on the other, architecture, as an embodiment of the body-subject, eludes any form of measuring grasp.

Le Corbusier's *Modulor* as well as the *Athens Charter* appear as a major point of reference for the architecture and city planning designs of the 1960s. Between the city's functional division and the anthropometric model of the *Modulor* there is an immediate connection with regard to the mechanistic grasp on architecture and man. With a group of Japanese architects who called themselves Metabolists, the universal concept of measure obtained from the anatomical body was replaced by the concept of "biotechnical agents", whose measurements change according to their different states of development. Among these Metabolists was Kisho Kurokawa, whose writings and buildings are discussed by Tobias CHEUNG in relation to the influence of the so-called life sciences on architecture. While in the 19th century it was especially sensory physiology that played a decisive role in architectural theory, this was substituted in the second half of the 20th century by molecular-biological cell theories. With examples taken from a number of sources, Cheung shows how Kurokawa adapted central concepts of molecular biology. In addition, Kurokawa drew on the visualizations of cell structures resulting from experimental procedures in the 1950s and 1960s. Ideas of living systems made up of cells as the smallest building blocks of life, which develop according to the genetic code of these cells and the biochemical metabolic processes between them, are applied by the Metabolists to architecture and the city. That led to cellular megastructures with mobile, exchangeable capsules. Here, concepts of architecture obtained from life itself seem to correspond to the nature of man. Developing from cells, man makes a claim to be a builder of cells.

Returning again to the modern and physiological concepts of the body, the contribution by Heleni PORFYRIOU foregrounds the influence of 19th-century sensory-physiological and anatomical ideas on Camillo Sitte's major work *Städte-Bau nach seinen künstlerischen Grundsätzen*. Without Sitte having made such sources especially clear, a number of connections can be made to the perception theory of Hermann von Helmholtz. In the 19th century the discussion on the perception of space reached a climax. If Immanuel Kant located this perception in the perceiving subject, and thus made out of the objective notion of space a subjective one, then it was the task of sensory physiology to trace spatial perception back to the anatomical features of the sensory organs. While there was disagreement in the details about which part in the perceptual process, and to what extent beyond the organic conditions, experience could be asserted, the perception of space as a whole was traced back to an interaction between visual, tactile, and motoric or kinesthetic sensations. The relation between space and a perceiving, and above all corporeal, subject, which is to say, a body-subject, is reflected in the aesthetic debates from the last third of the 19th century. Camillo Sitte thus belongs to a phalanx of artists, art historians, and estheticians who do not simply relate architecture and city planning to an observing subject, but give an account of built space on the basis of its anatomical and physiological features. Hence, their image of the body proved to be an essentialist one. Over the last few years, connections to sensory physiology have been identified for empathy aesthetics,[30] as well as for Alois Riegl,[31] August Schmarsow,[32] and indeed Camillo Sitte.[33] Porfyriou rightly speaks, with respect to the end of the 19th century, of an unresolvable field of interconnected scientific and artistic insights and practices.

If Beatrix ZUG-ROSENBLATT has already discussed the connections between sensory physiology and the architectural theory of space in the work of August Schmarsow elsewhere, and there too speaks in connection with Schmarsow of an "anthropology of space"[34], the present paper foregrounds the influence of Hegelian aesthetics on Schmarsow's definition of architecture as a shaper of space. According to Zug-Rosenblatt, it is particularly Hegel's conception of architecture, explicated by means of the element of the wall as enclosure either of the spirit-subject itself or its objectified form as divine image, that is adopted by Schmarsow. Under the influence of the empirical sciences, however, Schmarsow modifies this conception of architecture by substituting Hegel's spirit-subject for a body-subject. Likewise, Schmarsow relocates the three dimensions of length, width, and height, in which for Hegel enclosure and demarcation in architecture occurs, into this body-subject. Moreover, he attempts to show that three-dimensional architectural space is an objectification of the vertical, horizontal, and depth axis inherent in the body, which should ultimately underlie all perception of space. What remains to be problematized, however, is the derivation of the Cartesian coordinate system from the body. The extent to which Schmarsow here goes beyond Hegel to address Kant's pre-critical and critical concepts of space, as well as Gottfried Semper's formal authorities from his *Stil in den technischen und tektonischen Künsten,* has been developed by others.[35] That the vertical body axis was already associated with the soul in the art theory of the 16th century, and in this way acquired a special significance, is pointed out by Paolo Sanvito in his contribution. Beyond the axiality of the body, architectural space — like the perception of space in general — is predicated on the sensory modalities of sight and touch. Furthermore, in Schmarsow, movement and movement sensations become central. They correlate the dimension of depth and rhythm as a temporalizing of space. Zug-Rosenblatt discusses Wilhelm Wundt's "physiological psychology" as an important source for Schmarsow.

For Harry Francis MALLGRAVE, the 19th-century shift away from Hegel's idealism and toward the physical body represents a prerequisite for a reformist architecture, such as that of Hellerau. At the center of Hellerau is the rhythmically moving body of eurhythmics and modern expressive dance. Hellerau thereby *embodies* the multimodal, kinesthetic body-subject that aesthetics and art history via sensory physiology had put at the basis of the production and reception of architecture. Accordingly, for Mallgrave the garden city is representative of an architecture that corresponds to man's evolutionary makeup. In this respect, here too an essentialist image of the body can be determined. On the basis of neuroscience, this image is shown to be an image of the 'cerebral' body. It draws on concepts of an embodied mind, and in this way simultaneously claims to overcome the old schism between mind and body. Made productive for architecture, it traces approaches within architectural theory that emphasize sensory perception.[36] Here, one can see parallels between, on the one hand, the 19th-century connections between aesthetics and sensory physiology, and, on the other, those between art history, architectural theory, and neuroscience in the 21st century. If in the 19th century the leading science, physiology,[37] served a content-aesthetics to bring a scientific and evidential force to its symbol theory,[38] by referring it back to the physiological laws of the body, something similar can be noted for the current neuroaesthetics. Now neuronal processes turn out to be a prerequisite for aesthetic judgment, even for the creation of meaning. The poststructuralist floating signifier seems to have been immobilized in the body.[39] Revealingly, the evidential force of neuroscientific knowledge is based on visualizations of the body that have also found their way into theories of art and architecture: images of neuronal excitement made visible via magnetic resonance imaging. If these images are themselves the object of controversial discussions, they simultaneously refer to the underlying conflict between essentialist images of the body on the one hand and constructivist images of the body influenced by social and cultural factors on the other.

The next three contributions examine anthropomorphism in architecture from different perspectives. They raise questions about animism, the function and representation of the human body in architectural sculpture, and the transitoriness of the built environment. With the example of architectural sculpture Paolo SANVITO investigates anthropomorphic and animistic tendencies in the architecture of the early modern period. In the art theory of the 15th century, ideas passed down from antiquity of an animate matter, which are taken up in the panpsychic tendencies of early modern natural history, as well as of an animating act of creation transferred to the arts, yield conceptions of a likewise animate architecture. The same conception is found in Michelangelo's definition of architectural sculpture as the "living skin" of the building body. As is shown by the repertoire of gesture and facial expression, and in general by a lively decorative sculpture that does not shy away from the grotesque or monstrous, the corresponding animation of architecture, which extends far beyond purely anthropomorphic conceptions, remained popular into the 17th century. In this connection, a central position can be assigned to Cosimo Fanzago, whose sculptural motifs refer to the natural-philosophical and physiognomic discourses circulating in the late 16th and early 17th centuries in Naples. Fanzago's masks, characterized by an ambiguous laugh, lead Sanvito to speak of an *"architecture rigolante"*. Circulated and standardized via pattern books, such lively ornament paved the way for the style of the Baroque, which was simultaneously accompanied by a kind of domestication of the affective vocabulary of the body, until the underlying idea of a living building 'body' was eventually abandoned.

In parallel Sanvito traces the formation of an art historical theory, extending from August Schmarsow, via Aby Warburg, to Georg Weise, which shifts the motoric to-move and the affective to-be-moved of the body to the center of the production and reception of the arts — and thereby partly refers to the art theory of the early modern period. Under the influence of Warburg it was clearly Weise's intention to link the animated architectural sculpture of the early modern period to the panpsychic and magical currents of natural philosophy. If Sanvito prolongs the historical line from the art theory and architectural sculpture of the 15th and 16th centuries, via modern approaches of empathy aesthetics and reception theory, to the current development of an organic architecture and neuroaesthetics, this raises further questions: firstly about the extent to which, in the modern and postmodern periods, projections of body sensations onto built space are also or still accompanied by animistic ideas; and secondly about the historical transformations of images of the body, which through the centuries have been triggered by anatomy, physiology, molecular biology, and more recently by neuroscience — all of them having their own specific methods of visualizing the body, which in turn effect both the theory and the practice of the arts.

At the end of the 19th century the relation between building and architectural sculpture was considered in a new way. In her study of relief sculpture, Claire BARBILLON[40] raises the problem of the extent to which precisely the representation of the human body initiates an emancipation of architectural sculpture from the underlying building. By being subordinated to architecture, architectural sculpture essentially serves as a decorative element that takes up and emphasizes the structure and rhythm of the building and its façade. That was even true of the caryatids and atlantes — the representations of the body that are used as apparently load-bearing elements or to emphasize the vertical — which were revived in historicism. In contrast, new ways of representing the body in low and high relief point in a new direction. The movement and expressivity of the body that entered sculpture with the realistic and naturalistic currents of the 19th century as a whole, led to architectural sculpture becoming independent of architecture. Exemplary in this respect is the sculpture *La Danse* by Jean-Baptiste Carpeaux, one of the four allegorical figure groups commissioned for the ground floor façade of the Paris Opéra. The intertwining bodies moving both vertically and in a circle project out into the space of the street. Auguste Rodin with his *Porte de l'Enfer* goes as far as to fragment the animated bodies extracted from the material. Rodin's expressive modeling is connected with an animation of the sculpture. However, with Adolf von Hildebrand's epoch-making relief theory, which heavily influenced the sculpture of the early 20th century, architectural sculpture is reintroduced into the structural framework of architecture.

The transitoriness of matter, which affects the human body as well as architecture, is considered by Tanja JANKOWIAK in relation to the house and museum of Sir John Soane. Here, anthropomorphism is taken up in an overarching analogy between nature and architecture with respect to processes of growth and decay taking place in time. In a tour through the building complex with its living spaces and collection spaces containing spolia, architectural fragments, and sculptures, as well as sarcophagi, a history of architecture takes shape in which space and time are condensed. Soane's intricate arrangement of spatial openings, perspectives, mirrors, and skylights produces an architectural narrative that goes far beyond a mere staging of the collection. Rather, the individual

KIRSTEN WAGNER & JASPER CEPL

rooms — some of which are laid out like archaeological excavations or burial sites — and the objects gathered in them relate to each other in such a way that the finiteness of the built is correlated with the finiteness of life. The concentration or accumulation of time, which is generally associated with the collection of things, can simultaneously be interpreted as an attempt to suspend time's passage.

In the sense of an interruption the contribution of the philosopher Sven-Olov WALLENSTEIN[41] leads to a critical history of the body in relation to the work of Michel Foucault. Foucault's reception in architecture itself initially foregrounded not the body, but — starting with *Des espaces autres* — space.[42] Foucault's remarks on architecture tend to be indirect rather than direct. That was even the case when in the early 1970s, as part of individual or joint studies, he dealt with the institutions and building types of prison and hospital, or the residential architecture of the 19th century. Architecture here is treated above all as a spatial order. A spatial order, however, that is simultaneously also an order of the body. As Wallenstein's passage through Foucault's writings shows, Foucault's image of the body is itself subject to change. The body's repression by power is confronted, as regards the existential experiences belonging to the body, with something that is not subsumed in the discourse of power and its materialities such as architecture. The early Foucault finds this above all in a literature that is able to articulate these experiences. In a critical examination of phenomenology, however, bodily experiences, even though they elude discourse, cannot be traced back to a natural, essentialist body. The body is always — as also the phenomenological body-subject that emerged from the anthropological and sensory-physiological discourses of the 19th century — to be historicized. If the concept of experience remains central, in later writings the generative nature of power is foregrounded. The body is not only an object of control for discipline and biopower, the latter also contribute to the body's production in an entirely constructive sense.

With the hospital, the medical historian Philipp OSTEN turns to a modern institution already examined by Michel Foucault.[43] The fact that the hospital is not wholly, or only in a certain historical phase, absorbed into the space of discipline becomes evident with the hospital buildings and designs for Berlin from the mid-19th to the mid-20th centuries discussed by Osten. These are bound up with manifold conflicting discourses and practices of dietetics, hygiene, and technology-based medicine, as well as of architecture and city planning, which not only define the hospital in a variety of ways, but also the body (of the patient). Here, according to Osten, the relation between architecture and body remains precarious. At precisely the point at which the architecture of the hospital makes reference to the body, it does not refer to a concrete body, but an abstract body constituted through the discourses of hygiene and statistical medicine, as well as new image-producing processes and medical practices. This leads to a number of connections to the contribution of Indra Kagis McEwen. With their pavilion-like architecture, the hospital buildings of the 19th century still show the clearest references to the space of discipline. They combine the forms of the military camp and the factory, whose spatial orders serve the division and separation of bodies, their control as well as their self-disciplining and productivity. At the same time, this space is forced open by historicist and sacral borrowings. Following ventilation in the 19th century, in the first half of the 20th century sunlight was added as a determining factor of hospital architecture, which led to terraced façades. Finally, new holistic approaches in medicine, which took greater account of environmental influences, were associated in the post-war period with a critique of a hospital architecture that was based on function and efficiency alone. These approaches find their echo in an organic, biomorphic formal language.[44] For Osten, an architecture addressing the concrete body is given form in the *Cellules* of the Israeli artist Meir Eshel. Here, art and utopia provide the framework within which an *anthropological* architecture in its immediate reference to the body can be implemented.

Irene NIERHAUS draws on Foucault's concepts of body/discipline and population/regulation to examine the housing of the post-war period. If the rebuilding of the cities destroyed during World War II is linked to a naturalizing of urban space, then that is especially true for the housing of the 1950s and early 1960s. Green areas, which in the city evoke a space of nature and landscape, have a fundamental role in the newly emerging decentralized residential complexes. Hygiene, light, and air remain the determining discourses of a spatial order that serves the surveillance of the individual body and the biopolitical control of the population in equal measure. The naturalization of space corresponds to a naturalization of the social. This becomes visible in an exemplary way in public art, with its images of fauna and flora, the seasons and life cycles, mother and child. Thus, in the housing of the post-war period one encounters a natural appearing social order with, at its center, the patriarchal family. Corresponding images of family life are reproduced and disseminated via media. To break through these orders requires interventions on the level of concrete urban space as well as of media. Nierhaus reconstructs such interventions with the examples of three films, by Claude Faraldo, Federico Fellini and Pier Paolo Pasolini. At the center of these films is a body produced via social practices of embodiment, which in its sexuality withdraws from the spatialized social order and thereby undermines it. With the caves, ruins, and dumps, as well as with the urban periphery, these bodies are assigned to spaces that resist the homogenized and geometrized spaces of discipline and biopower. However, in the sense of Foucault, the sexual body does not refer to an essentialist body. It is no less generated by power, and as soon as it tries to liberate itself it is occupied by it in new and different ways.

The present volume closes with a kind of visual manifesto on anthropomorphism and biomorphism in architecture by Günther FEUERSTEIN. Beyond the

20   KIRSTEN WAGNER & JASPER CEPL continued relevance of the anthropomorphic in architecture, Feuerstein's contribution also shows the extent to which images of the body in architecture participate in the reproduction of orders of the body and of gender.

We would like to thank the Deutsche Forschungsgemeinschaft and the Fritz Thyssen Stiftung für Wissenschaftsförderung for their support, which made the conference and the present volume possible. Further thanks go to the Internationale Bauakademie Berlin and Hans Kollhoff for kindly inviting us to hold the conference in the Roter Saal inside the 'mockup' of the Bauakademie, to the Wasmuth Verlag, to Geoffrey Steinherz for his copyediting and to Benjamin Carter for his diligent translations.[45] Finally, we would like to dedicate this book to the memory of the architect and cultural historian Tanja Jankowiak.

NOTES

1   The present volume has its origins in the conference "Images of the Body in Architecture. Anthropology and Built Space" hosted by the Sonderforschungsbereich 447 "Kulturen des Performativen" in April 2010. The conference was the result of a cooperation between the Institute for Cultural History and Theory of the Humboldt-Universität zu Berlin and the Fachgebiet für Architekturtheorie of the Technische Universität Berlin.

2   Conversely, the Greek word *demas* for body, from the root *dem-*, to which the verb *demo* is related, meaning to build something in layers from the ground up to create a well formed whole, shows an early conception of the human body in terms of the built, or as well joined from parts. See on this Maria KARVOUNI, "*Demas*. The Human Body as a Tectonic Construct", in: *Chora 3. Intervals in the Philosophy of Architecture,* edited by Alberto PÉREZ-GÓMEZ and Stephen PARCELL, Montreal: McGill-Queen's University Press, 1999, pp. 101–124.

3   Ibid., pp. 105.

4   See Rudolf LÖBL, *TEXNH – TECHNE. Untersuchung zur Bedeutung dieses Wortes in der Zeit von Homer bis Aristoteles,* VOL. 1: *Von Homer bis zu den Sophisten,* Würzburg: Königshausen & Neumann, 1997, pp. 6ff.

5   Klaus HEINRICH, *anthropomorphe. Zum Problem des Anthropomorphismus in der Religionsphilosophie,* Basel and Frankfurt am Main: Stroemfeld / Roter Stern, 1986.

6   KARVOUNI, "*Demas*. The Human Body as a Tectonic Construct", p. 106.

7   Rudolf Löbl, *TEXNH – TECHNE. Untersuchungen zur Bedeutung dieses Worts in der Zeit von Homer bis Aristoteles,* VOL. II: *Von den Sophisten bis Aristoteles,* Würzburg: Königshausen & Neumann, 2003, p. 2.

8   See Edward Twitchell HALL, *The Hidden Dimension,* Garden City, NY: Doubleday, 1966.

9   This text is related to a built history of the *Habitations humaines* conceived by Garnier for the 1889 Exposition Universelle in Paris, a row of eclectic models ranging from prehistoric and non-European dwelling and settlement forms to the historical Gothic and renaissance forms of 'modern' civilizations.

10 See *Architecture, espace pensé, espace vécu,* edited by Philippe BONNIN, Paris: editions Recherches, 2007.

11 See Nold EGENTER, *The Present Relevance of the Primitive in Architecture,* Lausanne: Structura Mundi, 1992 · EGENTER, "The Deep Structure of Architecture. Constructivity and Human Evolution", in: *Architectural Anthropology,* edited by Mari-Jose AMERLINCK, Westport, CT and London: Bergin & Garvey, 2001, pp. 43–81.

12 See Amos RAPOPORT, "Architectural Anthropology or Environment-Behavior Studies?", in: *Architectural Anthropology,* ed. AMERLINCK, pp. 27–41 · Grant HILDEBRAND, *Origins of Architectural Pleasure,* Berkeley, Los Angeles, and London: University of California Press, 1999.

13 On the body as an object of historical anthropology see Richard VAN DÜLMEN, *Historische Anthropologie. Entwicklung, Probleme, Aufgaben,* Cologne, Weimar, and Vienna: Böhlau, 2000 · Christoph WULF, *Anthropologie. Geschichte, Kultur, Philosophie,* Reinbek bei Hamburg: Rowohlt Taschenbuch Verlag, 2004 — On the cultural history of the body, from the early modern period up to the present see *Histoire du corps,* 3 VOLS., edited by Alain CORBIN, Jean-Jacques COURTINE, and Georges VIGARELLO, Paris: Seuil, 2005 — On the manifold approaches to the body in cultural history, historiography, and the social sciences see Maren LORENZ, *Leibhaftige Vergangenheit. Einführung in die Körpergeschichte,* Tübingen: edition diskord, 2000.

14 Hans BELTING, *Bild-Anthropologie: Entwürfe für eine Bildwissenschaft,* Munich: Wilhelm Fink, 2001.

15 Michel FOUCAULT, *Les mots et les choses,* Paris: Gallimard, 1966.

16 See Jonathan CRARY, *Techniques of the Observer. On Vision and Modernity in the Nineteenth Century,* Cambridge, MA and London: The MIT Press, 1990.

17 Exemplary in this respect is *Polyclet.* See [Johann] Gottfried SCHADOW: *Polyclet, oder, Von den Maassen des Menschen nach dem Geschlechte und Alter, mit Angabe der wirklichen Naturgrösse nach dem rheinländischen Zollstocke, und Abhandlung von dem Unterschiede der Gesichtzüge und Kopfbildung der Völker des Erdboden, als Fortsetzung des hierüber von Peter Camper ausgegangenen,* Berlin: L. Sachse & Co., 1834.

18 August SCHMARSOW, *Das Wesen der architektonischen Schöpfung. Antrittsvorlesung, gehalten in der Aula der K. Universität Leipzig am 8. November 1893,* Leipzig: Karl W. Hiersemann, 1894, p. 5.

19 On the shift in the meaning of anthropomorphism in the 19th century see Ralf BECKER, "Anthropomorphismus II", in: *Archiv für Begriffsgeschichte,* VOL. 50, 2008, pp. 152–185.

20 For an overview see Anthony VIDLER, *The Architectural Uncanny. Essays in the Modern Unhomely,* Cambridge, MA and London: The MIT Press, 1992.

21 See the exemplary study *Sexuality and Space,* edited by Beatriz COLOMINA, New York: Princeton Architectural Press, 1992.

22 See on this the study by Rob IMRIE, "Architect's Conceptions of the Human Body", in: *Environment and Planning D: Society and Space,* VOL. 21, 2003, pp. 47–65.

23 See on this Joseph RYKWERT, "Körper und Bauwerk | Body and Building", in: *Daidalos,* no. 45, 1992, pp. 100–109 · Marco BUSSAGLI, *L'uomo nello spazio. L'architettura e il corpo umano,* Milan: Medusa Edizioni, 2005.

24 See on this Bruno REUDENBACH, "In mensuram humani corporis. Zur Herkunft der Auslegung und Illustration von Vitruv III 1 im 15. und 16. Jahrhundert", in: *Text und Bild. Aspekte* *des Zusammenwirkens zweier Künste in Mittelalter und früher Neuzeit,* edited by Christel MEIER and Uwe RUBERG, Wiesbaden: Ludwig Reichert, 1980, pp. 651–688 · REUDENBACH, "Die Gemeinschaft als Körper und Gebäude. Francesco di Giorgios Stadttheorie und die Visualisierung von Sozialmetaphern im Mittelalter", in: *Gepeinigt, begehrt, vergessen. Symbolik und Sozialbezug des Körpers im späten Mittelalter und in der frühen Neuzeit,* edited by Klaus SCHREINER and Norbert SCHNITZLER, Munich: Wilhelm Fink, 1992, pp. 171–198.

25 Indra Kagis MCEWEN, *Vitruvius: Writing the Body of Architecture,* Cambridge, MA and London: The MIT Press, 2003.

26 See Frank ZÖLLNER, *Vitruvs Proportionsfigur. Quellenkritische Studien zur Kunstliteratur des 15. und 16. Jahrhunderts,* Worms: Wernersche Verlagsgesellschaft, 1987 · ZÖLLNER, "Anthropomorphismus. Das Maß des Menschen in der Architektur von Vitruv bis Le Corbusier", in: *Ist der Mensch das Maß aller Dinge? Beiträge zur Aktualität des Protagoras,* edited by Otto NEUMAIER, Möhnesee: Bibliopolis, 2004, pp. 307–344.

27 On this see *Figura Umana. Normkonzepte der Menschendarstellung in der italienischen Kunst 1919–1939,* edited by Eckhard LEUSCHNER, Petersberg: Michael Imhof, 2012.

28 Jacques BERTILLON, *Identification anthropométrique. Instruction signalétique,* 2 VOLS., Melun: Imprimerie administrative, 1893.

29 See on this the writings of Gustav Fechner and Adolf Zeising.

30 See on this the seminal study prepared by Harry Francis MALLGRAVE and Eleftherios IKONOMOU: *Empathy, Form, and Space. Problems in German Aesthetics, 1873–1893,* Introduction and translation by Harry Francis Mallgrave and Eleftherios Ikonomou, Santa Monica: Getty Publications Program, 1994.

31 Mechthild FEND, "Körpersehen. Über das Haptische bei Alois Riegl", in: *Kunstmaschinen. Spielräume des Sehens zwischen Wissenschaft und Ästhetik,* edited by Andreas MAYER and Alexandre MÉTRAUX, Frankfurt am Main: Fischer Taschenbuch Verlag, 2005, pp. 166–202.

32 Beatrix ZUG, *Die Anthropologie des Raumes in der Architekturtheorie des frühen 20. Jahrhunderts,* Tübingen and Berlin: Ernst Wasmuth, 2006.

33 Heleni PORFYRIOU, "Camillo Sitte und das Primat des Sichtbaren in der Moderne", in: *Kunst des Städtebaus. Neue Perspektiven auf Camillo Sitte,* edited by Klaus SEMSROTH, Kari JORMAKKA, and Bernhard LANGER, Vienna, Cologne, and Weimar: Böhlau, 2005, pp. 239–256 · Gabriele REITERER, "Wahrnehmung – Raum – Empfindung", in: ibid., pp. 225–237.

34 ZUG, *Die Anthropologie des Raumes in der Architekturtheorie des frühen 20. Jahrhunderts.*

35 See Harry Francis MALLGRAVE, *Gottfried Semper. Architect of the Nineteenth Century. A Personal and Intellectual Biography,* New Haven and London: Yale University Press, 1996 · Jasper CEPL, "Ein Blick zurück auf neue Räume — August Schmarsows *Barock und Rokoko*", in: *Stadt Land Fluß. Urbanität und Regionalität in der Moderne. Festschrift für Gertrude Cepl-Kaufmann zum sechzigsten Geburtstag,* edited by Antje JOHANNING and Dietmar LIESER with the collaboration of Jens KNIPP, Neuss: Ahasvera, 2002, pp. 97–108 · Cornelia JÖCHNER, "Wie kommt Bewegung in die Architekturtheorie? Zur Raum-Debatte am Beginn der Moderne", in: *Wolkenkuckucksheim. Internationale Zeitschrift zur Theorie der Architektur,* VOL. 9, 2004, no. 1.

36 See in detail on this Harry Francis MALLGRAVE, *The Architect's Brain. Neuroscience, Creativity and Architecture,* Chichester and Malden, MA: Wiley-Blackwell, 2010.

37 See *Physiologie und industrielle Gesellschaft. Studien zur Verwissenschaftlichung des Körpers im 19. und 20. Jahrhundert,* edited by Philipp SARASIN and Jakob TANNER, Frankfurt am Main: Suhrkamp, 1998.

38 See on this the physiologically motivated reformulation of the symbol theory of Friedrich Theodor Vischer by his son Robert VISCHER, *Ueber das optische Formgefühl. Ein Beitrag zur Aesthetik,* Leipzig: Hermann Credner, 1873.

39 See on this the critique of poststructuralism by John ONIANS, *Neuroarthistory. From Aristotle and Pliny to Baxandall and Zeki,* New Haven and London: Yale University Press, 2007, p.1.

40 In connection with the present volume see Claire Barbillon's pertinent study on proportion theories and measurement concepts in the arts of the 19th century: Claire BARBILLON, *Les canons du corps humain au XIXe siècle. L'art et la règle,* Paris: Odile Jacob, 2004.

41 Against the background of Foucault's writings Sven-Olov Wallenstein has produced two studies on modern architecture: Sven-Olov WALLENSTEIN, "Foucault and the Genealogy of Modern Architecture", in: WALLENSTEIN, *Essays, Lectures,* Stockholm: Axl Books, 2007, pp.361–404 · WALLENSTEIN, *Biopolitics and the Emergence of Modern Architecture,* New York: Princeton Architectural Press, 2009.

42 On the reception of Foucault in architecture see Daniel DEFERT, "Foucault, der Raum und die Architekten", in: *Politics/Poetics. Das Buch zur Documenta X,* Ostfildern-Ruit: Cantz, 1997, pp.274–284 · Jean-Louis VIOLEAU, "Du panoptisme aux réseaux. Foucault et les architectes", in: *Michel Foucault, la littérature et les arts,* edited by Philippe ARTIÈRES, Paris: Editions Kimé, 2004, pp.159–186.

43 On hospital architecture in the joint study directed by Michel FOUCAULT (with Blandine BARRET KRIEGEL, Anne THALAMY, Francois BEGUIN, and Bruno FORTIER) *Les machines à guérir. Aux origines de l'hôpital moderne* (1976), Brussels: Pierre Mardaga, 1979. See especially the contributions "La machine à guérir" by François Béguin and "Architecture de l'hôpital" by Bruno Fortier.

44 On the organic architectural designs of the 1960s as well as on cell architecture see the contribution by Tobias Cheung in this volume.

45 Benjamin Carter is responsible for the translations of the editor's introduction as well as the contributions by Günther Feuerstein, Irene Nierhaus, Philipp Osten, Frank Zöllner and Beatrix Zug-Rosenblatt.

INDRA KAGIS MCEWEN

Whose Body?

INTRODUCTION

The body that is the topic of theoretical discourse in architecture — and the body whose images are, of course, the topic of this publication — is, conventionally at least, nobody's body in particular. In view of this, is asking "whose body?" just a pointless provocation? If I thought so, I would not ask the question.

Obviously, "the body" of architectural discourse is not my body, my mother's or my father's, my children's or that of any of my siblings or ancestors. It is neither yours, nor that of any of *your* children or ancestors. "The body" is independent of persons, and can therefore have no relatives.

The body is neither *a* body, nor a plurality of bodies. Thus, for instance, "the body" as such was nowhere to be found in Mexico City on May 6th, 2007, even with a choice of 18,000 naked bodies, crouching on all fours in the Zócalo early that morning. They had gathered there at the behest of Spencer Tunick, the American artist who makes a specialty of bringing large numbers of people together in different locations all over the world in order to pose and photograph them without their clothes on.[1] The 18,000 bodies whose living flesh carpeted the vast expanse of Mexico City's great central plaza in 2007 remains the all-time record for the number of participants in such installations.

By contrast, only 2,500 people showed up for a pre-dawn shoot in Montreal in May 2001, eager to surrender their identities to Tunick's project of forming, as he told CBC news, "a sea of pink with brown and yellow and tan [...] pure bodies blocking out the pavement, a sea of bodies."[2] If "the body" has no identity, neither did any of the bodies Tunick photographed in Montreal, where the image of countless bodies sprawled like corpses along one of the city's main thoroughfares evoked a rather chilling, though surely unintentional reminder of the mass carnage photographed in liberated concentration camps at the

IN / KIRSTEN WAGNER AND JASPER CEPL (EDITORS) /
IMAGES OF THE BODY IN ARCHITECTURE: ANTHROPOLOGY AND BUILT SPACE /
TÜBINGEN · BERLIN / ERNST WASMUTH VERLAG / 2014 / PP. 25–46

end of World War II. Though stripped of identity, none of these bodies is "the body".

Tunick has claimed that he is "trying to create flesh architecture", and appears to take great care not only with composition and structure but also with such matters as the color-coordination of available flesh. Like most architects these days, he does his planning on a computer. "On my website, you can apply to be a model, and you give your skin tone on a colour chart [...] I can then play off your flesh tone against the other end of the spectrum, or group you with people of the same colour", he told *The Telegraph* in a 2006 interview.[3]

In June 2009, a shoot at Montauk Point, Long Island, on the American Atlantic coast with 300 participating bodies, was one of Tunick's rarer non-urban ventures. Afterwards, he complained about the trouble he had making himself heard in this particular context, because of the noise of the surf. "For the Montauk work it was very difficult to communicate because of the sea, and the sound of the crashing waves", he said later in an interview.[4] It follows that if no one had heard the artist's instructions, there would have been no "flesh architecture" created on this Long Island beach that early June morning — just a crowd of cold, naked people milling around wondering what they were doing there.

More recently, on the 1st of March 2010 in Sydney, Australia, Tunick overcame the problem of audibility by the simple expedient of using a microphone. The work, called *Mardigras: The Base,* involved filling up the stairs of Sydney Opera House with the naked bodies of some 5,000 gay, lesbian and straight participants as part of Sydney's gay and lesbian festival. You can hear the artist giving orders, loud and clear on the videos posted on the internet. "You gotta spread out!" he shouts, "I need you to fill up the stairs." Then, "you have to lay down, hands down; don't have a smile on your face."

And everybody does exactly as they are told.[5] People want to obey instructions, Tunick explains to an interviewer, adding that there are not too many rebels. The scenario for his Sydney shoot included photographing naked gays embracing naked straights as a testament to mutual tolerance and affection.

Participating in Tunick's installations means convening well before dawn, at an hour when the early morning chill makes nakedness particularly uncomfortable. So why do people do it? "It feels tribal", said one enthusiastic participant in the Sydney event, "a gathering of humanity".

Now, whether or not you accept Tunick's claim to being an architect, the necessity of his being *heard* in order to exercise his *métier* raises a crucial point, which in a rather roundabout way brings me back to the question that is the title of this paper. For his "flesh architecture" to take shape, people have to hear and obey the architect's instructions which, he points out, they are glad to do.

As already intimated, none of the many individual bodies that actually supply the flesh for Tunick's installations is of much help in understanding the nature of the unitary body that for so long furnished architects with legitimating metaphorical underpinning. Nor, for that matter, are any of these bodies, in and of themselves, much help in answering the question "whose body?" Nevertheless, people in large numbers assemble when and where they are asked to. They happily put their naked flesh on display because someone has made them believe that it is a good idea.

Perhaps, then, the nature and authority of the artist's *instructions* point to a more fruitful avenue of inquiry. And that is why I would now like to turn my attention from flesh to the *word*.

WRITING THE BODY OF ARCHITECTURE[6]

Vitruvius, whose *De architectura* has been credited as the source of so many images of the body in architecture never actually furnished any himself, for indeed all Vitruvius ever in fact supplied concerning bodies were words.

It is generally agreed that only ten drawings, at most, originally accompanied Vitruvius' text. All of these were of a technical, how-to nature: the schema for the entasis of columns, for instance, or a diagram showing how to draw an ionic volute — explanatory images which he appears to resort to with reluctance only when words completely fail him. There are no pictures of human bodies, nor any reference to any images of bodies that may have since been lost.[7]

Inspired by Vitruvius, Leonardo may have intended to draw "the body" — but Vitruvius never did. Moreover, for all the iconic status of Leonardo's famous image, one of his aims in drawing it appears to have to prove that Vitruvius' circle-and-square schema was not entirely accurate.[8] But as I said, Vitruvius himself drew no body images. This was not an oversight.

Vitruvius' purpose, as he repeatedly claims, was to "*write* the body of architecture" (not to draw it) — the perfect body of architecture, as he insists at one point: *emendatum*, "without a flaw".[9] This is how he concludes his treatise, writing at the end of book 10, his book on machinery:

> *In this scroll I have given as complete an account as I could of the principles of the machines I consider most useful in times of peace and war. Now in the previous nine I brought together the ones for the other subjects and parts, so that the whole body of architecture might have all its members developed in ten scrolls.*[10]

It is usual to understand that Vitruvius' claim to have written the body of architecture is simply that he has written a comprehensive compilation — that that, and nothing more, is what he means by referring to his work as a *corpus*.

There are many reasons to disagree. One of them is the deployment (often extremely laborious) of his material into ten *volumina* or scrolls — a deliberate aspect of his intention to write a *corpus* whose referent was not only comprehensive but also, as I see it, quite literally corporeal (**FIG. 1**).[11] Vitruvius knew that ten was *perfectus* — complete, finished. Here is what he writes at the beginning of Book 3, just after the passage Leonardo meant to illustrate with his celebrated drawing:

> *Moreover [the ancients] deduced the standards of measure that all works obviously require from the parts of the human body: finger, palm, foot, cubit. And they arranged these into the perfect number the Greeks call* teleon *["that which has been brought to fulfillment"]. The ancients determined ten to be the perfect number; for it was, in fact, discovered from the hands and the number of fingers. Indeed if nature completes both palms with ten fingers, it was also Plato's opinion that the number ten is perfect because individual units, called* monades *in Greek, complete the decade. But as soon as these go over to make eleven or twelve, they cannot be perfect until they reach another decade. For units are fragments of ten."*[12]

1
THE TEN SCROLLS THAT COMPRISED THE TEN "BOOKS" OF *DE ARCHITECTURA* AT THE TIME OF ITS WRITING. (MODEL BY AUTHOR)

Ten is the sum of the first four integers, and so a "perfect" number. With its units, arrayed in triangular configuration as shown (**FIG. 2**), it was the *tetractys*: worshipped by Pythagoreans as the "organizing idea of cosmic events", the "circle and limit of all the numbers", the key to the whole order of nature, the agent of unity, the container and content of time. It was also, as Vitruvius stresses, the "number" of the human body, a testament to its wholeness, its completion, its perfection — and, perhaps most importantly, to its role in ordering the cosmos.[13] Ten, Vitruvius intimates, is not *a* body: it is *the* body — the *real* body, in the best Platonic tradition: the pure form, of which particular bodies are mere appearances and whose images — including Leonardo's — are just flickering shadows at the back of a cave. Here, it is worth recalling Plato's opinion that only men not taken in by such shadows are fit to rule.

Following upon this, neo-Pythagorean theories of kingship of the late Hellenistic period made rationality the distinguishing characteristic that separated the ruler from the ruled. The test of a king's legitimacy was his ability, like the royal eagle's (or like that of Plato's philosopher), to stare straight into the sun.[14]

It is only through architecture, Vitruvius would have us believe, that the mathematical truth of this *real* body can acquire a spatial dimension in the world of appearances.

2
TEN PEBBLES
LAID OUT IN THE
TRIANGULAR
FORM OF THE
PYTHAGOREAN
TETRACTYS

DINOCRATES

In the preface to Book 2 of *De architectura,* Vitruvius introduces Dinocrates, an architect mentioned in a number of ancient sources but never described as Vitruvius describes him — never described elsewhere at all, for that matter which, of course, means that his physical appearance must be of particular relevance to

Vitruvius' argument.[15] Vitruvius presents him as a muscleman — tall, handsome and exceptionally well-built — which might at first glance lead the reader to believe that he is abandoning the word for the flesh. Not at all. Vitruvius is setting Dinocrates up as a straw man, whose imposing corporeality ultimately serves as strategic underpinning for the far greater power of the word.

The story is well known. As Vitruvius tells it, the Macedonian architect Dinocrates, unable to obtain an introduction to Alexander the Great by conventional means, adopts the unconventional expedient of disguising himself as Hercules by donning a "costume" which consists of a freshly applied coat of oil, a lion skin slung over the left shoulder, and a club. The Macedonian's "towering stature, appealing good looks and majestic build" ensure the outfit's immediate impact.

Having thus caught Alexander's attention, Dinocrates presents his project: to form Mount Athos into the shape of a statue of a man who holds a walled city in one hand, and reservoir of water in the other. The project is duly admired, but ultimately rejected. Alexander does not want a sculptor, he wants an architect. Moreover, Alexander points out, the site of the city would not be able to sustain its population. Yet he keeps Dinocrates with him, and they go on to found the city of Alexandria in Egypt.

"And so", concludes Vitruvius, "commended by his appearance and the stateliness of his body, Dinocrates came to fame."

"As for me, Imperator", Vitruvius says, addressing Augustus Caesar, for whom he wrote his treatise, "nature has not given me stature, age has spoiled my appearance and bad health has sapped my strength. Deserted by these defenses, it is therefore with the help of knowledge and writings that I hope to gain recognition."[16]

It is clear that Vitruvius' self-deprecating evocation of his own decrepitude is a rhetorical tactic meant to enhance the Herculean potential of the *real* body of ten scrolls that is *De architectura*.

Like his contemporary Leonardo, the Sienese architect Francesco di Giorgio Martini (1439–1501) was in love with body images. As it happens, Francesco di Giorgio was Vitruvius' earliest translator. But when he translated the Dinocrates story he ended it with the foundation of Alexandria and, tellingly enough, omitted Vitruvius' concluding paragraph about the supremacy of the word.[17] It is therefore not surprising to discover that he either missed, or deliberately ignored the rhetorical point of the anecdote with which Vitruvius opens book II of *De architectura*.

The drawing of Dinocrates that appears in the Magliabechiano manuscript of the second of Francesco di Giorgio's two treatises on architecture conflates Dinocrates and his Mount Athos project in a single graceful image (FIG. 3). Worth noting is that the city cradled in the architect's left arm is a fortress, and very much in keeping with the kind of work for Francesco di Giorgio himself was known. The text which the drawing is meant to illustrate outlines the Dinocrates story more or less as Vitruvius tells it, omitting, of course, Vitruvius' concluding message about the book's Herculean potential being at least the equal of, if not superior to that of the Macedonian architect's muscle-bound frame.

Preparing the ground for his own concluding message, Francesco di Giorgio says that what Alexander admired in Dinocrates' project was *"la similitudine della città al corpo umano"*.[18] This is Francesco's own interpolation, for Vitruvius says no such thing. Moreover it is from Alexander's alleged admiration of the

3
FRANCESCO DI
GIORGIO MARTINI /
TREATISE ON
ARCHITECTURE /
MAGLIABECHIANO
MANUSCRIPT /
DINOCRATES

resemblance of the city to the human body that Francesco draws the conclusion that all the principal parts of cities and other buildings should reflect some part of a man's body, and that each should have the same proportional relation to the city overall as the parts of the body have to the body, overall.

Francesco had already drawn similar conclusions from an earlier reference to the Dinocrates story, which appears at the beginning of his first treatise.[19] Here, however, it is not Dinocrates who is drawn in the margin, but a charming boyish figure whose body parts are made to correspond to the different parts of a fortified city (FIG. 4): on his head is a *rocca* or castle (because, explains Francesco, the head rules the body), at his elbows and feet appear defensive towers labelled *torrone,* in his chest there is a church, and, in the centre at his stomach, a circular piazza. Francesco's specialization was military architecture, and there

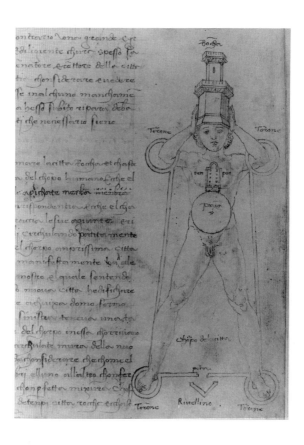

4
FRANCESCO
DI GIORGIO
MARTINI /
TREATISE ON
ARCHITECTURE /
SALUZZIANO
MANUSCRIPT /
"FORTRESS
MAN"

was nothing charming or boyish about the many, virtually invulnerable fortresses he built for the Duke of Urbino in the Marches of east central Italy where he exercised his profession.

And so, Francesco's text concludes, "just as in the body all its members relate to one another [...] with perfect proportions, so must the same be observed in the composition of temples, cities, fortresses and castles." If the principle cannot be derived from the Dinocrates story, as Francesco di Giorgio would claim, it most certainly does derive from Vitruvius. But for Vitruvius its importance is relevant, above all and especially, to the design of temples. Otherwise, the prescription is mentioned only twice in *De architectura*.[20] For Francesco di Giorgio, whose pages overflow with images of lovely boys and girls, the body metaphor is a panacea (see also FIG. 7, below).

But to return to Dinocrates. We have seen Francesco di Giorgio invoke the Dinocrates story twice. On both occasions, his appearance is meant to justify the prescription that "the composition of temples, cities, fortresses and castles" be based on the proportions of the human body. Although the principle may indeed be called Vitruvian, Dinocrates has nothing to do with its justification in Vitruvius' own version of the story. As already noted, Vitruvius' point in introducing Dinocrates' extraordinary physique is rhetorical enhancement of the "perfect body of architecture", that is his own book: the ten scrolls that make up *De architectura*.

Dinocrates appears only once in Vitruvius. He makes no fewer than three appearances in the work of Francesco de Giorgio Martini. I have already discussed two of them.

The third of these, being the earliest, is actually the first. It appears in the dedicatory preface to a book of drawings he presented to the famous renaissance warlord, Federico da Montefeltro, Duke of Urbino in about 1475.[21] The dedication is in Latin, and this time, Francesco does not present Dinocrates to model the relation between "the body" and architecture, but rather to model the reciprocity of architecture and ambition.

Thus, writes Francesco in his preface, Alexander the Great delighted in Dinocrates as a man of genius expert in the attack and defense of cities, and other matters essential for preserving sovereignty (*imperium*), and defeating enemies. So too, he says, did Julius Caesar honor Vitruvius. The reference here is to Vitruvius' early career as a military architect in Caesar's service during his conquest of Gaul, rather than to the author of *De architectura,* which Vitruvius dedicated to Caesar's successor, Augustus.[22]

So too, he hopes, will Federico da Montefeltro who (as Francesco puts it) has lighted up all Italy with his immortal exploits, allow the brilliance of his (Federico's) own genius to recognize the genius of others: by which of course he implies his (Francesco's) own.

Evidence for this "genius" (*ingenium,* in Latin) is the little codex its author here presents to the Duke. As Martin Warnke showed in his *The Court Artist* of 1985, an increasingly popular term for the "genius" shared by both patron and artist, was the Italian word *virtù*.[23]

Whatever the term — *ingenium* or *virtù* — Francesco di Giorgio's point is that like must recognize like. "Love" is the word he actually uses: "You who shine so brilliantly with your own genius cannot help but love the genius of others."[24]

In this, if not in the matter of word versus flesh discussed earlier, Francesco di Giorgio demonstrates perfect agreement with at least one crucial aspect of Vitruvius' presentation of Dinocrates; or rather, with how Vitruvius has Dinocrates present himself.

When, thanks to the Herculean disguise, Alexander finally takes appreciative notice of him and asks him who he is, Dinocrates answers, "Dinocrates, the Macedonian architect who brings you ideas and designs worthy of your renown."[25]

Presenting a king (or a duke or an emperor) with "ideas and designs worthy of [his] renown" is precisely what Francesco di Giorgio is doing with his little codex. It is also precisely what Vitruvius is doing when he presents *De architectura* to Augustus Caesar. What each seeks is *recognition.*

Vitruvius has Alexander "recognize" Dinocrates by having the architect appear before him as the king's own preferred mythical persona, namely Hercules, whom Alexander claimed as his ancestor.

What is important here, as I have argued elsewhere, is that Vitruvius makes Dinocrates appear as the king's double.[26] This double declares himself an architect with ideas and designs worthy of the king's renown.

Thus, through a subtle game of mirrors and the slippery logic of rhetorical persuasion, Vitruvius has architecture itself slide into the role of Hercules: unconquered conqueror, slayer of monsters, friend to mankind — a Herculean role which the king cannot, given the argument, properly perform without the help of an architect.

The encounter is successful, even though the Mount Athos project is not, for as we saw, "From then on, Dinocrates never left the king", and they go on to found the city of Alexandria in Egypt, named, of course, after Alexander, who was later buried there.

When, after his conquest of Egypt in 30 BC, Augustus Caesar was in Alexandria, he visited the tomb of Alexander where, according to his biographer Suetonius:

> *He had the sarcophagus and body of Alexander the Great brought forth from its shrine, and after gazing on it, showed his respect by placing upon it a golden crown and strewing it with flowers; and being asked if he wished to see the tomb of the Ptolemies [who succeeded Alexander] as well, he replied, "My wish was to see a king, not corpses".[27]*

As we saw, Vitruvius makes sure his audience understands that his own flesh and blood body has strictly nothing Herculean about it. The body he hopes Augustus, will "recognize", in the same way that Alexander "recognized" the Herculean body of Dinocrates, is the book Vitruvius is presenting to him: the 10 scrolls that constitute his own perfect body of architecture. And, just as Dinocrates/Hercules doubled Alexander, so does Vitruvius mean these ten scrolls to double the current world ruler: his dedicatee, Augustus Caesar.

How exactly this works will, I hope, bring us a little closer to answering the question, "whose body?"

In about 100 BC, St. John the evangelist began his gospel with the majestic verses that proclaim that, in the beginning was the word, that the word was God and that the word became flesh. Like St. Paul and the other evangelists, St. John wrote in Greek. The Greek word he used in his prologue was *logos: en archei ên ho logos* — "in the beginning was the word".

The primacy of the word — of *logos* — was, of course, not a Christian invention, if we recall Plato and his successors. Nor was the notion of the "word" becoming flesh. Indeed, it was in the centuries immediately preceding St. John that there developed, in Hellenistic and Roman political theory, the tradition of regarding the ruler as the embodiment or agent or representative on earth of the Law, or Reason, or Logos of God.[28]

On this view, the ruler was alternatively *nomos empsychos,* or *logos empsychos*: the "living law" or the "living logos". Even Cicero, whom Vitruvius names as one of his favorite authors, gave voice to the theory when discussing the merits of monarchy in his *Republic,* although, Cicero, who wrote in Latin, did not use the word *logos,* of course. The word he used was *ratio.*[29] And *ratio,* as it happens, is the noun that appears in *De architectura* more frequently than any other — a grand total of 331 times.[30] The word *locus* is the next most frequent and trails behind with only 295 occurrences.

One of the 331 times *ratio* appears is at the end of Vitruvius' first preface, where he dedicates his work to the new ruler of the Roman world. "For in these scrolls", he concludes, "I have laid out all the principles of the discipline *(omnes disciplinae rationes)*."[31] These principles, or *rationes,* as Vitruvius is at all points eager to demonstrate, are founded in nature — the same that govern the natural order.[32] Moreover, he has assembled them in a single well-ordered *corpus* whose number was ten: the key, as we saw, to the whole order of nature, the agent of unity, the container and content of time; also, the "number" of the human body, a testament to its wholeness, its completion, its perfection — and to its role in the ordering the cosmos. But whose body? Not every body can bring order to the world.

Vitruvius was active during the tumultuous years of almost uninterrupted civil strife that marked the transition from republic to empire and the advent of the de facto monarchy of a single, all-powerful man: Julius Caesar's adoptive son and heir, who went by the name of Octavian.

Octavian was hailed for bringing the civil wars to an end, and in January of 27 BC, full of gratitude, the Roman senate conferred on him unprecedented honors, one of which was the attribution of the name by which he is known to posterity: Augustus.

"Augustus", a name resonant with numinous power, had never before been given to any human. Its multiple evocations covered a range of meanings all pointing to a special relation to the gods, and the god-given power to set the world to rights.[33] Vitruvius presented his treatise to this "Augustus" shortly afterwards, addressing him in his first preface with these, the very first lines of *De architectura*:

> *When your divine mind and power (divina tua mens et numen), Imperator Caesar, were seizing command of the world, and all your enemies had been crushed by your invincible strength and citizens were glorying in your triumph and victory; when all subjected peoples awaited your nod and the senate and the Roman people, now free of fear, were being guided by your most noble thoughts and counsels . . .[34]*

There is no question that Vitruvius' terms, particularly his choice of the expression *divina mens et numen,* were dictated by a new imperial ideology, and that this ideology reflected (or was reflected in) the kingship theories just alluded to.

5
THE STATUE OF
AUGUSTUS FROM
PRIMA PORTA /
C. 19 BC /
VATICAN
MUSEUMS /
BRACCIO NUOVO

Even more explicit in this regard is the figured cuirass of what is probably the most famous of the countless statues made of the new ruler. The portrait statue, which stands just over two meters high, is commonly referred to as the Prima Porta statue of Augustus, named after the site on the northern outskirts of Rome where it was found (**FIG. 5**).[35]

An armed conqueror, yet barefoot, he is represented with his right hand raised in a gesture of *adlocutio,* or public address.[36] The emperor does not brandish a sword, or trample a fallen enemy: he speaks. The reason for the choice of pose is elaborated by the relief carving at the centre of his breastplate, where a barbarian surrenders an eagle-tipped standard to a Roman military man. They stand on the right and left, respectively, of the emperor's navel (**FIG. 6**).

6
THE STATUE OF
AUGUSTUS FROM
PRIMA PORTA /
DETAIL

The representation refers to the recovery in 20 BC of Roman standards that had been captured by the Parthians — a nation at the eastern limit of the Roman world — in three humiliating defeats earlier in the century. According to the Roman historian Dio Cassius, Augustus "received [the standards] as if he had conquered the Parthian in war, for he took great pride in the achievement, declaring that he had recovered without a struggle what had formerly been lost in battle."[37]

Thus, the event was broadcast as a diplomatic, not a military victory — a victory for *ratio,* in other words: for reason, for the *logos,* for the *word.*

But that is far from all. The historical event, depicted as the willing submission of the barbarian to superior Roman reason — or, if you like, the barbarian's submission to the irresistible power of the emperor's word — is, simultaneously, a world-ordering, cosmic event.

Embedded in the order of nature, the surrender of the standards is situated between the earth, represented as a mother with two small babies reclining at the emperor's groin and the sky that extends its canopy over his chest. Between the sun rising over Augustus's right breast, heralded by a new dawn, and Diana, the moon goddess riding a stag on his left hip. It is situated halfway between the East, represented by a defeated Galatian captive huddled on the emperor's left flank, and the West, whose representative is the humiliated Spaniard slumped against the other side of his body.

The figured cuirass whose contours, we are meant to believe, duplicate the perfect, muscular torso of the man who is wearing it, is the whole Roman world: *corpus imperii,* the body of empire, as the Augustan poets put it, animated by the living word, the *logos empsychos* that is the divine mind and power of the man Vitruvius addresses in the opening lines of his treatise.[38] The man he hopes will "recognize" him, the way Alexander the Great "recognized" Dinocrates; the man whose world-ordering body Vitruvius means to double with his own "perfect body of architecture".

But if Augustus is here presented as the living word, how far would — *could* — that imperial word actually carry? How could its audibility, so to speak — its reception and acceptance — be guaranteed? How could the word become *fact*? Vitruvius' answer was, through the *logos empsychos,* the perfect body of *De architectura.*

The rhetoric of the statue was perhaps irresistible, and its ideology no doubt subscribed to by all right-thinking Romans of the day: certainly by Vitruvius, at any rate. What Vitruvius understood, and what he meant his treatise to demonstrate, was that without architecture, the rhetoric of the Prima Porta statue would remain just that. By laying out, as he puts it, all the *rationes* of his discipline and showing that, just like the Roman right to rule, these *rationes* were founded in nature, he shows how, through architecture, the imperial ideology of world dominion could acquire the incontestable factuality of spatial extent.

The American philosopher John R. Searle has recently shown "how we are free, in theory, to reject institutional reality are but not free to reject what is physically real."[39] Understood in these terms, the task Vitruvius set himself was

INDRA KAGIS MCEWEN

to demonstrate how the physical reality of architecture would place the institutional reality of Roman rule beyond all challenges.

Thus, if we look to *De architectura* — the canonical referent, after all, for matters concerning "the body" and architecture — to find an answer to the question "whose body?" it seems to me that the only reply Vitruvius can give is "the body of the king".

But is this *the* answer, universally valid for all times and places? Of course not. Nevertheless, as long as Vitruvius was invoked at the ultimate arbiter on matters corporeal, the ideology tended to remain part of the package, though not always in a direct or obvious way.

CONSEQUENCES

The early modern period, and the "re-discovery", so called, of Vitruvius, brought with it a flood of body images. Francesco di Giorgio Martini, as already noted, was the author of countless drawings meant to underwrite the body metaphor. Whose body is behind his parade of lovely, youthful figures? The question is worth asking if we are to maintain a critical distance from their seductive magic.

His "fortress man" is particularly suggestive (**FIG. 4**), begging to be considered in terms of Francesco's ten-year attachment to the warlord, Federico da Montefeltro, for whom he built so many fortresses throughout the Marches, as already noted.

Vitruvius described his 'Vitruvian man' — the one eventually drawn by Leonardo — at the beginning of his third book, on temples, right after the assertion that just as in a well-shaped man, "in sacred dwellings, the symmetry of the members ought to correspond completely, in every detail and with perfect fitness to the entire magnitude of the whole".[40]

For Vitruvius, the chief architectural locus of the body's — which is to say the king's — power was the temple, because Roman power, so it was held, rested in Rome's privileged relation with the gods.[41] Indeed, Augustus made a major point of being famous for his piety, in large part through tireless temple-building.[42]

Francesco di Giorgio's almost verbatim citation of Vitruvius' text on the corporeal referent for proportion runs alongside his fortress man with only a passing reference to temples. The image, and the chapter on *fortezze* which it introduces, leave no doubt that the overriding preoccupation of this late quattrocento reader of Vitruvius was, as he puts it, *città, rocche e castella*.

Thus, it is surely no accident that, a few pages further along, at the bottom of one of several folios bristling with designs for impregnable fortresses is where Francesco di Giorgio chooses to place the drawing of a pretty naked youth, arms outstretched, poised with insouciant elegance inside Vitruvius' circumscribing circle and square. Francesco locates his own take on the 'Vitruvian man' of *De architectura* book 3, chapter 1 squarely in the realm of military architecture (**FIG. 7**). What Francesco is affirming here is that, in the war-torn Italian peninsula of his time and in the wake of the gunpowder revolution, fortresses (not temples) were indeed the chief architectural *loci* of a prince's power.

In the introduction to his chapter on fortifications in his second treatise, Francesco argues passionately and at some length that the divine order of things has ordained that some must dominate, and others be dominated.[43] That is why, he concludes, a prince needs fortresses: instruments, one must assume, of the natural hierarchy and its divine decree.

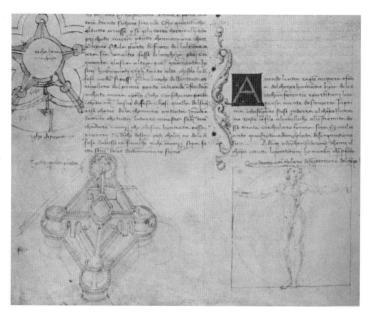

7
FRANCESCO
DI GIORGIO
MARTINI /
TREATISE ON
ARCHITECTURE /
SALUZZIANO
MANUSCRIPT /
"VITRUVIAN
MAN"

Another early renaissance reader of Vitruvius — even earlier than Francesco di Giorgio and, like him a firm believer in natural hierarchies — was Antonio Averlino, commonly known as Filarete, a name which, of course, means "lover of virtue".[44] His treatise on architecture was written for another victorious warlord, Francesco Sforza, Duke of Milan, who had seized the city by force in 1450.[45]

According to Filarete, Adam was the first architect. The first building was Adam's own body (**FIG. 8**).[46] Architecture was founded in the proportions of that body, which was perfect because God had made it in his own image. The most ornate of the architectural orders, the one with the leafy capital conventionally known as "Corinthian", Filarete renames "Doric", calling it Adam's column, because it is the largest and the finest in the hierarchy of orders he calls *qualità* or "qualities".[47]

INDRA KAGIS MCEWEN

These grand, foliated Adamic columns are like *signori,* he explains later on, and, just as lords need servants to support them, such columns must always stand at the tops of buildings, sustained below by the lesser "qualities".[48] "The body" that, in Filarete's treatise, begins innocently enough as Adam's body very

quickly becomes the body of a lord. Other bodies that appear in his treatise tend, unequivocally, to drive the point home.

Thus, Filarete presents the reader with statues of kings enthroned, or on horseback, crowning impossibly over-scaled monuments whose structural underpinning consists almost exclusively of what Filarete calls "figures in the place of columns", a usage clearly derived from Vitruvius' caryatids and, especially, his Persian prisoners.

One of the most extravagant projects in a treatise that is full of them, is a multi-storey building Filarete calls Casa Areti, or Casa della virtù (**FIG. 9**). Here, "figures in the place of columns" appear as support for the roof portico, while at the very top stands the figure of *virtù* itself.[49]

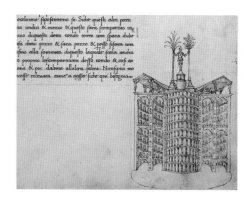

9
FILARETE /
TREATISE ON
ARCHITECTURE /
MAGLIABECHIANO
MANUSCRIPT /
"CASA DELLA
VIRTÙ"

Filarete's *virtù* is a winged man in full armor, his head haloed in a sunburst, with a figure of Fame flying above it (**FIG. 10**). His feet are balanced on the point

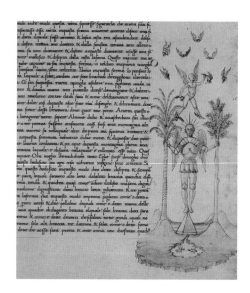

10
FILARETE /
TREATISE ON
ARCHITECTURE /
MAGLIABECHIANO
MANUSCRIPT /
"*VIRTÙ*"

of a diamond which, as the author explains in another context, ranks first as the hardest and most transparently "virtuous" in the hierarchy of stones: *diamante* in Italian, in Latin *adamanta* — from *adamas,* the Greek word for "invincible".[50]

The *virtù* Filarete exalts here is not conventional goodness, of course, but military excellence: the sum of the soldierly qualities of courage, decision and manliness. Francesco Sforza's *virtù* was what the court humanists invoked to justify the warlord's otherwise entirely illegal claim to Milan.[51] This, clearly, is the quality Filarete, the virtue-loving architect, loves. His treatise was written for the man who possessed it.

The central theme of Filarete's treatise is the project for a city (**FIG. 11**), the first ideal city of the Renaissance, so it is claimed. It is, of course, a fortified

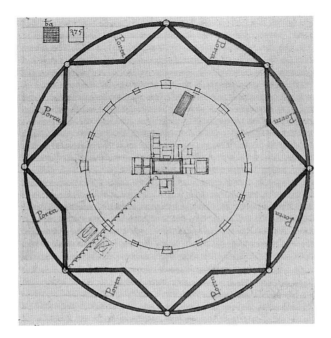

11
FILARETE /
TREATISE ON
ARCHITECTURE /
MAGLIABECHIANO
MANUSCRIPT /
THE PLAN OF
SFORZINDA

city but unlike Francesco di Giorgio, Filarete nowhere suggests that its shape is drawn from the human body. But calling it Sforzinda after his patron, the Duke, could hardly have made its referent more obvious.

Until the 18th century, Vitruvius presided over an architectural universe grounded in the aristocratic assumption of allegedly natural hierarchies. For all their ongoing poetic appeal, these hierarchies and the concomitant embrace of microcosmic-macrocosmic correspondences as legitimating underpinning for the corporeal referent in architecture began to lose credibility over two centuries ago. Asking "whose body?" is a reminder of how unjust the Vitruvian universe could be.

NOTES

1   Spencer Tunick has been documenting installations such as this one — over 75 to date — since 1994. For more information you may visit the websites www.artnet.com/awc/spencer-tunick.html and www.spencertunick.com

2   www.cbc.ca/canada/story/2001/05/26/tunick010526.html

3   www.telegraph.co.uk/culture/art/3652386/In-the-studio-Spencer-Tunick.html

4   http://flavorwire.com/26939/exclusive-spencer-tunick-corrals-300-naked-people-in-front-of-montauk-lighthouse

5   www.guardian.co.uk/artanddesign/video/2010/mar/01/naked-art-spencer-tunick-sydney

6   On this topic see, in general, Indra Kagis MCEWEN, *Vitruvius: Writing the Body of Architecture,* Cambridge, MA and London: The MIT Press, 2003.

7   Philippe FLEURY, introduction, *Vitruve: de l'architecture, livre I,* Paris: Les belles lettres, 1990, pp. lxii–lxvii · McEwen, *Vitruvius,* pp. 32–33 and 156–157, with references.

8   On Leonardo's famous image (Accademia, Venice, no. 228) see, among countless others, Carlo PEDRETTI, *Leonardo architetto,* Milan: Electa, 1981, pp. 160–162 · Frank ZÖLLNER, *Vitruvs Proportionsfigur. Quellenkritische Studien zur Kunstliteratur im 15. und 16. Jahrhundert,* Worms: Wernersche Verlagsgesellschaft, 1987, pp. 77–87 · Pierre GROS, "La géométrie platonicienne de la notice vitruvienne sur l'homme parfait (*De architectura* III, I, 2–3)", in: *Annali di architettura,* VOL. 13, 2001, pp. 15–32 · Most recently: Toby LESTER, *Da Vinci's Ghost. The Untold Story of the World's Most Famous Drawing,* London: Profile Books, 2011.

9   "Corpus emendatum architecturae": VITRUVIUS, *De architectura,* IX.8,15. See also II.1,8, IV.pref. 1, V.pref. 5, VI.pref. 7, VII.pref. 10, VII.pref. 14, X.pref. 4, and X.16,12. Here, as elsewhere, the Latin text cited is from the 10-volume French edition of *De architectura* (*Vitruve: de l'architecture,* Paris: Belles lettres, 1969–2009). All translations from the Latin are my own.

10   VITRUVIUS, *De architectura,* X.16,12.

11   McEwen, *Vitruvius,* pp. 42–43.

12   VITRUVIUS, *De architectura,* III.1,5.

13   J. E. RAVEN, "Polyclitus and Pythagoreanism", in: *Classical Quarterly,* VOL. 45, 1951, pp. 147–152 · McEwen, *Vitruvius,* pp. 43–48, with references.

14   E. R. GOODENOUGH, "The Political Philosophy of Hellenistic Kingship", in: *Yale Classical Studies,* VOL. 1, 1928, pp. 55–102 · Glenn F. Chesnut, "The Ruler and the *Logos* in Neo Pythagorean, Middle Platonic and Late Stoic Political Philosophy", in: *Aufstieg und Niedergang der römischen Welt,* PART 2: *Principat,* VOL. 16/2, edited by Wolfgang HAASE, Berlin and New York: Walter de Gruyter, 1978, pp. 1310–1332.

15   McEwen, *Vitruvius,* pp. 91–154.

16   VITRUVIUS, *De architectura,* II.pref., 4.

17   Francesco DI GIORGIO MARTINI, *La traduzione del* De architectura *di Vitruvio,* edited by Marco BIFFI, Pisa: Scuola Normale Superiore, 2002, p. 6. There are many gaps in Francesco's translation, which dates from about 1485. See further Gustina SCAGLIA, *Il "Vitruvio Magliabechiano" di Francesco di Giorgio Martini,* Florence: Gonelli, 1985.

18   Francesco DI GIORGIO MARTINI, Codex Magliabechiano, II.1,141 (c. 1490), Florence, Bibliote-

ca Nazionale Centrale, fol. 27v · See also DI GIORGIO MARTINI, *Trattati di architettura ingegneria e arte militare,* edited by Corrado MALTESE, 2 VOLS., Milan: Il Polifilo, 1967, VOL. 2, p. 362.

19 Francesco DI GIORGIO MARTINI, Codex Saluzziano 148 (c. 1485), Turin, Biblioteca Reale, fol. 3r: "come el corpo ha tutti i membri l'uno all'altro conferenti e le partizioni con perfetta misura, così in nelle composizioni de' tempi, città, rocche e castella osservare si debba". DI GIORGIO MARTINI, *Trattati di architectura,* VOL. 1, p. 4.

20 Its relevance to the design of temples is repeatedly stressed in opening paragraphs of *De architectura,* book 3, the first of Vitruvius' two books on religious architecture. The only two other appeals to a body referent for the principle of commensurability in architecture occur in book 1: *De architectura,* I.2, 2; I.2, 4.

21 Francesco DI GIORGIO MARTINI, *Opusculum de architectura,* Harley ms. 3281, British Museum, Department of Prints and Drawings 197B.21 · See A. E. POPHAM and Philip POUNCEY, *Italian Drawings in the Department of Prints and Drawings in the British Museum: The 14th and 15th Centuries,* 2 VOLS., London: British Museum, 1950, VOL. 1, p. 33, where the preface is reprinted.

22 VITRUVIUS, *De architectura,* I.pref.

23 Martin WARNKE, *The Court Artist,* translated by David McLintock, Cambridge: Cambridge University Press, 1985, pp. 35, 135 and passim.

24 *Qui cum ipse ingenio plurimum floreas aliorum ingenia non amare nequeas.*

25 VITRUVIUS, *De architectura,* II.pref., 2.

26 MCEWEN, *Vitruvius,* pp. 95–112.

27 SUETONIUS, *Divus Augustus,* 18, 1.

28 CHESNUT, "The Ruler and the *Logos* in Neo Pythagorean, Middle Platonic and Late Stoic Political Philosophy", p. 1312.

29 CICERO, *De republica,* 1.56–60.

30 L. CALLEBAT, P. BOUET, Ph. FLEURY, and M. ZUINGHEDAU, *Vitruve. De architectura. Concordance. Documentation bibliographique, lexicale et grammaticale,* 2 VOLS., Hildesheim, Zürich, and New York: Olms-Weidmann, 1984, S. V. "ratio".

31 VITRUVIUS, *De architectura,* I.pref. 3.

32 MCEWEN, *Vitruvius,* pp. 47–48.

33 Ibid., p. 10, with references.

34 VITRUVIUS, *De architectura,* I.pref., 1.

35 Vatican Museums, Braccio Nuovo (INV. 2290).

36 Richard BRILLIANT, *Gesture and Rank in Roman Art,* New Haven: The Academy, 1963, p. 67 · John POLLINI, "The Augustus from Prima Porta and the Transformation of the Heroic Ideal", in: *Polykleitos, the Doryphoros, and Tradition,* edited by Warren G. MOON, Madison, WI: The University of Wisconsin Press, 1995, pp. 265–266.

37 DIO CASSIUS, *Roman History,* LIV.8, 2.

38 As for example by OVID in ca. 10 AD: *Tristia,* II, 226. See Dietmar KIENAST, "Corpus imperii", in: *Romanitas, Christianitas. Untersuchungen zur Geschichte und Literatur der römischen Kaiserzeit,* edited by Gerhard WIRTH with the collaboration of Karl-Heinz SCHWARTE and Johannes HEINRICHS, Berlin: Walter de Gruyter, 1982, pp. 1–17.

39 John R. SEARLE, *Making the Social World: The Structure of Human Civilization,* Oxford: Oxford University Press, 2010. See N. J. ENFIELD, review in: *Times Literary Supplement,* September 3, 2010, p. 3.

40 VITRUVIUS, *De architectura,* III.1,3.

41 McEwen, *Vitruvius,* pp. 183–198 · See Mary BEARD, "Religion", in: *The Cambridge Ancient History,* VOL. 9: *The Last Age of the Roman Republic, 146–143 B.C.,* edited by J. A. CROOK, Andrew LINTOTT, and Elizabeth RAWSON, 2nd edition, Cambridge, New York, Melbourne, Madrid, and Cape Town: Cambridge University Press, 1994, pp. 729–768.

42 Pierre GROS, *Aurea templa: Recherches sur l'architecture religieuse de Rome à l'époque d'Auguste,* Rome: École française de Rome, 1976.

43 DI GIORGIO MARTINI, Codex Magliabechiano, fols. 46v–47v · DI GIORGIO MARTINI, *Trattati di Architectura,* ed. MALTESE, VOL. 2, pp. 414–417.

44 John ONIANS, "Filarete and the *qualità*: Architectural and Social", in: *Arte Lombarda,* VOL. 38/39, 1973, pp. 116–118 · See also Indra Kagis McEwen, "*Virtù-vious*: Roman Architecture, Renaissance Virtue", in: *Cahiers des études anciennes,* VOL. 48, 2011, pp. 255–283.

45 Lauro MARTINES, *Power and Imagination: City-States in Renaissance Italy,* Baltimore: Johns Hopkins University Press, 1988, pp. 140–148.

46 FILARETE, Codex Magliabechiano, Florence, Biblioteca Nazionale Centrale, II.1,140, fol. 4v · Antonio AVERLINO detto IL FILARETE, *Trattato di architettura,* edited by Anna Maria FINOLI and Liliana GRASSI, 2 VOLS., Milan: Il Polifilo, 1972, VOL. 1, pp. 23–24 · Antonio di Piero AVERLINO, known as FILARETE, *Treatise on Architecture,* translated with an introduction and notes by John R. SPENCER, 2 VOLS., New Haven and London: Yale University Press, 1965, VOL. 1, p. 10.

47 FILARETE, Codex Magliabechiano, fol. 3r · FILARETE, *Trattato di architettura,* VOL. 1, p. 18 · FILARETE, *Treatise on Architecture,* VOL. 1, p. 8 · ONIANS, "Filarete and the *qualità*".

48 FILARETE, Codex Maglibechiano, fol. 55v · FILARETE, *Trattato di architettura,* VOL. 1, pp. 214–215 · FILARETE, *Treatise on Architecture,* VOL. 1, pp. 94–96.

49 FILARETE, Codex Magliabechiano, fols. 144r–145r · FILARETE, *Trattato di architettura,* VOL. 2, pp. 536–540 · FILARETE, *Treatise on Architecture,* VOL. 1, pp. 247–250.

50 FILARETE, Codex Magliabechiano, fol. 143r · FILARETE, *Trattato di architettura,* VOL. 2, p. 533 · FILARETE, *Treatise on Architecture,* VOL. 1, p. 246 — On diamonds and precious stones in general: FILARETE, fol. 17v · FILARETE, *Trattato di architettura,* VOL. 1, pp. 74–76 · FILARETE, *Treatise on Architecture,* p. 52. On their properties, PLINY, *Natural History,* 20.1.2 and 37.15.4.

51 Gary IANZITI, *Humanistic Historiography under the Sforzas: Politics and Propaganda in Fifteenth-century Milan,* Oxford: Clarendon Press, 1988.

IMAGES

Author: FIGS. 1 and 2 · Francesco DI GIORGIO MARTINI, Codex Magliabechiano, II.1,141, Florence, Biblioteca Nazionale Centrale, fol. 27v: FIG. 3 · Francesco DI GIORGIO MARTINI, Codex Saluzziano 148, Turin, Biblioteca Reale, fol. 3r: FIG. 4 and fol. 6v: FIG. 7 · Vatican Museums, Rome, Braccio Nuovo, INV. 2290: FIGS. 5 and 6 · FILARETE, Codex Magliabechiano, Florence, Biblioteca Nazionale Centrale, II.1,140, fol. 4v: FIG. 8; fol. 144r: FIG. 9; fol. 143r: FIG. 10; fol. 43r: FIG. 11

FRANK ZÖLLNER

Anthropomorphism: From Vitruvius to Neufert, from Human Measurement to the Module of Fascism

ANTHROPOMORPHISM AS A FORM OF THOUGHT (*DENKFORM*)

As is well known, anthropomorphism belongs to the oldest and most prominent forms of thought in the history of culture. However, a glance at how the notion of an anthropomorphic God has been received within religious history shows the degree to which this multifaceted form of thought is a problematic construct. Although in many religious doctrines God is imagined as a white adult male, and the transferral of the human form to a higher being seems to be a constitutive element of religion in general,[1] the fragility of anthropomorphic thought was already remarked on and criticized in antiquity.[2] In the canonical writings of Judaism and Christianity, as well as Islam, the information as to whether or not God can be imagined in human form is nothing if not contradictory.[3] This has inevitably led to lively controversies: for example, in the early church at the turn of the 4th to the 5th century, when the so-called "anthropomorphites" were criticized for their image of God.[4] The consequence of this critique was a monotheistic, *logos*-oriented and strictly transcendental idea of God that tended towards scepticism in relation to an anthropomorphic God.[5]

Be that as it may, from a rationalist point of view, "the inadequacy of anthropomorphism for a coherent interpretation of the world" is evident.[6] Thus, some thinkers have considered anthropomorphism as a primitive stage of religion, or at least one that should be overcome.[7]

IN / KIRSTEN WAGNER AND JASPER CEPL (EDITORS) /
IMAGES OF THE BODY IN ARCHITECTURE: ANTHROPOLOGY AND BUILT SPACE /
TÜBINGEN · BERLIN / ERNST WASMUTH VERLAG / 2014 / PP. 47–75

Although anthropomorphism was and still is an idea afflicted with all sorts of contradictions and controversies, it has repeatedly played a role in relation to architecture — both as a form of thought and as an argumentative support.[8] Particularly in theoretical reflections on buildings and their parts — that is, when

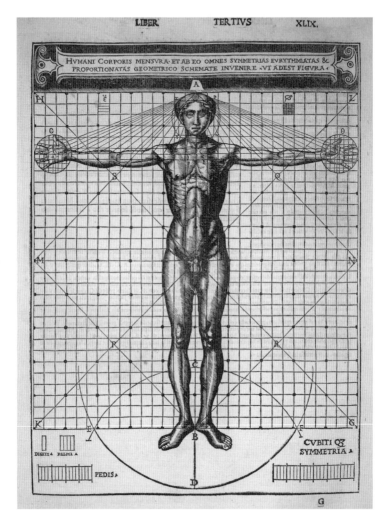

1
CESARE
CESARIANO /
"HOMO AD
QUADRATUM"
AFTER
VITRUVIUS /
1521

architecture is considered in the medium of language — architects, architectural theorists and laypeople have made frequent use of the metaphor of the human body, which was considered as an immediate symbolic model and copy of architecture or its parts. Both the body and the building were defined and metaphorically transcribed with the help of measurements, numbers, proportions and geometric figures. Hence, the anthropomorphic metaphor has two different forms of expression: firstly, the form or the image of the body itself; and, secondly, its numeric or abstracting translation into numbers and geometric figures.

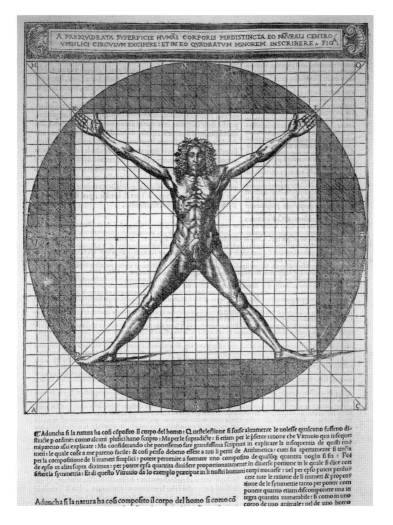

2
CESARE
CESARIANO
/ "HOMO AD
CIRCULUM"
/ AFTER
VITRUVIUS /
1521

VITRUVIUS' PROPORTIONAL FIGURE

All elements of the anthropomorphic metaphor can already be found in Vitruvius' *De architectura libri decem* (**FIGS. 1–3**),[9] the only architectural treatise to have come down to us from antiquity, which provided architectural theory from the

15th to the 18th century with its most important point of reference. Vitruvius initially describes anthropomorphism with the example of Dinocrates[10] and with a study of the Doric column.[11] However, the most comprehensive as well as the most prominent remarks on human measurement as architectural measurement are found at the beginning of his third book. There he writes that the design of religious architecture is based on symmetry and proportion, and that this design corresponds to the right organization of the human body.[12] He even derives the individual measurements themselves, as well as the two geometric figures of the circle and the square, from a well-formed body stretching out its arms and legs, while the navel forms the body's middle point.[13]

Since Rudolf Wittkower's book *Architectural Principles in the Age of Humanism,* published in 1949, Vitruvius' so-called "homo ad quadratum" (**FIG. 1**) together with his 'alter ego', the so-called "homo ad circulum" (**FIG. 2**), have been understood as symbols of renaissance architecture.[14] However, on closer inspection it becomes clear that Wittkower retroactively prefixed this figure to his interpretation of renaissance architecture as an emblem that was closer to the symbolically inflected understanding of 20th-century architecture than to the architectural conceptions of the early modern period.

Indeed, the figure described by Vitruvius had no direct influence on the architecture of the 15th and 16th centuries.[15] The anthropomorphic understanding of architecture was not something one could apply directly to architecture since, as a rule, buildings are not actually given the form of the human body.[16] Only the underlying abstract idea of a design could be considered in anthropomorphic terms.

In the following, I shall discuss the importance of this metaphorically meant reference for architects and theorists with examples taken from architectural theory. In doing so, I would like to show how and why the importance of the anthropomorphic view of architecture in the architectural theory of the 16th to the 19th century began a steady decline, and was ultimately called into question. To conclude, I shall examine the resurgence of anthropomorphism in modern and German Fascist conceptions of order.

Vitruvius' discussion of human body measurements relies heavily on ancient building practices and Greek metrology (the science of measurement). This dependency is partly the result of his rootedness in the practice of engineering and building, and partly due to his reception of ancient Greek sources of architectural theory that are now lost.[17] Accordingly, Vitruvius defines measurements as values that approximate the real dimensions of individual body parts.

In the first and third book Vitruvius expressly mentions, as examples of anthropomorphic measurements, *digitus, palmus, pes,* and *cubitus* (finger, palm, foot, and cubit or ell) among others. He also indirectly mentions the fathom by indicating that the distance between the fingertips of the outstretched arms of a well-proportioned man corresponds to the height of the same man from head to toe. This measurement, which to all appearances was not even illustrated in the lost original manuscript of *De architectura*,[18] has been correctly illustrated up to the present with the figure of the so-called "homo ad quadratum" (**FIG. 2**). Since the Renaissance, however, the so-called "homo ad circulum" has been interpreted, probably incorrectly, as a figure with outstretched arms and spread legs (**FIG. 1**). In his description of the "homo ad circulum", Vitruvius may well have been thinking of a man with his arms stretched upwards (**FIG. 3**). Visualized

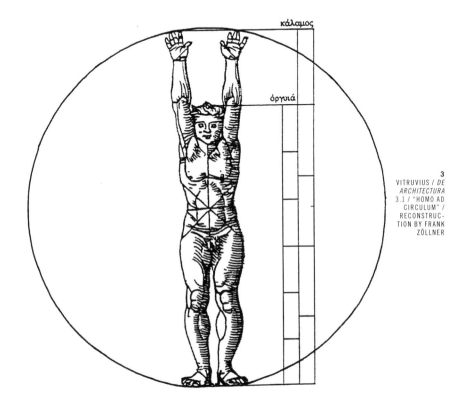

3
VITRUVIUS / *DE ARCHITECTURA* 3.1 / "HOMO AD CIRCULUM" / RECONSTRUCTION BY FRANK ZÖLLNER

in this way, the dimension would also correspond to a measurement that was common at the time.[19]

Almost all of the individual measurements mentioned by Vitruvius were part of the anthropomorphic system of measurement that was used in numerous areas of human life — although with local variants that differed considerably.[20] Only with the Metre Convention of 1875 was the human-based measurement system replaced by a geomorphic system obtained from the earth's circumference — one ten-millionth of the length of the earth's meridian along a quadrant. This departure from good old anthropomorphism was a decisive event whose consequences have still not been fully accepted by architectural theory.

A certain regret concerning the loss of anthropomorphic measurement can be felt — to mention just one example — in a book that was first published in 1936 by a student of Walter Gropius, Ernst Neufert: the *Bauentwurfslehre* (first published in English in 1970 as *Architects' Data*). This "handbook for the building specialist, client, teacher and student", which has been translated into fifteen languages and is now in its 40th German edition (2012), is probably the most influential architectural handbook in the world, and it expressly defines "Der Mensch als Maß und Ziel" (literally, "man as measure and goal". In the English translation of the *Bauentwurfslehre,* this section has been translated as "Man: the universal standard").[21]

In this chapter (on which more will be said at the end of this essay) Neufert states categorically:

Even today many people would have a better understanding of the size of an object if they were told that it was so many men high, so many paces long, so many feet wider or so many heads bigger. These are concepts we have from birth, the sizes of which can be said to be in our nature. However, the introduction of metric dimensions put an end to that way of depicting our world.[22]

Of course, we are born with nothing of the sort! The anthropomorphic systems of measurement that circulated in the most varied forms up to the introduction of the metre as well as the duodecimal system with its complicated fractional calculations were simply not very practical — not to mention the various weight and capacity measurements and the coinage systems. But let us return to the history of anthropomorphism and its steady demise.

ANTHROPOMORPHISM AND LEVEL OF THEORY (*THEORIENIVEAU*)

The metaphorically meant comparison between body and architecture was also formulated in the Middle Ages, and independently of Vitruvius.[23] There, however, the comparison did not serve as a planning schema, but merely as the basis for the subsequent interpretation of a building.[24] Also to be placed in this tradition of anthropomorphic projection are the art and architectural theorists of the Quattrocento.

One example is the Sienese architect, engineer and painter Francesco di Giorgio Martini (1439–1501). Although the anthropomorphic comparison between building and body can be seen in the various versions of his extensive writings on the theory of architecture, it is especially evident in the early and intellectually less developed version of his architectural treatise. When, around 1480, he made a direct comparison between a building's plan and elevation and the human figure, he was simply combining a medieval view of anthropomorphism with Vitruvius' proportional figure.[25] Although, from the point of view of an anthropomorphic idea of architecture, Vitruvius' proportional figure did not offer anything essentially new to the Sienese engineer and architect, it provided him with the opportunity to give an antique cast to medieval anthropomorphism. Similar approaches and motifs can also be found in the art theoretical writings of Lorenzo Ghiberti[26] and Antonio Averlino, called Filarete.[27]

As a figure of thought and argumentative support, anthropomorphism thus made an appearance in the early stages of theory formation, and particularly among those theorists for whom, due to their status as craftsmen, it was a means to social advancement.

Evidence of this is also to be seen in anthropomorphism's dwindling effectiveness towards the end of the Quattrocento, attested to in an exemplary way by Francesco di Giorgio's abovementioned treatise, the second version of which gave less prominence to anthropomorphism than the first, which represented a more primitive level of theory.

The only claim of relevance anthropomorphism still had towards the end of the 15th century was as a rather naïve argumentative support. One might think of Leonardo da Vinci, who used the metaphor of the building as a body in a number of drafts of his letters in order to vie with the professional architects in Milan.[28] However, this decidedly low level of theory formation obviously did not achieve the desired effect since, as is well known, Leonardo got the short end of the stick in relation to the local Lombard architects.[29]

The description of Vitruvius' proportional figure in Cesare Cesariano's Vitruvius commentary published in 1521[30] is another example of a lower theoretical level. Cesariano came from a modest social background and suffered unspeakably at the hands of his extraordinarily vicious stepmother, whose machinations he mentions in his Vitruvius commentary — not without bitterness. There, he describes how, equipped with a compass, straightedge and his Vitruvius commentary, he acquired the courage to escape the poverty and the schemes of his stepmother[31] — of all things with the instruments that guarantee the right measurement in architecture. Cesariano attempted to advance his social standing with the Vitruvius commentary.

Cesariano describes his understanding of the anthropomorphic system of measurement in detail with the example of Vitruvius' proportional figure (FIGS. 1–2). In doing so, he explains in concrete terms the significance of the anthropomorphic measurement for architectural design and on-site measurement, also mentioning the necessary instruments. Accordingly, the man in the square illustrates the "symmetriata quadratura"; that is, he shows the possibility of determining, with the help of geometry and the anthropomorphic measurements, the size of all planes (FIG. 2). The measuring instruments Cesariano individually names are measurement standards of various dimensions such as the *bacculo ligneo,* with the length of an ell, and longer measuring instruments such as the six-foot *trabucco,* the fathom (Greek: *orguia*) illustrated in Vitruvius' "homo ad quadratum", and the ten-foot *pertica,* the longest standard measuring bar.[32] While describing these instruments, Cesariano emphasizes that the measurements required for surveying land or buildings are taken directly from the human body.

Cesariano's text manifests an understanding of anthropomorphic measurements that is immediately compatible with the views of Vitruvius. This precise understanding is explained above all by the circumstance that Cesariano was a practically trained architect and surveyor. He therefore possessed detailed knowledge of surveying practice, which, in relation to the instruments used and the measurements derived from anthropomorphism, was largely identical to the practice at the basis of Vitruvius' formulation.

Although his illustrations of the Vitruvian man cannot be counted among the most beautiful of the genre, it becomes clear in the accompanying text that, as a theorist, Cesariano took the derivation of architectural measurements from the human body especially seriously. As was the case for the theorists of the Quattrocento, his practical training made him especially susceptible to the theoretical concept of anthropomorphism.

MUSICAL HARMONY VERSUS ANTHROPOMORPHISM

Whereas the architectural theorists of the early Renaissance, who were still practically trained, used Vitruvius' proportional figure to procure the sanction of antique theory, the succeeding generations of architects and theorists show a slightly more detached attitude to anthropomorphism. For them musical proportion was more important than the direct metaphorical derivation of architectural measurements from the body. Hence, the leading architectural theorists of the Renaissance — Leon Battista Alberti in the 15th century[33] and Andrea Palladio in the 16th century[34] — based their ideas on musical harmony. For these theorists, who either had a higher social standing (Alberti) or a higher level of theory as a result of intellectual advancement (Palladio), the metaphor of human measurement hardly played a role anymore.

In the place of the metaphorically intended comparison with human measurement, attempts were increasingly made to derive whole buildings and their parts from measurement ratios that exactly corresponded, or were thought to exactly correspond, to musical intervals such as the fourth, fifth or octave. A well-known example is the church of San Francesco della Vigna in Venice, for whose reconstruction one simply postulated certain proportions, as an aid to conviction, so to speak.[35]

The extent to which theory formation left anthropomorphism behind while also being raised to an abstract level is shown by the author of the most important Vitruvius commentary of the 16th century, Daniele Barbaro, a significant humanist and prominent member of the Venetian patriciate. In the second edition of his Vitruvius commentary, which was first published in Latin in 1556 and then in Italian in 1567, the proportional figure is no longer even accorded an illustration. Moreover, Vitruvius' anthropomorphic measurements have been entirely replaced by a proportional system based on musical harmonies[36], without any relation to ancient systems of measurement.

Barbaro's proportional system eventually found its most complete theoretical reception and practical deployment in the Vincentian architect Andrea Palladio, whose architectural treatise no longer accorded anthropomorphism any importance. This was above all due to the fact that intellectually agile authors such as Palladio, as well as his mentors Alberti and Barbaro, replaced an anthropomorphically conceived building ideology with the rational proportional conception of music theory. Music theory could indeed be converted into building practice,[37] as well as be plausibly related to cosmic harmonies considered from a similar musical standpoint.[38]

THE PROVISIONAL END OF ANTHROPOMORPHISM

A far more radical questioning of the anthropomorphic conception of architecture took place in the French architectural theory of the 17th century. This break was carried out most clearly by Claude Perrault's French Vitruvius translation first published in 1674 and again in 1684.[39] In the footnotes to Vitruvius' text, Perrault presents his own views on proportion, which are decisively opposed to all previously known traditional conceptions, and hence also to those of Vitruvius himself. Perrault categorically rejects a traditional theory of proportion that could be applied to architecture like a law of nature. In his commentary on the origin of the Doric column, whose proportions Vitruvius derived from the length of the human foot (see above), he even explicitly goes against the hitherto prevailing conception. As he writes, proportions in architecture have nothing natural about them; they do not follow incontrovertible rules such as those derived from the dimensions of the stars or from the parts of the human body. Rather, architects establish the proportions of a building based on an agreement ("consentement") determined by tradition and custom.[40] Hence, the foundation of beauty is not human measurement but the power of human custom. Perrault's uncompromising rationality, which also placed him in strong opposition to his period's absolutist academic doctrine of art, is yet to be surpassed.

Of course, Perrault's break with the anthropomorphic theory of proportion did not go uncontested.[41] Nevertheless, his influence can still be felt in theories from the 18th to the 20th century.[42] Accordingly, Bernardo Galliani, in his 1758 Vitruvius commentary, pays little attention to human proportions. In fact

Galliani explicitly opposes an all too serious conception of anthropomorphism, even criticizing the commonplace circulated by Pietro Cataneo in 1567 that the proportional figure directly underlies the ground plan of Christian church architecture (**FIG. 4**).[43]

4
PIETRO
CATANEO /
TREATISE ON
ARCHITECTURE /
1567 /
CHURCH PLAN

The renunciation of man as the measure of all things was further reinforced by the introduction of the metre in the 19th century. Although the human body was still occasionally compared with the building and its parts,[44] the importance of architectural anthropomorphism was on the wane, even as a nonbinding metaphor. Thus, at the beginning of the 19th century, Jean-Nicolas-Louis Durand (1760–1834) contested the relation between the human body and architecture, rejecting for example the derivation of the proportions of a column from the measurements of the human body. He suggested using arbitrary proportions.[45]

Other theorists, such as Eugène Emmanuel Viollet-le-Duc (1814–1879) and Auguste Choisy (1841–1909), formulated a concept of proportion that was dependent on structural analysis and geometry.[46] In the 18th century, English theorists began to argue along similar lines.[47] Although in Anglo-American culture anthropomorphic measurement and duodecimal calculation remained significant into the 20th century, an empirical, rationally determined attitude led to the renunciation of anthropomorphism as a figure of thought.[48]

56

Another reason for the renunciation of anthropomorphism in the 18th and 19th centuries should be searched for in industrialization, which favoured an empirical and functional conception of architecture. Nevertheless, in the 20th century the serial production of single building units accompanying industrialization seems to have stimulated the renaissance of an anthropomorphic theory of proportion. It is entirely in this sense that we should examine probably the best-known attempt to revive architectural anthropomorphism: namely, the *Modulor* (**FIG. 5**) of the Swiss painter and architect Le Corbusier. Indeed, one of

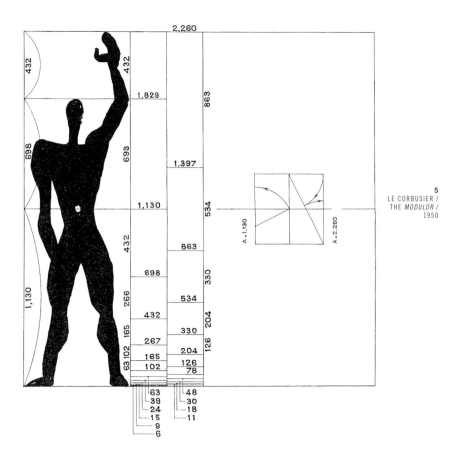

5
LE CORBUSIER /
THE *MODULOR* /
1950

the basic concepts of the *Modulor* is its relation to serial production and the standardization of architectural parts.[49]

Already in the years between 1910 and 1911, Le Corbusier anticipated the *Modulor* in his reflections on a proportional system based on the golden section.[50] However, as Eckhard Leuschner has recently been able to show, the *Modulor* should also be understood in the context of certain ideas of the 1920s and 30s about harmony and order.[51] Le Corbusier developed rather more concrete steps towards the *Modulor* in 1943 in Paris. Finally in America, in April 1947, he made his proposals public. The definitive text version of the *Modulor* was completed in November 1948.[52]

Le Corbusier's description of the *Modulor's* genesis has become the subject of legend. According to Le Corbusier, the proportional figure was conceived during Germany's occupation of France as a reaction to the mental hardship and material needs of the time.[53] As a system of measurement Le Corbusier intended the

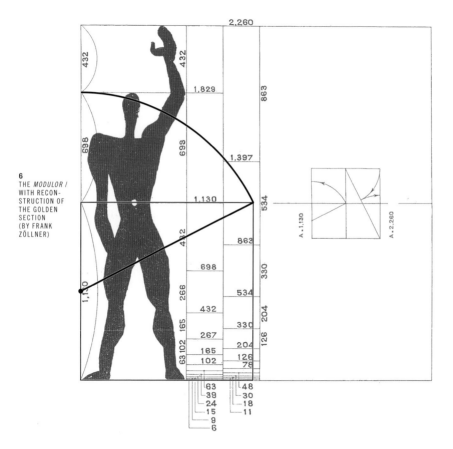

6
THE *MODULOR I*
WITH RECON-
STRUCTION OF
THE GOLDEN
SECTION
(BY FRANK
ZÖLLNER)

Modulor to take into account man's average dimensions while also being based on nature's mathematical law of proportion. To achieve this he transferred the golden section to the dimensions of the human body. The figure's height was initially determined at 175 cm, but subsequently changed to 183 cm. With his arm raised above his head, the figure has a height of 226 cm; the distance from navel to toe now measures 113 cm.[54]

The artist provides two explanations for the growth of his proportional figure: firstly, well-built policemen in English detective novels were six feet tall, which corresponds in the metric system to a height of 183 cm; secondly, this measurement would give rise to a larger number of correspondences between the metric system and the anthropomorphic measurements of Anglo-American culture.[55] Especially the first of these two explanations gives us reason to suspect that Le Corbusier did not take the *Modulor* quite as seriously as its later adherents (see below). Indeed, Le Corbusier's allusion to the size of policemen in detective novels testifies to a rather relaxed attitude in his treatment of "natural laws", which in the general idea of measurement dealt with here are taken entirely seriously as "innate" (see above) and eternal.

The relation of the dimensions selected by Le Corbusier to one another corresponded approximately to the proportions of the golden section. The Swiss architect developed the number and proportion series while crossing the Atlantic in a "terrible storm" and in a heavy sea swell. As a system, however, the number series of the golden section, devised "in the tumult of the waves", which seems to have impressed Le Corbusier like an event of nature,[56] presents several problems. As is well known, the golden section leads to irrational number relationships, which are hardly suited to architectural practice. Hence, the golden section was rarely used in architecture.

Le Corbusier's use of the golden section was not his only recourse to an earlier tradition. Like Vitruvius before him, Le Corbusier derives the size of the body from the height of a grown man. The man with the raised arm was also an old acquaintance since this is surely what Vitruvius meant with his "homo ad circulum" (FIG. 3). As anthropomorphic measure, this was also common in ancient and Byzantine metrology, as well as in modern building practice. Thus, with his propagation of the golden section as well as his proportional figure, Le Corbusier stood in a long-outlived tradition.

Le Corbusier's *Modulor* was directed expressly against the introduction of the metre and the decimal system. For Le Corbusier the metre was abstract, bloodless and unfeeling, and its use had brought about the slackening of architecture.[57] Le Corbusier's polemic probably conceals an attempt to defend modern architecture against its critics. Due to its renunciation of ornament and its machine-like quality, this architecture had been described as cold, empty, boring and soulless since the 1930s — for instance, by the German philosopher Ernst Bloch, who emigrated to the USA in 1938.[58]

Hence, anthropomorphism's resurrection in the form of the *Modulor* could be understood as a utopia expressing the desire for a human architecture. Be that as it may, Le Corbusier enlists anthropomorphism in one of his attempts to legitimize the rationality of his architecture which had been characterized as "technoid" with a coolly calculated combination of "eternal" laws of proportion and organic looking natural forms. His argumentation can be summarized approximately as follows: the spiral form of the sea snail found on the beach is governed by the same measurement ratios of the golden section as the *Modulor* and therefore the male body. Accordingly, the mathematics of nature to be found in the proportions of the sea snail and the body served the Swiss architect in his "self-styling as a poet of architecture"[59].

THE MODULE OF FASCISM

Twentieth-century anthropomorphism is made up not only of attempts at the theoretical legitimization and poetical heightening of rationalist and functionalist architecture; it also acts as a banner for certain ideas about order that result from industrial standardization and the assembly of architectural components as well as the political motives of the time. To finish, I would like to consider the latter connection with the example of the anthropomorphic ideas of Ernst

DAS MASS ALLER DINGE

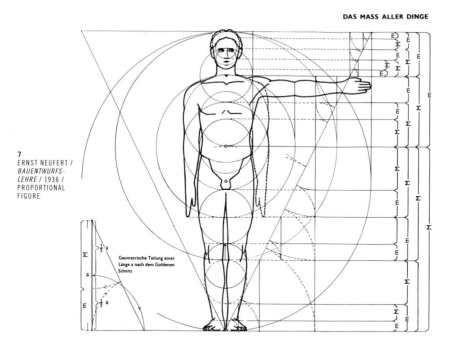

7
ERNST NEUFERT /
*BAUENTWURFS-
LEHRE* / 1936 /
PROPORTIONAL
FIGURE

Geometrische Teilung einer
Länge a nach dem Goldenen
Schnitt

Neufert (1900–1986) mentioned at the beginning, which are a central component of both his *Bauentwurfslehre,* first published in 1936, and his *Bauordnungslehre,* first published in 1943.[60]

Neufert's ideas on the theory of proportion, first stated in 1936, have remained unchanged in all 39 editions of his *Bauentwurfslehre* that have appeared up to the present. Only their position and weight within the book, which has been continuously extended over the years, has been slightly modified. While in the early editions the section "Der Mensch als Maß und Ziel" was a key part of the introduction of the *Bauentwurfslehre*, modern editions have shifted these programmatic remarks to the second chapter, thus slightly weakening their fundamental significance.[61]

Originally, however, Neufert placed the greatest value on the anthropomorphic foundation of his conception of architecture and his ideas about standardization. This is shown, for example, by a previously overlooked prepublication of the *Bauentwurfslehre*.

In the spring of 1935 the section "Der Mensch als Maß und Ziel" had already been published in the *Monatshefte für Baukunst und Städtebau* as a prelude to the later book publication. Already here, the guiding themes are human measurement and the demand for the standardization of all architectural components.[62]

The proportional figure already included as an illustration in the 1935 prepublication as well as in all editions of the *Bauentwurfslehre* (**FIG. 7**) is based largely on the related theories of Albrecht Dürer and supplemented by the measurement system of the golden section. For this, Neufert draws on Adolf Zeising's text *Der Goldene Schnitt* from 1884 as well as more concretely on Ernst Mössel's speculations on the laws of measurement governing earlier architecture, which appeared in 1926 and 1931.[63] Neufert writes the following about Mössel's now outdated theories[64]:

According to Ernst Mössel's extensive and very precise (calculated) investigations, the vast majority of classical buildings can be seen to be based on the Golden Section. The pentagon or pentagram has a natural relation to the Golden Section. However, its special measurement ratios found less use.[65]

These remarks have been omitted from more recent editions of the *Bauentwurfslehre*. Its editors clearly recognized that Mössel's obscure proportional measurements based on the golden section could no longer provide the theoretical grounding for a serious architectural handbook. In the newer editions Mössel's remarks have been replaced by Le Corbusier's *Modulor*.[66] Yet even in current editions numerous diagrams of a broad range of obscure measurement procedures such as the pentagram are presented without in each case an explanation being added.[67]

However, a number of more detailed explanations are found in Neufert's *Bauordnungslehre*. In it he not only takes seriously Le Corbusier's humorous six-foot justification of the *Modulor*,[68] but he also once again advances the proportion series of the golden section, now with the help of racist neologisms, as an eternally valid law of measurement and beauty:

> *Through the natural selection derived continuously over millions of years from his own sense of beauty, man forms himself into an ideal of the beauty that dwells in him [...]. Beyond this, this proportion series seems, in the sense of Greek thought, to represent the general law of nature's germination [allgemeine Sprossungsgesetz der Natur] independent of man and his feelings.*[69]

How elastically one can interpret anthropomorphism and its supposedly 'natural' laws of proportion is also shown by the concrete development of Neufert's anthropomorphic ideas of measurement in the 1930s and 40s. If his 1936 *Bauentwurfslehre* was still largely of a technical nature, in a number of essays as well as in his 1943 *Bauordnungslehre,* he also adds ideological elements that Walter Prigge has recently seen as having a "symbolic relation to the Fascist articulation of body ideals".[70]

In the 1940s, namely, Neufert developed his proportional figure into a special modular system, the so-called *Oktameter.* In doing so, he changed a few concrete measurements of the figure. Man's body height remained the same as that of the proportional figure of 1936 at 175 cm; however, the height of the shoulders increases from 143 to 150 cm. In this way, man as "the measure of all things" becomes more compatible with the module of the *Oktameter* of 12.5 or 125 cm. This module, which is found in the most varied body parts and positions (**FIG. 8**), did not correspond to a 'natural' law of proportion, but to the "system measurement" ("Systemmaß") of brick that was developed at the time as an industrial standard.[71] Furthermore, the *Oktameter* module was also compatible with the 250 cm unit spacing ("Achsmaß/Tafelmaß") that the *Luftwaffe* had initially developed for the construction of aircraft hangars and that was also used in the construction of housing for workers building the *Autobahn,* as well as in timber construction. It eventually became a general construction standard.[72]

In 1943, in his foreword to the *Bauordnungslehre,* the Minister of Armaments and War Production for the Third Reich, Albert Speer, explained the deep political and strategic importance of standardization in the *Oktameter* with the following words: there should now be no "parliamentary discussion" in questions of construction since "total war demands the concentration of all our forces, even in the building industry. Extensive standardization for the economization of technical resources and for the development of rational serial production is the precondition for an increase in output, which is necessary for the accomplishment of our great building tasks"[73]. Neufert himself used a similar choice of words when describing the essence of standardization in the building industry as follows: "[T]he emphasis lies on the identification of corresponding, rational building constructions on the basis of found measurement ratios, as they are required by total war."[74] With these remarks, in retrospect, Speer's and Neufert's ideas about order and the theory of proportion acquire a rather macabre relevance, since on 18 February of the same year, in his famous speech in the Berlin Sportpalast, the Reich Propaganda Minister Joseph Goebbels had used very similar words. His speech peaked in ten rhetorical questions addressed to the mesmerized audience, the most famous of which is still: "Do you want total war? If necessary, do you want a war more total and radical than anything that we can even imagine today?"[75] Neufert himself would not have been indifferent to this question, since already in a 1942 text, "Systematische Baunormung im Aufbruch", he had stated only a little less vigorously that the purpose of the

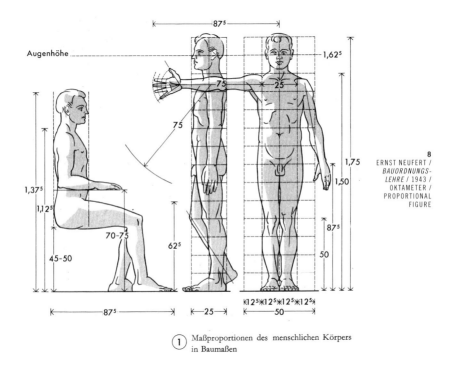

8
ERNST NEUFERT /
*BAUORDNUNGS-
LEHRE* / 1943 /
OKTAMETER /
PROPORTIONAL
FIGURE

(1) Maßproportionen des menschlichen Körpers in Baumaßen

anthropomorphic standardization of the *Oktameter* is "the accomplishment of our enormous tasks in the East".[76]

According to Neufert, the architects of the day, by using standardized numbers, would stand in the great tradition of the ancients.[77] With regard to the concrete numbers used for the aims of standardization, Neufert also employed anti-Semitic undertones, discouraging the use of the number seven since it is used in "many ritual activities, especially in the case of Jews everywhere".[78] Accordingly, in Neufert's *Oktameter,* it was man or his measurement and module that was adapted to the desirable standards, not the other way round.

The standards propagated in those years and their legitimization in laws of measurement stood under the sign of the "enormous construction tasks in the East"[79] and thus in relation to the "Generalplan Ost",[80] which had a racist "Vernichtungskrieg"[81] as its condition, and the conquering of "Lebensraum" in the East as its goal.[82]

Of course, this connection does not discredit the figure of thought of anthropomorphism as such, but it does feed a suspicion that prompts me in conclusion to ask: Was it human measurement that determined architectural design, or was it the real or supposed necessities of design that has determined our idea of human measurement? Rather than man being the measure of all things, was it not rather the things — or, as in the case just treated, the political circumstances — which dictate our idea of human measurement?

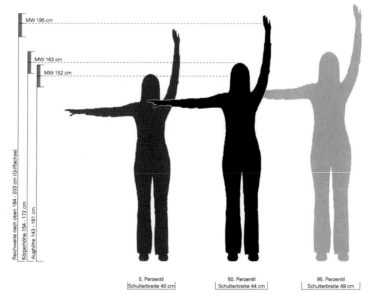

Körpermaße der Frau entsprechend DIN 33402-2, M 1:20
5., 50. (MW = Medianwert) und 95. Perzentil, Altersgruppe 18 bis 65 Jahre

9
PROPORTIONAL
FIGURE / FROM
RAUMPILOT /
2010

MW 195 cm

MW 163 cm

MW 152 cm

Reichweite nach oben 184 - 203 cm (Griffläche)
Körperhöhe 154 - 172 cm
Aughöhe 143 - 161 cm

5. Perzentil
Schulterbreite 40 cm

50. Perzentil
Schulterbreite 44 cm

95. Perzentil
Schulterbreite 49 cm

During the work on the present essay, an architectural handbook has been published under the title *Raumpilot* that may possibly replace Neufert's *Bauentwurfslehre*. Here too, under the heading "Anthropometrie", human measurement forms an important foundation for further considerations on the planning and building of architecture. However, these remarks are now freed of ideological ballast, and human measurement is no longer illustrated with a naked male, ideal and standardized body, but with clothed figures of both sexes (FIGS. 9–10). The selected measurements, without being subjected to an ideological system, consider man or woman — and thus not only the perfect man — in his or her real activities.[83]

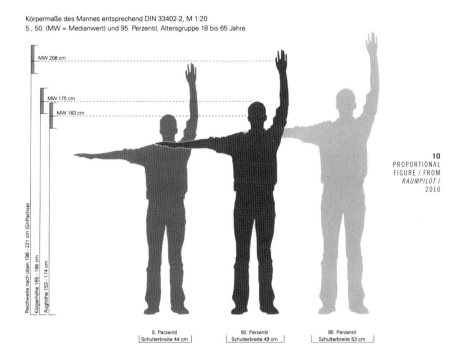

Körpermaße des Mannes entsprechend DIN 33402-2, M 1:20
5., 50. (MW = Medianwert) und 95. Perzentil, Altersgruppe 18 bis 65 Jahre

MW 208 cm
MW 175 cm
MW 163 cm

Reichweite nach oben 196 - 221 cm (Griffachse)
Körperhöhe 165 - 186 cm
Aughöhe 153 - 174 cm

5. Perzentil
Schulterbreite 44 cm

50. Perzentil
Schulterbreite 49 cm

95. Perzentil
Schulterbreite 53 cm

10
PROPORTIONAL
FIGURE / FROM
RAUMPILOT /
2010

This essay relates to my earlier publications on the same theme (see notes 8 and 19). In most cases I have modified my previously published positions and provided updated bibliographic information. The considerations on anthropomorphism oriented to the history of religion as well as the remarks on Ernst Neufert's ideas about order are treated for the first time here.

For their suggestions, I would like to thank Christoph Kleine, Heinz Mürmel, Hubert Seiwert (Leipzig), Martin Behet, Roland Bondzio (Münster and Leipzig) and Christoph Schnoor (Auckland).

1   See *Encyclopædia of Religion and Ethics,* edited by James HASTINGS, 13 VOLS., Edinburgh: T.& T.Clark, 1908–1926, VOL.1, pp.573–578 (F.B.JEVONS) · Stuart Elliott GUTHRIE, *Faces in the Clouds: A New Theory of Religion,* Oxford: Oxford University Press, 1993 · *Die Religion in Geschichte und Gegenwart. Handbuch für Theologie und Religionswissenschaft,* 4th edition, edited by Hans Dieter BETZ, Don S. BROWNING, Bernd JANOWSKI, and Eberhard JÜNGEL, 9 VOLS., Tübingen: Mohr Siebeck, 1998–2007, VOL.1, cols. 525–526 (Gebhard LÖHR) · *Lexikon für Theologie und Kirche,* 3rd edition, edited by Walter KASPER, with Konrad BAUMGARTNER, Horst BÜRKLE, Klaus GANZER, Karl KERTELGE, Wilhelm KORFF, and Peter WALTER, 11 VOLS., Freiburg: Herder, 1993–2001, special edition 2006, VOL.1, cols. 734–737 (Hans-Walter SCHÜTTE).

2   See XENOPHANES (25, fr.15) with his often-quoted remark: "But if horses or oxen or lions had hands or could draw with their hands and accomplish such works as men, horses would draw the figures of the gods as similar to horses, and the oxen as similar to oxen, and they would make the bodies of the sort which each of them had." (XENOPHANES of Colophon, *Fragments. A Text and Translation with a Commentary* by J. H. LESHER, Toronto: University of Toronto Press, 2001). For further sceptical positions regarding anthropomorphism, see Esther J. HAMORI, *"When Gods Were Men". The Embodied God in Biblical and Near Eastern Literature,* Berlin and New York: Walter De Gruyter, 2008, pp.35–64 · Andreas WAGNER, *Gottes Körper. Zur alttestamentlichen Vorstellung der Menschengestaltigkeit Gottes,* Gütersloh: Gütersloher Verlagshaus, 2010, especially pp.43–44.

3   See *Anthropomorphism and Interpretation of the Qur'ān in the Theology of al-Qāsim ibn Ibrāhīm,* edited with translation, introduction and notes by Binyamin ABRAHAMOV, Leiden, New York, and Cologne: E. J. Brill, 1996, pp.1–18 · WAGNER, *Gottes Körper,* pp.41–51 · Othmar KEEL, "Warum im Jerusalemer Tempel kein anthropomorphes Kultbild gestanden haben dürfte", in: *Homo pictor,* edited by Gottfried BOEHM, Munich and Leipzig: K. G. Saur, 2001, pp.244–282 · Angelika BERLEJUNG, *Die Theologie der Bilder. Herstellung und Einweihung von Kultbildern in Mesopotamien und die alttestamentliche Bilderpolemik,* Freiburg (Switzerland): Universitätsverlag | Göttingen: Vandenhoeck & Ruprecht, 1998, pp.3–5, 35–39, 286–288.

4   On this see the case study by Dimitrij BUMAZHNOV, *Der Mensch als Gottes Bild im christlichen Ägypten. Studien zu Gen 1,26 in zwei koptischen Quellen des 4.–5. Jahrhunderts,* Tübingen: Mohr Siebeck, 2006 · In general see also *Historisches Wörterbuch der Philosophie,* edited by Joachim RITTER, Karlfried GRÜNDER, and Gottfried GABRIEL, 13 VOLS., Basel: Schwabe, 1971–2007, VOL. I, cols. 375–378.

5   Ibid.

6 Martin SCHEWE, *Rationalität contra Finalität. Spinozas Anthropomorphismuskritik als Element seiner Methodenlehre,* Frankfurt am Main, Bern, and New York: Peter Lang, 1987, p. 73: „die Unzulänglichkeit von Anthropomorphismen für eine schlüssige Interpretation der Welt" · See also WAGNER, *Gottes Körper,* p. 46.

7 Julian HUXLEY, *Ich sehe den künftigen Menschen. Natur und neuer Humanismus,* Munich: List, 1965 (first in English under the title *Essays of a Humanist,* London: Chatto & Windus, 1964) · See also *Religion in Geschichte und Gegenwart,* col. 524 · WAGNER, *Gottes Körper,* p. 46 · Fritz MAUTHNER, *Wörterbuch der Philosophie. Neue Beiträge zu einer Kritik der Sprache,* 2 VOLS., Munich and Leipzig: Georg Müller, 1910, VOL. 1, p. 26, and VOL. 2, p. 91.

8 See Paul von NAREDI-RAINER, *Architektur und Harmonie. Zahl, Maß und Proportion in der abendländischen Baukunst,* Cologne: DuMont, 1982 · Frank ZÖLLNER, *Vitruvs Proportionsfigur. Quellenkritische Studien zur Kunstliteratur des 15. und 16. Jahrhunderts,* Worms: Wernersche Verlagsgesellschaft, 1987 · John ONIANS, *Bearers of Meaning. The Classical Orders in Antiquity, the Middle Ages and the Renaissance,* Princeton: Princeton University Press, 1988, pp. 162–165 and passim · Bruno REUDENBACH, "Die Gemeinschaft als Körper und Gebäude. Francesco di Giorgios Stadttheorie und die Visualisierung von Sozialmetaphern im Mittelalter", in: *Gepeinigt, begehrt, vergessen. Symbolik und Sozialbezug des Körpers im späten Mittelalter und in der frühen Neuzeit,* edited by Klaus SCHREINER and Norbert SCHNITZLER, Munich: Wilhelm Fink, 1992, pp. 171–198 · Joseph RYKWERT, *The Dancing Column. On Order in Architecture,* Cambridge, MA and London: The MIT Press, 1996 · Marcus FRINGS, *Mensch und Maß. Anthropomorphe Elemente in der Architekturtheorie des Quattrocento,* Weimar: VDG, 1998 · Ivan MUCHKA, "Anthropomorphismus in der Architektur um 1600", in: *Rudolf II, Prague and the World,* edited by Lubomír KONEČNÝ, Beket BUKOVINSKÁ, and Ivan MUCHKA, Prague: Artefactum, 1998, pp. 57–63 · *Body and Building. Essays on the Changing Relation of Body and Architecture,* edited by George DODDS and Robert TAVERNOR, Cambridge, MA and London: The MIT Press, 2002 · Frank ZÖLLNER, "Anthropomorphismus. Das Maß des Menschen in der Architektur von Vitruv bis Le Corbusier", in: *Ist der Mensch das Maß aller Dinge? Beiträge zur Aktualität des Protagoras,* edited by Otto NEUMAIER, Möhnesee: Bibliopolis, 2004, pp. 306–344 · Annette HOMAN, *Spielräume des Glaubens. Anthropomorphismus in der Architekturtheorie und die Umwandlung von St. Maximin in Trier,* Berlin: wvb Wissenschaftlicher Verlag Berlin, 2005, pp. 77–96 (overview).

9 On Vitruvius and his reception, see Lucia A. CIAPPONI, "Vitruvius", in: *Catalogus Translationum et Commentariorum: Mediaeval and Renaissance Latin Translations and Commentaries. Annotated Lists and Guides,* 9 VOLS. (so far), Washington, DC: Catholic University of America Press, 1960–, here VOL. 3, 1976, edited by F. Edward CRANZ in association with Paul Oskar KRISTELLER, pp. 399–401 · Georg GERMANN, *Einführung in die Geschichte der Architekturtheorie,* Darmstadt: Wissenschaftliche Buchgesellschaft, 1980 · L. CALLEBAT, P. BOUET, Ph. FLEURY, and M. ZUINGHEDAU, *Vitruve. De architectura. Concordance. Documentation bibliographique, lexicale et grammaticale,* 2 VOLS., Hildesheim, Zurich, and New York: Olms-Weidmann, 1984 · Heiner KNELL, *Vitruvs Architekturtheorie. Versuch einer Interpretation,* Darmstadt: Wissenschaftliche Buchgesellschaft, 1985 · Pier Nicola PAGLIARA, "Vitruvio da testo a canone", in: *Memoria dell'antico nell'arte italiana,* edited by Salvatore SETTIS, 3 VOLS., Turin: Giulio Einaudi, 1984–1986, VOL. 3, pp. 3–85 · FRINGS, *Mensch und Maß,* pp. 19–23.

10 Vitruvius, *De architectura*, II.pref.

11 Ibid., IV.1,6. On this see Onians, *Bearers of Meaning*.

12 "Aedium compositio constat ex symmetria, cuius rationem diligentissime architecti tenere debent. Ea autem paritur a proportione, quae graece αναλογια dicitur. Proportio est ratae partis membrorum in omni opere totoque commodulatio, ex qua ratio efficitur symmetriarum. Namque non potest aedi ulla sine symmetria atque proportione rationem habere compositionis, nisi uti [ad] hominis bene figurati membrorum habuerit exactam rationem." Vitruvius, *De architectura libri decem*, translated and annotated by Curt Fensterbusch, Darmstadt: Wissenschaftliche Buchgesellschaft, 1981, III.1 (p.136). On this see also Zöllner, *Vitruvs Proportionsfigur*, passim · *Vitruve*, edited by Pierre Gros, pp.55–78 · Giacomo Berra, "La storia dei canoni proporzionali del corpo umano e gli sviluppi in area Lombarda alla fine del Quattrocento", in: *Raccolta Vinciana*, VOL.25, 1993, pp.159–310 · Frings, *Mensch und Maß*, pp.19–56 · Burkhardt Wesenberg, "Vitruv und Leonardo in Salamis. Vitruvs Proportionsfigur und die metrologischen Reliefs", in: *Jahrbuch des Deutschen Archäologischen Instituts*, VOL.116, 2001 (published 2002), pp.357–380 · Indra Kagis McEwen, *Vitruvius. Writing the Body of Architecture*, Cambridge, MA and London: The MIT Press, 2003.

13 Vitruvius, *De architectura*, III.1,3: "Item corporis centrum medium naturaliter est umbilicus. Namque si homo conlocatus fuerit supinus manibus et pedibus pansis circinique conlocatum centrum in umbilico eius, circumagendo rotundationem utrarumque manuum et pedum digiti linea tangentur. Non minus quemadmodum schema rotundationis in copore efficitur, item quadrata designatio in eo invenietur. Nam si a pedibus imis ad summum caput mensum erit eaque mensura relata fuerit ad manus pansas, invenietur eadem latitudo uti altitudo, quemadmodum areae, quae ad normam sunt quadratae."

14 Rudolf Wittkower, *Architectural Principles in the Age of Humanism*, London: The Warburg Institute, University of London, 1949. On Rudolf Wittkower see *Klassiker der Kunstgeschichte*, edited by Ulrich Pfisterer, 2 VOLS., Munich 2008, VOL. 2, pp.107–123 (Alina Payne).

15 Zöllner, *Vitruvs Proportionsfigur*. On this thesis, see also the reviews in the *Newsletter of the Society of Architectural Historians of Great Britain* (Winter 1988, by John Onians), the *Archiv für Kulturgeschichte* (VOL.71, 1989, pp.511–513, by Günter Binding), and in the *Journal of the Society of Architectural Historians* (VOL.52, 1993, pp.359–360, by Carolyn Kolb, and my response, ibid., VOL.53, 1994, p.377).

16 On possible exceptions to this rule, see for example Suzanne Preston Blier, "Houses Are Human. Architectural Self-images of Africa's Tamberma", in: *Journal of the Society of Architectural Historians*, VOL.42, 1983, pp.371–382 · Jan Pieper, "Häuser des Narziß. Architektur nach des Menschen Bild und Gleichnis | Houses of Narcissus. Architecture According to the Image of Man", in: *Daidalos*, no.45, 1992, pp.30–47 · Günther Feuerstein, *Biomorphic Architecture*, Stuttgart and London: Axel Menges, 2002, with 2 supplements published as *Zoon. Anthropomorphes Bauen. Architektur als Wesen*, Vienna: Grafisches Zentrum HTU, 2003 and 2004.

17 Vitruvius, *De architectura*, I.2,4; III.1,1–9; II.3,3; III.1,7; VI.8,9 · On ancient metrology see Friedrich Hultsch, *Griechische und römische Metrologie*, second edition, Berlin: Weidmannsche Buchhandlung, 1882, pp.30–74 · Eivind Lorenzen, *Technological Studies in Ancient Metrology*, Copenhagen: Nyt Nordisk Forlag, 1966 · Thomas Thieme, "Metrology and Planning in the Basilica of Johannes Stoudios", in: *Le Dessin d'architecture dans les sociétés antiques. Actes du colloque de Straßbourg 26-27 January 1984,* Leiden: E. J. Brill, 1985, pp. 291–308 · Eric FERNIE, "Historical Metrology and Architectural History", in: *Art History,* VOL. 1, 1978, pp. 383–399 · ZÖLLNER, *Vitruvs Proportionsfigur,* pp. 23–43 · VITRUVE, *L'architecture,* ed. GROS, VOL. 3, pp. 55–78 · WESENBERG, *Vitruv und Leonardo.*

18 WESENBERG, *Vitruv und Leonardo.*

19 ZÖLLNER, *Anthropomorphismus* · Frank ZÖLLNER, "Vitruvs Proportionsfigur. Eine Metapher für Maß und Geometrie", in: *Entwerfen. Architektenausbildung in Europa von Vitruv bis Mitte des 20. Jahrhunderts,* edited by Ralph JOHANNES, Hamburg: Junius, 2009, pp. 145–161.

20 VITRUVIUS, *De architectura,* 1.2, 4 and III.1, 5–8.

21 Ernst NEUFERT, *Bauentwurfslehre. Grundlagen, Normen, Vorschriften über Anlage, Bau, Gestaltung, Raumbedarf, Raumbeziehungen, Maße für Gebäude, Räume, Einrichtungen, Geräte; mit dem Menschen als Maß und Ziel. Handbuch für den Baufachmann, Bauherrn, Lehrenden und Lernenden,* weitergeführt von Peter NEUFERT und der PLANUNGS-AG NEUFERT MITTMANN GRAF, 33rd, completely revised and redesigned edition, Braunschweig and Wiesbaden: Friedr. Vieweg & Sohn, 1992. The 39th German edition was published in 2009 on behalf of the newly founded Neufert-Stiftung · Quoted after: Ernst and Peter NEUFERT, *Architects' Data,* 3rd edition, edited by Bousmaha BAICHE and Nicholas WALLIMAN, Oxford: Blackwell Science, 2000, p. 1 · On Neufert and his *Bauentwurfslehre* see Gernot WECKERLIN, "Die Angst des Architekten vor dem leeren Blatt. Architekturhandbücher als Medien im künstlerischen Prozess", in: *Imaginäre Architekturen. Raum und Stadt als Vorstellung,* edited by Annette GEIGER, Stefanie HENNECKE, and Christin KEMPF, Berlin: Dietrich Reimer, 2006, pp. 102–119, esp. p. 111 (on the numerous editions of the *Bauentwurfslehre*).

22 NEUFERT, *Bauentwurfslehre,* 1992, p. 24: „Noch heute haben wir einen besseren Begriff von der Größe einer Sache, wenn wir erfahren: sie war soviel Mann hoch, soviel Ellen lang, um soviel Fuß breiter oder soviel Köpfe größer. Das sind Begriffe, die uns angeboren sind, deren Größe uns sozusagen im Blute liegt. Das Metermaß hat dem allen aber ein Ende gemacht."

23 See for example the source material in Victor MORTET, *Recueil de textes relatifs à l'histoire de l'architecture et à la condition des architectes en France en Moyen Age,* 2 VOLS., Paris: Alphonse Picard et fils, 1911–1929, VOL. 1, pp. 157–161 and VOL. 2, pp. 183–188 · Hans LIEBESCHÜTZ, *Das allegorische Weltbild der heiligen Hildegard von Bingen,* Leipzig and Berlin: B. G. Teubner, 1930, pp. 31–34 · Günter BANDMANN, *Mittelalterliche Architektur als Bedeutungsträger,* Berlin: Gebr. Mann, 1951, p. 65 · See also Bruno REUDENBACH, "In mensuram humani corporis. Zur Herkunft der Auslegung und Illustration von Vitruv III.1 im 15. und 16. Jahrhundert", in: *Text und Bild. Aspekte des Zusammenwirkens zweier Künste in Mittelalter und früher Neuzeit,* edited by Christel MEIER and Uwe RUBERG, Wiesbaden: Ludwig Reichert, 1980, pp. 651–688, 675–676 · FRINGS, *Mensch und Maß,* pp. 57–62.

24 See MORTET, *Recueil,* VOL. 1, pp. 159–160 note 3. The argumentation of these and the following remarks follows in large part ZÖLLNER, *Vitruvs Proportionsfigur,* pp. 44–76.

25 Francesco DI GIORGIO MARTINI, *Trattati di architettura ingegneria e arte militare,* edited by Corrado MALTESE, 2 VOLS., Milan: Il Polifilo, 1967, VOL. 1, p. 20. See Lawrence LOWIC, "The Meaning and Significance of the Human Analogy in Francesco di Giorgio's Trattato", in: *Journal of* *the Society of Architectural Historians,* VOL. 42, 1983, pp. 360–370 · ZÖLLNER, *Vitruvs Proportionsfigur,* pp. 72–76 · REUDENBACH, "Gemeinschaft als Körper und Gebäude", pp. 171–176 · Francesco Paolo FIORE and Manfredo TAFURI, *Francesco di Giorgio architetto,* Milan: Electa, 1993, no. XX.4, pp. 363–365 · FRINGS, *Mensch und Maß,* pp. 199–287.

26 Lorenzo GHIBERTI, *Denkwürdigkeiten (I Commentarii),* edited by Julius von SCHLOSSER, 2 VOLS., Berlin: Julius Bard, 1912, VOL. 1, pp. 227–231, esp. p. 228 · Klaus BERGDOLT, *Der dritte Kommentar Lorenzo Ghibertis,* Berlin: VCH, 1988, pp. 550–554, 562–568, and XXXI–XXXII, LXI, LXVII, LXXVI–LXXVII, XCI–XCIV.

27 Antonio AVERLINO detto IL FILARETE, *Trattato di architettura,* edited by Anna Maria FINOLI and Liliana GRASSI, 2 VOLS., Milan: Il Polifilo, 1972, VOL. 1, pp. 20, 21, and 18 (fols. 3v–4r and 6r) · FRINGS, *Mensch und Maß,* pp. 153–198.

28 *The Literary Works of Leonardo da Vinci,* edited by Jean Paul RICHTER, 2 VOLS., third edition, London: Phaidon, 1970 (first edition: London: Sampson Low, Marston, Searle & Rivington, 1883), VOL. 2, § 1347A (i. e. Codex Atlanticus, fol. 270r [new count 730r]).

29 Richard SCHOFIELD, "Amadeo, Bramante and Leonardo and the 'tiburio' of Milan Cathedral", in: *Achademia Leonardi Vinci. Journal of Leonardo Studies,* VOL. 2, 1989, pp. 68–100.

30 Cesare CESARIANO, *Di Lucio Vitruvio Pollione de Architectura Libri Dece traducti de latino in Vulgare [...],* Como: Gotardus de Ponte, 1521, fols. 48r–50v.

31 Ibid., fols. 91v–92r. See also Carol Herselle KRINSKY, *Cesare Cesariano and the Como Vitruvius Edition of 1521,* Ph.D. Thesis, New York University, 1965 (Ann Arbor: University Microfilms, 1965), pp. 297–300 · Paolo VERZONE, "Cesare Cesariano", in: *Arte Lombarda,* VOL. 16, 1971, pp. 203–210.

32 CESARIANO, *Vitruvio,* fols. 48v and 143.

33 Leon Battista ALBERTI, *De re aedificatoria,* Florence: Nicolaus Laurentius Alamanus, 1485, used in the edition of Max THEUER, Wien and Leipzig: Heller, 1912, 9.5–6 (musical harmony) and 7.5 (anthropomorphism). See also Peter Hugh SCHOFIELD, *The Theory of Proportion in Architecture,* Cambridge: Cambridge University Press, 1958, p. 57 · *Leon Battista Alberti,* edited by Joseph RYKWERT and Anne ENGEL, Milan: Electa, 1994, pp. 292–299 (Paul von NAREDI-RAINER) and pp. 300–315 (Robert TAVERNOR).

34 Andrea PALLADIO, *I Qvattro libri dell'architettvra,* Venice: Dominico de' Franceschi, 1570, pp. 6 (1.1, anthropomorphism). On the problem of the proportional system in Palladio see WITTKOWER, *Architectural Principles,* pp. 110–124 · Deborah HOWARD and Malcolm LONGAIR, "Harmonic Proportion and Palladio's *Quattro Libri*", in: *Journal of the Society of Architectural Historians,* VOL. 41, 1982, pp. 116–143 · Branko MITROVIĆ, "Palladio's Theory of Proportions and the Second Book of the *Quattro Libri dell'Architettura*", in: *Journal of the Society of Architectural Historians,* VOL. 49, 1990, pp. 279–292.

35 See Antonio FOSCARI and Manfredo TAFURI, *L'armonia e i conflitti. La chiesa di San Francesco della Vigna nella Venezia del '500,* Turin: Giulio Einaudi, 1983, pp. 208–209.

36 Daniele BARBARO, *I dieci libri dell'architettvra di M. Vitrvvio. Tradotti & commentati [...],* Venice: Francesco de' Franceschi & Giouanni Chrieger, 1567 (reprint, edited by Manfredo TAFURI and Manuela MORRESI, Milan: Il Polifilo, 1987), pp. 96–108 · See Diego Horacio FEINSTEIN, *Der Harmoniebegriff in der Kunstliteratur und Musiktheorie der italienischen Renaissance,* Ph.D. Thesis, Universität Freiburg, 1977, pp. 135–143 · ZÖLLNER, *Vitruvs Proportionsfigur,* pp. 155–169 · On

Daniele Barbaro see also Manfredo Tafuri, *Venezia e il Rinascimento,* Turin: Giulio Einaudi, 1985, pp. 179–198.

37 Howard and Longair, "Harmonic Proportion and Palladio's *Quattro Libri*".

38 Wittkower, *Architectural Principles,* pp. 110–124.

39 Claude Perrault, *Les dix livres d'architecture de Vitruve,* second, revised edition, Paris: Jean Baptiste Coignard, 1684 · See Wolfgang Herrmann, *The Theory of Claude Perrault,* London: A. Zwemmer, 1973 · Antoine Picon, *Claude Perrault, 1613–1688, ou la curiosité d'un classique,* Paris: Picard, 1988, pp. 115–135 · Henry Millon, "The French Academy of Architecture. Foundation and Program", in: *The French Academy. Classicism and its Antagonists,* edited by June Hargrove, Newark: University of Delaware Press | London and Cranbury, New Jersey: Associated University Presses, 1990, pp. 68–77.

40 Perrault, *Les dix livres d'architecture de Vitruve,* pp. 104–105; see also ibid., p. 11 · On Perrault and his theory see also Schofield, *Theory of Proportion in Architecture,* pp. 27–73 · Walter Kambartel, *Symmetrie und Schönheit. Über mögliche Voraussetzungen neueren Kunstbewußtseins in der Architekturtheorie Claude Perraults,* Munich: Wilhelm Fink, 1972 · Alberto Pérez-Gómez, *Architecture and the Crisis of Modern Science,* Cambridge, MA and London: The MIT Press, 1983, pp. 32–39.

41 Pérez-Gómez, *Architecture and the Crisis of Modern Science,* pp. 39–47 · Hanno Walter Kruft, *Geschichte der Architekturtheorie. Von der Antike bis zur Gegenwart,* 4th edition, Munich: C. H. Beck, 1995, pp. 148–150.

42 On this see Schofield, *Theory of Proportion in Architecture,* pp. 76–80.

43 *L'architettura di M. Vitruvio Pollione,* translated with comment by Berardo Galiani, Naples: Stamperia Simoniana, 1758, p. 94 and plate 4 · Pietro Cataneo, *I qvattro primi libri di architettvra,* Venice: Aldus [Manutius], 1554, fol. 35, and idem, *L'architettvra di Pietro Cataneo,* Venice: Aldus [Manutius], 1567, pp. 75–76.

44 See for example Joseph Gwilt, *An Encyclopædia of Architecture. Historical, Theoretical and Practical,* a new edition, revised, with alterations and considerable additions by Wyatt Papworth, London: Longmans, Green, and Co., 1867; reprint 1982 (New York: Bonanza Books), pp. 796 and 802 · Kruft, *Geschichte der Architekturtheorie,* p. 328.

45 J. N. L. [Jean-Nicolas-Louis] Durand, *Précis de leçons d'architecture données à l'Ecole Royale Polytechnique,* Paris: chez l'auteur, a l'École Royale Polytechnique, 1817–1819, pp. 8–14 and p. 5 (first edition: *Précis des leçons d'architecture données à l'Ecole polytechnique,* 2 vols., Paris: chez l'auteur, a l'École Polytechnique, an x [1802] and an xiii [1805]).

46 Eugène Emmanuel Viollet-le-Duc, *Dictionnaire raisonné de l'architecture française du xie au xvie siècle,* 10 vols., Paris: Librairies-Imprimeries Réunies, 1854–1868, vol. 7, p. 534 · Auguste Choisy, *Histoire de l'architecture,* 2 vols., Paris: Gauthier-Villars, 1899, vol. 2, p. 764, after Kruft, *Geschichte der Architekturtheorie,* pp. 323 and 328.

47 Schofield, *Theory of Proportion in Architecture,* pp. 76–80 · Heinz Bienefeld, "Bedeutung und Verlust des Schönen in der Kunst. Proportion und Material als Wesensmerkmale der Architektur", in: *Das Münster,* vol. 46, 1993, pp. 115–118.

48 See for example Edward Cresy, "Principles of Proportion", in: Gwilt, *An Encyclopædia of Architecture,* p. 766.

49 Le Corbusier, *Der Modulor*, VOL.1: *Darstellung eines in Architektur und Technik allgemein anwendbaren harmonischen Maßes im menschlichen Maßstab*, 5th edition (reprint of second edition 1956), Stuttgart: Deutsche Verlagsanstalt, 1985, pp.115–117 (first German edition: Stuttgart: Cotta, 1953; original French edition: *Le Modulor. Essai sur une mesure harmonique à l'échelle humaine applicable universellement à l'architecture et à la mécanique*, Boulogne-sur-Seine: Éditions de l'Architecture d'Aujourd'hui, 1950) · See Stanislaus von Moos, *Le Corbusier. Elemente einer Synthese*, Frauenfeld and Stuttgart: Huber, 1968, pp.398–406 · Kruft, *Geschichte der Architekturtheorie*, pp.328 and 463–464 · Le Corbusier, *Une Encyclopédie*, Paris: Centre Georges Pompidou, 1987, pp.259–261 · On the first variations, see also Le Corbusier, *Sketchbooks*, 4 VOLS., New York: Architectural History Foundation | Cambridge, MA and London: The MIT Press, 1981–1982, VOL.2: *1950–1954*, 1981, passim · On the reception see Eva-Marie Neumann, "Architectural Proportion in Britain 1945–1957", in: *Architectural History*, VOL.36, 1996, pp.197–221.

50 On the genesis of the Modulor, see the essay by Christoph Schnoor in this volume.

51 Eckhard Leuschner, "Wie die Faschisten sich Leonardo unter den Nagel rissen. Eine architekturgeschichtliche Station auf dem Weg des 'Vitruvianischen Menschen' zum populären Bild", in: *Beständig im Wandel. Innovationen — Verwandlungen — Konkretisierungen. Festschrift für Karl Möseneder zum 60. Geburtstag*, edited by Christian Hecht, Berlin: Matthes & Seitz, 2009, pp.425–440, esp. pp.431–433.

52 Le Corbusier, *Le Modulor*.

53 Le Corbusier, *Der Modulor*, pp.36 and 176.

54 Ibid., pp.36–68.

55 Ibid., p.56.

56 On this see Niklas Maak, *Der Architekt am Strand. Le Corbusier und das Geheimnis der Seeschnecke*, Munich: Carl Hanser, 2010, p.127.

57 Le Corbusier, *Der Modulor*, pp.19, 20, 223, and 33.

58 Ernst Bloch, *Das Prinzip Hoffnung*, 3 VOLS., Frankfurt am Main: Suhrkamp, 1974 (first edition: 1959), VOL.2, pp.858–863, esp. p.861 with a critique of Le Corbusier.

59 Maak, *Der Architekt am Strand*, p.127.

60 On Neufert in general and on his *Bauentwurfslehre* see Anka Ghise-Beer, *Das Werk des Architekten Peter Neufert. Ein Beitrag zu Entwicklungstendenzen in der Architektur der ersten Nachkriegsjahrzehnte*, Ph.D. Thesis, Universität Wuppertal, 2000, pp.17–21. See also the literature quoted below in notes 66 and 70–72.

61 Ernst Neufert, *Bauentwurfslehre. Grundlagen, Normen und Vorschriften. Handbuch für den Baufachmann, Bauherrn, Lehrenden und Lernenden*, Munich: Bauwelt-Verlag, 1936, p.6; idem, *Bauentwurfslehre*, 1992, pp.24–25. On the history of the editions see ibid., p.IV. Not until the 30th edition from 1979 was the *Bauentwurfslehre* "significantly" revised and "significantly" expanded (still by Ernst himself), as was the 33rd edition from 1992.

62 Ernst Neufert, "Der Mensch als Maß und Ziel", in: *Monatshefte für Baukunst und Städtebau* (Bauweltverlag Berlin), VOL.19, no.5, 1935, appendix: "Bauwelt-Tafeln" with the subtitle "Neufert Entwurfslehre" and with the proportional figure as a signet on each plate (these plates were added to the *Monatshefte für Baukunst und Städtebau*, which appeared until 1942, up to the 23rd issue in 1939). The title *Bauentwurfslehre* used from 1936 onward appears for the first time in an announcement at the end of the journal, ibid., VOL. 20, no. 6, 1936: "Neufert. Bauentwurfslehre. Handbuch für den Baufachmann, Bauherrn, Lehrenden und Lernenden. 267 Tafeln mit 3600 Zeichnungen".

63 Ernst MOESSEL, *Die Proportion in Antike und Mittelalter,* Munich: C. H. Beck, 1926; idem, *Urformen des Raumes als Grundlagen der Formgestaltung,* Munich: C. H. Beck, 1931.

64 On this see Konrad HECHT, *Maß und Zahl in der gotischen Baukunst,* 3 parts in a single volume, Hildesheim and New York: Georg Olms, 1979.

65 NEUFERT, *Bauentwurfslehre,* 1936, p. 39: „Nach den eingehenden und sehr genauen (rechnerischen) Untersuchungen von Ernst Moessel lassen sich weitaus die meisten klassischen Bauten nach dem Goldenen Schnitt bestimmen. Das Fünfeck oder Pentagram (Drudenfuß) hat natürliche Beziehungen zum Goldenen Schnitt. Seine besonderen Maßverhältnisse fanden aber weniger Verwendung."

66 On Ernst Neufert and Le Corbusier see Thilo HILPERT, "Menschenzeichen. Ernst Neufert und Le Corbusier", in: *Ernst Neufert. Normierte Baukultur im 20. Jahrhundert,* edited by Walter PRIGGE, Frankfurt and New York: Campus, 1999, pp. 131–143.

67 See the section on "Maßverhältnisse" in: NEUFERT, *Bauentwurfslehre,* 1992, pp. 34–37: "Grundlagen" (pp. 34–35), "Anwendung" (p. 36), and "Anwendung Modulor" (p. 37).

68 Ernst NEUFERT, *Bauordnungslehre. Handbuch für rationelles Bauen nach geregeltem Maß,* third edition, Wiesbaden and Berlin: Bauverlag, 1965, p. 36: Le Corbusier's "beautiful man", the "police constable", "always" measures six foot.

69 Ernst NEUFERT, *Bauordnungslehre,* edited by the Generalbauinspektor für die Reichshauptstadt Reichsminister Albert SPEER, Berlin, Amsterdam, Prague, and Vienna: Volk und Reich Verlag, 1943, pp. 44 and 46: „Durch diese über Millionen Jahre immer wieder aus dem eigenen Schönheitsempfinden heraus geleitete Zuchtwahl bildet sich der Mensch selbst zu dem in ihm wohnenden Schönheitsideal heran [...]. Darüber hinaus scheint diese Proportionsreihe im Sinne griechischen Denkens das vom Menschen und seinem Empfinden unabhängige, allgemeine Sprossungsgesetz der Natur überhaupt darzustellen." · NEUFERT, *Bauordnungslehre,* 1965, p. 41. This section was changed in the new edition from 1965; however, the quoted remarks and the racist vocabulary (natural selection, law of germination) remain the same in both editions.

70 Walter PRIGGE, "Zwischen bauhaus und BAUHAUS", in: *Ernst Neufert,* ed. PRIGGE, pp. 7–13, here p. 12 · On this see in general also LEUSCHNER, "Wie die Faschisten sich Leonardo unter den Nagel rissen".

71 Ernst NEUFERT, "Das Oktameter-System", in: *Der Soziale Wohnungsbau in Deutschland,* VOL. 1, 1941, pp. 453–465 · Gerd KUHN, "Die Spur der Steine. Über die Normierung des Ziegelsteins, das Oktametersystem und den Maßstab Mensch", in: *Ernst Neufert,* ed. PRIGGE, pp. 335–357. On the brick measurement see also NEUFERT, *Bauentwurfslehre,* 1992, pp. 53–55.

72 Ernst NEUFERT, "Baunormung als Ganzheit", in: *Die Bauindustrie,* VOL. 9, 1941, pp. 1377–1386 · *Wohn- und Tagesunterkünfte für Bauarbeiter nach den Richtlinien der Deutschen Arbeitsfront.* Vorwort von Reichshauptamtsleiter Albert Speer (*Schriftenreihe des "Amtes für Schönheit der Arbeit",* VOL. 10), Berlin: Verlag der deutschen Arbeitsfront, 1940 · Wolfgang VOIGT, "Triumph der Gleichform und des Zusammenpassens. Ernst Neufert und die Normierung in der Architektur", in: *Bauhaus-Moderne im Nationalsozialismus. Zwischen Anbiederung und Verfolgung,* edited by Winfried NERDINGER, Munich: Prestel, 1993, pp. 179–193.

73 Albert SPEER, "Vorwort", in: NEUFERT, *Bauordnungslehre*, 1943, p.3: „der totale Krieg zwingt zur Konzentration aller Kräfte auch im Bauwesen. Weitgehende Vereinheitlichung zur Einsparung technischer Kräfte und zum Aufbau rationeller Serienfertigung ist die Voraussetzung zu einer Leistungssteigerung, die zur Bewältigung unserer grossen Bauaufgaben erforderlich ist [...]".

74 Ibid., p.11: „der Schwerpunkt liegt auf der Herausarbeitung entsprechender, rationeller Baukonstruktionen auf den gefundenen Maßbeziehungen, wie sie der totale Krieg erfordert." · See also Ernst NEUFERT, "Die Pläne zum Kriegseinheitstyp", in: *Der Wohnungsbau in Deutschland*, VOL.3, 1943, pp.233–240, here p.233: „Der totale Krieg fordert gebieterisch die Beschränkung unserer Lebensbedürfnisse auf das unbedingt Notwendige."

75 Iring FETSCHER, *Joseph Goebbels im Berliner Sportpalast 1943: "Wollt ihr den totalen Krieg?"*, Hamburg: Europäische Verlagsanstalt, 1998, pp.63–98, here p.95: „Wollt ihr den totalen Krieg? Wollt ihr ihn, wenn nötig, totaler und radikaler, als wir ihn uns heute überhaupt erst vorstellen können?" — On the preparations for "total war" from 1937 on, see also Joachim C. FEST, *Hitler*, 2 VOLS., Frankfurt am Main, Berlin, and Wien: Ullstein, 1978, VOL.2: *Der Führer*, pp.739 and 924 (first edition as *Hitler. Eine Biographie*, 1 VOL., Berlin: Propyläen, 1973).

76 Ernst NEUFERT, "Systematische Baunormung im Aufbruch", in: *Der deutsche Baumeister*, VOL.4, 1942, no.12, pp.9–12, here p.11: „für die Bewältigung der gewaltigen Aufgaben im Osten". — *Der Deutsche Baumeister* was a National Socialist journal.

77 Ibid., p.12. On Fascism's relation to antique culture see Klaus WOLBERT, *Die Nackten und die Toten des "Dritten Reiches"*, Gießen: Anabas, 1982, p.66 and passim · See also Daniel ZAIDAN, *Bildende Künste im Dritten Reich. Eine kritische Auseinandersetzung mit einem vernachlässigten Kapitel deutscher Kunstgeschichte*, Hamburg: Diplomica, 2008, which (p.55) rightly speaks of an imagined "parallel ethos between National Socialism and antiquity". See for example also Friedrich PAULSEN, "Ostgermanischer Holzbau", in: *Monatshefte für Baukunst und Städtebau*, VOL.20, 1936, pp.365–368, here p.368: "The Greek temple and eastern Indo-Germanic timber construction are based on the same racial laws of formation." [„Der griechische Tempel und der indogermanische Holzbau des Ostens unterliegen ein und denselben rassischen Bildungsgesetzen."] (It was in this journal in 1935 that Neufert first published his "Bauentwurfslehre", see above).

78 NEUFERT, *Bauordnungslehre*, 1943, p.31: „bei vielen kultischen Handlungen, vor allem bei Juden überall".

79 On this see additional articles in the journal *Der deutsche Baumeister* from 1942. Besides technical articles and National Socialist themes (see for example Adolf Hitler's motto for the 10th issue) the journal as a whole contains numerous comments on the "Osteinsatz"; see esp. Erich BÖCKLER, "Der Osten als Bauaufgabe" in VOL.4, 1942, no.5, pp.1–8.

80 *Der "Generalplan Ost". Hauptlinien der nationalsozialistischen Vernichtungspolitik*, edited by Mechthild RÖSSLER and Sabine SCHLEIERMACHER, Berlin: Akademie-Verlag, 1993 · Bruno WASSER, *Himmlers Raumplanung im Osten. Der Generalplan Ost in Polen 1940-1944*, Basel, Berlin, and Boston: Birkhäuser, 1993 · Isabel HEINEMANN, *"Rasse, Siedlung, deutsches Blut". Das Rasse- und Siedlungshauptamt der SS und die rassenpolitische Neuordnung Europas*, Göttingen: Wallstein, 2003, pp.359–381.

81 With this term I refer to the so-called "Wehrmachtsausstellung" ("Vernichtungskrieg. Verbrechen der Wehrmacht 1941-1944" [1st exhibition 1995-1999, 2nd revised exhibition 2001-2004]) of the Hamburg Institut für Sozialforschung; on this see the overview by Wiebke GRÖSCHLER, *Der Wandel eines Täterbilds. Von der ersten zur zweiten "Wehrmachtsausstellung"*, Cologne: PapyRossa, 2008.

82 On this see FEST, *Hitler*, pp. 933–939.

83 Thomas JOCHER and Sigrid LOCH, *Raumpilot. Grundlagen*, edited by the WÜSTENROT STIFTUNG, Stuttgart and Zürich: Karl Krämer, 2010, pp. 11–30. I am grateful to Roland Bondzio for the information.

IMAGES

Cesare CESARIANO, *Di Lucio Vitruvio Pollione de Architectura Libri Dece traducti de latino in Vulgare [...]*, Como: Gotardus de Ponte, 1521, fol. 49r: FIG. 1 and fol. 50r: FIG. 2 · Frank Zöllner: FIG. 3 · Pietro CATANEO, *L'architettvra di Pietro Cataneo*, Venice: Aldus [Manutius], 1567, p. 76: FIG. 4 · *Le Modulor*, Boulogne-sur-Seine: Éditions de l'Architecture d'Aujourd'hui, 1950: FIG. 5 and FIG. 6 (© FLC/VG Bild-Kunst, Bonn 2014; FIG. 6 with reconstruction by Frank Zöllner) · Ernst NEUFERT, *Bauentwurfslehre. Grundlagen, Normen und Vorschriften. Handbuch für den Baufachmann, Bauherrn, Lehrenden und Lernenden*, Munich: Bauwelt-Verlag, 1936: FIG. 7 · Ernst NEUFERT, *Bauordnungslehre*, edited by the Generalbauinspektor für die Reichshauptstadt Reichsminister Albert SPEER, Berlin, Amsterdam, Prague, and Vienna: Volk und Reich Verlag, 1943: FIG. 8 · Thomas JOCHER and Sigrid LOCH, *Raumpilot. Grundlagen*, edited by the WÜSTENROT STIFTUNG, Stuttgart and Zürich: Karl Krämer, 2010: FIG. 9 and FIG. 10

1
REBECCA HORN /
MESSKASTEN /
1970 /
STAATSGALERIE
STUTTGART

ECKHARD LEUSCHNER

Measuring Beauty: Ideal Proportions and the Human Figure ca. 1930

"'Why did you measure that overcoat?' I asked, with some curiosity.
'Parbleu! To see how long it was', replied my friend imperturbably. I was vexed. Poirot's
incurable habit of making a mystery out of nothing never failed to irritate me."
Agatha CHRISTIE, *The Murder on the Links* (1923)

Poor Hastings. Although Poirot answered his question, he still felt that he had learned nothing new. And, indeed, little is said if someone claims to be measuring something or somebody in order to establish how long, high, dense, loud, light, etc. a person or a thing is. As points of interest the parameters and instruments chosen for the measuring process and the assumptions or intentions of the person doing the measuring are equally or more important. This observation not only applies to criminology but also to the fine arts, including architecture and architectural history.

The *Messkasten* (Measuring Box), an early work by Rebecca Horn (FIG. 1),[1] consists of a black metal frame, the vertical elements of which are perforated at regular intervals, and horizontal aluminum rods of the same length placed in the holes. These rods can be moved forward to the center of the box or away from it. A photo of the work in operation shows the artist herself standing upright in the center of the box with her arms attached to her body. As long as she is fixed in the construction, each of the rods has a point of contact with her body. If two of the four lines of rods are set back and allow her to exit (or escape) from the *Messkasten,* the other two lines remain in the measuring position, thus defining the profile of the person measured and representing an outline of his or her individual physical self.

IN / KIRSTEN WAGNER AND JASPER CEPL (EDITORS) /
IMAGES OF THE BODY IN ARCHITECTURE: ANTHROPOLOGY AND BUILT SPACE /
TÜBINGEN · BERLIN / ERNST WASMUTH VERLAG / 2014 / PP. 76–98

In the — fairly limited — reference to Horn's oeuvre it has been pointed out that in this work the later dealings of the artist with the relationship of body and space are already announced. One might even assume that the construction of the box alludes to Leonardo da Vinci's *Vitruvian Man* and the geometrization of the human body in renaissance thought, or that the *Messkasten* is based on artistic practices of the early modern period, namely the transfer or replication of three-dimensional objects through systematic marking of measuring points.[2] However, Horn's *Messkasten* is unlikely to exhaust itself in references to art history or outdated studio practices. At this point, therefore, we are facing a methodological problem: the ways in which 20th-century art continued to rely on artistic practices and measuring methods of the kind just mentioned need to be researched more precisely.

METROLOGY AND THE ARTS

Artists of the early modern period did a lot of measuring. They applied theses activities either to individual human models, whose dimensions or 'body types' they established, or to exemplary ancient sculptures, whose proportions they considered to be canonical standards of beauty.[3] In the 19th century, concepts of beauty and the beautiful remained closely associated with the idea of the harmonious relations of individual body parts to each other, i.e. the mathematically quantifiable proportions that artists found (or, rather, thought they could find) in the most celebrated ancient works.[4] Until the early 20th century, art academies based their images of the human figure on binding canonical proportional charts, and, by teaching students to take and memorize the measurements of the most revered sculptures of antiquity (or, as it were, of casts), generations of artists learned the importance of absolute and relative measures and practiced the transfer of such metrological knowledge to their own works. Not coincidentally, the original meaning of the ancient Greek word *canon* (yardstick or ruler) is closely related to this practice.[5] In the Romantic movement, rulers served both as an elementary means of image construction and as symbols of an all-encompassing metaphysical order, a spiritual correspondence of microcosm and macrocosm. In a painting by Georg Friedrich Kersting representing the painter Caspar David Friedrich in his studio,[6] measuring tools are shown hanging on the wall; since the artist is represented working on a landscape picture and although the window is closed and barred, these tools describe the artist's work as a mental rather than a technical process.

A major reason for artists to move away from the age-old practice of determining absolute or relative measures of the human body was their growing awareness of the differences between the physical measures of an object or person and the dimensions of a representation on a picture plane or in a piece of sculpture. Artists or art critics such as Adolf von Hildebrand, Hans von Marées, and Konrad Fiedler discovered the autonomy of the artistic image.[7] Not much later, some painters went even further and said farewell to all 'rational principles' or 'objective rules' formerly considered to be the essence of artistic creation. As an international avant-garde movement, Expressionism swept away the last remnants of such notions.

In his famous essay on the history of proportion, first published in 1921 as "Die Entwicklung der Proportionslehre als Abbild der Stilentwicklung" ("The History of the Theory of Human Proportions as a Reflection of the History of Styles"), Erwin Panofsky explains it as a "modern, subjective viewpoint that a work of art is something utterly irrational."[8] According to Panofsky, to contemporary viewers it is "uninteresting, if not distressing, when the historian tells him that a rational system of proportions, or even a definite geometrical scheme, underlies this or that representation." And, indeed, clear indications of an aversion to the artistic imitation of fixed measures or 'natural' proportions can be found in many works of avant-garde painters active in the first years of the 20th century, for example in Umberto Boccioni's painting *Volumi orizzontali* from 1912. In this picture, Boccioni added exact quantifications of the spatial dimensions represented, denoting both body measures of the sitter and certain distances between her and buildings in the background or other objects. He thus mocked all expectations of a proper representation of 'real' spatial relations and distances in his canvas.[9]

While pre-World War I artists displayed an ever more skeptical attitude towards concepts of fixed measures in art (including theories of ideal human proportions), a lot of measuring went on in the late 19th century. Both in the natural sciences and in the growing industrial production, there was a metrological boom, as both reacted to a tremendous need for the standardization of virtually every part of modern life. A quick survey of manuals on metrology published in the early 20th century is sufficient to understand the extraordinary variety of measuring instruments and procedures, all of which claimed to enhance or optimize human life by prescribing standard measures or *étalons*. State institutions guaranteed the accuracy of measuring units, the best known of which is the *mètre* standard introduced after the French Revolution (*mètre étalon*). The newly established metrical system resulted in a farewell to previous metrological units that had been based on body analogies such as the foot or the yard — at least in the countries that adopted the French system. It is well known that Marcel Duchamp created his *Trois stoppages étalon* as a laconic commentary on the normative tendencies of his time. He cut three rulers in the forms of threads that he experimentally threw to the ground and thus created 'artistic' étalons.[10] The questions Duchamp's *Stoppages* asked were manifold: Do 'objective measures' exist? Can (or should) art have any binding measures or rules? Can art devise methodological or metrological alternatives to those employed by science?

In his already mentioned essay on the history of proportional theories in art, Panofsky pointed out that in his own era probably only anthropologists and criminologists (and some enthusiasts — *Schwärmer* — among artists) remained interested in human proportions. He was right in the sense that both criminal investigation and anthropology were important fields of research in which human beings were still subjected to measuring procedures. However, regarding the renewed interest of avant-garde artists in concepts of measure and proportion in the early 1920s, Panofsky was decidedly uninformed. Hardly an epoch of 20th-century art has created more depictions of measuring tools, rulers, goniometers, anatomical charts, etc. than the generation active in the years between the start of World War I and the mid-1930s. Some of these images can be explained as visual expressions of the new post-World War I ideology of the *retour à l'ordre*. For example, in the Italian *Novecento,* images of rulers and compasses are frequent features. In this movement in the 1920s, which was sponsored by Margherita Sarfatti, Mussolini's mistress, artists such as Mario Sironi turned away from the abstractions of the pre-war avant-garde and sought a new foundation of art.[11] They represented measuring instruments not only because such details appear

2
MARIO SIRONI /
THE STUDENT /
1922–24 /
PAINTING /
PRIVATE
COLLECTION

in portraits of artists and architects created during the Italian Renaissance,[12] but probably also because rulers represented their patriotic 'rectitude'. *The Student* by Sironi (**FIG. 2**) is a strongly geometricized figure in the manner of Piero della

ECKHARD LEUSCHNER

Francesca, and thus alludes to the orderly pursuit of artistic activity. In addition to that, the woman's left forearm rests on a table next to a goniometer, thus illustrating the origin of a major measuring unit, the yard, in a body part.[13] Although Sironi's painting can hardly be reduced to its political implications, it was meant to visualize the convergence of the current artistic and political ideals in Italy.

Other images of measuring tools created in or soon after Word War I, especially those by Giorgio de Chirico, cannot be connected as easily with the *retour à l'ordre*. Despite some superficial similarities, the *Novecento* movement had little to do with the metaphysical art of De Chirico, whose pictures abound with representations of rulers, yardsticks and anatomical charts, all of which evoke the grand traditions of academic training in 19th-century art schools, even though they also contain images of factories and steam trains and thus defy all demands for lofty academic clarity and 'perfect measures'. With this irritating display of metrological skepticism, De Chirico's *Metafisica* was a major source of inspiration for the Surrealists.

Still Life in the Studio, painted by Otto Dix in 1924 (**FIG. 3**), represents the corner of a room, probably an artist's studio. Coarsely grained boards form the

3
OTTO DIX / *STILL LIFE IN THE STUDIO* / 1924 / PAINTING / KUNSTMUSEUM STUTTGART

floor, and the walls are covered with raw, partially cracked or smeared-on plaster.[14] In this composition, the artist has arranged items related to his professional activities in a most unsystematic manner; even the spatial arrangement is meant to look inharmonious. Only upon closer inspection, one recognizes that there is a living nude model among the studio junk: a naked middle-aged woman with a dark cloth over her groin and large, sagging breasts. She has her head thrown back and raises her right arm with bent hand. Her face betrays the effort of this gesture, while the absence of a narrative context makes her pose look totally unmotivated. Next to the woman, on a chair, is a life-sized doll with a slightly damaged skin of fabric and a light blue cloth draped over her waist and left arm, whose splayed fingers seem to echo the gesture of the life model. Where the doll's head should be, only an elongated stub remains. Even closer to the viewer is a blank easel turned diagonally away, on which, quite prominently, a red-painted T-square is leaning.

Certain details of Dix's provocative picture, such as the studio utensils, were probably meant as allusions to the traditional standards and shared convictions of the artistic sphere. However, just as in the case of De Chirico, Dix's arrangement of measuring tools was hardly intended to be an allegory in praise of the Fine Arts or metrological exactitude. The worn out shape of the studio doll,[15] moreover, should not be attributed to the depredations of moths or heavy use, but to Dix's interest in pictures by Matthias Grünewald, especially the latter's representations of the tortured body of Christ on the Cross. In this context, the blood-red measuring tool may well be an (ironic) transfer of Passion symbolism to the 'passion' of the artist's models in the studio. Dix, in fact, displayed a skeptical attitude vis-à-vis the academic figure and the classical instruments of the artistic creation of beauty, and he searched for alternative means of expression, which he found in Northern paintings of the late medieval period, especially in depictions of the suffering Christ. These non-beautiful models or prototypes of his art were an obvious choice, since, in the sense of a dilemma addressed by Friedrich Nietzsche, the Christ of the Passion, unlike the pagan gods of Greek antiquity, is just not beautiful.

Did traditional concepts of the beautiful or theories pertaining to the visual construction of beauty have any effect on the arts of the 1920s and 1930s? One does not have to search long to find that, side by side with the outspoken or implicit refutations of the traditional academic standards just cited, the period witnessed a new enthusiasm vis-à-vis Pythagorean concepts of harmony, proportion, and measure. The ex-Futurist and former Cubist Gino Severini was one of the first painters of his era to develop a profound taste for geometry as a ruling principle of art, and he propagated his new creed in 1921 in *Du cubisme au classicisme. (Esthétique du compas et du nombre),* a publication that had repercussions in all parts of Europe, notably at the Bauhaus.[17] The first generation of Italian Futurists active before World War I had declared that art museums should be destroyed, while at the same time retaining the criterion of beauty by declaring a racing car to be a thousand times more beautiful than the Nike of Samothrace.[18] In a related attitude, Le Corbusier in the early 1920s proclaimed that the high technical standards of Greek temples defined them as "machines", comparing them with the best cars of his own era.[19] While such linear derivations of modern technology from ancient art and architecture had a provocative touch, the reference to "Greek foundations" of current consumer culture soon became fashionable in certain strata of society. Around 1930, Ernst Zoberbier's

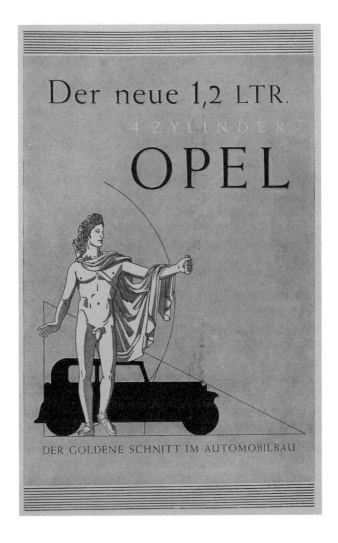

advertisement for Opel cars (FIG. 4) depicted the ancient statue of the *Apollo Belvedere* together with a schematic representation of the car company's most recent product, thus paralleling the golden section with the allegedly harmonious design of an automobile.[20]

The Zoberbier advertisement is a clear indicator of the fact that, on closer inspection, age-old artistic concepts of measure and proportion, even 'ideal beauty', remained important factors in the arts and popular cultures of the 1920s. There are other cases in point. For example, in 1928 the Hollywood company MGM promoted the film star Anita Page as a realization of perfect beauty (FIG. 5)

by comparing her body measurements as indicated in a photographic representation with the "Ideal screen type drawn from photographs of 13 leading stars".[21] In this diagram, beautiful body parts of other female film stars were indicated, but — according to the film advertisement — only Page managed to combine all such beauty features in a single figure of physical perfection.

In 1929, the exhibition *Der Schöne Mensch in der Neuen Kunst* (Human Beauty in Recent Art) took place in Darmstadt.[22] The cover of the catalogue (**FIG. 6**) was designed by the artist Hermann Keil (1889–1962), who was also one of the show's

6
HERMANN KEIL /
COVER OF
*DER SCHÖNE
MENSCH IN DER
NEUEN KUNST /*
1929

organizers. Keil's image is a typical example of the more progressive currents in German art and visual culture of the period in question. The orange, black, and grey shades on a white background echo the constructivist aesthetics of El Lissitzky and László Moholy-Nagy. Combined with diagonals or right angles, a decidedly contemporary letter type was chosen. The center of the cover is a photograph of a female torso by Alexander Archipenko with extra long, footless legs.[23] The Archipenko torso is positioned in front of the flat relief-like contours of an ancient Egyptian woman. Of these two pieces of art, the first stresses the absolute modernity of the 'beauty' theme, the other, as an art historical reference, the constancy of the same phenomenon throughout history. In addition to that, the modern torso and the Egyptian relief also connected the current

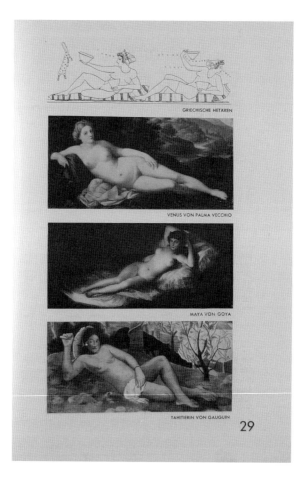

7
FOUR FEMALE
NUDES
FROM
*DER SCHÖNE
MENSCH IN DER
NEUEN KUNST*

fashion of representing the body as a fragment (e.g. lacking a head or arms) with older artistic traditions — in this case not with Greek or Roman art, but, rather, Egyptian works (Germany was still subject to Nefertiti mania[24]).

The Darmstadt exhibition was originally intended to be called *Der nackte Mensch in der Neuen Kunst* (The Naked Human Being in Recent Art), but in the course of its preparation the organizers appear to have lost their courage to use this title. Either for fear of censorship or due to a concern for greater systematic depth, they introduced a title change. Not stopping there, they also supplemented the artistic representations of nudes sent in by German and international artists with historic photos and documents on the theory and practice of "human beauty" in art through the centuries. This combination of an art show and a theoretical approach is more manifest in the catalogue than it must have been in the exhibition itself, especially since the artworks on view were limited to the media of painting and sculpture, whereas the catalogue also contains artistic photography, which was completely excluded from the actual event. In addition to the photos, the catalogue also exemplified the idea of beauty standards 'through the ages' by combining similar images from art history such as reclining female nudes from ancient Greece, by Palma Vecchio, Francisco Goya, and Paul Gauguin (FIG. 7).

Several of the artists represented in the show may have reacted to the Call for Participation under the first project title. Even though no particularly unsightly nude was exhibited, this fact may account for the great diversity of formal and stylistic approaches. Among the participating painters (Otto Dix was conspicuous for his deliberate absence), there were some veterans of German Expressionism such as Ernst Ludwig Kirchner, Otto Müller and Max Beckmann, but also representatives of the Italian *Novecento* such as Mario Tozzi and Ubaldo Oppi, and a few machine aesthetes such as Amédée Ozenfant and Willi Baumeister. The sculpture displayed ranged from a nude by Charles Despiau to an almost abstract figure by Étienne Béothy. Male nudes were outnumbered by females, while individualized images or portraits remained an exception. In the majority of cases, artists looked for the 'blueprint' of the human body. Therefore it was no accident, that someone such as Béothy participated, a Paris-based sculptor who was already preparing his book *La série d'or* (published in 1939), in which he would proclaim the golden ratio not only as the fundamental law of nature, but also as the principle on which all artistic and industrial design should be based.[25]

Klaus Wolbert, one of the few scholars to have taken notice of the Darmstadt exhibition, limited his analysis to a few aspects.[26] He stressed the international scope of the show (which included, among others, works by Marc Chagall, Auguste Herbin, and Jean Metzinger) and — given the proximity of the exhibition to the year 1933 — pointed out the conspicuously small number of racial or even strongly political undertones of the project. Regarding the art-theoretical background, he qualified the comments on "beauty" in the catalogue as a somewhat naive, largely unhistorical compilation, bound together by the then already obsolete idea of 'eternal' beauty standards.

Wolbert's claim that the exhibition represented a conventional, canon-related concept of beauty appears to be evident at first glance, but one should also acknowledge the innovative character of the Darmstadt project. Since the

Blaue Reiter exhibition in 1911, *Der Schöne Mensch* has perhaps been the most important attempt by contemporary artists in Germany to explore the various relations between art and 'non-art' in the sense of self-assessing and positioning their own activities. In the entire catalogue, as a matter of fact, there is no authoritative single definition of "beauty" that claims ultimate validity. Above all, perhaps no other self-organized exhibition by artists in the 1920s took more notice of what Theodor Adorno would a few years later call "culture industry",

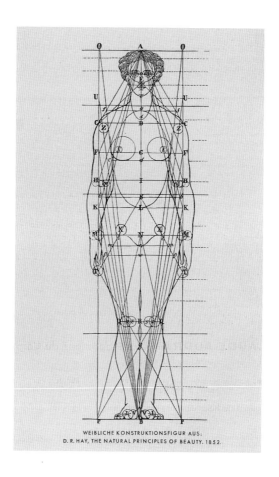

8
DIAGRAM FROM
DAVID RAMSAY
HAY'S *NATURAL
PRINCIPLES
OF BEAUTY* AS
ILLUSTRATED
IN *DER SCHÖNE
MENSCH IN DER
NEUEN KUNST*

WEIBLICHE KONSTRUKTIONSFIGUR AUS:
D. R. HAY, THE NATURAL PRINCIPLES OF BEAUTY. 1852.

i.e., the ever-growing presence of quick profit imagery in mass media such as fashion and leisure magazines, advertising and the film industry. Indeed, the producers of these 'popular images', unlike most avant-garde painters or sculptors, did not hesitate to indulge in traditional normative concepts of 'perfect measures', ideal bodies and absolute beauty. Avant-garde artists active in the late 1920s could hardly overlook this trend.

ECKHARD LEUSCHNER

'Natural' or 'canonical' standards of human beauty were a major theme in the catalogue of the Darmstadt show. Compiled and introduced by Paul Westheim, there are relevant quotations from Vitruvius[27] and Leon Battista Alberti,[28] and diagrams or proportional charts from Albrecht Dürer's *Four Books on Human Proportion* (1528), David Ramsay Hay's *Natural Principles of Beauty*[29] (1852) (**FIG. 8**) and Johann Gottfried Schadow's *Polyklet* (1834),[30] one of the most widely used manuals for artists on human growth and standard proportions in the 19th century. Famous pieces of ancient sculpture such as the *Venus de Milo* and the *Apollo Belvedere* were illustrated as eternal beauty standards. In another illustration of the Darmstadt catalogue, two contemporary men were shown studying a more or less willing young woman in a swimsuit and compar-

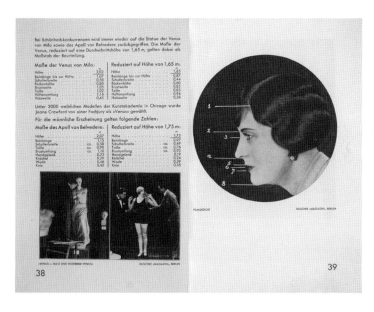

9
A MEASURING
PROCESS /
PAGE FROM *DER
SCHÖNE MENSCH
IN DER NEUEN
KUNST*

10
"FILM FACE" /
PAGE FROM *DER
SCHÖNE MENSCH
IN DER NEUEN
KUNST*

ing her proportions to those of the ancient Venus (**FIG. 9**). Additionally, a photo of an American beauty contest demonstrated, as the catalogue asserted,[31] that attempts to define the natural standards *(Naturwert)* and a canon of beauty were still taking place. In more or less the same line, a photographic profile of a young woman defined the characteristics of the perfect "film face" (**FIG. 10**).[32] Slightly out of touch with the rest of the catalogue, but closely related to contemporary Weimar culture, an article by the sports apostle Hans Suren promoted physical education as a means of individually achieving an ideal figure.[33] In keeping with the sports and gymnastics movement of the time, he demonstrated that physical beauty consists in the continuous process of its acquisition, i.e. in a permanent performative act of self-beautification.

In the scant research on the 1929 exhibition, the picture credit in the lower margin of several illustrations in the Darmstadt catalogue, "Klischee: Das Magazin", has not yet stirred any scholarly interest. *Das Magazin,* in fact, was one of the most widely read illustrated journals published in the days of the Weimar Republic, a periodical intended for a liberal, 'modern' clientele with a penchant for light intellectual entertainment and the American Way of Life. In the July 1928 issue of *Das Magazin,* the article "Schönheit nach Maß" (Beauty to Measure) can be found (**FIG. 11**).[34] It revolves around the (probably) fictional character of Kiki, a young woman whose likeness is given in a photo of a fashionable girl hold-

11 / 12 / 13
PAGES FROM
THE "BEAUTY
TO MEASURE"
ARTICLE IN *DAS
MAGAZIN* /
1928

ing a tape measure in her hand. According to the article, one of Kiki's admirers compared her beauty to that of the *Venus de Milo.* To her, this compliment sounded like an insult: "Look at these hips! Not to mention the waistline".[35] At first glance, such a reaction reads as a fundamental critique of the traditional ideals of female beauty. And, indeed, Kiki's aversion to the 'old-fashioned' beauty standards as exemplified by the *Venus de Milo* needs to be seen in the context of the androgynous ideal of the 1920s, the *garçonne.* Yet, as far as Kiki was concerned, her own efforts to reach that new ideal were short-lived. Much to her relief, she received the first prize for slenderness in a beauty contest, and at about the same time another of her male friends who had some mathematical competence converted the dimensions of the *Venus de Milo,* a sculpture more than two meters high, to Kiki's own body size. He found that her proportions were almost identical to those of the sculpture in the Louvre — from then on, she was quite satisfied with being compared to the classical Venus (**FIG. 12**).[36] For the time being (at least according to *Das Magazin*), old and contemporary beauty standards were thus reconciled. In the same article, another famous piece of sculpture was proposed as a standard for the male body: the *Apollo Belvedere.* In an illustration (**FIG. 13**), a woman applies a tape measure to this ancient exemplar of male beauty (or, rather, a cast), and a contemporary athlete is shown right under that image as a "modern Apollo". The article's closing remark is: "Proportions matter more than anything else! All things proportioned are beautiful."[37]

Popular imagery can be analyzed in terms of its immediate commercial, social or political function, but it also sheds light on the 'high' culture or the arts in general of a particular period. One aspect of the "Schönheit nach Maß" article is especially obvious: concepts of measure and proportion were an important element of contemporary discourses on physical attraction or beauty, and many of the concepts in question closely resemble those of the previous centuries. It looks as if the cultural mainstream of the 1920s never turned away from these 'outdated' ideas, whereas a lot of avant-garde artists (as exemplified by the participants of the Darmstadt show) began to return to them. The enthusiasm for 'natural' beauty standards, needless to say, was not shared by all artists connected with the 1929 event. In the catalogue of the Darmstadt exhibition, there is a section with statements by contemporary artists in which more nuanced opinions regarding ideal figures or artistic "beauty" than those of the historic authorities already cited are pronounced. For example, the Expressionist painter Reinhold Ewald criticized the concept of "eternal" proportions in a material sense and pointed out that Dürer's pedantry in questions of measure and scale would never do justice to the dynamics of the natural world.[38]

When analyzing the exhibition *Der Schöne Mensch* in a larger context, one is hardly surprised to find that the more 'progressive' anatomy books used for the education of artists in the 1920s no longer contained references to ancient sculpture, canonical modules or fixed formulas for the construction of beauty. It is enough to cite just one example, the *Plastische Anatomie* (Plastic Anatomy) of Siegfried Mollier which — despite its claim to teach the representation of the human body to future artists — did away with all former artistic ideals and more than anything resembles a medical textbook (**FIG. 14**).[39] However, both in

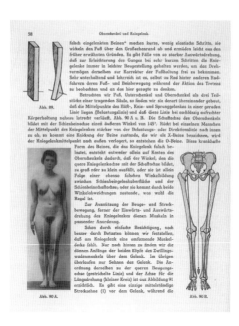

14
PAGE FROM
SIEGFRIED
MOLLIER'S
*PLASTISCHE
ANATOMIE /
1924*

the education of artists and in the popular 'learning how to draw' textbooks for *dilettanti,* the didactic means and educational aims were not as clearly defined as these 'progressive' authors preferred. In Germany and elsewhere, the authority of plaster casts and proportional charts remained considerable, and this situation changed little until the 1950s. In textbooks on fashion, comics and web design, 'natural measures' and fixed proportions of the human figure can still be found today. Not surprisingly, the Surrealists (who were almost completely absent from the Darmstadt show) mocked the eternal beauty standards of the human figure — one of these was Max Ernst who, in a cover design for an English edition of the poems of Paul Eluard, reproduced and 'reworked' a proportional chart that he must have found in a book on artistic or medical anthropometry.[40] However, artists such as Ernst were dealing with concepts and convictions that, as they saw, were quite alive, and it would be a simplification to interpret (and underestimate) these beauty concepts as ultimate ramifications of 19th-century academic classicism.

Only against this complicated cultural background can the artistic practice and theories of the avant-garde 'champion' of the human figure in post-World War I Germany, Oskar Schlemmer, be fully understood. None other than Schlemmer had the last word in the artists' statements collected in the Darmstadt catalogue: "Unless the signs deceive us, a renaissance of the human figure in art is close. After the Futurists in their manifestos have sworn death to the moon and even death to the nude in the arts; [...] after Verism and Neue Sachlichkeit represented human beings in a Biedermeier manner (*verbiedermeiert*) or with a penetrating naturalism; after such a course of development, the ideals which guided a Hans von Marées throughout his life, the ideals which cultivate the high style in art, should actually be revived. Their highest object will always be man, i.e. man as represented by the means of artistic beauty (*der kunstschöne Mensch*). These formations will always be, in Goethe's sense, 'antique' (*antikisch*), arising from the ideal symmetry of abstraction, measure and rule on the one hand and of nature, feeling, idea on the other. An exhibition entitled 'Der Schöne Mensch' will have to take special care to represent man as a product of art, as a likeness (*Gleichnis*) created by the means of art, i.e. form and color, that represents a special world, incomparable to the beauty of photography or the mere beauty of nature".[41]

Putting Schlemmer's statement in other terms, he tried to define his own position by clearly distinguishing between art on the one hand and 'popular' or 'natural' imagery on the other. Since this distinction was not one of mere traditionalism, he did not wish to return to the inflexible beauty concepts that had prevailed prior to Hildebrand and Fiedler, and it was not by chance, that he mentioned Hildebrand's artist-friend Hans von Marées. It is unclear whether Schlemmer, when writing his statement, was aware of the fact that the authors of the Darmstadt catalogue were planning to illustrate proportional charts and similar historic indicators of 'eternal beauty', but it seems unlikely. If he had been asked to comment on the published catalogue, Schlemmer would probably have pointed out that the combination of images of contemporary beauty contests and age-old diagrams representing the 'natural principles of beauty' was irrelevant for his own concept of the beautiful, as neither had any bearing upon the beauty of art.

If seen from this angle, Schlemmer's text not only indicates the tensions be-tween 'high' and 'low' in the arts and visual cultures of ca.1930, it also echoes the anthropological approach of the course that he himself had devised for his Bauhaus teaching, the "Menschenlehre". This course was meant to be much more than just an anatomy lesson or an introduction to the academic principles of figure creation; it was, rather, the ambitious attempt at a synthesis of the physical and spiritual natures of man. Schlemmer's famous drawing *Mensch im Ideenkreis* (Man in the Circle of Ideas) (**FIG. 15**) was intended to describe the basic capacities

15
OSKAR
SCHLEMMER /
DER MENSCH IM
IDEENKREIS /
1928–29
DRAWING

of the human body and, at the same time, to convey a generalized image of man, metaphysical and free of all contingencies, in a word: a-historical.[42] The fact that the human figure in his *Mensch im Ideenkreis* is shown running, i.e. mov-ing in space not unlike a "Human Figure in Motion" by Eadweard Muybridge, clearly distances him from the upright and immobile figures as represented in the anatomical charts of the old art academies. Yet Schlemmer's artistic quest for the "allgemeingültiger Typus der Gestalt"[43] (universally valid type of form) was undertaken in a spirit not unlike that of the early modern classicists upon whose convictions the first art academies were built, i.e. their concepts of an eternal, ideal beauty of man.[44]

It goes without saying that in the time span between Oskar Schlemmer and Rebecca Horn a lot of new art has been produced and a great many changes in culture and society have occurred. The word "changes" does not only refer to the racial and eugenic measuring practices in the Nazi period or the almost complete abandonment of the 'figure' in Western avant-garde art of the 1950s or even the 'pure proportions' of the cubic boxes created by American Minimalists such as Donald Judd or Sol LeWitt in the 1960s. The *Messkasten* by Rebecca Horn (**FIG. 1**), if considered in all its complexities, contains references to both the artistic tradition of measuring the human figure and the concepts of the body current in 1970. It therefore points to the tensions between the physical self and the norms of artistic creation that more often than not reflect gender-specific, ethical or racial norms outside the artistic sphere. Whatever Kiki was told, there are no 'natural proportions' or 'natural values' of the human figure, each measuring of a body, artistic or not, already being conditioned by the parameters chosen and the assumptions or intentions of the person performing it. A measuring process is a social act. Art and art history remain good places for the critique of such acts.

NOTES

1   See Anette Kuruszynski, "'Und verstehe die Freiheit, aufzubrechen, wohin er will'. Autonomie und Befreiung im Schaffen von Rebecca Horn", in: Rebecca Horn, *Bodylandscapes. Zeichnungen, Skulpturen, Installationen, 1964–2004,* Ostfildern-Ruit: Hatje Cantz, 2004, pp. 136–143, here pp. 138–139.

2   See the examples cited in Jane Andrews Aiken, "Leon Battista Alberti's System of Human Proportions", in: *Journal of the Warburg and Courtauld Institutes,* vol. 43, 1980, pp. 68–96.

3   See Jürgen Fredel, "Ideale Maße und Proportionen. Der konstruierte Körper", in: *Die Beredsamkeit des Leibes. Zur Körpersprache in der Kunst,* edited by Ilsebill Barta Fliedl and Christoph Geissmar, Salzburg and Vienna: Residenz-Verlag, 1992, pp. 11–42.

4   See Eckhard Leuschner, "Proportion", in: *Lexikon Kunstwissenschaft. Hundert Grundbegriffe,* edited by Stefan Jordan and Jürgen Müller, Stuttgart: Reclam, 2012, pp. 280–283.

5   See Eckhard Leuschner, "Rules and Rulers. Robert Morris, Canonical Measures and the Definition of Art in the 1960s", in: *Münchner Jahrbuch der Bildenden Kunst,* vol. 60, 2009, pp. 139–160.

6   See Hubertus Gassner, "Komposition: Hyperbeln — Symmetrien und Gitterstrukturen — Rhythmische Folgen — Bildpaare und Serien", in: *Caspar David Friedrich. Die Erfindung der Romantik,* edited by Hubertus Gassner, Munich: Hirmer, 2006, pp. 271–289, here pp. 272–273.

7   See especially Adolf von Hildebrand, *Das Problem der Form in der bildenden Kunst,* Strassburg: J. H. Ed. Heitz (Heitz & Mündel), 1893.

8   Erwin Panofsky, "Die Entwicklung der Proportionslehre als Abbild der Stilentwicklung", in: *Monatshefte für Kunstwissenschaft,* vol. 14, 1921, pp. 188–219. Quoted after: Erwin Panofsky, "The History of the Theory of Human Proportions as a Reflection of the History of Styles", in: Panofsky, *Meaning in the Visual Arts: Papers in and on Art History,* Garden City, NY: Doubleday Anchor Books, 1955, pp. 55–107, here p. 55.

9   See Uwe M. Schneede, *Umberto Boccioni,* Stuttgart: Gerd Hatje, 1994, pp. 111–113.

10 Herbert MOLDERINGS, *Kunst als Experiment. Marcel Duchamps "3 Kunststopf-Normalmaße",* Munich and Berlin: Deutscher Kunstverlag, 2006.

11 Elena PONTIGGIA, "L'idea del classico in Margherita Sarfatti e Massimo Bontempelli", in: *Arte e letteratura. Dal futurismo ad oggi,* edited by Vittorio FAGONE and Daniela GALANTE, Bergamo: Lubrina, 1998, pp. 65–71.

12 See Ingrid Leonie SEVERIN, *Baumeister und Architekten. Studien zur Darstellung eines Berufsstandes in Porträt und Bildnis,* Berlin: Gebr. Mann, 1992.

13 Mario Sironi cited in *Piero della Francesca e il Novecento,* edited by Maria Mimita LAMBERTI and Maurizio FAGIOLO DELL'ARCO, Venice: Marsilio, 1991.

14 On the painting by Dix see *Grünewald in der Moderne,* edited by Brigitte SCHAD and Thomas RATZKA, Cologne: Wienand, 2003, p. 54.

15 The doll might also refer to fetish practices in the manner of Kokoschka's life-sized Alma doll. See *Oskar Kokoschka und Alma Mahler: Die Puppe. Epilog einer Passion,* Frankfurt am Main: Städtische Galerie im Städel, 1992.

16 For Nietzsche's view of a fundamental conflict between the Christian religion and all concepts of beauty see, among others, Hans MAIER, "Mensch und Übermensch. Nietzsche und das Christentum", in: *Wagner — Nietzsche — Thomas Mann. Festschrift für Eckhard Heftrich,* edited by Heinz GOCKEL, Michael NEUMANN, and Ruprecht WIMMER, Frankfurt am Main: Vittorio Klostermann, 1993, pp. 83–96.

17 Piero PACINI, "Gino Severini: la riscoperta della Divina Proporzione e del Numero d'Oro", in: *Figura umana. Normkonzepte der Menschendarstellung in der italienischen Kunst von 1919 bis 1939,* edited by Eckhard LEUSCHNER, Petersberg: Michael Imhof, 2012, pp. 68–79.

18 Manfred HINZ, *Die Zukunft der Katastrophe. Mythische und rationalistische Geschichtstheorie in italienischen Futurismus,* Berlin: De Gruyter, 1985, p. 64 and passim.

19 LE CORBUSIER, *Vers une architecture,* edited by Jean-Louis COHEN, Paris: Flammarion, 2005, pp. 106–107. (First as LE CORBUSIER-SAUGNIER, *Vers une architecture,* Paris: G. Cres, [1923]).

20 On Zoberbier's advertisement design, see Esther Sophia SÜNDERHAUF, *Griechensehnsucht und Kulturkritik. Die deutsche Rezeption von Winckelmanns Klassizismus 1840–1945,* Berlin: Akademie Verlag, 2004, pp. 254–255.

21 For the photo of Anita Page as the "ideal screen type", see Robert DANCE and Bruce ROBERTSON, *Ruth Harriet Louise and Hollywood Glamour Photography,* Berkeley and Los Angeles: University of California Press, 2002, p. 129.

22 *Der Schöne Mensch in der Neuen Kunst,* edited by the Interessengemeinschaft fortschrittlicher Künstler Hessens, Darmstadt: Mathildenhöhe, 1929.

23 According to the 1929 catalogue, this work was not included in the exhibition (the photo credit was for the Flechtheim Gallery in Berlin). See the catalogue entry for Archipenko's torso by Christa LICHTENSTERN in *Canto d'amore. Klassizistische Moderne in Musik und bildender Kunst, 1914–1935,* Bern: Kunstmuseum Basel, 1996, pp. 152–153.

24 For the early reception of the bust of Nefertiti — on display in Berlin since 1923 — see Claudia BREGER, "Die Berliner Büste der Nofretete. Imperiale Phantasien im deutschen archäologischen Diskurs des 20. Jahrhunderts", in: *Der Körper der Königin. Geschlecht und Herrschaft in der höfischen Welt,* edited by Regina SCHULTE, Frankfurt am Main: Campus, 2002, pp. 279–301.

25 Etienne Béothy, *La série d'or,* Paris: Chanth, 1939. On the book, see Alfred Meurer, *Der Bildhauer Etienne Béothy. Werk und Ästhetik,* Weimar: VDG, 2003, pp. 74–86, and Claire Barbillon, *Les canons du corps humain au XIXe siècle. L'art et la règle,* Paris: Odile Jacob, 2004, pp. 263–273.

26 Klaus Wolbert, "Der Schöne Mensch in der Neuen Kunst. Internationale Ausstellung", in: *Die Darmstädter Sezession 1919–1997. Die Kunst des 20. Jahrhunderts im Spiegel einer Künstlervereinigung,* edited by Sabine Welsch and Klaus Wolbert, Darmstadt: Institut Mathildenhöhe, 1997, pp. 168–175.

27 *Der Schöne Mensch in der Neuen Kunst,* p. 31.

28 Ibid., p. 32.

29 David Ramsay Hay, *The Natural Principles of Beauty As Developed in the Human Figure,* Edinburgh: William Blackwood and Sons, 1852 · *Der Schöne Mensch in der Neuen Kunst,* p. 36.

30 Johann Gottfried Schadow, *Polyklet oder von den Massen des Menschen,* Berlin: published by the author, 1834 · *Der Schöne Mensch in der Neuen Kunst,* p. 37.

31 *Der Schöne Mensch in der Neuen Kunst,* p. 37: „Das starke Interesse für die menschliche Schönheit als Naturwert drückt sich heute auch in den Versuchen aus zu Normalmaßen und einem Kanon zu gelangen. Ihnen dienen jene Schönheits-Konkurrenzen, wie sie besonders Amerika liebt und veranstaltet."

32 Ibid., p. 39.

33 Hans Suren, "Schönheit des Körpers", in: *Der Schöne Mensch in der Neuen Kunst,* pp. 15–17, and idem, "Körpertypen und Körperbildung", ibid., pp. 18–20.

34 Author unknown, "Schönheit nach Maß", in: *Das Magazin,* VOL. 47, July 1928, pp. 2485–2490.

35 Ibid., p. 2485: „Die Venus von Milo! Entsetzlich — diese Hüften! Von dem Taillenumfang gar nicht zu reden! Kiki hatte sie noch ganz genau vor Augen, wie sie sie im Louvre gesehen hatte: riesengroß, schön, harmonisch, aber unmöglich! Jedenfalls für eine moderne Frau! Und nun versuchte sich Kiki zu einem Garçonnetyp hinunterzutrainieren".

36 Ibid., pp. 2487–2488: „Wie würde sie denn eigentlich aussehen, wenn sie 2,02 m groß wäre? Sie rennt zu einem Freunde — Mathematik war immer ihre schwächste Seite gewesen — und lässt es sich ausrechnen. Ihr wurde schwarz vor Augen — es waren die Maße der Venus von Milo".

37 Ibid., p. 2489: „Auf die Proportion kommt es in erster Linie an! Alles, was proportioniert ist, ist schön. Wirklich schöne Menschen wissen natürlich lange bevor sie sich vor den Spiegel gestellt und gemessen haben, daß sie gut gebaut sind, denn viele Blicke haben ihnen das schon unzählige Male gesagt. Aber es ist angenehm, eine Erkenntnis, die man bereits hat, eines Tages schwarz auf weiß bestätigt zu sehen. Darum messt euch!"

38 *Der Schöne Mensch in der Neuen Kunst,* p. 53 (R. Ewald): „Solche Proportionen (sc. der antiken Ägypter und Griechen) sind nicht örtlichmessender Natur, auch nicht Umformungen oder Stilisierungen gemessener Orte des Stoff-(Modell-)Körpers, auch nicht Dürersche Pedanterie- und Geometrie-Konflikte, sondern an ihrer Entstehung ist das fließende Leben an sich schuld, das sich im Kunstphantom festigt."

39 Siegfried Mollier, *Plastische Anatomie. Die konstruktive Form des menschlichen Körpers,* Munich: J. F. Bergmann, 1924.

40 Max Ernst, "Thorns of Thunder" (1936), illustrated in Werner Spies, *Max Ernst Collages: the Invention of the Surrealist Universe,* translated by John William Gabriel, New York: Abrams, 1991, fig. 529 · See also Ernst's painted fusions of human and animal forms such as "Figure anthropomorphe" (1931), illustrated in *Max Ernst. Retrospektive zum 100. Geburtstag,* edited by Werner SPIES, Munich: Prestel, 1991, p. 162.

41 *Der Schöne Mensch in der Neuen Kunst,* p. 54 (Oskar SCHLEMMER): „Wenn die Zeichen nicht trügen, so bereitet sich eine Renaissance der Menschendarstellung in der Kunst vor. Nachdem die Futuristen damals in ihren Manifesten Tod dem Mondschein und auch Tod dem Nackten in der Kunst geschworen hatten; […] nachdem sodann Verismus und Neue Sachlichkeit den Menschen zwar darstellten, aber verbiedermeiert oder in penetranter Naturalistik; — so müssten nach solchem Entwicklungsverlauf eigentlich notwendigerweise die Ideale wiederaufleben, die einen Hans v. Marées ein Leben lang beherrschten, die Ideale, die sich um den hohen Stil in der Kunst bemühen. Deren höchster Gegenstand wird immer der Mensch, der kunstschöne Mensch sein. Es werden immer Formungen sein, die im Goetheschen Sinne ‚antikisch' sind, Schöpfungen, entsprungen aus der Verbindung und aus dem idealen Gleichmaß von Abstraktion, Maß, Gesetz einerseits, andrerseits aus Natur, Gefühl, Idee. Eine Ausstellung ‚Der schöne Mensch' wird bedacht sein müssen, den Menschen als Produkt der Kunst aufzuzeigen, als das mit den Mitteln der Kunst, aus Form und Farbe geschaffene Gleichnis, das eine Sonderwelt repräsentiert, unvergleichbar dem bloß Fotografie- oder bloß Naturschönen".

42 On Schlemmer's "Menschenlehre", see Oskar SCHLEMMER, *Der Mensch. Unterricht am Bauhaus. Nachgelassene Aufzeichnungen,* Mainz: Florian Kupferberg, 1969 · Birgit SONNA, *Oskar Schlemmer. Der neue Mensch. Körperkult und Lebensreform,* Ph.D. Thesis, Regensburg 1992, especially pp. 167–171 and 230–232 · Rainer K. WICK, "Schlemmers Menschenbild", in: WICK, *Bauhaus. Kunst und Pädagogik,* Oberhausen: Athena, 2009, pp. 297–312.

43 Karin von MAUR, *Oskar Schlemmer,* VOL. 1, Munich: Prestel, 1979, p. 74.

44 It is (involuntarily?) ironic that the picture in the picture on the wall to the left represents an academic, immobile figure — Schlemmer inscribed it with the title "art".

IMAGES

Rebecca HORN, *The Glance of Infinity,* Zurich, Berlin, and New York: Scalo, 1997, p. 54: FIG. 1 (© VG Bild-Kunst, Bonn 2014) · *Sironi. Mario Sironi (1885–1961),* edited by Jürgen HARTEN and Jochen POETTER, Cologne: DuMont 1988, cat. no. 86: FIG. 2 (© VG Bild-Kunst, Bonn 2014) · *Grünewald in der Moderne,* edited by Brigitte SCHAD and Thomas RATZKA, Cologne: Wienand, 2003: FIG. 3 (© VG Bild-Kunst, Bonn 2014) · *Kunst! Kommerz! Visionen!: Deutsche Plakate 1888–1933,* edited by the DEUTSCHES HISTORISCHES MUSEUM, Heidelberg: Edition Braus 1992, p. 523: FIG. 4 · Robert DANCE and Bruce ROBERTSON, *Ruth Harriet Louise and Hollywood Glamour Photography,* Berkeley and Los Angeles: University of California Press, 2002, p. 129: FIG. 5 · *Der Schöne Mensch in der Neuen Kunst,* Darmstadt: Mathildenhöhe, 1929, Cover: FIG. 6, p. 29: FIG. 7, p. 36: FIG. 8, p. 38: FIG. 9, p. 39: FIG. 10 · *Das Magazin,* VOL. 47, 1928, pp. 2485: FIG. 11, p. 2488: FIG. 12, p. 2490: FIG. 13 · Siegfried MOLLIER, *Plastische Anatomie. Die konstruktive Form des menschlichen Körpers,* Munich: J. F. Bergmann, 1924, p. 58: FIG. 14 · *Bauhaus,* edited by Jeannine FIEDLER and Peter FEIERABEND, Cologne: Könemann, 1999, p. 285: FIG. 15

CHRISTOPH SCHNOOR

Space and the Body:
Concepts of the Corporeal in
Le Corbusier's Work

"Taking possession of space is the first gesture of living things, of men and of animals, of plants and of clouds, a fundamental manifestation of equilibrium and of duration."[1]

"Architecture, sculpture and painting are specifically dependent on space, bound to the necessity of controlling space, each by its own appropriate means. The essential thing that will be said here is that the release of aesthetic emotion is a special function of space."[2]

INTRODUCTION: BODY AND SPACE

Le Corbusier had explored the concept of space since at least 1910. But only late in his career, in 1948, did he draw attention to the fact that the phenomenon of space was one of the driving forces of his work. Architecture was not silent or passive for him. It was something he invested with an astonishing range of human activities: touching, domination, caressing, and even wounding.[3] Although such a notion had already been present in *Vers une architecture,* it was only in his 1948 publication *New World of Space* that Le Corbusier brought such a humanization of architecture together with the notion of space, stating that "the release of aesthetic emotion is a special function of space."[4] The architecture he humanizes, personifies, strongly affects the beholder. He brings it into proximity with a human body that occupies and shapes space. Thus, he touches on the direct relationship between the human body and space, a relationship that, in its various aspects, manifested itself throughout his career. One finds the manifold notions of the human body in his work appear at times in dichotomies, or as a

IN / KIRSTEN WAGNER AND JASPER CEPL (EDITORS) /
IMAGES OF THE BODY IN ARCHITECTURE: ANTHROPOLOGY AND BUILT SPACE /
TÜBINGEN · BERLIN / ERNST WASMUTH VERLAG / 2014 / PP. 99–130

field of overlapping topics. To a certain extent, these aspects of one theme — visual perception, the anthropomorphic, the anthropometric, the mechanic, the organic, the erotic and the idea of metamorphosis — are all and ever present in his work. But they occur with ever changing intensity at different times.

Rather than attempting to disentangle this web of concepts and influences, this essay examines the varying spatial implications of Le Corbusier's image of the human body. Six 'snapshots' are presented out of his work that reveal varying degrees of a human body spatiality at a particular stage of his career.

These are: urban space as perceived through the eye and body of the *flâneur*; the body interpreted as a standardized 'apparatus' with a machine-like quality that does not resonate spatially; the body's naked form influencing the shape of

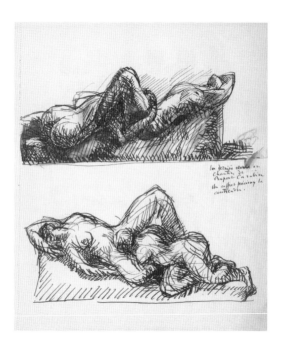

1
LE CORBUSIER /
DEUX NUES
FÉMININS
(TWO FEMALE
NUDES) /
STUDY AFTER
A SCULPTURE
BY RUPERT
CARABIN / 1917 /
PEN ON PAPER

buildings in plan and section; the body as an organism that anthropomorphizes the city; the body interpreted mathematically in the *Modulor*; the Cabanon as a point of concurrence of bodily aspects that are both spatial and non-spatial.

Generally speaking, from early manifestations in nude drawings — as separate from architecture — to Le Corbusier's late work, the body becomes more overt through his career as theme for and influence on his architecture and urban designs. In later life, when he aimed at a synthesis of the arts, one can observe such a synthesis on the level of forms, but intellectually concepts are still unresolved and tensions remain.[5]

CHRISTOPH SCHNOOR

The human body appeared as a distinctive topic in Le Corbusier's work as early as 1908, when as Charles-Édouard Jeanneret, he studied life drawing in Vienna.[6] Taking classes with a relatively unknown artist called Karl Stemolak, he wrote to his parents "from Stemolak I learn to see"[7]. After his stay in Vienna, several early manifestations of nude sketches and gouaches are notable, apparent particularly around 1913 and 1917 (FIG. 1).[8] These studies are often of an explicitly erotic nature. In the later ones, the sea-shell appears as both a direct attribute of the female figure and is also used, in his works of that period, to suggest female and sexual symbolism.[9]

On a theoretical level, we find a first encounter with the human body in his discussion of urban design — the unfinished treatise *La Construction des villes*. Here, in the research of theories of perception, the link between the eye and body of the urban flâneur is explored in depth. During 1910, Le Corbusier intensively worked on *La Construction des villes,* a study his teacher Charles L'Eplattenier had asked him to write.

To prepare himself Le Corbusier deeply delved into the German discourse on *Stadtbaukunst,* the "art of urban design", then in its heyday. He produced a lengthy manuscript that heavily relied on this discourse. Starting an apprenticeship at Peter Behrens' Berlin office in November 1910, he was more or less forced to abandon the unfinished manuscript, which he never published.[10]

Yet this first take on urban aesthetic laid the intellectual foundation for much of his future work. More than just advocating the aesthetic principles of spatial enclosure laid down by Viennese architect and theorist Camillo Sitte, Le Corbusier brings together aspects of the 'practical aesthetics' of perception of the urban realm, as investigated by German language writers on urban design themes.[11]

His study can be called a 'double reception' of Sitte's research and theories: on the one hand, it was a direct reception of Sitte's ideas, on the other hand it was a reception via those architects and art historians who had read and digested, and occasionally criticized Sitte's ideas: Paul Schultze-Naumburg, Albert Erich Brinckmann and Karl Henrici, as well as Theodor Fischer, to name just a few. But none of these writers, including Le Corbusier, was as versed in the physiological background of questions on visual perception as Sitte was.[12]

While Sitte's view seems to be mostly a bird's-eye view of the urban square, Schultze-Naumburg and Henrici actually take the observer into the streets, exploring what the *flâneur* sees while walking through urban spaces. Karl Henrici deserves special mention because rather than disconnecting the eye of the passerby from his body, he manages to link those two aspects in order to discuss the effects of visual perception of the streetscape on bodily perception: thus his categories of *langweilig* and *kurzweilig,* of pleasant and tedious, could be called 'functional' in a corporeal sense, inasmuch as Henrici stresses the direct link between visual perception and bodily comfort or discomfort.[13] In Le Corbusier's words:

> *It is in wandering a city's streets that one will either find a reason for enthusiasm, daydreams and enjoyment or feel a dreary lethargy, creeping in to paralyse our legs and leave for ever a hateful memory of the city thus glimpsed.*[14]

Eagerly picking up the cues from Henrici, Le Corbusier's investigations into the necessary sensorial qualities of a cityscape achieve a very direct quality, much closer to the human body than the counterparts of argumentation taking place in *Urbanisme* in 1925, when he speaks on matters of urban perception. Proof of his early understanding of the importance of Henrici's arguments is the fact that for *La Construction des villes,* he patiently translated Henrici's article on pleasant and tedious streets in full, summarizing:

> *According to Henrici, a street is boring when the passerby walking there feels that the street is longer than it is in reality; if the opposite is true, the street is pleasing. The skill of the city designer* [traceur des rues] *is therefore to play with optical illusions to obtain advantages or disadvantages* [FIG. 2]:

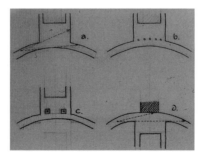

2
LE CORBUSIER /
SKETCH OF A
PASSERBY'S LINES
OF SIGHT IN A
CURVED STREET
WITH MONUMENTAL
BUILDING / 1910 /
AFTER KARL HENRICI'S
*BEITRÄGE ZUR
PRAKTISCHEN ÄSTHETIK
IM STÄDTEBAU*
(P. 91–92)

> *the less street surface and façade is visible, the shorter the street is believed to be. If, however, the street creates a negative misapprehension in the pedestrian walking there, the street is boring. Yet the more street surface and side walls are visible, the longer, more spacious and important the street will appear; being shorter in reality than its clever proportions lead one to believe, the street will surprise the passerby agreeably and be an entertaining street.*[15]

In *La Construction des villes,* Le Corbusier engages with definitions of space as such. The manuscript contains some of the very few instances in which he clearly explained his attitude towards space, to which he repeatedly refers using

CHRISTOPH SCHNOOR

the term *corporalité*. Is this a literal translation from the German *Körperlich-keit*, a term which plays a major role in the early 20th century *Wirkungsästhe-tik* movement, which investigates the aesthetics of perception?[16] Even if this were the case, Le Corbusier did not employ it to denote the physical presence of buildings as we would now understand them — as architectural objects.

In fact, he consistently uses the term *corporalité* when referring to the idea of a tangible three-dimensional space, something which is apparently not adequately conveyed by the term *espace*. The word *corporalité* is rarely used in French, although it is interesting to note Voltaire's use of the term in connection with something ostensibly intangible: he writes of the "corporalité des âmes", or physicality of souls. He means precisely the same thing the young Le Corbusier was seeking to express: actually being able to feel something which in itself is intangible.[17]

Fifteen years later, in *Urbanisme*, Le Corbusier drops the issue of spatial considerations in urban design. However, in *La Construction des villes* he clearly accepted space as a key part of urban design aesthetics. If *corporalité* was indeed his translation of Albert Erich Brinckmann's term *Körperlichkeit* in *Platz und Monument* (another book that Le Corbusier thoroughly studied in 1910), this would be an indirect appropriation of art historian Heinrich Wölfflin's concept of perception in which the observer or rather, the participant of urban spaces is able to *feel* the appropriateness of the proportional relationship of buildings to space through his own bodily perception.[18]

It is plausible to assume that the repertoire of the visual and tactile perception of urban situations which Le Corbusier developed during his research in the libraries in Munich and Berlin and 'on site' in various, predominantly German, towns and cities, formed a fertile background for his spatial explorations in his houses, notably the 1920s villas, such as the Villa Savoye.

He was fascinated with Auguste Choisy's interpretation of the Acropolis as *pittoresque* composition.[19] This became a main source for his idea of the architectural promenade. But it is crucial to note that Le Corbusier's reading of Choisy fell on fertile ground on his visit in 1911 because he was already prepared by earlier readings and observations of the perception of urban space: the *promenade architecturale* also relates to Le Corbusier's 1910 research on Sitte and the urbanism of the enclosed space.[20]

Taking this idea further, it is suggested that particular urban situations, which he studied from books and from nature, served as models to be translated into particular architectural moments in his buildings.

Thus, the interior of the Maison La Roche-Jeanneret, translated as a picturesque medieval town square — an adaptation of lessons learned from Schultze-Naumburg and Fischer — intensified, on a domestic scale, the experience of visual and bodily engagement a *flâneur* would have in an 'urban theatre', in the well-composed streets and squares of vernacular or traditional towns. The compact, even compressed superimposition of spaces around the entry of the Maison La Roche (**FIG. 3**) echoed the treatment of adjacent squares at a different level,

linked through spatially complex figures, including flights of stairs, as recorded by Jeanneret from Fischer's and Schultze-Naumburg's observations and designs. The Villa Savoye, on the other hand, may have profited from Henrici's reflection on the pedestrian, i.e. vertical versus the vehicular or horizontal connection in overcoming height distances. Henrici's notes accompanying a small drawing

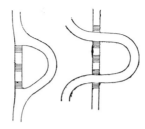

(**FIG. 4**) which shows the superimposition of a ramp with a flight of stairs, reads as an anticipation of the Villa Savoye: "With such ensembles in the open, it is

CHRISTOPH SCHNOOR

important that both motifs, the serpentine and the steep ramp, stair or terrace, are seen in tandem: that is where stimulating overlaps of the different lines can be encountered."[21] But Le Corbusier's translation of this into the Villa's interior was more than a compositional device in that it overlaid movements of the body within the house at different speeds and with different intentions: the servant stair and the gentle ascent of the ramp that would lead a visitor to the main storey are visibly put in contrast to each other to enhance the aesthetic impact through a functional device (**FIG. 5**).

5
LE CORBUSIER /
VILLA SAVOYE /
POISSY / RAMP
AND SPIRAL
STAIRS

Thus, with his early urban analyses, Le Corbusier discerns a direct relationship between eye and body. He lays a foundation stone for future investigations by establishing a link between the bodily sensations such as delight or tiredness, conveyed to the passerby by his stroll through a city, with his visual perception of walking through urban spaces. In this, the human body is not depicted as an image nor described as an organism or mechanism as happens elsewhere in Le Corbusier's work. Rather, the body is implied as a main influence on his architecture, since the architecture forms the result of his patient recording and analyzing, and of a *mis en scène,* via design, of the spatial qualities which he understood would have a profound effect on the visual and bodily sensations of any visitor to his villas, for example the La Roche or Savoye.[22]

THE BODY AS STANDARDIZED "APPARATUS" OF MODERNIZATION

Although the notion of the body moving through space clearly finds its expression in Le Corbusier's built work of the 1920s, in his written work at the same time the human body is given attention primarily as a means of modernization. Le Corbusier develops views which respond to contemporary changes and challenges: the speeding up of every aspect of life, an increasing demand for affordable products that require standardized fabrication, and an understanding of the human body that frees it from traditional bounds.

Modern Man, as seen particularly in the 1920s, is equipped with a body that needs to be trained, improved and maintained. According to this view, the idea of the body often approximates that of a mechanical object, even a machine: a view that Le Corbusier embraces. However his requests for the renewal of architecture are less driven by health and hygiene requirements — issues then frequently discussed[23] — but by discussions of a mechanistic nature of human being.

In his immediate environment, his brother Albert Jeanneret and the physician Pierre Winter contribute to Le Corbusier's view on the human body as a mechanic organism. This mechanistic body is remarkably disconnected from all its other aspects, including the idea of a spatial realm in relationship with the body — which he had already actively embraced in 1910.

Le Corbusier argues that the body is a mechanic tool and needs mechanized tools: human beings have typified needs and it is necessary to design standardized tools for them. His discussions in *Vers une architecture* on standardization and type — Parthenon vs. automobile — are legend,[24] more to the point here are those in *L'Art décoratif d'aujourd'hui* (The Decorative Art of Today) of 1925. Determined to research the human basis for mechanical objects that assist our daily actions, Le Corbusier declares: "To search for the human scale, for human function, is to define human needs."[25] The proximity of this statement to the *Modulor* which asks for the ultimate basis of human scale is obvious. Le Corbusier continues that these human needs are not numerous, and that "they are very similar for all mankind, since man has been made out of the same mould from the earliest times known to us."[26] He cites the *Larousse* dictionary, aiming to show that the anatomy of the human body could be described through just three images: through the structure, the nervous system, and the arterial system — "the whole machine is there".[27] Thus, the body is understood as a well-functioning apparatus.

CHRISTOPH SCHNOOR

Le Corbusier keeps alive such a view of the body over the next 30 years, as a letter of 1956 shows in which he tries to persuade his wife Yvonne to quit smoking by sending her an anatomical drawing which shows how the nicotine poisoned her body (FIG. 6).

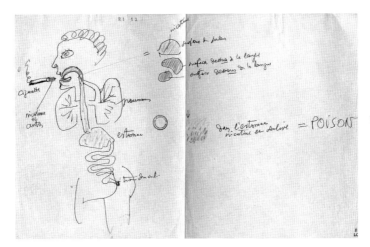

6
LE CORBUSIER /
YVONNE POISONS
HERSELF WITH
SMOKING /
DRAWING IN A
LETTER OF 1956

In *L'Art décoratif d'aujourd'hui*, Le Corbusier continues in search of universal aspects of the body: "These needs are type, that is to say they are the same for all of us; we all need means of supplementing our natural capabilities, since nature is indifferent, inhuman (extra-human), and inclement; we are born naked and without sufficient armour."[28] In other words, human beings are all similar; therefore their needs are mostly the same and have to be answered accordingly. Le Corbusier clearly rejects any attempt to cater to individual needs through 'body-tools':

> *In speaking of decorative art, we have the right to insist on the type-quality of our needs, since our concern is with the mechanical system that surrounds us, which is no more than an extension of our limbs; its elements, in fact, artificial limbs. Decorative art becomes orthopaedic [...]: the client is a man, familiar to us all and precisely defined.*[29]

The key word is the "type-quality of our needs". Le Corbusier cites his conversation with "one of the big names in charge of the 1925 Exhibition" who "proclaimed the need of each individual for something different, claiming different circumstances in each case: the fat man, the thin man, the short, the long, the ruddy, the lymphatic, the violent, the mild, the utopian, and the neurasthenic", and so on.[30] Le Corbusier accuses his counterpart of confusing the "tool-object" with a "sentiment-object". He assumes that the reaction to individual bodily needs would lead to an *objet d'art* rather than to a well-adapted tool-object. He does admit that, in the end, "only *poetry,* that is to say, happiness, carries authority." But he sees the individual sentiment-object as unrealistic and demands a clear distinction between the elevated life of the spirit and the tools of daily life. The life of the spirit he sees as a highly individual activity, but one equally detached from the secondary level of his tools, which might be described as the life of the body.[31] Thus, the tools that organize our daily life, secondary to the "Sistine Chapel, that is to say works truly etched with passion"[32], are to be standardized and not to be filled with sentiment. They have to be treated as what they are, nothing more than tools. Does separation of tool and poetry also mean a separation between mind and body? This seems to be the case here.

The view of modern man as closely linked to the machine appears in accordance with Le Corbusier's conviction of the 1920s that Taylorism, the American version of "Scientific Management", was the future for urban planning and politics.[33] On the level of the human being, Dr Pierre Winter's contributions in *L'Esprit nouveau* point at the related 'scientific management' of the body through sports. Winter asserts that contemporary man has neglected his body and is not living according to its needs: "Man is ignoring his physiological limits. He is a creature of habit, he adapts to situations. He has got used to overworking, to insomnia, to overeating, to an excessive or languished sex life, and to toxins."[34] This has to be rectified through sports. One of the important requirements for modern man is to put order into everyone's individual life. "If everyone fathoms out, methodically, their daily use of time, in a sense of Taylorization of actions and gestures, […] one could, by adding up all the minutes gained, find the necessary time for sports, to deal with our body."[35] A certain 'mechanistic' attitude towards the body cannot be denied but Winter nevertheless attempts to balance his demands for sports; he does not wish to create *homme-machines,* "body monsters" who cannot think.[36]

Albert Jeanneret was advocating a position a step ahead, not only of Winter's position, but also of his brother's thinking: whereas, in *L'Art décoratif d'aujourd'hui,* Le Corbusier separates the needs of body and mind from each other, Albert Jeanneret advocates, in two consecutive 1920 issues of *L'Esprit nouveau,* rhythmic dance, *eurhythmics,* as an integrative art for modern man. He points out:

> *The human body has become an expressive power again, since great artists have revealed the beauty of its forms and the purity of its plastic intentions. The problems resolved by mechanics make wish for this rhythmical machine which the human body is, or rather for this harmonization to be established between body and spirit, the same possibility of precision.*[37]

Albert Jeanneret is close to Winter in picturing the human body as a "rhythmical machine" but he also claims a close link between the body, sports and art. Since, as a student of eurythmics, he experienced the almost utopian link between a highly modern idea of dance movement — Émile Jaques-Dalcroze's eurhythmics — and Heinrich Tessenow's architecture as well as Adolphe Appia's stage sets for the Hellerau Institute, Albert Jeanneret was able to evoke this powerful link between the 'modern' body and art, combined with a quest for precision which, as he argues, is a precondition for modern life, which contemporary men and women usually fail to develop: "Rarely is the harmonization between body and spirit strived for."[38] He demands an education which fosters concentration and precision in thought and movement; this could be achieved by eurhythmics. Albert Jeanneret thus brings together body and mind — in its movement through the space on stage.

Since Le Corbusier had visited Hellerau as early as 1910 and seen Tessenow's theatre finished in 1913, he would have been able to 'inhale' not just the atmosphere of the Dalcroze Institute but also the extremely up to date way in which the human body was freed of conventions in terms of dance movement and clothing. This experience may not have challenged his later collectivist view of the human body because he could have argued that the dance movements of *eurhythmics* were not individual expressions of the dancers but universal expressions of the human condition. Nevertheless, his early investigations of the body moving through urban space, as undertaken in *La Construction des villes,* were closer to Albert's requests for a *eurhythmic* education combining the understanding of space, movement, and time. But the closeness of body and mind as studied in *La Construction des villes* seems to have disappeared in Le Corbusier's *L'Art décoratif d'aujourd'hui.* The question remains as to whether a reintegration of these two realms happens later in his life.

BODY INFLUENCES BUILT SPACE: ORGANIC FORMS AND *WOHNLEIB*

Despite such an overtly expressed mechanistic view, the rhythmical machine of the body starts to influence Le Corbusier's architecture in the 1920s, leaving imprints on the floor plans of his houses. Curves in the plans appear mainly as an indication of a direct relationship to the human body: they either relate to the movement of the body through a space or to the body in its natural state. As always, there are exceptions to this, the most famous being the curve which the Savoyes' car 'carved' into their weekend house in Poissy.

Where the curve does relate to the movement of the human body through space, it either relates directly to movement as 'action' as in the curving of a staircase (such as in the Villa Stein-de Monzie in Garches) or it may hark back to the early investigations on the body's movement through a city, as does the ramp in the Villa La Roche of 1923–24. There are also complex deformations of shapes such as the staircase in the Pavilion Suisse in Paris (1930–32) and its adjacent column that can be read as being affected by the impact of the *idea* of movement through this space.[39]

In spaces in which the body interacts directly with the architecture, Le Corbusier allowed it to affect the perceived 'mass' of the building. In these cases it is as if the body was leaving a direct imprint on the building itself when naked, particularly when bathing: the body seems to be extending the walls which contain bathtubs, showers, and the toilet, in order for them to adapt to the human figure. This happens in many of his houses of the 1920s, particularly so in the villas Stein-de Monzie (**FIG. 7**) and Savoye. Le Corbusier also displayed a version

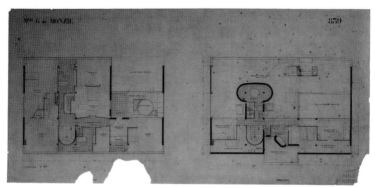

7
LE CORBUSIER /
VILLA STEIN-
DE MONZIE /
GARCHES /
1ST AND 2ND
FLOOR PLANS

of Henri Matisse's bronze *Nu couché* of 1907, a reclining female figure, on a shelf in the Villa Stein-de Monzie, "perhaps as a statement: his architecture was in harmony with the body."[40] The organic forms of these rooms go beyond the Cartesian order of many of his 1920s-buildings, bringing them closer to what von Moos has, adapting a remark by Lewis Mumford, called "the animal feeling" in Le Corbusier's paintings.[41]

Since in *L'Art Décoratif d'aujourd'hui,* the body was presented as organism akin to an apparatus, one could expect to find that his paintings of women followed this lead. But, as von Moos has pointed out in comparing Le Corbusier's nudes to contemporary paintings of Fernand Léger, Le Corbusier's figurative work "does not celebrate man as an abstract, archaic idol" as Léger's so often does. Instead, Le Corbusier's women are highly expressive; "nobody would compare them to mechanical dolls"; much rather a "sense of parody and pathos, despair and frantic vehemence permeates this work".[42] Likewise, Le Corbusier's machine-analogies used in *L'Art décoratif d'aujourd'hui* and other places are actually surprisingly moderate, considering to what high degree the human body was generally seen, during the 1920s, as something mechanical, which needs to function, be adjusted, and optimized.[43] While the human body is not depicted as a mechanical *poupée,* nevertheless "in certain photographs of his architec-

CHRISTOPH SCHNOOR

ture in the late 1920s, Le Corbusier employed wooden *poupées* in the manner of Man Ray, presumably to suggest a fantastic environment of competing scales."[44] Instead of depicting mechanical qualities in his drawings and paintings of the nude figure, a return to the classical is visible in at least some of Le Corbusier's nude drawings and paintings, such as *La pêcheuse d'huitres* of 1928 or his voluptuous Algiers women, similar to a tendency that many artists in the 1920s and 1930s followed. But central to this particular aspect of Le Corbusier's image of the body and to this essay as a whole must be the sense of ambiguity. Niklas Maak has pointed at a particular instance in a painting of 1931, entitled "femme, homme et os" — "woman, man and bone". The sexes of the figures depicted are ambiguous, even oscillating when regarding the work. Maak convincingly shows that it is unclear which of the two figures — who are in an ambivalent embrace — is man and which is woman, because attributes of both sexes seem to apply to both figures.[45] This ambiguity appears in conjunction with aspects of distortions, either of objects or of the bodies themselves. Von Moos has read these contorted bodies as expressing crisis: "On many of these paintings after 1930, monstrous forms and compact heaps of stacked arms and legs, often badly compressed between roping and all sorts of objects, reflect a convulsive state, a crisis."[46]

The fact that Le Corbusier started to draw and paint human, mostly female figures in large numbers from 1928 onwards may be a symptom of a general shift of his worldview, might even be seen as a crisis of his devotion to architecture as a standardized mechanical object, the *machine à habiter*. After the Villa Savoye had been designed to form a peak of this movement, Le Corbusier introduced more natural forms and materials into his architectural and painterly vocabulary. It is indeed the Villa Savoye which is the swansong on the somehow disembodied architecture of the 1920s. Those 'stylistic' elements of the *International Style* — the white, cubic, undecorated form — had already been left behind, at least in part, at the moment of their canonization by Henry-Russell Hitchcock and Philip Johnson.[47] Triggered also by a growing dissatisfaction with the technical difficulties experienced with his houses, particularly the Villa Savoye, Le Corbusier sets out to 'rematerialize' his architecture: *pilotis* grow fat and acquire bone-shapes, the rubble-wall which serves as background of his own studio in the Rue Nungesser-et-Coli, begins to appear in further designs, timber is introduced as building material, the outlines of his buildings start to move off the Cartesian grid, and the *béton brut* of the Unité is not far away. The rift of the 1920s between the mechanistic and the spatial aspect of the body is overcome — in part — through a growing corporality of Le Corbusier's architecture.

This becomes particularly visible in his own apartment in the Rue Nungesser-et-Coli in Paris of 1933, where Le Corbusier takes the idea of the spatial imprint of the body on architecture a decisive step further. The whole building seems to fit around the body of its author and owner. Le Corbusier chose to respond to municipal building height restrictions by translating them into vaulted ceilings of his apartment in the Immeuble Molitor, therefore allowing himself more space for studio and dining room (**FIG. 8**). But this is not simply a pragmatic

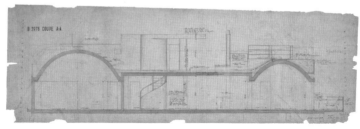

decision. It has the effect of moving towards a fundamentally different quality of space, much closer to Hugo Häring's idea of the *Wohnleib* (dwelling body) than the *machine à habiter*.[48] What Le Corbusier discussed in *La Construction des villes* twenty years earlier he appears to take up here: the idea of *corporalité* as a distinct embodiment of space. In the Immeuble Molitor, the space almost turns into an organic body surrounding man comfortably, like a womb. It is striking to see how Le Corbusier arrives at creating this cave-like shelter while towering high over Paris. Fittingly, it has also been argued that the eastern wing of his apartment in the Immeuble Molitor had his wife, Yvonne, "or the feminine, for its thematic source."[49] This example foreshadows the chapel at Ronchamp which has, times and again, been described as a motherly womb. It is remarkable that this modernist architect's work was, at times, most archaic and elementary in capturing the human need for a protective, even womb-like shelter.[50]

The organic-mechanistic side of Le Corbusier's approach to the human body does not disappear in the Immeuble Molitor; here, a number of sanitation objects reveal this aspect. Arthur Rüegg has observed how the sink, placed against a narrow window made of glass-blocks, is not just functional but full of symbolism. Although "[p]opular opinion would hardly have found the sink's surface-mounted tangle of pipes either attractive or practical", it stands to reason that Le Corbusier created this provokingly crude piece intentionally. It can be read as an "anatomical specimen in which the blood vessels supply a beautifully formed organ. The system's form seems to be a metaphor of its function."[51] This metaphor works in two ways. The sink in its closeness to an 'anatomical specimen' highlights the organic side of bathroom equipment as much as, by likening it to an organ, it points out the 'machine' nature of organisms.

This presentation of the mechanic side of the human organism goes along with a blurring of boundaries between the public and the private in a very direct, even blunt manner. Le Corbusier drags the functions of the human organism into view or in the open, because he understands the human body as an apparatus whose functions should not be concealed but celebrated. He repeatedly displays bathroom furniture (sinks, washbasins, bathtubs, bidets), if in the almost sacred overtone of the hand-wash basin in the Villa Savoye, which has been compared to a stoup, or in the invasion of the bedroom of his own apartment by a bidet. As Colin Rowe has observed, "with Le Corbusier, apparently there was always the greatest anxiety (amounting sometimes to fetishism) to positively celebrate the triumph of running water."[52]

THE CITY AS ORGANISM? *URBANISME* AND *VILLE RADIEUSE*

Such observations on the organic nature of his architecture directly relate to a thought expressed by Le Corbusier in *Urbanisme:*

> *One could say that the further the works of mankind are removed from our direct grasp, the more they tend towards pure geometry: a violin or a chair that both touch our body are of a less pure geometry, but the city is of pure geometry. Free, man strives for pure geometry. He pursues what is called order.*[53]

This claim directly explains his attitude to architectural forms as just described — the naked body impresses itself on walls, via bathtubs and other objects close to the body. But in terms of urban design this assertion appears as a major contradiction in Le Corbusier's work, one that cannot easily be resolved: For in *Urbanisme* the city is, on the one hand, understood as a technical tool: "La ville est un outil de travail."[54] Its illustration, the *Ville contemporaine,* is conceived accordingly, as a work of pure order and geometry, and thus Le Corbusier's — misled — arguments against Sitte and picturesque urbanism are well covered by this dictum;[55] however, another notion slowly develops in Le Corbusier's thinking and calls into doubt this very idea: the city understood as organism. After a first snippet of presence in 1910, the idea of the organic with regard to the city matures, becoming a central element of his argumentation in the book *La ville radieuse* of 1935.[56] Rather than following Alberti's notion of the city as a house, which would accord with the idea of the human body in space as expressed in 1910, Le Corbusier increasingly compares the city with a living organism. But he does not distinguish clearly either between botanical, zoological, or human organisms, or between a functional or formal understanding of the organic in general.

The analogy of city and organism is introduced as appendix to *Urbanisme,* at odds with the rest of the book.[57] Under the heading *Confirmations, Incitations, Admonestations* (confirmation, incitation, admonition), Le Corbusier shows eight figures to demonstrate the organic character of a city's structure, choosing most diverse organisms: the development of a sponge, various spinal columns of fish, partitions of different shell types, and even a comparison of the brains of mammals (**FIG. 9**). He does so in order to show developments from

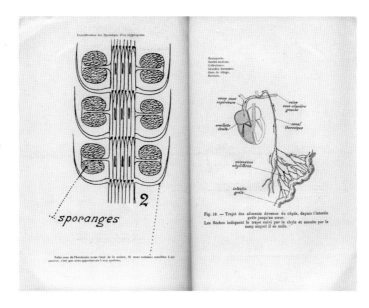

the simple to the complex, from the primal to complete, but also in order to prove how our sense for harmony stems from nature, saying: "Because we belong to its system, we are receptive to its works."[58] This caption is written under the drawing of a sporangium of a fern plant which resembles later designs for new-town developments with the separation of different classes of traffic. The drawing clearly is placed there with exactly this intention, despite being functionally completely unrelated. The same is true for another diagram showing the progress of nutrients of the chyme from the intestines to the human heart; above the drawing, Le Corbusier has written "transport, kinetic centre, collector roads, traversing roads, shunting yard, services".[59] He uses human metabolism, in direct translation, as a kind of instruction manual for how the city should be understood.[60] He could not claim more clearly that the (human) organism and a city are analogous in their function and therefore in their form. Such conflation of a functional with a formal analogy is astounding in its simplicity — but not uncommon amongst urban designers.[61]

The earliest inspirations for interpreting the city as organic may be found in Le Corbusier's 1910 reading of Schultze-Naumburg's *Kulturarbeiten: Der Städtebau,* particularly in the criticism of the regular grid of a city.[62] Le Corbusier closely follows Schultze-Naumburg's claim that the organic form of a city possesses advantages over the grid: a separation of vehicular and pedestrian traffic as much as the non-orthogonal connections through the city which allow shortest connections between different parts of the city (**FIG. 10**).[63]

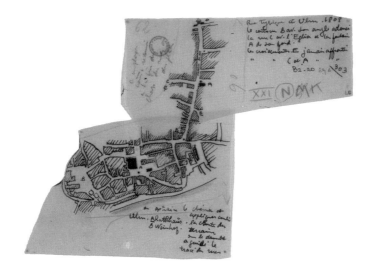

10
LE CORBUSIER /
TRACING OF
THE STREET
MAP OF ULM /
1910 / AFTER
DER STÄDTEBAU /
1909

In Schultze-Naumburg's words:

One can recognize that, in such plans which do not resemble an ossified geometric diagram but real organic growth, such difficulties [of prolonged paths between points a and b] will not arise. Here, the streets run through the city like great arteries; the main points are connected by main streets; countless small commercial passageways, pedestrian and road bridges, and thoroughfares always provide interconnections via the most direct, natural route.[64]

Le Corbusier's early reception of this idea of the organic is related to formal, aesthetic aspects and to the perception of the urban spaces by the *flâneur*, also avoiding the analogy of human or floral organisms with the functioning of a city. And whereas the *Ville contemporaine*, despite Le Corbusier's assertions of its functional nature, is strongly based on aesthetic considerations, closely following Marc-Antoine Laugier's requests for the redevelopment of Paris,[65] it is in the appendix of *Urbanisme,* that the conflation of functional and formal analogies into one idea of the 'organic city' appears. This analogy between organism and city shows a misunderstood functionalism in that the workings of a city are equated with completely unrelated functions of biological systems. On a symbolic level, this 'bio-morphism' is understandable and has a long tradition (for example in India), but on a functional level it is not sufficiently based in reality, particularly when used as the starting point of urban form.

In the book *La ville radieuse* of 1935, Le Corbusier presents two fundamentally different versions of the new city: on the one hand his designs for Algiers and Rio de Janeiro of around 1930, "linear viaducts treated as large landscape sculptures"[66], are based on vaguely biomorphic, and extremely long-stretched high-rise buildings, which, in many cases, carry motorways on top. One of these drawings for Algiers he calls a "lesson in nature, in urban biology"[67]. These designs, partly inspired by his drawings of voluptuous Algerian women,[68] directly contradict his claim that "the further the works of mankind are removed from our direct grasp, the more they tend towards pure geometry", as quoted above. It seems that here, Le Corbusier ignored his own understanding of scale relationships. The designs display Le Corbusier's technique of taking any artistic material at hand from one discipline and, through metamorphosis, turning it into something completely new.[69]

On the other hand, he presents a design for the *Ville radieuse* proper. This is accompanied by a kaleidoscopic range of arguments for the new city. As a programmatic statement of his new direction of work, he opens the book *La ville radieuse* with the following words: "I am attracted to the natural order of things. [...] I look for primitive men, not for their barbarity but for their wisdom. America, Europe, farmers, fishermen."[70] Le Corbusier's argument is that the city needs to be based on natural laws. Praising the natural, but also symbolic elements that were creating life on earth, Le Corbusier says: "The apotheosis of a great day. A pastoral symphony. Nature! This prodigious spectacle has been produced by the interplay of two elements, one male, one female: sun and water."[71] Having established these "laws of nature and the laws of men", Le Corbusier extends the biological analogy by comparing the city to an organism which, in his description, resembled a self-organizing organism of protozoa. First he sees an "amorphous, quivering, but purposeless mass", formed by multiplying single cells. "Then an intention appeared, an axis began to form in the centre of this motionless agglomeration. A current, a direction became apparent. An organism was born. [...] Life was pursuing its natural impulse towards organi-

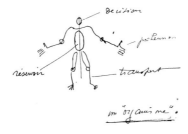

11
LE CORBUSIER /
THE ANTHROPO-
MORPHIC MODEL
FOR THE CITY /
FROM *THE
RADIANT CITY*

zation."[72] In a little drawing (FIG. 11) he turns the accumulation of protozoa into a human figure. He uses captions marking the head of the figure as "decision", the rump as "reservoir", the hand as "grip", and the legs as "transport", calling the

CHRISTOPH SCHNOOR

whole figure "an organism".[73] Thus in *La ville radieuse,* Le Corbusier brings the analogy to a point which he had neither reached nor attempted in *Urbanisme* ten years earlier: In its physiological functions the human being has become the anthropomorphous city.

Thus, Le Corbusier establishes the need for an organic structuring of the city. Nevertheless, his design proper of the *Ville radieuse,* unlike the anthropomorphic outlines that shaped his projects for Algiers and Rio, is very similar to the *Ville contemporaine,* in which the *blocs à redents* meander in an orthogonal order as do the roads, on the 'English landscape garden' spreading out underneath and between the buildings. It must appear that the 'organic' in the *Ville radieuse* is a notion, not a formal device. The plans for the city attempt to explain the relationship between the "common cell" and those parts of the body that would 'drive' the whole organism, and to overcome a problem Le Corbusier sees in his own *Ville contemporaine:* "Any concentrically designed city (all cities created in the past of ground plans determined by 'donkey tracks'; also my own 1922 project for a modern city of 3 million inhabitants) makes regular, organic development impossible: a biological defect."[74] The accompanying drawing, entitled "Biological organization of the city. Permanent possibility of extension", is relatively schematic and avoids translating the sketch of the human figure directly into a city that looks like a human being. Nevertheless, Le Corbusier places areas of the city in such a way that they present an abstract anthropomorphism, if that paradoxical formulation is permitted.[75]

But as much as this might be an ideal and symbolic symbiosis of human and city form (if one agrees with such a proposition), the dwellings of the *Ville radieuse* show the split of a 'whole body' into eye without body. In a sketch in *La ville radieuse,* Le Corbusier shows the 'workings' of a high-rise building, with the supply of gas, electricity, communication through telephone and fresh, well-tempered air. In his apartment, shown as a small figure, the inhabitant is represented by a colossal eye which dominates the whole drawing. This eye, as the central organ of the inhabitant, demonstrates that the connection of eye and body in Le Corbusier's early reading of Henrici is finally split apart. Henrici's technique, based on the correspondence between the experience of the eye — in seeing — and the body — in walking through a city —, was continued and put to the test by Le Corbusier in houses like La Roche or Savoye. But here the body does not feel any more what the eye sees. Le Corbusier separates the technical (or purely utilitarian) needs and the *besoins sentimentals,* the sentimental needs: "I express them insofar as they concern us, architects, in two words: visual drama and architecture."[76] This separation, happening simultaneously with Le Corbusier's proclamation of the city as anthropomorphic, is similar to the already observed split of the "tool-object" and "sentiment-object" in *L'Art Décoratif d'aujourd'hui.* One intention of integration is accompanied by another act of separation.

From 1943 to 1946, Le Corbusier worked on developing the system, a "grille de proportion", of dividing surfaces, based on the golden section and using measurements of the human body as dividers. His collaborators, Gerald Hanning, Elisa Maillard, and later his associate, André Wogenscky, contributed to answering the complex mathematical questions attached to this problem, until on the way to the United States in December 1945 Le Corbusier finished, on board of the Vernon S. Hood, his presentation of the system. In February 1946, it was christened "Modulor".[77] Having originally based it on the average height of 1,75 m of a French man, he faced the problem that the divisions obtained by the *Modulor* could not be translated into feet, yard, and inches. It was crucial for him to achieve this because the imperial system is based directly on the human body's measurements; thus he could strengthen the link back to primitive and ancient societies whose builders would use their own bodies to determine dimensions.[78] Le Corbusier's collaborator, Marcel Py, solved the problem by suggesting that in English detective stories, the 'good' men always were six foot tall.[79] The *Modulor* was mathematically not exact — and Le Corbusier knew this. In fact, he had asked René Taton, a mathematician, to clarify this for him.[80]

It seems strange that the *Modulor* should have appeared so suddenly and without any perceptible forewarning: nevertheless, Le Corbusier did not claim that it had been conceived 'on the spot'; rather, it related back to his early interest in questions of system, order, and mathematics: "More than these thirty years past, the sap of mathematics has flown through the veins of my work, both as an architect and painter; for music is always present in me."[81] A decade earlier, Matila Ghyka had published his book on the golden section, *Le nombre d'or,* which had a strong effect on Le Corbusier.[82] Niklas Maak sees Ghyka's book as the true origin of the *Modulor*.[83] It may have been the trigger, but it was by no means Le Corbusier's earliest occupation with the golden section. His own notes document that he was interested in the origin and workings of the golden section (and in what would become his *tracés régulateurs*) as early as 1911. One of his German travel notebooks gives testimony of this. He takes notes of the golden section and of a contemporary book by Alhard von Drach on medieval rules of triangulation.[84] Although not mentioned by Le Corbusier, those notes point to Hendrik Petrus Berlage's *Grundlagen und Entwicklung der Architektur,* a book that Le Corbusier might very well have read during his time in Behrens' office. All of the notes on those pages correspond with respective discussions in Berlage's *Grundlagen.* But Berlage, who investigated possibilities of an application of proportional rules, also warned about the system of triangulation, noting that "it should be understood that the geometry alone does not turn someone into an artist, since the artistic idea is not generated by the geometrical idea. Non-artists will not be able to create anything with this system but artists may be able to do everything with it."[85] This warning comes very close to Le Corbusier's own qualification that "the 'Modulor' is a working tool [...]. The 'Modulor' does not confer talent, still less genius. It does not make the dull subtle: it only offers them the facility of a sure measure."[86]

The possibilities of the *Modulor* are exemplarily put to the test in Le Corbusier's Duval Factory (**FIG. 12**) in Saint-Dié, France, of 1951, which demonstrates

12
LE CORBUSIER /
DUVAL FACTORY /
ST.-DIÉ

how the idea of the machine, the cosmic order, the poetry, and the natural come together in relative harmony, in a well-rounded and complete application of the *Modulor*. Le Corbusier proudly points out that "1. it is proportioned entirely by the Modulor, 2. the section is strongly expressed, 3. the ceilings, wood work, plumbing, etc. are intensely coloured in accordance with the robust character of the concrete. The factory of St.-Dié was finished before the Unité at Marseilles. Both express a rude health, their colour schemes being pushed to a most powerful intensity."[87]

The Duval Factory is situated towards the north of the small town of St.-Dié in the Vosges, just outside the area that would have been covered by Le Corbusier's reconstruction plan for the city. But it does not fulfil the series of expectations one might have about a factory building by Le Corbusier. First of all and in contrast to his plan for St.-Dié, the building supports the street edge and thus spatially frames the street. Secondly, the building consists of a box, three stories high, supported by a massive concrete floor-slab which partly rests on a ground floor of dressed stone and is partly suspended on rows of pilotis. This suspended area is compositionally offset by a rooftop floor which leads onto a roof garden.

Brise-soleils form the dominant theme of the façade, consisting of 14 bays, three stories high, which frame the bulk of the building. Behind these brise-soleils are offices as well as production areas. The fact that Le Corbusier unifies these different functions in the façade treatment plays down the recognizable presence of the factory. In section, Le Corbusier uses a split-level to achieve the full floor height necessary for production. The façade is compositionally intricate in that Le Corbusier employs three different, and independent rhythms belonging to the *Modulor*. The brise-soleils, a complex system of window frames behind, and the concrete structure of the building are all offset against each other in such a way that tension between the elements is created without upsetting the eye. Le Corbusier himself uses the analogy of a piece of music in asserting that in their independence, "all belong to the same range and all are of the same family. I imagine that the music played here by the architect will be firm and subtle, shaded, like Debussy's."[88] In this building, the *Modulor* has undoubtedly been successful in creating tension as well as harmony, a unity in variation as Le Corbusier always strived for. This is supported by the harmonious interplay of rough concrete, wooden window frames and roughly dressed stone walls.

The Duval Factory is an unusual modernist factory building in that is does not distinctively reveal its function. This is particularly surprising given the importance that modernist architects placed on the imagery of factories, even in buildings that were not themselves factories — as in Walter Gropius' Bauhaus in Dessau of 1926. And Le Corbusier himself well and truly applied the factory aesthetics even to private dwellings, for example to Amedée Ozenfant's studio in Paris of 1922. For the Duval Factory nevertheless, it seems that the *Modulor* helped Le Corbusier in 'humanizing' the factory, in turning it into a warm, approachable building that works well in breaking down the scale of a factory to human scale elements. This undoubtedly makes the building successful.

But it should also be noted that the anthropomorphic adaptations in plan and in section, displayed in earlier buildings, are not employed here. And it is with respect to the spatial aspects of the human body, that the Modulor takes an odd position. The Duval factory shows this. On one hand it could be argued that the *Modulor* is the crowning moment of Le Corbusier's attempt at synthesizing nature and geometry, as opposed to the relationship between body and perceptual space, which Le Corbusier had explored around 1910. Thus, the *Modulor* could exemplify a synthesis of body and measured space: von Moos has claimed that the *Modulor* brings together in one system what Le Corbusier had started very early in his career: "to discover nature with the help of geometry and to use geometry as a cabalistic key — not to an intellectual understanding alone, but ultimately to a pantheistic experience of nature".[89] Nevertheless, Le Corbusier's original intention to find a "grille de proportion" should not go unnoticed: the *Modulor* is useful to orthogonally divide surfaces or planes, even spaces. But despite its being derived from the Fibonacci series, the spiralling series of natu-

120

ral numbers, by virtue of its nature the *Modulor* has a strong bias to orthogonal systems such as the Duval Factory — or Le Corbusier's Museum of Unlimited Growth of 1939. And contrary to William Curtis' praise that the *Modulor's* "dynamic and telescoping proportions were well suited to the spatial ambiguities, complex curvatures and rhythmic, textured facades of Le Corbusier's late style"[90], the organic, in part anthropomorphic forms in his architecture are not, at least not explicitly, incorporated into the architectural elements governed by the more anthropometric *Modulor*. They stay natural, one could say, wild and untamed by a controlling device. A contradictory aspect of the *Modulor* appears. Orthogonal forms are ordered and set into a system that links architecture to the microscopic as well as to the universal. But although based on the human body and its proportions, and despite its rich possibilities of variation, Le Corbusier does not use the Modulor to categorize or tame his organic formal creations.

THE CABANON — ACHIEVED SYNTHESIS AND REMAINING TENSIONS

Does a full synthesis indeed happen in Le Corbusier's late work? Can such a synthesis between the various 'characters' which the body was able to assume be found in works like La Tourette, Chandigarh, the Harvard Visual Arts Center, or even the project for the Venice Hospital? Is there an instance that shows how the 'animal' feeling and the 'cerebral' aspect of the Modulor come together?

The Visual Arts Center seems to recommend itself since its "sole objective [was] to bring to the present generation the taste and the desire to combine the work of the hands with that of the mind, which is Le Corbusier's most important social vow."[91] Certainly, it combined organic and Cartesian forms in plan; by help of its ramp street it allowed the link of visual and bodily perception that he had investigated forty years earlier. Also, in its vaguely anthropomorphic plywood wrap, the assembly hall in the Millowner's Association acts at the same time, similarly to the Catalan vaults in the Maisons Jaoul, as a body extension and as an architectural embrace to the body. But a much smaller project comes to mind.

In a photo by Brassaï of 1952, Le Corbusier presented himself as a Noble Savage at Cap-Martin.[92] He did so by posing in short swimming trunks, right next to his recently finished hermit's hut, the Cabanon. This image has been read as pure marketing of an architect who wished to be seen as the pioneer of a synthesis of natural principles of building with industrial production.[93]

There is more to it. Since, in the 1920s, Le Corbusier presented himself as the avant-garde architect with hat and bowtie, is this a reconciliation with nature and therefore with the body? The hut itself is an essential piece for understanding Le Corbusier's attitude towards the human body. Most of the published photographs create the illusion of a solitary structure situated in wilderness, thus concealing its slightly mendacious nature: the fact that it was directly attached to Thomas Rebutato's restaurant at Roquebrune-Cap-Martin, and that trains on the Nice–Ventimiglia line were passing by only a few meters above the building. On the other hand, the wilderness of the Mediterranean Sea in front of the hut is simple reality.

Can the Cabanon be seen as representing, in its double nature, the ambivalent aspects of Le Corbusier's own attitude towards the human body — the supposedly natural body and the body as a machine? In order to answer this, we need to recall Colin Rowe's remark about the versatility of the image of the noble savage as a "superlative role-player" who could, among other things be "a classical shepherd, a Red Indian, someone discovered by Captain Cook, a *sans sculotte* of 1792, [...] a liberated hippy, a scientist, an engineer and, in the end, a computer."[94] So, if the noble savage turned into this empty 'container' for representing educated naivety alongside with intuitive wisdom, he may have done something for Le Corbusier, as well: in representing himself as noble savage, Le Corbusier was enabled to play with the double notion of naturalness and wisdom, nature and technology.

The Cabanon was a little hut, about 4 m in the square, consisting of a single room with a somewhat separated toilet and a hand wash-basin integrated into the main space of the room, containing a bed, a cupboard, and a desk. With its outside lined with rough sawn boards the Cabanon pretended to be a log cabin.

But the inside was treated as if the whole building was a fine piece of furniture rather than a primitive hut, completely lined with plywood. Le Corbusier had assigned the Corsican cabinet-maker Charles Barberis to manufacture "the ingenious, yet pragmatical combination of traditional and modern production methods and materials (solid wood, plywood)."[95] Even Jean Prouvé was involved in the design by being asked to produce the windows for the Cabanon. And the *arbre sanitaire,* the water-providing column, sophisticated through its design process, but simple and rustic in appearance, contained a semicircular chrome steel basin imported from Sweden.[96]

The Cabanon's crude outside, the attachment to Rebutato's restaurant which provided a supply of freshly cooked food, and the specific care given to the simple appearance are all aspects which resonate with Le Corbusier's arguments for human-limb objects, not made for poetry — because that is what the mind possesses — but as well-designed tools to make everyday life easier. But the carefully designed and especially crafted plywood lining and the *armatures* defy this notion of simple tools because they elevate the simplicity to a higher realm; in short, they symbolize simplicity. Arthur Rüegg has described the *arbre sanitaire* in the cabin as "reminiscent of a life close to nature that embodies Spartan, simple, essential values."[97] The apparently simple tools carry with themselves all the poetic and cultural connotations attached to them. This tiny building that was not included in Le Corbusier's *Œuvre Complète* speaks of individuality as much

CHRISTOPH SCHNOOR

as of repetition, of a sheltered inside space and the natural space outside (as in a snail's shell), both linked not by interstitial spaces but by precisely defined apertures (**FIG. 13**).[98] Here, Häring's *Wohnleib* has taken a simultaneously crude and

sophisticated form; considering the inside lining we remember Le Corbusier's 1925 comment that "we all need means of supplementing our natural capabilities" since "we are born naked and with insufficient armour".[99] Additionally, the Cabanon brings together the *Modulor* with debates of the relationship of man to society as well as the relationship of the human body to nature.

It must seem that the synthesis of conflicting positions is attempted and achieved — and at the same time, in its Janus-face the Cabanon shows a deep rift that cannot be bridged. As a hut for an intellectual mind that enjoys the simple but protected life of a monk served for by an immediately available infrastructure, it is an image for Le Corbusier's desired return to nature — but with a lifeline. Is it the fulfilment of a dream about the biological metaphor of cells being part of a much larger organism, or is it rather the dream of an architect who could be the primitive man for a few weeks but who could just as easily, whenever he decided to, leave his hut and take the train back to Paris within minutes? As Adolf Behne said: "[T]he deciding factor is the attitude towards society. The human being stands between nature and society. He opts for human community and thus places himself in a certain state of tension with nature. He opts for nature and is in a certain state of tension with society."[100] In these terms, the Cabanon is both: attached to a restaurant, it opted for community which it simultaneously denied by apparently opting for nature, as it presented itself to the viewer.

Thus the Cabanon may stand as Le Corbusier's very personal comment on the role of architecture in relationship to the human body. The Cabanon addresses many aspects of Le Corbusier's interpretation of the body and, in its smallness, even makes visible the realization that Le Corbusier has opened a vast richness of debates with his work that could, by their very nature, not be unified in a system of thought. The tensions in his attempted synthesis can only remain. But as much as their logical inconsistencies, it is the strength of his work that Le Corbusier plays out such ambivalences, as the Cabanon in all its minuteness, ably demonstrates.

NOTES

1   Le Corbusier, *New World of Space. The Foundations of His Work,* New York: Reynal and Hitchcock, 1948, p. 7.

2   Ibid., pp. 7–8.

3   Ibid., p. 8.

4   Ibid.

5   A research and travel grant by Unitec New Zealand enabled me to conduct research for this essay in Berlin and Paris during spring 2010. I am thankful to Jasper Cepl and Kirsten Wagner for their invitation to write on this topic and for their inspiring questions and suggestions. I would like to specifically thank Johan Linton and Mary McLeod for their comments and advice. I also want to thank Kim Sanderson for her translations as indicated below.

6   Charles-Édouard Jeanneret used the pseudonym Le Corbusier since 1920 for his writings and architecture, exclusively since 1928. In order to simplify reading, the name Le Corbusier will be used from here on.

7   H. Allen Brooks, *Le Corbusier's Formative Years. Charles-Edouard Jeanneret at La Chaux-de-Fonds,* Chicago and London: The University of Chicago Press, 1997, p. 121.

8   See Brooks, *Formative Years,* pp. 372–376, and Françoise Ducros' catalogue entry "Still Life and Genre Scenes", in: *Le Corbusier before Le Corbusier,* edited by Stanislaus von Moos and Arthur Rüegg, New Haven and London: Yale University Press, 2002, pp. 267–269.

9   Ducros, "Still Life and Genre Scenes", p. 269: "These [nudes] were to change again, in 1928, becoming more imaginary than real, while the shell, associated with the natural world of the beach, will figure again, among objects eliciting a poetic reaction."

10   See Le Corbusier, *La Construction des villes. Le Corbusiers erstes städtebauliches Traktat von 1910/11,* edited by Christoph Schnoor, Zurich: gta, 2008.

11   Nowhere in the manuscript is there a mention of Schmarsow, Wölfflin or any other art historian concerned with theories of perception, therefore it has to be assumed that he only studied ideas of perception through the 'practical aesthetics' of a Sitte, Henrici or Schultze-Naumburg.

12   See Heleni Porfyriou, "Camillo Sitte. Optically Constructed Space and Artistic City Building" in this volume · Gabriele Reiterer, *AugenSinn. Zu Raum und Wahrnehmung in Camillo Sittes Städtebau,* Salzburg: Anton Pustet, 2003.

13 K. [Karl] HENRICI, *Beiträge zur praktischen Ästhetik im Städte Bau. Eine Sammlung von Vorträgen und Aufsätzen,* Munich: Georg D.W. Callwey, [1904].

14 LE CORBUSIER, *La Construction des villes,* p. 290. Translation from the French by Kim Sanderson.

15 Ibid., p. 295. Translation from the French by Kim Sanderson.

16 See Francesco PASSANTI on Jeanneret's use of the term *corporalité* in his essay "Architecture: Proportion, Classicism, and Other Issues", in: *Le Corbusier before Le Corbusier,* ed. VON MOOS and RÜEGG, pp. 69–98, here p. 84.

17 This meaning of *corporalité* is illustrated in É. [Émile] LITTRÉ, *Dictionnaire de la langue française,* Paris: L. Hachette, 1863–1872, 4 VOLS., here VOL. 1, 1863, p. 816: "Qualité de ce qui est corporel." Littré gives a quote from Voltaire as an example: "Arnobe parle […] positivement de la corporalité des âmes". The quote (with no omission indicated by Littré) is from *Oeuvres completes de Voltaire,* 92 VOLS., [Kehl]: Société Littéraire Typographique, 1785, here VOL. 41, p. 336.

18 Albert Erich BRINCKMANN, *Platz und Monument. Untersuchungen zur Geschichte und Ästhetik der Stadtbaukunst in neuerer Zeit,* Berlin: Ernst Wasmuth, 1908 (reprint with an afterword by Jochen Meyer, Berlin: Gebr. Mann, 2000), and Heinrich WÖLFFLIN, *Prolegomena zu einer Psychologie der Architektur,* Munich: Wolf, 1886 (new edition with an afterword by Jasper Cepl, Berlin: Gebr. Mann, 1999).

19 See Robin MIDDLETON, "Auguste Choisy, Historian: 1841–1909", in: *International Architect,* VOL. 1, no. 5, 1981, pp. 37–42.

20 As has been pointed out by: Richard ETLIN, *Frank Lloyd Wright and Le Corbusier. The Romantic Legacy,* Manchester and New York: Manchester University Press, 1994.

21 HENRICI, *Beiträge zur praktischen Ästhetik im Städte Bau,* p. 104: „Bei solchen offenen Anlagen ist es für den Eindruck von Bedeutung, dass man die beiden Motive, das der Serpentine und das der steilen Rampen-, Treppen- oder Terrassenbildung, in ihrem Zusammenhange erkennt; da ergeben sich belebende Ueberschneidungen der verschiedenartigen Linien".

22 As a logical consequence of this procedure, these villas are open to interpretations such as that of Beatriz COLOMINA, who investigates the photographic and filmic qualities of the Villa Savoye in her essay "The Split Wall: Domestic Voyeurism", in: *Sexuality and Space,* edited by Beatriz Colomina, New York: Princeton Architectural Press, 1992, pp. 73–130.

23 On the relationship between modernism and the sanatorium see Beatriz COLOMINA, "The Medical Body in Modern Architecture", in: *Anybody,* edited by Cynthia C. DAVIDSON, Cambridge, MA and London: The MIT Press, 1997, pp. 228–239.

24 See Francesco PASSANTI, "The Vernacular, Modernism, and Le Corbusier", in: *The Journal of the Society of Architectural Historians,* VOL. 56, 1997, pp. 438–451.

25 LE CORBUSIER, *L'Art décoratif d'aujourd'hui,* Paris: G. Crès, 1925. English translation: *The Decorative Art of Today,* translated by James I. Dunnett, London: The Architectural Press, 1987, p. 72.

26 LE CORBUSIER, *The Decorative Art of Today,* p. 72.

27 Ibid.

28 Ibid.

29 Ibid.

30 Ibid.

31 Ibid., p. 73.

32 Ibid., p. 76.

33 Mary MᴄLᴇᴏᴅ: "'Architecture or Revolution': Taylorism, Technocracy, and Social Change", in: *Art Journal*, ᴠᴏʟ. 43, 1983, pp. 132–147, here p. 133: "An important dimension of this ideological stance was Taylorism, the American system of Scientific Management. Like many European professionals, Le Corbusier saw Taylorism as a means of breaking with prewar society, a key to social renewal. The term 'Taylorism' appears in almost every one of his books from *Après le cubisme* (1918) to *La Ville radieuse* (1935); *Ville Contemporaine* and *Plan Voisin*, premised upon speed, efficiency, and economy, were architectural visions of the American industrial utopia made manifest."

34 Pierre Wɪɴᴛᴇʀ, "Le sport", in: *L'Esprit Nouveau*, ɴᴏ. 16, Mai 1922, pp. 1951–1952, here p. 1951: "*L'homme ignore ses limites physiologiques.* Il est un animal qui s'habitue, s'adapte. Il s'est habitué au surmenage, à l'insomnie, à la suralimentation, à l'excès ou au rationnement sexuel, aux poisons." Translation by author.

35 Ibid., p. 1952: "Mettre de l'ordre dans notre vie individuelle et notre vie sociale. Si chacun étudiait avec méthode son emploi du temps journalier, dans le sens de taylorisation de ses actes, de ses gestes… […] Si chacun, raisonnablement, faisait cela, on pourrait en totalisant toutes les minutes gagnées, trouver le temps nécessaire pour le sport, pour s'occuper du corps." Translation by author.

36 Pierre Wɪɴᴛᴇʀ, "Le sport", in: *L'Esprit Nouveau*, ɴᴏ. 15, February 1922, p. 1755–1758, here p. 1757.

37 Albert Jᴇᴀɴɴᴇʀᴇᴛ, "La Rythmique", in: *L'Esprit Nouveau*, ɴᴏ. 2, November 1920, pp. 183–189 and ɴᴏ. 3, December 1920, pp. 331–338, here p. 183: "L'homme redemande à son corps la puissance suggestive d'action. Les manifestations plastiques se multiplient, en même temps que les manifestations sportives. Le corps humain redevient valeur expressive, parce que de grands artistes ont révélé la beauté de sa forme et la pureté de ses intentions plastiques. Les problèmes résolus de la mécanique font désirer pour cette machine rythmée qu'est le corps humain, ou plutôt pour cette harmonisation à établir entre le corps et l'esprit, la même possibilité de précision." Translation by author.

38 Ibid., p. 184.

39 This provoking analysis is provided by Peter Eɪsᴇɴᴍᴀɴ, *The Formal Basis of Modern Architecture*, Ph.D. Thesis, Cambridge, 1963 (reprint: Baden, Switzerland: Lars Müller Publishers, 2006).

40 Françoise Dᴜᴄʀᴏs, catalogue entry "Still Life and Genre Scenes", in: *Le Corbusier before Le Corbusier*, ed. ᴠᴏɴ Mᴏᴏs and Rᴜᴇɢɢ, pp. 267–269.

41 Stanislaus ᴠᴏɴ Mᴏᴏs, *Le Corbusier: Elements of a Synthesis*, revised and expanded edition, Rotterdam: 010 Publishers, 2009, p. 269.

42 Ibid., p. 282.

43 See for example the extensive catalogue: *Puppen. Körper. Automaten. Phantasmen der Moderne*, edited by Pia Mᴜᴌʟᴇʀ-Tᴀᴍᴍ and Katharina Sʏᴋᴏʀᴀ, Cologne: Oktagon, 1999.

44 Daniel Nᴀᴇɢᴇʟᴇ, "The Image of the Body in the Œuvre of Le Corbusier", in: *Le Corbusier & the Architecture of Reinvention*, London: Architectural Association, 2003, pp. 16–39, here p. 31.

45 Niklas Mᴀᴀᴋ, *Der Architekt am Strand. Le Corbusier und das Geheimnis der Seeschnecke*, Munich: Carl Hanser, 2010, pp. 82–86.

46 ᴠᴏɴ Mᴏᴏs, *Le Corbusier: Elements of a Synthesis*, p. 282.

47 Henry Russell Hɪᴛᴄʜᴄᴏᴄᴋ and Philip Jᴏʜɴsᴏɴ: *The International Style: Architecture since 1922*, New York: W. W. Norton, 1932.

48 See Hugo HÄRING, "Arbeit am Grundriß", in: *Baukunst und Werkform,* VOL. 5, 1952, no. 5, pp. 15–22.

49 Peter CARL, "Le Corbusier's Penthouse in Paris, 24 Rue Nungesser-et-Coli", in: *Daidalos,* NO. 28, 1988, pp. 65–75, here p. 68.

50 On Ronchamp in this context, see NAEGELE, "The Image of the Body in the Œuvre of Le Corbusier", and MAAK, *Der Architekt am Strand.*

51 Arthur RÜEGG: "Transforming the Bathroom", in: *Charlotte Perriand. An Art of Living,* edited by Mary MCLEOD, New York: Harry N. Abrams, in association with the Architectural League of New York, 2003, pp. 114–129, here p. 116.

52 Colin ROWE, *The Architecture of Good Intentions,* London: Academy Editions, 1994, p. 60.

53 LE CORBUSIER, *Urbanisme,* Paris: G. Crès, 1925, p. 22. Translation by author.

54 Ibid., "Avertissement", p. I.

55 For a closer discussion of this complex relationship between Sitte and Le Corbusier see Christoph SCHNOOR, "Kritische Einführung", in: LE CORBUSIER, *La Construction des villes,* pp. 17–227, here pp. 37–39.

56 LE CORBUSIER: *La ville radieuse: éléments d'une doctrine d'urbanisme pour l'équipement de la civilisation machiniste,* Boulogne-sur-Seine: Éditions de l'Architecture d'Aujourd'hui, 1935. English translation: *The Radiant City,* London: Faber and Faber, 1967.

57 This might explain the fact why these pages do not form part of the English translation under the title *The City of To-morrow and its Planning,* translated by Frederick Etchells, New York: Payson & Clarke, 1929. It appears that Etchells or his editor saw Le Corbusier's annex as unfitting or irrelevant to the main body of the book.

58 LE CORBUSIER, *Urbanisme,* Appendix (p. 290): "Notre sens de l'harmonie nous vient de la nature. Si nous sommes sensibles à ses œuvres, c'est que nous appartenons à son système".

59 LE CORBUSIER, *Urbanisme,* Appendix (p. 291): "Transports. Centre moteur. Collecteurs. Grandes traverses. Gare de triage. Services".

60 See the contribution of Tobias CHEUNG, "Kurokawa's Metabolic Space" in this volume.

61 Similar to Le Corbusier's image of the fern sporangium are the 'organic' town layouts of German architect Hans Bernhard Reichow, as discussed in: Werner DURTH, *Deutsche Architekten. Biographische Verflechtungen 1900–1970,* Braunschweig and Wiesbaden: Friedrich Vieweg & Sohn, 1986.

62 Paul SCHULTZE-NAUMBURG, *Kulturarbeiten,* edited by KUNSTWART, VOL. IV: *Städtebau,* Munich: Georg D. W. Callwey | Kunstwart-Verlag, [1906]; 2nd enlarged edition 1909, p. 66–71.

63 LE CORBUSIER, *La Construction des villes,* p. 290–295.

64 SCHULTZE-NAUMBURG, *Städtebau,* p. 66: „Man wird erkennen, dass auf einem solchen Plan, der nicht wie eine erstarrte geometrische Figur, sondern wie ein organisches Wachstum aussieht, solche Schwierigkeiten nicht entstehen können. Hier durchlaufen die Strassen wie grosse Schlagadern die Stadt; die Hauptpunkte sind durch Hauptstrassen verbunden, zahllose kleine Verkehrskanäle, Stege, Brücken und Durchgänge vermitteln immer auf direktestem und natürlichstem Wege die Verbindung untereinander." Translation by Kim Sanderson.

65 [Marc Antoine LAUGIER], *Essai sur l'architecture,* Paris: Duchesne, 1753. On Le Corbusier's aesthetic urbanism, see Francesco PASSANTI, "The Aesthetic Dimension in Le Corbusier's Urban

Planning", in: *Josep Lluís Sert. The Architect of Urban Design, 1953–1969,* edited by Eric Mumford and Hashim Sarkis, New Haven and London: Yale University Press | Cambridge [MA]: Harvard University Graduate School of Design, 2008, pp. 25–37.

66   William Curtis, *Le Corbusier. Ideas and Forms,* New York and London: Phaidon, 1986, p. 120.

67   Le Corbusier, *The Radiant City,* p. 245.

68   See von Moos, *Le Corbusier: Elements of a Synthesis,* p. 269.

69   Also see Naegele's reference to Le Corbusier's tendency towards the colossal in his "The Image of the Body in the Œuvre of Le Corbusier", p. 27.

70   Le Corbusier, *The Radiant City,* p. 6.

71   Ibid., p. 78.

72   Ibid., p. 81.

73   Ibid.: "décision / réservoir / préhension / transport // un *'organisme'*". Caption, not translated from the French.

74   Ibid., p. 168.

75   It should be obvious that the human being was not the only source of this organizing model, rather that Le Corbusier's deep interest in the Syndicalists and their idea of a meritocracy organized in the form of a pyramid, in addition to their valuing of representation, had an effect on the form of the *Ville Radieuse.* See William Curtis, *Ideas and Forms,* pp. 119–120.

76   Le Corbusier, *The Radiant City,* p. 36.

77   See Johan Linton, "Le Corbusier et l'esprit mathématique", in: *Le symbolique, le sacré, la spiritualité dans l'œuvre de Le Corbusier,* edited by the Fondation Le Corbusier, Paris: Éditions de la Villette, 2004, pp. 55–66. For a detailed account of the history of the *Modulor,* see also Johan Linton, *Om Arkitekturens Matematik. En studie av Le Corbusiers Modulor,* Göteborg: Master thesis Chalmers Tekniska Högskola, 1996.

78   Le Corbusier, *The Modulor. A Harmonious Measure to the Human Scale Universally Applicable to Architecture and Mechanics,* translated by Peter de Francia and Anna Bostock, London: Faber and Faber, [1954]. First edition in English (from the 2nd French edition of 1951). Also see Emma Dummett, *Green Space and Cosmic Order: Le Corbusier's Understanding of Nature,* Ph.D. Thesis, University of Edinburgh, 2007, pp. 39–40.

79   Six foot is $30{,}48 \times 6 = 182{,}88$ — this is sufficiently close to 183 cm which works as a number of the Fibonacci series. See Linton, "Le Corbusier et l'esprit mathématique", p. 57.

80   See Frank Zöllner, "Anthropomorphism: From Vitruvius to Neufert, from Human Measurement to the Module of Fascism" in this volume.

81   Le Corbusier, *The Modulor,* p. 129.

82   Matila Ghyka, *Le nombre d'or. Rites et rythmes pythagoriciens dans le développement de la civilisation occidentale,* Paris: Gallimard (éditions de la "Nouvelle Revue française"), 1931.

83   Maak, *Der Architekt am Strand,* pp. 107–117.

84   He notes: "un livre de recherches sur la mise en formule des proportions architecturales: 'Das Hüttengeheimnis vom gerechte[n] Steinmetze-grund' livre qui contient les recettes égyptiennes et gothiques" p. 7–8. This is: Alhard von Drach: *Das Hütten-Geheimniß vom Gerechten Steinmetzen-Grund in seiner Entwicklung und Bedeutung für die kirchliche Baukunst des deutschen Mittelalters, dargelegt durch Triangulatur-Studien an Denkmälern aus Hessen und den Nachbargebieten,*

Marburg: Elwert, 1897. LE CORBUSIER (Ch.-E. Jeanneret), *Les voyages d'Allemagne. Carnets,* edited by Giuliano GRESLERI, Milan: Electa | Paris: Fondation Le Corbusier, 1994, pp. 126–127.

85 Hendrik Petrus BERLAGE, *Grundlagen und Entwicklung der Architektur. Vier Vorträge gehalten im Kunstgewerbemuseum zu Zürich,* Berlin: Julius Bard, 1908, pp. 21–22: „Nur mache man sich recht klar, dass die geometrische Grundlage allein noch nicht den Künstler macht, weil die künstlerische Idee durch die geometrische Idee nicht gezeugt wird. Nichtkünstler können mit jenem System nichts, Künstler mit ihm alles machen, in der Voraussetzung, dass sie das Mittel beherrschen und nicht dessen Sklave werden."

86 LE CORBUSIER, *The Modulor,* p. 131.

87 LE CORBUSIER, *Œuvre Complète,* VOL. 5: *1946–1952,* edited by Willy BOESIGER, Zurich: Editions Girsberger, 1953, p. 13.

88 LE CORBUSIER, *The Modulor,* p. 163.

89 VON MOOS, *Le Corbusier: Elements of a Synthesis,* p. 312.

90 CURTIS, *Ideas and Forms,* p. 164.

91 LE CORBUSIER, *Œuvre Complète,* VOL. 7: *1957–1965,* edited by Willy BOESIGER, Zurich: Artemis, 1965, p. 54.

92 Bruno CHIAMBRETTO: *Le Corbusier à Cap-Martin,* Marseille: Edition Parenthèses, 1987, p. 5.

93 Niklas MAAK, "The Beaches of Modernity: Le Corbusier, Ronchamp and the 'objet à réaction poétique'", in: *Le Corbusier. The Art of Architecture,* edited by Alexander VON VEGESACK, Stanislaus VON MOOS, Arthur RÜEGG, and Mateo KRIES, Weil am Rhein: Vitra Design Museum, 2007, pp. 293–324.

94 Colin ROWE and Fred KOETTER, *Collage City,* Cambridge, MA and London: The MIT Press, 1978, p. 17.

95 Arthur RÜEGG, "The equipment", in: *Le Corbusier. L'interno del Cabanon | The Interior of the Cabanon, Le Corbusier 1952 – Cassina 2006,* edited by Filippo ALISON, Milan: Electa, 2006, pp. 55–64, here pp. 56–58.

96 Ibid.

97 Ibid., p. 60.

98 Bruno CHIAMBRETTO, in *Le Corbusier à Cap-Martin,* has analyzed the Cabanon as a snail's shell and Niklas MAAK, in *Der Architekt am Strand,* pp. 39–42, takes this comparison further.

99 LE CORBUSIER, *The Decorative Art of Today,* p. 72.

100 Adolf BEHNE, *Der moderne Zweckbau,* Munich: Drei Masken, 1926, p. 53:
„Das Entscheidende ist die Stellung zur Gesellschaft!
Der Mensch steht zwischen Natur und Gesellschaft. Er entscheidet sich für die menschliche Gemeinschaft und steht dann in einer gewissen Spannung zur Natur. Er entscheidet sich für die Natur und steht in einer gewissen Spannung zur Gesellschaft." English quote after: BEHNE, *The Modern Functional Building,* translated by Michael Robinson with an introduction by Rosemarie Haag Bletter, Santa Monica: Getty Research Institute, 1996, p. 129. It is of course not without irony to quote Behne in this manner since he saw Le Corbusier as a clear and un-ambiguous rationalist. See BEHNE, *The Modern Functional Building,* pp. 130–135.

TOBIAS CHEUNG

Kurokawa's Metabolic Space

For Kisho Kurokawa, the task of future architects is to build spaces that emerge from living things and the "flux" of their "life-worlds" (*seikatsu ryudosei;* 生活流動性).[1] Living architecture and the architect as an engineer of life — these are key themes in his writings. Within the same perspective, cybernetic feedback technology is nothing else than the logic and order of life transformed into man-built spaces and their various devices and installations. Bodies, houses, and cities are in Kurokawa's terminology all cell-like simple or composed "capsules". Streets, highways, and railroads as well as escalators, corridors, and halls represent the mediating elements that, through linear interconnected structures, combine the capsule-elements on different scales and levels with various environments. For Kurokawa the resulting "linear cities" with seemingly unlimited growth potential replace concentric urban structures.[2] In Kurokawa's "metabolic space" (メタボリック・スペース),[3] Patrick Geddes' Garden City and Rudolf Virchow's "cell state" begin to move by expanding their borders outside of the proper body and merging with other bodies and environmental structures. From life processes to "metabolic spaces", capsules as the most condensed "space modules" grow — like in Constantinos Doxiadis' urban vision[4] — into houses, metapolises (basic urban settlements), metropolises, megalopolises, ecumenopolises (in which people commute by air routes), and cosmopolises (that connect urban settlements via satellite communication). Each agglomeration corresponds to a certain scale and undergoes major pattern changes that Kurokawa calls "metamorphosis":

> *The single housing unit, the moment it is part of an urban unit, undergoes a metamorphosis and will complete a decisive change when transformed into a megalopolis from a metropolis. The transformed house structure may be described as a meta-architecture. In the same manner, a single urban*

IN / KIRSTEN WAGNER AND JASPER CEPL (EDITORS) /
IMAGES OF THE BODY IN ARCHITECTURE: ANTHROPOLOGY AND BUILT SPACE /
TÜBINGEN · BERLIN / ERNST WASMUTH VERLAG / 2014 / PP. 131–165

unit, the moment it becomes an element of a metropolis, begins to undergo metamorphosis, and, while being transformed from a megalopolis into ecumenopolis, will undergo a decisive change. The urban unit thus transformed, may be described as a metapolis.

$$House \rightarrow Urban\,Unit \rightarrow Metropolis \rightarrow Megalopolis \rightarrow Ecumenopolis$$

Meta-architecture   Metapolis

In other words, a meta-architecture, as a house unit within the megalopolis, is a super-house equipped with feed-back and control mechanisms, in order to function as part of that megalopolis. A metapolis, while being part of [an] ecumenopolis, is a super-urban unit equipped with feed-back and control mechanisms so as to serve as part of that ecumenopolis.[5]

The two themes: 1) *architecture and the life sciences* and 2) *architecture and agent models* structure the different sections of this essay. Other themes of Kurokawa's architectural program, more frequently discussed, concern the close relation between growing economies and urban development, models of recyclable

architecture (with building components that can be replaced according to their different life-cycles),[6] and the compatibility of Japanese traditional architecture with post-modern architecture. One striking image that Kurokawa, born in Nagoya, evokes himself, is that of the atomic bombs that have turned Japan into black earth without cities — the same earth on which now grows the "metabolism" of vast urban areas.[7] I will discuss some of these aspects in the last section.

In *Homo movens* (first published in Japanese in 1969), Kurokawa draws on major themes from Michel Ragon's *Où vivrons-nous demain?* (1963, translated into Japanese in 1965).[8] He criticizes the "new art of building" cities of the Athens Charter, published in 1943 by an influential group of avant-garde architects — among them Le Corbusier and Walter Gropius — after the fourth meeting of the Congrès Internationaux d'Architecture Moderne (1933).[9] The title of the congress was *The Functional City*. The Athens Charter focused on the "path of communication" of "urban agglomerations" that secure their "exchanges" and closely connect them with their "particular area" — topics that also frequently occur in Kurokawa's writings.[10] However, for Kurokawa, the Charter is still based on the old industrial model of non-overlapping anatomical zones with functional properties, already outlined in *The Declaration of La Sarraz* of the first conference (1928). According to this declaration, the "primary functions" of urbanism — dwelling, working, and recreation — are mapped with specific zones that are clearly separated from each other.[11] Kurokawa thus joins Asger Jorn's and Henri Lefebvre's critique of urban functional segregation.[12] In Kurokawa's view, such urban models do not represent the order of life that really generates urban space, but architectural norms that have been established according to standardized anatomical images of the human body from Leonardo da Vinci's *Vitruvian Man* to Le Corbusier's *Modulor,* echoed in the famous series of Le Corbusier's Unités d'Habitation (1947–1965).[13]

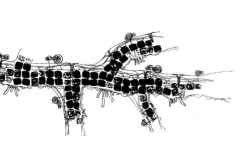 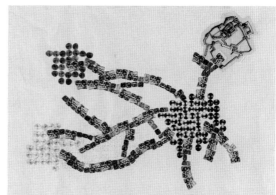

Kurokawa's conceptual point of departure is Jean Gottmann's investigation of a five hundred mile long urban area of about thirty seven million people stretching from Boston in the north to Washington, published in 1961.[14] Gottmann calls this urban area "megalopolis". It is basically characterized by interrelations between the "processes that caused the local population to grow, those that attracted certain kinds of people to the megalopolis, and those that supplied the swelling crowds with the means to live and work together".[15] He refers to the order of such "areas" as "colloidal mixtures", a term also used by biochemists in the 1950s to explain the structure and the origin of molecular components of cells and organisms:

> In this area, then, we must abandon the idea of the city as a tightly settled and organized unit in which people, activities, and riches are crowded into a very small area clearly separated from its non-urban surroundings. Every city in this region spreads out far and wide around its original nucleus; it grows amidst an irregularly colloidal mixture of rural and suburban landscapes; it melts on broad fronts with other mixtures, of somewhat similar though different texture, belonging to the suburban neighborhoods of other cities.[16]

Travelling through North America, Western Europe, and some Mediterranean countries, Gottmann reports that he finds everywhere the "nebulous structure of urbanized regions", in which cities are "expanding one toward another" and a "deep transformation of modern modes of life and habitat" is taking place.[17] Kurokawa, who also describes himself as a frequent traveler, observes a similar structure between Osaka and Tokyo. It is this Japanese megalopolis that fascinates him and for which his metabolic space is made.

DESIGN, ORGANISMS AND METABOLIC SPACES

Metabolism. The Proposals for New Urbanism is the title of a manifesto of five young Japanese architects — besides Kurokawa, Kiyonori Kikutake, Masato Otaka, Fumihiko Maki, and Kiyoshi Awazu — and the architecture critic Noboru Kawazoe for the World Design Conference presented in Tokyo from May 12 to 15, 1960.[18] *Metabolism* (besides *Symbiosis*) is also the title that Kurokawa has chosen for his own architecture.[19] In the preface of their manifesto, the group of Japanese architects emphasized that metabolism as an architectural form of order is not just a "natural historical process", but an expression of the active "development" of society through "design and technology".[20] For Kurokawa, design is an order generating process that expresses a certain form or style. In contrast to the ontotheological conception of cosmic design, in which *one* God creates the design for *one* world, Kurokawa considers design to be the title for all kinds of agent-dependent processes that impose a certain shape and order on things. In this scheme, every human is a "hero", a potential designer of himself and of his environment. Life is nothing else than design of matter, and technology is the realization of possible designs of matter. Human technology is not a natural process, and yet life as a natural process exposes what technology *in nuce* is: design.[21]

Kurokawa normally employs the *katakana* transcription of metabolism (メタ
ボリズム), used to write non-Chinese loanwords, and not the *kanji* term in Chi-
nese characters (*shinchintaisha,* 新陳代謝), which can already be found in Japanese physiology textbooks of the 1920s.[22] This is a first hint that Kurokawa refers
to contemporary debates in the life sciences. Asked about the title of his architecture as metabolism, Kurokawa's standard response is that the group members
just screened a dictionary for a somewhat convenient title of their program.[23]
Some major English dictionary editions of the 1950s and 1960s in the main library of the University of Tokyo refer to the following aspects of *metabolism*:

*The sum of the physiological processes concerned at the building up of sub-
stance (protoplasm) of plants or animals and its destruction in furnishing
the energy for their living.* — Webster's New Practical Dictionary, 1951[24]

*Process in a cell or organism by which nutritive material is built up into liv-
ing matter* (constructive ~, anabolism) *or by which protoplasm is broken
down to perform special functions* (destructive ~, katabolism). — New
Desk Standard Dictionary, 1951[25]

*The sum of the processes concerned in the building up of protoplasm and
its destruction incidental to life; the chemical changes in living cells, by
which the energy is provided for the vital processes and activities, and new
material is assimilated to repair the waste. Metabolism may be regarded
as including two aspects: constructive (termed anabolism or assimilation)
or destructive (catabolism or dissimilation). Both forms consist in a series
of steps. In anabolism these are in the main synthetic, resulting in building
up of the nutritive substances into the more complex living protoplasm.
In catabolism they are mainly destructive, decomposing and oxidizing the
constituents of protoplasm into simpler bodies with a liberation of energy.
Anabolism and catabolism go together, but one may predominate and obscure the other.* — Webster's New International Dictionary of the English
Language, 1952[26]

*The sum of the processes or chemical changes in an organism or a single cell
by which food is built up (anabolism) into living protoplasm and by which
protoplasm is broken down (catabolism) into simpler compounds with the
exchange of energy.* — The American College Dictionary, 1962[27]

The lemmas refer to "constructive" and "destructive" processes ("anabolism"
and "catabolism") through chemical reactions and the exchange of "energy"
within "living protoplasm", itself regarded as the physical carrier of the processes
within cells. With the exception of living protoplasm, Kurokawa frequently em-

ploys all these terms to explain his architecture. He also uses the relatively new dictionary entries *metabolite* (a product of metabolism), *metabolic* and *metabolize*, in *katakana*. Further on, his writings contain images of various components of the cell cytoplasm — like nuclei, chromosomes, DNA, and Golgi apparati — that have been made visible through experimental techniques in the 1950s and 1960s (such as gene sequencing, electron microscopes, and centrifuges). The dictionary entries represent an earlier research period than these images.

Within a more concrete historical framework, Kurokawa refers to John Desmond Bernal's *The Physical Basis of Life,* a lecture given in 1947 for the Physical Society of London, first published as a monograph in 1951 and translated into Japanese in 1952.[28] In the 1920s and 1930s, Bernal's experimental research focused on the x-ray crystallography of organic substances such as proteins, enzymes, and viruses. From 1932 to 1938, he was a member of the Cambridge Theoretical Biology Club, together with Dorothy and Joseph Needham, Conrad Hal Waddington, and Joseph Henry Woodger. The group, inspired by Alfred North Whitehead's concept of processual reality, mainly discussed systemic aspects of organismic order, especially integrative models of genetics, embryology, and evolution.[29]

Like John Haldane, Alexander Oparin, André Lwoff, and Alexandre Dauvillier,[30] Bernal outlined in *The Physical Basis of Life* a speculative model[31] of the physico-chemical processes of the evolution and "stepwise catalysis"[32] of organic molecules. The notion of "life" refers for Bernal to the "totality of cyclical processes involving mostly compounds of carbon and nitrogen accessible to our observation on this earth".[33] With references to Erwin Schrödinger's *What is Life? The Physical Aspect of the Living Cell* (1943) and Ilya Prigogine's *Étude thermodynamique des phénomènes irréversibles* (1947), Bernal explained processes of life through "a close analogy to those of a chemical factory", only that, "instead of the materials being poured from one reaction vessel to another, the individual molecules diffuse from one enzyme to the next, the rates are fixed, and a number of them circulate in these cycles, making use of a certain fraction of the available energy of the reaction, to reverse the entropy again".[34] The reversion of entropy leads to a "stable process of conversion" between chemical substances as a first step of the production of organic agents.[35] For Kurokawa, the main effect of the organizing work of the architect as a space designer is what Bernal's organisms accomplish: the reversion of entropy.[36]

While the steady interactions between complex molecules in a "general medium" during the "long stage of chemical evolution" characterize in Bernal's model the origin of the "internal economy" of life, "living things" with a concrete "external shape" occur when a "section of this medium" is separated out that is "sufficiently large to contain a self-maintaining system of reactions with the medium".[37] Organisms are "kinds of complex chemical molecules",[38] and the first "section" that constitutes a metabolic inside-outside-difference within the general medium is a "cell". Infrared spectroscopy, x-ray crystallography, ultra-centrifuges, and electron microscopes visualize the highly differentiated, dense-ly structured interior of these cells as "little worlds", in which the "whole set of chemical reactions" that characterizes the "large volume of pre-organic life" is "concentrated"[39, 40] Such cells exist as self-maintaining living systems within the mega-structure of agglomerations of cells in entire organisms. Kurokawa adopts Bernal's definition of these "living systems". He quotes the following passage of *The Physical Basis of Life*:

> *We begin to see now that the material aspects of a living system are but the struts and levers of a machine, the particular function of which is to effect energy interchanges, and that growth and assimilation are but means of achieving a metabolism consisting of enzyme-promoted energy changes. Thus in a very physical sense process takes precedence over structure.*[41]

In *The Dynamic State of Body Constituents,* published in 1942 and translated into Japanese in 1955,[42] Rudolf Schönheimer defined in a similar way the "inter-mediary metabolism" of "biological systems" through "*one* great cycle of closely linked chemical reactions".[43] For Schönheimer and Bernal, solid structures or frameworks support a steady state of dynamic metabolic interactions — trans-formations, conversions, exchanges, regenerations, and formations — within cells of organisms, between their boundaries, and with the outer milieu. These organismic models inform Kurokawa's notion of metabolic space.

Cells are for Kurokawa productive and reproductive, genetically designed units. Like Wiener's cybernetic automata, they carry with them traces of their history and origin, and these traces or memories are part of their potential to develop, maintain, and transform themselves.[44] Genetics and metabolism con-stitute the past and the future of every existing organismic unit, which is, in Bernal's terms, a "fossil" that "carries in it by inference all the evidence of its pre-decessors".[45] Kurokawa calls the production, reproduction, diversification, and complexification of metabolic units "biopoiesis", a term that he borrows from Bernal. In "The Problem of Stages in Biopoiesis" (1959), published in the *Pro-ceedings of the First International Symposium on: The Origin of Life on the Earth* held at Moscow in August 1957, Bernal defined "*biopoiesis* or life-making" as a process of "embodiment within a certain volume of self-maintaining chemical processes".[46]

For the logic of the production of collections of cell-like individual agents as multiagent systems, Kurokawa refers in general to models of emergent proper-ties in complex systems that have been discussed by Benoît Mandelbrot and in the chaos debates of the 1960s and 1970s.[47] While Kurokawa calls drastic design changes during transforming processes, in analogy to the caterpillar-butterfly-development, "metamorphosis", he mentions Alfred Koestler's essay "The Tree and the Candle" (1973) in order to show how nature modularizes processes of complexification into cells as units or "holons" that possess at the same time a tendency to maintain their autonomy and a property to transcend their individuality into higher orders.[48] Hierarchical and modular orders are thus both aspects of complex living systems.[49] Tokyo is for Kurokawa a "holon of three hundred cities".[50]

Through models of cell-like codeable units, holonic hierarchical orders, and emergent "metamorphoses", Kurokawa explains the transformations of processes that constitute agents. He does not, like Le Corbusier in the *Modulor,* define a "new harmonious measure to the human scale universally applicable to architecture and mechanics".[51] Rather, Kurokawa highlights that measures change according to the different developments and states of agents. Megalopolises grow through the activity of these agents, and cities die when they do not support their metabolism. For Kurokawa, the human is itself a megastructure that has to be understood through its simpler, modular units. He describes the human body as a "symbiotic complex made up of a plurality of living things in dynamic relationship with each other".[52] This body lives again in "symbiosis" with other living beings and its entire environment. Kurokawa's "metabolism" is therefore also a "philosophy of symbiosis" or of "coexistence".[53]

Another cell-based metatheory of the origin and evolution of living things, to which Kurokawa refers, can be found in Pierre Teilhard de Chardin's *The Phenomenon of Man* (1955). Teilhard de Chardin begins his origin-of-life-discourse with a theory of matter in which the "Within" of all elements — energies, forces, wills — are "co-extensive" and in a dynamic exchange with their "Without".[54] This becomes most apparent through the "double related involution" of the "coiling up of the molecule upon itself" in the form of the "cell" and the "coiling up of the planet upon itself" in form of the earth as a system-like entity.[55] For Teilhard de Chardin, it is "in and by means of the cell that the molecular world 'appears in person' […], touching, passing into, and disappearing in the higher constructions of life".[56] Through "cells", that are "at the same time so single, so uniform and so complex", the "stuff of the universe" reappears "once again with all its characteristics — only this time it has reached a higher rung of complexity and thus, by the same stroke […] advanced still further in *interiority,* i.e. in consciousness".[57]

In Teilhard de Chardin's cosmology, complexification as cellularization finally tends to a kind of supreme consciousness that represents a fusion point of the "Universal" and the "Personal" in an "impersonal" or "hyper-personal" "noosphere".[58] Kurokawa criticizes this orthogenesis. In *Homo movens* (1969), he contrasts the image of an impersonal unification with that of an ongoing diversification "of mutually independent individual spaces, determined by the free will of individuals".[59] Teilhard de Chardin's first five "elemental movements of life" — reproduction, multiplication, renovation, conjugation, and association — reappear in Kurokawa's metabolic space, but not the sixth one: "con-

　　　　　　　　　　　　　　　　　　　　TOBIAS CHEUNG

trolled additivity", that is to say a regulating activity that results in the evolution of the mind and its specific sphere.[60]

It is not in Teilhard de Chardin's *Phenomenology,* but in Peter Brian Medawar's *The Future Man* (1960) in which Kurokawa finds a reflection of his image of a "heterogeneous society where all of its members are highly individualized and evolving in different directions".[61] In 1960, Medawar received the Nobel Price for the discovery of acquired immunological tolerance through the injection of foreign cells into young animals. Kurokawa does not refer to this aspect of Medawar's work. However, his recurrent references to the plasticity, transformability, and collectivity of capsule-lives that fuse with other capsules or become a part of them are an echo of the convergent discourses on the origin of life, cell metabolism, genetics, and immunology. Further on, works like Majory Stephenson's *Bacterial Metabolism* (1949) and Kenneth Thimann's *The Life of Bacteria: Their Growth, Metabolism, and Relationships* (1955) are part of the cell-orientated framework within which Kurokawa's metabolism emerges.[62]

Bernal did not just cooperate with Koestler and refer to cybernetic machines. As a crystallographer who was interested in the structure and spatialization of organic substances, he published essays on the relation between the natural sciences and architecture.[63] He also developed the model of a space capsule — which reappears in the first article of Kurokawa's Capsule Manifesto in *Homo movens*.[64]

CYBORGS, RHIZOMES, AND THE *HOMO MOVENS*

For Kurokawa, there is no categorical difference between organisms and biotechnical agents. Cybernctic models of the brain and complex feedback processes are for him part of the evolving logic that nature itself set into motion when the first organisms appeared on earth.

While he mentions John von Neumann's digital "thinking machines" as an indicator of the future "symbiosis between man and machine"[65] — other examples within the flourishing cyborology of the time would have been W. Ross Ashby's feedback systems in *Design For a Brain* (1948) or W. Grey Walter's turtle-like (analogue) *Machina speculatrix* (1950)[66] —, Kurokawa highlights the work of the Japanese medical engineer Kazuhiko Atsumi who in 1959 transplanted "a mechanical heart into a goat" and kept it alive for 344 days.[67]

From Atsumi, Kurokawa adopts the term "biomation" to indicate "the application of technology to biology", or, in Atsumi's words, "the mating of the automation of man-made technology and the *bio* of living things", which "will give birth to the technology of a new human society".[68] It is in this context that the notion of "symbiosis" or "co-existence", to which Kurokawa refers in his later writings as a specific order of community life,[69] first occurs in *Homo movens* for the "co-existence between machines and humans" (*kikai to ningen no kyosei*, 機械と人間の共生).[70]

Ontologies of biotechnic agents are for Kurokawa part of an "information society" (*joho shakai*, 情報社会), a term that he borrows from Tadao Umesao, a Japanese cultural anthropologist. In his seminal essay on "Information Societies" (1963), Umesao outlined a historical three stage meta-scheme of the development of societies and compared this scheme with the development of different layers of germ cells: The entoderm represents the agricultural age, which produces the inner organs, the mesoderm the industrial age, which produces the muscles, and the ectoderm the information age, which produces the brain and sensibility.[71] The succession of the three phases expresses the "self-realization" (*jiko jitsugen*, 自己実現) of human beings.[72] Within a neo-Marxian framework, the root of the human is for Umesao a "homo economicus" (ホモエコノミクス),[73] who changes reality through production processes and work. While Kenzo Tange refers for the order of economic processes to Walt Whitman Rostow's non-communist manifesto,[74] Kurokawa combines Umesao's model with Daniel Bell's liberal theory of economic growth, based on mass consumption as a driving factor of product diversification, job growth, and social changes.[75] However, Kurokawa also refers to Jean Baudrillard and a shift from a product-orientated society to a value-orientated society of "symbolic exchanges".[76]

Kurokawa's "homo movens" (ホモ・モベンス)[77] is a member of a mass consumption society, and yet he is a kinesthetic product of a certain experience of the world of urban regions, whose perceptions the Italian futurists painted and about which Paul Virilio will write his dromology.[78] For Kurokawa, humans are moving metabolic agents, whose first cities were based on the speed of their legs, and who subsequently invented new tools and spaces of movement until they transform in the information age into "nomads" of megalopolises.[79] However, Kurokawa goes further than Umesao and follows the path of Atsumi's metahistory. After the information age, there is a fourth step, the "post-machine age" (Kurokawa)[80] or the "biomation age" (Atsumi)[81]. This is Atsumi's version of it:

In order to increase the efficiency of their labor, human beings used primitive tools in the agricultural age, and mechanical, electric, and optical equipment during the industrial age. "Information" has become the most important "device" in this age. The biomation society is still in the embryonic stage, growing steadily as we proceed to develop the field of bioengineering.

Since the invention of the steam engine, various technologies have been developed, making an important contribution to human welfare by replacing human labor with automated machines. Thus, the history of engineering can be defined as the history of automation.

The remarkable progress of automation technology in the information age could bring us great advantages. On the other hand, uniformity, stan-

dardization, and a tendency toward dehumanization have been pointed out as the demerits of the information age.

One of the keys to negate such faults of the information society will be "biomation", the hybridization of artificial automation technology with bioorganisms, a gift of nature. Through biomation, the so-called "mechanic" civilization of human beings will be drastically transformed into "organic" civilization.

With the arrival of the "biomation" society, we will increasingly put emphasis on softness, preciseness, dynamism, multiplication, individuality, and totality, rather than rigidity, hugeness, stability, simplicity, uniformity, and partiality.[82]

Kurokawa's *homo movens* is a biomated agent, a hybrid of the technic space of the megalopolis in which he moves. The inner flow of his perceived life-world seems to resemble Henri Bergson's *élan vital,* and yet Kurokawa's life-worlds are based on a double process of inside-outside movements that change, through stimuli and systemic reactions, both sides of the exchange, the inner and the outer world. Existential desires and structured space coexist for Kurokawa in a dynamic field of mutual interactions, and the field of meaningful signs is not fixed. It changes together with the agents and their environment.

In his essay on Gilles Deleuze and Felix Guattari (1988), Kurokawa defines the world in which the *homo movens* exists as a "rhizome world", that unfolds its latent complexity through an immanent process of stimuli-reaction-events.[83] This post-modern rhizome world is also the metabolic space of the megalopolis, the home of the *homo movens* who left, in Kurokawa's perspective, Le Corbusier's metropolis of the industrial machine age:

The concept of the rhizome as explained by Deleuze and Guattari in RHIZOME, extrait de MILLE PLATEUX *(1980), is a dynamic, varied and plural form. They liken modern society to a tree. A tree has roots, a trunk, branches, and leaves; each part has an unchanging function, and each exists in a hierarchy within the whole. This they offer as a symbol for modern society, modern cities, and Modern Architecture. In contrast, a rhizome is an interlocking web. It is a conjunction of dynamic relations-producing bulbs here and there, interweaving with great complexity, reaching outward in its continuing growth. It represents the principle of dynamic, varied pluralism that absorbs the hierarchical structure of the tree.*[84]

Within this rhizome world, the *homo movens* is the transient carrier, the *être passager,* of the circulation and distribution of data as goods that move through the communication channels of "network cities" and the various new media or "data transfer technologies" (データ送信技術) of radios, televisions, phones, and computers.[85] He is part of the "flux between humans, things and energy"[86], and

Kurokawa wants to construct his car-like[87] mobile homes, according to the principles of his Capsule Manifesto.[88]

METABOLIC ARCHITECTURES: CAPSULE TOWERS
AND THE MEGALOPOLIS

Kurokawa's metabolic architecture is composed of cell-like minima, the "capsules", and "capsule" clusters of various levels of complexity or intensity. Degrees of intensity characterize the compactness or denseness of space that is composed of capsules. Between capsules and megalopolises, there are different forms of dense spatial arrangements with multifunctional properties. These intermediate spatial arrangements are not horizontally divided into spatial zones, but use fusions of horizontal and vertical structures — like the tower-shaped urban centers that Louis Kahn planned for midtown Philadelphia (1953).[89]

While Kikutake refers to a "tower shape community" of different "ocean" cities, one of them called "Unabara" in Sagami Bay — entirely moveable cities with a "network" of capsule-like "living units" attached to "living cylinders" — and Tange develops the plan of an urban agglomeration above the Tokyo Bay with interconnected marine towers as "vertical core systems" and "pilotis areas" as "spatial links between private and public areas", Kurokawa[90] and Arata Isozaki sketch their tower communities above the ground of Tokyo.[91]

4
KISHO
KUROKAWA /
HELICAL CITY
PLAN FOR
TOKYO / 1961

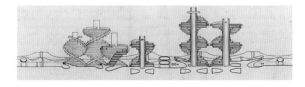

5
ARATA ISOZAKI /
CLUSTERS IN THE
AIR PROJECT /
1960–62

Through references to new technologies with flexible user interfaces, the metabolist group of 1960 joins the overall debate on megastructures — a term first used by Maki in *Investigations in Collective Form* (1964).[92] Megastructures are

TOBIAS CHEUNG

fusion points of the mass and the individual through transportation systems that characterize the city visions of Antonio Sant'Elia *(Futurist City)*, Constant *(New Babylon)*, Doxiadis *(Ecumenopolis)*, Paolo Soleri *(Acropolis)*, and the Situationist International[93] (founded in 1957).[94] These visions inform the capsule architectures of the Groupe d'étude d'architecture mobile (GEAM) and the Archigram group. Kurokawa often refers to these two movements.[95] However, in the 1960s and 1970s, capsule architectures are also related to models of self-sustaining submarines, aircraft carriers, oil platforms, and orbital capsule spaces.[96]

The GEAM (1958–1962) and the Archigram group (1961–1974) emerge as critical platforms of urban development after the collapse of the CIAM conference cycle. The GEAM movement was founded by Yona Friedman, Paul Maymont, Frei Otto, Eckhard Schulze-Fielitz, Werner Ruhnau, and David Georges Emmerich. Friedman's *L'Architecture mobile* and *La Ville Spatiale,* both published in 1958, were the GEAM group's two manifestos.[97] After several reconstructable houses with prefabricated box-sets of design elements had already been developed in the US during the last years of the Second World War,[98] Friedman sketched prefabricated *Panel Chains* (1945) and *Movable Boxes* (1949) for people who lost their homes during the war. Friedman's "ville spatiale" — visualized in his urban models of *Tunis spatial* (1958), *Paris spatial* (1958), and *Venise monégasque* (1959) — is based on a "spatial infrastructure" for collective purposes. This infrastructure has the form of a skeletal, metal "space-frame grid" of several levels. The grid is filled with mobile, user-dependent elements as ground plates and partition walls for individual, cell-like "space design". These "cells" represent complete homes in themselves or become functional within modular apartments. The "habitat" is thus determined by the "habitant" of a "mobile society" through "convertible forms" and "convertible surfaces" within a "three dimensional skeleton".[99]

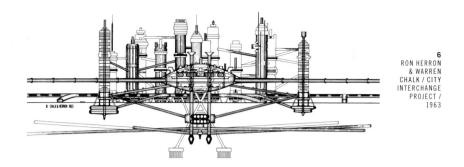

6
RON HERRON
& WARREN
CHALK / CITY
INTERCHANGE
PROJECT /
1963

The British Archigram group — Peter Cook, Michael Webb, Ron Herron, Dennis Crompton, Warren Chalk, Bryan Harvey, and David Greene — continued to sketch megastructures and elements of mobile urban architectures.[100] However, their 1963 exhibition *The Living City* at the Institute of Contemporary Arts in London displayed organic models of a playful mobility and adaptability that belong to the growing economies of the post-war-period,[101] put into pop art images, in which quasi-autonomous cell-like capsules or "living pods", prefabricated and yet individually designed by set choices, freely move between local vertical docking stations.[102] Cook called such cities "Plug-in Cities".[103] Analogue to Kikutake's floating cities in the ocean, Herron sketched a *Walking City* (1964) for solid ground. Models of the *Living City* exhibition, Cook's *Plug-in-City* (1964), Herron's *Walking City,* and Greene's design of a *Living Pod for capsule living* (1966) were published in the Archigram magazine that appeared in ten issues between 1961 and 1974.[104]

After Kikutake's transformable *Sky House* (1958, Tokyo),[105] Chalk's model of a capsule tower in 1964 and Tange's modular *Shizuoka Press and Broadcasting Center* (1967, Tokyo), Kurokawa developed many projects of prefabricated capsule apartment houses.[106]

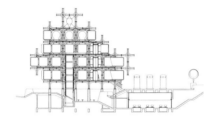

7
KISHO
KUROKAWA /
TAKARA
BEAUTILLON /
OSAKA / 1970

For the Osaka World Exposition in 1970, Kurokawa planned the Takara Beautillion Building (**FIG. 7**) and the Capsule House in the Theme Pavilion.

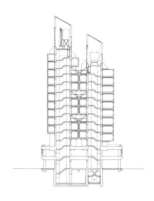

8
KISHO
KUROKAWA /
NAKAGIN
CAPSULE
TOWER /
SECTION /
1972

With the Nakagin Capsule Tower (**FIGS. 8, 9**) in Tokyo (Ginza), built in 1972, Kurokawa finally realized a plug-in project of capsules stacked into a vertical tower "for the use of businessmen living in distant suburbs of the city" or as a "hotel space for businessmen staying in Tokyo for brief periods".[107]

The individual capsules (**FIG. 10**) contain a bed and bedding, storage space for clothing, a desk for office work, a bathroom, telephone and audio units. Kuro-

kawa also designed "service items" for the capsules, such as sheets, blankets, and even tooth-brushes.[108] Capsules with specific functions could be "linked by access doors".[109] Through these links, capsules form "ordinary dwellings" with living rooms, bedrooms, and kitchens.[110] 144 capsules were prefabricated through a mix of "modules": modules of proportion[111], size, time, length of durability, and gravity scales. The interior design of each capsule depends on the set choice of the habitant.[112] Like Le Corbusier, Kurokawa thus made use of prefabricated, standardized forms, but his main emphasis is on the flexibility and plurality of individualized basic capsule-elements (**FIG. 11**) that mediate between the user and its environment in a post-industrial biomation society.[113]

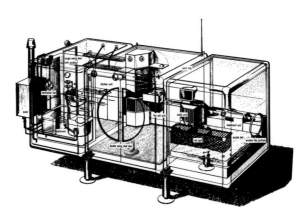

11
KISHO
KUROKAWA /
NAKAGIN
CAPSULE
TOWER /
EXPERIMENTAL
LEISURE
CAPSULE /
1971–72

CONCLUDING REMARKS: METABOLIC SPACE, BUDDHISM, AND JAPANESE CULTURE

Within a larger historic framework, Kurokawa's *homo movens* and his metabolic space are part of the environments that already characterize the *flâneurs* of Baudrillard and Benjamin, or, in other words, the *homo movens* resembles the modern subjects that experience world and otherness within the highly differentiated and ordered techno-spaces in which they exist: in big cities, and, from the 1950s on, in megalopolises with dense media communication networks.[114] These relations result from movements — of contracting fibres, of the whole body-subject, of data — transporting the agents from one place to another, and joining their bodies in bigger groups and clusters.

While Patrick Geddes' and Lewis Mumford's megalopolises represent unnatural, misfitted, confusing and exploiting environments,[115] Kurokawa's *homo movens* is a transformable desire machine that enjoys the ever-changing, stimulant, and complex life-worlds of vast urban settlements. Against Geddes' and Mumford's view of the megalopolis as a necropolis that tends to destroy the vitality of its own inhabitants, Tokyo is for Kurokawa not a suffocating city recalling the burnt earth of Nagoya, but a region of a renascent, flowering posturban life.[116] For Kurokawa, megalopolitans are biotechnic agents, and growing

TOBIAS CHEUNG

complexities represent for them nothing else than a field of multiplied events, experiences, and options to which they can adapt through new designs. Kurokawa's *homo movens* is neither sick nor, as Franz Kafka's New York protagonist in *Der Verschollene* (1912), lost in urban labyrinths. Rather, the *homo movens* always embodies the shifting foundations of his environment. He possesses no ultimate form, and the shapeless megalopolis mirrors his metabolic and "nomadic" existence.[117]

In his phenomenology of a playful megalopolitan, Kurokawa mentions Johan Huizinga's *Homo Ludens: A Study of the Play-Element of Culture* (1938),[118] but his image of the *homo movens* is closer to Henri van Lier's "human statue" *(stature humaine)* in *Les arts de l'espace* (1959).[119] Van Lier, a Belgian philosopher and anthropologist, criticized Le Corbusier's attempt to map the human statue through a single norm.[120] Rather, the human statue is for Lier a transformable, multidimensional being, itself able to unfold various functional needs according to the dynamic spatial interfaces in which it exists.[121] With references to Jean-Paul Sartre, Gaston Bachelard, and Martin Heidegger, Lier characterizes humans through their faculty of spatial design. Humans are thrown-into-the-world and have to build a "home" *(habitation)*, a concrete space in which they can dwell. Architecture thus is the first of all plastic arts, a skill that is as necessary as the act of design itself.[122] Van Lier's architecture, influenced by Friedman's visions[123] and Tange's Tokyo Bay project,[124] is a "mobile" and "synergetic" architecture. For van Lier, future cities grow and transform like crystals or corals. Their inside-outside-interfaces should be like "chemically conditioned walls" that "regularize themselves according to external variations".[125] Van Lier locates his urban vision in a comparative cultural perspective: while stable, fixed structures are representative for the "skeleton" *(ossature)*-architecture of the Occident, mobile architecture is more favored by "oriental vegetability", especially in Japan. However, the "industrial design" of the coming age should be informed by both cultural spheres. It should be "really international" *(vraiment international)* and express the multiple "sentiments of existence" of human agents.[126]

While van Lier ends his cultural discourse with this claim for an international industrial design, Kurokawa goes further in his comparison of occidental and oriental patterns. Metabolic space is also for Kurokawa an intercultural space par excellence in which various designs of living beings, cities, and machines melt into each other. However, Kurokawa is not so much interested in the processes through which different cultures merge into meta-spaces or become variations of one of Italo Calvino's cities and their hypertexts. Rather, he mainly focuses on cultural patterns that favour the existential needs and desires of the future inhabitant of megalopolises. And these patterns are, for him, part of Eastern Buddhistic cultures. Kurokawa thus binds his discourse of metabolic space to the renascent national identity debates of an economically growing Japan.[127] Through Kurokawa's cultural turn, the West occurs as a cultural sphere of iterative dualisms and of a logocentrism that philosophers like Maurice Merleau-Ponty, Deleuze, and Jacques Derrida "deconstructed".[128]

Recurrent themes in Kurokawa's Eastern Culture discourse are Buddhistic notions of eternal change *(samsara)* and of identity (as a relation between self and non-self), the Genroku era of Edo period culture (1688–1703), and the urban architecture of Kyoto during this period. In Kurokawa's Edo Kyoto, grids, sliding-doors, and floors (which are extended beyond wooden walls (called *engawa,* 縁側)) of traditional townhouses, the *machiya,* construct a semi-permeable space of multiple exchanges along streets.[129] The semi-permeable space (to which Kurokawa refers as "media" or "*en*-space"[130]) represents also the ambivalent and undetermined state of "co-existence" between its agents. While Kurokawa relates (within his culture discourse) the notion of "co-existence" *(kyosei)* to Jodo-Buddhism,[131] he refers for his identity concept of self-as-non-self to the school of the Indian Buddhist monk Nagarjuna.[132] For Kurokawa, the individual existence of humans is not based on the awareness of a non-contradictory substance (for example, René Descartes' *cogitatio*). Rather, the substantival self (which Kurokawa mentions in Sanskrit as *ātman* and in Japanese as *jiga*) relies on a more fundamental processual non-self (*anātman* or *muga*) that is composed of various interacting entities such as physical parts, affects, sensations, perceptions, volitions, and consciousness. Kurokawa thinks that the notion of a processual non-self fits better than any dualism to the dynamics of metabolic spaces in which human agents express their multiple desires. Desires, stimulated and triggered by events, represent the seemingly unlimited productivity and creativity of the non-substantival human condition of existence. The complex, multilayered, interconnected, and commercialized spaces of megalopolises are the best playground for the coming-into-being of these desire-evoking events.

In Kurokawa's philosophy of symbiosis or coexistence, the *homo movens* gradually transforms into Basho's figure of the eternal traveller, who is nowhere at home and whose home is at the same time every place through which he moves — a figure that corresponds to the Buddhist image of floating self — and which is again related to the frequent travels of local landlords, who had to visit the Shogun in New Edo every one or two years. Kurokawa thus creates a dense package and long lists of the Japaneseness of the future East Asian *homo movens.*

In a final stroke, Kurokawa relates this package to two historical beginnings of the Japanese culture: the first, already highlighted by Tange and Kawazoe in *Ise: Prototype of Japanese Architecture* (1965), represents the architecture of the Ise shrine, an ensemble of buildings that date at least back to the fifth century BC, as an example for a Shintoist (and thus typical Japanese) tradition of a modular, easily renewable architecture, and the second focuses on the invasion of Korean nomadic tribes as common ancestors of the Japanese.[133] Both thesis are controversial, the latter one almost certainly a myth with little archeological evidence.[134]

Kurokawa's cultural construction of the *homo movens* who inhabits the metabolic space of megalopolises is problematic, and yet it is both part of a Western discourse about the seemingly modern style of Japanese traditional architecture (that dates back to Frank Lloyd Wright and Bruno Taut)[135] and a reaction to a post-war world order that is still dominated by the West.[136] However, Kurokawa is clearly aware of the danger of renascent nationalisms. He often highlights that the Japanese culture is just a part of the global "symbiosis" of "regional cultures":

> *I don't think that Japanese culture is superior to any other culture, and I am strongly opposed to an exclusivist tribalism, nationalism, racism or historicism. For me the goal of architecture for the new age is a symbiosis of universal order and regional cultures in which fluid, intermediary space and abstracted, cultural traditions and intellectualised expression become valuable.*[137]

In the seminal *Space Design* issue on capsule architecture (1969), the reader finds a page filled with lemmas about the Japanese character 囚 *(shu)*, which means prisoner. In the encircled center of this character, there is again the character for man 人 *(hito)*. The image evokes a tension, because in Kurokawa's capsule manifesto of the same issue, the capsule is not something that encloses the subject into a walled dwelling, but a permeable, membrane-like skin through which he is able to communicate and interact with his environment. Kurokawa and the other capsule-architects thus point to the notion of a designed technospace which does not alienate the subject from its natural environment, but which reinforces and multiplies its interfaces and expressive potentials. In this perspective, Kurokawa's vision of a capsulized built space is not opposed to the nature of humans, but an expression of how humans are related to space. Humans are capsule-builders, they always exist as metabolic and biotechnic agents within capsules, and their activity produces the space of megalopolises.

NOTES

1   Kisho Kurokawa, メタボリズムの発想, Tokyo: Hakuba, 1972, p.59. Unless otherwise indicated, translations are those of the author of this essay. Japanese names are written in the following order: given names precede surnames. The *kanji* character of Kurokawa's given name (紀章) can be read in two different ways: *Noriaki* and *Kisho*.

2   Kisho Kurokawa, *Intercultural Architecture. The Philosophy of Symbiosis,* London: Academy Editions, 1991, p.58: "The concentric expansion of large cities has reached the limit of structural growth. Linear cities must be constructed to reform the concentric urban structure with its single-celltype public and service centres located in the heart of the city. In the linear city, nature and urban life exist in parallel; there is no city centre and there is considerable growth potential." Kurokawa (ibid.) refers to Hishino New Town (1967, Aichi prefecture) and Fujisawa New Town (1976,

Kanagawa prefecture) as examples for linear city projects that have been built. For the Hishino New Town project, see Kisho KUROKAWA, "Project of Hishino 1967", in: *Kenchiku Bunka*, VOL. 6, 1967, pp. 93–128 — Linear city models were first developed by Arturo Soria y Mata for Madrid in the 1880s. In the 1920s and 1930s, Nikolai Alexander Milyutin and Ernst May developed linear city projects for the urban planning programs in the Soviet Union. See also Kisho (Noriaki) KURO-KAWA, "Report on the Town Planning of U.S.S.R", in: *Kokusai Kentiku*, VOL. 26, 1959, pp. 57–61.

3   Kisho KUROKAWA, "量産設計方法論メモ. メタボリック・スペースの追求", in: *Kenchiku*, VOL. 9, 1962, pp. 92–112, here p. 92.

4   See Constantinos A. DOXIADIS, *Ekistics. Introduction to a Science of Human Settlements*, London: Hutchinson, 1968.

5   KUROKAWA, *Intercultural Architecture*, p. 72.

6   This is a recurrent theme among the Japanese metabolists. See Kisho KUROKAWA, *Metabolism in Architecture*, London: Studio Vista, 1977, pp. 31–32: "Although Metabolism emphasizes the principle of replaceability and changeability of parts, the reasons for doing so derive from a philosophy entirely different from the use-and-discard approach sometimes justified by economics in mass-consumption societies. I know of many instances in which entire buildings have been wastefully destroyed because portions of them were no longer serviceable. If spaces were composed on the basis of the theory of the metabolic cycle, it would be possible to replace only those parts that had lost their usefulness and in this way to contribute to the conservation of resources by using buildings longer."

7   See KUROKAWA, *Metabolism in Architecture*, p. 23.

8   See Michel RAGON, *Où vivrons-nous demain?*, Paris: R. Laffont, 1963.

9   See Kisho KUROKAWA, ホモ・モペンス, Tokyo: Chuokoron, 1969, pp. 6–10 · KUROKAWA, 現代建築の創造/CIAM. 崩壊以後, Tokyo: Shokokusha, 1971 · KUROKAWA, 都市革命. 公有から共有へ, Tokyo: Chuokoron-Shinsha, 2006 — For the CIAM meetings and documents, see *Congrès Internationaux d'Architecture Moderne. Dokumente 1928–1939*, edited by Martin STEINMANN, Basel and Stuttgart: Birkhäuser, 1979 · Eric MUMFORD, *The CIAM Discourse on Urbanism, 1928–1960*, Cambridge, MA and London: The MIT Press, 2000.

10   See LE CORBUSIER (Charles-Édouard Jeanneret-Gris), "The Charter", in: LE CORBUSIER, *The Athens Charter*. With an introduction by Jean Giraudoux and a new foreword by Joseph Lluis Sert, translated by Anthony Eardley, New York: Grossman Publishers, 1973, pp. 39–110, here p. 43.

11   CIAM, "The Declaration of La Sarraz", in: Ibid., pp. 6–8, here p. 7.

12   See Asger JORN, "Contre le fonctionnalisme" (1958), reprinted in: Mirella BANDINI, *L'esthétique, le politique. De Cobra à l'internationale situationniste (1948–1957)*, translated by Claude Galli (1st Italian edition: Rome: Officina edizioni, 1977), Arles: Editions Sulliver | Marseille: Via Valeriano, 1998, pp. 218–223 · Henri LEFÈBVRE, *Critique de la vie quotidienne*, VOL. 1: *Introduction*, Paris: B. Grasset, 1947 and VOL. 2: *Fondements d'une sociologie de la quotidienneté*, Paris: L'Arche, 1961 · LEFÈBVRE, *La révolution urbaine*, Paris: Gallimard, 1970.

13   See KUROKAWA, *Intercultural Architecture*, pp. 74–75.

14   Another influential urban development study is Raymond VERNON's *Metropolis 1985*, published in 1960 and translated into Japanese in 1968. See Raymond VERNON, *Metropolis 1985. An Interpretation of the Findings of the New York Metropolitan Region Study*, Cambridge, MA: Harvard

University Press, 1960; and VERNON, 大都市の将来. 蠟山政道監訳, Tokyo: Tokyo Daigaku Shuppankai, 1968.

15 Jean GOTTMANN, *Megalopolis. The Urbanized Northeastern Seaboard of the United States,* Norwood, MA: The Plimpton Press, 1961, pp. 9–10.

16 Ibid., p. 5.

17 Ibid., pp. 776–778. Denis de Rougement writes about Europe (quoted in RAGON, *Où vivrons-nous demain?,* p. 41): "Le continent européen est devenu Megalopolis: une maison tous les cent mètres en moyenne, à quelque distance des autoroutes à six pistes, lesquelles permettent d'aller aussi vite d'une ville à l'autre que les trains-express (quelques-uns déjà souterrains). Les avions long-courriers atterrissent verticalement sur les rares terrains vagues conservés dans les faubourgs."

18 For the metabolist movement, see Kisho KUROKAWA, "メタボリズム方法論", in: *Kindai-Kentiku,* VOL. 14, 1960, pp. 50–63 · Günter NITSCHKE, "The Metabolists of Japan", in: *Architectural Design,* VOL. 34, 1964, pp. 509–524 · Noboru KAWAZOE, "Metabolism (1)", in: *The Japan Architect, VOL. 44,* no. 159, December 1969, pp. 101–108 · Noboru KAWAZOE, "Metabolism II", in: *The Japan Architect,* VOL. 45, no. 160, January 1970, pp. 97–101 · Yasuo UESAKA, "A Review of his Metabolist Philosophy and Arts since Expo '70", in: *Architecture Plus,* VOL. 2, 1974, pp. 96–107 · Charles JENCKS, *The Language of Post-Modern Architecture,* New York: Rizzoli International Publications, 1977 (with a focus on "postmodern" architecture) · KUROKAWA, *Metabolism in Architecture,* pp. 41–45 · Michael F. ROSS, *Beyond Metabolism: The New Japanese Architecture,* New York: Architectural Record, 1977 · Daniel STEWART, *The Making of a Modern Japanese Architecture. 1868 to the Present,* Tokyo and New York: Kodansha International, 1987, pp. 175–185 · Patrizia RANZO, Silvana DE MAIO, and Diana DE MAIO, *La metropoli come natura artificiale. Architetture della complessità in Giappone,* Naples: Edizioni Scientifiche Italiane, 1992, pp. 37–41 and 66–67 · Alain GUIHEUX, *Kisho Kurokawa. Architecte. Le métabolisme 1960–1975,* Paris: Éditions du Centre Pompidou, 1997 · Hajime YATSUKA and Hideki YOSHIMATSU, メタボリズム. 一九六〇年代―日本の建築アヴァンガルド, Tokyo: INAX, 1997 · Noboru KAWAZOE, "The Thirty Years of Metabolists", in: *Thesis. Wissenschaftliche Zeitschrift der Bauhaus-Universität Weimar,* VOL. 44, 1998, no. 6, pp. 146–151 · Cherie WENDELKIN, "Putting Metabolism Back in Place. The Making of a Radically Decontextualized Architecture in Japan", in: *Anxious Modernisms. Experimentation in Postwar Architectural Culture,* edited by Sarah Williams GOLDHAGEN and Réjean LEGAULT, Montréal: Canadian Centre for Architecture | Cambridge, MA and London, The MIT Press, 2000, pp. 279–299 · Raffaele PERNICE, "Metabolism Reconsidered. Its Role in the Architectural Context of the World", in: *Journal of Asian Architecture and Building Engineering,* VOL. 3, 2004, pp. 357–363 · PERNICE, "The Transformation of Tokyo During the 1950s and Early 1960s. Projects Between City Planning and Urban Utopia", in: *Journal of Asian Architecture and Building Engineering,* VOL. 5, 2006, pp. 253–260 · PERNICE, *Metabolist Movement between Tokyo Bay Planning and Urban Utopias in the Years of Rapid Economic Growth 1958–1964,* Ph.D. Thesis, Waseda University, Tokyo, 2007 · Rem KOOLHAAS and Hans Ulrich OBRIST, *Project Japan. Metabolism Talks…,* edited by Kayoko OTA with James WESTCOTT (AMO), Cologne: Taschen, 2011 · *Metabolism. The City of the Future: Dreams and Visions of Reconstruction in Postwar and Present-Day Japan,* edited by Mami HIROSE, Hitomi SASAKI, Naotake MAEDA, Miho TAGOMORI, Ami TAMAYAMA, Yuri YOSHIDA, and Ayako YOSHIDA, Tokyo: Mori Art Museum, 2011.

19 In "The Growth of the City", Ernest Watson Burgess mentions that the dynamics of "social organization and disorganization" in metropolitan areas like New York resembles "processes of metabolism". See Ernest W. BURGESS, "The Growth of the City: An Introduction to a Research Project", in: Robert E. PARK, Ernest W. BURGESS, and Roderick D. MCKENZIE, *The City,* Chicago and London: The University of Chicago Press, 1925, pp. 47–62, here p. 53; and ibid.: "How far is the growth of the city, in its physical and technical aspects, matched by a natural but adequate readjustment in the social organization? What, for a city, is a normal rate of expansion, a rate of expansion with which controlled changes in the social organization might successfully keep pace? […] These questions may best be answered, perhaps, by thinking of urban growth as a resultant of organization and disorganization analogous to the anabolic and catabolic processes of metabolism in the body. In what way are individuals incorporated into the life of a city?"

20 Noboru KAWAZOE, *Metabolism. The Proposals for New Urbanism,* Tokyo: Bijutsu Shuppan, 1960, p. 5.

21 Design as a process that is based on the creation of forms, models of functional interfaces, and technology is also one of the key themes of Kikutake's writings. See Kiyonori KIKUTAKE, 建築の心, Tokyo: Inoueshoken, 1973, pp. 59–65 — For the larger context of design debates, see John A. WALKER, *Design History and the History of Design.* With a contribution by Judy ATTFIELD, London: Pluto Press, 1989.

22 In 共生の思想 *(kyosei no shiso),* Kurokawa also uses the *kanji* form. He refers to a "principle of life as a process of metabolism" (新陳代謝をする生命の原理). See Kisho KUROKAWA, 共生の思想, Tokyo: Tokumashoten, 1996, p. 22.

23 See Charles JENCKS, "Introduction", in: KUROKAWA, *Metabolism in Architecture,* pp. 8–22, here p. 9. However, Kurokawa himself remarks (in: Kisho KUROKAWA, *The Philosophy of Symbiosis,* London: Academy Editions, 1994, p. 24): "I consciously selected the terms and key concepts of metabolism and metamorphosis because they were the vocabulary of life principles. Machines do not grow, change, or metabolize of their own accord. 'Metabolism' was indeed an excellent choice for a key word to announce the beginning of the age of life." — For other possible sources of the term, see KOOLHAAS and OBRIST, *Project Japan. Metabolism Talks…,* p. 234.

24 *Webster's New Practical Dictionary,* Springfield, MA: G. & C. Merriam, 1951, p. 403.

25 *New Desk Standard Dictionary,* New York: Funk & Wagnalls, 1951, p. 16.

26 *Webster's New International Dictionary of the English Language,* 2nd edition, unabridged, Springfield, MA: G. & C. Merriam, 1952, p. 1544.

27 *The American College Dictionary,* New York: Random House | Tokyo: Kinokuniya Book-Store, 1962, p. 764.

28 See J. D. [John Desmond] BERNAL, 生命の起原: その物理學的基礎. 山口清三郎, 鎮目恭夫譯, Tokyo: Iwanamishoten, 1952.

29 See Conrad Hal WADDINGTON, *Towards a Theoretical Biology,* 4 VOLS., Edinburgh: Edinburgh University Press, 1968–1972.

30 See John B. S. HALDANE, "The Origin of Life", in: *The Rationalist Annual,* VOL. 148, 1929, pp. 3–10 · Alexander I. OPARIN, *The Origin of Life,* New York: Macmillan, 1938 · André LWOFF, *L'Évolution physiologique,* Paris: Herrmann, 1943 · Alexandre DAUVILLIER, *Genèse, nature et évolution des planètes,* Paris: Hermann, 1947. — J. D. [John Desmond] BERNAL (*The Physical Basis* *of Life,* London: Routledge and Kegan Paul, 1951, p.11) himself refers to these authors. He (ibid., p.6) calls the title of his lecture an "unconscious echo" of Thomas Henry HUXLEY's lecture *On the Physical Basis of Life* (1901) and mentions (ibid., p.67) also Edmund B. WILSON's *The Physical Basis of Life* (1923).

31 See BERNAL, *The Physical Basis of Life,* p.9: "It is probable that even a formulation of this problem is beyond reach of any one scientist, for such a scientist would have to be at the same time a competent mathematician, physicist, and experienced organic chemist, he should have a very extensive knowledge of geology, geophysics and geochemistry and, besides all this, be absolutely at home in all biological disciplines."

32 Ibid., p.13.

33 Ibid.

34 Ibid., p.46. See also ibid., p.15.

35 BERNAL (ibid., p.28) describes this production as a "play" with a prologue and three acts: "The process is one which we can imagine as taking the form of a play divided into a prologue and three acts. The prologue introduces the scene on the surface of the primitive earth, and the first group of actors of an entirely inorganic kind which must start the play. The first act deals with the accumulation of chemical substances and the appearance of a stable process of conversion between them, which we call life; the second with the almost equally important stabilization of that process and its freeing from energy dependence on anything but sunlight. It is a stage of photosynthesis and of the appearance of molecular oxygen and respiration. The third act is that of the development of specific organisms, cells, animals and plants, from these beginnings. All we have hitherto studied in biology is really summed up in the last few lines of this act, and from this and the stage set we have to infer the rest of the play."

36 See KUROKAWA, ホモ・モベンス, pp.170–171.

37 BERNAL, *The Physical Basis of Life,* pp.43–44.

38 See ibid., p.19: "Living organisms as we know them are composed of thousands of kinds of complex chemical molecules — sugars, amino acids, purines — molecules out of which are composed the far more complicated macro-molecules of the proteins and nucleic acids and such microscopically visible structures as membranes and fibres."

39 Ibid., p.54.

40 See ibid., pp.53–54: "The evolution of organisms must have been preceded by a period of the evolution of the cell. But the story of that evolution is certainly the most difficult part of the whole unravelling of biological processes, because it is at the same time the furthest removed from synthetic chemistry and analytical biology. Nevertheless in recent years, thanks to the new methods described above, much deeper understanding of the cell is becoming possible. The most striking general feature is the dual construction. The cell consists, inside a membranous envelope, of two parts, a nucleus itself provided with a membrane, and an external cytoplasm. Each of these volumes in turn contains other finer parts. The nucleus contains filamentous processes of varying number, the chromosomes, together with the associated nucleoli and centromeres, while the cytoplasm contains a world of particles of varying dimensions, particularly the mitochondria, the golgi bodies and a number of smaller plastids, including chloroplasts in the plants and microplasts and other so-called organelles. Many, if not all, these constituents appear to be self-reproducing.

Therefore even in single-celled organisms there is a considerable differentiation. Protoplasm is therefore far from a structure-less substance".

41 Ibid., p.23. In *Notes on Media Space* (1973), Kurokawa quotes Bernal's definition of metabolism from the Japanese translation of *The Physical Basis of Life* (by YAMAGUCHI and SHIZUME). See BERNAL, 生命の起原, p.24; and Kisho KUROKAWA, "中間体 (メディア・スペース) に関するノオト", in: *Kenchiku Bunka,* VOL.28, 1973, pp.75–106, here p.75: 「生物系の物質的な側面は一種の機械の骨組と連結杆にほかならない。その特殊な機能はエネルギーの交換を営むことであり、成長と同化作用は酵素によって促進されるエネルギー変化から成る新陳代謝を達成する手段である」". In the translation of Yamaguchi and Shizume, 成長 is written 生長. See also KUROKAWA, *Metabolism in Architecture,* p.180.

42 Rudolf SCHÖNHEIMER, *The Dynamic State of Body Constituents,* Cambridge, MA: Harvard University Press, 1942 · SCHÖNHEIMER, 生体の動態. 野島德吉訳, Tokyo: Nayashoten, 1955.

43 SCHÖNHEIMER, *The Dynamic State of Body Constituents,* p.64.

44 See Norbert WIENER, *The Human Use of Human Beings: Cybernetics and Society* (1st edition: Boston: Houghton Mifflin, 1950), New York: Avon Books, 1967, pp.137–138: "One thing at any rate is clear. The physical identity of an individual does not consist in the matter of which it is made. Modern methods of tagging the elements participating in metabolism have shown a much higher turnover than was long thought possible, not only of the body as a whole, but of each and every part of it." And ibid., p.166: "I repeat, to be alive is to participate in a continuous stream of influences from the outer world, in which we are merely the transitional stage." Wiener's *The Human Use of Human Beings,* first published in 1950, was translated into Japanese in 1954, and his *Cybernetics or Control and Communication in the Animal and the Machine* (1948) in 1957.

45 BERNAL, *The Physical Basis of Life,* p.16. See Kisho KUROKAWA, *From Metabolism to Symbiosis,* London: Academy Editions, 1992, p.10: "The theory of Metabolism is based on two principles: diachronicity, or the symbiosis of different time periods, and the processes and changes that a creature undergoes as it lives, and synchronicity. The first aim of the Metabolism movement was to introduce this regenerating process into architecture and city planning, the name being expressive of the conviction that a work of architecture should not be frozen once it is completed but should be apprehended instead as a thing — or as a process — that evolves from past to present and from present to future. Another way to express this process of evolution from past to present to future is to call it a symbiosis of the three time periods. Although anticipated future conditions are taken into consideration as much as possible, a building is given a particular form within the context of the present. But historically speaking, architecture has at times found its present in the past or has enclosed in it an image of the future." — For further references in the life sciences, see Robert P. WAGNER and Herschel K. MITCHELL, *Genetics and Metabolism,* New York and London: John Wiley & Sons, 1955 · Melvin CALVIN, "Chemical Evolution", in: *Proceedings of the Royal Society of London. Series A, Mathematical and Physical Sciences,* VOL.288, 1965, pp.441–466 · Earl D. HANSON, "Evolution of the Cell from Primordial Living", in: *The Quarterly Review of Biology,* VOL.41, 1966, pp.1–12 · Soraya DE CHADAREVIAN, "Sequences, Conformation, Information: Biochemists and Molecular Biologists in the 1950s", in: *Journal of the History of Biology,* VOL.29, 1996, pp.361–386.

46 J. D. [John Desmond] BERNAL, "The Problem of Stages in Biopoiesis", in: *Proceedings of the First International Symposium on: The Origin of Life on the Earth. Held at Moscow 19–24 August 1957,* edited for the Academy of Sciences of the U.S.S.R. by A. I. OPARIN, A. G. PASYNSKIĬ, A. E.

BRAUNSHTEĬN, and T. E. PAVLOVSKAYA, English-French-German Edition, edited for the International Union of Biochemistry by F. CLARK and R. L. M. SYNGE, New York, London, Paris, and Los Angeles: Pergamon Press, 1959, pp. 38–53, here pp. 39–40.

47 See KUROKAWA, *From Metabolism to Symbiosis*, p. 15.

48 For Koestler, human agents are holons. See Arthur KOESTLER, *The Ghost in the Machine*, London: Hutchinson & Co., 1967, p. 56: "No man is an island — he is a holon. A Janus-faced entity who, looking inward, sees himself as a self-contained unique whole, looking outward as a dependent part. His *self-assertive tendency* is the dynamic manifestation of his unique *wholeness*, his autonomy and independence as a holon. Its equally universal antagonist, the *integrative tendency*, expresses his dependence on the larger whole to which he belongs: his *'partness'*."

49 See KOESTLER, *The Ghost in the Machine*, p. 58: "Organisms and societies are multi-levelled hierarchies of semiautonomous sub-wholes branching into sub-wholes of a lower order, and so on. The term 'holon' has been introduced to refer to these intermediary entities which, relative to their subordinates in the hierarchy, function as self-contained wholes; relative to their superordinates as dependent parts."

50 Kisho KUROKAWA, *Each one a Hero. The Philosophy of Symbiosis*, Tokyo, New York, and London: Kondansha International, 1997, p. 100. See Arthur KOESTLER, "The Tree and the Candle", in: *Unity Through Diversity: A Festschrift for Ludwig von Bertalanffy*, edited by William GRAY and Nicholas D. RIZZO, New York: Gordon and Breach, 1973, pp. 287–314. Koestler first develops his holon theory in *The Ghost in the Machine* (1967). Kurokawa (*Intercultural Architecture*, p. 147) refers also to Koestler's concept of creativity.

51 The subtitle of Le Corbusier's book.

52 KUROKAWA, *Each one a Hero*, p. 131.

53 See ibid., p. 20.

54 See Pierre TEILHARD DE CHARDIN, *The Phenomenon of Man*, translated by Bernard Wall (first published in French as *Le phénomène humain*, Paris: Editions du Seuil, 1955), New York: Harper Perennial Modern Thought, 2008, p. 56.

55 Ibid., p. 73.

56 Ibid., p. 81.

57 Ibid., p. 87.

58 Ibid., p. 260. TEILHARD DE CHARDIN (ibid.) calls this point also "Omega Point".

59 See KUROKAWA, ホモ・モベンス, p. 153 · KUROKAWA, *Metabolism in Architecture*, p. 79.

60 See TEILHARD DE CHARDIN, *The Phenomenon of Man*, pp. 104–108 and p. 180.

61 KUROKAWA, *Metabolism in Architecture*, p. 79. Medawar was also a member of the Theoretical Biology Club.

62 Noboru Kawazoe wrote for the Metabolism manifesto (1960) a poem with the title "I want to be kabi (bacteria)". See KAWAZOE, *Metabolism. The Proposals for New Urbanism*, p. 51.

63 See John D. BERNAL, *The Freedom of Necessity*, London: Routledge & Kegan Paul, 1949, pp. 191–213.

64 See KUROKAWA, ホモ・モベンス, p. 143 · KUROKAWA, *Metabolism in Architecture*, p. 75. — For Bernal's model of a space habitat, see J. D. [John Desmond] BERNAL: *The World, the Flesh and the Devil. An Inquiry into the Future of the Three Enemies of the Rational Soul*, London: Kegan Paul,

Trench, Trubner & Co. | New York: E.P.Dutton & Co., 1929, 2nd edition, Bloomington: University of Indiana Press, 1969.

65 Kurokawa, *Intercultural Architecture,* p.126.

66 See William R.Ashby, "Design for a Brain", in: *Electronic Engineering,* VOL.20, 1948, pp.379–383 · W.Grey Walter, "An Electro-Mechanical 'Animal'", in: *Dialectica,* VOL.4, 1950, pp.206–213; and "An Imitation of Life," in: *Scientific American,* VOL.182, no.5, 1950, pp.42–45. — Norbert Wiener's *The Human Use of Human Beings,* first published in 1950, has been translated into Japanese in 1954. In the poem "I want to be kabi (bacteria)", Kurokawa's metabolist colleague Kawazoe combines the life of a bacteria with the vision of a mobile "brain wave receiver" through which its carrier "conveys directly and exactly what other people think and feel of him and vice versa" (Kawazoe, *Metabolism. The Proposals for New Urbanism,* p.51). This vision echoes William Grey Walter's comparison of the electrical stimulus-response-mechanisms in amoeba and human brains in *The Living Brain* (see W.Grey Walter, *The Living Brain,* New York: W.W.Norton, 1953, reprint 1958, p.20). For Walter, as for Kawazoe and Kurokawa, the only difference between the single bacteria-cell and the human brain is the complexification of interdependent communication units. Walter's emphasis on stimulus-reaction-schemes — to which Kurokawa refers in the context of multiplied stimuli in big cities that intensify and modify the life activity of its agents — are again part of the behavioristic debates about the end of classic psychology.

67 Kurokawa, *Intercultural Architecture,* p.126 · Kazuhiko Atsumi, "History of artificial organs in Japan", in: *Journal of Artificial Organs,* VOL.8, 2005, pp.1–12.

68 Kurokawa (ibid.) quotes from Kazuhiko Atsumi: "New Concept — BIOMATION — Its Revolutionary Impact on Industry and Society", in: *Symposium Proceedings: The Social Impact of Advanced Technology. Discoveries International Symposium,* The Ohio State University, May 10–13, 1982, [Tokyo]: The Honda Foundation, 1984, pp.15–43. — In the Capsule Manifesto of *Homo movens* (ホモ・モベンス, p.154), Kurokawa drew a clear distinction between the intentions and the free will of humans and technical things that can only serve as "devices" for their desires. See Kurokawa, *Metabolism in Architecture,* p.79.

69 See Kurokawa, *From Metabolism to Symbiosis.*

70 See Kurokawa, ホモ・モベンス, pp.97–99.

71 Tadao Umesao, "情報社会産業論", in: *Chuokoron,* VOL.905, 1963, pp.46–58, here p.53.

72 Ibid.

73 Ibid., p.58.

74 See Kenzo Tange, 日本列島の将来像, Tokyo: Kodansha, 1966, p.16 · W.W. [Walt Whitman] Rostow, *The Stages of Economic Growth. A Non-Communist Manifesto,* Cambridge: [Cambridge] University Press, 1960. — Kurokawa (in *The Philosophy of Symbiosis,* p.18) criticizes Rostow's five-stage model as a theory that only explains developments in certain Western societies.

75 See Kurokawa, ホモ・モベンス, pp.18–22.

76 See Kurokawa, *Intercultural Architecture,* pp.138–152.

77 Kurokawa first uses the word in a book with the same title (*Homo movens,* 1969). At the end of this book, he mentions that the term was first employed by the sociologist Michitaro Tada with whom he had many discussions. See Kurokawa, ホモ・モベンス, p.175.

78 Kurokawa often quotes Nippon Hoso Kyokai (NHK) reports on transformations of daily life activities in big cities in Japan. The reports are entitled *nihonjin no seikatsu jikan,* 日本人の生活時間. See KUROKAWA, ホモ・モベンス, p.115 · Kisho KUROKAWA, 行動建築論. メタボリズムの美学, Tokyo: Sho-kokusha, 1969.

79 See KUROKAWA, ホモ・モベンス, p.56–60. The "nomad" is a frequent theme in Kurokawa's writ-ings. See Kisho KUROKAWA, ノマドの時代. 情報化社会のライフスタイル, Tokyo: Tokumashoten, 1989.

80 KUROKAWA, *Each one a Hero,* p.126.

81 Kazuhiko ATSUMI, "Biomedical Engineering: The Future Medicine in the Biomation Age of the 21st Century", in: *Journal of Perinatal Medicine,* VOL.15, 1987, Supplement 1, p.159.

82 Ibid.

83 In *La ville cybernétique,* Nicolas Schöffer describes these stimuli-reaction-events, with a refer-ence to Stéphane Lupasco's energy models, as activators of latent, undetermined "potentialities" of the involved agents (Nicolas SCHÖFFER, *La ville cybernétique,* Paris: Tchou, 1969, p.109): "Cette organisation, ou plutôt organicité, de la cité ne se manifeste pas seulement sur le plan expansion-nel, mais aussi dans son fonctionnement quotidien, car les rapports entre l'individu et son envi-ronnement subissent constamment des impulsions indéterminées, provoquées par d'autres indi-vidus ou groupes d'individus ou par des phénomènes naturels. Ce sont des virtualités potentielles (suivant le vocabulaire de Lupasco) qui s'actualisent ou vice versa, selon les lois statisticiennes du hasard."

84 Kisho KUROKAWA, "Toward a Rhizome World or 'Chaosmos'", in: *The Japan Architect,* VOL.376, 1988, pp.8–11, here p.9. — See also KUROKAWA, *From Metabolism to Symbiosis,* p.13: "Deleuze and Guattari see man and machine, society and technology, not as essentially opposed entities but as states of existence that are intimately interwoven in a rhizome-like web."

85 KUROKAWA, ホモ・モベンス, pp.20–41. Kurokawa mentions Bell only as a "professor of Columbia University" (p.20).

86 Ibid., p.86.

87 For the positive connotation of cars in Kurokawa's writings, see KUROKAWA, メタボリズムの発想, pp.60–61. — See also Reyner BANHAM, "A Home is not a House", in: *Art in America,* VOL.53, 1965, pp.70–79, here p.72: "The present mobile home is a mess, visually, mechanically, and in its relationship to the permanent infrastructure of civilization. But if it could be rendered more com-pact and mobile, and be uprooted from its dependency on static utilities, the trailer could fulfil its promise to put a nation on wheels."

88 See KUROKAWA, ホモ・モベンス, pp.143–173. — A brief, first version of the "Capsule Manifesto" already appeared in the journal *Space Design* in March 1969, about six months before *Homo mov-ens.* See Kisho (Noriaki) KUROKAWA, "Capsule Declaration 1969 (カプセル宣言)", in: *Space Design,* VOL.3, 1969, pp.50–53. An English translation of the enlarged version can be found in KUROKAWA, *Metabolism in Architecture,* pp.75–85. In the *Space Design* issue of 1969, Noboru Kawazoe, Kiyoshi Awazu, Toshio Nakamura, and Fumihiko Maki also wrote short essays about capsule architectures.

89 See Louis I. KAHN, "Toward a Plan for Midtown Philadelphia", in: *Perspecta,* VOL.2, 1953, pp.10–27 · KAHN, "Order in Architecture", in: *Perspecta,* VOL.4, 1957, pp.[58]–[65].

90 See Kisho KUROKAWA, *From the Age of the Machine to the Age of Life,* London: BookArt, 1998, p.28: "Based loosely on the DNA molecule, the spirals intersect rather than run in parallel and the centres are open horizontals rather than tightly packed. Life sciences give the new iconography,

but they are reinterpreted visually and functionally." — See also KUROKAWA, *From Metabolism to Symbiosis*, p. 14: "The concept of the helix city, an important part of the founding of Metabolism in 1960, took the double helix of the DNA molecule as its pretext. This was realized in the 1970 Toshiba pavilion. In 1963 the Metabolist movement announced plant cells to be the models for a city that allows growth and change. We conceived of cities built on lakes and the ocean, and in the late sixties, I proposed a design of a factory floating on the ocean, which I called the Metabonate. Its special feature was that it could always be updated with the very latest technological advances. The roofs of buildings were roads, while the lake provided for access by boats. The residences were based on a double helix structure. The first use of this plan was the Nitto Food Main Cannery, built in 1963. The structure of the capitals of its columns allowed for future extension, as the architecture of Metabolism was based on a growing biological model."

91 See Kiyonori KIKUTAKE, "Ocean City", in: KAWAZOE, *Metabolism. The Proposals for New Urbanism*, pp. 6–39, pp. here 12–27 · Kenzo TANGE Team (Kenzo Tange, Koji Kamiya, Arata Isozaki, Sadao Watanabe, Noriaki Kurokawa, Heiki Koh): "A Plan for Tokyo, 1960 — Toward a Structural Reorganization", in: *the japan architect,* [VOL. 36], April 1961, pp. 8–38, here p. 30: "In our plan for Tokyo, we have devised means of unifying the core system and the *pilotis*. As we envision them, the cores of buildings take the place of columns, creating 'column-less' *pilotis* areas under the buildings. This system is unified with the cyclical transportation we propose. Each link of the transportation system contains a unit of area with multi-level parking space. People would enter the parking space in their cars, get out of the vehicles, and then ride up into buildings in elevators situated in vertical cores. In this way the unit urban area and the highway system would intermesh, and there would be spatial order as well as a speed hierarchy linking, first, streets, interchanges, parking spaces, and buildings and, second, high speed, low speed, human speed, and immobility. Urban space would be restored to life." — For further references to the works of Tange, Kiyonori and Isozaki, see Philip DREW, *The Architecture of Arata Isozaki,* London and New York: Granada Publishing, 1982 · *Arata Isozaki. Architecture 1960–1990,* edited by Kate NORMENT, New York: Rizzoli, 1991 · Manfred SPEIDEL, "Städte im Wasser für Japan. Die metabolistischen Konzepte Kiyonori Kikutakes", in: *Der Traum von der Stadt am Meer. Hafenstädte aus aller Welt,* edited by Gisela JAACKS, Hamburg: Museum für Hamburgische Geschichte, 2004, pp. 175–189 · Zhongjie LIN, *City as Process. Tange Kenzo and the Japanese Urban Utopias, 1959–1970,* Ph.D. Thesis, University of Pennsylvania, 2006 · Zhongjie LIN, "Urban Structure for the Expanding Metropolis: Kenzo Tange's 1960 Plan for Tokyo", in: *Journal of Architectural and Planning Research,* VOL. 24, 2007, pp. 109–124 · Ken T. OSHIMA, *Arata Isozaki,* London: Phaidon, 2009 · Antje WAGENKNECHT, "Kiyonori Kikutake: Künstliche Inseln für Japan", in: *OAG Notizen,* May 2009, pp. 2–16.

92 Fumihiko MAKI, *Investigations in Collective Form,* St. Louis: The School of Architecture. Washington University, 1964, pp. 3–8 · See Noboru KAWAZOE and Masato OTAKA, "Toward Group Form", in: KAWAZOE, *Metabolism. The Proposals for New Urbanism,* pp. 52–69 — On Maki's architecture, see Jennifer TAYLOR with James CONNER, *The Architecture of Fumihiko Maki. Space, City, Order and Making,* Basel, Berlin, and Boston: Birkhäuser, 2003, pp. 12–24 — For the larger context of debates about megastructures, see Reyner BANHAM, *Megastructure. Urban Futures of the Recent Past,* London: Thames and Hudson, 1976 · Sarah DEYONG, "Planetary Habitat: The Origins of a Phantom Movement", in: *The Journal of Architecture,* VOL. 6, 2001, pp. 113–128 · Ruth EATON, *Die* *ideale Stadt. Von der Antike bis zur Gegenwart,* translated by Nikolaus G. Schneider, Berlin: Nicolai, 2001, pp. 218–223.

93 See Bandini, *L'esthétique, le politique. De Cobra à l'internationale situationniste (1948–1957)* · Eaton, *Die ideale Stadt,* pp. 223–232.

94 Interactive architecture and art as well as new interfaces between mass and individual production processes, through which engaged users co-design their objects, were major issues of various movements from pop art to painting in the 1960s. In this context, Kurokawa refers to the works of the Italian Gruppo T (founded in Milan in 1959 and active until 1962, with its core members Giovanni Anceschi, Davide Boriani, Gianni Colombo, and Gabriele de Vecchi) and the kinaesthetic, mobile art of Alexander Calder. See Kurokawa, ホモ・モベンス, pp. 5–6.

95 In *The Creation of Contemporary Architecture. After the Collapse of CIAM* (1971, in Japanese), Kurokawa reconstructs the emergence of the metabolism group within a dense field of other architecture movements. For his account on GEAM and Archigram, see Kurokawa, 現代建築の創造, pp. 102–115 and pp. 169–178.

96 Banham (*Megastructure,* pp. 21–28) mentions Hans Hollein's and Paolo Soleri's capsule models. Besides GEAM and Archigram, the Team 10, a subgroup formed during the last CIAM conference including Jaap Bakema, Georges Candilis, Giancarlo De Carlo, Aldo van Eyck, Alison and Peter Smithson, and Shadrach Woods, represents another community of architects that focuses on urban architectures. All these groups hold conferences and are in close contact. Kurokawa joined the Team 10 meetings in Royaumont (1962) and Urbino (1966). Within the context of urban city design, Kurokawa also refers to the Italian Radical Design movement of Archizoom and Superstudio.

97 In 1965, a new group on future urban architecture emerged, the Groupe International d'Architecture Prospective (GIAP), around Friedman, Michel Ragon, Walter Jonas, Paul Maymont, Georges Patrix, Ionel Schein, and Nicolas Schöffer. The last conference of this group was held in 1967. For the history and context of both groups and the Futurist movement, see Reyner Banham, *Theory and Design in the First Machine Age,* London: The Architectural Press, 1960, pp. 99–138 · Larry Busbea, *Topologies. The Urban Utopia in France, 1960–1970,* Cambridge, MA and London: The MIT Press, 2007.

98 In the 1930s and 1940s, various issues of *The Architectural Forum* focused on prefabrication. See, for instance, VOL. 77, September 1942: Walter F. Bogner, "Prefabrication", pp. 78–81; Paul Thiry, "Housing Unit, Details", pp. 82–83; Charles H. Warner Jr., "Prefabricated, Demountable House", pp. 84–86; Ralph Rapson and David B. Runnels, "A Fabric House", pp. 87–89; Louis Skidmore, Nathaniel A. Owings, and John E. Merrill, "Flexible Space", pp. 100–103 · See also the whole chapter on "Prefabrication", in: *The Architectural Forum,* VOL. 77, December 1942, pp. 49–60 — Kenneth Frampton (*Modern Architecture. A Critical History,* London: Thames and Hudson, 1980, reprint 1982, pp. 239–240) refers to Richard Buckminster Fuller's models of prefabricated bathrooms (1938–1940) and various capsule-designs of houses and cars that Fuller published in his journal *Shelter.*

99 See Günther Kühne, "Mobiles Planen. Mobiles Bauen", in: *Bauwelt,* VOL. 49, 1958, pp. 491–493, here p. 492 · Yona Friedman, *L'architecture mobile suivi de la théorie des systèmes compréhensibles,* [first privately printed in 1958], Brussels: Centre d'Études Architecturales, 1971, pp. 7–8:

"L'architecture mobile opère de deux façons:

1 – par la convertibilité des formes et usages de constructions (conviennent ici les constructions permettant une réutilisation après leur déplacement, les constructions démontables, temporaires ou celles à amortissement rapide);

2 – par la convertibilité des surfaces ou espaces utilisés, sans changement de la structure portante des constructions, ceci par le moyen d'un système de plates-formes, réseaux de voierie, d'alimentation et de canalisations qui soit transformable et déplaçable dans et sur les structures portantes."

100 See FRAMPTON, *Modern Architecture,* pp.269–297 · Simon SADLER, *Archigram. Architecture without Architecture,* Cambridge, MA and London: The MIT Press, 2005 · Hadas A. STEINER, *Archigram. The Structure of Circulation,* New York and London: Routledge, 2009.

101 For Banham, the playful aspect of the Archigram models "celebrates disorder, fun, chance, consumerism, entertainment" (BANHAM, *Megastructure,* p.92).

102 In *Archigram,* no.5, 1965, Crompton writes about a computerized interface between the organic and inorganic functioning of the city: "The mechanism is at once digital and biological, producing rational and random actions, reactions and counter-reactions. The computer programme is a conglomeration of rational reasoning, intuitive assumption, personal preference, chance, sentiment and bloody mindedness which is assimilated and interpreted". See SADLER, *Archigram,* p.120. The Archigram movement also focused on the nomad-theme in *Archigram,* no.8, 1968. For a more detailed reconstruction of the movement, see Bernard RUDOFSKY, *Architecture without Architects: A Short Introduction to Non-Pedigreed Architecture,* New York: Museum of Modern Art, 1965 · BANHAM, *Megastructure,* pp.89–98 · *Archigram,* edited by Peter COOK, London: Studio Vista, 1972 · SADLER, *Archigram.*

103 For Archigram's Plug-in models, see Herbert LACHMAYER and Dennis CROMPTON, *A Guide to Archigram 1961–74 | Ein Archigram-Program 1961–74,* London: Academy Editions, 1994, pp.110–117 · SADLER, *Archigram,* p.14: "Forging ahead with the building of the future, Plug-In City reworked two slightly repressed motifs to be found in modernism: those of megastructure and the 'building-in-becoming'. They had been tried in theory in Le Corbusier's Algiers project (1931) and in the Soviet linear city projects of the 1920s; megastructures existed in built form in Karl Ehn's Karl-Marx-Hof in Vienna (1927) and Le Corbusier's Unité d'Habitation in Marseilles (1947–1953). Plug-In City combined elements of all of these precedents — the principle of collectivity, of interchangeable apartment units, and the incorporation of rapid transport links." For mutual influences between the Metabolist and the Archigram movement, see ibid., pp.17–18.

104 See LACHMAYER and CROMPTON, *A Guide to Archigram 1961–74.*

105 See WENDELKIN, "Putting Metabolism Back in Place. The Making of a Radically Decontextualized Architecture in Japan", p.283: "The house featured a large central space resting high above the site on piers and could be expanded by what he called 'movenets' plugged in beneath the floor to provide bathrooms, storage space, and removable children's rooms for an expanding and contracting family. Its use of clip-on modules foreshadowed later ideas about flexibility and growth in Metabolist projects."

106 Kurokawa already sketched a *Prefabricated Apartment House* in 1962. See KUROKAWA, *Metabolism in Architecture,* p.92. Ibid., pp.92–133, Kurokawa mentions also the *Discotheque Space Capsule* (1968), the *Toshiba Ihi Pavilion* (1970), the *Capsule House in the Theme Pavilion* (1970), the

Takara Beautillion Building (1970), the *Capsule Village* (1972), the *Koito Building* (1974), the *Big Box* (1974), the *Concrete Capsule House* (1975), the *Sony Tower* (1975), and the *Um Al-Kanhazeer Project* (1975). Donald Shepherd's "portakabins" for temporary accommodation were built into Cedric Price's multiple purpose community *Inter Action Centre* (1971) in London. For the larger context of megastructure-capsule-projects, see Justus DAHINDEN, *Stadtstrukturen für morgen. Analysen. Thesen. Modelle,* Stuttgart: Gerd Hatje, 1971.

107 See KUROKAWA, メタボリズムの発想, p.184 · Kisho (Noriaki) KUROKAWA, "Nakagin Capsule Tower Building", in: *The Japan Architect,* VOL.47, no.190, October 1972, pp.18–38 · KUROKAWA, *Intercultural Architecture,* pp.105–109.

108 KUROKAWA, メタボリズムの発想, p.105.

109 Ibid.

110 Ibid.

111 Kurokawa (*Metabolism in Architecture,* p.88) mentions Le Corbusier's *Modulor* for modules of proportion. For other modules, see KUROKAWA, メタボリズムの発想, p.28.

112 See ibid., p.105: "Utilities, interior fittings, television sets and the like were all assembled and installed at the factory and all capsules were then attached to a concrete shaft at the site. The 144 capsules were attached at the rate of five to eight a day and all work was finished in thirty days." See Jencks, "Introduction", in: KUROKAWA, *Metabolism in Architecture,* pp.17–19.

113 For Le Corbusier, norms and standards serve to remove "obstacles" in an industrial machine age. See LE CORBUSIER (Charles-Édouard Jeanneret-Gris), *The Modulor 1 & 2: A Harmonious Measure to the Human Scale Universally Applicable to Architecture and Mechanics,* Cambridge, MA: Harvard University Press, 1980, pp.111–112: "The reality of the industrial civilization calls for abundance, punctuality, efficiency. The work of man, the use of machines, and the benefits of organization will make the wheel turn (the production cycle), providing nourishment both spiritual and material. A civilization will come into being by virtue of its own sensitivity, its reason, the cleverness of its hands, and its tools, the machines. Standardization reduces the obstacles, sweeping them away before the majesty of the rule."

114 The literary topos of the *flâneur* is closely related to changing images of urban space. See Matthias KEIDEL, *Die Wiederkehr der Flaneure. Literarische Flanerie und flanierendes Denken zwischen Wahrnehmung und Reflexion,* Würzburg: Königshausen & Neumann, 2006, p.28: „Zu den Auslösern der literarischen Flanerien zählen also wie bei Baudelaire massive Veränderungen des Stadtbildes." — For similarities between Baudelaire's flâneur and Kurokawa's *homo movens,* see Marshall BERMAN, *All That Is Solid Melts Into Air. The Experience of Modernity,* New York: Penguin Books, 1982, pp.131–171 · BAUDELAIRE's *Le peintre de la vie moderne* (1863, quoted from Sven BIRKERTS, "Walter Benjamin. Flâneur: A Flanerie", in: *The Iowa Review,* VOL.13, 1982–1983, pp.164–179, here p.167): "To be away from home and yet to feel at home anywhere; to see the world, to be at the very center of the world, and yet to be unseen of the world, such are some of the minor pleasures of those independent, intense and impartial spirits, who do not lend themselves easily to linguistic definitions [...] Thus the lover of universal life moves into the crowd as though into an enormous reservoir of electricity. He, the lover of life, may also be compared to a mirror as vast as this crowd; to a kaleidoscope endowed with consciousness, which with every one of his movements presents a pattern of life [...] It is an ego at thirst for non-ego".

115 See J. Arthur Thomson and Patrick Geddes, *Life: Outlines of General Biology*, 2 vols., London: Williams & Norgate, 1931, vol. 2, pp. 1387–1392 · Lewis Mumford, *The Culture of Cities,* New York: Harcourt, Brace and Co., 1938, pp. 223–299 · Helen Elizabeth Meller, *Patrick Geddes: Social Evolutionist and City Planner,* London and New York: Routledge, 1993 · Volker M. Welter, *Biopolis: Patrick Geddes and the City of Life,* Cambridge, MA and London: The MIT Press, 2002. — Mumford's *The Culture of Cities. Its Origins, Its Transformations, and Its Prospects* (1938) has been translated into Japanese in 1955. In *The City in History,* first published in 1961, Mumford compares the metabolism of organisms with that of cities. For him, however, the equilibrium, that has to be maintained for living processes, limits growth and the patterns of inside-outside-relations. See Lewis Mumford, *The City in History. Its Origins, Its Transformations, and Its Prospects,* New York: Harcourt, Brace & World, [1961], p. 556: "Now, in every organism, the anabolic and catabolic processes, the creative and destructive, are constantly at work. Life and growth depend, not on the absence of negative conditions, but on a sufficient degree of equilibrium, and a sufficient surplus of constructive energy to permit continued repair, to absorb novelties, to regulate quantities, and to establish give-and-take relations with all the other organisms and communities needed to maintain balance. The negative factors in metropolitan existence might have provided the conditions for a higher development if the very terms of expansion had not given them the upper hand and tended to make their domination permanent, in ever more destructive processes." See also ibid., pp. 544–545.

116 See Thomson and Geddes, *Life: Outlines of General Biology,* vol. 2, pp. 1387–1392 · Mumford, *The Culture of Cities,* pp. 223–299 · Meller, *Patrick Geddes* · Welter, *Biopolis.* — However, for Tange and other metabolists, the metabolist movement was also a reaction against the post-war city-planning of Tokyo. See Kikutake in Kawazoe, *Metabolism. The Proposals for New Urbanism,* p. 13: "Tokyo, a huge city, is worn out with bad sickness. She has lost the proper control […], because of her mammoth like scale. On the contrary, she is even trying to conceal her illness and to justify the present situation by depending on the adaptability of [the] inhabitant." · Yatsuka and Hideki, メタボリズム, pp. 10–18 · Wendelkin, "Putting Metabolism Back in Place. The Making of a Radically Decontextualized Architecture in Japan", pp. 288–291.

117 See Kurokawa, ホモ・モベンス, pp. 46–50 · 見えがくれする都市|江戸から東京へ, edited by Fumihiko Maki, Yukitoshi Wakatsuki, Hidetoshi Ono, and Tokihiko Takatani, Tokyo: Kajimashuppankai, 1980.

118 The original Dutch title is: Johan Huizinga, *Homo ludens. Proeve eener bepaling van het spelelement der cultuur.* First English translation: *Homo Ludens: A Study of the Play-Element in Culture,* Boston: Beacon Press, 1955. Huizinga refers to the notion of "play" as a basic, order-creating property of animals and humans. See Huizinga, *Homo ludens,* p. 1: "Play is older than culture, for culture, however inadequately defined, always presupposes human society, and animals have not waited for man to teach them their playing."

119 As far as I know, Kurokawa does not mention van Lier.

120 Henri van Lier, *Les arts de l'espace. Peinture, sculpture, architecture, arts décoratifs,* Paris: Casterman, 1959, 5th edition 1971, p. 249: "L'harmonisation à la stature humaine varie donc en architecture, sans disparaître jamais. Ses variations procèdent même du souci de la réaliser mieux […] Peu importe le mètre, le pied-pouce ou tout autre étalon, l'essentiel est l'épreuve sentie; et le plus dogmatique des théoriciens souligne que son Modulor est un ruban tangible entre les mains et les bras de l'architecte, lequel invente dans le contact vivant de la mesure."

121 The relation between creation, function and architecture is one of the key elements of Kikutake's writings. See KIKUTAKE, 建築の心, pp. 59–65.

122 See VAN LIER, *Les arts de l'espace,* p. 252.

123 See BUSBEA, *Topologies,* pp. 18–26.

124 See VAN LIER, *Les arts de l'espace,* p. 284.

125 Ibid., p. 285: "Faisons la part du rêve d'anticipation, il reste de nouveau un principe revolutionnaire: celui d'une architecture qui ne s'édifie plus, mais qui croît, se transforme comme les cristaux ou les coraux, créant un espace plus varie, plus soupie que celui des voiles ou des tentes, plus synergique aussi, puisque ses parois, chimiquement conditionnées, s'autoréguleraient selon les variations extérieures."

126 Ibid., p. 286.

127 See Jacqueline E. KESTENBAUM, *Modernism and Tradition in Japanese Architectural Ideology, 1931–1955,* Ph.D. Thesis, Columbia University, New York, 1996 · Jörg H. GLEITER, "DisOrientiert: Japan, der Westen und der Ästhetizentrismus", in: *Thesis. Wissenschaftliche Zeitschrift der Bauhaus-Universität Weimar,* VOL. 44, 1998, no. 6, pp. 8–16 · Florian URBAN, "Talking Japanese", in: *Architecture and Identity,* edited by Peter HERRLE and Erik WEGERHOFF, Berlin: LIT, 2008, pp. 91–102 · For Kurokawa's Eastern turn, see KUROKAWA, *Each one a Hero,* pp. 22–23.

128 See KUROKAWA, *The Philosophy of Symbiosis,* p. 30 · KUROKAWA, *From Metabolism to Symbiosis,* p. 11: "In Western philosophy, which is the basis on which Modern architecture is built, humanity and technology, religion and technology, art and science are regarded as fundamentally opposed to each other. An extension of this dualism is the belief that the human being is composed of body and spirit, two opposing and mutually exclusive entities. This is the fundamental dualism of Western culture, from which its dialectic, philosophy and principle of majority rule were born [...] The philosophy of Metabolism, by contrast, sought to transcend the Western opposition between man and technology, and began from the assumption that man and machine could live in symbiosis."

129 See KUROKAWA, ホモ・モベンス, pp. 117–122. Kurokawa published a whole book on street architecture. See Kisho KUROKAWA, 道の建築: 中間領域へ, Tokyo: Maruzen, 1983. In *The Death and Life of Great American Cities* ([New York]: Random House, [1961]) Jane JACOBS also focussed on city-street-interfaces in Western cities. Kurokawa translated Jacobs' book into Japanese. See Jane JACOBS, アメリカ大都市の死と生. ジェン・ジェコブス著. 黒川紀章訳, translated by Kisho KUROKAWA, Tokyo: Benseishuppan, 2006.

130 *en* (縁) is here the first kanji of the compound *engawa* (縁側). It means in general *relation* or *connection.*

131 See KUROKAWA, *Each One a Hero,* p. 280 · KUROKAWA, *From Metabolism to Symbiosis,* p. 16: "The concept of symbiosis is also intimately linked with the very root of Buddhist thought. Buddhism is not so much a religion as a way of living, and this is why symbiosis was able to transcend the bounds of religion and become the basis of Japanese culture as a whole." — Kurokawa's main reference is the kyōsei-movement of Benkyo Shiio, who was also the principal of Kurokawa's Tokai High School in Nagoya. See KUROKAWA, *The Philosophy of Symbiosis,* pp. 37–38. — For Shiio's notion of kyōsei, see Egaku MAEDA, "Rev. Shiio Benkyo and His Thought of *Kyosei*", in: *Journal of Indian and Buddhist Studies,* VOL. 45, 1997, pp. 676–681.

132 1st–2nd century BC. Within this context, Kurokawa often refers to Hajime Nakamura's work on Indian Buddhism. Nakamura was a professor of the University of Tokyo during Kurokawa's studies at this university. See KUROKAWA, *Each one a Hero,* p. 23.

133 See KUROKAWA, ホモ・モベンス, pp. 110–112 and pp. 120–121 · KUROKAWA, *Metabolism in Architecture,* p. 32. — Besides the Ise shrine, Kurokawa also often mentions the Katsura Palace in Kyoto as a typical example of Japanese architecture. See KUROKAWA, *The Philosophy of Symbiosis,* p. 20 · KUROKAWA, *Each one a Hero,* p. 48.

134 For the Ise shrine and its role in the process of reshaping Japanese national identity, see Noboru KAWAZOE, "The Ise Shrine", in: *Japan Quarterly,* VOL. 3, 1962, pp. 285–292 · Kenzo TANGE and Noboru KAWAZOE, *Ise: Prototype of Japanese Architecture,* Cambridge, MA: The MIT Press, 1965 · Robert Treat PAINE and Alexander SOPER, *The Art and Architecture of Japan,* Harmondsworth: Penguin Books, 1955, 3rd edition 1981, p. 282 · Hajime YATSUKA, "Japan, the Object of Dual Aestheticization", in: *Thesis. Wissenschaftliche Zeitschrift der Bauhaus-Universität Weimar,* VOL. 44, 1998, no. 6, pp. 18–27 · Jonathan M. REYNOLDS, "Ise Shrine and a Modernist Construction of Japanese Tradition", in: *The Art Bulletin,* VOL. 83, 2001, pp. 316–341. — For the Nomad thesis, see Gari LEDYARD, "Galloping along with the Horseriders: Looking for the Founders of Japan", in: *Journal of Japanese Studies,* VOL. 1, 1975, pp. 217–254 · Walter EDWARDS, "Event and Process in the Founding of Japan: The Horserider Theory in Archeological Perspective", in: *Journal of Japanese Studies,* VOL. 9, 1983, pp. 265–295. — Kurokawa's nomad thesis is based on Namio EGAMI's essay "The Formation of the People and the Origin of the State in Japan", in: *Memoirs of the Research Department of the Toyo Bunko,* VOL. 23, 1964, pp. 35–70.

135 Frank Lloyd Wright worked in Japan from 1917–1922, and Bruno Taut from 1933–1936. After Taut's writings on Japanese architecture, Walter Gropius published in 1960 with Kenzo Tange and Yasushiro Ishimoto an influential book on *Tradition and Creation in Japanese Architecture,* based on the Katsura palace in Kyoto. For Kurokawa's critique of Taut's and Gropius' vision of Japanese architecture, see KUROKAWA, *Intercultural Architecture,* pp. 27–28.

136 Within this context, KUROKAWA (*From Metabolism to Symbiosis,* p. 13) refers to Lévi-Strauss' structuralism: "the structuralism of Levi-Strauss, who saw each culture as having its own distinct character that can at the same time be linked to every other culture in a single global structure. In this way, Levi-Strauss relativized 'superior' Western civilization. We live in a time when the gaps that separate Japan, for example, from Islamic civilization, from the rest of Asia, from Africa, or from Europe, are all felt as equal."

137 KUROKAWA, *From Metabolism to Symbiosis,* p. 19.

IMAGES

Kisho KUROKAWA, *Metabolism in Architecture,* London: Studio Vista, 1977, p. 58: FIG. 1 and p. 59: FIG. 3 · Kisho KUROKAWA, ホモ・モベンス, Tokyo: Chuokoron, 1969, p. 3: FIG. 2 · Kisho KUROKAWA, *From the Age of the Machine to the Age of Life,* London: BookArt, 1998, p. 28: FIG. 4 and p. 57:

FIG. 11 · *Arata Isozaki. Architecture 1960–1990,* edited by Kate Norment, New York: Rizzoli, 1991, p. 34: FIG. 5 · Simon Sadler, *Archigram. Architecture without Architecture,* Cambridge, MA and London: The MIT Press, 2005, p. 78: FIG. 6 (© VG Bild-Kunst, Bonn 2014) · Kisho Kurokawa, *From Metabolism to Symbiosis,* London: Academy Editions, 1992, p. 61: FIG. 7 and p. 60: FIG. 8 · Kisho (Noriaki) Kurokawa, "Nakagin Capsule Tower Building", in: *The Japan Architect,* VOL. 47, no. 190, October 1972, pp. 18–38, here p. 32: FIG. 9 and p. 37: FIG. 10.

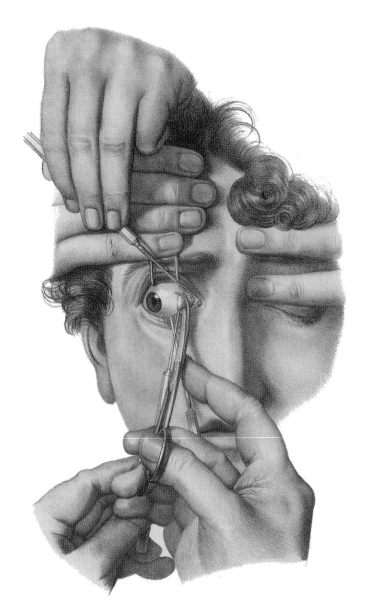

DRAWING BY
NICOLAS HENRI
JACOB /
FROM JEAN-
BAPTISTE MARC
BOURGERY /
*TRAITÉ COMPLET
DE L'ANATOMIE
DE L'HOMME /
ATLAS* / VOL. 7 /
1840

HELENI PORFYRIOU

Camillo Sitte: Optically Constructed Space and Artistic City Building

The description of city building according to artistic principles undertaken by Camillo Sitte in his famous book *Der Städte-Bau*[1] is formulated on the basis of the effect that urban space has on the observer. But an aesthetic analysis based on purely visual terms is not an exclusively Sittian choice. On the contrary, it is amply subscribed to by Romantic aesthetics and is typical of a series of artistic theories of the second half of the 19th century.[2] These theories — based on the principle of the artistic perception of the observer — can be ascribed to the broader context of early 19th-century epistemological discoveries placing vision in the context of the functioning of the human body (FIG. 1), thus giving rise to models of subjective vision in a great number of disciplines.

Daniel Wieczorek[3] and George R. Collins and Christiane Crasemann Collins[4] have already underlined the connections between the procedures of *Der Städte-Bau* and the artistic theories of the period; while more recent research has provided further insight.[5] However, the opening of Sitte's archive along with the publication of his writings on art history and theory allow us to improve our analysis of Sitte's approach and enhance our understanding of his work.[6]

The aim of this essay is, therefore, to take a step forward in an attempt to place Sitte's contribution within the founding movement, in modernity, of a science of art based on the functioning of the human body, thus resulting, hopefully, in a broader understanding of art and science in the 19th century, as part of a single interlocking field of knowledge and practice.[7] In fact, the labeling of Sitte as "romantic" by 20th-century historiography[8] stressed the separation between art and science, while missing the point that the principles of artistic city building introduced by Sitte were based on an optically constructed space, founded on the functioning of the body which he investigated in physical, psychological, and anatomical terms.

IN / KIRSTEN WAGNER AND JASPER CEPL (EDITORS) /
IMAGES OF THE BODY IN ARCHITECTURE: ANTHROPOLOGY AND BUILT SPACE /
TÜBINGEN · BERLIN / ERNST WASMUTH VERLAG / 2014 / PP. 166–188

The discovery that perception and, more broadly, knowledge are conditioned by the physical and anatomic functioning of the human body, of the eye to be precise, dates back to the 19th century.

In the 17th and 18th centuries observation is already "perceptive knowledge" but is rarely considered a form of knowledge exclusively based on vision. On the contrary, tactile and optical perception are not autonomous and make up an indivisible sensory knowledge, which is often inseparable from rational knowledge. In other words, "the senses are conceived more as adjuncts of a rational mind and less as physiological organs"[10].

In this sense the *camera obscura* — its monocular opening is the perfect embodiment of the philosophical concept of the "monad" and of a single point of

2
CAMERA
OBSCURA /
1646

view (**FIG.2**), not of the binocular body of the human subject — becomes the epistemological paradigm of a time that denies sensory evidence in favour of representations that this same apparatus can offer.[11]

Between 1810 and 1840, in the space of a few decades, dominant theories and practices concerning vision break with the classic regime. Starting from Johann Wolfgang von Goethe's *Theory of Colors* (1810), the studies of empirical sciences — on physiological optics, physical optics, and physiological psychology — prove that vision is subjective and based on rules and parameters that can be quantified and deduced from scientific research on the functioning of the eye (**FIG.3**). Consequently, perception is remodelled as dynamic, temporal and synthetic, 'freeing' the observer from the static condition assumed by the paradigm of the *camera obscura*.

For Goethe and the physiologists of the period "whatever the healthy corporal eye experienced was in fact optical truth"[12]. The new objectivity accorded to subjective phenomena by 19th-century epistemology has several implications: The observer becomes a privileged source of scientific knowledge of the world and at the same time an object of study. The physiological basis of vision allows the existence of optical techniques or practical procedures for the external modification of perception and consequently also of aesthetic perception — since it too is tied to the specificity of human corporeality.

Yet, starting from the mid-19th century, an immense quantity of studies carried out in scientific, philosophical, psychological, and artistic circles leads to the conclusion that vision, like any other sense, cannot continue to claim essential objectivity and certainty. From the 1860s on, the work of Hermann von Helmholtz, Gustav Fechner, and many others — founders of the theory of subjective vision — define, in parallel, the outlines of a general epistemological crisis in

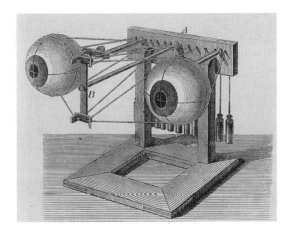

3
OPHTALMOTROP /
APPARATUS FOR
MEASURING EYE
MOVEMENT

which visual experience does not possess any of the guarantees that originally sustained its privileged relationship with the bases of knowledge in modernity.

Starting from the late 1870s, "attention" begins to be an issue, indicating the generalized crisis of the state of the perceptive subject. According to classic theory the observer is in general a passive receiver of stimuli that come from external objects, which form perceptions reflecting the external world. However, in the last decades of the 19th century, new conceptions of perception begin to take shape in which the subject (like a dynamic psycho-physical organism) actively builds the world around it through a stratified ensemble of sensory and cognitive processes referable to superior and inferior cerebral centres. This type of dynamic theories of cognition and perception implies the notion that subjectivity is a temporary assemblage of mobile and variable components. In this sense, various studies on attention have attempted (in a convincing though not complete fashion) to distinguish two forms of the "state of attention". The first is conscious and voluntary attention, task-oriented and often associated with superior and more developed behavior. The second is automatic or passive attention (which includes, according to scientific psychology, the area of customary activity, among others).

THE TRANSPOSITION OF THE NOTIONS OF SUBJECTIVE VISION IN SITTE'S AESTHETIC ANALYSIS

Sitte's interest in visual perception and representation issues dates back to his studies at the University of Vienna, where he studied art history and archeology with Rudolf von Eitelberger, whose insistence on close attention to the visual properties of works of art became a characteristic trait of the Vienna School, known later on for its attempt to put art history on a scientific basis. His relationship with Eitelberger remained close throughout the years. On his recommendation, in 1875, Sitte was offered the post of director of the State School of Applied Arts in Salzburg, for which he was very grateful to his former teacher, as he wrote in the articles published after Eitelberger's death in 1885.[13]

Sitte also studied anatomy and the physiology of vision with Ernst Wilhelm von Brücke,[14] one of the most versatile physiologists of his time and a friend of Helmholtz. Sitte's writings on Piero della Francesca's theory of perspective (1879), on the new methods of perspective construction (1879–1884), and on the practical value of the golden section (1880) clearly reveal where his interests lie.[15]

Trained as both a painter and an architect, Sitte was called to Vienna in 1883 to organize the new State School of Applied Arts, where not only did he create a flourishing didactic center, like the one in Salzburg, but he also turned his home into "a model of arts and crafts activities and intellectual and musical soirees — very similar to [...] William Morris' Red House"[16].

Furthermore Sitte was well acquainted with both Helmholtz's and Fechner's work, as is evident from his comments in the above-mentioned article on the golden section of 1880,[17] while the copy of Fechner's book *Vorschule der Ästhetik* found with Sitte's personal notes (now at the library of the University of Technology) further supports this fact.[18]

Given his background, it is not surprising that Sitte considers visual perception as a privileged source of knowledge regarding space and that he founds the empirical approach of his *Der Städte-Bau* on the physiological mechanism of vision.[19] The preface of his book already states, in fact, that "the author adhered to the principle of discussing only those [places] which he has seen himself, and what he has himself observed of aesthetic effect"[20]. "Only that which a spectator can hold in view, what can be seen is of artistic importance: for instance, the single street or the individual plaza."[21]

In his subsequent examination of numerous "lovely old plazas and whole urban layouts", eclectically selected among different European cities and period styles, Sitte is engaged in "seeking out the basis of their beauty"[22] that "attracts the eye of the observer", "creates pleasant impressions", "stimulates the interest" and "makes one happy" because "the innate, instinctive aesthetic sense that worked such obvious wonders for the old masters without resort to narrow aesthetic dogma or stuffy rules"[23] has been lost. These hidden principles must be re-discovered by a "critical and strictly scientific knowledge *(streng wissenschaftlich)*"[24]. For this purpose he introduces a form of contrast between urban spaces that produce pleasant or, on the contrary, unpleasant effects, investigating, like Fechner before him, the visual habits or patterns, memory patterns and space patterns that produce pleasant or unpleasant effects.

Sitte was in fact familiar with Fechner's work regarding aesthetics and with the experiments he conducted seeking to determine by actual measurements which shapes, dimensions, and proportions are naturally pleasing or unpleasing to our senses — or, in other words, what determines "the bad impression of monotony, uniformity, boredom, emptiness, bareness, and poverty"[25]. As their common vocabulary also indicates, Sitte's empirical investigation on pleasing or unpleasing urban forms and proportions closely reflects Fechner's approach, and may be considered as part of the scientific quest of his time to define innate or acquired categories relating to the psychophysical perception of space.[26] For Sitte, as for Helmholtz, perception embodied the internal construction of the external object. However, while Helmholtz maintained that these internal experiences, considered as "unconscious inferences", belonged to the individual's history,[27] for Sitte "this subconscious power"[28] belonged to innate or culturally acquired patterns.

Similarly, Sitte introduces another opposition between the characteristics of picturesque urban design and the practical system of planning. The former give rise to aesthetic perception and create spaces expressing artistic needs, while the latter regards spaces that meet material, everyday needs.

This distinction echoes the division suggested by Arthur Schopenhauer, who effected an anatomical separation of aesthetic perception from the part of the nervous system that is simply responsible for the body's subsistence. Schopenhauer is, in fact, the first to elaborate the notion of autonomous artistic perception,[29] basing it on physical structure and the functioning of the human body, and, furthermore, is the first to suggest that there are corporal techniques or practical procedures able to "increase the attention", that is, able to modify artistic perception externally. In this sense for Schopenhauer (and later for Henri Bergson) "the essential effect of attention is to render perception more intense"[30]. We can therefore suggest that it is the concept of "attention" that allows Sitte to introduce this distinction in his approach and to place artistic perception within the realm of the physiology of vision.

Passive attention or lack of attention takes place in those areas of the city characterized by habitual, practical activities (such as residential neighborhoods), where "the city may appear in its work clothes"[31], as Sitte says. On the other hand, conscious or voluntary attention, which, according to Schopenhauer, leads to "losing oneself in perception"[32], and gives rise to aesthetic perception, takes place in public areas, in few major plazas and thoroughfares which should, according to Sitte, "be a pride and joy to the inhabitants"[33]; places where, as Sitte points out, our forefathers concentrated all they could in terms of works of civic art. This is how it was in ancient times, comments Sitte, and could still be so today because "the artist only needs for his purpose a few main streets and piazzas and is willing to turn all the rest over to traffic and to everyday material needs"[34]. In this sense, Sitte's decision to deal exclusively with public spaces (piazzas) as the privileged site for the exercising of art can be more clearly understood.

But also when comparing cityscapes of the past with modern ones, Sitte is still preoccupied with the notion of "attention". In fact he compares and contrasts techniques of spatial configuration that respectively intensify or decrease the observer's attention, thus producing in the first case "artistic", "harmonious" or "pleasant effects" and in the latter "unpleasant", "monotonous", "dull"[35], or "commonplace effects". What Sitte criticizes in modern city layouts is that the observer's state of inattention is permanent. Urban spaces, be they public squares or residential neighborhoods, no longer "stimulate our interest"[36] or "enhance the susceptibility of the cerebral nervous system"[37], to put it in Schopenhauer's words. The result, Sitte comments, is a reduction of artistic sensibility "to such an extent that only the most powerful effects can still make any impression"[38].

According to Sitte, the responsibility for the total lack of artistic effects in modern cities lies with modern town planning, which is exclusively concerned with aspects of viability and hygiene. These aspects only require a two-dimensional understanding of the city that refers to a geometric and abstract space.

It is "the use of T-square and compass on the drafting board"[39] and the "mechanical" conception of urban projects "without any organic relation to their surroundings"[40], Sitte says, that prevent the creation today of unique spaces, like the ones of the past. He continues: "Industrial production is yet again the trademark of modernism; in this field, as in others, cheap repetition of a single standard model is the characteristic feature of our time"[41].

The artistic perception of urban space should therefore be based on three-dimensional effects.

In point of fact, Sitte's artistic principles are essentially aimed at increasing three-dimensional solidity.

As previously noted, the first and basic argument of Sitte's book is that urban space was and must be created optically. Old masters, he writes, were committed to "judging and arranging everything right on the spot for its actual effect"[42], and elsewhere he claims that "old planning was not conceived on the drafting board, but instead developed gradually *in natura,* allowing for all that the eye notices *in natura* and treating with indifference that which would be apparent only on paper"[43]. "In Baroque plans", he further notes, "everything was well thought out and judged as to its eventual appearance"[44]. The three-dimensional character of an optically constructed urban space was therefore of primary importance for Sitte and is tirelessly emphasized throughout his book. In fact "Sitte single-handedly gave city planning back to architects"[45], as George Collins and Christiane Crasemann Collins put it, and "made civic art a truly spatial art *(Raumkunst)*"[46]. Thus, while architecture and buildings represent solid elements, piazzas and streets are the principal urban elements, characterized as voids.

Enclosure and continuity are the indispensable qualities of these principal urban elements as Sitte demonstrates by investigating the pleasant or unpleasant effects of old and modern townscapes through the eyes of the observer. In this respect he writes that "formerly the empty spaces (streets and plazas) were a unified entity of spaces calculated for their impact"[47]. "Ancient arcades [...] run uninterruptedly along the whole curve of a street as far as the eye can see, or they encircle a plaza enclosing it completely; [...] Their whole effect is based on continuity"[48].

But if three-dimensionality, continuity, and enclosure are the properties/qualities of physiologically perceived space, picturesque composition, according to Sitte, is the ultimate principle that comprises all, amalgamating diversities in an overall architectural effect.

It is the relationship of the parts with each other and with the whole. The relationships of dimension, scale, and proportion between the piazzas and the buildings surrounding them, and between the spaces themselves and the whole make up the overall effect. This effect derives, in other words, from unity within diversity, combining opposing impressions, contrasting a building to its environment, where irregularities "produce a harmonious effect because each motif is modelled in great clarity and each superstructure is given its counterpart, a balance being assured within the overall composition"[49]. In the "art of space", says Sitte, "the comparative relationships alone are important"[50].

"Everything is based on the reciprocity of effects. Each factor works on the other and determines its value"[51], as Hildebrand wrote shortly afterwards, conceptualizing Sitte's description. And yet the evaluation of both was apparently rooted in the redefinition of visual perception as temporal and dynamic effected in the first half of the 19th century. As proved by scientific experiments, perception is not virtually instantaneous, but comprises in an image a temporal unfolding of opposing, successive, or simultaneous impressions confined to the same external cause. "The eye", as Goethe wrote in 1810, "cannot for a moment remain in a particular state determined by the object it looks upon. On the contrary, it is forced to a sort of opposition, which, in contrasting extreme with extreme, intermediate degree with intermediate degree, at the same time combines these opposite impressions, and thus ever tends to be whole"[52].

In this sense, a picturesque urban compositional arrangement, considered as an external cause, forces the eye to contrast and combine a great number of opposing impressions, implying that the greater the stimulus, the greater the attention and the higher the result of aesthetic perception.[53]

In fact, scientific discoveries regarding the physiological mechanisms of binocular vision (that is, the manner of perceiving solid objects or space) had already demonstrated, since 1830, that pronounced spatial effects depended on closed views and on significant variations of the angle of convergence of the optical axes. Since 1850, the creation of popular new optical devices, like the stereoscope, greatly contributed to the spread of these scientific discoveries (FIG. 4).

4
HOLMES
STEREOSCOPE /
1870S

Nineteenth century knowledge about the perception of space evolved together with the stereoscope.[54] Whether Sitte owned a stereoscope (not improbable) or not, his artistic principles are the counterpart, in the art of urban space, of these scientific discoveries. In fact, both the 'realism' of the stereoscope and Sitte's *Der*

　　　　　　　　　　　　　　　　　　　　　　　　　HELENI PORFYRIOU

Städte-Bau are tied to the 19-century massive reorganization of knowledge that allowed for the emergence of an optically constructed space.[55]

Using two flat images, the stereoscope could represent three-dimensional effects similar to those of the real, tangible world. In stereoscopic images the 'vividness', three-dimensionality, or tangibility of the perceived scene depended on two factors: a) on closed views and b) on the presence of objects (or obtrusive forms) in the near or middle ground, which by necessitating significant changes in the angle of convergence of the optical axes, increased the impression of three-dimensional solidity. "Our eyes", writes Crary, "follow a choppy and erratic path into the depth of the stereoscopic image"[56]. The space created by the stereoscope is "an assemblage of local zones of three-dimensionality"[57], not a homogeneous and metric space as that implied by the perspectival model of vision associated with the Renaissance.[58]

It is astonishing how much these findings echo Sitte's own artistic principles. In fact, George Collins and Christiane Crasemann Collins point out that "for Sitte the ultimate in beauty was apparently a panorama of somewhat kaleidoscopic pieces in a closed but asymmetrical pictorial arrangement [...] essentially a late-Impressionist mode of vision"[59]; or as Sitte put it:

> *The striking picturesqueness of Amalfi, for example, is due mainly to its really grotesque confusion between interior and exterior motifs, so that one finds oneself at the same time inside a house and on the street, and at one spot simultaneously on the ground level and on an upper floor, depending on the interpretation one wishes to give the peculiar structural combinations. It is this which leaves the* collector of vistas in a transport of delight [...].[60]

Collins' intuition seems to find confirmation in Crary's words, who suggests that both the 'realism' of the stereoscope and the 'experiments' of certain impressionist painters were equally tied to a much broader transformation of the observer resulting in the emergence of this new optically constructed space.[61] Similarly, Sitte's predilection for the picturesque compositional arrangement and his determination to fracture the city into a series of spatial tableaux *(Stadtbild)* are indebted to and embedded in these 19th-century epistemological discoveries leading to the emergence of an optically constructed space. Such an understanding allows us to place Sitte and his art of space (as he defines it) in modernity, throwing new light on the reasons that led Albert Brinckmann to criticize him strongly and leading more contemporary architects and planners to periodical reappraisals of his work.[62]

If the discovery, therefore, of physiological space and of an optically constructed space is the direct consequence of 19th-century scientific studies on subjective vision, the discovery of urban space is the outcome of Sitte's *Der Städte-Bau.*

Notwithstanding his familiarity with physiological perception and experimental psychology, in his book Sitte refers explicitly only on one occasion to "the physiological mechanism that gives rise to the perception of space on which all architectural effects are based" in order to recall as he says "the act of seeing"[63]. There are only a very few other occasions in which we can grasp his cognitive references. One of the most significant regards the quantitative relationships between acoustic and visual stimuli and perceptions, when Sitte refers to the acoustic studies of the physiologist Helmholtz, though once again without quoting either the author or his source.[64]

The lack of a clear explanation on Sitte's part about the scientific knowledge on which his theory is based leads us to suppose that these notions were widespread and fashionable in the period in question. The artistic theories based on visual perception, formulated in those years by Conrad Fiedler, Adolf von

5
THE EFFECT ON
PERCEPTION
OF A VIEWER'S
DISTANCE
FROM THE
OBJECT — IN
THIS CASE, THE
PORTICO OF
S.ANDREA AT
MANTUA —
ACCORDING TO
THE THEORY
EXPOUNDED
BY HERMANN
MAERTENS

Hildebrand, Heinrich Wölfflin, and Alois Riegl, seem to indicate that. More specifically Hermann Maertens' formulations demonstrate that these scientific investigations on the physiology of vision were broadly acknowledged, since they were already being applied in the town planning field.

In a series of works published between 1877 and 1890, Maertens — architect and mathematician — introduced a scientific method for the assessment of spatial aesthetics.[65] On the basis of Helmholtz's theory of physiological optics,

Maertens calculated the limits of the ocular field of vision and the proportional relationship between buildings and their surrounding space, formulating aesthetic rules and tables applicable to the plastic arts and above all to architecture and town planning.[66] His results regarding questions of scale and artistic urban layout were widely used and considered as "aesthetic rules" by the foremost figures in the town planning field. For example by Joseph Stübben (1893, 1890) Charles Buls (1906) and Albert Brinckmann (1908, 1920), who unhesitatingly referred to Maertens as an authority.[67]

As Brian Ladd has pointed out, the consensus obtained by Maertens' formulae even within local administrative bodies was due to the fact that his aesthetic rules not only reflected the taste of the period for monumental planning (isolating big cathedrals and providing them with perspective vistas) but were also in line with some of the building regulations governing public hygiene.[68]

The typical aesthetic decision formulated on the basis of Maertens' "laws" assumes an observer standing at a fixed point and looking at a single monument

(FIG. 5). The static nature of Maertens' observer and the universal application of his formulae regardless of the individual character of each place led Sitte to consider his work useless; he does not even mention him. "All our so-called aesthetic town planning ordinances illustrate this weak, meager, and unfortunate taste"[69], he affirms. After all, Sitte's predilection for the picturesque compositional arrangement presupposes a dynamic experience of space, which is in contrast with the static nature of Maertens' observer.

Sitte's preoccupation with the city as the terrain of phenomenological aesthetics could not but have sociological implications, as is made evident already by his initial choice to analyze only public spaces, piazzas, and streets. A choice not only due to the fact, as he says that, "only that which a spectator can hold in view, what can be seen, is of artistic importance"[70] — and not elements such as a street network, that "can never be comprehended sensorially, can never be grasped as a whole except in a plan of it"[71] — but also to the fact that these places had "a vital and functional use […] for [the] community life"[72] of the past and "were of primary importance to the life of every city"[73]. In the past, public spaces represented places charged with meaning, places that reflected "the pleasure that the inhabitants take in their city"; from which stemmed "their attachment to it, their pride in it, in short, their feeling of belonging"[74]. He continues by claiming that "major plazas and thoroughfares should wear their 'Sunday best' in order to be a pride and joy to the inhabitants, to awake civic spirit and forever to nurture great and noble sentiment within our growing youth"[75].

An approach such as that employed by Sitte, which defines the cities of the past as the expression of the collective spirit and recognizes the social value of art, acknowledging the educational function of artistic city building as "this type of artistic endeavor, above all (others), that affects formatively everyday and every hour the great mass of the population"[76], implies that spatial organization is indissolubly linked to social organization.

The meanings Sitte attributes to places are not simply sociological or aesthetic — they are also psychological. He writes in this respect, "An undeviating boulevard, miles long, seems boring […] it is unnatural […] and it remains uninteresting in effect, so that, mentally fatigued, one can hardly await its termination"[77]. The uniformity and repetitive nature of spaces in modern cities make one lose "all sense of orientation"[78]. The enclosure and harmonious proportions of certain piazzas invite a pause, while others induce discomfort and anxiety.[79] These are only a few examples showing that for Sitte the question of urban morphology considered in aesthetic terms is also charged with meanings based on the existential experience of the city.

In this context the example of agoraphobia,[80] which Sitte presents as a "nervous disorder" experienced by "numerous people […] whenever they have to walk across a vast empty place"[81], underlines once more not only the synchronism of the research of the period, but also the spirit with which Sitte describes and perceives space as both physiological-aesthetic and psychological-existential.

The inseparability of psychology and biology is a dominant feature common to many 19th-century philosophers interested in vision, from Schopenhauer to

Fechner. Seeing with the eyes and through the eyes, that is with the physical eye and the psychological eye, becomes in those years a single scientific notion. Once more, we see that Sitte's approach shares the same background and preoccupations regarding subjective vision that dominated 19th-century culture and science.

Similarly we can appreciate to what extent art and science were part of a single interlocking field of knowledge and practice and how misinterpreting his picturesque approach as "romantic" stressed the separation between art and science, thus making us miss the point: that Sitte's contribution to a science of art was based on the physiological body, both as a physical and psychological entity.

HUMAN ANATOMY AND BODILY PERCEPTION

Sitte's understanding of urban space as a living place replete with existential connotations implies and requires not only a visual perception but also a corporeal experience.

> *Enchanting* recollections *of travel form part of our most* pleasant reveries. *Magnificent town views, monuments and public squares, beautiful vistas all parade before our* musing eye, *and we* savour *again the delights of those sublime and graceful things in whose* presence *we were once so* happy.
> *To* linger*! If we could but linger again in those* places whose beauties *never wane; surely we would then be able to endure many difficult hours with a* lighter heart, *and carry on, thus* strengthened, in the eternal struggle of this existence. […] *Anyone who has* enjoyed the charms *of an ancient city would hardly disagree with the idea of the strong influence of* physical setting on the human soul. *Perhaps most effective in this sense are the ruins of Pompeii. Here in the* evening, *starting homeward after a long day's work, one is* powerfully drawn *to ascend the flights of steps of the Temple of Jupiter in order* to view *from its podium over and over again the noble spectacle that is spread* before his eyes, *and out of which surge* rich harmonies like the most beautiful music — *pure and sonorous. In such a situation we do indeed comprehend the words of Aristotle, who summarizes all* rules of city planning *in observing that a city must be so designed as to* make its people *at once* secure and happy.[82]

This short paragraph, an extract from his introduction, encapsulates all Sitte's tools and aims.

This emotion-filled description conceives perception as comprising not only optical stimuli, but also acoustic, atmospheric, tactile, physic and psychic stimuli, as well as recollections, memory-based images, etc.

The polyphony of the senses comprised in Sitte's perception finds its counterpart in the multiform research he undertook in his quest for principles. His investigation in different fields of artistic creation, ranging from painting, sculpture, and the decorative arts, to architecture, stage sets, city planning, and music, is best expressed in his vast eight-volume historical project, yet to be published at the time of his death, based on his research on Darwinism, art history, and cultural history.[83]

Moreover, the 19th-century discovery that perception and, more broadly, knowledge are conditioned by the physical and anatomic functioning of the human body, in other words the physiological basis of his scientific investigation, leads Sitte to pay attention not only to perception (or visual perception) but also to the relationship between the anatomic functioning of the human body and its artistic expressions.

As we have already mentioned, Sitte studied anatomy in Vienna in the winter semesters of 1871–72 and of 1872–73 with Ernst von Brücke, founder of the Institute of Physiology, whose pupils included, among others, Sigmund Freud. Throughout his life Brücke dealt with questions regarding the theory of art, which formed an integral part of his work on physiology. Sitte also probably attended the lectures of anatomy of Joseph Hyrtl[84] who, following the method of anatomic reconstruction, assembled the skeletons of the Laocoön group in

6
JOSEPH HYRTL /
"LAOCOÖN
GROUP" /
1850–60 /
ANATOMISCHES
MUSEUM
VIENNA

the 1850s (**FIG. 6**), demonstrating in a visually impressive way the thesis that the functional mechanics of the body are directly related to the artistic expression of postures. In 1889 the anatomic museum of the University of Vienna opened,

180   HELENI PORFYRIOU

showing as its main attraction, among skulls of various nationalities, the bone preparation of the famous Laocoön group by Hyrtl. That same year, and only four days after the opening of the anatomic museum, which was followed attentively by Viennese scholars, Sitte in his role as director of the State School of Applied Arts of Vienna gave an inspiring lecture at the Association of Engineers and Architects on "Town-schemes with respect to squares and monument-settings in Vienna". The lecture, which concerned the Ringstraße area, was much acclaimed by the numerous experts present. On the same occasion Sitte also announced the publication of his book, which came out four months later.

In 1893 Sitte wrote a review "The Beauty of the Arm", of a book by his old master of anatomy, Brücke.[85] Discussing the anatomic and artistic position of the arms in the Laocoön group and in other sculptures, Sitte comments: "In all these cases nature was faithfully reproduced with all its zigzagging and no geometrical corrections were carried out."[86]

The hidden principles underpinning the "beauty of the arm" or the "beauty of the body", the "beauty of the Laocoön group" or the "beauty of old urban layouts" are to be found, according to Sitte, in following nature. In fact "to go to school with Nature and the old masters also in matters of town planning" is the fundamental idea expressed in his *Der Städte-Bau* too, as he himself notes in the preface of the 3rd edition in 1900.

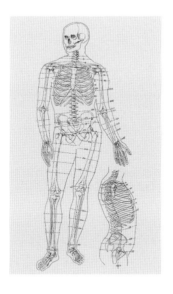

Sitte's fascination with the body and its structure is further evident in the autograph collection of 41 drawings of a topographic anatomy of the human body (**FIG. 7**). Dated 1900–02, and probably prepared for publication, since there is a layout and subtitles, these drawings reveal a medical rather than an artistic interest. Though seemingly intended for use as references in the courses on free design held by Sitte, the unusual relationship they introduce between bones, skeleton, and skin cannot pass unnoticed, as has been highlighted by Robert Stalla.[87]

This last consideration, evoking Juhani Pallasmaa's *The Eyes of the Skin*[88], reconnects the human body to the corporeal perception of space (as Merleau-Ponty put it, "it is depth that gives flesh to things") and reveals a somehow neglected element in the understanding of Sitte: that is, the importance arts and crafts tradition and practice had in his life. Sitte, who theorized the human scale as measure of the city, not only conceived corporeality as a mode of perception but also as a depository of human wisdom, where "any natural sensitivity", "traditional artistic creativity", or "artistic instincts", like those of "children's placing of their monuments [or] of building snowmen"[59] is rooted.

NOTES

1   Camillo SITTE, *Der Städte-Bau nach seinen künstlerischen Grundsätzen,* Vienna: Carl Graeser, 1889. English edition: "City Planning According to Artistic Principles", translated by George R. Collins and Christiane Crasemann Collins, in: COLLINS and CRASEMANN COLLINS, *Camillo Sitte: The Birth of Modern City Planning,* New York: Rizzoli, 1986, pp. 130–302. All references make use of this edition. — In the first edition (New York: Random House, 1965), Sitte's text and in the commentary were published in two separate volumes.

2   By Conrad Fiedler, Alois Riegl, or Theodor Lipps · See Otto PÄCHT, "Art Historians and Art Critics – VI: Alois Riegl", in: *The Burlington Magazine,* VOL. 105, 1963, pp. 188–193 · Michael PODRO, *The Manifold of Perception: Theories of Art from Kant to Hildebrand,* Oxford: Clarendon, 1972 · *Empathy, Form, and Space. Problems in German Aesthetics, 1873–1893,* edited by Harry Francis MALLGRAVE and Eleftherios IKONOMOU, Santa Monica: Getty Publications Program, 1994.

3   Daniel WIECZOREK, *Camillo Sitte et les débuts de l'urbanisme moderne,* Brussels and Liège: Pierre Mardaga, [1981]. Italian translation: *Camillo Sitte e gli inizi dell'urbanistica moderna,* translated by Laura Majocchi, Milan: Jaca Book, 1994. All references make use of the Italian edition.

4   COLLINS and CRASEMANN COLLINS, *Camillo Sitte: The Birth of Modern City Planning.*

5   See *Formationen der Stadt. Camillo Sitte weitergelesen,* edited by Karin WILHELM and Detlef JESSEN-KLINGENBERG, Basel, Boston, and Berlin: Birkhäuser – Verlag für Architektur | Gütersloh and Berlin: Bauverlag, 2006 · Heleni PORFYRIOU, "Camillo Sitte und das Primat des Blicks", in: *Kunst des Städtebaus. Neue Perspektiven auf Camillo Sitte,* edited by Klaus SEMSROTH, Kari JORMAKKA, and Bernhard LANGER, Vienna, Cologne, and Weimar: Böhlau, 2005, pp. 239–256 · Gabriele REITERER, *AugenSinn. Zu Raum und Wahrnehmung in Camillo Sittes* Städtebau, Salzburg and Munich: Anton Pustet, 2003 · Michael MÖNNINGER, *Vom Ornament zum Nationalkunstwerk. Zur Kunst- und Architekturtheorie Camillo Sittes,* Braunschweig and Wiesbaden: Friedr. Vieweg & Sohn, 1998.

6   See Camillo SITTE, *Gesamtausgabe,* edited by Klaus SEMSROTH, Michael MÖNNINGER, and Christiane Crasemann Collins, VOLS. 1, 4, and 5, Vienna, Cologne, and Weimar: Böhlau, 2008 (VOLS. 1 and 4) and 2010 (VOL. 5).

7   An approach brilliantly discussed in Jonathan CRARY, *Techniques of the Observer. On Vision and Modernity in the Nineteenth Century,* Cambridge, MA and London: The MIT Press, 1990, pp. 1–24. Jonathan CRARY, "Unbinding Vision", in: *October,* VOL. 68, 1994, pp. 21–44.

8   Among the most recent essays on the subject: Wolfgang SONNE, "Political Connotations of the Picturesque", in: *Sitte, Hegemann and the Metropolis. Modern Civic Art and International Exchanges,* edited by Charles C. BOHL and Jean-François LEJEUNE, New York: Routledge, 2009, pp. 123–140. More dated but relevant for the stylistic declinations of Sitte's work are Heleni POR-FYRIOU's essays on: "Artistic Urban Design and Cultural Myths: The Garden City Idea in Nordic Countries, 1900–1925", in: *Planning Perspectives,* VOL. 7, 1992, pp. 263–302 · "L'impatto di Sitte nei paesi nordici", in: *Camillo Sitte e i suoi interpreti,* edited by Guido ZUCCONI, Milan: Franco Angeli, 1992, pp. 175–183 · "Sulla declinazione classicista di Camillo Sitte nella storia urbanistica dei paesi nordici", in: *Storia Urbana,* no. 62, 1993, pp. 79–104.

9   This section is basically a synthesis of the stimulating arguments of Crary (particularly *Techniques of the Observer,* chapter 2–3) relevant for our reasoning.

10   CRARY, *Techniques of the Observer,* p. 60.

11   On the "camera obscura" see also Svetlana ALPERS, *The Art of Describing: Dutch Art in the Seventeenth Century,* Chicago: University of Chicago Press, 1983. Although the work of Crary critically supersedes Alpers' approach, her description of an "empirical mode of seeing" remains equally suggestive.

12   CRARY, *Techniques of the Observer,* p. 98.

13   COLLINS and CRASEMANN COLLINS, *Camillo Sitte: The Birth of Modern City Planning,* pp. 336–337. Eitelberger, through his publications, had a major impact in the development of medieval art history in Austria and was co-founder in 1864 of the Imperial Austrian Museum for Art and Industry. His writings on the Ringstraße may have influenced Sitte. For more information see Robert STALLA (with the collaboration of Andreas ZEESE), "'Künstler und Gelehrter' — Der Universalist Camillo Sitte. Ein Eitelberger-Schüler im Umfeld der 'Wiener Schule für Kunstgeschichte'", in: Camillo SITTE, *Gesamtausgabe,* VOL. 5: *Schriften zu Kunsttheorie und Kunstgeschichte,* pp. 9–86, here pp. 13–20 and pp. 76–84, and ibid.: Camillo SITTE, "Rudolf v. Eitelberger (1885)", pp. 314–321 and SITTE, "Rede am Grabe Eitelberger's (1885)", pp. 321–322.

14   Ibid., pp. 23–27.

15   These writings of Sitte can be found ibid. See pp. 143–150, pp. 429–434, and pp. 435–446 respectively.

16   COLLINS and CRASEMANN COLLINS, *Camillo Sitte: The Birth of Modern City Planning,* p. 26.

17   Camillo SITTE, "Über den praktischen Wert der Lehre vom goldenen Schnitt", in: Camillo SITTE, *Gesamtausgabe,* VOL. 5: *Schriften zu Kunsttheorie und Kunstgeschichte,* pp. 435–446.

18   See Karin WILHELM, "Ordnungsmuster der Stadt. Camillo Sitte und der moderne Städtebaudiskurs", in: *Formationen der Stadt,* ed. WILHELM and JESSEN-KLINGENBERG, pp. 15–95, here pp. 40–42.

19   All studies on *Der Städte-Bau* agree on this point independently of the depth of their analysis.

20 SITTE, "City Planning According to Artistic Principles", p.139. Following the fashion of the Grand Tour, Sitte, like Goethe and Schinkel, undertook many trips to Italy and Greece.

21 Ibid., pp.229–230.

22 Ibid., p.138.

23 Ibid., p.158.

24 Camillo SITTE, "Gottfried Semper", obituary, in: *Salzburger Gewerbeblatt*, VOL.3, 1879, pp.22–24, here p.23. See also WIECZOREK, *Camillo Sitte et les débuts de l'urbanisme moderne*, p.154.

25 Gustav Theodor FECHNER, *Vorschule der Ästhetik*, 2 parts in 1 volume, Leipzig: Breitkopf & Härtel, 1876, part 1, p.53: „den missfälligen Eindruck der *Monotonie, Einförmigkeit, Langweiligkeit, Leere, Kahlheit, Armuth*".

26 See SITTE, "City Planning According to Artistic Principles", p.158 (emphasis added): "Thus we are presented with a mystery — the mystery of the *innate, instinctive* aesthetic sense that worked such obvious wonders for the old masters without resort to narrow aesthetic dogma or stuffy rules."

27 Helmholtz recognized for example that the perception also of illusions arose chiefly from the individual's history (not from stimuli).

28 See SITTE, "City Planning According to Artistic Principles", p.159 (emphasis added): "[…] to peer into the workings of this *subconscious power* of creation in order to find out what the basis of its success might be and to put this into words. […] to understand the situation intellectually, for it is only too obvious […]".

29 Ernst Mach, in 1885, credited Goethe and Schopenhauer for having founded a modern physiology of senses. For Mach, space is the outcome of our perception, "a function of our brain" as Schopenhauer had said. On Schopenhauer in this context, see CRARY, *Techniques of the Observer*, pp.75–85; on Mach see WIECZOREK, *Camillo Sitte et les débuts de l'urbanisme moderne*, pp.174–175.

30 CRARY, *Techniques of the Observer*, p.85 note 46. See also Jonathan CRARY, "Spectacle, Attention, Counter-Memory", in: *October*, VOL.50, 1989, pp.97–107.

31 SITTE, "City Planning According to Artistic Principles", p.230.

32 Arthur SCHOPENHAUER, quoted in: CRARY, *Techniques of the Observer*, p.84.

33 SITTE, "City Planning According to Artistic Principles", p.230.

34 Ibid.

35 It is interesting to notice that Sitte and Fechner use the same terms (pleasant, monotonous, dull, etc.) as mentioned before.

36 SITTE, "City Planning According to Artistic Principles", p.186.

37 Arthur SCHOPENHAUER, *The World As Will and Representation*, New York: Dover, 1958, VOL.2, p.368.

38 SITTE, "City Planning According to Artistic Principles", p.244.

39 Ibid., p.209.

40 Ibid., p.213.

41 Ibid., p.214.

42 Ibid., p.213.

43 Ibid., pp.187–188.

44 Ibid., p.219.

45 COLLINS and CRASEMANN COLLINS, *Camillo Sitte: The Birth of Modern City Planning*, p. 66.

46 Ibid., p. 67.

47 SITTE, "City Planning According to Artistic Principles", p. 225.

48 Ibid., p. 224.

49 Ibid., p. 188.

50 Ibid., p. 180.

51 WIECZOREK, *Camillo Sitte et les débuts de l'urbanisme moderne*, p. 169.

52 Johann Wolfgang VON GOETHE, *Theory of Colours*, Cambridge, MA and London: The MIT Press, 1970, p. 13, in: CRARY, *Techniques of the Observer*, p. 99.

53 See SITTE, "City Planning According to Artistic Principles", p. 186: "It is generally realized from personal experience that these irregularities do not have an unpleasant effect at all, but on the contrary, they enhance naturalness, they stimulate our interest, and, above all, they augment the picturesque quality of the tableau."

54 On the stereoscope and the physiological mechanisms of binocular vision see CRARY, *Techniques of the Observer*, pp. 117–130.

55 Helmholtz's detailed investigation of vision permitted him to refute Immanuel Kant's earlier theory of space (considering it as a mental attribute) by showing exactly how the sense of vision created the perception of space. Space, according to Helmholtz, was an acquired, not an innate concept.

56 CRARY, *Techniques of the Observer*, p. 126.

57 Ibid.

58 In this context Sitte's writings on Piero della Francesca's theory of perspective (1879), on the new methods of perspective construction (1884), and particularly the one on the golden section (1880) should be better evaluated in relation to his comments about space perception and proportion. See SITTE, "City Planning According to Artistic Principles", pp. 179–180, 186–190.

59 COLLINS and CRASEMANN COLLINS, *Camillo Sitte: The Birth of Modern City Planning*, p. 375 note 163.

60 SITTE, "City Planning According to Artistic Principles", pp. 246–247 (emphasis added).

61 CRARY, *Techniques of the Observer*, p. 126.

62 COLLINS and CRASEMANN COLLINS, *Camillo Sitte: The Birth of Modern City Planning*, pp. 125–127 · WIECZOREK, *Camillo Sitte et les débuts de l'urbanisme moderne*, p. 182 · Heleni PORFYRIOU, "Space as place, lo spazio come luogo nell'urbanistica moderna" in: *Progettare nella città esistente per la società esistente. Atti del Convegno Internazionale di Urbanistica*, edited by Patrizia GABELLINI, [s.l.]: Danibel, 1993, pp. 156–169. For a recent critical evaluation of Sitte's work and interpreters see *Sitte, Hegemann and the Metropolis. Modern Civic Art and International Exchanges*, ed. BOHL and LEJEUNE.

63 SITTE, "City Planning According to Artistic Principles", p. 271.

64 Ibid., p. 179: "In general, it is wrong to assume that the size effect of a public square as we perceive it increases in proportion to the actual size of the square. In other areas of human perception where analogous phenomena have already been carefully studied [his reference is to Helmholtz's work] it has become apparent in every case that when a stimulus is steadily increased, perception cannot keep pace with it, but finally levels off." — The scientific coherence of Sitte's *Der Städte-*

Bau based on the physiological mechanisms of vision is discussed in an acute way in WIECZOREK, *Camillo Sitte et les débuts de l'urbanisme moderne,* pp. 152–162.

65 Among Hermann MAERTENS most important writings see: *Der Optische-Maassstab oder die Theorie und Praxis des ästhetischen Sehens in den bildenden Künsten. Auf Grund der Lehre der physiologischen Optik für Architekten, Maler Bildhauer etc.,* Bonn: Max Cohen & Sohn (Fr. Cohen), 1877 · *Skizze zu einer praktischen Aesthetik der Baukunst und der ihr dienenden Schwesterkünste in einem neuen Systeme zusammengestellt,* Berlin: Ernst Wasmuth, 1885 · *Optisches Maaß für den Städtebau,* Bonn: Max Cohen & Sohn (Fr. Cohen), 1890.

66 Brian K. LADD, "Urban Aesthetics and the Discovery of the Urban Fabric in Turn-of-the-Century Germany", in: *Planning Perspectives,* VOL. 2, 1987, pp. 270–86. See also Brian LADD, *Urban Planning and Civic Order in Germany, 1860–1914,* Cambridge, MA and London: Harvard University Press, 1990.

67 See COLLINS and CRASEMANN COLLINS, *Camillo Sitte: The Birth of Modern City Planning,* p. 350 note 50.

68 LADD, "Urban Aesthetics", p. 275.

69 SITTE, "City Planning According to Artistic Principles", p. 190.

70 Ibid., p. 229.

71 Ibid.

72 Ibid., p. 154.

73 Ibid., p. 143.

74 Ibid., p. 270.

75 Ibid., p. 230. — It is important not to undervalue Sitte's empirical method of analysis and confuse it with his idealism, evident in these quotations. See for example Gerhard FEHL, "Camillo Sitte als 'Volkserzieher' — Anmerkungen zum deterministischen Denken in der Stadtbaukunst des 19. Jahrhunderts", in: *Städtebau um die Jahrhundertwende. Materialien zur Entstehung der Disziplin Städtebau,* edited by Gerhard FEHL and Juan RODRÍGUEZ-LORES with the collaboration of Ilse BAUMGARTEN, Cologne, Stuttgart, Berlin, Hannover, Kiel, Mainz, and Munich: Deutscher Gemeindeverlag | W. Kohlhammer, 1980, pp. 172–221. — For a critical reading see SONNE, "Political Connotations of the Picturesque". For many decades the artistic theories and elaborations of many "romantic" scholars from Schopenhauer to Riegl have been marginalized and considered as systems of a transcendental mode of perception. Recent studies, on the contrary, have reopened the debate re-evaluating similar contributions, thus establishing a new cultural history and art history. Apart from Crary, see Michael PODRO, *The Critical Historians of Art,* New Haven and London: Yale University Press 1982 · Margaret IVERSEN, *Alois Riegl: Art History and Theory,* Cambridge, MA and London: The MIT Press, 1993.

76 Ibid., pp. 249–250. — Sitte had a strong interest in pedagogical issues as well. Evidence is given in the three hundred boxes of notes, found at his death, for a *magnum opus* intended for publication in eight volumes. Volume eight was supposed to collect his pedagogical writings. See COLLINS and CRASEMANN COLLINS, *Camillo Sitte: The Birth of Modern City Planning,* pp. 30–31. It is not of secondary importance to recall, in this context, that the work of Johann Friedrich Herbart — who undertook one of the earliest attempts to quantify the movement of cognitive experience and was thus considered "a spiritual father of stimulus-response psychology" — was directly tied to his pedagogical theories, which were influential in Germany during the mid 19th century. See CRARY, *Techniques of the Observer,* pp. 100–102.

77 Ibid., p. 224.

78 Ibid., p. 235.

79 WIECZOREK, *Camillo Sitte et les débuts de l'urbanisme moderne,* pp. 178–179.

80 COLLINS and CRASEMANN COLLINS, *Camillo Sitte: The Birth of Modern City Planning,* p. 379 note 186 · WILHELM, "Ordnungsmuster der Stadt", in: *Formationen der Stadt,* ed. WILHELM and JESSEN-KLINGENBERG, pp. 56–65.

81 SITTE, "City Planning According to Artistic Principles", p. 183.

82 Ibid., p. 141 (emphasis added).

83 See COLLINS and CRASEMANN COLLINS, *Camillo Sitte: The Birth of Modern City Planning,* pp. 30–31 · STALLA, "'Künstler und Gelehrter' — Der Universalist Camillo Sitte".

84 In 1845, Hyrtl was appointed professor of anatomy at the University of Vienna. In 1847, he published the widely read *Handbuch der topographischen Anatomie, und ihrer praktisch medizinisch-chirurgischen Anwendungen* (Handbook of Topographical Anatomy), 2 VOLS., Vienna: J.B.Wallishauser, 1847, which organized the study of anatomy by region of the body, the first textbook of applied anatomy ever issued. In his academic career, Hyrtl also improved and expanded the Anatomical Museum.

85 Camillo SITTE, "Die Schönheit des Armes", in: *Beilage zur Allgemeinen Zeitung,* no. 214, September 15, 1893, pp. 4–6, review of Ernst BRÜCKE, *Schönheit und Fehler der menschlichen Gestalt* (Vienna: Wilhelm Braumüller, 1891); now in: Camillo SITTE, *Gesamtausgabe,* VOL. 5: *Schriften zu Kunsttheorie und Kunstgeschichte,* pp. 331–340.

86 Ibid., p. 335: „In allen diesen Fällen wurde die Natur mit ihrer Zickzackbrechung getreulich nachgebildet und keine geometrische Correctur vorgenommen."

87 STALLA, "'Künstler und Gelehrter' — Der Universalist Camillo Sitte", p. 60.

88 Juhani PALLASMAA, *The Eyes of the Skin. Architecture and the Senses,* Chichester: John Wiley & Sons, 2005.

89 See SITTE, "City Planning According to Artistic Principles", p. 159: "It is significant that when children at play follow unhindered their own artistic instincts in drawing or modeling, what they create bears a resemblance to the unsophisticated art of primitive peoples. [...] The parallel is to be seen in their favourite winter pastime of building snowmen. These snowmen stand on the same spots where, under other circumstances and following the old method, monuments or fountains might be expected to be located."

IMAGES

Jean-Baptiste Marc BOURGERY, *Traité complet de l'anatomie de l'homme,* 8 VOLS., Paris: C.-A. Delaunay, 1832–1844, *Atlas,* vol. 7, 1840, plate B: FIG. 1 · Athanasius KIRCHER, *Ars magna lvcis et vmbrae. In decem Libros digesta [...],* Rome: Hermann Scheus, 1646, plate 28 (facing p. 807): FIG. 2 · Hermann HELMHOLTZ, *Handbuch der physiologischen Optik,* Leipzig, Leopold Voss, 1867, p. 526: FIG. 3 · Jonathan CRARY, *Techniques of the Observer. On Vision and Modernity in the Nineteenth*

Century, Cambridge, MA and London: The MIT Press, 1990, p. 134: FIG. 4 · *Formationen der Stadt. Camillo Sitte weitergelesen,* edited by Karin WILHELM and Detlef JESSEN-KLINGENBERG, Basel, Boston, and Berlin: Birkhäuser – Verlag für Architektur | Gütersloh and Berlin: Bauverlag, 2006, p. 36: FIG. 6 · Camillo SITTE, *Gesamtausgabe,* edited by Klaus SEMSROTH, Michael MÖNNINGER, and Christiane Crasemann Collins, VOL. 5: *Schriften zu Kunsttheorie und Kunstgeschichte,* Vienna, Cologne, and Weimar: Böhlau, 2010, p. 423: FIG. 7

BEATRIX ZUG-ROSENBLATT

Architecture as Enclosure of Man: August Schmarsow's Attempt at a Scientific Grounding of the Hegelian Principle

Towards the end of the 19th century the art historian August Schmarsow proposed a theory of architecture that would establish a close connection between architecture and man in his physical manifestation and mental condition. In his inaugural lecture as Professor of Medieval and Modern Art History at Leipzig University in 1893, in which he first presented his theory of architecture to a broad public, Schmarsow describes architecture's task as forming enclosures for man:

Every spatial creation is first and foremost the enclosing of a subject; and thus architecture as a human art differs fundamentally from all endeavours in the applied arts.[1]

According to Schmarsow architecture is concentrated on man, or more precisely it surrounds him. This requires that man is recognized and considered in his essence. The subject, man, is the centre for which the enclosure or the space is formed. With this basic principle Schmarsow draws on Georg Friedrich Wilhelm Hegel, who, in his *Aesthetics,* had already defined the task of architecture as creating "enclosures of a subject".[2]

For its vocation lies precisely in fashioning external nature as an enclosure shaped into beauty by art out of the resources of the spirit itself, and fashioning it for the spirit already explicitly in the present, for man, or for the divine images which he has framed and set up as objects. Its meaning this

IN / KIRSTEN WAGNER AND JASPER CEPL (EDITORS) /
IMAGES OF THE BODY IN ARCHITECTURE: ANTHROPOLOGY AND BUILT SPACE /
TÜBINGEN · BERLIN / ERNST WASMUTH VERLAG / 2014 / PP. 189–206

enclosure does not carry in itself but finds in something else, in man and his
needs and aims in family life, the state, or religion, etc., and therefore the
independence of the buildings is sacrificed.[3]

Hegel's grounding of the principle of enclosure is only at first glance an attempt to define architecture anthropologically according to man's aims and needs. Although Hegel does speak of these things and their relation to man's social, political, and religious condition, he does not mean the fulfilment of functions, such as protection against the elements. This becomes clear when one asks about the needs of a religious statue, which Hegel also understands as a subject for which an enclosure is erected, namely the classical temple.[4]

Hegel grounds the principle of enclosure with his philosophy of spirit. According to Hegel, art, including architecture, belongs to the sphere of the absolute spirit.

The absolute appears [...] as living, real and hence also human subject, as
the human and finite subjectivity, as the spiritual, as the absolute substance
and truth, which makes the divine spirit living and real in oneself.[5]

The facticity of art is derived from the spiritual condition of man, who has the need to double himself as spirit. Through artistic shaping and intuition, the spirit takes pleasure in itself.[6] Art is absolute knowledge because the spirit comes to know itself through the reflection on a symbol that it establishes itself. Compared with other forms of absolute knowledge — religion and philosophy — art, according to Hegel, is characterized by its spiritual and sensual articulation.[7]

In Hegel's view, architecture is fundamentally a symbolic art. It symbolizes something that lies outside itself; that is, it falls into the spheres of the social, political, and religious, etc. For Hegel, the fact that one can use architecture — its functionality — is of less importance. In Hegel's introduction to classical and romantic art forms, the symbolic character of architecture is only modified, not restricted, even if especially Romantic architecture produces self-contained buildings which also exist for themselves, regardless of whether they were built for a particular function or purpose.[8] Since the art forms mentioned should also describe different architectural epochs, Hegel implicitly accords architecture a development that follows its own interests and guidelines. Romantic architecture is distinguished by the fact that, besides fulfilling concrete aims, it formulates its own themes:

But, as we said already, a wall as such does not have supporting as its sole
principle, for on the contrary it serves to enclose and connect and for this
reason is a preponderating feature in romantic architecture.[9]

Walls serve to connect spaces. In Romantic architecture, therefore, the joining together of the spaces or the system of the spaces becomes a separate theme.

This task is posited by architecture itself, which consequently stands independently for itself.

Enclosures are symbols. One encloses to be able to demarcate, separate, and shape what is enclosed from the surrounding area. An enclosure is a space in the sense of a demarcated area. The element for the creation of an enclosure is the wall:

> *Walls are of course necessary for an enclosure. But as has been shown in examples already, walls can also stand independently without completely forming an enclosure, for which a roof above is essential and not merely an enclosure of side-spaces. But such a roof must be carried. The simplest means for this consists of columns, the essential and also strict function of which in this connection is to be load-bearing, walls are strictly a superfluity. For load-bearing is a mechanical relation and belongs to the province of gravity and its laws.[10]*

The roof as a necessary component of enclosure calls for the support, which has a mechanical function. In this way Hegel can establish a relation between the principle of enclosure as the proper architectural principle and the principle of support and load bearing. The latter principle should be understood as being subordinate or secondary, since it serves the creation of the enclosure.

Whereas the wall is essential for the enclosure and the connection,[11] the columns fulfil the function of support:

> *The column has no other purpose but to be a support and, although a row of columns set up beside one another in a straight line marks a boundary, it does not enclose something as a solid wall or partition does but is moved in front of a proper wall and placed by itself independently.[12]*

Since columns only demarcate, they do not fulfil the architectural principle in the proper sense. Hence, the demarcation must follow from the principle of enclosure. That which is enclosed is thereby demarcated and separated from the surroundings. But something that is demarcated is, in Hegel's terminology, not yet enclosed. Only via the principle of support and load bearing are columns linked with the principle of enclosure, and they are only characterized as an architectural element via their supporting function. The basic form of architecture, and consequently the original enclosure, is the fully enclosed house.[13]

> *If we look more closely at a house and examine its mechanical proportions, we have, as said above, on the one hand architecturally formed masses carrying a load, and, on the other, those being carried, both being bound together to give support and stability. To these is added, thirdly, the purpose of enclosing, and demarcating, in the three dimensions of length, breadth, and height.[14]*

The idea of defining space according to the three dimensions, which will become characteristic of Schmarsow's theory of architecture, was already anticipated by Hegel. Schmarsow adopts Hegel's basic principle that architecture is concerned with the enclosure of a subject.

The reference to Hegel's *Aesthetics* is pointed out by Heinrich Wölfflin in his review of Schmarsow's inaugural lecture, without, however, mentioning Hegel by name. For Wölfflin, it is "certainly remarkable that an art historian once again attempts a psychological form of aesthetic enquiry; and if the lecturer, as historian, finally offers a hand in friendship to his 'old companion' architecture, one might think such an act of reconciliation might be more fitting between the long estranged disciplines of art history and aesthetics."[15] In this review Wölfflin describes the basic idea of Schmarsow's inaugural lecture as the notion that the essence of architecture is not the handling of the enclosing wall — here Wölfflin implicitly compares Schmarsow's ideas with Hegel's remarks — but the demarcated space,[16] and that the intention to fashion an enclosing whole as seat of the subject is therefore crucial, so that common to all forms of architecture is that they are spatial formations. Architecture, according to Schmarsow, is the shaper of space according to the ideal forms of human spatial intuition. As emphasized by Wölfflin, Schmarsow shifts space to the centre of his considerations.

In his inaugural lecture Schmarsow grounds the principle of the "enclosure of a subject" with his theory of space. For this it is necessary to establish man as subject and to grasp an enclosure as a space in the sense of a delimited area. Under these conditions Schmarsow is able to ground the principle of spatial enclosure by means of a theory of the constitution of space. The difference between Hegel and Schmarsow can be seen in the different ways in which they ground this principle: in the case of Hegel, with his metaphysics of the spirit, hence philosophically; Schmarsow, on the other hand, wanted to develop a (natural-) scientific foundation and based his enquiry on the intuition of space. Schmarsow updates Hegel by abandoning his metaphysics and orientating himself to the exact sciences of his time.

How is space constituted in order for the principle of man's enclosure to be valid? That is the fundamental question that Schmarsow must answer. He has to ground a theory of space which has man at its centre. Space must unfold around man. Evidence that Schmarsow is indeed formulating such an argument can be seen in the development of his inaugural lecture. The thesis that the principle of architecture is to fashion a spatial enclosure of a real or ideal subject[17] is introduced by Schmarsow prior to the discussion of the constitution of space on the basis of human corporeality, since Schmarsow is of the view that the intuition of space is a consequence of man's corporeal and mental constitution:

The intuited form of space, which surrounds us wherever we may be and which we then always erect around ourselves and consider more neces-

sary then the form of our own body, consists of the residues of sensory experience to which the muscular sensations of our body, the sensitivity of our skin, and the structure of our body all contribute. As soon as we have learned to experience ourselves and ourselves alone as the center of this space, whose coordinates intersect in us, we have found the precious kernel, the initial capital investment so to speak, on which the architectural creation is based[18].

The starting point for Schmarsow is the determination of intuited space according to the three dimensions of height, breadth, and length. In this he follows Hegel,[19] who thinks space in the dimensions of length, breadth, and height, which must be shaped.

Schmarsow bases his remarks concerning the genesis of intuited space on the mathematical model of the orthogonal Cartesian coordinate system. This idea is maintained by Schmarsow in all his subsequent writings.

Psychologically, the intuited form of three-dimensional space arises through the experiences of our sense of sight, whether or not assisted by other physiological factors. All our visual perceptions and ideas are arranged, are ordered, and unfold in accordance with this intuited form; and this fact is the mother lode of the art whose origin and essence we seek.[20]

Schmarsow faces the task of explaining the "faculty of the intuited form of space", which he considers the foundation of architecture.[21] According to this strategy, the three dimensions of space must be relocated in man's body and his physical sensations. Schmarsow's central idea is that the spatial axes intersect within man's body. This is a problematic and implausible thesis. It is difficult to see how the spatial axes, which belong to a mathematical model, the Cartesian coordinate system, should have their origin in man's body.

Schmarsow derives the dimension of height from man's upright posture. Verticality becomes part of man's experience through the upright form of his body. Schmarsow pays particular attention to the fact that this verticality can be felt, so that the idea of the vertical is indeed obtained from the orientation of the human body. Schmarsow thinks the vertical axis always and exclusively in relation to the body.

Although the claim that the idea of the vertical axis is obtained from man's physical sensations cannot be denied a certain plausibility, Schmarsow states further that all spatial axes can be related to man's body. This is based on the idea of the body's constitution with the orientations already placed in it. Under physical constitution one should understand not only the body's corporeal structure, but also man's sensations in relation to his own body as well as the non-identity of right and left placed in man's organism.

Next to the vertical line, whose living bearers resolve space by our bodily orientation into above and below, front and back, left and right, the most important direction for the actual spatial construct is the direction of free movement — that is, forward — and that of our vision [...] defines the dimension of depth.[22]

The dimension of depth begins in man's body and extends away from him in accordance with the direction of his gaze, which at the same time generates the orientation "forward" and "backward". It corresponds to the direction of sight and is the direction in which motion is possible. The designations "forward" and "direction" become synonyms. The notion of "direction" requires man's body, which is to a certain extent the starting point of direction. Man "grasps" breadth by stretching out his arms to the right and left and thereby establishing a minimal measure between himself and other objects. These designations of direction also require a reference to the human body. The measurement of "breadth" is based on man's physical constitution.

However, Schmarsow's strategy cannot solve the problem: "Moreover, the contemplation of the two horizontal axes can alternate."[23] Depending on the direction of the gaze, spatial "depth" can be seen as "breadth" and vice versa. That differs from the Cartesian coordinate system whose directions are clearly defined. It should therefore be noted that Schmarsow does not manage to determine three orthogonal axes that have their origin in man's physical constitution. He cannot plausibly derive the three dimensions of intuited space from man's corporeality.

Following from Schmarsow's thesis that the spatial axes intersect in the human body is the thesis that each person is the zero point of another coordinate system. Although man is the central point of, in each case, another coordinate system, it does not follow, however, that he simultaneously also creates his own space, but only that space no longer has a single centre. Each person becomes the spatial centre of both perception and motion to which all directions refer. How the relations in space are determined depends in each case on the concrete point of reference that man is. As a result, different people are able to construct and perceive different relations in "the same space"; despite being only one space, not only their position but also their evaluation of the "places" in the space are distinct. In each case, the putting-oneself-in-relation to the space is different.[24]

Man's body is grasped as an instrument to distinguish and determine the directions in space. Corporeality is essentially based on man's self-awareness, since only in the reflection on one's own body can its instrumentality be grasped. For Schmarsow the "I" is the centre in which the axes intersect. Not only corporeality but also man's self-awareness is seen as the foundation of spatial sensation.

The intuited form of space presupposes man's self-perception and self-awareness. For Schmarsow man is the "I", the zero point of the space. The zero point of the spatial axes is the "place" of the "I", is the "here" based on which a "there" can be determined. Also depth as a direction is related to the "here" of the subject. Depth corresponds to the open space in which man can move. The accessibility of things creates a spatial relation to man. Here the measurements of the human body are fundamental. Even today common measurements of space and length are based on the names of body measurements such as ell and foot, or oriented to the potentialities of the body, such as the German *Schritt* (step) *Wegstunde* (the distance travelled in an hour) or *Tagwerk* (the amount of work achieved in a day).[25]

The body is an instrument for the registering and processing of sense data, corporeal sensations, and motion data. This results in an intuition of space. Besides verticality, another corporeal sensation mentioned by Schmarsow is the sensation of the muscles, but also the stretching out of arms and legs, which in combination with touch can create sensations of space. Sense perceptions are supplied to man through a large number of receptors. In Schmarsow's commentary, the two most important senses for the sensation of space are those of sight and touch. Of particular importance for Schmarsow's theory of space, however, is man's movement. By moving, man can change his posture — he can stand up or lie down — as well as his position in relation to his surroundings. He can move in the world. Hence, besides sight, movement is essential for the perception and use of spatial depth. Schmarsow expands on the idea of motion as the equivalent of spatial depth in a later essay, "Über den Werth der Dimensionen im menschlichen Raumgebilde" (On the Value of Dimensions in Human Spatial Formation) from 1896, in which he refers to the "physiological psychology" of Wilhelm Wundt.

Wundt takes three-dimensional space as a given,[26] even when he wants to show how man's spatial representation is formed, since representations are intellectual constructs that man forms on the basis of his sensations and his psychical and physiological disposition. In his theory Wundt attempts to prove that "our representation of space always results from the combination of a qualitative manifold of peripheral sense perceptions with the qualitatively uniform sensations of motion, which though their intensive gradation pertain to a general measure."[27] Wundt derives the tactile and visual representations of space from his theory of local signs and their relation to motion representations. Under the latter, Wundt also understands the innervations or movements of the muscles caused by both touching and looking.

Schmarsow adopts Wundt's idea that the representation of space can only be produced through the unity of sense perception and motion. Accordingly, in his theory of space in "Über den Werth der Dimensionen im menschlichen Raumgebilde",[28] Schmarsow remarks that the depth of space can only be perceived when man sets himself in motion and — either concretely or imaginatively — measures the expanse of space.[29]

Besides the claim about the equivalence of "depth" and motion representation, Schmarsow also borrows the models for other theorems developed in
"Über den Werth der Dimensionen im menschlichen Raumgebilde" from Wundt's *Grundzüge der physiologischen Psychologie* (Principles of Physiological Psychology), namely the thesis that tactile space generates the representation of a
plane, the idea of the distance layer, and the view that motion representation is
the unity of a spatial and temporal form of intuition.

Schmarsow claims that tactile space and visual representation create the representation of a plane. The corresponding remarks by Wundt refer to the explanation of the genesis of tactile representations of space:

> *The local signs of the sense of touch form a two-dimensional continuum
> that allows the development of the representation of a plane. But the con-
> tinuum of the local signs still contains in and of itself nothing of the repre-
> sentation of space.*[30]

This initially sounds like a confirmation of Schmarsow's remarks concerning the genesis of the dimension of breadth from tactile space. However, Wundt
continues:

> *We therefore assume that this is the result of a reference to the simple con-
> tinuum of the muscle sensations and the corresponding central innerva-
> tions. These provide, in their* intensive *gradation, a uniform measure for
> both dimensions of the qualitative system of the local signs, and thus con-
> vey the intuition of a constant manifold whose dimensions are similar to
> one another. The form of the plane in which the local signs are ordered
> is initially completely undefined. It changes with the form of the surface
> touched. Due to the basic principles of movement of the limbs, however,
> such changes of position are preferred in which the organ of touch moves
> in a straight line* towards or counter to the objects. *To the extent that the
> straight line becomes the determining element of tactile space, the latter
> receives the form of an* even *space in which the planes changing in their
> curvature, which we perceive through touch, are traced back to three recti-
> linear dimensions.*[31]

By paraphrasing Wundt, Schmarsow overlooks the fact that motion representation is also the decisive foundation for the development of tactile representations of space. Schmarsow's interpretation of motion representation in the
sense of man's movement in space, and his use of motion representation exclusively for the genesis of optical depth through the gaze do without a foundation
in Wundt's physiological psychology.

In order to explain spatial vision, Wundt has to adopt, besides the two-dimensional visual field that he can experimentally prove, the further dimension
of the "direction of the lines of sight", in order for a total of three dimensions

BEATRIX ZUG-ROSENBLATT

result. The directions of the lines of sight and the straight line as the shortest distance result from the physiology of the eye muscles.

> *The constitution of the lines has, however, its physiological cause in the character of our muscles, their principle of rotating around fixed axes, which also gives rise to the even constitution of tactile space. For this reason, visual space is also an* even *space, in which* three *dimensions are required for the construction of the plane of the visual field.*[32]

Wundt also requires motion in order to be able to prove the third dimension of space. Schmarsow borrows this idea when, in "Über den Werth der Dimensionen im menschlichen Raumgebilde", he speaks of a distancing layer.[33] In front of this is a "personal space", which is characterized by the idea that perception and constitution arise from man's body. Behind the distancing layer is space in general. Like a screen the distancing layer provides an "image" of a general and objective space whose depth can only be grasped through movement in space. However, the model that Schmarsow develops here operates according to two different concepts of space, which raises the question of which spatial concept architectural space is to be assigned to.

> *For the human individual, depth is the actual life axis of every spatial formation because it is the axis of his movement in space on the natural ground and all his activity with the natural tools of his body.*[34]

From motion as the foundation of the dimension of depth, Schmarsow derives "rhythm" as a decisive criterion for architecture. Again Schmarsow's model is Wundt, who thinks motion representation — on which Schmarsow considers rhythm to be based — as the unity of the spatial and temporal forms of intuition: "The temporal and spatial forms of intuition are united in motion representation."[35] Schmarsow takes this thesis as a starting point when he claims that through the "rhythmic movement" of walking the control of "successivity in space and time" is achieved.[36] This idea seems to be confirmed by Wundt when he writes:

> *Each movement is conceived as a temporal succession; and at the same time, the image is formed of the distance covered. Thus tactile and motion representations form the foundation of all the other representations of the senses.*[37]

It should be pointed out, however, that in Wundt's psychology motion representation is also the foundation of tactile representations of space, and is therefore not used exclusively for the genesis of optical depth, as in the case of Schmarsow. Schmarsow borrows ideas from Wundt's physiological psychology, without taking into account the full range of his argument. Therefore, a defence of Schmarsow's theses cannot be based on Wundt's physiological psychology.

Schmarsow treats the human body as an instrument that is able to perceive the dimensions of space by gathering various impressions and sense perceptions and assimilating them for an intuition of space. He sees the intuition of space as a product of the psyche. He wants to explain the genesis of this psychological data with the help of man's psychology and physiology. Schmarsow's approach is an anthropological one that draws on physiological and psychological investigations. For Schmarsow, anthropology does not only include psychology, but also physiology, which is concerned with man's biological organization and the processing of stimuli.[38] He therefore takes up anthropology, which in the 18th century was closely related to empirical psychology, which for its part included a physiology of corporeal phenomena.

In his inaugural lecture Schmarsow describes his method as a "genetic approach" and as an "aesthetics from within". With the choice of the word "genetic"[39] Schmarsow links himself with the physiologists of his time who held the view that the intuition of space was acquired empirically.[40] The "aesthetic from within" that Schmarsow hoped to achieve also takes into account man's physiological and psychical organization and results from the unity of empirical science, whose basis Schmarsow sees as psychology and aesthetics in the sense of a theory of perception and a theory of art. Schmarsow sees himself as an esthetician[41] who sets store in art-theoretical explanations. In this respect too he can be placed in the tradition of Hegel.

In principle, man's body is a reliable means of perceiving space, one that is available to everybody. This thesis provides the basis for the general validity and the objectivity of Schmarsow's theory of space. However, Schmarsow does not deal with the problem of sensory illusion, which fundamentally challenges his approach. Although he admits the appearance of sensory illusion,[42] he does not comment on its implications for the perception of space. He is of the view that the intuition of space can be generated only on the basis of empirical data.

Schmarsow emphasizes that for the development of the intuition of space man's physical as well as mental constitution are crucial. Man is thus the mental and corporeal-sensory centre of space, which forms around him. Schmarsow describes this with words that one has to have learnt in order to feel oneself the centre of space;[43] only then would it be possible to be able to stretch space around one. Man does not only erect the space of experience around himself, but similarly also the space of architecture. In both cases the generation or the creation of space is based on the same law.

Consequently, there is no difference between the perception and the constitution of space in everyday life and the perception and constitution of an "architectural space". Architectural space is essentially characterized by the three dimensions of height, breadth, and depth. In this sense it is no different from the space of experience. In his inaugural lecture Schmarsow uses a concept of space that applies to both the space of experience as well as architectural space. Valid for both is Schmarsow's remark that the law of the three spatial axes is contained in every spatial idea.[44]

But how is architectural space distinguished from the space of experience? This question is not answered by Schmarsow in his inaugural lecture. Nevertheless, the principle of enclosure would only be completely grounded if Schmarsow could show that man, on the basis of his sensations and representations, does not only constitute a space, whose centre he is, but that as a result a space around man is also demarcated. Such a space encloses man when there is also a boundary that separates and distinguishes this space from other spaces. Such a space can be shaped by architecture. But this is precisely what Schmarsow does not set out in his inaugural lecture. With his theory of space he is not able to demarcate the space around man from its surroundings. He reacts to this problem likewise in his essay "Über den Werth der Dimensionen im menschlichen Raumgebilde", in which he presents his model of personal space and general space, but which ultimately cannot rectify these difficulties.[45]

Schmarsow does not manage, with the help of his theory of space, to establish the space of architecture as an area marked off from a general space. He therefore fails in his intention to ground the basic principle of the spatial enclosure of a real or ideal subject as an architectural principle on the basis of psychology and physiology.

Only the boundary allows space to be shaped. According to Schmarsow, the task of architecture is the sensually visible indication, designation, delimitation of a spatial section in general space.[46] Architecture is the shaper of space. Man attempts to define the chosen spatial section by marking off and drawing boundaries. This could be a line in the sand or a fortification wall. The signs able to define a boundary are manifold. It is a symbolic procedure that man can interpret independently of the signs used.[47] Architecture is concerned with defining the desired spatial section through the drawing of boundaries. Thus the defining of the boundary is part of architecture.

For Schmarsow the spatial enclosure is primarily the wall at the edges.[48] Accordingly, all kinds of walls and fences are "spatial formations" and therefore belong to architecture's beginnings. Schmarsow borrows the idea of the wall as a basic element of an enclosure from Hegel, who writes:

The final point for our consideration is enclosure, i.e. walls and partitions. Columns are indeed load-carrying and they do form a boundary, but they do not enclose anything; on the contrary, they are the precise opposite of an interior closed on all sides by walls. Therefore if such a complete enclosure is required, thick and solid walls must be constructed too.[49]

For Schmarsow, the basic principle that the wall is also to be defined as a boundary implies that it must be visible:

Only later did art become aware that the wall must not be transparent if it is to enclose a self-contained interior space; that neither a nearly invisible glass window nor a row of columns with openings between them can do what a simple hung carpet can do. The same logic was applied to the permanent roof.[50]

In this passage it becomes clear that Schmarsow ultimately also draws on Hegel's idea that part of an enclosure is the roof above; in Hegel's *Aesthetics* we read:

Walls are of course necessary for an enclosure. But as has been shown in examples already, walls can also stand independently without completely forming an enclosure, for which a roof above is essential and not merely an enclosure of side-spaces.[51]

For both Schmarsow and Hegel the wall is the element with which an enclosure is formed. As already mentioned in connection with Hegel's definition of Romantic architecture, the characteristic of this epoch concluding the development of architecture is that not only is the wall the main element, but also that architecture finds its own themes. One theme is the problem of the connection of spaces, independent of concrete use and architectural purpose. Therefore the central question of Romantic architecture is: what spatial systems are possible?

To finish, I would like to present an architecture that not only deals with this problem as its concept, but which demonstrates the basic principle of enclosure. *Raumnotation V* by the architect Imke Woelk is the diagram of an exhibition architecture and shows a configuration of dots. In the accompanying caption, these dots are defined as fixtures to which posts can be mounted, which are then stretched with fabric. Characteristic for this diagram is that the dots are defined, but do not cover the whole plane, so that there is not a homogenous field of dots. Nor do these dots have the same value, since they are drawn in different sizes.

Connecting the different dots with stretched fabric creates subspaces, which are demarcated from the surroundings. Wall-like elements, the lengths of fabric, are the element of the creation of space. The resulting spaces are enclosed and demarcated by the stretched fabric.

One might start by joining the dots that have the same size. The application of this principle already creates a broad range of spatial systems. But dots of different sizes can also be put into relation to one another — by being joined with a length of fabric. One should bear in mind, however, that the size of the dot, hence the pole, allows different spans. Smaller dots, due to their smaller intervals, allow a fine demarcation of space; larger dots create larger subspaces. Through the distance of the dots to one another and through the corresponding sizes of the posts, certain areas are excluded from the spatial formation; they cannot be fitted with stretched fabric as wall-like elements.

On the basis of these considerations, *Raumnotation V* can be interpreted as maintaining a variability in the structure of the partitioning of the main space while simultaneously affording the largest possible variation in the resulting spatial orders. This variability is of particular importance in an exhibition ar-

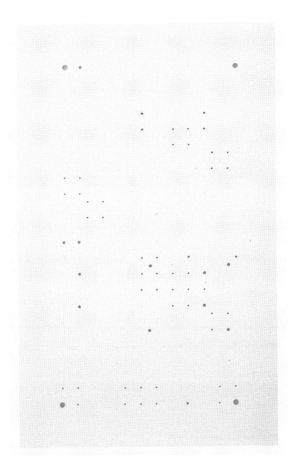

1
IMKE WOELK /
RAUMNOTATION V

chitecture since the classification and linking of the subspaces influences the presentation of the exhibited works. *Raumnotation V* reacts to this task with the notation of possible spatial orders.

Spatial systems are a modern interpretation of the concept of enclosure. Architecture creates enclosures — for these it might be demanded that they take into account man in his essence.

NOTES

1   August Schmarsow, *Das Wesen der architektonischen Schöpfung. Antrittsvorlesung, gehalten in der Aula der K. Universität Leipzig am 8. November 1893,* Leipzig: Karl W. Hiersemann, 1894, p. 15: „Jede Gestaltung des Raumes ist zunächst Umschließung eines Subjekts, und dadurch unterscheidet sich die Architektur als menschliche Kunst wesentlich von allen Bestrebungen des Kunsthandwerks." Quoted (here and below) after the English translation, "The Essence of Architectural Creation", in: *Empathy, Form, and Space. Problems in German Aesthetics, 1873–1893,* Introduction and translation by Harry Francis Mallgrave and Eleftherios Ikonomou, Santa Monica: Getty Publications Program, 1994, pp. 281–297, here p. 288. In the given quote, the translation by Mallgrave and Ikonomou emphasizes the aspect of creative action ("spatial creation", "enclosing"). A translation closer to Schmarsow's formulation might be: "All shaping of space is first of all enclosure of a subject; this is essentially what distinguishes architecture as a human art from all endeavours in applied art."

2   Georg Wilhelm Friedrich Hegel, *Ästhetik,* Berlin and Weimar: Aufbau-Verlag, 1976, VOL. 2, p. 52: „Umschließungen eines Subjektes". Quoted (here and below) after the English edition: G. W. F. Hegel, *Aesthetics. Lectures on Fine Art,* translated by T. M. Knox, 2 VOLS., Oxford: Clarendon Press (Oxford University Press), 1975, VOL. 2, p. 662 (translation modified).

3   Hegel, *Aesthetics,* p. 633, and *Ästhetik,* p. 26: „Denn ihr [that is: architecture's] Beruf liegt eben darin, dem für sich schon vorhandenen Geist, dem Menschen oder seinen objektiv von ihm herausgestalteten und aufgestellten Götterbildern die äußere Natur als eine aus dem Geiste selbst durch die Kunst zur Schönheit gestaltete Umschließung heraufzubilden, die ihre Bedeutung nicht mehr in sich selbst trägt, sondern dieselbe in einem anderen, dem Menschen und dessen Bedürfnissen und Zwecken des Familienlebens, des Staats, Kultus usf. findet und deshalb die Selbständigkeit der Bauwerke aufgibt."

4   See ibid., p. 662, and *Ästhetik,* p. 52.

5   Constanze Peres, *Die Struktur der Kunst in Hegels Ästhetik,* Bonn: Bouvier Verlag Herbert Grundmann, 1983, p. 105: „Das Absolute erscheint […] als lebendiges, wirkliches und somit auch menschliches Subjekt, als die menschliche und endliche Subjektivität, als geistige, die absolute Substanz und Wahrheit, den göttlichen Geist in sich lebendig und wirklich macht."

6   See ibid., p. 38.

7   See ibid., p. 22.

8   See Hegel, *Aesthetics,* VOL. 2, p. 634, and *Ästhetik,* p. 27.

9   Ibid., p. 666, and *Ästhetik,* p. 56: „Die Wand aber hat, wie wir bereits sahen, nicht das Tragen als solches zu ihrem alleinigen Prinzip, sondern dient wesentlich zur Umschließung und Verbindung und macht deshalb in der romantischen Baukunst ein überwiegendes Moment aus."

10   Ibid., p. 656f., and *Ästhetik,* p. 47: „Zu einer Umschließung sind nämlich einerseits zwar Mauern nötig; Mauern aber können auch selbständig, wie schon früher an Beispielen gezeigt ist, dastehen, ohne die Umschließung vollständig zu machen, zu welcher wesentlich eine Bedeckung von oben und nicht nur ein Umschließen der Seitenräume gehört. Eine solche Bedeckung nun aber muss getragen werden. Das Einfachste hierfür sind Säulen, deren wesentliche und zugleich strenge Bestimmung in dieser Rücksicht in dem *Tragen* als solchem besteht. Deshalb sind Mauern, wo es aufs bloße Tragen ankommt, eigentlich ein Überfluss. Denn das Tragen ist ein mechanisches Verhältnis und gehört ins Gebiet der Schwere und ihrer Gesetze."

11   See ibid., p. 666, and *Ästhetik*, p. 56.

12   Ibid., p. 666, and *Ästhetik*, p. 56: „Die Säule hat keine andere Bestimmung als die des Tragens, und obschon eine Reihe von Säulen, in gerader Linie nebeneinandergestellt, eine Abgrenzung markiert, so umschließt sie doch nicht wie eine feste Mauer oder Wand, sondern wird ausdrücklich von der eigentlichen Wand fortgerückt und frei für sich hingestellt."

13   See ibid., p. 685, and *Ästhetik*, p. 72.

14   Ibid., p. 665 (translation slightly modified), and *Ästhetik*, p. 55: „Nehmen wir das Haus näher in seinem mechanischen Verhältnis zu sich selbst, so erhalten wir nach dem eben Gesagten auf der einen Seite *tragende*, architektonisch gestaltete Massen, auf der anderen Seite *getragene*, beide aber zu Halt und Festigkeit verbunden. Hiezu kommt drittens die Bestimmung des *Umschließens* und Abgrenzens nach den drei Dimensionen der Länge, Breite und Höhe."

15   Heinrich WÖLFFLIN, Review of: SCHMARSOW, *Das Wesen der architektonischen Schöpfung*, in: *Repertorium für Kunstwissenschaft*, VOL. 17, 1894, pp. 141–142: „[Es] ist […] gewiss bemerkenswerth, dass ein Kunsthistoriker wieder einmal eine ästhetisch-psychologische Fragestellung versucht und wenn der Vortragende zum Schluss als Historiker der ‚alten Freundin' Architektur die Hand zu erneutem Bündniss reicht, so möchten wir meinen, ein derartiger Act der Versöhnung wäre mit besserem Recht zwischen den lange getrennten Disciplinen der Kunstgeschichte und der Aesthetik inscenirt worden."

16   See ibid., p. 141.

17   See SCHMARSOW, "The Essence of Architectural Creation", p. 288, and *Das Wesen der architektonischen Schöpfung*, pp. 15–16.

18   Ibid., pp. 286–287, and *Das Wesen der architektonischen Schöpfung*, p. 11: „Sobald aus den Residuen sinnlicher Erfahrung, zu denen auch die Muskelgefühle unseres Leibes, die Empfindlichkeit unserer Haut wie der Bau unseres ganzen Körpers ihre Beiträge liefern, das Resultat zusammenschießt, das wir unsere räumliche Anschauungsform nennen, — der Raum, der uns umgibt, wo wir auch seien, den wir fortan stets um uns aufrichten und notwendig vorstellen, notwendiger als die Form unsers Leibes, — sobald wir uns selbst und uns allein als Centrum dieses Raumes fühlen gelernt, dessen Richtungsaxen sich in uns schneiden, so ist auch der wertvolle Kern gegeben, das Kapital gleichsam des architektonischen Schaffens begründet".

19   See HEGEL, *Aesthetics,* VOL. 2, p. 688, and *Ästhetik*, p. 74.

20   SCHMARSOW, "The Essence of Architectural Creation", p. 286, and *Das Wesen der architektonischen Schöpfung*, p. 10–11: „Die psychologische Tatsache, daß durch die Erfahrungen unseres Gesichtssinnes, sei es auch unter Beihülfe andrer leiblicher Faktoren, die Anschauungsform des dreidimensionalen Raumes zu Stande kommt, nach der sich alle Wahrnehmungen des Auges und alle anschaulichen Vorstellungen der Phantasie richten, ordnen und entfalten, — dieser Tatbestand ist auch der Mutterboden der Kunst, deren Ursprung und Wesen wir suchen."

21   On the relation of Schmarsow's theory of space to the discussion of his time, see Beatrix ZUG, *Die Anthropologie des Raumes in der Architekturtheorie des frühen 20. Jahrhunderts*, Tübingen and Berlin: Ernst Wasmuth, 2006, p. 19.

22   SCHMARSOW, "The Essence of Architectural Creation", p. 289, and *Das Wesen der archititek-*

tonischen Schöpfung, p.16: „Nächst dem Höhenlot, dessen lebendiger Träger mit seiner leiblichen Orientierung nach oben und unten, vorn und hinten, links und rechts bestimmend weiter wirkt, ist die wichtigste Ausdehnung für das eigentliche Raumgebilde vielmehr die Richtung unserer freien Bewegung, also nach vorwärts und zugleich unsers Blickes [...] also die Tiefenausdehnung." The translation by Mallgrave and Ikonomou does not make sufficiently clear that the physicality of man is the basis of the perception of space. The following translation may be closer to Schmarsow's argument: "Besides the vertical axis, whose living bearer, with his corporeal orientation upwards and downwards, forwards and backwards, to the left and to the right, continues to operate in a determining way, the most important extension for a proper spatial formation is the direction of our free movement — hence forwards — and also our gaze [...] — hence the extension in depth."

23 Ibid., p.290, and SCHMARSOW, *Das Wesen der architektonischen Schöpfung*, p.17: „Die Betrachtung der beiden Horizontalaxen kann ferner miteinander abwechseln."

24 On Schmarsow's phenomenology, see ZUG, *Die Anthropologie des Raumes in der Architekturtheorie des frühen 20. Jahrhunderts*, pp.21–22.

25 See ibid., p.25.

26 See Wilhelm WUNDT, *Grundzüge der physiologischen Psychologie*, third, rewritten edition, 2 VOLS., Leipzig: Wilhelm Engelmann, 1887, VOL. 2, p.83 (first edition: 1874).

27 Ibid., p.207: „unsere Raumvorstellung überall aus der Verbindung einer qualitativen Mannigfaltigkeit peripherischer Sinnesempfindungen mit den qualitativ einförmigen Bewegungsempfindungen, welche sich durch ihre intensive Abstufung zu einem allgemeinen Größenmaß eignen, hervorgeht."

28 August SCHMARSOW, "Über den Werth der Dimensionen im menschlichen Raumgebilde", in: *Berichte über die Verhandlungen der Königlich-Sächsischen Gesellschaft der Wissenschaften zu Leipzig. Philologisch-Historische Classe*, VOL. 48, 1896, pp.44–61.

29 On the differences of this theory of space to the conception in the inaugural lecture, see ZUG, *Die Anthropologie des Raumes in der Architekturtheorie des frühen 20. Jahrhunderts*, pp.26–30.

30 WUNDT, *Grundzüge der physiologischen Psychologie*, VOL. 2, p.32: „Die Localzeichen des Tastsinns bilden ein Continuum von zwei Dimensionen, welches damit die Möglichkeit gewährt, die Vorstellung einer *Fläche* zu entwickeln. Aber das Continuum der Localzeichen enthält an und für sich noch nichts von der Raumvorstellung."

31 Ibid., p.32–33: „Wir nehmen daher an, dass diese erst durch die Rückbeziehung auf das einfache Continuum der Muskelempfindungen und der diesen entsprechenden centralen Innervationsempfindungen entstehe. Diese geben in ihrer *intensiven* Abstufung für die beiden Dimensionen des qualitativen Systems der Localzeichen ein gleichförmiges Maß ab und vermitteln so die Anschauung einer stetigen Mannigfaltigkeit, deren Dimensionen einander gleichartig sind. Die Form der Fläche, in welche die Localzeichen geordnet werden, ist zunächst völlig unbestimmt. Sie wechselt mit der Form der betasteten Oberfläche. Durch die Bewegungsgesetze der Gliedmaßen sind aber solche Lageänderungen bevorzugt, bei welchen sich das Tastorgan *geradlinig* den Gegenständen entgegen oder an ihnen hinbewegt. Indem so die Gerade zum bestimmenden Element des Tastraumes wird, erhält der letztere die Form eines *ebenen* Raumes, in welchem die in ihrer Krümmung wechselnden Flächen, die wir durch Betastung wahrnehmen, auf drei geradlinige Dimensionen zurückgeführt werden."

32 Ibid., p. 194: „Die Beschaffenheit der Richtlinien hat aber ihren physiologischen Grund in der Eigenschaft unserer Muskeln, ihre Ansatzpunkte um feste Axen zu drehen, woraus auch die ebene Beschaffenheit des Tastraumes hervorgeht. Darum ist der Gesichtsraum gleichfalls ein *ebener* Raum, in welchem zur Construction der Sehfeldfläche *drei* Dimensionen erfordert werden."

33 See SCHMARSOW, "Über den Werth der Dimensionen im menschlichen Raumgebilde", p. 54.

34 August SCHMARSOW, "Raumgestaltung als Wesen der architektonischen Schöpfung", in: *Zeitschrift für Ästhetik und Allgemeine Kunstwissenschaft*, VOL. 9, 1914, pp. 66–95, here p. 74–75: „Und diese dritte Dimension ist die eigentliche Lebensachse jedes Raumbildes für das menschliche Individuum, weil sie die Richtungsachse all seiner Ortsbewegung auf dem natürlichen Grunde und all seiner Betätigung mit den natürlichen Werkzeugen seines Leibes ist."

35 WUNDT, *Grundzüge der physiologischen Psychologie*, VOL. 2, p. 3: „Die zeitliche und die räumliche Form der Anschauung sind in der Vorstellung der Bewegung vereinigt."

36 See SCHMARSOW, "Über den Werth der Dimensionen im menschlichen Raumgebilde", p. 55.

37 WUNDT, *Grundzüge der physiologischen Psychologie*, VOL. 2, p. 3: „Jede Bewegung wird aufgefasst als eine zeitliche Succession, und zugleich entsteht damit das Bild der zurückgelegten Raumstrecke. So bilden die Tast- und Bewegungsvorstellungen die Grundlage zu allen anderen Sinnesvorstellungen."

38 See ZUG, *Die Anthropologie des Raumes in der Architekturtheorie des frühen 20. Jahrhunderts*, p. 17.

39 See SCHMARSOW, *Das Wesen der architektonischen Schöpfung*, p. 6, and "Über den Werth der Dimensionen im menschlichen Raumgebilde", p. 45.

40 See ZUG, *Die Anthropologie des Raumes in der Architekturtheorie des frühen 20. Jahrhunderts*, pp. 30–31.

41 See SCHMARSOW, *Das Wesen der architektonischen Schöpfung*, p. 26.

42 See SCHMARSOW, "Über den Werth der Dimensionen im menschlichen Raumgebilde", p. 50.

43 See SCHMARSOW, *Das Wesen der architektonischen Schöpfung*, p. 11.

44 See ibid., p. 11.

45 See ZUG, *Die Anthropologie des Raumes in der Architekturtheorie des frühen 20. Jahrhunderts*, pp. 26–34.

46 See SCHMARSOW, *Das Wesen der architektonischen Schöpfung*, pp. 11–12.

47 See ibid., p. 12.

48 See ibid., p. 16.

49 HEGEL, *Aesthetics*, VOL. 2, p. 671, and *Ästhetik*, p. 61: „Die letzte Bestimmung, nach welcher wir uns umzusehen haben, betrifft die *Umschließung*, die *Mauern* und *Wände*. Säulen tragen und umgrenzen wohl, aber sie umschließen nicht, sondern sind gerade das Entgegengesetzte des von Wänden rings eingeschlossenen Innern. Soll deshalb solch eine vollständige Einschließung nicht fehlen, so müssen auch dichte, solide Wände aufgeführt werden."

50 SCHMARSOW, "The Essence of Architectural Creation", p. 295, and *Das Wesen der architektonischen Schöpfung*, pp. 26–27: „Später dringt die Kunst zu dem Bewußtsein durch, daß die Wand nicht durchsichtig sein darf, wenn sie einen Innenraum abschließen soll als Raumganzes für sich,

daß weder die fast unsichtbare Glasscheibe noch die Säulenreihe mit offenen Intervallen als Ae-
quivalent fungiert und nicht leistet, was schon der Teppich vermag. Sie handelt dann ebenso kon-
sequent in der festen Abschließung nach oben".

51 HEGEL, *Aesthetics,* VOL. 2, p. 656, and *Ästhetik,* p. 47: „Zu einer Umschließung sind nämlich einerseits zwar Mauern nötig; Mauern aber können auch selbständig, wie schon früher an Beispielen
gezeigt ist, dastehen, ohne die Umschließung vollständig zu machen, zu welcher wesentlich eine
Bedeckung von oben und nicht nur ein Umschließen der Seitenräume gehört."

IMAGE

Imke WOELK, *Architekturprojekte 2003 bis 2004,* Rome: Deutsche Akademie Villa Massimo, 2003,
p. 14.

HARRY FRANCIS MALLGRAVE

New Hellerau: Design in the Biological Age

1.

In many architectural histories over the past century, Hellerau has been justly celebrated as Germany's first garden city and a model of progressive thinking. It has been exalted for its ecological sensitivity, response to individual needs, community organization, artistic emphasis, and pedagogical reforms. Looking at this experiment from our vantage point of a little more than 100 years since its foundation, it can also be cited for one other distinction. It is one of the first attempts to conceive a living environment from an embodied biological perspective. In this regard it is a worthy metaphor for another new era rushing in upon us today.

The conception of Hellerau — a creation of Karl Schmidt, Richard Riemerschmid, and Wolf Dohrn — drew upon two important intellectual pedigrees. One was the half-century of psycho-physiological experimentation undertaken by Hermann von Helmholtz, Ernst Mach, Johann Friedrich Herbart, Carl Stumpf, Wilhelm Wundt, and Gustav Theodor Fechner. The second, no less significant line, was that body of *Einfühlungstheorie* promulgated by Friedrich Theodor Vischer, Karl Köstlin, Hermann Lotze, Robert Vischer, Johannes Volkelt, Heinrich Wölfflin, August Schmarsow, and Theodor Lipps. The idea that body and

IN / KIRSTEN WAGNER AND JASPER CEPL (EDITORS) /
IMAGES OF THE BODY IN ARCHITECTURE: ANTHROPOLOGY AND BUILT SPACE /
TÜBINGEN · BERLIN / ERNST WASMUTH VERLAG / 2014 / PP. 207–225

Geist could be modulated or brought into some kind of sympathetic accord was of course a rejection of the Hegelian idealism that had dominated so much of 19th century Germanic philosophy, and one can only imagine the buoyed sense of freedom that accompanied the first tentative glimpses of a physiologically-based understanding of the human condition. In this regard the simple intellectual ambition and verve of the period from Helmholtz to Lipps has been much underappreciated, despite the acclaim it has found in recent years.

It was under Lipps that Dohrn took his doctorate in 1902, and eight years later Dohrn resigned as the executive director of the Deutsche Werkbund to devote himself full-time to the project of realizing a new town oriented around and in harmony with art. That music should be the centerpiece of Hellerau was suggested by the Czech composer Richard Batka in the early phase of the design process, but the decisive event took place in 1909 when Dohrn witnessed the production of a troupe of musicians and dancers led by the Swiss musicologist Émile Jaques-Dalcroze. The event proved electric. Dohrn was convinced he had found his Phidias, and through a series of negotiations he pleaded with Dalcroze to relocate his base to Hellerau. The clincher was his promise — against the hesitation of Schmidt — to build a new theatre and institute to house the activities. Although Riemerschmid strenuously vied for the commission, the job went to Heinrich Tessenow, who composed his classical design out of simple squares, rectangles, and triangles, decorated with one yin/yang symbol in the pediment. When the college was fully operational in 1913, its two-week musical festival attracted 5,000 visitors, and overnight Hellerau became a cultural rival to Bayreuth.

Much has been made of the international fascination with Hellerau and Dalcroze in the few years between 1910 and 1914.[1] Among the many thousands of intellectuals who made the pilgrimage to observe the "New Olympus" were Ebenezer Howard, Martin Buber, George Bernard Shaw, Max Reinhardt, Rainer Maria Rilke, Serge Diaghilev, Thomas Mann, Stefan Zweig, Oskar Kokoschka, Emil Nolde, Hugo Ball, Karl Ernst Osthaus, Raoul Hausmann, Kurt Schwitters, Heinrich Wölfflin, Max Klinger, Wilhelm Worringer, Julius Meier-Graefe, Franz Kafka, and Upton Sinclair. Architects were no less curious visitors. Charles-Edouard Jeanneret (later Le Corbusier), whose brother Albert was an instructor employed by Dalcroze, visited the town twice in 1910–1911, and the second time he was even offered a job by Tessenow.[2] Henry van de Velde, along with most of the architects involved with the Deutsche Werkbund, monitored the experiment closely, as did Ludwig Mies van der Rohe, who visited the town while his future bride Ada Bruhn was a student at the institute. Another visitor of interest was Alma Mahler, the widow of the Austrian composer and later the wife of Walter Gropius. In retrospect, it seems entirely possible that this town might have dramatically altered the theoretical premises of German modernism — if the experiment had not been crushed by the catastrophe of World War I.

The importance of Hellerau, however, rests not with its buildings but rather with the approach to musical education installed by Dalcroze. The overall system was called "rhythmic gymnastics" or "eurhythmics", and it began not with learning musical instruments but with a series of body movements and rhythmic marches that he termed "plastic exercises" — carefully choreographed or sequenced dances. The aim was for one to find one's natural biological rhythm as a prelude to tapping into the source of one's creative powers. The daily regimen entailed gymnastics, ear training, music theory, piano improvisation, choral and ensemble rehearsals, and of course "plastic" dancing. All were integrated with regular "sun baths" and "air baths".

Dalcroze was forthright in articulating the theoretical underpinning to his method. He viewed music not as an end to itself but rather as a means to expand upon one's natural sense of well-being — that is, to harmonize the body movements with the neural activities of the brain and thereby bring about a "coordination between the mind which conceives, the brain which orders, the nerve which transmits and the muscle which executes."[3] It is an embodied theory of social health that seeks to align the body with our neurological centers of activity and thus enhance the working efficiency of the brain. The key is to tap into the body's natural rhythm, "for the body", as he goes on to say, "can become a marvellous instrument of beauty and harmony when it vibrates in tune with artistic imagination and collaborates with creative thought."[4] One early enthusiast of Dalcroze's method credited him with reopening a door that had long been closed: the discovery of "one of the secrets of Greek education".[5] Another likened his plastic dances to the "beautiful abstractions of colour and line" that were contemporaneously being explored by Wassily Kandinsky.[6] Indeed, the intellectual successor to Hellerau, as few have noted, was the Bauhaus, for the simple reason that the pedagogical theories of Itten, Kandinsky, Klee, and most especially Moholy-Nagy were based on similar biological premises.

2.

In this essay I am employing Hellerau as a metaphor. It is a metaphor for the fact that our physical environment relates to a larger social and cultural environment. And in this relationship the mental and physical health of the individual housed within a physical environment contribute in no insignificant way to the health of the community as a whole. I have also used the adjective "biological" in the title to this essay, which I know evokes a sense of unease with many people. Some view it as a harbinger to some 'brave new world', while others take it as an affront to the creative autonomy of the architect. Yet architectural theory in the early 1990s lost much of its luster in the face of the embarrassing collapse of poststructural affectations, and the well-intentioned arguments of many "green" advocates have more often than not failed to produce a compelling vision of what our future built environment should be. Sustainability, as a concept, is entirely a valid one, but I argue that so far it has been too narrowly construed. If sustainability wants to become a serious ethic it has to be given biological substance. It has to be given a "human face".

Such a statement is of course not new, and I confess that what I mean by such a statement is not very different from what Aldo van Eyck some years ago referred to as "man's homecoming". We assiduously pare down every facet of our energy consumption and we scold others for their lack of ecological sensitivity, but in the end we give preciously little reflection to the nature of the human habitat. We suffer this omission because we still operate under the premise that the human brain — like human life — is infinitely malleable and able to adjust to every quirky convolution that the enthusiastic young designer is able to generate with the latest parametric software. The psychologist Steven Pinker has referred to this as the "blank slate" syndrome: the belief that human beings can all be assigned dreary cells in brute Corbusian towers and still be expected to smile. If science has taught us anything in the last few decades, it is that the opposite is the case. As biological organisms, we are born with involved genetic codes and marvelously complex neurological structures that have been selectively crafted for our pursuits over the course of millions of years. The built human habitats of the past 10,000 years can do little to alter this evolutionary fact.

A biological approach to design is actually nothing new. Architects, we all should agree, are ostensively in the business of creating healthy and aesthetically pleasing environments, and indeed one of the first architects to take note of our "neurological entity" and "brain physiology" was the modernist Richard Neutra, who advocated a similar position in 1954 with his book *Survival through Design*. In this regard he was even preceded by a few years by László Moholy-Nagy's various yet determined efforts to devise a "biological theory" for design.[7] Neutra, however, was explicit in his morality and trenchant in his desire to move beyond what he referred to as "the *pure* aesthetics of a bygone brand of speculation."[8] Citing the need for the architect to undertake new research in the areas of "sensory significance" as well as to become familiar with the evidence already offered by the biological sciences, he noted:

> It is in this era of brain-physiological research that the designer, who wields the tools of sensory and cerebral stimulation professionally, can perhaps be recognized as a perpetually and precariously active conditioner of the race and thus acquire responsibility for its survival. He acts, in a way, as a guardian of such survival, and students, as practitioners, will gain in moral stature when they come to consider what is entrusted to them.[9]

In retrospect, Neutra's arguments were perhaps a little too grounded in the pessimism of the post-war years, but the kernel of his argument remains entirely

HARRY FRANCIS MALLGRAVE

correct. Architects should know a little more about the biological nature of the human beings for whom they design. The more apprehensive among us will no doubt counter with the objection that the "revolution" in our understanding of the human organism (which has taken place largely in the last two decades) is still a little too new, and perhaps the whole matter needs a little more "peer review". Two responses can overcome such timidity. First, the genetic and neuro-scientific evidence that has been amassing, while wildly liberating (rather than constricting) in its philosophical implications, constitutes some of the most "peer reviewed" evidence that has ever been produced by the scientific community. Second, in the last few years we have probably learned more about our biological beings — Heidegger's *Dasein* — than we have in all of human history. If disciplines as remote as art history, psychology, and phenomenology are rushing to affix the prefix "neuro" to their newly minted fields, why are architects supposed to await further clarification? As architects, we extol the virtues of creativity and imagination, and now for the first time we are observing how the whole process works on an MRI screen. As designers, we seek the pleasurable appeal of the people for whom we craft our products, and now for the first time we are beginning to understand how they actually perceive, navigate, and make their judgments about the built environment. As artists, we take pride in the proficiency and uniqueness of our creations, and now for the first time we are beginning to understand that powerful Darwinian (selectionist) urge of ours to make something "special". Antonio Stradivari no doubt felt this urge.

3.

For reasons that will soon become evident, I think that embodiment is an excellent word to circumscribe this biological body of evidence that will soon find its way into architectural design. Once again, the idea is not a new one. When Leonardo da Vinci in the 1480s embarked on a series of sketches attempting to locate Vitruvian man within a geometric order, he was of course re-codifying the embodied classical notion that every building should have "an exact system of correspondence to the likeness of a well-formed human being".[10] In other words, man is the measure of all things architectural and proportions drafted from human bodies invested design with both a visual vitality and a cosmic genealogy. Leon Battista Alberti laid the metaphysical basis for these drawings with his duality of "beauty" and "ornament". The former was an idea in a Platonic sense, but the latter, like his preceding discussion of slender and buxom women, was conspicuously sensual in its cosmic or cosmetic physicality, not unlike the rouge that one applies to one's cheek. The mediating concept bridging this divide for Alberti was none other than the arch of *concinnitas*, a nod to Vitruvian *symmetria* but also a notion curiously presaging Dalcroze's fascination with eurythmy.

For Cicero *concinnitas* was that rhetorical flourish obtained when words are fashioned together in such a way as to produce a style or *symmetria,* which disappears when they are changed although the thought remains the same. For Alberti, capturing this elusive rhythm "is the main object of the art of building, and the source of her dignity, charm, authority, and worth."[11]

Even as the worldview of renaissance theory began to fade, architects of the 17th- and 18th-centuries simply pursued another variation on the theme of architectural embodiment. The rationalist Claude Perrault is credited with promulgating the French declaration of independence from Italian ideas. Notwithstanding, few have noted that the crucial footnote in his translation of Vitruvius is attached to the passage in which the Roman architect is praising the Hellenic Hermogenes for having achieved the quality of *asperitas* in his designs — that is, by removing an inner row of columns from a double colonnade.[12] For Perrault this word (*aspreté* in archaic French, asperity in English) meant nothing less that the "lively aspect" or "visual tension" biologically induced by a colonnade when the retina and brain respond to the visual contrast of sunlit columns and shadows in deep relief. Similarly, in Perrault's later treatise on column orders he rejected Alberti's notion of musical harmonies not on theoretical grounds, but for the anatomical reason that the eye and the ear process their stimuli differently. Nearly a century later, in 1764, Julien-David Le Roy accepted Perrault's anatomical explanation by arguing, in essence, that the beauty of a Greek colonnade lay not with its proportions but rather with the neurological effects it has on the walking spectator taking in the experience.[13]

Le Roy's argument was probably also informed by Edmund Burke's *A Philosophical Inquiry into the Origin of Our Ideas of the Sublime and Beautiful* (1757), the first major treatise of the British picturesque movement. With its inductive approach, picturesque theory was inherently anti-classical in its demeanor, and nowhere is this better illustrated than in Burke's insistence that Vitruvian man "never supplied the architect with any of his ideas" — first on the basis that such a strained position was unnatural, and second for the reason that a man thus portrayed did not resemble a house.[14] Yet the Lockean empiricism underlying his reasoning was at the same time predicated on the senses, and this sensuous foundation demanded not a metaphysical but a physiological and emotional explanation. Hence the perception of beauty and sublimity was in large part the psychological result of how the optic nerve responds physically to perceived objects. Beautiful objects tend to relax the retinal muscles and thereby make us happy, while sublime ones induce tension, awe, and sometimes pain. Burke's follower, Uvedale Price, built an entire aesthetic system precisely on this "coquetry of nature," by arguing for a new aesthetic field of picturesque impressions situated somewhere in between "the languor of beauty" and "the tension of sublimity."[15] The architectural recipient of this theory of sensory embodiment was no less than the wildly inventive classicist John Soane.

Of course the 19th century with its new industrial reality struggled to mediate the gaping divide between the machine precision of tools and industrial
forms and sensory-based approaches to design. Karl Friedrich Schinkel, for one,
was obsessed with the contradiction, even to the point of inventing forms of
"pure radical abstraction."[16] His dissatisfaction with this solution — a crisis perhaps intensified by his reading of Schopenhauer's vitalism — at least allowed his
student Karl Bötticher to proffer a way out. A building now became an *"ideal organism"*.[17] It is ideal in the sense that the powerful forces of gravity (materiality)
are temporarily held in abeyance and articulated by the ornamental ingenuity
of the architect. From this highly animate perspective, a building reverted to an
Albertian "form of body", one again pregnant with gravitational energy.

Even Bötticher's antagonist, Gottfried Semper, eventually came round to
such a viewpoint, and it is therefore not surprising that the goal of his "Practical
Aesthetics" was to overturn once and for all the unembodied *Geist* of Hegelian idealism. Semper, with his friendship with Friedrich Theodor Vischer, also
brings us to the inception of *Einfühlungstheorie* that presages the phenomenon
of Hellerau. On another continent, Emerson's sensuous philosophy espoused
a material animism that redounded through the "organic" theory of Horatio
Greenough to the "living force" of Louis Sullivan's ornamentation. *Concinnitas,*
in the sense that Alberti intended, is an appropriate word to apply to his rhythmic and inspired creations.

4.

Within philosophical and psychological circles of the 20th century, the notion
of embodiment has enjoyed an uneasy existence. That line of psycho-physiological research that commenced with Helmholtz and others finds its splendid
culmination in the work of Gestalt psychologists, who in their endeavor to find
"the brain correlates of perceptual facts" were the first to suggest some kind of
isomorphism between mind and body. Nevertheless, their efforts were offset by
the popular but now starkly antiquated speculations of Freudian psychology on
the one hand, and by the equally defunct "black box" of behavioral psychologists
on the other. By defining the mind as the unknowable other world, behaviorists
in fact foreswore the idea of embodiment altogether.

The idea of embodiment was also central to the phenomenological schools
of Henri Bergson and Edmund Husserl, as well as to the hermeneutics of Heidegger. But once again these schools were often overshadowed in academic
settings by the semiotic musings of logical positivism and structuralism. The
turning point, if this is the right word, was the work of Maurice Merleau-Ponty,
who in fact attempted to marry the work of the Gestalt psychologists with the
insights of Husserl. In *Structure of Behaviour* (1942) he first attempted to do

away with the Cartesian dualism of mind and body, but this work was simply a prelude to his better known *Phenomenology of Perception* (1945), which more concretely surveyed the embodied nature of the perceptual field. He was even more explicit in the posthumously published manuscript *The Visible and Invisible*. Here he provided the idea of embodiment with an apt metaphor — that of flesh:

> *We have to reject the age-old assumptions that put the body in the world and the seer in the body, or, conversely, the world and the body in the seer as in a box. Where are we to put the limit between the body and the world, since the world is flesh?*[19]

Flesh, for Merleau-Ponty, not only captured the idea of our essentially embodied condition as sentient beings, but also the fact that we always experience expressive sounds, expressive movements, and expressive gestures, rather than meaningless forms in space and time. In a curious note to the text, he even takes the idea of "flesh" back to Robert Vischer's concept of *Einfühlung*, by which he means "that my body is made of the same flesh as the world (it is perceived), and moreover that this flesh of my body is shared by the world, the world *reflects* it, encroaches upon it and it encroaches upon the world."[20] We empathize or "feel ourselves into" things because the brain, body, and world form a continuum in which we, as organisms, cannot set ourselves apart.

Within a few years, the idea of embodiment would begin to find its way into biological circles, beginning with Gerald Edelman's path-breaking book *Neural Darwinism* (1987), in which this Nobel-Prize winner attempted to explain neurologically the rise of human consciousness. Edelman later defined embodiment, quite simply, as "the view that the mind, brain, body, and environment all interact to yield behavior", which he distinguished from Cartesian "dualistic consciousness".[21] Edelman's effort was soon followed by Antonio Damasio's *Descartes' Error* (1994), in which the highly respected neurologist presented an embodied view of emotion that seemingly put to rest the idea that the mind and body can in any way be divorced. The fact that he and his team of neuroscientists at UCLA were at the same time using PET scans to depict neurologically the implication of emotion in all of our "rational" or cognitive processes also provided graphic evidence to buffer his case.

Support for the idea of embodiment also came from other circles. In 1980 George Lakoff and Mark Johnson published their now classic study *Metaphors We Live By*, in which they demonstrated that much of our everyday language is structured by conceptual metaphors related to aspects of our corporeal being, such as when we say "we *rise* in the morning" or "*fall* asleep at night". In tapping into the growing body of neurological evidence in the late-1990s, the same two authors produced their much acclaimed *Philosophy in the Flesh: The Embodied Mind and its Challenge to Western Thought* (1999). Over its 600 pages, the authors argue that not only is the mind fully integral to our biological organism, but that our acts of reflection about the world — our very process of thinking — are "crucially shaped by our bodies and brains, especially by our sensorimotor system."[22] The underlying idea here is that while language is a rather late development of *Homo sapiens,* earlier humans and even earlier species of hominids, over the course of millions of years, were able to make weapons, aim and throw spears, and establish camps for hunts and other migrations. These neurological circuits relating to force, movement, and direction were the same circuits that language eventually took over to fashion more complex (yet still often corporeally related) concepts.

Also in the 1990s the biologist Francisco Varela and the philosopher Evan Thompson collaborated on a model of consciousness that they called "radical embodiment", which sought to draw intersubjectivity (made possible by the discovery of mirror neurons) into the embodied equation of organismic regulation and the sensorimotor coupling of neocortical and subcortical structures of the brain. The key point is that "the processes crucial for consciousness cut across the brain-body-world divisions rather than being located simply in the head."[23] In a more recent study, *Mind in Life* (2007), Thompson has drawn upon sources in molecular biology, evolutionary theory, complexity theory, neuroscience, and cognitive psychology to fashion an approach that he calls neurophenomenological. Thus the ghost of Husserl still lingers, but this is not what you might call your father's phenomenology. Nevertheless such contemporary evidence, along with the research carried out over the last two decades along a score of other scientific fronts, hold enormous implications for architecture — ramifications for which we, limited by space to just a few instances, can now turn.

5.

In 1976 the British geographer Jay Appleton published a small book entitled *The Experience of Landscape.* In surveying both landscape paintings and 18th-century picturesque gardens, he noted their general focus on a few themes — open grassland with scattered clumps of trees, water, high ground for "prospect" as well as protected areas or shelters for "refuge". He speculated that there might be a biological basis for this preference, and that people might "relate pleasurable sensations in the experience of landscape to environmental conditions favourable to biological survival."[24] A few years later, and working from his own research, the biologist Gordon H. Orians noted the very same thing.[25] In conducting studies on the park systems on various continents, he too was struck by the similarity of landscapes that people tend to visit to find peace and relaxation. Orians concluded that we relax in these settings simply because our brains, molded by millions of years of survival on African savannahs, are biologically at home in them. In 1984, the sociobiologist Edward O. Wilson defined this inborn affiliation that we have with nature as "biophilia".[26]

The work of Appleton, Orians, Wilson, and others coalesced in the early 1990s into the new field of evolutionary psychology. The premises of this field, as articulated by three of its founders, are interesting:

1) Within universal human nature there are genetically evolved components or psychological mechanisms of behavior;

2) These mechanisms are adaptations formed over long periods of evolutionary time;

3) The present-day human brain is largely a creation of the Pleistocene hunter-gatherer era (1.8 million to 12,000 years ago).[27]

With these simple tenets, the Standard Social Science Model, as they described it, was summarily tossed. All of this might seem incidental to architecture until we take into account a short study published in 1984. A young psychologist, Roger S. Ulrich, in analyzing the recovery rates of hospital patients who had undergone gall-bladder surgery, arranged forty-six patients of comparable health into two groups: one who had a view of stands of trees outside their window; the other who had a view of a brick wall. His finding startled the medical profession. The patients with the view of trees had fewer post-operative complaints, took fewer pain medications, and were discharged one day earlier than patients who had the view of the brick wall.[28] It seems that when someone places a potted plant on an urban window sill, it is more than a cultural affectation.

Biophilic design, not unrelated to evidence-based design, has now come to architecture. Initially, its defining characteristics were the abundant use of natural light, water, plants, views and vistas, green facades and roofs, and landscapes restored to more natural conditions. Literally, it is a greener architecture, and this is especially true at an urban scale, where many cities are today actively extending forested or other green areas into or near their downtown areas. The health benefits for urban residents having regular contact with nature are now well documented: reduction of stress and blood pressure, enhanced attention and focus, and — not surprisingly — a happier outlook on life.[29]

Research regarding biophilic design, first applied to healthcare and school design, has since expanded its horizons into other building types. The topics of investigation have similarly expanded. In one recent book, for instance, architects and researchers considered such themes as order and complexity, curiosity and enticement, sensory variability, patterned wholes, fractals, biomimicry, ornament, scale, and proportion.[30] In some ways these topics resemble a second-coming of the early work of Christopher Alexander, except that now — as with Alexander's later work — the basis is biological rather than sociological. This is not to say that this new field of biophilic design is either fixed in its parameters or does not have its critics.[31] Nevertheless, it has already in a rather quiet way revolutionized the way many designers approach problems. Hospital design, for instance, has become a highly specialized field requiring familiarity with the extensive research studies, and deaths from such things as incidental infections are now being dramatically reduced where such research is applied.

6.

If evolutionary psychologists have in recent years weighed in on such issues as ornament, proportions, and the experience of art, it is interesting that many of the same issues have also come to the fore within the neurosciences. The term "neuroaesthetics" was first coined by the neurobiologist Semir Zeki in 1999, and over the past decade he has been joined in his MRI studies of aesthetic issues by teams of researchers across the globe. Zeki made his reputation with his decades of work on unraveling the workings of the brain's visual cortex. His research, together with that of others, has brought to light the fact that the visual cortex (within the brain's occipital lobe) takes its stream of stimuli off the optic nerve, separates it into such components as lines, shapes, colors, and motion, and then disperses this data to other areas specialized in processing these attributes. There are additional processing areas of the brain, as we have recently learned, that respond only to faces, others only to human bodies, and still others to landscapes and buildings. Two things about this new visual model are remarkable. One is that nowhere in the brain are the components of our images ever put back together, and, second, the processing of these disparate elements is not entirely synchronous in time. Locations, for example, are perceived before color, which is perceived before form, motion, or orientation. Where, then, resides our consciousness or sense of a "now"?

Zeki takes a biological line with respect to art. If the brain has the Darwinian task of acquiring knowledge about the world to ensure our survival, then artistic behavior must be an extension of this task. And if the role of the brain is to seek out those permanent and characteristic properties of objects, art must in some way exploit this "parallel-processing perceptual system" of the brain. Hence, and with shades of Richard Neutra, he reports that "there can be no satisfactory theory of aesthetics that is not neurobiologically based."[32]

Zeki has written extensively on art — too extensively to be discussed in detail here. He has considered Wagnerian opera, the sculptures of Michelangelo, and the paintings of Vermeer, Cézanne, Mondrian, and Malevich. With regard to the last two artists he was one of the first to recognize that not only were they often describing their efforts in quasi-biological terms but they were also intuitively exploiting the neurological workings of the human brain. In Mondrian's case, we now know that certain neurons respond only to vertical or horizontal lines, and these areas are distinct from those that respond to the diagonal lines favored by Malevich. In speaking of how the brain processes forms, Zeki has also resurrected the term *Einfühlung*, which he defines as that "link between the 'pre-existent' forms within the individual and the forms in the outside world which are reflected back."[33]

Such a statement should seem startling, if only because it reminds us of Alberti. Is our sense of beauty truly inborn and universal? Do we in fact have a biological propensity for certain forms? And if so, how are these propensities mediated by how the individual artist develops particular areas of the brain? In Berlin, for example, we have two buildings close in time and place: Hans Scharoun's Philharmonic Hall, and Ludwig Mies van der Rohe's New National Gallery. Both architects came to prominence within a narrow circle in the early 1920s, and both worked with similar vocabularies at the Weißenhof exhibition of 1927. Yet why did Mies (with obvious De Stijl influence) design exclusively with straight rectilinear lines and scarcely any suggestion of interior space, while Scharoun composed with forceful parabolic lines and a decidedly different sense of space? Would a MRI have been able to discern differences within their neural structures? Such questions are not far from being definitively answered, and Zeki even goes so far as to suggest that certain proportions may be biologically preferred.[34] Still another team of neuroscientists have recently argued from their studies that the golden ratio does indeed evoke a distinct neurological footprint.[35]

The field of neuroaesthetics has exploded, entirely in line with the proliferation of the new scanning technologies across the globe. Some teams are studying the details of our perceptual thinking, others the neurological processes implicated with aesthetic behavior, while still others are plotting the location and sequencing of the areas of the brain involved with artistic judgment and the perception of beauty. If much of this work has been focused on such traditional arts as painting and music (which can be accommodated by existing scanning technologies), research in how we experience or negotiate our built environments has also begun in a few instances. The architect who ignores this already rich bounty of research is turning his back on a treasury of themes now open for exploration.

7.

Neuroaesthetics is also not without its critics, and two criticisms in particular are of interest to us. One is the Western focus on what constitutes the nature of art, and the second is the fact that too much emphasis is being placed on the cognitive aspects of aesthetic judgments. For instance Ellen Dissanayake, who approaches the matter from an ethological or bioevolutionary perspective, argues that human aesthetic sensibilities were cultivated in pre-paleolithic phases

HARRY FRANCIS MALLGRAVE

of hominid evolution, and first appeared in ceremonies or rituals surrounding such events as birth, puberty, death, the warding off of evil, and good hunting. Such events, she argues, tend to short-circuit "cognitive labeling and classifying processes", and, as biological events, are rather grounded more in emotional than in conceptualized experience. She also invokes the idea of *Einfühlung* as an explanation for how it is that we somatically project or feel ourselves into artistic form.[36] In a related way, Nancy Aiken returns to Konrad Lorenz's idea of "fixed-action patterns" (reflexive behavior genetically triggered by certain stimuli) to explain the body's "releaser" response to the configuration of certain lines, shapes, colors, and sounds — once again calling to mind the theories of the early Bauhaus masters.[37]

Support for such views is also coming from neuropsychologists and new models of emotion. Lisa Barrett and a team of colleagues, for example, have recently proposed a theory of emotion derived from MRI studies, and it is important to note that we are defining "emotion" in a biological sense as "the process by which the brain determines or computes the value of a stimulus".[38] In Barrett's model, the process begins with a core emotional state of pleasure or displeasure centered in the brainstem and limbic area that largely precedes conscious activity. Once emotionally focused, the brain continues to process sensory information from the stimulus as well as somatic-visceral information from the body and produces — within the cerebral cortex — an affective conscious feeling bound to a particular situational meaning.

Two aspects of Barrett's model are particularly notable. One is the extent to which emotional activity floods the areas of the prefrontal cortex — the long presumed, privileged seat of "reason". Second is the discovery of two disassociative but interdependent neural streams of emotional activity, which also, and not coincidentally, are involved with aesthetic judgments. Without going into the details of the brain's anatomy, they involve two areas of the prefrontal cortex, two older areas of the cortex buried deep within the brain and often described as parts of the paralimbic system (the insula and anterior cingulate cortex), and the amygdala (an emotional module within the limbic system).[39] Such a model suggests that not only might we largely evaluate our built environments at a precognitive level but also that our conscious reflection of what we experience is strongly biased by these emotional responses.

This model has to be considered in line with another remarkable discovery of the last few years — that of "mirror neurons". In the early 1990s a team of Italian scientists, led by Giacomo Rizzolatti and Vittorio Gallese, were probing the brains of macaques with electrodes in the effort to map cortical activity involved with such simple actions as picking up an object. They found this pattern but they also found something else, which was that this pattern of neural activity appeared not only in monkeys engaged in the act but also in other monkeys who were simply watching their companions pick up the object. What they discovered — a fact since documented with an abundance of follow-up studies — is that the primate brain, and most particularly the human brain, comes equipped with pre-programmed neural templates that allow us, in a precognitive and embodied way, to recognize the actions of others by rehearsing or simulating their activities in our own sensorimotor cortex (the area of the brain involved with the movement and sensations of our bodies).[40] These templates are groups of neurons that fire in unison in parts of the occipital, temporal, and parietal lobes, but most especially in the premotor cortex of the frontal lobe. If I watch you dig a hole or play piano, the same neural areas that are active for you are also active in my brain, the more so if I have dug a hole before or know how to play piano. And, as has now become clear from further studies, I not only simulate your motor activity but also discern the intentions behind your activity through my neural simulation.[41]

Mirror neuron systems have since, quite fittingly, been endowed with the appellation "empathy theory", in honor of Robert Vischer. And the latter's aesthetic definition of the term in 1871 as a projection of our "own bodily form — and with this also the soul — into the form of an object" remains substantially correct, if we accept the fact that the form of an object actually does reside in our neocortex.[42] The discovery of mirror neurons has also been used to explain a number of other things, everything from the conceptual origin of language to the particular metaphoric structure of language of which Lakoff and Johnson spoke. The noted neurologist V. S. Ramachandran has argued that the human refinement of the mirror-neuron system, the ability to mime internally the complex actions of others, led to that "great leap forward" of our Cro-Magnon ancestors. In his words, "I think that, somewhere around 50,000 years ago, maybe the mirror neurons system became sufficiently sophisticated that there was an explosive evolution of this ability to mime complex actions, in turn leading to the cultural transmission of information, which is what characterizes us humans."[43]

Gallese has since offered an "interactionist" theory of meaning, which can only be described as yet another assault on one of the more sacred foundations of Western philosophy — the presumption that abstract thought is a distinct representational activity unique to human beings and bound to language. The starting point of his argument is the biological premise that we, like all other living matter, are organisms exposed to environmental energies (mechanical, electromagnetic, and chemical stimuli), which our sensory responses to the world (tactile, audio, olfactory, and visual systems) transduce into action potentials of neural clusters (the firing of neural maps in different regions of the brain), similar to the way the mirror-neuron system evolved. The biological reason for such systems is the organism's need to create informational codes or what Gallese also calls "control strategies", which model the interaction between the organism and the environment. This neurological coupling of objects or environments with events allows us simultaneously to perceive and store knowledge. The challenge of neuroscience in this regard is to explain "how the localized patterns of activation of different neural cortical networks can enable the capacity to distinguish, recognize, categorize and, ultimately, conceptualize objects, events and state of affairs in the real world."[44]

This would seem to be an ambitious task, but already several brain-imaging experiments related to the mirror-neuron system are suggesting answers to the problem. One of the key findings is that the recognition of man-made objects (including our constructed habitats) takes place not only in the object-recognition areas of the occipito-temporal cortex but also in areas of the motor cortex that were earlier presumed to be involved only with the control of action and not the representation of objects. This suggests that such factors as how the objects are to be handled, manipulated, and used "appear to comprise a substantial part of their representational coding".[45] We perceive and conceptualize such objects through our body actions, and moreover, "the same *sensorimotor* circuits that control the ongoing activity of the organism within its environment also map objects and events in that very same environment, thus defining and shaping their representational content".[46] What this means is that perception (a firing of cross-modal neural patterns) is already an abstraction of an object's use value, what Mark Johnson has called "a model of and a model for possible experience and action". Concepts, Johnson goes on to say, "have to be understood as the various possible patterns of activation by which we can mark significant characteristics of our experience".[47] If some apes also have the sensorimotor ability to associate certain tools with use, then it must also be conceded that they too have this presumably "higher" cognitive power of conceptualization. Saying this in a simpler way, perceiving (as the Gestalt psychologists long ago realized) is thinking.

Gallese, in collaboration with the art historian David Freedberg, has also applied his neurobiology to the artistic experience and the results not surprisingly challenge many of our assumptions — specifically, "the primacy of cognition in responses to art. We propose that a crucial element of aesthetic response consists of the activation of embodied mechanisms encompassing the simulation of actions, emotions and corporeal sensation, and that these mechanisms are universal."[48] Their argument once again takes us back to empathy-theory, and in its own way validates what Friedrich Schiller was suggesting many years ago when he noted that the object of the play impulse is "living form", that is, sensuous form combined with reason.[49] Because we have the ability with our mirror neurons "to pre-rationally make sense of the actions, emotions and sensations of others" — motor simulation and emotional resonance must be primary, not secondary, to the artistic experience. If we come upon a twisted Romanesque column, as Theodor Lipps noted a century ago, our bodies respond emotionally (in a somatic and visceral act of simulation) as if we ourselves were twisting. The taut profile of a Doric column encourages us to stand upright, as Heinrich

Wölfflin might have said. Such an outlook does not preclude the relevance of cultural factors in the understanding or appreciation of artistic form, but it profoundly calls into question many of the aesthetic premises of both modern and postmodern theory, which were intentionally abstract or disembodied.

Such a realization also provides us with a good moment to conclude this essay. Architects in recent years have enjoyed quoting themselves, their decentered conditions, their political angst, and of course Palladio or Schinkel. No one will deny them the judicious exercise of their play instincts and intra-professional gamesmanship. But architects sometimes need to be reminded that people do not experience their buildings in these highly conceptualized ways. If neuroscience has taught us anything about ourselves over the past two decades, it is the fact that we are multi-sensory, embodied beings who, like all living organisms, take in the world in much more holistic and visceral way. The same is true for architecture — as the work of someone like Peter Zumthor will surely attest. When the visual cortex begins the processing of an image, as MRIs demonstrate, the tactile areas of the somatosensory cortex become activated. When we hear a distant cough in a Gothic cathedral, we form a sense of the room's spatial dimension and stimulate activity in the parahippocampal areas. When sunlight filters through a well-placed window, we feel an increase in our body's vitality, as anyone recovering from an illness can attest. These are ageless lessons that too easily, it seems, get lost from view in our world of abstract form-making or in the often comic-book realism of our virtual renderings. Yet they are essential lessons bound to our health and well-being; this is the new quintessential fact of our biological age.

HARRY FRANCIS MALLGRAVE

NOTES

1   The German literature on Hellerau is vast. See, in particular, Wolf DOHRN, *Die Gartenstadt Hellerau,* Jena: Eugen Diederichs, 1908 · Hans-Jürgen SARFERT, *Hellerau. Die Gartenstadt und Künstlerkolonie,* Dresden: Hellerau-Verlag, 1995 · Karl Lorenz, *Wege nach Hellerau. Auf den Spuren der Rhythmik,* Dresden: Hellerau-Verlag 1994.

2   See Marco DE MICHELIS, "Modernity and Reform, Heinrich Tessenow and the Institut Dalcroze at Hellerau", translated by Vicki Bilenker, in: *Perspecta,* VOL. 26, 1990, pp. 143–170.

3   Émile JAQUES-DALCROZE, "Rhythm as a Factor in Education", translated by P. and E. Ingham, in: *The Eurhythmics of Jaques-Dalcroze,* Introduction by M. E. SADLER, Boston: Small Maynard and Company, 1913, pp. 15–25, here p. 18.

4   Ibid., p. 21.

5   M. E. SADLER, "The Educational Significance of Hellerau", in: *The Eurhythmics of Jaques-Dalcroze,* pp. 11–14, here p. 11.

6   Michael T. H. SADLER, "The Value of Eurhythmics to Art", in: *The Eurhythmics of Jaques-Dalcroze,* pp. 60–64, here pp. 63–64.

7   See László MOHOLY-NAGY, *Von Material zu Architektur,* Munich: Albert Langen, 1929 (reprint: Mainz and Berlin: Florian Kupferberg, 1968) · MOHOLY-NAGY, *Vision in Motion,* Chicago: Paul Theobald, 1947.

8   Richard NEUTRA, *Survival through Design,* New York: Oxford University Press, 1954, p. 118.

9   Ibid., p. 244.

10   VITRUVIUS, *De architectura,* III.1,1.

11   Leon Battista ALBERTI, *On the Art of Building in Ten Books,* translated by Joseph Rykwert, Neil Leach, and Robert Tavernor, Cambridge, MA and London: The MIT Press, 1988, p. 303.

12   Claude PERRAULT, *Les dix livres d'architecture de Vitruve,* second, revised edition, Paris: Jean Baptiste Coignard, 1684, p. 79 note 16.

13   Julien-David LE ROY, *Histoire de la disposition et des formes différentes que les Chrétiens ont données à leurs Temples, depuis le Règne de Constantin le Grand, jusqu'à nous,* Paris: Desaint & Saillant, 1764, pp. 59–63. The passages were later included in the second edition of *Les Ruines des plus beaux monuments de la Grece* (Paris: Louis-François Delatour, 1770).

14   Edmund BURKE, "A Philosophical Inquiry into the Origin of Our Ideas of the Sublime and Beautiful", in: *The Works of Edmund Burke,* 6 VOLS., here VOL. 1, London: George Bell & Sons, 1913, p. 121.

15   Uvedale PRICE, *Essays on the Picturesque as Compared with the Sublime and the Beautiful,* London: J. Mawman, 1810, 3 VOLS., VOL. 1, p. 87.

16   Goerd PESCHKEN, *[Karl Friedrich Schinkel.] Das architektonische Lehrbuch,* Berlin: Deutscher Kunstverlag, 1979, p. 150.

17   Karl BÖTTICHER, *Die Tektonik der Hellenen,* 3 VOLS., Potsdam: Ferdinand Riegel, 1852.

18   Wolfgang KÖHLER, *Dynamics in Psychology,* New York: Washington Square Press, 1965, p. 62.

19   Maurice MERLEAU-PONTY, *The Visible and the Invisible,* edited by Claude LEFORT, translated by Alphonso Lingis, Evanston: Northwestern University Press, 1968, p. 138.

20   Ibid., p. 248.

21 Gerald M. Edelman, *Wider Than the Sky. A Phenomenal Gift of Consciousness,* New Haven and London: Yale University Press, 2004, p. 156.

22 George Lakoff and Mark Johnson, *Philosophy in the Flesh. The Embodied Mind and its Challenge to Western Thought,* New York: Basic Books, 1999, p. 22.

23 Evan Thompson and Francisco J. Varela, "Radical Embodiment. Neural Dynamics and Consciousness", in: *Trends in Cognitive Sciences,* vol. 5, 2001, pp. 418–425, here p. 424.

24 Jay Appleton, *The Experience of Landscape,* London, New York, Sydney, and Toronto: John Wiley & Sons, 1975, p. vii.

25 Gordon H. Orians, "Habitat Selection. General Theory and Applications to Human Behavior", in: *The Evolution of Human Social Behavior,* edited by Joan S. Lockard, New York: Elsevier, 1980, pp. 49–66; and "An Ecological and Evolutionary Approach to Landscape Aesthetics," in: *Landscape Meanings and Values,* edited by Edmund C. Penning-Rowsell and David Lowenthal, London: Allen and Unwin, 1986, pp. 3–22.

26 Edward O. Wilson, *Biophilia. The Human Bond with Other Species,* Cambridge, MA and London: Harvard University Press, 1984.

27 See *The Adapted Mind. Evolutionary Psychology and the Generation of Culture,* edited by Jerome H. Barkow, Leda Cosmides, and John Tooby, Oxford, New York, etc: Oxford University Press, 1992, p. 5.

28 Roger S. Ulrich, "View through a Window May Influence Recovery from Surgery", in: *Science,* vol. 224, 1984, pp. 420–421.

29 The scientific body literature here is immense. Some of the better studies are Stephen Kaplan and Rachel Kaplan, *Cognition and Environment. Functioning in an Uncertain World,* New York: Praeger, 1982 · Gordon H. Orians and Judith H. Heerwagen, "Evolved Responses to Landscapes", in: *The Adapted Mind. Evolutionary Psychology and the Generation of Culture,* edited by Jerome H. Barkow, Leda Cosmides, and John Tooby, New York: Oxford University Press, 1992, pp. 555–579 · Roger S. Ulrich, "Biophilia, Biophobia, and Natural Landscapes", in: *The Biophilia Hypothesis,* edited by Stephen R. Kellert and Edward O. Wilson, Washington, DC: Island Press, 1993, pp. 73–137 · Stephen Kaplan, "The Restorative Benefits of Nature. Toward an Integrative Framework", in: *Journal of Environmental Psychology,* vol. 15, 1995, pp. 169–82 · Rachel Kaplan, Stephen Kaplan, and Robert Ryan, *With People in Mind. Design and Management of Everyday Nature,* Washington: Island Press, 1998 · Rachel Kaplan, "The Nature of the View from Home. Psychological Benefits", in: *Environment and Behavior,* vol. 33, 2001, pp. 507–542 · Agnes E. van den Berg, Terry Hartig, and Henk Staats, "Preference for Nature in Urbanized Societies. Stress, Restoration, and the Pursuit of Sustainability", in: *Journal of Social Issues,* vol. 63, 2007, pp. 79–96, here p. 91.

30 Stephen R. Keller, Judith H. Heerwagen, and Martin L. Mador, *Biophilic Design. The Theory, Science, and Practice of Bringing Buildings to Life,* New York: John Wiley & Sons, 2008. See also Stephen S. Kellert, *Building for Life. Designing and Understanding the Human-Nature Connection,* Washington, DC: Island Press, 2005.

31 See especially Jaak Panksepp and Jules B. Panksepp, "The Seven Sins of Evolutionary Psychology", in: *Evolution and Cognition,* vol. 6, 2000, pp. 108–131.

32 Semir Zeki, "Artistic Creativity and the Brain", in: *Science,* vol. 293, 2001, pp. 51–52.

33 Semir Zeki, *Inner Vision. An Exploration of Art and the Brain,* Oxford: Oxford University Press, 1999, p. 104.

34 Ibid., pp. 104–116.

35 See Cinzia Di Dio, Emiliano Macaluso, and Giacomo Rizzolatti, "The Golden Beauty: Brain Response to Classical and Renaissance Sculptures", in: *PLoS One,* vol. 2, 2007.

36 Ellen Dissanayake, "Aesthetic Experience and Human Evolution", in: *Journal of Aesthetics and Art Criticism,* vol. 42, 1982, no. 2, p. 152. See her chapter on this theme in *Homo Aestheticus: Where Art Comes From and Why,* Seattle: University of Washington Press, 1992.

37 Nancy E. Aiken, *The Biological Origins of Art,* Westport, CT: Praeger, 1998.

38 Joseph LeDoux, *Synaptic Self. How Our Brains Become Who We Are,* New York: Penguin, 2002, p. 206.

39 See Lisa Feldman Barrett, Batja Mesquita, Kevin N. Ochsner, and James J. Gross, "The Experience of Emotion", in: *Annual Review of Psychology,* vol. 58, 2007, pp. 373–403. See Oshin Vartanian's discussion of Barrett's model in "Conscious Experience of Pleasure in Art", in: *Neuroaesthetics,* edited by Martin Skov and Oshin Vartanian, Amityville, NY: Baywood Publishing, 2009, pp. 264–270.

40 The original paper of the discovery was published in 1992. For a more recent recounting of the discovery, see Giacomo Rizzolatti and Laila Craighero, "The Mirror-Neuron System", in: *Annual Review of Neuroscience,* vol. 27, 2004, pp. 169–187.

41 Giacomo Rizzolatti, Leonardo Fogassi, and Vittorio Gallese, "Mirror in the Mind", in: *Scientific American,* vol. 295, no. 5, November 2006, pp. 54–61.

42 Robert Vischer, "On the Optical Sense of Form", in: *Empathy, Form, and Space. Problems in German Aesthetics, 1873–1893,* edited by Harry Francis Mallgrave and Eleftherios Ikonomou, Santa Monica: Getty Publications Program, 1994, p. 92.

43 V. S. Ramachandran, *A Brief Tour of Human Consciousness,* New York: Pi Press, 2004, p. 38.

44 Vittorio Gallese, "A Neuroscientific Grasp of Concepts. From Control to Representation", in: *Philosophical Transactions of the Royal Society of London,* vol. 358, 2003, p. 1234.

45 Ibid., p. 1235.

46 Ibid., p. 1236.

47 Mark Johnson, *The Meaning of the Body. Aesthetics of Human Consciousness,* Chicago: University of Chicago Press, 2007, p. 159.

48 David Freedberg and Vittorio Gallese, "Motion, Emotion and Empathy in Esthetic Experience", in: *Trends in Cognitive Sciences,* vol. 11, 2007, pp. 197–203.

49 See the 15th letter of Friedrich Schiller's *The Aesthetic Education of Man: A Series of Letters,* first published in 1795.

IMAGES

Based on photographs taken from: *The Eurhythmics of Jaques-Dalcroze,* Introduction by M. E. Sadler, Boston: Small Maynard and Company, 1913, unnumbered plates facing pp. 60 and 64, respectively.

PAOLO SANVITO

The Building as a Living Work of Art in the Time of Cosimo Fanzago

ILLUSTRATIVE AND FIGURATIVE VERSUS VITALISTIC AND ORGANICISTIC CONCEPTS
OF ARCHITECTURE AT THE THRESHOLD BETWEEN RENAISSANCE AND BAROQUE

> "Se tu haueßi ueduto l'Aurora di Michel Agnolo,
> laquale non ha il Diauolo dentro come gli antichi idoli"
> Anton Francesco DONI, *Disegno,* 1549, 11r

> "Uti in hominis corpore e cubito pede palmo digito ceterisque particulis symmetros est
> eurythmiae qualitas, sic est in operum perfectionibus."
> VITRUVIUS, I.2,4

INTRODUCTION: THE POLARITY FIGURATION/VITALISM AT THE ORIGIN OF WESTERN ART

This essay aims to show how, in the early modern period, a paradigmatic change in architectural sculpture, stemming from its vitalistic and animistic interpretation, contributed to invigorate and, in more than a metaphorical sense, animate late cinquecento and baroque ornamentation. Later in the 17th century, this turnabout would lead to an unprecedented general and decisive re-vision of European architecture as dominated by organicism and vitalism.

In 15th-century art theory a normative definition of architecture according to vitalistic and animistic principles was based primarily on the assumption that the building material — metals or mud, for example — was infused with the life of the natural universe. In Vitruvius' much-commented treatise, which heavily influenced the positions of 15th-century theory, this assumption had been clearly expressed with specific regard to the typology of the temple, where straw

IN / KIRSTEN WAGNER AND JASPER CEPL (EDITORS) /
IMAGES OF THE BODY IN ARCHITECTURE: ANTHROPOLOGY AND BUILT SPACE /
TÜBINGEN · BERLIN / ERNST WASMUTH VERLAG / 2014 / PP. 227–262

or live plants are involved as such material.[1] Even Heinrich Wölfflin followed this interpretation in his dissertation of 1886. When analyzing plant decoration in capitals, he asserted that the column "widens at the top, because its function is to take on weight [from above], with the widest surface, and not because of pressure."[2]

According to this theoretical tradition the affinity of primitive buildings to nature was necessarily determined by their construction materials: wood, straw, bones, or other organic fragments, clay, etc., or even entire animals, which might have been attached to them, whether alive or dead. In fact, from the age of ancient Mediterranean civilizations animal corpses, plants, and trophies had, as a matter of course, been fixed to buildings, not just as decoration, but often with ritual intent (for instance, various body parts of the sacred bull were used in Minoan buildings of Crete; the same animal became sacred to Hera in classical Greece). Similarly, as late as the early 16th century, the humanistic physician Paracelsus understood some forms of life to be contained in such forms of matter as salt, precious stones, gems, metals, minerals, roots, aromatic substances, resin, bones, water etc.[3] What can be recognized in Paracelsus is what August Riekel has called the "panpsychic trend of cinquecento philosophy, as Cusanus already enunciates it, as continued exemplarily by Bernardino Telesio (Bruno was one of his adepts) and which reaches its climax with Paracelsus and Bruno."[4] Panpsychism "found a place in his system for the ubiquitous *spiritus*" and thus "provided a new theoretical basis (with precedents in Presocratic and Stoic thought) for the cosmic vitalism that had always been prominent in the occultist worldview."[5] For Girolamo Cardano all objects were also endowed with a soul, but only the "higher forms" (i.e. mankind) possessed at the same time spirit (*mens*).[6]

In addition, in early modern popular, 'folkloric', or magical thought, still current among early modern philosophical circles, buildings were assumed to embody the same vigor which had been breathed into man by the act of divine creation. But the popular or traditional link of architecture to natural matter is neither crucial nor sufficient enough for explaining the general cultural shift of the early modern era towards the vivification or vitalization of architectural works. There are more profound driving forces at work. Important among these was the neo-platonic view of artistic creation as a divine act: the act of giving life *par excellence*; of giving motion to inanimate objects. Indeed, already in the 15th century, art theory mirrored theology in linking the production of *any* architectural artefact to divine creation, *a fortiori* with regard to clay, air, watercourses, or wells. Accordingly, a building, even if not sacred and consecrated, could become endowed with a limited level of earthly life (in most cases, apparently, with *anima,* though not with *mens,* if we recall Cardano's view).

Georg Weise, one of Aby Warburg's closest disciples (an acquaintance from the latter's influential appointment at the University of Hamburg) was perhaps

PAOLO SANVITO

the first art historian, during and immediately after World War II, who tried to link the gestural repertoires of quattrocento and cinquecento architecture to those of international Gothic,[7] especially in northern and central Europe, where the gothic style was of particularly long duration. His *Manierismo* of 1971, of course, had an impact on Barasch's seminal *Gestures of Despair* of 1976 and even, indirectly, on Marchand's more recent *Gebärden in der Florentiner Malerei* of 2004.[8]

Since then, much contemporary research has focused on the challenge of representing or reproducing life from the animal world, or from the realm of nature, in the artistic research of the early modern period. However, the present investigation does not address the problem of how, or where, or why the realistic, figurative character of art works of that period is sometimes more, sometimes less obvious. Indeed, renaissance artists always remained free to keep the fictional representation of life at an arbitrary level. A wide range of disparate illustrative versus vitalistic responses to these issues is evident in the sculptural decoration at Bomarzo and Pratolino, for example, and in other sculpture cycles in similar complexes or earlier, in Guido Mazzoni's sculptured passion plays. Architectural treatises and monuments present an immense corpus of works dealing with the problem of fictional imitation. The interest of this paper, on the contrary, is to address works, realistic or not, which were intended as an emanation of the supra-ordinate intelligence of an ultra-mundane soul and thus, in their essence, were pervaded by it. Exemplary in this respect are many early works by Michelangelo, whose neo-platonic education during his early youth in Florence must be considered neither coincidental nor tangential.[9] But Michelangelo was only the first of an important lineage of architects who dealt with their buildings in terms of life-embodiment.

The early modern organicist vision of architecture could be seen as anticipating today's *human ecology*. It is in closer harmony with an architecture deeply preoccupied with contemporary organic concerns than, say, Zuccari's generation of late-mannerist onomatopoetic-illustrative academicism. In fact, for more updated and inspiring reflections on the significance of a *New Organic Architecture,* I should refer to the comprehensive study of that title by David Pearson,[10] containing many examples from the time of the Viennese Secession onwards. The intuitive or preliminary stage of organicism before the advent of functionalism in the 20th century — a stage prior to the recent 'human ecological' one — refers to the intimate relationship between both the living person and the artificial product of human crafts to their natural environment. This is already present in high renaissance aesthetics, where the artistic or architectural work is considered as one of the infinite components of a living world. Thus, it is possible to see Michelangelo's generation, and a large deal of early cinquecento culture, as presenting something of a unique occasion for innovatively addressing environmental questions concerning the relationship of a building to its environs. However, this would involve further fundamental issues of architectural theory, either early modern or contemporary, which could be the task of a further investigation, independent from the present one.[11]

What Michelangelo has possibly introduced to Western art for the first time is the definition of architectural sculpture as a metaphorical "living skin" applied to the building body, or *corpo della fabbrica* (as it is tellingly called in Italian); a view which found many followers. According to Alina Payne, one of the most prominent was Palladio, in whose oeuvre "the ornamental screen is understood to swell and contract as if it were a muscle."[12] When addressing this specific phenomenon in Michelangelo's work, however, we are confronted with a flood of representations of the face or of masks on the surfaces of his buildings. They mostly grin at the viewer, with an intense expression and flashing gaze, as for example in the pediment of the Chapel at Castel Sant'Angelo's *Cortile d'onore* (a chapel which has been already defined as "facelike").[13] Sometimes this motif receives a peculiar satyric-demonic spirit or seal with connotations of evil, as it does in the mask of a drawing for the tomb of Julius II (London, British Museum 1895–9–15–496c). One can surely attribute such masks and gestures partially

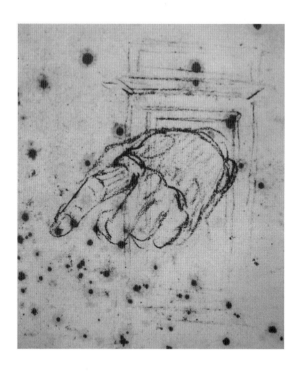

1
MICHELANGELO
BUONARROTI /
"HAND" IN THE
SOCLE FOR
THE RICETTO /
LAURENZIANA
LIBRARY /
DRAWING /
CASA
BUONARROTI
FLORENCE

to Michelangelo's typically intense striving either for a dynamic of form or for tortured expressive force, for instance in his drawing (FIG. 1) of a hand in the

PAOLO SANVITO

socle for the Laurenziana or in a frieze of masks by his pupil Silvio Cosini, in Michelangelo's New Sacristy (**FIG. 2**). But something similar can also be found

2
SILVIO COSINI
/ FRIEZE
OF MASKS /
INNER WALL /
FLORENCE/ NEW
SACRISTY

in the drawings of many representative architectural handbooks and treatises throughout Europe. One example is Serlio, whose work has been widely investigated. But also in the treatises of some of his less-studied followers in France, after Fontainebleau, one can find comparable solutions for the same problem, as in the publication by the sculptor Hugues Sambin on *Termes,* i.e. Caryat-

3
HUGUES
SAMBIN / *OEVVRE
DE LA DIVERSITE
DES TERMES,
DONT ON VSE EN
ARCHITECTURE,
REDUICT
EN ORDRE* /
1572 / FIG. 1
("PORTRAIT
DU 1. TERME")
AND FIG. 14
("PORTRAIT DU
14. TERME")

ids, published in 1572 (**FIG. 3**).[14] Slightly later portal models by Wendel Dietterlin seem also comparable — almost overcharged with great populations of living creatures, as in his so-called *Toscana* portal.[15] According to Manfredo Tafuri's inspiring interpretation, with Dietterlin animism indeed reached "the highest qualitative peak of monstrosity."[16] In such examples the ultimate frontier of formal experimentation is probably attained, at least in this historical period. Later, a new aesthetic would be based on different principles. In fact, it is possible to observe that by the end of the Cinquecento a decisive turn was taking place, a gradual but definitive rebound from the characteristic mannerist decorative style of Michelangelo and its followers, who by 1600 had almost all passed away.

In his Porta Pia, in 1561, Michelangelo still deliberately quotes the exuberant portals from Serlio's *Primo* and *Extraordinario Libro*;[17] and Buontalenti, Ammannati, and Cellini remain posthumously faithful to Michelangelo. Also the latter's typical *finestra inginocchiata* (kneeling window, first example 1517) shall continue to be reused and requoted among the followers: for example later in Palazzo Pitti, but also by the classicist Vignola in Casino di Villa Giulia; or by Ammannati in Palazzo Giugni (before 1577); by Buontalenti in Palazzo Non-

4
BERNARDO
BUONTALENTI /
WINDOW FROM
THE GROUND
FLOOR OF
PALAZZO
NONFINITO IN
BORGO DEGLI
ALBIZZI / 1593 /
FLORENCE /
ORIGINAL
DRAWING

finito in Borgo degli Albizzi after 1593 (**FIG. 4**). Buontalenti's Palazzo Serguidi with its several masks on the kneeling windows, including many bat- or dragon-like monsters, has also to be mentioned here. This repertoire should be compared for example with Buontalenti's great stair of the choir in S. Trinita,[18] with its bat form, today displaced and reconstructed in S. Stefano (**FIG. 5**). Giorgio Va-

5
STAIRS FROM
THE CHOIR IN
S. TRINITA /
RECONSTRUCTED
IN S. STEFANO /
FLORENCE

sari calls the upper volutes of the kneeling window *spallette* (little shoulders),[19] whereas the lower ones are referred to as legs. Francesco Bocchi later judges these windows as being "come le donne assai [=ad satis, enough] (sono) ornate, che contente della bellezza naturale sprezzano ogni ornamento esteriore", obviously, therefore, personifications of real women.

In art history, the iconographic formulas of masks with putto, satyr, or Eros faces are taken as trans-historical. Already present during the Middle Ages, they were continuously used throughout the period of the Baroque, for in-

stance in Francesco Borromini's vaults of the second, fourth, and extern naves in S. Giovanni in Laterano (**FIG. 6**). Even before the Baroque, particularly shortly after 1600 in Naples, they appeared especially in the work of Cosimo Fanzago,[20] with masks made of human faces — for instance in the cornice of the table of the main altar in Ss. Severino e Sossio and in the decoration of S. Maria di Costantinopoli (**FIG. 7**) — or of sirens' and satyrs' faces — see the fourth right chapel in

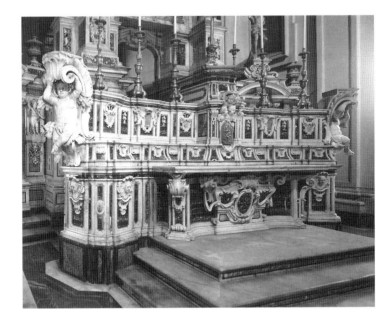

S. Maria delle Grazie a Caponapoli, by the Fanzaghian Francesco Pagano, dated 1715 (**FIG. 8**).[21] Already in Michelangelo's work the mask had not simply been a

grotesque or a combinatory element of a grotesque, because it was integrated by him into ornament as a living monster, ostentatiously pushing aside the illusion of something not living or exsanguinous (examples come from a set of drawings for Pope Julius della Rovere's monument). But the iconographic and stylistic formulas, minted and spread by Michelangelo's followers throughout the 16th as well as in the early 17th century, eventually mutated into a new international ornamental code, which changed the understanding of the function of these iconographies by only *seeming* to quote Michelangelo's ornamental vision, and indeed forcing it out of its own boundaries. In the course of that generation, the creation of new forms gave way to a simultaneous boom in the publication of handbooks or template-books, which codified ornamentation according to new formulas and principles (in the pattern books of Central Europe). This standardization of templates or models extended into the late 17th century, and necessarily entailed the phase of academicism and late classicism, which, around 1600–1630, immediately preceded the conventional development of baroque style in the 1630s. The codified ornamental vocabulary finds its systematic application before the conventional beginning of this style, for example in the Sebeto

Fountain, 1601 (**FIG. 9**), with Michelangelo Naccherino, either working alone or with Bernini's father Pietro (a veritable Tuscan on his turn, born in Sesto near Florence in 1562).

In fact, some of their work of this period would be developed later by Fanzago. Certain scholars also recognize the participation of the sculptor Girolamo D'Auria in Fanzago's projects,[22] but this complex cooperation of two workshops resulted moreover from the intense productivity of Fanzago's workshop itself. During his youth he had become acquainted with Florentine ornamentation, especially in Rome and after 1608 in Naples through the mediation of Pietro Bernini, one of his mentors.

Thus, on the one hand, his work must be referred back to the tradition of Michelangelo. On the other hand, however, in the early decades of the Seicento, he developed an innovative corpus of ornaments and architectural sculptural motifs, which, carried to their extremes, finally established a singular personal style, a stylistic *sphragís,* which at the same time became specific for a veritable artistic dynasty, the Fanzaguesque (Sebeto Fountain, or the later Monteoliveto Fountain (**FIG. 10**)) influencing further artistic workshops of the time, like those

10
COSIMO
FANZAGO AND
FRANCESCO
D'ANGELO /
MONTEOLIVETO
FOUNTAIN /
NAPLES /
AFTER 1668

of Domenico Antonio Vaccaro, Andrea Falcone, and Ercole Ferrata (in Naples, in S. Severino e Sossio, or in the Cappella Firrao in S. Paolo Maggiore, built in the 1640s by Vaccaro, and in further examples in Bari and Apulia).[23] It has been rightly suggested that, because of the expansion of the so-called "Spanish districts" to the west of the city centre at the turn of the 16th and 17th centuries, Naples was transformed into the largest and most relevant urban agglomeration in Italy, which obviously meant more available space for new art.[24] According to Weise, even the roots of the Southern German Baroque ornamentation are to be found in Fanzago's work.[25] There is no doubt that, at the end of the 16th and the beginning of the 17th century, Fanzago, along with other decorators, *invented* a style anew in Naples.

To describe this style, one might be tempted to adopt the same formula applied to architects of the French Revolution: *architecture parlante*. And yet, the disguise of physiognomical forms by masks, their antics and risible grimaces might lead one, rather, to speak of *architecture rigolante,* as indeed one could for the forms of the late Cinquecento. One might recall the *Fontana del Nettuno* in the convent of S. Martino, the pseudo-pediments of the door in the cloister courtyard and also in the entrance porch, dated much later (1623–1631), where we find the typology which Fanzago reuses to effect in the decoration of later large building enterprises, as, for example, at S. Maria degli Angeli alle Croci. Here the architectural surfaces appear as satyr-like laughing grimaces. Did Fanzago also intend them as such? But laughter and smiles can, of course, be accounted for in two entirely different ways: positively as attributes of joy or gladness; or negatively, as laughter with a malign, vicious, or dark source, related to demonic or other evil powers, or eventually to sadism, as partially expressed in the Italian lemma *riso amaro* (bitter laughter). Ernst Kris has often pointed out the significance and function of showing laughter, in art as well as psychology, as a specific "nature" mask provided by the human body under normal as well as under pathological conditions. This perspective makes the close tie between the mask and the representation of laughter obvious.[26]

Nowhere does the literature on Fanzago ever seem to have identified or analyzed the sources of his many new inventions. Are they still accessible, or must we assume absolute novelty for his work, entirely unrelated to earlier artists' models? If so, what was the source of his inspiration? It is unbelievable that, since the publication of Weise's many articles, not a single serious monograph has appeared in print, with exception of an overly general one on "Neapolitan Baroque *and* Cosimo Fanzago" *(Napoli barocca e Cosimo Fanzago)*.[27]

ART HISTORY IN THE TRADITION OF WARBURG AND WEISE AND ITS BACKLASH IN THE DECRYPTION OF ARCHITECTURAL ORNAMENT

In order to frame this stylistic change correctly, we should look at the ornamental style generally adopted after 1600, a style called *Ohrmuschelstil* in Central Europe (see Godfridt Müller's *Nevws Compertament Bvchlein* of 1621 or Friedrich Unteutsch's *Zieratenbuch* of 1650)[28] that, according to Erik Forssman, was essentially irrational and *antivitruvianisch*.[29] Weise, significantly, referred it back to Fanzago. Considering this style, ornament so entirely engulfed constructions that they dissolved in un-architectural altars and superficial wall decoration. Its formal and compositional principle was the decomposition of human body surfaces and flesh, of cartilages and muscles. Although represented, these are only recognizable when isolated as fragments. Two features of the *Ohrmuschelstil* are of particular relevance here. First, any naturalistic or realistic representation of bodies and facial characteristics is entirely abandoned (see Müller, *Bvchlein*, plate 1: instead of a face, intensely expressive eyes emerge from the ornament, with a piercing gaze remaining identifiable, as in the tradition of Michelangelo). Second, and unlike mannerist ornament, it is grounded far more deeply in organicism and naturalism, with a preference for representations of *"das Häßliche und Kranke"*[30] — the ugly and the sick, a phenomenon never seen before in earlier styles.[31] Later, in the fully baroque style after 1630, religious and mythological iconographies on the contrary remained, in keeping with the well-known normative repertoire of Mannerism.

The masks from this period could therefore even be used in 'laboratory experiments' for verifying the approach of 'neuroaesthetics', which today proposes to ground esthetical judgement in the anatomical, or rather in the neuronal structure of the body (see Harry Francis Mallgrave's contribution to this volume). Thus the constants of physiognomical configurations in figurative styles would be explainable by a specific correspondence of the viewer's reactions to the vividly sculptured glances, especially those of fright (see masks models, such as those published by Godfridt Müller, Friedrich Unteutsch, or Gabriel Krammer[32]). Forssman even argues that "female beauty" on the whole must have seemed "questionable" at the time, and that "hence one shortened the arms of naked figures to become volutes, ungainly bulged out the belly or depicted it as if opened up, tore up the thighs and treated them as mere muscular mass"; to him the *Ohrmuschelstil* shows the "struggle between Vitruvian rule and German will for expression" ("Kampf zwischen vitruvianischer Regel und germanischem Ausdruckswillen").[33] A certain nationalistic view adopted by German art historians, before or after the end of the Third Reich, may not be irrelevant to such peculiar critical visions (already mentioning the abused word *germanisch* had become somewhat controversial, even sometimes ominous, among German speakers around the world after 1945). Even the unimpeachable Wilhelm Worringer had claimed in 1908: "The German is [...] a born artist of expression."[34] (Whether such a statement is defensible is not the concern of this paper.) Forssman's explanations draw on the slogan of the time around 1600 as a "savaged and disorganized epoch"[35] to illustrate the context of such "decomposition" of the surface of human bodies. But he does not determine more precisely how, and why, and to which degree the epoch was "savaged" (apparently in a sociological and political sense). In any case, his arguments do not identify a historical context, nor even a causal explanation for all the phenomena he mentions. For him, monstrosity and menace are not explicable in terms of the prevailing cultural climate. He does not discuss the predominant dark (and for Weise at least partially occult) forces, which he assumes as the background of artistic trends.[36] But this was exactly what Weise (in the same years as Forssman!) was trying to do in a number of writings where he named ideological and political circumstances concerning the intellectual generation of around 1600, which could be taken as the root and origin of the artistic trends under discussion.[37] These were primarily the antinaturalistic and abstract decorative styles predominating through the 17th century. For examples, see the epitaph of Domenico Fontana in the atrium of S. Anna dei Lombardi, dated 1627, with two little protruding teeth,[38] and in the altar in S. Domenico Maggiore by Domenico Antonio Vaccaro.[39] Cherubs' wings transform themselves in volutes and melt into unique, completely fantastic shapes (very much like in Fanzago's fountains).

But in the period of Fanzago's maturity, during the 1640s and until his death in 1678, there is a turn in aesthetic orientation: Weise recognizes the advent of an artistic mentality "more refined, sentimental, and affectionate" in Naples.[40] For example the later altar decoration from S. Tommaso d'Aquino is doubtless "fanzaguesque", but probably only produced in his workshop and deeply rooted in it and characterized by such gentleness.[41] The "savage" forms are abandoned towards the maturity of the baroque style, which, as I demonstrated, acted at the same time as a neutralization of the *Ohrmuschelstil*.[42]

It is long overdue to recognize Weise's research as decisive for establishing new hermeneutical approaches in art history. Drawing to some extent on literary and theoretical sources, he demonstrated, perhaps systematically for the first time, how and to what extent the meanings and rationale of various architectural patterns — especially the anthropomorphization of things and beings of the natural world — were based on vitalistic and animistic ideas. He did this also on the score of theoretical sources of the early modern era: since his overt assertions on this subject in the essays on vitalism and panpsychism (1959 and 1960, see note 36), a vigorous branch of art theoretical reflection has taken up the question of animistic thought in artistic circles or has attributed its notions to some of the different styles spread in the Cinquecento and the Baroque. As already pointed out, this hermeneutical approach had a large impact on the research being done from the early 1960s to recent times on the High Renaissance and especially Michelangelo's architectural and sculptural ornamentation: for example, in Giulio Carlo Argan's *Il barocco in Francia, in Inghilterra, nei Paesi Bassi*; the thought-provoking conference *Manierismo, barocco, rococo: concetti e termini* (Rome 1960),[43] or in Tafuri's *Manierismo*.[44] Architecture and sculpture were thus considered to be inextricably intertwined and dominated by animistic significance, as certain contemporary cinquecento observations testify: those of a Florentine painter and theoretician, for instance, who wrote in 1509 that the aim of art was "to make a dead thing appear alive"[45]. Gian Paolo Lomazzo's treatise on painting, sculpture, and architecture, which stresses the importance of the use of anatomy and muscularity to express robustness, can be named here as well.[46]

The reception of some principles from ancient, especially Platonic, philosophy — like the idea of the world's soul, *anima mundi,* which sees the entire world as a unique, immense living being[47] — or their intricate elaborations, for example in Nicholas of Cusa, hint further back to the foundations of the early modern era in Florence, where animism found its first Italian formulations.[48] These concepts were further developed by Giordano Bruno and his generation, obviously by his contemporary Johannes Kepler and all the major early modern philosophers. According to Brian P. Copenhaver, Bruno "gave matter a privileged, divinised status"[49]: it is our task to find out where unequivocal positions in the philosophical writings, especially in the early Seicento, and how the arts, including poetry such as that of Giovan Battista Marino (1569–1625) and that of contemporary *petrarchismo,* responded to them.[50] In the Sonnet xciv, *Pianta gentil,* by Luigi Tansillo, a tree branch unbinds the golden hair lichens of the beloved mistress, but remains captured in them.[51]

Two or three decades before Weise, Warburg's teacher August Schmarsow had already laid the foundations for such interpretations, for instance in his *Grundbegriffe der Kunstwissenschaft* of 1905, where he postulated that architecture meant spatial creation "in terms of the spatial will" ("im Sinne des Raumwillens") of man, whose directional movement forward fundamentally determined the spatial experience of architecture.[52] There is, incidentally, a close correspondence between Schmarsow's spatial categories and the practice of renaissance architects, although his theories were in no way exclusively formulated to explain them, nor formulated in keeping with spatial visions that necessarily fall between 1400 and 1600.

Even in the same generation as Schmarsow, Wölfflin's 1886 dissertation had also addressed the psychological impact of architecture.[53] In Schmarsow's *Grundbegriffe* we also find an analysis of Michelangelo's gesture of chiselling as an intentional contrast to organically pulsing bodies. This transmission of ideas is explicable by the fact that Schmarsow's intuitions were crucial to Warburg's theories of emotion, including his famous concept of *Pathosformel.* Movement and emotion were obviously seen by these scholars as closely related to each other and later inspired Weise, who was a veritable *familiaris* of Warburg's research, particularly of his investigations of the emotional value of gestures in the early modern era. Living between Italy and Germany until 1978, he was able to continue and verify some of his teacher's theories especially concerning the art of the 17th century, which Warburg unfortunately had no occasion to investigate. We must finally acknowledge that an international dialog on animism in the arts has been dominant for several decades — especially in the theory and history of architecture (and obviously such trends were already acknowledged during the early phase at the Warburg Institute). One of its protagonists was Weise who, after his "rehabilitation" in the post-war period (the Nazis had marginalized him), with his extensive studies on Fanzago, Michelangelo, and the Baroque, also played the role of an intercultural mediator. Analyzing this international network of reciprocal influences could be worthwhile, but is far beyond the scope of this essay.

EVIDENCE FOR VITALISTIC IDEAS OF ART IN PHILOSOPHICAL WRITINGS. EARLY MODERN PNEUMATOLOGY AND COSMOLOGY

To find out more about philosophy's influence on the theory and practice of art before and around 1600, one has to consider the accordant writings in natural philosophy and especially cosmology. Concerning the vitalistic ideas that flourish in the artistic circles of that time, it also requires a close reading of the debate on new formulations in the field of pneumatology, the theory of languages, political theory, and theory about the structure of human sociality. Many aspects of the cultural and political climate around 1600 in Italy were extremely complex and multi-layered. An age of crisis and insecurity was beginning: the deep financial crisis hitting the Spanish Empire had begun to depress a great part of the country's pivotal provinces (Milan, the Kingdom of Naples, and Genoa, which was still independent, but acted as the official banker of the Spanish crown).

Artistic patterns of the time have been described, not least with regard to Fanzago, as "not only bizarre, [...] but also fearful and oppressive, an expression of occult and terrifying forces".[54] Such insights could make us assume a negative socio-political attitude in artists as well as in philosophers. Actually, this cultural disposition could be exemplified in the Sepolcro del Cavalier Marino in S. Domenico Maggiore (**FIG. 11**). The detail shows a sequence of monstrous skulls of demons, the façade of the monument itself consists of an enormous sea-monster mask. Just as in philosophy utopian societies did not exalt the *status quo,* depicting threatening and fearful subject matter on façades reflected a denunciation of negative positions, nihilistic thought, or fatalism. (Parenthetically, it is intriguing to consider that such positions might reveal a curious similarity to socio-political conditions in Italian society today and in some ways could be an encouragement to approaches and analytical strategies in current cultural studies).[55]

Significantly, Fanzago, who is universally recognized as having, for a while, played a key role in and outside of Italy, settled in Naples, living from time to time in the immediate vicinity of other key personalities like Bruno, Campanella (under arrest from 1600 on), Caravaggio, or Marino, who were explicitly de-nouncing the critical condition in which Italian culture and its reference models found themselves. For the latter Fanzago had to realize two (!) different sepul-chres, of which one is extant in Bruno's Dominican church (the already men-tioned **FIG. 11**). A couple of streets away, Giambattista della Porta wrote mainly

on physiognomy, physics, and pharmacology. He is the author of the impressive *De ea naturalis physiognomoniae parte quae ad manuum lineas spectat libri duo* (printed first in Strasbourg, 1606, and in Naples, 1614). His *Caelestis physiogno-mia,* which established an intimate relationship between the forms of the hu-man body and the shapes and movements of the planets and stars, appeared even earlier in Naples, namely in 1603. With this and other related writings he provided the theoretical ground for the development of contemporary, and even of later artistic studies of faces and grimaces and simultaneously assured its dif-fusion at large, since della Porta was closely related to the Accademia dei Lincei in Rome.[56]

Decades before the above mentioned art historical studies on baroque archi-tecture (by Weise, Tafuri, and others) which reflected this circulation of ideas between the artistic and philosophical circles of that time, Ernst Cassirer had al-ready familiarized Aby Warburg with Bruno's works. Later, in the last two years of his life, Warburg realized Bruno's importance both for cosmology *and* ico-nography; to him many decorative cycles in Naples at least testified that Bruno's presence must have influenced the artistic trends of the time.[57] However, several studies on this subject are about to appear, whose conclusions can hardly be anticipated by the present contribution.[58]

While Weise's and Warburg's endeavours have attained (at least partially) their aims, our hermeneutics today can benefit from many further studies. As a result, panpsychism can be considered as an immediate effect, among others, of a transnational cultural debate on soul, life, pneumatology, cosmology, and the function of visual expression. Its influence penetrated the thought of the mature Renaissance, be it in Italy (where, initially, Pico, Achillini, and Ficino, among others, met), or more specifically in Naples (with the meeting of Bruno, Campanella, Telesio, and even Galileian adepts), or even in Central Europe (as in Prague, for example, where Brunian and Keplerian theories encountered each other during Bruno's visit). New interpretive tools can also be provided by the recent reflection on art media history by Hans Belting.[59]

For art history, clarification is still needed as to whether, and exactly how the activity of philosophers in major artistic centres on the continent seriously affected the turbulent artistic transformations of their time: this essay presents some definitive positions on this problem, and especially on Bruno's role, in the second to last paragraph on "animism beyond philosophy". The contexts and media through which the philosophers' and natural philosophers' influence reached artists and their debates (or how opportunities for exchange were possible) has not yet been satisfactorily analyzed and explained.

THE NEW ANTI-SCHOLASTIC VIEW OF NATURE AND ITS FORMAL REPRESENTATION IN THE WORK OF MICHELANGELO. PANPSYCHISM IN MICHELANGELO'S BUILDINGS

The example of the "kneeling window" discussed earlier is not the only case of an architectural element perceived as alive in Michelangelo's architecture. If his contemporaries knew that his *Aurora* "did not have the Devil inside" ("non ha il Diavolo dentro"), it must then have an angelic spirit with it.[60] It actually has been proven that Michelangelo projected his buildings according to anthropomorphic principles.[61] As it is well known, the Sacrestia Nuova — his complex experiment where he for the first time on a large scale tried to substitute columns for the human figure — led him to the peculiar, architecturally heterodox compositional idea of the binary column. The constitutive parts of architecture 'originated' in parts of the human body, as is recognizable in the ground plan with eyes drawn for S. Giovanni dei Fiorentini: the eyes on the plan are *axially oriented* according to the building axis and symmetrical on both sides of it, as they are in bodies. The 'organism' of the building must, apparently, be endowed with sight, although we cannot know whether these eyes always find their ultimate form in windows.[62] Let us recall the numerous façades he constructed after the model of the human (or sometimes animal) face. As Vasari wrote, "like the face of man", the building is provided with eyes, tongues, arms, and teeth.[63]

Only a few years after Michelangelo's drawing, in accordance with widely-accepted Aristotelian theories (especially pneumatology) Lomazzo called the axis of a represented figure its *anima*. We find the same concept in Michelangelo's *Letter to an unknown prelate,* possibly Cardinal Rodolfo Pio da Carpi, dated 1550–1560, dealing with the axes of a centrally-planned church. This letter has been thought to refer to S. Giovanni dei Fiorentini, because of its suggested reference to a centrally-planned church. The axiality shared by the human body and buildings is essential for both of them, and both are objects of constant interest to Michelangelo concerning the principles and the significance of life as well as of motion, one of whose fundamentals seems to be the symmetry derived from the human body and assimilated by the buildings. Michelangelo was not, as Summers noted, "running off into Vitruvian commonplaces" here, "rather the axiality shared by architecture and by the human body was essential."[64] Vasari wrote as well that the façade of an ideal building should be endowed with *decoro* and *maestà,* and should be subdivided exactly like the human face, with the portal in the centre at the bottom, and the windows one right and one left, in *parità* (meaning here "balance", not "equality").[65]

The drawing of the Palace of Altopascio[66] of the late 1540s — years of intense interest in anatomy for Michelangelo — is symmetrically structured, with a literal transposition of the traditional anthropomorphic metaphor. In the letter mentioned earlier, he writes:

> *What is in the very center always is as free as you like, just as the nose, which is in the middle of the face, need not conform to either one or the other eye. But one hand is quite obliged to be like the other, and one eye like the other with regard to position and correspondence. For it is an established fact that the members of architecture resemble the members of man. Whoever neither has been nor is a master at figures, and especially at anatomy, cannot really understand architecture.*[67]

Summers accordingly considers the architectural image of the human body as generally "based upon analogy [...], which gave on to a kind of metaphysical fantasy, a fantasy that was, however, unfailingly anthropomorphic, or perhaps better, always subject to the reasons [...] discoverable in the living human body."[68]

A last and most imposing example for an architecture conceived as a living body is the Capitol complex at Rome. According to Vasari, the staircases of its Palazzo dei Senatori are to be seen as "arms and legs"[69]; exactly the way they can be seen in many similar contemporary palace designs. But in my opinion, only the bulky *cordonata* (the paved ramp, planned and built posthumously, and not present in Vasari's time) could actually be imagined as the "legs of the Capitol", being located below the "belly" of the square. In fact, the perfectly oval pavement of the square is its "belly". Because the Senatorial Palace, even as Vasari puts it, beholds *(guarda)* the square in front of "himself", "he" must have eyes which make him the head of the entire monumental complex. The interpretation of the oval as an architectural belly is confirmed by further textual evidence in other sources, where the meaning of circular ground plans is considered as originating in the human body,[70] including the example of the Pantheon. The oval or (etymologically) egg-form originates in the figure of a human torso beginning from the clavicle down to pelvis.[71] The oval pavement of the Campidoglio is indeed governed by the same axis which extends to the top of the Palazzo dei Senatori and, remarkably, is continued out to the city itself through the long axial Via Capitolina. Even the trapezoid ground plan of the square which opens only narrowly towards the city centre, releasing a compressed gaze from inside the square towards Rome, bears out Weise's interpretation of Michelangelo's conceptualization of forces of motion, characterized by a "forced compression of movements and poses" ("compressione forzata dei movimenti e delle pose"), or as Stephen Campbell precisely puts it, with his understanding of michelangelesque "excess in representation", when he talks "of the image as a substitute that might eclipse what it stands for."[72]

ANIMISM BEYOND PHILOSOPHY IN BRUNO, KEPLER, AND CAMPANELLA

Returning to the animate presence of spirit in artefacts as expressed in natural philosophy, certain characteristics of natural philosophy in general should be added here. The peculiarity of the early modern period is indeed that only then did nature begin to be considered, rather high-handedly, as existing independently from human, civilized, or social life. Concurrently, a deep awareness of empathy and intimacy with the world dominated in the 16th century. An important form of the new renaissance individualism is embedded in this new relation to nature, expressed in literature and in other artistic media, which, as early as the 15th century, allowed individuals to emancipate themselves from ecclesiastical and monarchic hierarchies. Renaissance natural philosophy was therefore panpsychistic, pananimistic; in it, nature in all its parts was alive. Confirmed by theory in the correspondence of microcosm and macrocosm, every single natural being (including humans) corresponds and mirrors the overall structure of nature.

The sense of nature's intimate vitality persisted until the end of the 16th century. It culminated in Giordano Bruno's concern with the emotions, but had already appeared in Campanella's concept of *anima universalis*. But similar visions characterize and even mutate, soon after, into the atomistic positions of Bruno's (neo-platonic, neo-plotinian) thought itself, which was completely integrated into his vision of the pantheistic tradition. In his *Sigillus sigillorum* of 1583 (in part, a mnemotechnical treatise on the use of images) we read, for example, "because the soul exists ubiquitously, and it is an entire entity and at the same time entire in any parts of the universe, subsequently thank to the specific condition of physical matter, you will be able to perceive the world in any object even if smallest and severed, let alone a representation of the world"[73]. In later seicento and baroque art, however, nature is constituted by dead, mechanically detachable fragments of lifeless corpses or matter, in which assuming a spiritual presence would make no sense. Also the influence of the "golden age of anatomy" in the artistic practice and its discoveries around 1500 had been fading away, neutralizing the interest in the sciences and the mechanics of the human body. Yet animistic and pantheistic principles were still alive and had unsuspected consequences. First, occult and obscure forces, no longer confined to the netherworld, now pervaded the whole of worldly life and, at the end of the 16th century, threatened early modern individuals with collective psychoses and fears of witchcraft and demonic persecution. A second consequence was the progressive obscurity and degeneration of social-educational conditions.[74] The described monstrous features seem to affect more deeply by far the Central European styles, such as the *Ohrmuschelstil,* which is also known in a Central-Southern Italian diffusion. In any case, what matters is less the geographical diffusion of stylistic phenomena than their "iconology", or most intimate sense. A sense of obscurity and oppression was, no doubt, widespread in absolutist Europe, where political powers were becoming increasingly menacing and invisible well beyond the borders of Italy.

In this respect, the decisive lack of ambiguity in Bruno's postulation, in his *Sigillus sigillorum,* of the transferability or osmosis of diverse figures, of presences and life forms in the world, could be interpreted as pointing to pantheism, or, as one scholar argued, even to "pananimism", and simultaneously as a warning against a take over by negative forces: "Finally all things create all things, and therefore, as they get created and shaped by all things, hereby we can be pushed forward (advanced) finding, examining, considering, discussing and remembering about all things through all things."[75]

In this respect, one should also recall Bruno's preoccupation with the role of figures and images. This is obvious in his late work *De Imaginum, signorum, & Idearum compositione,* which deals with the *spiritus phantasticus.*[76] In fact, the entire theory of the *spiritus phantasticus,* as such, favours a panpsychistic interpretation of the world and thus of the visual arts in general, whether sculptural or pictural, as osmotic between the worlds of the three worlds called *archetypus, physicus,* and *umbratilis:* "Itaque formae, simulacra, [i.e.: statues] signacula, vehicula sunt et vincula veluti quaedam, quibus favores rerum superiorum inferioribus tum emanant."[77] Forms, *simulacra,* symbols or signs are the vehicles and at the same time channels, the "ropes", through which superior beings — alive, but transcendent ones — share and communicate their contents to inferior ones in the natural world.

A similar position is even more unequivocal in Campanella whose treatise *De sensu rerum* came with a truly explanatory subtitle, which has been translated as: "A remarkable tract of occult philosophy in which the world is shown to be a living and truly conscious image of God and all its parts and particles thereof to be endowed with sense perception, some more clearly, some more obscurely, to the extent required for the preservation of themselves and of the whole in which they share sensation."[78] According to his view, if the natural world is sentient, the matter which gives life to animals must be considered as sentient as well: the heavens are sentient, and so too is the earth.

Kepler's theories, developed over a long period until his late maturity, are comparable in this point. In his *Mysterium cosmographicum* (1596) he remained faithful to a "traditional conception of force as a soul animating the celestial bodies."[79] But according to David Skrbina,[80] in 1621 Kepler changed his mind and decided that "force was a better term than 'soul'", adopting a more, albeit not entirely, matter-centered vision (see his *Harmonies of the World*).[81] Confirmation of these trends in the *Weltanschauungen* concerning the "natural world" is to be found in the rich and vivacious visions of landscape in art throughout the 16th century, markedly different from the "idealistic" landscapes of baroque painters, where the natural countryside is degraded to a mere stage set for human or respectively animal actors: an instrument for conveying their personalities and the narrative of their vicissitudes. The same process is noticeable in physiognomy, as Ernst Kris has shown,[82] where human and animal laughter or frightening grimaces are likewise intentionally used as a form of mask to conceal the authentic face, in art as well as in gesture as the expression of the human psyche: it does not matter, in this regard, whether or not laughter is a sign of normal or even of pathological conditions (which it surely sometimes can be). Without interruption, from 1500 through the mature Baroque, mannerist and *Ohrmuschelstil* masks therefore convey much of the sense of universal malaise pervading the whole period. Research by physicians and physiognomists before and during the first 'scientific revolution' of 1580–1620 surely helped to increase awareness of this topic in figurative artists, as Kris proposed in an article of 1926 on "Style rustique", which begins with an analysis of mature Flemish mannerists, like Hans Vredeman de Vries (see the plates of his *Caryatidum* of about 1565).[83] John Onians made an attempt similar to Kris' in a very short essay, in which he wrote that

> the main reason why architects began to use forms which were increasingly organic and specifically anthropomorphic, was that as they drew more freely they naturally tended to select preferentially from the charcoal and ink marks those forms which the brain recognised as corresponding to human templates. This tendency is already clear in Michelangelo [...] and directly underlies much that is new in his architecture, especially of the Medici Cha-

*pel. One such feature is the cornice in which eggs and darts become masks
[sculpted by his assistant Silvio Cosini] and another the series of face capitals on the pilasters, but perhaps the most significant is the baluster-like
element in the attic.*[84]

The definitive stylization and schematization of decorative patterns in baroque ornament corresponds to a decrease or neutralization of magical thought
and of beliefs in the vitality of artistic creation. In Italy and interestingly at the
centre of the artistic debate, in Rome, the formal repertoire transforms itself at
the latest with Pietro da Cortona into a purely decorative one, deposited on the
surface with a mitigated purpose of emotional effect. This might be related to
the increasing predominance of the major post-reformational orders, or also
with the dominance of Aristotelian attitudes towards architecture. Bit by bit, art
abandons the habit of projecting life into the artistic object, as it has been practiced since the early and mature Renaissance.

THE SOUTHERN ITALIAN CONTRIBUTION TO LATE MANNERIST AND EARLY BAROQUE DECORATION. POSSIBLE REFLECTIONS IN CENTRAL EUROPEAN CIRCLES

The fund of the monstrous forms, only systematized by recent scholarship, leads
to the justifiable assumption that this was obviously the basis of the first Italian Baroque of the 17th century. Whether of local, Flemish, or Tuscan origin, or
stemming from what Weise called the Spanish *estilo monstruoso*,[85] or from the
so-called *Knorpelstil* (cartilage style),[86] or from the *Ohrmuschelstil*, the Baroque
was in any respect, as Frederick Antal has claimed, the first international style of
Europe. In this regard, we must again recognize a sort of renunciation, or at least
the waning of the corporeal in representations of nature in artistic figuration.
Forssman expressed the opinion that in all the cases where "the *Ohrmuschel*-
ornamentation has a character of realism, it is [nevertheless] not derived from
the repertoire of nature."[87] It is an anti-naturalistic, even 'surrealistic' ornament
and transcends reality: in fact, not only do anthropomorphic remembrances
no longer play an important role, every allusion to anatomy denies the logic of
anatomy itself. In some cases it is obsessively nightmarish and menacing, as in
the above described Sepolcro del Cav. Marino in S. Domenico Maggiore, where
the most monstrous elements are located at the viewer's eye level, or in the Bat
and Mask on the epigraph at the rear entrance portal of the Cortile del Salvatore
in Via Giovanni Paladino, in the University buildings of Naples. In the Tuscan
decorative tradition, a portal is of course already generally understood (literally
or metaphorically) as a mouth through which what is foreign enters the body of
the building (recall the Palazzo Zuccari at Rome), but in the Neapolitan example

its grimace is more menacing than any mouth. Similar physiognomical decoration is found in numerous examples from Southern Germany: in the Ingolstadt Münster, for example, the *Rollwerk* applied to the nose of a large mask functions as *cimasa*-moulding of the choir stalls.[88] Relevant again in this context are August Schmarsow's ideas when he speaks of the "menschliche Dimension im Raumgebilde" ("human dimension in the figuration of space"), with special reference to the sculptural-plastic, or glyptical, arts of the early modern period.[89]

In summary, the pivotal mutation that occurred around 1600 can not simply have been a revival, as such, of fantastic and animal creatures from the traditional repertoire, as would be the case of a spontaneous evolution from earlier traditions. On the contrary, the abrupt change after the beginning of the 17th century consists either in increasing exaggeration of any facial expression or, alternatively, in the sinister erasure which accompanies a perturbing annihilation of the vibrancy of the eyes and gaze in faces. Such phenomena could be explained not only by an appeal to the history of medicine, physiognomy, and other natural sciences, but also ideologically, in reference to the adverse political-cultural momentum of that period, or philosophically, by the reception, and sometimes vulgarization, of nihilistic theories adopted by some of the most influential contemporary thinkers, together with the role of materialistic scientific theories. Which of them could therefore provide an ultimately convincing interpretation of the advent of the new exuberant decorative style, detached from the mannerist tradition, which pervaded the various trends of the 17th century?

More than the question of a thorough analysis of these styles, which is beyond the scope of this essay, we could address the question of their cultural-historical significance. In the 1950s, the historian of philosophy, Lorenzo Giusso, proposed that only after the acceptance of the Galileian concept of nature, with Descartes' later exaltation of the aniconic and his strong dependence on monotheistic Catholic orthodoxy, did the negative attitude towards pagan or non-Christian myths and mythologies (however they might be defined) as well as panpsychism lose its influence. This interpretation could explain the abrupt change in the ornamental styles.[90] More recently, the historian of philosophy, Georg Toepfer, has seen it differently. For him, architecture was a primary model for a rationalistic and materialistic approach to the comprehension of the body and all living organisms:

It is hardly surprising that materialist approaches played a significant role in the development of early organism models. By dispensing with the soul as a central regulatory and organizing principle for the living creature, they were forced to explain the complex vital functions based on the interaction of the parts. Terminologically, this change manifested itself in the increased use of terms taken from craft and architecture for the description and analysis of vital processes. Thus, at the end of the sixteenth century, G. Bruno uses metaphors taken from the field of architecture when he speaks of the body of a living creature ('composizione d'uno animale'; 'architettura'; 'edificio').[91]

Yet, for all these reasons, it seems necessary to re-orient the approach of art history to much early baroque or pre-baroque ornamentation, to artistic workshops in Italy and to their context. In fact, in spite of the valuable work of Oreste Ferrari in Naples and Rome, of Raffaello Causa and, more recently, of Nicola Spinosa in Naples, the present knowledge of parts of the Italian architectural and sculptural heritage, especially in the Neapolitan area and the rest of the Kingdom, is still too fragmentary.

NOTES

1 See VITRUVIUS, *De architectura*, II.1,5: "The hut of Romulus on the Capitol is a significant reminder of the fashions of old times, and likewise the thatched roofs of temples on the Citadel." (*The Ten Books on Architecture,* translated by Morris Hicky Morgan, Cambridge, MA: Harvard University Press | London: Humphrey Milford, Oxford University Press, 1914, p. 40). See also, for the liveliness of the capitals, VITRUVIUS, IV.1,9 (ibid., p. 104), with the famous episode of the maiden of Corinth and the origin of the Corinthian capital.

2 Heinrich WÖLFFLIN, *Prolegomena zu einer Psychologie der Architektur* (first edition: Munich: Wolf, 1886), new edition with an afterword by Jasper Cepl, Berlin: Gebr. Mann, 1999, p. 37–38: „Die Säule breitet sich oben aus, weil es zweckmäßig ist, die Last breit zu fassen, nicht weil sie gequetscht wird; sie behält immer noch Kraft genug, sich (unmittelbar unter dem Abacus) wieder zusammenzuziehen." And p. 38: „Das heißt die Säule weiß genau, was sie zu tragen hat und handelt demgemäß."

3 *The Hermetic and Alchemical Writings of Aureolus Philippus Theophrastus Bombast of Hohenheim Called Paracelsus the Great. Now for the First Time Faithfully Translated into English,* edited with a biographical preface, elucidatory notes, a copious hermetic vocabulary, and index by Arthur Edward WAITE, 2 VOLS., London: James Elliot and Co., 1894, VOL. 1, p. 136–137 · David SKRBINA, *Panpsychism in the West,* Cambridge, MA and London: The MIT Press, 2005, p. 67.

4 See, for the panpsychistic tendency of cinquecento philosophy, August RIEKEL, *Die Philosophie der Renaissance,* Munich: Ernst Reinhardt, 1925, p. 80: „Die panpsychistische Tendenz der Renaissancephilosophie, wie sie sich schon mit Cusanus ankündigt und mit Paracelsus und Bruno ihren Höhepunkt erreicht"; and further, ibid.: „So werden von Paracelsus außer dem Gedanken der Einheit, der ja schon von Cusanus vorbereitet wurde, vor allem die Gedanken der Variabilität und der Allbeseelung ausgesprochen."

5 Brian P. COPENHAVER, "Astrology and Magic", in: *The Cambridge History of Renaissance Philosophy,* edited by Charles B. SCHMITT, Quentin SKINNER, Eckhard KESSLER, and Jill KRAYE, Cambridge, New York, Melbourne, Madrid, Cape Town, Singapore, and São Paulo: Cambridge University Press, 1988, 7th printing 2007, p. 264–300, here p. 292.

6   Girolamo CARDANO, *De subtilitate libri XXI,* Nuremberg: Johann Petreius, 1550 · See *The First Book of Jerome Cardan's De Subtilitate,* translated from the original Latin with text introduction and commentary by Myrtle Marguerite CASS, Williamsport, PA: The Bayard Press, 1934, p. 116.

7   A kind of systematical record of all kinds of motion, of movement, gesticulation, demeanor, and gait, of how they can be found in the later Renaissance is already provided by Weise's studies as early as the 1950s (see notes 20, 25, 37, 44, and 61 for bibliographic details).

8   Moshe BARASCH, *Gestures of Despair in Medieval and Early Renaissance Art,* New York: New York University Press, 1976 · Eckard MARCHAND, *Gebärden in der Florentiner Malerei: Studien zur Charakterisierung von Heiligen, Uomini Famosi und Zeitgenossen im Quattrocento,* Münster: LIT, 2004.

9   See several studies by André CHASTEL: *Marsile Ficin et l'art,* Geneva: E. Droz | Lille: R. Giard, 1954; third edition 1996 · *Art et Humanisme à Florence au temps de Laurent le Magnifique. Études sur la renaissance et l'humanisme platonicien,* Paris: Presses Universitaires de France, 1959 · *The Myth of the Renaissance, 1420–1520,* translated by Stuart Gilbert, Geneva: Editions D'Art Albert Skira, 1969 — And more recently on the same subject: Joanne SNOW-SMITH, "Michelangelo's Christian Neoplatonic Aesthetic of Beauty in his Early Oeuvre: The Nuditas Virtualis Image", in: *Concepts of Beauty in Renaissance Art,* edited by Francis AMES-LEWIS and Mary ROGERS, Aldershot and Brookfield, VT: Ashgate, 1998, pp. 144–162.

10   David PEARSON, *New Organic Architecture. The Breaking Wave,* Berkeley and Los Angeles: University of California Press, 2001.

11   Also, if we search for life reenactment in contemporary artistic visions, one of the pioneers has been Yves Klein with his formula of the painting as *living object.* Vanessa Beecroft's very architectural performances are also worth mentioning in this context.

12   Alina PAYNE, "Reclining Bodies: Figural Ornament in Renaissance Architecture", in: *Body and Building. Essays on the Changing Relation of Body and Architecture,* edited by George DODDS and Robert TAVERNOR, Cambridge, MA and London: The MIT Press, 2002, pp. 94–113, pp. 340–343 (notes), and pp. 375–378 (bibliography), here p. 113.

13   David SUMMERS, *Michelangelo and the Language of Art,* Princeton: Princeton University Press, 1981, p. 435.

14   Hugues SAMBIN, *Oevvre de la diversite Des termes, dont on vse en architecture, reduict en ordre,* Lyon: Iean Dvrant, 1572, unpaged (14th Terme): "En ce Terme n'y a sinon la poursuite d'une composite retrassée après l'antique, qui est toutefois bien plaisante, à cause que l'ouvrier a prins peine de l'enrichir de beaux ornemens, et de la naïve proportion." The first Terme "est appellé tuscan" (or rustique).

15   Wendel DIETTERLIN, *Architectvra. Von Außtheilung, Symmetria vnd Proportion der Fünff Seulen, und aller darauß volgender Kunst Arbeit, von Fenstern, Caminen, Thürgerichten, Portalen, Bronnen und Epitaphien [...],* Nuremberg: Balthasar Caymox, 1598, p. 30r. This essay, because of a lack of space, deliberately does not deal with the work by the Neapolitan architect Pirro Ligorio (Naples 1510–Rome 1583) — a peculiar case for the entire Renaissance and a model for the following 17th century as well.

16   Manfredo TAFURI, *L'architettura del Manierismo nel Cinquecento europeo,* Rome: Officina Edizioni, 1966, p. 315: "Col Dietterlin l'animismo raggiunge i più alti vertici — alti anche in senso qualitativo — del mostruoso; [...] fallimento di ogni sforzo ordinatore, naufragio orrendo di ogni utopica humanitas." Tafuri recurs to Weise's ideas, but at the same time criticizes him, *passim*, and not coherently (p. 301): To him "il pampsichismo nel Telesio, Bruno e Campanella" is "teso a risolvere la struttura dell'universo in leggi di omogeneità e unità, sia pure a sfondo vitalistico."

17 Giulio Carlo Argan, in: Argan and Bruno Contardi, *Michelangelo architetto,* Milan: Electa, 1990, p. 301.

18 Amelio Fara, *Bernardo Buontalenti,* Milan: Electa, 1996, p. 136.

19 Argan, *Michelangelo architetto,* p. 85.

20 See Georg Weise, "Il repertorio ornamentale del barocco napoletano di Cosimo Fanzago e il suo significato per la genesi del Rococò", in 5 parts (which I will refer to as: parts i to v), in: *antichità viva,* VOL. 13, 1974, part i: no. 4, pp. 40–53 (here p. 45) and part ii: no. 5, pp. 32–41; VOL. 14, 1975, part iii: no. 1, pp. 24–31 (FIG. 26: main altar in S. Maria in Portico, Naples) and part iv: no. 5, pp. 27–35; VOL. 16, 1977, part v: no. 5, pp. 42–51. Borromini also treats his architectural elements as if they were lively in the composition of the lantern of the dome in S. Ivo alla Sapienza. And to compare the relationship of sculpture and stucco in Borromini, see Paolo Portoghesi, *Borromini,* Milan: Electa, 1990, FIG. 408, where both sculpture and stucco *adhere* on the architectural surface, without being rooted in the body of the building.

21 Weise, "Il repertorio ornamentale del barocco napoletano di Cosimo Fanzago...", part ii, p. 34, FIG. 7. See also the right volute of the *altare maggiore,* S. Giacomo degli Spagnoli, p. 40, FIG. 33: It derives from the "motivo in parola" (a mask usually accompanied by the spiral volutes) which is of ancient Roman origin.

22 Most recent researches on D'Auria, with reference to older studies, in: *Giovanni da Nola, Annibale Caccavello, Giovan Domenico D'Auria. Sculture 'ritrovate' tra Napoli e Terra di Lavoro 1545–1565,* edited by Riccardo Naldi, Naples: Electa Napoli, 2007.

23 Decoration in stucco relief of the Dome in S. Paolo Maggiore, Cappella Firrao, by Aniello and Nicola Falcone, contract 1641, with putti. See also Gaetana Cantone, *Napoli barocca e Cosimo Fanzago,* Naples: Banco di Napoli, 1984, plate 69 (Cappella Cacace in S. Lorenzo Maggiore). — There is a large number of discordant hypotheses on Cosimo Fanzago's early period. According to Francesco Rossi's "hypothesis" (*Allgemeines Künstlerlexikon,* VOL. 36, Munich and Leipzig: K. G. Saur, 2003, pp. 564–566), he is supposed to have received an artistic education for a short period in Rome before he moved to Naples in 1608 (aged sixteen), where, as a supplement to his education, he is supposed to have been immediately sent to the workshop of a relative, a Pompeo Fanzago (p. 564). The latter however is not at all mentioned there, as an artist, except as a relative of Cosimo's. Hence there is no guarantee that this historical version is reliable, given that an artist active in Naples would have normally been mentioned primarily in artistic documents and sources. — See also, for Apulian monuments, Vincenzo Cazzato, Marcello Fagiolo, and Mimma Pasculli Ferrara: *Atlante del Barocco in Italia,* VOL.: *Puglia 1: Terra di Bari e Capitanata,* Rome: De Luca, 1996, p. 55.

24 Antonia Nava Cellini, "La scultura dal 1610 al 1656", in: *La scultura del Seicento a Napoli,* edited by Francesco Abbate, Turin: Scriptorium, 1997, pp. 15–55, here p. 38: "partendo dalla visione esagitata del [Santuario del] Gesù Vecchio e del Gesù Nuovo e dal clima appena di poco più contenuto della Certosa", Fanzago ends up in a contrast with the last phase, the one of the Tesoro di

S. Gennaro. Other contemporary artists and comrades in arms with Fanzago were Giuliano Finelli (Cappella Antinori, S. Apostoli, or Cappella del Tesoro di S. Gennaro) and Ercole Ferrata (long active in Rome as well).

25 See Georg WEISE, "L'Italia e il problema delle origini del 'Rococò'", in: *Paragone. Arte,* VOL. 5, no. 49, 1954, pp. 35–42, here p. 41 · WEISE, "Il repertorio ornamentale del barocco napoletano di Cosimo Fanzago…", part v, and especially FIG. 4 and FIG. 6 with comparisons of Aversa (Northern Neapolitan County) with Zwiefalten (Suabia).

26 Ernst KRIS, *Ricerche psicoanalitiche sull'arte.* Prefazione all'edizione italiana di Ernst H. Gombrich, translated by Elvio Fachinelli, Turin: Giulio Einaudi, 1988, p. 226.

27 CANTONE, *Napoli barocca e Cosimo Fanzago.*

28 *Nevws Compertament Bvchlein,* Braunschweig: Godfridt Müller, 1621 · Friedrich UNTEUTSCH, *Neues Zieratenbuch, den Schreinern Tischlern oder Küstlern und Bildhauer sehr dienstlich,* Nuremberg: Paulus Fürsten, [1650] · Similar ornaments in: Joseph FURTTENBACH, *Architectura civilis: Das ist: Eigentliche Beschreibung wie man nach bester form, und gerechter Regul, Fürs Erste: Palläst, mit dero Lust: und Thiergarten, darbey auch Grotten: So dann Gemeine Bewohnungen: Zum Andern, Kirchen, Capellen, Altär, Gotshäuser: Drittens, Spitäler, Lazareten und Gotsäcker aufführen unnd erbawen soll,* Ulm: Jonas Saur, 1628. — Erik FORSSMAN, *Säule und Ornament. Studien zum Problem des Manierismus in den nordischen Säulenbüchern und Vorlageblättern des 16. und 17. Jahrhunderts,* Stockholm: Almquist & Viksell, 1956, p. 146 quotes also: Donath HORN, *Neues und Wohl Inventiertes Ziraten Buch, allen Liebhabern die sich der Schneidkunst bediene[n],* Nuremberg: Johan Hoffmann, no date but circa 1660–1670 · Joseph BOILLOT, *Novveaux povrtraitsz et figures de termes pour vser en l'architecture,* Langres: Jean des Preyz, 1592. German edition: *New Termis Buch von allerley grossen vierfüssigen Thieren zugerichtet […],* [Strasbourg?]: [Antoine Bertram?], 1604, containing, „echt manieristisch", fifty five animal herms; and Ioannes PHRYS [Hans VREDEMAN DE VRIES], *Theatrvm Vitæ Hvmanæ,* Antwerp: Petrus Balt, 1577 · Rudolf ZÖLLNER'S Ph.D. Thesis (Universität Kiel 1959) *Deutsche Säulen-, Ziraten- und Schild-Bücher 1610 bis 1680. Ein Beitrag zur Entwicklungsgeschichte des Knorpelwerkstils* is only available as a typescript.

29 FORSSMAN, *Säule und Ornament,* p. 188: „ein barockes Aufbäumen gegen das […] vitruvianische Dogma".

30 Ibid., p. 191: „Im Vergleich zum manieristischen Ornament, das immer konstruiert wirkt, ist das Ohrmuschelornament ungleich organischer und […] naturnäher. Mit dem Naturalismus der barocken Bildkunst hängt es zusammen, daß sie auch das *Häßliche und Kranke* darzustellen wagt, das früher in so krasser Form nicht darstellungswürdig war."

31 See also ibid., p. 190.

32 Gabriel KRAMMER, *Architectvra: Von Den Fvnf Sevlen Sampt Iren Ornamenten Vnd Zierden Als Nemlich Tvscana Dorica Ionica Corintia Composita; In Rechter Mas Teilvng Vnd Proportzion […],* Cologne: Iohan Buxenmacher, 1610.

33 FORSSMAN, *Säule und Ornament,* p. 201: „Leibliche Schönheit muß der Zeit fragwürdig, ja sündig erschienen sein, so daß man nackten Figuren die Arme zu Voluten verkürzte, den Bauch unschön herauswölbte oder wie geöffnet darstellte, die Schenkel aufriß und wie bloße Muskelmaterie behandelte." See also WEISE, "Il repertorio ornamentale del barocco napoletano di Cosimo Fanzago…".

34 Wilhelm Worringer, *Die altdeutsche Buchillustration,* Munich and Leipzig: R. Piper 1908, p. 8: „Der Deutsche ist […] ein geborener Ausdruckskünstler."

35 Forssman, *Säule und Ornament,* p. 190: "verwilderten und desorganisierten Epoche".

36 Some interesting contributions to the threat stimulus in art is offered by Nancy E. Aiken in her *The Biological Origins of Art,* Westport, CT: Praeger, 1998, especially chapter 7, even though the actual consideration of artistic devices is very reduced. I thank Harry Francis Mallgrave for his friendly hints to this and further recent studies in this research area.

37 To this regard we could also refer to some of Weise's interpretations, e. g. in Georg Weise, "Vitalismo, animismo e panpsichismo nella decorazione del Cinquecento e del Seicento", in: *Critica d'arte,* vol. 6, 1959, pp. 375–398, here p. 386: "Sembra sia destino dell'arte tedesca il condurre le diverse fasi stilistiche fino alle ultime conseguenze, proprio nel momento in cui negli altri paesi si delineano già le premesse di un nuovo periodo evolutivo." But these could also be the effects of the competitive relationship between centre (Toscana) and periphery (Bavaria, Alpine region, Kingdom of Sicily).

38 Weise, "Il repertorio ornamentale del barocco napoletano di Cosimo Fanzago…", part I, p. 47, plate 15, and p. 45: "Predomina a partire dalle prime decadi del Seicento un intensificato gusto plastico e aggettante, liberatosi dalla tradizione classico-rinascimentale del vincolamento dei motivi formali ai dettami di una disposizione planimetrica e aspirante alla bellezza dei ritmi lineari. Quasi esclusivamente il nuovo sistema decorativo si basa sull'elemento [nuovo] antinaturalistico e astratto delle curve e volute."

39 Weise, "Il repertorio ornamentale del barocco napoletano di Cosimo Fanzago…", part III, fig. 26.

40 Ibid., part V, p. 48: "più ingentilita, sentimentale e affettuosa".

41 Ibid., "[…] continuità del repertorio formale [senza] ogni parentela con gli elementi formali costitutivi del fenomeno stilistico della rocaille."

42 It is to this context that Weise's following remark applies: "In tutti i settori della produzione architettonica e decorativa la transizione a forme più pieghevoli e aggraziate mi sembra essersi verificata a Napoli un po' prima che nelle altre parti dell'Europa occidentale." And: "Gli esempi caratteristici si potrebbero annoverare, a mio avviso, pure tra le facciate delle chiese e cappelle così come tra gli altari". Weise, "Il repertorio ornamentale del barocco napoletano di Cosimo Fanzago…", part V, p. 49. — His influence was acknowledged by: Paolo Portoghesi, *Borromini nella cultura europea,* Rome: Officina Edizioni, 1964 · Manfredo Tafuri: *L'architettura del Manierismo nel Cinquecento europeo,* Rome: Officina Edizioni, 1968 · Eugenio Battisti, "Simbolo e classicismo", in: *Archivio di filosofia,* 1958, p. 215–233 · Battisti, *Rinascimento e Barocco,* [Turin]: Einaudi, 1960 · Battisti, *L'antirinascimento,* Milan: Feltrinelli, 1962 (Weise is an "amico carissimo" for Battisti; see ibid, p. 12) · Giulio Carlo Argan, "Il barocco in Francia, in Inghilterra, nei Paesi Bassi", in: *Manierismo, barocco, rococo. concetti e termini,* Rome: Accademia Nazionale dei Lincei, 1962, pp. 329–336 · Robert J. Clements, *Michelangelo's Theory of Art,* New York: University Press, 1961 · Stephen J. Campbell, "'*Fare una Cosa Morta Parer Viva*': Michelangelo, Rosso, and the (Un) Divinity of Art", in: *The Art Bulletin,* vol. 84, 2002, pp. 596–620.

43 See *Manierismo, barocco, rococo. concetti e termini,* Rome: Accademia Nazionale dei Lincei, 1962. The conference was held in Rome in April 1960.

44 TAFURI, *L'architettura del Manierismo nel Cinquecento europeo*. See, for evidence of the international dialog initiated by Weise, also Georg WEISE, *Il Manierismo. Bilancio critico del problema stilistico e culturale,* Florence: Leo S. Olschki, 1971, p. xii, in which relations to further historical circles are indicated: "non posso fare a meno di ricordare la stretta collaborazione e l'intesa spirituale che da ormai più di dieci anni mi unisce al mio amico Francesco Pugliese-Carratelli [Rome-Naples]". — With *Gotik in der Renaissance. Eine kunsthistorische Studie* (Stuttgart: Ferdinand Enke, 1921) August SCHMARSOW had paid, probably for the first time, great attention to the case of Ghiberti and his Gothic roots; he compared Gothic cathedrals with Brunelleschi's works and a chapter is dedicated to Botticelli and Leonardo, pp. 71–91. On Schmarsow's theories about the sequence of historical periods and their transitional phases, see Ernst ULLMANN, "August Schmarsows Beitrag zur Architekturtheorie", in: *Künstlerisches und kunstwissenschaftliches Erbe als Gegenwartsaufgabe: Referate der Arbeitstagung vom 16. bis 18. April 1975,* edited by the Abteilung Dokumentation und Information der Sektion Ästhetik und Kunstwissenschaften der Humboldt-Universität zu Berlin, 2 VOLS., Berlin: Humboldt-Universität zu Berlin, 1975, VOL. 1, p. 130–139, here p. 133: „Es ist nicht der Name, sondern die Auffassung als eine Zeit der Wiedergeburt des ganzen Menschen, woran mir gelegen ist" (quoting SCHMARSOW's essay "Zur Beurtheilung der sogenannten Spätgotik", in: *Repertorium für Kunstwissenschaft,* VOL. 23, 1900, pp. 290–298.)

45 See CAMPBELL, "*'Fare una Cosa Morta Parer Viva'*: Michelangelo, Rosso, and the (Un)Divinity of Art" · Francesco LANCILOTTI, *Trattato di pittura composto per Francesco Lancilotti [...] da rarissima stampa con nuova impressione a novella richiamata; con prefazione, fac-simile, bibliografia mazochiana ed annotazioni storiche e filologiche dal marchese Filippo Raffaelli,* Recanati: R. Simboli, 1885, p. 4 (verses from the poem *Ch'alla figura manchi solo il moto,* "composto per [=by] Francesco Lancilotti pittore fiorentino" as it introduces itself): "Ch'alla figura manchi solo el moto", "Fare una Cosa Morta Parer Viva, / quale iscienza è più bella che questa? / O felice colui che quì arriva!" Argan's interpretation of the Sacrestia Nuova in San Lorenzo proceeds from the same paradigm of the building as a living body (ARGAN, *Michelangelo architetto,* pp. 88): "Era in questo primo ordine che si poneva imperiosamente il problema del rapporto tra le forme innaturali del lessico architettonico e le forme umane delle figure statuarie, e va detto subito che l'artista ha scartato ogni riferimento alla realtà naturale: i tempi del giorno erano immagini concettuali, le statue dei duchi umanistici *elogia*." Serlio's *bugnato rustico,* which he considers compatible with all the classical orders, becomes in this case "parte opera di natura, & parte opera di artefice", as he writes in his *Regole generali di architettura sopra le cinque maniere de gli edifici [...]* (Venice: Francesco Marcolini, 1537), fol. XIIIv (facsimile in Sebastiano SERLIO, *On Architecture,* VOL. 1: *Books I–V of 'Tutte l'opere d'architettura et prospetiva',* translated from the Italian with an introduction and commentary by Vaughan HART and Peter HICKS, New Haven and London: Yale University Press, 1996). This will enable him to sketch the numerous awkward portals of the later *Libro extraordinario* of 1551, a veritable 'Libro delle porte', partly natural, partly artificial.

46 Gian Paolo LOMAZZO, "Trattato dell'arte della pittura, scoltura et architettura", in: LOMAZZO, *Scritti sulle arti,* 2 VOLS., edited by Roberto Paolo CIARDI, Florence: Marchi & Bertolli, [1973]–[1974], here VOL. 2, [1974], pp. 9–592, here p. 120: "La robustezza fa gl'atti gagliardi, duri e rigidi, come guardar fieramente e posar forte su le gambe e sempre portar la vita ben composta insieme, cioè non lasciar dilatare le membra [...]."

47 WEISE, "Vitalismo, animismo e panpsichismo nella decorazione del Cinquecento e del Seicento", p. 398.

48 RIEKEL, *Die Philosophie der Renaissance,* p. 60, sees Cusanus as „von einem neuplatonisch-mystischen Monismus ausgehend, der sich zum Renaissance-Pantheismus durchdringt", his pantheism being „auf der Entwicklungslinie zum Panpsychismus", and Riekel further elaborates that the „monistisch-panpsychistische Pantheismus der Renaissance" begins with Cusanus (albeit tentatively). Riekel (p. 68) sums up the latter's philosophy thus: „Nichts ist ohne das Andere, alles fließt zurück zu der göttlichen Urform des Seins."

49 COPENHAVER, "Astrology and Magic", p. 293.

50 See Hans HESS, *Die Naturanschauung der Renaissance in Italien,* Marburg an der Lahn: Kunstgeschichtliches Seminar, 1924.

51 Tansillo is quoted several times in Alfred NOE, *Die Präsenz der romanischen Literaturen in der 1655 nach Wien verkauften Fuggerbibliothek,* 3 VOLS., VOL. 3: *Die romanischen Texte der "Musicales",* Amsterdam and Atlanta, GA: Rodopi, 1997, p. 353, which witnesses the diffusion of Italian (and Neapolitan) seicento poetry even in Central Europe.

Furthermore, Tansillo's poetic style strongly influenced Bruno, particularly in the sonnets. In his dialog *De gli eroici furori,* Bruno even introduces the character Tansillo, who serves as his alter ego and explains his poetics. See on this Pasquale SABBOTINO, "'Scuoprir quel ch'è ascosto sotto questi sileni'. La forma dialogica degli *Eroici furori*", in: *Bruniana & Campanelliana,* VOL. 5, 1999, pp. 367–380, here p. 378.

52 August SCHMARSOW, *Grundbegriffe der Kunstwissenschaft. Am Übergang vom Altertum zum Mittelalter kritisch erörtert und in systematischem Zusammenhange dargestellt,* Leipzig and Berlin: B. G. Teubner, 1905, p. 180. Schmarsow's „menschliche Dimension im Raumgebilde" ("Raumgestaltung als Wesen der architektonischen Schöpfung," in: *Zeitschrift für Ästhetik und allgemeine Kunstwissenschaft,* VOL. 9, 1914, pp. 66–95, here p. 75) also sounded particularly similar to Weise's later theories. In *Grundbegriffe der Kunstwissenschaft,* p. 268, Schmarsow observed about Michelangelo, „wie seine schöpferische Phantasie unter den Bann dieses technisch bedingten Werdeganges geraten ist. Gerade der Gegensatz des kristallinischen Materials und der organischen Formen, die sich daraus abheben, kann seinen Einfluß nicht verfehlen." And elsewhere (p. 203) he observes „ein fühlbarer Zusammenhang zwischen der innen wirkenden Dominante und der ungestalteten Raumweite [werde], wenn auch noch nicht hergestellt, doch angebahnt […]."

53 WÖLFFLIN, *Prolegomena zu einer Psychologie der Architektur.* Notwithstanding the brevity of this Ph.D. Thesis, we find there at least some very interesting general observations on the relationship between organicity and architecture, see p. 17–18: „Und so behaupte ich, daß alle die Bestimmungen, die die formale Ästhetik über die *schöne Form* gibt, nichts anderes sind, als *Bedingungen organischen Lebens.* Formkraft ist also […] eine vis plastica, um diesen in der Naturwissenschaft verpönten Ausdruck hier zu gebrauchen."

54 WEISE, "Vitalismo, animismo e panpsichismo nella decorazione del Cinquecento e del Seicento", p. 386: "non solo bizzaro, […] ma anche angoscioso e opprimente, espressione di forze occulte e terrificanti".

55 Even the recent political-historical film *Il Divo* (Italy 2008) is set in baroque halls and churches and related menacing décor. The central figure is the Italian politician Giulio Andreotti.

56 Giambattista DELLA PORTA, *Edizione nazionale delle opere di Giovan Battista della Porta,* VOL. 9: *De ea naturalis physiognomoniae parte quae ad manuum lineas spectat libri duo,* edited by Oreste TRABUCCO, Naples: Edizioni Scientifiche Italiane, 2003.

57 Warburg was preparing the conference *Ästhetischer Kongress* Hamburg in 1929 with the title "Perseus oder energetische Ästhetik als logische Funktion im Geschäfte der Orientierung bei Giordano Bruno". Weise, a devoted friend of Warburg's also in the latter's last years, might have discussed its subject with him, but there is no evidence for this. As documented in Warburg's notes from 1929 (now in the London Warburg Institute Archive), he contacted outstanding Neapolitan historians of religion and historians of philosophy, like Benedetto Croce, to discuss Bruno with them at length, and he begun studying the Neapolitan cosmologic and pneumatologic tradition and erudition. He also tried to investigate the years, milieu, and context of Bruno's own philosophical education and later production. The pivotal cultural function of Bruno's erudite Dominican convent, where no less a personality than Thomas Aquinas had resided, seemed to him — and still seems to be — an indispensable context to work on. Research on this has been done by Michele MIELE, "Ricerche su San Domenico Maggiore II: i rapporti col seggio di Nido", in: *Napoli nobilissima,* 5th series, VOL. 7, 2006, pp. 95–108, who in fact confirms Warburg's intuitions.

58 Different international research groups are working on Warburg's material, which is still mostly unordered and whose interpretation is a quite difficult task. See at present the temporary results of these researches in an issue on "Philosophy and Iconology", in: *Cassirer Studies,* VOL. 1, 2008. One of Warburg's major merits, however, though only hinted at in his notes, was his attempt to disclose a whole imaginative and iconographic heritage, as based on the speculative systems of soul, body, and the cosmos and on their transformation by the artists in late Cinquecento. Bruno, apparently, was for him one of the "seismographs", as he would call them — such an outstanding one, that Bruno ended up being killed by the "earthquake" itself. For us, he is certainly at least one of the main ambassadors of this period's bad conscience, pointing out restraints on freedom of speech and expression, and calling attention to the condition of despair in which whole social classes, the upper ones included, were about to find themselves at the time of Inquisition, civil war and Spanish dominion in the Kingdom of Naples, of Lombardy and, in part, of Liguria.

59 For example in the Deutsche Forschungsgemeinschaft research group "Bild, Körper, Medium". Or owing to the discovery of an *anthropology of images.* See for example Hans BELTING, *Bild-Anthropologie: Entwürfe für eine Bildwissenschaft,* Munich: Wilhelm Fink, 2001, p. 34: "Das Bild am Körper. Die Maske."

60 See Doni's quote at the very beginning of this contribution.

61 For the fundamental role of his art in this respect, but referring to the Spanish Renaissance, see again Georg WEISE, "Der monstruöse Stil der spanischen Renaissance-Ornamentik als kunstgeschichtliches und geistesgeschichtliches Problem", in: *Festschrift Ulrich Middeldorf,* edited by Antje KOSEGARTEN and Peter TIGLER, Berlin: Walter de Gruyter, 1968, pp. 364–369, here p. 367: „In Italien scheinen mir die ornamentalen Erfindungen Michelangelos und die Abwandlungen der Grotteske im Umkreis seiner Schule einen der wichtigsten Ausgangspunkte zu bilden."

62 SUMMERS, *Michelangelo and the Language of Art,* p. 429: "Leonardo [...] extracted the idea of axiality from his studies of human movement and [...] gave birth to [...] those organism to which Michelangelo's plans for S. Giovanni dei Fiorentini are still indebted", whereas Michelangelo's walls (for example in the New Saint Peter's church) "are fleshy and various, his spaces sculpturally contained and organically continuous rather than separate and related rhythmically."

63 Giorgio VASARI, *Le vite de' più eccellenti pittori, scultori e architettori nelle redazioni del 1550 e 1568,* edited by Paola BAROCCHI and Rosanna BETTARINI, 6 VOLS., Florence: G.C.Sansoni (VOLS. 1–3) and Studio per Edizioni Scelte (VOLS. 4–6), 1966–1988, VOL.1, 1966, p.79: "come la faccia dell'uomo". In the context of the same Florentine tradition is to be mentioned also the case of Giannozzo Manetti with his *Oratio de secularibus et pontificalibus pompis,* written for the dedication of the cathedral, in 1436, where the "figura ecclesiae" coincides with the *forma corporis,* which, in perfection, superates all other objects in the world. For this example see also SUMMERS, *Michelangelo and the Language of Art,* p.425.

64 Ibid., p.429.

65 VASARI, *Le vite,* VOL.1, p.79.

66 From this drawing it can be easily deduced that the Altopascio Palace is thought as representing the human body. Beside this, Michelangelo's *fantasia* for Pope Clement VII should be mentioned here: the creation, after the Pope's request, of a colossus behind Pallazzo Medici, whose "head would serve as the campanile of S. Lorenzo, which has great need of one", see *Il Carteggio di Michelangelo. Edizione postuma di Giovanni Poggi,* 5 VOLS., edited by Paola BAROCCHI and Renzo RISTORI, Florence: G.C.Sansoni (VOLS. 1–3) and S.P.E.S. (VOLS. 4 and 5), 1965–1983, here VOL.1, 1965, p.191 · See also Paola BAROCCHI, *Michelangelo e la sua scuola,* 3 VOLS., Florence: Leo S.Olschki, 1962–1964, VOL. [2]: *I disegni di Casa Buonarroti e degli Uffizi: Tavole,* folios 155v, 156r, 99r with similar drawings from the 1520s.

67 CLEMENTS, *Michelangelo's Theory of Art,* p.320. For the original quote from Michelangelo's famous letter on anthropomorphism in architecture (addressed to Cardinal Rodolfo Pio da Carpi) see Gaetano MILANESI, *Lettere di Michelangelo,* Florence: Le Monnier, 1875, p.554: "[E] i mezzi sempre sono liberi, come vogliono. Siccome il naso, che è nel mezzo del viso, non è obbligato nè all'uno, nè all'altro occhio, ma l'una mano è bene obbligata a essere come l'altra, e l'uno occhio come l'altro per rispetto degli lati e de' riscontri, e però [here – thus] è cosa certa che le membra dell'architettura dipendono dalle membra dell'uomo. Chi non è stato, o non è buon maestro di figure, e massime di notomia, non se ne può intendere." For the Altopascio drawing in general, see Frederick HARTT, *Drawings of Michelangelo,* London: Thames and Hudson, 1971, no.492, drawing Casa Buonarroti, 117Ar (the palace is identical with the Palazzo d'Ugolino Grifoni, realized by Bartolomeo Ammannati after Michelangelo's death).

68 SUMMERS, *Michelangelo and the Language of Art,* p.583.

69 VASARI, *Le vite,* VOL.1, p.8off.

70 SUMMERS, *Michelangelo and the Language of Art,* p.582 note 67: According to Summers, Lomazzo claims: "Square plans are derived from the human body (the example being Poggioreale in Naples) and oval plans from the shape of the torso from clavicle to pelvis governed by the vertical axis." Summers also draws attention to a chapter in Lomazzo's treatise entitled "Come ancora le misura, de Navi, Tempij, Edificij & L'altre cose sono tratte dal corpo humano". See LOMAZZO, "Trattato dell'arte della pittura, scoltura et architettura", p.87–90, here p.88–89, where he writes that the oblong or circular form derives from the uterus: "anco dalla linea della fontanella al pettignone [i.e. a line from the breast to the vagina — in Tuscan dialect] e dal diametro del corpo in mèzzo a quella, che forma un altro ovato, trassero gl'antichi la forma dei teatri". SUMMERS, *Michelangelo and the Language of Art*, p.435 proposes, referring to Realdo COLOMBO, *De re anatomica*, Venice: Nicolai Beuilacqua, 1559, p.194 on oval forms: "Michelangelo's anatomical study and speculation may have contributed to Colombo's formulation".

71 Tilmann BUDDENSIEG, "Criticism and Praise of the Pantheon in the Middle Ages and the Renaissance", in: *Classical Influences on European Culture, A.D. 500–1500,* edited by R.R.BOLGAR, Cambridge: Cambridge University Press, 1976, pp.259–267.

72 WEISE, *Il Manierismo*, p.90 · CAMPBELL, "*'Fare una Cosa Morta Parer Viva'*: Michelangelo, Rosso, and the (Un)Divinity of Art", p.608.

73 Giordano BRUNO, "Sigillus sigillorum" (1583), in: BRUNO, *Opera latine conscripta publicis sumptibus edita,* VOL.2, part 2, edited by F. TOCCO and H.VITELLI, Florence: typis successorum Le Monnier, 1890, pp.161–217, here p.196 (from a chapter on art, "De arte", p.195–196): "cum anima ubique praesens existat, illaque tota et in toto et in quacumque parte tota, ideo pro conditione materiae in quacumque re etiam exigua et abscisa mundum, nedum mundi simulacrum valeas intueri". Art is seen as one of the four main governors of the actions of the soul (*actuum rectores,* the others are: Love, Magic, Knowledge [Mathesis]).

74 We find similar hypotheses in: *Theologische Realenzyklopädie,* VOL.25, edited by Gerhard MÜLLER, Berlin and New York: Walter de Gruyter, 1995, p.216, s.v. "Okkultismus" · Paul MEISSNER, *England im Zeitalter von Humanismus, Renaissance und Reformation,* Heidelberg: F.H.Kerle, 1952, pp.283–285, and p.494: „England nimmt [...] kaum eine Sonderstellung ein, wenn auch Seelenängste nicht ein so erschütterndes Ausmaß annehmen, wie im Deutschland Luthers".

75 BRUNO, "Sigillus sigillorum", p.208: "Omnia tandem formant omnia et formantur ab omnibus, atque dum omnia per omnia formantur atque *figurantur* [italics: PS], ad inveniendum, inquirendum, iudicandum, ratiocinandum reminiscendumque de omnibus per omnia possumus promoveri." For a comment see Robert KLEIN, "L'immaginazione come veste dell'anima in Marsilio Ficino e Giordano Bruno", in: KLEIN, *La Forma e l'intelligibile. Scritti sul Rinascimento e l'arte moderna,* Turin: Giulio Einaudi, 1975, pp.45–74 and passim) · See also BRUNO, "De Umbris Idearum", in: BRUNO, *Opera latine conscripta publicis sumptibus edita,* VOL.2, part 1, edited by V. IMBRIANI and C. M. TALLARIGO, Naples: Dom. Morano, 1886, p.1–55, here p.25 and in "Explicatio triginta sigillorum", in: BRUNO, *Opera,* VOL.2, part 2, p.73–160, here p.138 (from the chapter "Daedali, qui decimusquartus est sigillus, explicatio"): "Quemadmodum omnis artifex, qui plurimos diversosque intendit effectus, vel pluribus intrumentis vel unico diversimode multiformiterque exagitato organo ad proprias proficiscitur functiones, haud aliter hic Daedalus". See also Bruno's treatise "De lampade combinatoria", ibd. pp.227–327, here p.303: "Si rhetoricus es vel poëta vel propheta, adde ex omnibus terminis qualiacunque occurrunt, assumptas metaphoras seu translationes [...]. Sic enim de omnibus onmia dici possunt, ut de homine serpens, planta, lectus, ovis, leo, lupus, radix, ramus, stirps, fructus, manus, cauda, dens, et alia centena millia."

76 Iordanus BRUNUS NOLANUS [Giordano BRUNO], *De Imaginum, signorum, & Idearum compositione. Ad omnia Inuentionum, Dispositionum, & Memoriæ genera Libri tres,* Frankfurt am Main: Apud Ioan.Vuechelum et Petrum Fischerum, 1591.

77 Giordano BRUNO, "De imaginum, signorum et idearum compositione" (1591), in: BRUNO, *Opera latine conscripta publicis sumptibus edita,* VOL.2, part 3, pp.85–322. Very important is chapter 5

("De imaginum momento physico, mathematico, logico iuxta universas modorum istorum acceptiones"), pp. 101–104.

78 See Thomas [Tommaso] CAMPANELLA, *De Sensu Rerum et Magia, Libri Quatuor, pars mirabilis occultæ philosophiæ, Ubi demonstratur, Mundum esse DEI vivam statuam, beneque cognoscentem; omnesque illius partes, partiumque particulas sensu donatas esse, alias clariori, alias obscuriori, quantus sufficit ipsarum conseruationi ac totius, in quo consentiunt; & fere omnium Naturæ arcanorum rationes aperiuntur,* edited by Tobias ADAM, Frankfurt am Main: Apud Egenolphum Emmelium, impensis Godefridi Tampachij, 1620 · For the translation of the subtitle cited, see Bernardino M. BONANSEA, *Tommaso Campanella. Renaissance Pioneer of Modern Thought,* Washington, DC: Catholic University of America Press, [1969], p. 156.

79 Max JAMMER, *Concepts of Force. A Study in the Foundations of Dynamics,* Cambridge, MA: Harvard University Press, 1957, p. 82.

80 SKRBINA, *Panpsychism in the West,* p. 82.

81 Johannes KEPLER, *Harmonies of the World,* in: idem: *Epitome of Copernican Astronomy & Harmonies of the World,* translated by Charles Glenn Wallis, Amherst, NY: Prometheus Books, 1995, p. 90. (First Latin edition: *Harmonices Mundi libri V,* Linz: Johann Planck for Gottfried Tampach, 1619).

82 KRIS, *Ricerche psicoanalitiche sull'arte,* p. 226.

83 Ernst KRIS, *Le Style rustique. Le moulage d'après nature chez Wenzel Jamnitzer et Bernard Palissy (1926), suivi de: Georg Hoefnagel et le naturalisme scientifique (1927),* translated by Christophe Jouanlanne, Paris: Macula, 2005, FIG. 130. (Original German edition: "Der Stil 'rustique'. Die Verwendung des Naturabgusses bei Wenzel Jamnitzer und Bernard Palissy", in: *Jahrbuch der Kunsthistorischen Sammlungen Wien,* Neue Folge, VOL. 1, 1926, pp. 137–208).

84 John ONIANS, "The Biological Basis of Renaissance Aesthetics," in: *Concepts of Beauty in Renaissance Art,* ed. AMES-LEWIS and ROGERS, pp. 12–27, here p. 21.

85 WEISE, "Vitalismo, animismo e panpsichismo nella decorazione del Cinquecento e del Seicento", p. 382.

86 Ibid, p. 385.

87 FORSSMAN, *Säule und Ornament,* p. 191: „Wo die Ornamentation Wirklichkeitscharakter hat, ist sie [gleichwohl] nicht von der Natur abgeschrieben."

88 The *Rollwerk,* again, has origins in early cinquecento engravers of the Mannerism, like Agostino Veneziano; see FORSSMAN, *Säule und Ornament,* p. 115.

89 SCHMARSOW, "Raumgestaltung als Wesen der architektonischen Schöpfung", especially p. 75 · See also as examples of the enormous diffusion of the Ohrmuschelstil WEISE, "Vitalismo, animismo e panpsichismo nella decorazione del Cinquecento e del Seicento", p. 393: epitaph for the family of Otto von Oye, Bielefeld, Neustädter Marienkirche · For examples in the Magdeburg cathedral, dating from the late Cinquecento, see Ernst SCHUBERT, *Der Magdeburger Dom,* Leipzig: Koehler & Amelang, 1984, plate 128: Christoph Dehne, bronze epitaph for Cuno von Lochow and his wife; plate 130: Hans Klintzsch, epitaph for Lewin von der Schulenburg; plates 131 and 132: Christoph Kapup, pulpit with St. Paul as atlas of the pulpit (with telamons); plate 142: Hans Klintzsch, epitaph for Werner von Plotho, with asses (instead of corbels), several sirens, and putti; plate 156: Christoph Kapup, epitaph for Ernst von Mandelsloh, with bust-corbels and herms-caryatids.

90 I thank Giuseppina Saccaro del Buffa (Storia della storiografia filosofica, University of Rome) for her inspiring words (written and spoken) on this subject. For Lorenzo Giusso there is a "baccanale di divinità e di mostri contorcentisi colle groppe denudate che s'incontra nell'opera di Bruno" (Lorenzo GIUSSO, *Scienza e filosofia in Giordano Bruno,* Naples: Conte, 1955, p. 29).

91 Georg TOEPFER, "Organismus", in: TOEPFER, *Historisches Wörterbuch der Biologie. Geschichte und Theorie der biologischen Grundbegriffe,* 3 VOLS., Stuttgart and Weimar: J. B. Metzler, 2011, VOL. 2, pp. 777–842, here p. 781: „Es ist nicht verwunderlich, dass materialistische Ansätze einen erheblichen Anteil an der Entwicklung der frühen Organismusmodelle haben. Indem sie auf die Seele als ein zentrales Organisations- und Regulationsprinzip der Lebewesen verzichten, sind sie darauf angewiesen, die komplexen Lebensfunktionen aus der Interaktion der Teile zu begründen. Terminologisch manifestiert sich diese Veränderung in der verstärkten Verwendung von Begriffen aus dem Handwerk und der Baukunst zur Beschreibung und Analyse von Lebensprozessen. So gebraucht G. Bruno Ende des 16. Jahrhunderts Metaphern aus dem Bereich der Architektur, wenn er vom Körper eines Lebewesens spricht (‚composizione d'uno animale'; ‚architettura'; ‚edificio')."· See also Giordano BRUNO: *Spaccio della bestia trionfante | Austreibung des triumphierenden Tieres. Italienisch–Deutsch,* translated and edited by Elisabeth BLUM and Paul Richard BLUM, in: Giordano BRUNO, *Werke, mit der kritischen Edition von Giovanni Aquilecchia,* edited by Thomas LEINKAUF, VOL. 5, Hamburg: Felix Meiner, 2009, p. 18 (first edition: Paris [actually: London]: [John Charlewood], 1584).

IMAGES

Paola BAROCCHI, *Michelangelo e la sua scuola,* 3 VOLS., Florence: Leo S. Olschki, 1962–1964, VOL. [2]: *I disegni di Casa Buonarotti e degli Uffizi: Tavole,* plate CXXXIII: FIG. 1 · Author's collection: FIG. 2 · Hugues SAMBIN, *Oevvre de la diversite Des termes, dont on vse en architecture, reduict en ordre,* Lyon: Iean Dvrant, 1572, unpaged: FIG. 3 · Florence, Uffizi, Gabinetto Disegni, N. 2409A: FIG. 4 · Author: FIGS. 5, 9, 10, and 11 · Istituto di Storia dell'Arte "Giulio Carlo Argan", Rome: FIG. 6 · Georg WEISE, "Il repertorio ornamentale del barocco napoletano di Cosimo Fanzago e il suo significato per la genesi del Rococò", parts II, in: *antichità viva,* VOL. 13, 1974, no. 5, pp. 32–41, here p. 34 (FIG. 7): FIG. 7 · Dipartimento di Storia dell'arte, Università di Roma I: FIG. 8

CLAIRE BARBILLON

The Relief and the Body: Relationships between Sculpture and Architecture around 1900

The relationships between sculpture and architecture are key to understanding the theoretical reflections on the arts at the turn of the 19th century. When Antoine Bourdelle asserts that "sculpture and architecture never separate their laws"[1], he seems to express a certainty that, viewed from the perspective of many particular cases of the late 19th century, appears unconfirmed. Actually, being a member of Rodin's studio and the author of the sculptural decor of the façade of the Théâtre des Champs Elysées in Paris, what Bourdelle expresses here is more a wish, a *petitio principii,* than a statement of fact. In effect, Bourdelle tries to break with the recent past of French sculpture when he states in a lecture at the Académie de la Grand Chaumière given in 1912:

> My work wants to break away from a disgraceful era, in which all sculpted
> work is not anymore coherent with its supports, whether they be architec-
> tural walls or pedestals. Hence, this solitary effort to create the unity of the
> sculptures with the whole building is burdensome.[2]

THE DEPENDENCY OF RELIEF FIGURES ON ARCHITECTURE

On the basis of Bourdelle's fundamental criticism, let us step back into the third part of the 19th century and examine the role the sculptured body plays in reliefs that are related to an architectural project: Do the human bodies carved in relief in major architectural settings stand for an integration of sculpture into architecture or do they rather represent the independence of sculpture?

IN / KIRSTEN WAGNER AND JASPER CEPL (EDITORS) /
IMAGES OF THE BODY IN ARCHITECTURE: ANTHROPOLOGY AND BUILT SPACE /
TÜBINGEN · BERLIN / ERNST WASMUTH VERLAG / 2014 / PP. 263–280

It is clear that for certain other elements of the architectural decor, such as flowers, plants, or geometrical figures, the same question would not arise.[3] Abstracts motifs or those made from lifeless elements always provide support, emphasis, and decoration in agreement with the rhythms of the façades: from the controlled ribs of Hausmannian façades in Paris to the most 'avant-gardist' buildings, such as Josef Maria Olbrich's Secession in Vienna (1897–98) which, though exuberant (with its golden ribbon underlining the enormous ball topping the building), introduces no distance or rupture between the bas-reliefs and the structure of the building. In the field of relief it seems that only the sculptured human figure can occupy a complex position with regard to the architectural matrix on which it depends.

The question obviously overlaps with that of the relief grading of the figure. But it is not identical with it, since, from the very bas-relief to the very high relief, a variety of shadings is possible, which coalesces with the factors of space, plan, and legibility, in relation to the architectural structure. Certain conventions, however, compel the sculptured body to a state of mere dependency on architecture whatever these nuances are: the caryatids (**FIG. 1**) and atlantes (**FIG. 2**) ornamenting Parisian façades during the second Empire and the third Republic provide one of the most significant examples for this hierarchical alliance

CLAIRE BARBILLON

between sculptors and architects. This was the subject of an exhibition which, before the opening of the Musée d'Orsay, contributed to the great surge of the rediscovery of 19th century French sculpture.[4]

In the context of eclecticism and historicism dominating the official taste in France at the end of the 19th century, public and other buildings in the better areas of the capital are decorated with these figures. They flank entrance doors or windows, support balconies, underline light protrusions and, from 1902 on, when corbelled constructions are allowed at the top of façades, mainly congregate at the higher storeys. The function of these female or male figures is two-fold: they carry, support, serve as arm-rest, but they also mark an axis of verticality on façades where parallel horizontal lines often prevail. We can speak

2
AIMÉ MILLET /
ATLANTES /
1897 / 15 RUE
DU LOUVRE -
PARIS - 1ST
ARRONDISSE-
MENT / (ARCHI-
TECTE: HENRI
BLONDEL)

here of a system in which the sculptured human body, mostly in high relief but sometimes as *ronde-bosse,* supports architecture. The dependency of sculpture on architecture is very obvious even if the body of an atlant or a caryatid is sheathed; i. e. that its lower part is encased, which converts a part of it from a morphological imitation to a geometrical and abstract form.

To some extent, Bourdelle could have been proud of the atlantes and caryatids multiplying on Parisian façades. But even leaving aside the stylistic options of their authors, often close to baroque pastiche, these works did not satisfy him.

They did not respond to the strict demand of his rule that a sculptural subject must conform to the building function. He actually wanted the sculptured figures on the façade of the Théâtre des Champs Elysées to give the impression of "a small book of marble"[5], explaining the spirit of the building.

A close correspondence of the sculptured reliefs to the buildings for which they are intended was also proclaimed by the architect Charles Garnier when establishing the program of the allegorical groups ornamenting the façade of the Paris Opéra (**FIG. 3**). This question actually was at stake in the debate raised about

one of these groups: the high relief *La Danse* by Jean-Baptiste Carpeaux (**FIG. 4**), nowadays kept by the Musée d'Orsay. *La Danse* was commissioned in 1865; the theme of dance was specified later on. Garnier differentiates between two types of relief: decorating sculpture on the one hand, architectural sculpture on the other. Regarding the four groups of the Opéra's façades, he opted for the second type. Unlike Carpeaux's work, the three other allegorical groups (by Eugène Guillaume, François Jouffroy, and Jean-Joseph Perraud) fit with Garnier's claim. But Carpeaux's was unabashedly and exceptionally exuberant. Garnier recalls:

> *I don't know which of us made the biggest sacrifice by giving in to the other, but I know that for my part, I was absolutely decided, if Carpeaux would not listen to me, to let him go and do as he pleased. I found his model superb, I was amazed by his so vivid composition, by the thrilling contours of his clay figures, and eventually I said to myself: "Well, if the monument is afflicted with the exuberance of my sculptor, this will only be a small mishap whereas it would be a big one if keeping stubbornly to my ideas. I would deprive France of a work which will certainly be a masterpiece."[6]*

CLAIRE BARBILLON

The work, shown to the public in 1869, caused a shock, as many critical voices testify. A certain M. de Salelles published an excessively polemical small booklet entitled *Le groupe de la Danse de M. Carpeaux jugé au point de vue de la morale*

4
JEAN-BAPTISTE
CARPEAUX /
LA DANSE /
1865–69 /
ECHAILLON
STONE /
NOW IN THE
MUSÉE D'ORSAY
PARIS /
(REPLACED BY
A COPY BY PAUL
BELMONDO)

ou Essai sur la façade du nouvel opéra (The group of the Dance by M. Carpeaux considered from moral standards or Essay on the façade of the new Opera House). The section on Carpeaux's sculpture starts with the motto "J'appelle un chat, un chat"[7] (I call a spade a spade), which gave a foreboding of the tone of the comments to follow. The author denounces the "lustful postures", the "cynic glances", the "rave fever of pleasure", the "frenzy"[8], and the "sensual and truly shameless postures"[9]. He polemicizes that without the magnetic power of the male figure, which frenetically excites the female ones, they would roll in dust. Denouncing their flabby, limp, and worn flesh, their falling breasts, their creased bellies, he goes so far to say that: "They smell of vice and stink of wine."[10]

Although this hypercritic stands out in his repulsive rejection of Carpeaux's work, several other critics generally shared his opinion. The widespread rejection arose not only out of Carpeaux's realism, not even of the freedom he took with regard to the program (Garnier had imposed) by increasing the number of figures. It was caused by the fact that the high relief occupies a space half way between the façade and the street space. Significantly, Carpeaux, in his preliminary drawings searched for a solution both in the field of relief — the *Départ des Volontaires* (1834–36) by François Rude — and in a group of *ronde-bosse* — the Laocoön.[11] Each of the delineated groups contains a specific tension originating in the contrast between a figure welling up against the pressure of a gyrating group. With such a composition, Carpeaux above all aimed to realize a formal experience. The imposed subject on this experience is only a pretext. This high-handedness is unacceptable for an opinion, which expects from a sculptured decor an illustration of the purpose of the building. De Salelles clearly expresses this point of view: "When we will have public Bacchanalia or Saturnalia, then, but only then, will this group be true […]. How could the authorities therefore allow something outside the Opera […], which her agents have the duty to prohibit inside?"[12]

The shock produced by Carpeaux's group — damaged by an ink-bottle thrown on it,[13] something very rare at the time — is due to the fact that this very high relief, protruding in public space, directly addresses those who come close to the Opera House. It even seems to question the building itself, to which it should have been subordinated. That is what Émile Zola suggests when interpreting *La Danse* as a satire of the corrupted contemporary society: "Carpeaux's group is the Empire; it is a violent satire of the contemporary dance, this furious dance of millions, of women for sale and men sold."[14] Zola, pursuing the metaphor, declares Garnier's building as a sort of negative to the sculptured group:

> On this silly and pretentious façade, right in the middle of this bastard architecture, of this style Napoleon III, shamefully vulgar, the true symbol of the reign erupts.
>
> The columns are of a deceptive heaviness; the other groups stand there, stiff, constrained, disguised to mock history; the whole monument with its cold lines, its bourgeois luxury, its air of a honorable man in his Sunday best, seems built to tell our grandsons: "Look at those statues of cardboard: your fathers were chaste. […]"[15]

The powerful novelty of *La Danse* can be even more appreciated when compared to other relief groups of the same sculptor. Shortly before, Carpeaux had conceived a group in relief on the theme of Flora (**FIG. 5**) for the new Pavillon de

5
JEAN-BAPTISTE
CARPEAUX /
LE TRIOMPHE
DE FLORE /
1866 / SOUTH
FAÇADE OF THE
PAVILLON DE
FLORE / LOUVRE
PARIS

Flore built by the architect Hector Lefuel. It has often been said that the fullness of the shapes and the illusion of motion of this group represent not only a tribute to Rubens but also prefigured *La Danse*. With regard to the relationship of the Flora group to the building's façade it is exactly the opposite. The group fits perfectly well in the layout and the proportions of the façade to which it supplies a central point. The squatting posture of Flora's body and the small size of the *putti* accompanying it are in harmony with the pavilion's elevation at large. Situated high, out of the beholder's range, the group does not allow an interpretation aside the one traditionally allotted to the allegory. From the perspective of the subject as well as of the form, the relief is in absolute accordance with the principles adopted by the architect, and, while not diminishing the sculptor's talent, answers the necessary submission of sculpture to architecture, as stated later by Bourdelle.

THE AUTONOMY OF HUMAN FIGURES, OR THE QUESTION OF THE RELIEF'S STRUCTURE

The adapted solutions by Carpeaux for high relief groups which he animates with figures are not consistent and thus can oscillate between an accord with the building where they are placed and an emancipation from it. About ten years after the episode of *La Danse,* Auguste Rodin received the order for a monument for a future Musée de Arts décoratifs from the French State. As noted by Rosalind Krauss, the *Porte de l'Enfer* (**FIG. 6**) — composed of 227 figures of all sizes,

more or less standing out from the background — shows the breakdown of the principle of spatio-temporal unity.[16] The narrative models of *Trajan's Column* in Rome or the more segmented one of Lorenzo Ghiberti's *Baptistery Doors* in

Florence[17] are questioned by the profusion, entanglement, and apparent disorder of the sculptured figures and the intenseness of their torments on the *Porte de l'Enfer*. Rodin takes the liberty of freeing himself from tradition. Instead, an individual rendition of the subject as well as an apparent deconstruction of the narrative model of Dante's *Divine Comedy* characterize his *Porte de l'Enfer*. What does the work gain by this deconstruction? Obviously, an increased expressivity of the figures, springing up one by one, or in small groups, from the shapeless matter of an uncertain background — an abyssal mystery which the references to literature, to Dante's text, will not elucidate, but which draws profoundly on the drives of desire and death —, a freedom of motion that Julius Meier-Graefe hailed as a "sculpture, the hitherto unmoved, was given life."[18] More than any other art form, the relief permits a variable spectrum from clear shape to diffuse shapelessness in as much as the figures are related to the background by fusions or tensions of infinite nuances.

The way the relief is elaborated differs from the door leaves to the two pillars. In their architectural organization more homogeneous through their buttress, the groups and figures of the pillars sustain the stern limits of the pillar's constraint. In contrast, the wider space of the leaves gives the sculptor an astonishing plastic freedom to vary greatly the degrees of recession or outpouring of the figures. In fact, the background operates metaphorically like a sea, whose waves drag down or spew forth the quivering bodies one after the other, unless it is a lake of fire — it is just this sculptural matrix deprived of any distinct figure that the Parisian public discovered in 1900 at the Pavillon de l'Alma.

The sculpture undermines the legibility of the architectural structure underlying the relief. This becomes quite evident in the version of the gate bearing the figures, particularly from the man who falls backwards clinging to the edge of the cornice, as if he were desperately trying to get over an obstacle. It is worth noting that many figures appearing in the *Porte de l'Enfer* — like the *Penseur,* the *Fugit Amor,* or the *Baiser* — were utilized several times as a *ronde-bosse* by Rodin.

In his analysis, Rudolf Wittkower, stressing the innovative aspect of the sculptor, insists on Rodin's method of working in depth, proceeding from profiles and not from faces, in a way totally opposed to the rules given by Adolf von Hildebrand in *Das Problem der Form in der bildenden Kunst*.[19] Wittkower describes Rodin's approach as a "conception of sculpture as matter, plastic mass, animated from within and radiating outward"[20]. This also applies to the bodies that emerge in the *Porte de l'Enfer*. Rodin himself exposes this principle in a dialog with Paul Gsell, in which he recalls the advice Benjamin Constant had given him in his youth: "[W]hen you do sculptural works in future never perceive forms in the plane, but always in depth… Always consider a surface as the extremity of a volume, as if it were a smaller or larger point turned in your direction"[21]. As Wittkower has pointed out, it is exactly this treatment of relief that Hildebrand, who had such a great impact on the next generation of sculptors, argued against. He writes: "It is a historical fact that, directly or indirectly, 20th-century sculptors were immensely indebted to Hildebrand."[22] That is what I have attempted to show regarding the generation of sculptors closely following Rodin's time in my contribution to the exhibition catalogue *Oublier Rodin? La sculpture à Paris, 1905–1914.*[23]

In 1928, the sculptor Robert Schmitz, looking back on his years of study in Paris, reported that the debates led about the art theories of Rodin and those of "Fiedler/Hildebrand", concerning the principles of creation in sculpture, had reached a peak before the war.[24] Albert E. Elsen, for his part, states that Hildebrand's treatise was the result of his dismay over the fashionable realism of the time in sculpture, and the work in relief which most epitomizes this realism for Hildebrand, even though he never mentioned it, was Rodin's *Porte de l'Enfer*.[25] More than any other concept Hildebrand had developed, the relief appears as the most central: "Throughout his research, always drawing on deductions from the principle of the view from the distance as a unique type of artistic vision, Hildebrand builds up the theory that the only form or really artistic representation is that in relief", sums up Roberto Salvini.[26]

In a whole chapter devoted to "La conception en relief"[27], Hildebrand maintains that the only way to organize a three-dimensional representation in space consists in assembling the objects to be represented according to a certain number of levels as if they were contained between two glass plates: "The total volume of the picture, depending on the kind of object, consists of a number of such imaginary strata placed one behind another"[28]. Works obeying this conception by organizing the figures in ordered layers offer a radical alternative to the apparently uncontrolled outburst of bodies in Rodin's *Porte de l'Enfer*.

THE RETURN OF THE PRIMACY OF ARCHITECTURE

The Musée d'Orsay's 2009 exhibition about the impact of Rodin on sculptors working in Paris in the years before the First World War made it possible to verify that the reliefs of Joseph Bernard, Georges Minne, Aristide Maillol, Wilhelm Lehmbruck, Manuel Martinez Hugué called Manolo, Julio González, Elie Nadelman, Alexander Archipenko, Raymond Duchamp-Villon, Jacob Epstein, and Otto Gutfreund — whether or not they had been practitioners in the studio of Rodin — were at the same time positioned against Rodin and in accordance with Hildebrand's principles. Two of them, Albert Bartholomé — in the *Monument aux Morts* at Père Lachaise, inaugurated in 1899 — and Antoine Bourdelle — with the series of reliefs of the façade du Théâtre des Champs Elysées — particularly applied those principles to reliefs within the scope of an architectural project. In both cases the human figure is the only motive chosen by the sculptors. Bartholomé's work, situated at the end of the principal avenue of Père Lachaise cemetery, is a cenotaph with a unique façade of two levels (**FIG. 7**).

In its final stone version, it measures 7 meters in height and 14 in width. Its massive structure, planned by the architect Jean Camille Formigé, allows the sculptured figures to spread out on two levels: on the lower level, a man, a woman, and a child, all of them naked and halfway between recumbent statue and medieval *"transi"*[29], seem protected in their eternal sleep by a naked female figure with arms wide open. On the upper level, a couple stands with their backs to us, on each side of a gaping door, a black break, an entrance to death. As a frieze and high relief, from their right as well as from their left side, figures disposed to proceed on two downward slanting diagonals are stooped with despair or defeated by their tears, overwhelmed or consentient.[30]

Although difficult to imagine today, Bartholomé's monument was a big success. More than 100,000 people were present at its unveiling ceremony on All Saints Day in 1899. Critics immediately hailed its universal range, its inclusive capacity of invoking remembrance of all who have passed away, not only the renowned dead, but also the unknown, the poor, all tumbled together in a common grave.[31] Some even go further in their analysis and maintain that the work attains this universality not only by its meaning but also by its form. Maurice Demaison underlines three aspects in this regard: firstly the "straight-forwardness" of the plan, secondly the "gravity of the layout", which thirdly, allows for the "so clear expression of a sentiment and a thought"[32]. These qualities confer on the monument "the privilege of being recognized by all"[33]. According to the underlying ideologies, we find references to Egyptian antiquity, medieval art, opposing those of the Italian Renaissance. And eventually, Bartholomé's style is opposed to that of Jules Dalou and Rodin.

When contemporaries comment on French Sculpture from the end of the 19th century, do not, to paraphrase Johann Joachim Winckelmann, the ideals of "noble simplicity and quiet grandeur" call for a comparison with Rodin? The critic Gustave Larroumet addresses this comparison when contrasting Bartholomé's *Monument aux Morts* with Rodin's aesthetic: "In its execution it [the *Monument aux Morts*] is as studied and static as M. Rodin's works are spontaneous and volitionally incomplete. It effuses an impression of deep calm, that of Eternal rest, whereas in M. Rodin's work passion is restless and tormented."[34] Arsène Alexandre, too, opposes both Dalou and Rodin to Bartholomé in an article commemorating the latter's death in 1928:

> *In sculpture, Rodin recaptured the rights of imagination, Dalou that of great decorative tradition, Bartholomé eventually that of the simplicity of silhouettes and the expressive sobriety of contours. Any sculptor of today whom we appreciate for his synthetic skills is indebted, without even knowing it, to the author of the Monument aux Morts.*[35]

This simplicity and this mastery of the layout of figures appears today as characteristic of the close alliance between the architectural structure of the monument and the organization of the sculptured bodies. This is what distinguishes Bartholomé from the Canovian model (**FIG. 8**). For even if the Cenotaph

8
ANTONIO CANOVA /
CENOTAPH TO
MARIA CHRISTINA
OF AUSTRIA /
1805 /
AUGUSTINER-
KIRCHE /
VIENNA

to Marie Christine of Austria, Duchess of Teschen, in the Augustinerkirche in Vienna, resembles it with the procession of the living towards the opening in the gate of death, the illusionistic character of the figures in Canova prevails over the structure.

CLAIRE BARBILLON

Returning to Bourdelle, he confirms the fundamental design of Bartholomé: both with the way he organized the reliefs of the façade du Théâtre des Champs Elysées (**FIG. 9**) and in his theoretical writings. His course on March 15, 1915, at

9
AUGUSTE PERRET
(ARCHITECT) /
BAS RELIEFS
BY ANTOINE
BOURDELLE /
THÉÂTRE DES
CHAMPS-
ELYSÉES /
15 AVENUE
MONTAIGNE -
PARIS - 8TH
ARRONDISSE-
MENT

the Académie de la Grande Chaumière is titled: "Laws of the Bas-relief, Pensive Apollon and the Muses." In an oftentimes poetical style, made of short, aphoristic sentences provoking meditation, he asserts strict subordination of figures to architectural balance: "The detail is informed by the masses. The shadows are matched with the total clarity of the walls. [...] Each particular detail is affected by the general disposition of the whole of the built monument."[36] Still, the sculptor does not feel bound by an ancillary dependency since his creative impetuosity is fed by a constant movement between this necessity, derived from the purpose of his work, and life, which maintains his inspiration. "I have often looked at life to recognize that it in its powerful vigor lays out all with perfect equality."[37] The confrontation between the representation of life, which can be seen as a naturalistic temptation, and the demanding requirements of the sculptor's assignment — to make understandable to the spectator the meaning of architecture — is a permanent conflict. Bourdelle acted it out in the confrontation with solid matter. Wittkower would not consider him a modeler like Rodin, but as the carver of marble depicted by Hildebrand. "The immolator is, for us, the sculptor", says Bourdelle, "he disembowels virgin marble."[38] What becomes of the human figure, the representation of the body, in this conflict? Bourdelle, in contrast to Carpeaux, subordinates it to the general structure of the artwork. "Be able to sacrifice the human body's details on the altar of the total temple", he said to his pupils. His own commentary about the frieze of *Pensive Apollon and the Muses* (**FIG. 10**) is clear on the sublimation of the human body: "The human face

departed in all respects from the female body, but then came marble law [...]; and this frieze is more a blossoming wall than mankind revealing itself under a stone mask."[39]

NOTES

1   Antoine Bourdelle quoted by Laure DALON in the title of her article "'La sculpture et l'architecture ne séparent jamais leurs lois': Bourdelle, un sculpteur architecte", in: *Livraisons d'histoire de l'architecture*, no. 12, 2006, pp. 9–19.

2   Antoine BOURDELLE, "15 mars 1912. Les lois du bas-relief. Apollon pensif et les muses", in: BOURDELLE, *Cours & Leçons à l'Académie de la Grande Chaumière*, edited by Laure DALON, 2 VOLS., here VOL. 2: *Leçons (1909–1922)*, Paris: Paris-Musées | Édition des Cendres, 2007, p. 200–203, here p. 203 (note 1): "Mon travail veut s'arracher d'une époque de honte où toute œuvre sculptée n'est plus cohérente avec ses supports, qu'ils soient des murs architectoniques ou des piédestaux. Aussi cet effort solitaire pour créer l'unité des sculptures avec le tout de l'édifice est-il accablant."

3   See Anne PINGEOT, "Le décor extérieur du Louvre sur la cour Carrée et la rue de Rivoli (1851–1936). Iconographie de niche", in: *La Revue du Louvre et des Musées de France*, VOL. 39, 1989, no. 2, pp. 112–125.

4 *Atlantes et cariatides sous le Second Empire et la IIIe République,* exhibition organized by the supervision of Anne Pingeot and Antoinette Le Normand at the Musée d'Art et d'Essai, Palais de Tokyo, November 1978 to February 1979. See *Le Petit Journal des Grandes Expositions,* no. 71: Anne PINGEOT and Antoinette LE NORMAND, *Atlantes et cariatides de Paris sous le Second Empire et la Troisième République,* Paris: Réunion des Musées Nationaux, 1978.

5 BOURDELLE, "15 mars 1912. Les lois du bas-relief. Apollon pensif et les muses", p. 201: "un petit livre de marbre".

6 Charles GARNIER, *Le Nouvel Opéra,* Paris, Éditions du Linteau, 2001, pp. 372–373 (first published in 2 VOLS., 1878 and 1881): "Je ne sais lequel de nous deux fit un plus grand sacrifice en cédant ainsi à l'autre; ce que je sais, c'est que, pour ma part, j'étais absolument décidé, si Carpeaux ne voulait pas m'écouter, à le laisser aller à sa guise. Je trouvais son modèle superbe; j'étais émerveillé de sa composition si vivante, du modelé palpitant de ses figures d'argile, et, somme toute, je me disais: 'Eh bien, si le monument pâtit un peu de l'exubérance de mon sculpteur, ça ne sera qu'un petit malheur; tandis que ça en ferait un grand si, m'entêtant dans mes idées, je privais la France d'un morceau qui sera certes un chef-d'œuvre.'"

7 M. C. A. DE SALELLES, *Le groupe de la Danse de M. Carpeaux jugé au point de vue de la morale ou Essai sur la façade du nouvel opéra,* Paris: Dentu, 1869, p. 9.

8 Ibid.: "Leurs poses lascives et leurs regards cyniques provoquent le spectateur. Emportées par la fièvre délirante du plaisir, elles vont tomber épuisées. Sans la puissance magnétique de l'homme qui les excite avec frénésie, elles rouleraient dans la poussière, où l'amour est déjà renversé sous leurs pieds alourdis."

9 Ibid.: "poses sensuelles et vraiment impudiques".

10 Ibid, p. 15: "Elles sentent le vice et puent le vin."

11 These drawings were shown by Laure DE MARGERIE, *La "Danse" de Carpeaux,* Paris: Éditions de la Réunion des Musées Nationaux, 1989, pp. 34–47.

12 DE SALELLES, *Le groupe de la Danse de M. Carpeaux,* p. 10: "Quand nous aurons des bacchanales et des saturnales publiques, alors, mais seulement alors, ce groupe sera vrai […].
Comment l'autorité pourrait-elle donc autoriser à l'extérieur de l'Opéra […], une chose que ses agents ont le devoir d'interdire à l'intérieur?"

13 See DE MARGERIE, *La "Danse" de Carpeaux,* p. 57.

14 Émile ZOLA, "Une allégorie" (first published in: *La Cloche,* April 22, 1870), in: ZOLA, *Oeuvres complètes,* edited by Henri MITTERAND, 21 VOLS., Paris: Nouveau Monde, 2002–2010, VOL. 3: *La naissance du naturalisme, 1868–1870,* edited by Colette BECKER and Jean-Louis CABANÈS, 2003, pp. 516–519, here p. 516: "le groupe de M. Carpeaux, c'est l'Empire; c'est la satire violente de la danse contemporaine, cette danse furieuse des millions, des femmes à vendre et des hommes vendus."

15 Ibid., p. 516: "Sur cette façade bête et prétentieuse du nouvel Opéra, au beau milieu de cette architecture bâtarde, de ce style Napoléon III, honteusement vulgaire, éclate le symbole vrai du règne.

Les colonnes ont une lourdeur mensongère; les autres groupes sont là, raides, figés, déguisés pour tromper l'histoire; le monument entier, avec ses lignes froides, son luxe bourgeois, son air de Prud'homme endimanché semble bâti pour dire à nos petits-fils: 'Voyez ces statues de carton: vos pères étaient chastes. […]'"

16 See Rosalind E. KRAUSS, *Passages in Modern Sculpture,* London: Thames and Hudson, 1977.

17 On Ghiberti's Baptistery doors see *The Gates of the Paradise. Lorenzo Ghiberti's Renaissance Masterpiece,* edited by Gary M. RADKE, New Haven and London: Yale University Press, 2007.

18 Julius Meier-Graefe, quoted in: Heinz R. FUCHS, *Plastik der Gegenwart,* Baden-Baden: Holle, 1970, p. 41: "Die Plastik, die bisher unbewegte, erhielt Leben!" (French edition consulted by the author: *Sculpture contemporaine,* translated by Pierre Wirth, Paris: Albin Michel, 1972, p. 39).

19 The first German edition of Adolf (von) Hildebrand's *Das Problem der Form in der bildenden Kunst* came out in 1893 (Strassburg: J. H. Ed. Heitz (Heitz & Mündel)). Contrary to what Jacques POULAIN maintains ("Préface. La culture de la forme dans des arts plastiques et l'esthétique de la perception", in: Adolf HILDEBRAND, *Le problème de la forme dans les arts plastiques,* translated by Eliane Beaufils, Paris and Montréal: l'Harmattan, 2002, pp. 7–23) a French translation was first published in 1903 by Georges M. Baltus under the title *Le Problème de la forme dans les arts figuratifs* (Paris: Vve. Emile Bouillon | Strasbourg: Heitz & Mündel, 1903). This translation did not receive the acclaim expected since it also seems unknown to Liliane BRION-GUERRY, who wrote the notes to the large extracts of the treatise of Hildebrand contained in the French edition of *Pure visibilité et formalisme dans la critique d'art au début du xxe siècle,* edited by Roberto SALVINI, translated by C. Jatosti, A. Pernet, E. Dickenherr, and A. Real-Charrière (Paris: Klincksieck, 1988). Nevertheless, Brion-Guerry calls attention to "une traduction française dans une thèse de doctorat parue à Strasbourg en 1912 mais devenue introuvable" (p. 55). (Original Italian edition: *La critica d'arte della pura visibilità e del formalismo,* Milan: Garzanti, 1977).

20 Rudolph WITTKOWER, *Sculpture. Processes and Principles,* London: Allen Lane, 1977, p. 242 (French edition consulted by the author: *Qu'est-ce que la sculpture? Principes et procédures, de l'Antiquité au xxe siècle,* translated by Béatrice Bonne, Paris: Macula, 1995, p. 263).

21 Ibid., p. 240 — For the original quote see August RODIN, *L'Art. Entretiens réunis par Paul Gsell,* Paris: Bernard Grasset, 1911, p. pp. 64: "Quand tu sculpteras désormais, ne vois jamais les formes en étendue, mais toujours en profondeur … Ne considère jamais une surface que comme l'extrémité d'un volume, comme la pointe plus ou moins large qu'il dirige vers toi."

22 Ibid., p. 248.

23 Claire BARBILLON, "Après la *Porte de l'Enfer,* la leçon d'Adolf von Hildebrand", in: *Oublier Rodin? La sculpture à Paris, 1905–1914,* edited by Catherine CHEVILLOT, Paris: Hazan, 2009, pp. 141–147 and 258 (notes).

24 See Martina RUDLOFF, "Mutter und Kind: 'Noch freier, noch abstrakter' als bei Rodin", in: *Wilhelm Lehmbruck,* edited by Martina RUDLOFF and Dietrich SCHUBERT, Bremen: Gerhard Marcks-Stiftung, 2000, pp. 9–18, here p. 15.

25 Albert E. ELSEN, *Origins of Modern Sculpture: Pioneers and Premises,* New York: Georges Braziller, 1974, p. 132.

26 Roberto SALVINI, "Introduction", in: *Pure visibilité et formalisme dans la critique d'art au début du xxe siècle,* ed. SALVINI, p. 7–59, here p. 19: "Continuant sa recherche, toujours au moyen de déductions du principe de la vision éloignée comme unique type de vision artistique, Hildebrand théorise que le seul mode de représentation vraiment artistique est la *représentation en relief*".

27 We prefer keeping the first translation by Georges M. Baltus, particularly because it was the only one the sculptors could know at the beginning of the 20th century.

28 Adolf Hildebrand, "The Problem of Form in the Fine Arts", in: *Empathy, Form, and Space. Problems in German Aesthetics, 1873–1893,* Introduction and translation by Harry Francis Mallgrave and Eleftherios Ikonomou, Santa Monica: Getty Publication Programs, 1994, pp. 227–279, here p. 250. For the original quote in German see Adolf Hildebrand: *Das Problem der Form in der bildenden Kunst,* third, improved edition, Strassburg: J. H. Ed. Heitz (Heitz & Mündel), 1903, here p. 75: "Das Gesamtvolumen eines Bildes besteht aber je nach der Art des Gegenständlichen aus mehr oder weniger solchen hintereinander gereihten imaginären Flächenschichten". See also Hildebrand, *Le Problème de la forme dans les arts figuratifs,* pp. 62–64.

29 A *"transi"* or cadaver tomb is a monument featuring an effigy in the form of a decomposing corpse. It is a depiction of a rotting cadaver, particularly characteristic of the later Middle Ages.

30 See the description of the monument published in *Revue encyclopédique,* vol. 5, 1895, p. 272–273, at the time of the exhibition of the model at the Salon du Champ-de-Mars (illustration: p. 273). The State and the City of Paris commissioned the artist to enhance the work by a third.

31 Roger Marx, quoted in: *Revue encyclopédique,* vol. 9, 1899, p. 922.

32 Maurice Demaison, "M. Bartholomé et le Monument aux Morts", in: *La Revue de l'Art ancien et moderne,* vol. 6, 1899, pp. 265–280, here p. 266: "cette œuvre si différente des autres par la simplicité du plan, la gravité de l'ordonnance et le don merveilleux d'exprimer si clairement un sentiment et une pensée".

33 Ibid., p. 265: "Le *Monument* de M. Bartholomé avait le privilège de s'imposer à tous."

34 Gustave Larroumet, *L'art et l'état en France,* Paris: Librairie Hachette et Cie, 1895, p. 144: "[...] comme exécution, elle est aussi étudiée et arrêtée que les œuvres de M. Rodin sont spontanées et volontairement incomplètes. Il s'en dégage une impression de calme profond, celle du repos éternel, alors que, chez M. Rodin, la passion s'agite et se tourmente."

35 Arsène Alexandre ("Sur Albert Bartholomé", in: *Le Figaro,* November 8, 1928, p. 52) quoted in Thérèse Burollet, "A propos du monument aux morts d'Albert Bartholomé: une nouvelle acquisition du musée de Brest", in: *La Revue du Louvre et des Musées de France,* vol. 24, 1974, pp. 109–116, here p. 113: "Dans la sculpture, Rodin reconquit les droits de l'imagination, Dalou ceux de la grande tradition décorative, Bartholomé enfin ceux de la simplicité des silhouettes et de la sobriété expressive du modelé. Tel sculpteur d'aujourd'hui que nous apprécions pour ses facultés *synthétiques* est, sans qu'il s'en doute, redevable à l'auteur du *Monument aux Morts.*"

36 Bourdelle, "15 mars 1912. Les lois du bas-relief. Apollon pensif et les muses", p. 200:
"Le détail s'informe des masses.
Les ombres se mesurent aux clartés totales des murs.
[...] Chaque détail particulier se ressent de l'ordre général de tout le monument bâti".

37 Ibid., p. 201: "J'ai eu beaucoup à regarder la vie pour voir dans elle qu'elle met tout dans son puissant élan avec égalité parfaite."

38 Ibid., p. 202: "l'immolateur est pour nous le statuaire, il éventre le marbre vierge."

39 Ibid., p. 203: "Le visage humain prêta tout avec tout du corps de la femme mais la loi du marbre est venue [...] et cette frise est bien plus un mur qui fleurit qu'une humanité qui s'essaie sous un masque de pierre."

IMAGES

Flickr: FIG. 1 (Patrick and Mary Jo, 2012) · Wikipedia Commons: FIG. 2 (Tangopaso, 2011), FIG. 5 (Marie-Lan Nguyen, 2008), FIG. 7 (JLPC, 2013), FIG. 8 (Andreas Praefcke, 2010), FIGS. 9 and 10 (detail of FIG. 9) (Coldcreation, 2013) · Library of Congress, Washington, D.C., Prints & Photographs Divison, LOT 13418, no. 272: FIG. 3 · Institut National d'Histoire de l'Art, Paris: FIG. 4 · 1886 — Collections patrimoniales numérisées de Bordeaux 3: FIG. 6

TANJA JANKOWIAK

The Transitoriness of Matter: Reflections on the Architecture of Sir John Soane

Sir John Soane (1753–1837) ranks as one of the most important English architects of his era. For many years, he held the prestigious Chair of Architecture at the Royal Academy in London. Apart from a number of country homes, he has to his name such buildings as the Dulwich Picture Gallery and the new design and reconstruction of large and significant institutions such as the Bank of England, Chelsea Hospital, and the Law Courts. However many of his buildings, the public buildings in particular, no longer exist. This is true of his new building for the Bank of England, which was razed to the ground in the 1920s, the Privy Council Chamber in Whitehall, and the New Law Courts.

At the same time, Soane is an architect who clearly reflected the changes in the conception of architecture which went on around him. Brought up with and formed by the ideal of classicism, Soane's relationship to the Picturesque caused him to challenge the classical canon, introducing completely different motifs, internal structures, and reflections into architecture and altering how it is perceived.

In his lifetime, in the late 18th and early 19th centuries, Soane's buildings were already the subject of controversy in the press and within his profession, sometimes attracting strong criticism. The deviations from classical rules of form and proportion were especially singled out for denigration; these the architect was said to sacrifice — a common complaint — to pompous self-portrayal and an architectonic language that aimed for showy effects. This two-pronged criticism even finds its way into the memorial speech held at the Institute of British Architects shortly after Soane's death in 1837, which referred to Soane's "aberrations of genius" and "too often an attempt at effect by ignoble means".[1]

IN / KIRSTEN WAGNER AND JASPER CEPL (EDITORS) /
IMAGES OF THE BODY IN ARCHITECTURE: ANTHROPOLOGY AND BUILT SPACE /
TÜBINGEN · BERLIN / ERNST WASMUTH VERLAG / 2014 / PP. 281–300

I will take as my starting point what is perhaps Soane's most eccentric building, his own house in Lincoln's Inn Fields, London, which can be regarded as a kind of laboratory of how he understood and related to architecture. For decades, he experimented here on different levels with a variety of motifs, perspectives, and preceptions, thereby repeatedly overstepping and interrupting temporal and spatial dimensions.

The building at nos. 12–14 Lincoln's Inn Fields not only served the architect and his family as a private residence, it also housed Soane's architectural practice and the multifarious collections, mostly of architectural fragments, sculptures, drawings, and paintings, which he assembled for decades.

The ensemble consists of three adjoining buildings or plots which, between 1792 and his death in 1837, the architect successively acquired, built on, enlarged, and partially demolished to enable further redesign. Soane made provision for

his house to be turned into a museum when he passed away. His wife and elder son had predeceased him and he had fallen out with the younger son. Today, it remains virtually the same as it was in 1837.

When viewed from the street the house looks quite restrained (FIG. 1). The brick façades of no. 12 and no. 14 have been kept simple.[2] Only one part of the façade stands out somewhat from the surrounding buildings, the central area at no. 13, added during some particularly comprehensive new construction work in 1812–1813: a portico of equally restrained design, with generous window arches of Portland stone, topped with caryatids.[3]

Entering the house through this portico, one first encounters various private and reception rooms looking onto the street. These follow the classic arrangement for an English residence of the period. On the ground floor, where the front room would be, is the sumptuous Library, which leads into a smaller dining room. Directly above the Library, again with large windows overlooking the street, is the Drawing Room, in which guests were received, and above that, on the top floor, each with a small balcony to the street, are the bedrooms of John Soane and his wife Eliza.

Continuing further inside the building, after leaving the Dining Room and turning left, one first comes upon a small Breakfast Room (**FIG. 2**). The comfortably furnished room has been decorated throughout in shades of golden yellow; it has a marble fireplace, several bookshelves and paneled walls. On the right, a window opens onto a small inner courtyard. Sunlight enters from above through several windows, through a small lantern at the center of the room and from elongated skylights, concealed along both sides of the cupola. The room has a clear and harmonious feel; it is based on a rectangular floor plan in the center of which, rising from a perfect square, is a flattened canopy dome. The family's breakfast table occupies a central position. Two glass doors[4] afford a

view of another room beyond the Breakfast Room. They mark the transition to a suite of rooms which transcend the classical arrangement of space in several respects.

Directly behind the Breakfast Room is the narrow, high-ceilinged room which Soane had already designed in 1808 to accommodate his burgeoning collections. The original version of this room, which Soane later[5] modified and renamed Dome, was completely isolated; a strange, dark room which admitted daylight only through a skylight set high above. Two intricate, hand-colored illustrations commissioned by Soane in 1811 from a colleague in his employment, the painter and architect Joseph Gandy, show the Dome in its idealized original state (FIG. 3). Considering that one has just been in the well appointed, comfortable Breakfast Room, it seems as if by crossing the threshold one has been transported into another world. The Dome marks the beginning of a type of spatial language which differs as much from that of the classical home, as it does from that in which private collections are normally housed.

Antique spolia and countless casts of antique architectural components — parts of capitals and friezes — fill the high, narrow space; they virtually cover the surface of the inner walls. Like the incrustations on a bed of mussels, these architectural fragments seem not just to fill the room, but to constitute it, to evolve from it. Bathed in a *lumière mystérieuse,* vaulted arches of stone only become visible on second glance: galleries on opposite sides of the wall, whose balustrades seem to be made up of friezes. Rising up from these are narrow steel supports, rendered seemingly fragile by their chased surfaces. Their task is to support shelves on which intact antique urns are neatly ranged. On one of the galleries a figure can just be made out in the gloom. It is pointing with an outstretched arm to the pieces shining in the lamplight on the front wall, where an arrangement of fragments, layered one above the other, projects into the room itself, crowned by an architectural model of the semi-derelict temple at Vesta. Another very similar formation also extends into the center from the opposite wall, which is in complete darkness.

Countless pieces of an antique collection are assembled here, mostly architectonic fragments or casts of fragments, whereby three-dimensional architectonic elements and stored items belonging to the collection merge with one another. The apparently arbitrary, incoherent distribution of the individual objects and fragments, their unusual and disparate abundance, and the dramatic lighting which blurs the spatial boundaries are reminiscent of a phantasmagoria, a dream image. Some kind of organizing principle appears to the observer to be missing: countless heterogeneous fragments are ranged together, jostling one another, on top of one another, without obeying any principle or context, in an apparently unclassified, seemingly associative, arrangement.[6]

Deep within the Soane family residence, the visitor seems to have entered not only a collection, but another organization of space and time, in which objects are assigned to one another using a different metric.

A second, idealized image of the earlier Dome also depicts rows of fragmented architectural elements highlighted on the illuminated front wall in strong relief. The room rises up to its full height before the viewer, who feels as if he himself were part of the image (**FIG. 4**). Pale sunlight shines through a colored glass lantern, its gentle glow visible on the stone floor below. We now appear to be

beneath the earth's surface; the space seems to have been carved out of subterranean rocks. Indeed, foundation walls are also visible, their plain, semicircular stone arches forming niches. Capitals, remains of friezes, and columns are lying on the ground; there are urns in the dark side niches as in the early Christian Roman catacombs. A somewhat higher stone arch frames a passageway which opens up before the observer in the center. A Roman gravestone emerges out of the darkness, surrounded by an aureole of shimmering golden light, in a small room at the end of the passage.

At this point, one has the impression of looking into an open grave — a burial ground or an archaeological excavation. The subject of the grave, which is simultaneously a disinterment, forms the starting point for a series of descriptions of the building which Soane wrote shortly after the two illustrations of the Dome were completed in 1812. He calls his commentary "Crude Hints Towards a History of My House Lincoln's Inn Fields".[7] It remains unclear whether this was more a kind of self-reflection or whether the text was written with the intention of publishing it later.

In his text, Soane has a fictitious archaeologist of the future discover the mysterious ruins at Lincoln's Inn Fields in the course of his excavation work. By means of the remains in the area of the Dome, the imaginary archaeologist speculates on the nature of his find: Could it be an antique temple? Or a mediaeval monastery? Or a magician's palace? He finally arrives at another theory: „[M]ay not those varieties in the Cavedium [...] have been fixed there in like manner to exemplify later changes in Architecture & to lay the foundation of an History of the Art itself — its origin — progress — meridian splendour & decline!"[8]

From this we can tell that as early as 1812, Soane was planning to turn the rear rooms of his London house into a kind of space for experimentation and reflection on architectonic narrative. He imagines the spaces in which he presents his collections as a material illustration of the history of architecture throughout its development, its prime and decline. Both in the collection itself and in the imaginary experiment upon which "Crude Hints" is based, present, past, and future are intricately woven together.

On the basis of Gandy's pictures and the concept of "Crude Hints", it appears that Soane is attempting to portray his collection not so much as a demonstration of architectural history using individual objects, but rather as an archaeological excavation site in which the different historical layers still exist in the unclassified disorder produced by the course of history. His aim does not seem to be to present a classified historical arrangement, but the 'archaeological excavation of history', as it would present itself to the archaeologist who comes across a newly-opened site.[9]

It seems as though Soane preferred to devise a space in which to experience and discover rather than conducting a rational historical classification, a space in which to convey the discovery of the historical, the palpable breath of history, not some estranged organization created long after. However, that alters our view of architecture as well, in which the goal is no longer to show the complete canon of rules of an epoch, but rather the feel for what the passage of time through the ages does to buildings. Time becomes palpable in the disorder of the fragments of past epochs.

On his *Grand Tour* as a young architect, Soane visited not just Rome and Sicily but also the archaeological sites at Herculaneum and Pompeii — where, since the 1750s, systematic excavations had been carried out — and the Temple of Paestum, which had only been rediscovered in 1752.

The excavations at Vesuvius itself were an example of how history came alive in a particularly impressive way for the travelers of those days, as a physical descent into the excavation sites, i.e. into history itself, as a new *dis*-covery of the past. As is the case with a ruin, it is possible to read and sense the passage of time, and hence the past, in the fragmented nature of the discovered. With the motif of the 'archaeological excavation site of history' — the grave which is simultaneously a disinterment — Soane and Gandy were taking up a theme

typical of the time: that of the Picturesque.[10] The architectural historian David Watkin speaks in this connection of the concept of the antique world in those days as a "buried past".[11] This metaphor can be easily recognized in Soane's and Gandy's presentation of Lincoln's Inn Fields, as can another typical motif of the time which belongs to this category, that of the ruin, which Soane brings into play in "Crude Hints".[12]

Depictions of ruins, in works by Giovanni Paolo Panini (1691–1765), Giovanni Battista Piranesi (1720–1778), and Hubert Robert (1733–1808), to name but a few, were rapturously received in England. Soane was a particular admirer of Piranesi. He became acquainted with him personally in Rome as early as 1778, was presented with several engravings as a gift, and later bought more for his collection — part of Soane's extensive collection of urns was also previously owned by Piranesi.

In its architectonic structure, with arches that rest on a substructure and the lighting effect with the fall of fractured sunlight from above, the Dome is reminiscent of an engraving of Piranesi's from 1770 showing the ruins of a sculpture gallery reputed to have been in Hadrian's Villa in Tivoli.

TANJA JANKOWIAK

Although Soane did not plan and build his house as a ruin, he still anticipated its inevitable decline as well as the burial of his own period and architecture, and he included this in his reasoning. In "Crude Hints", Soane imagined an "Antiquary", who would discover his house, then undergoing constant redesign and rebuilding, complete with collections, as an excavation site at some point in the distant future. For an architect, he thus adopted an astonishing outlook — the perspective of the future perfect, in which the building he is occupied with, at some point in time, *will have existed.*

This temporal perspective, the future perfect tense, is found in other architectural images of the period, for instance in a well known painting by Hubert Robert, his *Grande Galerie du Louvre en ruines,* which he exhibited in the Paris Salon in 1796 (**FIG. 5**).[13] A contemporary design for the reconstruction of the Grande Galerie of the Louvre is depicted here as a ruin. Following Sir William

Chambers[14] and Robert Adam,[15] Soane also adopted this idea. Even while his own new design for the Bank of England was being built between 1788 and 1833, he had two pictures made of it as an imaginary ruin (**FIG. 6, FIG. 7**). So the fascination for the 'transitoriness' of architecture amounts to more than a fascination for excavations of past architecture; it merges instead as a perspective on newly completed or yet to be completed work, with the architect's whole oeuvre. As we have just seen in the collection of fragments and pieces, time then becomes its most tangible at the point of decay and transience. The transitory nature, not only of his buildings but of his own person becomes an almost obsessive subject for Soane.

At first, this seems to contradict the fact that Soane makes every attempt to maintain his house and its rooms of collections in their current condition for as long as possible. Yet one could also say: Soane *has* to make sure that the house is preserved in exactly this form for as long as possible so that centuries later the imaginary architect will be able to discover the house as a material example of architectural history. In this respect, it was not so much the passage of time that was the architect's real enemy, but any possible transformative interventions made by any heirs or later owners. After Soane's wife and eldest son had died, he did not leave the house to his younger son, with whom he had fallen out, stipulating on his death that it should become a foundation which could be self-financing through partial leasing and would guarantee the maintenance of the building in its current condition. —

In the course of time, the architect converted the Dome into a whole series of largely crypt-like rooms, mainly devoted to antiquity, which ended up stretching right through to the rear of the house. Alongside this room, Soane designed another room, devoted to the second, at that time central historical building era: the medieval period.

This room (**FIG. 8**), known as Monk's Parlour, is also filled with collected pieces. However, here the house owner obviously prefers to strike a more humorous note. Alluding to the contemporary gothic novel and the bestseller of the same name, *The Monk,* Soane creates a sort of theme room — a gloomy study room

8
MONK'S
PARLOUR /
CREATED IN
1824

full of small format plaster casts of medieval architectural ornamentation. In contrast to the contents of the Dome, there are no valuable pieces among them. The figure of the Grim Reaper in the annex indicates just as unequivocally the

TANJA JANKOWIAK

largely anecdotal character of this room, as does the atmospherically presented view of the small courtyard adjoining it. One looks out of the dark, panelled, oppressively low-ceilinged room through colored glass onto a grave site — allegedly the grave of the monk's dog, in fact the grave of Fanny, the Soane family's dog. The view is completed by the presence of an artificial ruin in the courtyard, intended to suggest the medieval monastery of the monk and which — 'true to the original', so to speak — is composed of medieval fragments from the Palace of Westminster.

Two aspects of the spatial design, which are repeated elsewhere in the house, interest me here. One is the conscious dismantling of spatial boundaries, the other is the interruption of an ongoing spatial atmosphere as a way of playing with perception.

In this respect, in one section of the Monk's Parlour the ceiling has been knocked through, at which point the otherwise dark, low-ceilinged room opens into a narrow, high space, in which refracted light falls, filtered through a col-

9
PICTURE ROOM
RECESS

ored glass skylight (**FIG. 9**). A connection to the floor above is made via this intermediate space, leading to the adjoining Picture Room, the side wall of which folds out, where Soane's extensive collection of paintings is kept.

The break in uniform spatial geometry, whether caused by lighting effects or by interruption of conventional material spatial division, counts as a typical aspect of the staged perception of the Picturesque, which is prefigured in the English landscape garden and which Soane adopts here in his house. Along the way the architect plays with the viewer's expectations: for example, while standing in the Picture Room, one suddenly finds oneself looking down into the Monk's Room, revealed when the hinged walls hung with pictures swing open. As in the Dome, Soane again gives priority to the experience of architecture over classical architectonic structures.

Given the portrayal of the building so far, one could presume that the motifs described here are limited to the collection rooms to the rear of the house, perhaps owing their existence to the peculiarities of the collection. In fact, a

10
VIEW OF THE
CATACOMB /
LITHOGRAPHY /
1835 / FROM
SOANE'S
DESCRIPTION OF
1835

second glance at the living and reception rooms to the front of the house reveals that they, too, are affected by the motifs and design aspects described. It can be observed how elements of design spread from the collections area to the front of the house, until motifs inspired by and derived from the collection finally pass into Soane's architectural language, emerging as aspects of style.

One example of this is represented by the canopy dome[16] in the Breakfast Room (FIG. 2), which the architectural historian and long-time curator of the Soane Museum, John Summerson, has identified in its form as the lid of an antique urn enlarged to scale.[17]

The theme of the transitory, which in the Dome stood for the immediate experience of time, is integrated here into the living quarters of Soane's house in the form of an architectonic design element and simultaneously becomes a macabre game with different historical periods. Sheltered by the canopy dome, those who breakfast in Soane's Breakfast Room find themselves inside an urn even while still alive. This impression is intensified by the fact that Soane places in the Breakfast Room a small wall niche, which also serves as a connecting passage to the Dome, and stages, as in the Picture Room, a spatial breakthrough to the lower floor and the Catacomb below. As in the space between Picture Room and Monk's Parlour, Soane lets into this passage another skylight, through which the colored glass of refracted light falls.

In 1824–25, Soane converts the small room below the Breakfast Room into a burial chamber where he installs part of his extensive collection of urns (FIG. 10). In the adjacent area, at the center of the Dome, Soane simultaneously places a

11
SECTIONAL
PERSPECTIVE OF
THE DOME AREA
AND BREAKFAST
ROOM LOOKING
EAST / FRANK
COPLAND / 1818

recently acquired ancient Egyptian sarcophagus, the most valuable piece in his collection.

A sectional elevation (FIG. 11) shows us roughly how this configuration of rooms would have fitted together, albeit before the conversion work. We see the Breakfast Room, spanned by the canopy dome in the shape of an urn lid, and can imagine how, after the small rooms below were converted and the break-through was made, the room eventually became embedded, like an enlarged urn, in the Catacomb containing the objects from Soane's urn collection.

With the breakthrough of spatial boundaries, Soane achieves a continuum, on the one hand, between different layers of time, i.e. the present of the Breakfast Room, the past of the early Christian catacomb, and the future of his own death, and, on the other hand, between the culturally separate areas of life and death. In the Breakfast Room, Soane also begins to play with different spatial perspectives in which, with the help of numerous convex mirrors — 58 of them in the canopy dome alone — he fragments and distorts the perception of the room

for the viewer who is willing to become involved (**FIG. 12**).[18] Each of these mirrors creates an apparently enclosed image, which presents a different, narrowly defined section of the room.

Convex mirrors — especially in the form of a pocket mirror called *Claude Glass*[19] — were very fashionable at the time. Connoisseurs of landscape design and landscape painters would carry with them such a mirror with a black backing, in a small case. In the mirror, the surrounding landscape was shown divided into a series of two-dimensional images which, compared with the actual landscape, appeared to be drawn with clear lines. The black background toned down the intensity of color and the color spectrum. The resulting perception of the landscape was supposed to resemble the perception of a painting by Claude Lorrain (1600–1682).

In contrast, the convex mirrors of Soane's Breakfast Room, which divide up the room into separate images, are in a fixed position. For Soane, it is less a mat-

ter of creating a perception of space with the viewer's presence than creating a multitude of perspectives and simultaneously deliberate confusion, since he not only arranges his mirrors in abundance around the room, but also places them on opposing, slanted planes.

In other rooms in the house, Soane positions flat mirrors directly opposite one another. Rows of mirrors like these can be found in other places, including the Dining Room: for instance in the niches in which Soane has placed busts, which can thus be viewed both from the back and the front at the same time; as friezes along the top of the walls where they meet the ceiling; between picture frames and behind bookshelves set into the walls (FIG. 13).

When looking into these mirrors, it is no longer possible to clearly isolate material boundaries; they retreat into the background in the presence of the play with perspective. The spaces seem to multiply in the reflections created by the mirrors, thus stretching to infinity. The reflected objects also multiply in an almost eerie way, as does, for instance, the larger-than-life portrait of Soane painted by Sir Thomas Lawrence in 1828–29, in which the sitter is portrayed gently smiling.

Later on Soane creates a different kind of mirror installation in the center of his collection, in the Dome (FIG. 14). Soane places himself — as master of the

14
DOME WITH THE
BUST OF SOANE

collection and conjuror of the scene — in the form of his bust opposite a cast of the Apollo Belvedere (FIG. 15), which, since Winckelmann, had been the epitome of antique beauty and perfection and thus a classical ideal. Now, how does this juxtaposition work alongside the others already observed in the house? This question would be fair if the only view were the one shown in the photograph, which however does not reveal the space separating the bust of the collector from that of Apollo. In this space, on the floor of the large room of the Dome, Soane has placed the opened, Egyptian sarcophagus.

Thus, when the whole scene is viewed from the gallery, a very different final tableau emerges, one in which Soane and Apollo are irreparably separated from each other. If they try to close the gap, they inevitably fall into the open sar-

15
DOME AREA WITH
THE BUST OF
SOANE LOOKING
AT APOLLO

cophagus, which here symbolizes the grave of history. They can only approach each other as broken pieces, fragmented by the passage of time.

1   Margaret RICHARDSON, "Soane's Legacy", in: *John Soane Architect. Master of Space and Light,* edited by Margaret RICHARDSON and MaryAnne STEVENS, London: Royal Academy of Arts, 1999, p. 48.

2   Instead of the London stock brick of the surrounding buildings, Soane used Norfolk brick, so that his façades must certainly have stood out in terms of texture and color. See Helen DOREY, "12–14 Lincoln's Inn Fields", in: *John Soane Architect,* ed. RICHARDSON and STEVENS, pp. 150–173, here p. 150.

3   Because of its prominence, the façade design was the subject of a legal dispute with the authorities, which Soane finally won. See ibid., p. 164.

4   In fact, all the inner doors to the Breakfast Room are double doors. The outward-facing doors are clear glass and the inward-facing doors are mirror glass, which produces a number of different effects. See ibid., p. 167.

5   At the same time as the Breakfast Room was rebuilt, in 1812–13.

6   As in the metaphor Freud used when he compared the deep architectonic layers of the city of Rome to the psyche's structure, history here consists of architectonic fragments.

7   Brian Lukacher points out that, in his imaginative portrayal of Lincoln's Inn Fields, Soane may have been influenced by Louis-Sébastien Mercier's *Le Tableau de Paris* (1781–88), in which Paris is described also as a future ruin, or the opening chapter of the Comte de Volney's description of the graves of Palmyra, *Les Ruines* (1792). See Brian LUKACHER, *Joseph Gandy. An Architectural Visionary in Georgian England,* London: Thames & Hudson, 2006, p. 157.

8   Sir John SOANE, "Crude Hints towards an History of my House in L[incoln's] I[nn] Fields", in: *Visions of Ruin: Architectural Fantasies and Designs for Garden Follies,* edited by Helen DOREY, [London]: Sir John Soane's Museum, 1999, pp. 61–74, here p. 70. See also Colin DAVIES, "Architecture and Remembrance", in: *The Architectural Review,* VOL. 175, no. 1044, 1984, pp. 48–55, here p. 51. — On the term "cavedium" see John BRITTON, *A Dictionary of the Architecture and Archaeology of the Middle Ages [...],* London: Longman, Orme, Brown, Green, and Longmans, 1838, p. 130: "CAVEDIUM, Lat. *Cava-œdium,* an open place, or area of a house, analogous to the French *cour,* the Italian *cortile,* and the English quadrangle, cloister, or court. A reference to plans, &c. of any of the Pompeian houses will shew the meaning of the appellation. Vitruvius enumerates five different cavedia: the Tuscan, Corinthian, tetrastyle, displuviated, and testudinated. The cavedium is the quadrangular court of private houses, such as abound in Paris, and many continental towns: the open court of Hungerford market, London, is a modern cavedium; so also the cloistered quadrangle of cathedrals."

9   A classification, in the sense of a clear assignment of certain object groups and epochs, is not a priority at Lincoln's Inn Fields. Only in regard to the Monk's Parlour and the Yard or the Crypt and Catacomb is there anything resembling 'theme rooms' (in contrast to Thomas Hope's house in Duchess Street), while, for example, the so-called "Sepulchral Chamber" is not, in fact, a closed crypt based on an ancient Egyptian model, but part of the Dome, which is open to many other rooms on different sides, including the Breakfast Room or the breakthrough to the Upper Drawing Office and reception rooms. In addition, ancient Roman urns are not only placed in the Crypt or

Catacomb, but at the most unlikely points around the house, including the Library, etc. Given this, I cannot concur with Watkin, who quotes Hittorf's interpretation: "Hittorf, who grasped its [Lincoln's Inn Fields'] speaking-role, described how the varied architectural qualities of each object represented the particular character of the period of art to which it belonged so that an assembly of antique columns took the form of a colonnade; mediaeval fragments were arranged to suggest the oratory of a ruined monastery; tombs and funerary urns were displayed in a catacomb; the Belzoni sarcophagus had its own sepulchral chamber; while the bust of Shakespeare and the monument to Pitt were surrounded by appropriate works of art." David WATKIN, *Sir John Soane. Enlightenment Thought and the Royal Academy Lectures,* Cambridge: Cambridge University Press, 1996, p. 414.

10 See David WATKIN, *The English Vision. The Picturesque in Architecture, Landscape, and Garden Design,* London: John Murray, 1982 · J. Mordaunt CROOK, *The Dilemma of Style. Architectural Ideas from the Picturesque to the Post-Modern,* London: John Murray, 1989 · John SUMMERSON, *Architecture in Britain 1530 to 1830,* 9th edition, New Haven, CT and London: Yale University Press, 1993, pp. 288–301 · See also Hanno-Walter KRUFT, *Geschichte der Architekturtheorie,* Munich: C.H. Beck, 1991, pp. 298–302.

11 See WATKIN, *The English Vision,* p. 62 (italics added): "His [Gandy's] preoccupation with the funereal, like that of his master Soane, is deeply rooted in the *picturesque obsession with the buried past.*" Crook talks about the notion of architecture as an "embodied memory". He does not directly assign this metaphor to the Picturesque, but calls it an aesthetic aspect typical of the late 18th century. See CROOK, *The Dilemma of Style,* p. 13 (italics added): "Picturesque values (that is, architecture as scenery) and associationist aesthetics (that is, *architecture as embodied memory*) broke up the canonical harmonies of classicism."

12 See WATKIN, *The English Vision,* pp. 55–57.

13 See Victor I. STOICHITA, "Museum und Ruine. Museum als Ruine", in: *Totalität und Zerfall im Kunstwerk der Moderne,* edited by Reto SORG and Stefan Bodo WÜRFFEL, Munich: Wilhelm Fink, 2006, pp. 67–90. As a member of the Conservatoire de Museum National, Robert gave this new draft for the redesigning of the Grande Galerie his full support. The complete title of the representation of the Grande Louvre as an intact building, which he exhibited at the same time, was: *Project to light the museum gallery from above, and to divide it up without losing the view. (Projet pour éclairer la gallerie du Musée par la voute, et pour la diviser sans ôter la vue de la prolongation du local).* Robert illustrated and supported this redesigning of the Galerie du Louvre, a large space spanned by a long chain of round arches with lantern skylights, which was never built in Paris. See STOICHITA, "Museum und Ruine", pp. 67–69. This spatial form was taken up by Soane in his new building, the Dulwich Picture Gallery, which he began in 1811 and which opened in 1817, seven years before the National Gallery.

14 The first depiction of an architectural design not conceived as a ruin in the form of a picture of a ruin is attributed to Sir William Chambers, who in 1752 had such a depiction prepared for a mausoleum in Kew Gardens which he designed (but which was never realized) for the Prince of Wales. See WATKIN, *The English Vision,* p. 56.

15 Ibid., p. 57.

16 One stimulus may have been the cupola that Soane's teacher, George Dance the Younger, designed and built for the Council Chamber of the Guildhall in 1777–78. See Christopher WOOD-WARD, "'Wall, Ceiling, Enclosure and Light': Soane's Designs for Domes", in: *John Soane Architect,* ed. RICHARDSON and STEVENS, p. 62.

17   John Summerson has combined his thesis with a breakdown of the many references to sepulchral objects that appear — at a decorative level or in the form of transformations into architectonic elements — in Soane's work, whether in Lincoln's Inn Fields, in his earlier country house Pitzhanger Manor, in the Dulwich Picture Gallery, or the Bank of England. See John SUMMERSON, "John Soane and the Furniture of Death", in: *The Architectural Review,* VOL. 163, 1978, pp. 147–155. As Summerson shows, even the Breakfast Room of Soane's former country home, Pitzhanger Manor, and the first Breakfast Room at no. 12, Lincoln's Inn Fields are reminiscent of an ancient urn lid or the roof of a crypt. Summerson speculates that Soane modelled the form of his ceiling on one of the ancient graves in the Necropolis of Tarquinia (later Corneto). See SUMMERSON, *Architecture in Britain 1530 to 1830,* p. 287. See also *Soane and Death: The Tombs and Monuments of Sir John Soane,* exhibition catalogue, edited by Giles WATERFIELD, London: Dulwich Picture Gallery, 1996.

18   Soane had already been living alone in the house for many years when the mirrors in the Breakfast Room were installed. Helen Dorey dates this measure to some time after 1825. See DOREY, "12–14 Lincoln's Inn Fields", p. 167.

19   See Jurgis BALTRUSAITIS, *Der Spiegel: Entdeckungen, Täuschungen, Phantasien,* Gießen: Anabas, 1986, p. 290 and p. 294.

IMAGES

Stefan BUZAS: *Sir John Soane's Museum, London,* Tübingen and Berlin: Ernst J. Wasmuth, 1994, p. 23: FIG. 1; p. 34: FIG. 2; p. 57: FIG. 9; p. 37: FIG. 12; p. 29: FIG. 13; p. 46: FIG. 14; p. 43: FIG. 15 · *John Soane Architect. Master of Space and Light,* edited by Margaret RICHARDSON and MaryAnne STEVENS, London: Royal Academy of Arts, 1999, p. 160: FIG. 3; p. 162: FIG. 4; p. 167: FIG. 11 · Jean-Jacques LÉVÊQUE, *L'art et la Révolution française, 1789–1804,* Neuchâtel: Ed. Ides et Calendes, 1987, p. 28: FIG. 5 · Brian LUKACHER, *Joseph Gandy. An Architectural Visionary in Georgian England,* London: Thames & Hudson, 2006, p. 163: FIG. 6; p. 162: FIG. 7 · Tim KNOX: *Sir John Soane's Museum, London,* London: Merrell Publishers, 2009, p. 97: FIG. 8 · John SOANE, *Description of the House and Museum on the North Side of Lincoln's Inn Fields. The Residence of Sir John Soane [...],* London: [privately printed], 1835, plate 20: FIG. 10

SVEN-OLOV WALLENSTEIN

Foucault and the Body as a Site of Resistance

THE QUESTION

A frequently raised question in the discussion of Foucault, posed from different angles — by Habermas, by Marxists of various creeds, and also by liberal theorists — would be the following: where does the possibility of resistance come from and how can it be accounted for, ontologically, epistemologically as well as normatively? To speak the language of medieval thought: how can resistance at all *exist* (what is its *ratio essendi* or *fiendi*), how can we *know* its grounds (*ratio cognoscendi),* and why should we *choose to act* in terms of resistance *(ratio agendi)*? If there is a unilateral process of power and knowledge, as seemed to follow from the analysis of discipline that Foucault developed in the mid 1970s, namely a continuously unfolding history of grids, surveillance, and incarceration, then the genealogy of the modern subject and its corresponding forms of rationality would seem to generate a massive and totalizing story without any chance of escape, unless we would opt for some sheer irrationality. *How* can we resist, and if it is at all possible, *why* should we bother to?

The first and second question, which bear on the *that* and *how* of resistance, ask if there is something that precedes or exceeds the processes within which power and knowledge mould the subject, a resource that would be located in some other dimension, and if we might be able to understand it as a principle of acting without simply undoing ourselves. Following the trajectory of this idea — which extends from the early to the last phases of Foucault's work and cannot be contained within the limits of his discussions of discipline — will provide his path with a certain unity, although it will be the unity of a question and an answer that are both continually displaced. Using a vocabulary that is not

IN / KIRSTEN WAGNER AND JASPER CEPL (EDITORS) /
IMAGES OF THE BODY IN ARCHITECTURE: ANTHROPOLOGY AND BUILT SPACE /
TÜBINGEN · BERLIN / ERNST WASMUTH VERLAG / 2014 / PP. 301–318

Foucault's own, and that he in some, but not all, periods probably would not resist, we might speak of a series of different ontologies, even though this quest eventually leads to a questioning, if not abandonment, of the very idea of an ontology as the basis of the possibility of resistance.

The third question, the *why* of resistance, is equally labyrinthine. At first glance there seems to be no normative claim, no idea of an essence of man, freedom, utopia, or an ideal community in Foucault; and yet there is an appeal to the concept of "experience" that still contains an ethical claim, not in the sense of a set of rules, but of an *ethos,* a relation to the world. This appeal in fact remains constant from the first to the last texts, and it is linked to the very possibility of thinking as a relation to an Outside — to the "abstract hurricane" of which Deleuze speaks in his commentary to this theme.[1] How, Deleuze asks, can we make this outside into a relative interiority? Thinking is resisting to the form of the present, since it attempts to seize such an outside and make it into our own. To some extent this might seem like a return to the first and second question, or maybe a flight into abstraction, and yet, for Foucault in the end it turned out to be the most concrete of questions: how we can think, and why we should think, are issues closely aligned to the problem of resistance, in the sense that it holds open the possibility for a transformation of experience. As Deleuze suggests, there is something here like a response to Heidegger's question *Was heißt Denken?*[2], in the double sense that Heidegger gave to it: what *is* thinking, and what *calls forth* this thing called thinking, if we understand thinking not merely as a reflection on ideas and essences, but as relating precisely to an *ethos,* an abode or a way of being in the world, which as such already implies an ontology.[3]

MADNESS AND LANGUAGE

Foucault's early work grows out of his engagement with psychology and psychiatry, which also involves practical work at the clinic Saint-Anne. His first publication, the introduction to his and Jacqueline Verdeaux's 1954 translation of Ludwig Binswanger's *Traum und Existenz,*[4] draws on this, and already here we can see the emergence of an idea of experience that incorporates the lessons of phenomenology and psychoanalysis, while also attempting to transcend them. Foucault's project is to show how Binswanger, in taking his cues from Husserl as well as Freud, does so only in order to go beyond them towards a different conception of consciousness. In Binswanger, Foucault locates a dialectic between experience and institution, or anthropology and social history, his question becoming how we might link them together. Is there something like a common root, a shared historicity, of these two modes of analysis, which would bring together the subjective and objective in a third dimension that does not treat them as fixed forms, but can account for their mutual and conflicted emergence? For Foucault, this is the beginning of his long-standing and by no means simple critique of the psychiatric establishment, which at first is bound up with the idea that madness harbors a profound experience of a limit, that it has an enigmatic substance, not just consisting in dysfunction, disorder, and deviation. The question will resonate throughout Foucault's work, as we can see in one of the last texts, a sketch for a preface to *The Use of Pleasures,*[5] which returns us to the initial problem, although obviously in a form that has been inflected by three decades of work.

In this early period there are however rapid oscillations between opposed perspectives. That same year he publishes a book on psychopathology, *Maladie mentale et personnalité,* where the concepts of the normal and the abnormal are seen as effects of institutional practices. Investigating the formation of modern psychiatry, Foucault now contends that sickness results from social conditions and conflicts, and he ends with a positive appraisal of Soviet-style "materialist" psychiatry, with Pavlov as the guiding reference. In a rather stark opposition to the text on Binswanger, we now encounter a critique of the "irrealization" of the relation to the world, and of the emphasis of the inner life of the individual. In 1962 there was a new edition of the book, where "personnalité" in the title had become "psychologie", and Pavlov was replaced by summaries of sections from the recently published *History of Madness.* After this Foucault refuses to have the book printed again, and he never refers to either of the two editions, whereas the text on Binswanger remains with him. This arguably testifies to a more profound continuity, where the concept of "experience" remains to the end,[6] although it is never clarified, perhaps because it would have demanded a systematic confrontation with phenomenology.

This theme of an experience of limits reaches its first high point in the 1961 book on madness. Foucault would later distance himself from this book, and suggest that it was marked by a certain romanticism. But in spite of this — or perhaps because of it — many of his later problems are contained in this book, although in a somewhat blurred state.[7] This also applies to the problem of resistance, which in fact can be taken as the very center of Foucault's methodological concerns: is there a different experience outside of the archives of knowledge and the relations of power, something that could work as a leverage for a thought that is *of* its conditions, and yet cannot be reduced *to* them?

The project, Foucault says, is not to write a history of a certain phenomenon called "madness", but first, to write a history of reason from a negative point of view (how reason has become what it is through the exclusion of its other, in various shapes and forms), but then, and more radically, to attempt to let madness itself speak through the system of exclusion, to write its own history. The first would be a history of the self-constitution of reason through exclusion, the second an "archaeology of silence", a way to let otherness speak from its position of otherness. This language of otherness, he suggests, would demand a return to a moment before the division or "Decision" (*la Decision*, as he says dramatically), to a zero point in history when madness was a still undifferentiated unity, a not yet divided experience of the division.

Multiple methodological problems are obviously engaged here. Beyond all the empirical issues that surround such a task, there remains the fundamental question, as Derrida noted in his famous critique,[8] of how we could ever aspire to return to the genesis of historicity *as such* within an empirical history. For Derrida, the claim underlying Foucault's investigation was not simply to neutralize, suspend, or even dismantle the project of philosophy,[9] but to simply circumvent it by reinscribing it into a set of factual conditions. The most notable case of this is Cartesian *cogito*, which Foucault, in Derrida's reading, simply reduces to a reflection of a particular historical totality, the classical age, and even more drastically to the "great internment" of reason's other with the establishing of the Hôpital général in 1654. Against this, Derrida claims that we must retain the possibility of thought to transcend any finite constellation, not in the sense that it would be able to reach some positive infinity of ideas, but as a gesture or movement that makes it possible for the difference between finitude and infinity to appear at all. However, this debate on the reading of Descartes has by no means been settled, and Foucault's belated response to Derrida in 1972, in his essay "Mon corps, ce papier, ce feu",[10] provides a distinctively different approach to historical texts, although Derrida's main point about the paradox inherent in reducing historicity as such to empirical events remained unanswered; to some extent Foucault's later work can be said to take up this question again and again.

For the Foucault of the aftermath of *The History of Madness,* the possibility of transgression was however just as much rooted in an interpretation in modern literature and art, as is visible in the final sections of the book, with its references to Friedrich Nietzsche, Vincent van Gogh, and Antonin Artaud. Foucault now suggests that madness amounts to the absolute interruption of the work, the moment where it is abolished, which is simultaneously the founding of its temporal existence.[11] Madness is the *absence of the work,* not in the sense of something simply negative, but as the truth of the modern work, a moment of unreason that opens the pathway to the undivided experience of division. Here we find the traces of another experience, a resistance that articulates itself by withdrawing into silence, to the margins of discourse, and rather than seeing madness as an entity constituted by being imprisoned in a medical institution, Foucault draws on another idea from romanticism: art as the bearer of another truth, a negativity that cannot be reduced to rational ordering. The infinity and excess of language transgresses reason and order, it scrambles and disassembles the law of the Father, and literary writing is as the primordial reservoir for this resistance.

This motif unfolds in a series of essays:[12] "Hölderlin and the Question of the Father" (1962), "Preface to Transgression" (on Georges Bataille, 1963), the book-length study of Raymond Roussel in 1963, "Fantasia of the Library" (on Gustave Flaubert, first published as a postscript to the German translation of Flaubert's *La tentation de Saint Antoine,* in 1964), and "La prose d'Actéon" (on Pierre Klossowski, 1964). Foucault's literary essays may seem as asides in relation to his historical work, and yet, in all their obvious diversity, they display a cumulative movement that can be taken to culminate in the essay from 1966 on Maurice Blanchot, "La pensée du dehors".[13] In the latter he explicates this in terms of an idea of literature as the relation of language to the Outside, *le Dehors,* a dimension of emptiness that dissolves the subject into a space of pure dispersal (a concept also later crucial for Deleuze's interpretation, which traces this concept in its various forms throughout Foucault's work, not just as a negative void and absence, but as space of openness out of which thinking emerges).

The same year, in *The Order of Things,* he also provides a reflexive account of the archaeological possibility of these counter-discourses, which to some extent deprives them of their radical quality by inserting their counter-historical thrust in a historical narrative. Literature, Foucault now suggests, is born as the obverse side of modernity's anthropological humanism, harboring an experience of the being of language that already from the beginning will haunt modernity and signal its limit.[14] While on the one hand this continues to give literature an extremely important place, it also renders its claims relative, and from this point onward Foucault will once more start to shift the focus.

From our perspective here, we can note that this idea of resistance through literary writing only approaches the body indirectly and obliquely, and if ideas of density and materiality are always at stake, they tend to be ascribed to writing and language, and not the lived body. This largely has to do with Foucault's rejection of phenomenology, which however is not a simple event, but a long and complex exchange that runs parallel to his occupation of literature, the history of which remains to be written.

We have already seen how the early text on Binswanger engages phenomenology, and a decade later, in 1963, the first edition of *Naissance de la Clinique* undertakes an analysis of the emergence of modern medical discourse that is replete with a vocabulary that seems particularly to draw on Maurice Merleau-Ponty,[15] with its folds, hinges, crevices, and textures, and that lays out the medicalized body in front of us in a manner reminiscent of the phenomenology of perception. If the book on madness dealt with the problem of the constitution of the object "madness", this second book addresses another type of object-creation, in which the sick body is constituted as a visible form in and through a new experience of death and finitude. Foucault demonstrates how the very visibility of objects such as madness and sickness, even the body itself in all its complexity, is dependent on a "syntactic reorganization of visibility" that determines a new sense of *space* (distance, the discovery of the patient as an object), of *language* (a new type of medical discourse, a new mode of enunciation), and finally of *death* (which now, following the studies of Bichat, is understood as entering into the body as an immanent process, underway since the constitution of the organism rather than as the result of external influences). Modern medicine, he suggests, is born through the constellation of these three modes of seeing and speaking, of the visible and the discursive, which is the object of this "archéologie du regard médical", as the subtitle of the 1963 book indicates.

Here, the problem of resistance and the outside seems to have receded into the background. But in fact, in this case the book also ends with a set of enigmatic references to a "lyrical experience in search of its language, from Hölderlin to Rilke",[16] which indicates the extent to which the idea of a limit that was at stake in the book on madness is still operative, beneath the unfolding of medical discourse. Foucault's debate with phenomenology surfaces here too, in the question of how the subject should be understood. An obvious case of this is the subtitle of the book, *An Archaeology of Medical Perception (Une archéologie du regard médical),* with its emphasis on the gaze, *le regard,* which is removed from editions after 1972, with important parts of the vocabulary from the 1963 edition also being transformed.[17]

Perhaps Foucault is here attempting to evade a paradox in the argument as presented in 1963, where his use of a phenomenological vocabulary to analyze the new experience of body and death that emerges around the time of Bichat implies that it somehow would be a neutral tool, at the same as it is a part of the modern episteme and its analytic of finitude and factuality, whose validity Foucault wants to circumscribe. This conceptual struggle, I would like to suggest, is however not simply the result of an intellectual indecision or imprecision, or just a residue that eventually will go away, but rather points to a nucleus of Foucault's work, to which he will constantly return in various guises: experience and subjectivity, as a domain conditioned by language and the discursive, by power and disciplines, and that yet can never be reduced to them, not because of its relation to the transcendence of ideas and idealities, but because of a constitutive relation to finitude and death.

DISCIPLINED BODIES

The shift from the archaeology of knowledge and the investigation of rules of discourse to the genealogy of power relations, with the 1970 lecture at the Collège de France, *L'ordre du discours,* as the key transitional text, reintroduces the body as the very locus of the unfolding of power, but also as the major site for the emergence of resistance; the body is the relay between action and passion, the capacity to affect and to be affected. In *Discipline and Punish,* Foucault famously charts a development in which punishments become less focused on inflicting pain, since the body must be rendered productive, and violence is not effective. We move from the naked violence of visible punishment to a form of correctional techniques that assemble around the body.

This is a new form of political technology, which in turn produces the soul as a new object of knowledge, a soul that also becomes the "prison of the body" in a series of steps that can be mapped back on to Nietzsche's *Genealogy of Morals,* which seems to guide Foucault. Discipline, he suggests, is not primarily about prohibiting, just as power is not essentially repressive, but a positive organization of space and time, a partition and creation of segmented unities, a breaking down and analysis of movements down to their smallest detail (military exercise, control of body postures in school). Space and time, bodies and gestures, are analyzed in minute detail, and then reassembled so as to become parts of larger and more efficient unities.

The prison becomes one of the places for the creation of such "docile bodies", and it is in conjunction with this, that we find the development of discourses on the criminal. Disciplinary power thus encounters new forms of knowledge: the power/knowledge complex is intensified, new types of criminality emerge, and the focus on norm produces an infinity of possible deviations and perversions that do not pre-exist the norm. The object of the legal system can in this sense be understood as the production of increasing criminality, in forms that can integrate that criminality in widening discursive circuits, just as the apparatus of sexuality engenders an infinitely proliferating series of perversions that fluctuate around the phallic principle, not in terms of law and transgression, but as norm and deviation.

Prison, hospital, school, mental asylum, are all systems that produce normality by surveillance and the installing of technologies of micro-power. This should not be understood simply as the history of a series of concrete institutions — Foucault distrusts this word, since it gives the idea of some solid and reified, and cannot account for the exchange inside-outside — but a whole "diagram" of power actualized in them, as in the case of the Panopticon, which is one particular modality of a general diagram. In the formula given by Deleuze, the general principle of this diagram would be to influence the greatest number of subjects possible through minimal physical force, thus transferal of force to the object that subjectivizes itself, that is subjected by recognizing itself as such (I am a criminal, a pervert, a madman, but also a pupil, a worker, etc.).

But where, then, is resistance? If the complex of power/knowledge forms an interlocking totality, and there is nothing savage or free outside it, at least not in the sense that Foucault assumed in the romantic version of the history of madness, where should we locate a possible Outside? The theoretical model for resistance, in fact, can already be found in Nietzsche's genealogy of consciousness and conscience, in his reflections on the amount of "pre-historical work" that is required for the formation of a responsible agent, and in a kind of ontology of forces. This is the element or the milieu in which something like the creation of "docile bodies" becomes possible, an element that will subsist under any such body as a virtual double, or a kind of non-bounded multiplicity.

This background in Nietzsche is essential for Foucault, and it touches on a whole set of issues that have to do with the specific French reception of Nietzsche in the wake of Heidegger's two-volume *Nietzsche* (1961) and Deleuze's *Nietzsche et la philosophie* (1962). Deleuze's analysis was, in fact, the first to highlight genealogy as a critical analysis of power relations and to propose the *body* as a focal point of analysis. His reading of the will to power breaks both with Heidegger's interpretation, which situates the concept of power as the last answer to the metaphysical question of the being of beings, in the tradition of Aristotle's *dynamis* and *energeia,* as well as with earlier subjectivist readings that located will and power in the domain of individual psychology. In many ways it provides a conceptual underpinning for Foucault's historical analysis, and for the idea of the body as a site of resistance, not in the sense of a center of individual experience that precedes forming, but as a kind of sieve that determines, through the mechanisms of power and knowledge, which possibilities for affecting and being affected will be allowed; which also means to distribute a whole set of virtual bodily manifolds that remain unintegrated and subsist in a non-personal, non-*ego*logical space.

For Deleuze this model would to some extent be present already in Spinoza, who seems largely absent from Foucault's work. "Taking the body as a guide to philosophy" is the proposal that opens Deleuze's second book on Spinoza, *Spinoza, philosophie pratique.*[18] The idea that the soul, or more precisely a certain interpretation of the soul, constitutes the prison of the body, and that we are not aware of what a liberated body might be capable of outside of its relation to the soul understood in terms of its Aristotelian "form", is indeed one of the great themes of Spinoza's *Ethics*: "[A]nd in fact, no one has been able to determine what a body is capable of *(quid corpus possit),* that is, experience has not yet enlightened us as to what the body — to the extent that is not determined by the soul — can or cannot do according to the laws of nature, if the latter is considered solely as corporeal". (*Ethics,* Book III, Theorem 2, Remark)

This microphysical domain consists of assemblages of non- or pre-subjective bodies and affections, and it is precisely because of its unruly and shifting quality that power relations remain unstable and that a "distant roar of battle"[19] can always be heard behind the official eloquence of institutionalized discourses of knowledge. This does not mean that we should or could attempt to return to this pre-subjective level as if to some true or authentic life beneath the discursive order, a life that would be deformed by a simple external force — which, in this second phase of his work, is Foucault's critique of phenomenology and the idea of a "savage" and "vertical" being that we find, for instance, in Merleau-Ponty. But although there can never be a question of returning to some version of pre-reflective life, this very unruliness remains a source of resistance, and it

SVEN-OLOV WALLENSTEIN

indicates why it is, in fact, resistance that *comes first,* as Foucault often said. The diagram of power relations can only be actualized in the form of action *and* reaction, and by setting free a multiplicity of forces that only become integrated to the extent that they also escape integration.

Indeed there are also important differences between Deleuze's (and Guattari's) philosophical constructivism and Foucault's analytic of power as it unfolds in this phase of his work, and they seem to reflect the difference in temperament and style between the philosopher and the historian.[20] Foucault's questions bear upon how we have become the kind of subjects that we are (sexed, normalized, deviant) through interplay with technologies, discourses, and mechanisms of power. But he tends to remain silent when it comes to positive programs for new types of subject-formation, which is why many critics, and not only Habermas, feel that his work needs some kind of normative basis. Deleuze and Guattari, on the other hand, are fascinated with synthetic and universal-historical models, and their project is to discern the fault lines that always open up in every assemblage, and to conceptualize the tension inside every ordering and regimentation, between "micropolitics" (molecular becomings that swarm below the surface of forms, sexes, and subjects) and "segmentarity" (the hardened forms that produce binary spaces), as they put it in chapter nine of *A Thousand Plateaus.*[21] For Deleuze and Guattari, a society is held together less by its segmented forms than by flows and lines of flight that escape such orderings, which indicates the proximity to Foucault's idea that resistance *comes first.*

But in fact, Foucault becomes increasingly critical of such non-historical and ontological conceptions of desire (or any other term that holds the same position) as a productive force, and he will come to understand the idea of a "desiring subject" as a product of modern confessional technologies. On the other hand, he is symptomatically led to evoke a similarly straightforward idea of "pleasure" *(plaisir)* that is supposed to underlie the split between the sex-desiring subject and bodies-pleasures, and he proposes a rather naive dualism between *ars erotica* and *scientia sexualis* in the first volume of *The History of Sexuality.* (This is admittedly an aside in his argument, and yet with a distinct strategic importance, which is further complicated by his suggestion that *scientia sexualis* can, in fact, be understood as a particularly modern and subtle form of *ars erotica.*) Thus, this point of divergence between Deleuze and Foucault, which is also a point where Foucault begins to question his earlier work on discipline, is a key issue for an understanding of the transformation of resistance in his work.

FROM DISCIPLINE TO BIOPOLITICS AND SECURITY

The major shift that occurs, first in the 1977–78 lectures on *Security, Territory, Population,* and then in the lectures from 1978–79 on *The Birth of Biopolitics,*[22] is a move away from the idea of discipline as the prevalent structure of modern societies (another important and related change, that I will leave aside here, would be the abandonment of the "war" model for social relations in the lectures *"Society Must Be Defended"* from 1975–76). After the abandonment of the disciplinary model, it seems as if Foucault increasingly came to distrust any overarching theory, and what we find is a spectrum of questions, or multiple guidelines for further research. They intersect and resonate with each other, but also diverge in different directions, and the idea of biopolitics seems almost like a prism through which his earlier ideas are diffracted into several directions.

The concept of biopolitics is first presented in the final chapter of the introductory volume to *The History of Sexuality* (1976), and it also appears, in the same year, in the final section of *"Society Must Be Defended"*. A "society's 'threshold of modernity' has been reached", Foucault famously says, "when the life of the species is wagered on its own political strategies. For millennia, man remained what he was for Aristotle: a living being with the additional capacity for political existence; modern man is an animal whose politics places his existence as a living being in question."[23] In this conception, biopolitics — or biopower, as Foucault more often says here — is understood as the other side of an "anatomico-politics of the human body", in a way that still remains closely connected to discipline, and the structure of biopower seems in fact to be a result of, or even an aside within, the genealogy of gender.

Piecing together the various parts of this first presentation, we can see that biopower has a three-tier structure. On the lower or micro-level it works by individualization, or more precisely by *producing individuality* as the focal point of all the different techniques for monitoring the body politic, which now fractures into a *living multiplicity* of individuals. In this sense, individuality is produced by those very disciplinary techniques that at the same time *discover* it as their proper object. But this process also makes another object visible on the higher or macro-level, namely *population,* which is how individuals appear when they are treated as statistical phenomena, in terms of collective health and collective forms of reproduction and life. And finally, there is a crucial link between the production of sex as individuating force and the production of sex in relation to the population, or to the collective entity: the *family.* The family is the site of exchange between individuality and collectivity, the relay through which all individuals have to pass in order to become members of the reproductive body politic.

In this, life becomes the object of regulation and administration, but in the same movement, there emerges something inside life that resists, as can be seen in the various vitalist philosophies that develop from Nietzsche onwards, which continues and deepens the earlier theme of the resisting, multiple body. If life is a self-relation, then the power exerted *over* life is also an emancipation of a resistant force *inside* of life (which is where Deleuze locates the possibility of vitalism in Foucault's genealogy of sexuality). The terms "biopolitics" and "bio-power" should thus not be understood solely in terms of an action that imparts form to some amorphous mass, but, just as in the case of discipline, as a complex of action *and* reaction, control *and* resistance.

In *Security, Territory, Population* the analysis will however soon take a different direction, and "biopolitics" (which is now the term generally used) is absorbed in the theory of "governmentality", to the extent that Foucault, especially in the subsequent lectures *The Birth of Biopolitics,* when he moves ahead to discuss modern liberalism, almost seems to lose interest in the topic. As we will see, the first and second model of biopolitics do share some features, above all the idea of "population", but there are also important differences.

What is strikingly new in the 1977–79 analysis of biopolitics when compared to the preceding claims in *The History of Sexuality,* is the privileged status accorded to the liberal tradition.[24] If liberalism in the analysis of discipline had been treated largely as a surface phenomenon, in the sense that the autonomous individual as a bearer of rights and as capable of rational choices was implicitly understood as a product of processes of discipline, this freedom now appears as a correlate to what Foucault in *Security, Territory, Population* calls "apparatuses of security", and as part of a new type of governing for which life is a reservoir that must be tapped into rather than subjected to legal or disciplinary strictures.

Sovereignty, Foucault now says, is exerted over a *territory* and a multiplicity of political subjects; discipline is applied to singular *bodies,* to their affects and passions, and the grid "individual" is both a technique of application and an intended result; security, finally, relates to the *population* and its inherent dynamic, as a living entity following laws that politics must obey, and in this sense it constitutes the *physis* of politics.

In this second version, discipline becomes a radical construction of an idealized reality that runs parallel to everyday life, whereas, in *Discipline and Punish,* it was applied to physical bodies and operated through a segmentation and analysis of actual space; discipline now becomes something *ideal,* which makes it possible to oppose it to a security that operates in the *real.* Therefore the deployment of apparatuses of security means neither the exercise of sovereignty over subjects, nor the creation of an ideal space of discipline. It becomes instead what the Physiocrats called a *physical* process, within which exhaustive control no longer is an issue. In this way, Foucault suggests, and here he once more significantly modifies his earlier theses, the Panopticon, where the central tower and its possibility of continual inspection is what displaces the discontinuous violence of the sovereign, appears as an archaic rather than a modern model. In the apparatuses of security, the modus operandi is not panoptic *surveillance,* but to take a step back and *observe* the nature of events. The aim here is not to attain some immutable essence of things, but to ask whether they are advantageous or not, and how one can find a support in reality itself that makes it possible to channel them in an appropriate direction. In this respect we can say that the law operates in the *imaginary*, it imagines something negative; discipline is applied in a sphere which is *complementary* to reality; security, finally, tries to work with reality, by getting the components of reality to enter into new relations — which is what the Physiocrats meant, Foucault suggests, when they said that economy in fact is a *physics*, and that politics still belongs to nature.

This, Foucault concludes, is the decisive first step in what would become the tradition of liberalism, and it allows for a different understanding of the role of the idea of freedom in the development of capitalism. Correcting his earlier proposals, which seemed to suggest that the emergence of the idea of freedom and of liberal political thought must be understood in connection with the massive deployment of disciplinary techniques (the free individual being a result of processes of discipline), Foucault now claims that freedom should be located in correlation to the apparatuses of security, in the sense that these apparatuses could only become operative if one assumes a certain freedom, a freedom of circulation, lodged in that "political nature" within which they are to be deployed.

Liberalism, Foucault proposes, is thus first and foremost not an ideology, in the sense of a false, distorted, or imaginary representation of reality, but a technology of power, or a way to work *with* reality; liberalism, seen from the perspective here adopted — which does not preclude other perspectives, although it implicitly claims to *precede* them — does not provide us with a theoretical and/or ideological smoke-screen behind which other and more real things (actions, practices, material events) are taking place; instead, itself a practice, it is a way to make certain things real by working with, intensifying, tempering, or redirecting processes already underway in reality itself.

As we noted above, when the idea of biopolitics was first introduced at the end of the first volume of *The History of Sexuality* in 1976, the concept of population still seemed to hinge around the idea of a police-like control, a power exercised in a top-down manner through various decrees and administrative measures emanating from the state, which would be fundamentally opposed to what is normally perceived as the basic ideas of liberal theory. When Foucault later links biopolitics closely to liberalism, this is not because he necessarily disputes the traditional understanding of the latter, nor because he simply subscribes to it; with regard to the history of political doctrines, or any of the grand concepts of political theory (the state, nature, rights, etc.), his method is "nominalist", as he said on many occasions.[25] The point here is that the doctrine of liberty, when seen within the strategic field of political economy, is a way to extract utility, a material and intellectual surplus value, from the individual. In biopolitical terms, this means that the activities of the state will be related to a "life" that always precedes and overflows it, and where this surplus has its origin. On this level there is no contradiction, rather a strategic complementarity, so that freedom (the spontaneity of acting that must be left to itself) and the

　　　　　　　　　　　　　　　　　　　　　　SVEN-OLOV WALLENSTEIN

deployment of apparatuses of security (which themselves include and even multiply disciplinary technologies) increase and reinforce each other: the individual can be discovered as the locus and source of rights and actions, as a new type of political subject that must be given a calculated latitude in order to facilitate an increase in productivity, which comes about through the involuntary interplay of freedoms — the doctrine of *laissez faire* — which as its correlate has an "invisible hand" that guides them.

Unlike the body as it was understood within the spaces of discipline, this is a different dimension of life; it is no longer an unruly multiplicity that remains outside the diagram of power relations, whose irreducible vis-à-vis gives priority to resistance. It is instead a correlate to the apparatuses of security, from which they draw their very efficiency. This move seems to displace the ontology of life, admittedly not in one single move, but as a gradual shift inside the relation between *bios* and power.

On the one hand, if we start off from the complex that relates biopolitics to security and freedom, it becomes obvious that modernity for Foucault is anything but a continuous process of discipline and incarceration; rather it is a complex production of subjectivity in the context of a "governmentality" which increasingly transfers agency to the individual. On the other hand, if it is not simply a disappearance of the vitalist ontology that subtended the work on discipline, then at least it renders such an ontology questionable: life, nature, and the *physis* of politics now appear as correlates to security, and no longer as an other side of technologies of power that would be a source of resistance. Security seems more to work with a "functionalist" co-existence, and the ontology is itself inscribed in a historicizing move.

In one sense, this can be understood as a continuation of the earlier self-critique with respect to the ontological conception of madness as a radical outside, which is now developed so as to also encompass the idea of virtual multiplicities of forces that envelop stabilized power relations. As the analysis of biopolitics evolves, resistance in fact appears less central, and one may ask the question to what extent the analysis of neoliberal governmentality allows us at all to assume a critical distance to the present. If power in neoliberal societies is no longer exercised through normalization, but through diversification and individualization — or, as Deleuze would suggest some years after his systematic reading of Foucault in 1986,[26] in a way that transcends the individual as an entity still too substance-like and inflexible, towards the "dividual", where discipline as a fixed mold is replaced by a continual modulation and control in an open territory — would it not be possible to say that Foucault risks simply duplicating the power structures of the present? To what extent Foucault's lectures on biopolitics enable us to extricate ourselves from this must remain an open issue; it is however true that resistance as based on an ontology of multiplicity drawing on Spinoza and Nietzsche becomes problematic, and that the theory of the body that was the implicit basis for the analysis of discipline cannot as such be sufficient.

GOVERNING ONESELF

In the final works, separated from the work on biopolitics, liberalism and governmentality by a chronological hiatus that still remains to be filled,[27] Foucault famously returns to the Greeks, and to a "hermeneutics of the self" whose Greek origins he now traces in great detail. This hermeneutics of the self can no longer be understood as simply a modern avatar of Christian confessional technologies, as would seem to follow from the initial work on the history of sexuality. Rather we must see these technologies as made possible by a much longer historical development that takes us back to Plato. Sexuality and gender are now integrated in a problem of self-relation that has a much wider scope, and it becomes the terrain where he once more takes up the dialog with phenomenology and psychoanalysis begun in the work before the *History of Madness,* and where the problem of the constitution of "experience" comes to the fore again.

Perhaps there is here a final encounter with phenomenology, with Merleau-Ponty and Heidegger, as Deleuze suggests somewhat reluctantly, although it extends far beyond the limits of traditional phenomenology. This encounter would circle around the possibility of a historical ontology of subjectivity resulting from practices and technologies of the self, or processes of "subjectivation". In this becoming-subject, the deciphering of the self's interiority is not simply forced upon the subject by complexes of power and knowledge (within which you must confess who you are, scrutinize your motifs and display them before the authority of knowledge), but is just as much a way a subject constructs itself. This is done in a way that involves the body, its pleasures and pains, capacities and shortcomings, and Foucault analyzes such technologies of the self as they appear in Greek and Roman texts, ranging from sexual behavior, eating, and drinking, all the way up to techniques for attaining spiritual and philosophical truth. These are types of comportments that involve a dimension of "mastery over the self", *enkrateia,* and while they are always carried out in relation to the ideas of truth and relations of power that surround them, they nevertheless are not simple reflections, but form an agency of their own.

This many-faceted research on the history and modes of subjectivation, from the Greek ideas of the "use of pleasures" and "the care of the self" including the sketches for further developments that we can find in Foucault's lectures, shows that his concern is the *genesis* of subjectivity as a variable and changing form of self-relation. This undoubtedly involves an initial move of *de-transcendentalizing,* which, in order to constitute its own territory, had to oppose a certain idea of phenomenology. However, it also opens a different avenue for an expanded phenomenology that engages with the histories of technology and self-fashioning in a much more fluid way, in which *experience* is more a constantly shifting enigma than an idea of a universal form.

In the Greek and Roman texts discussed by Foucault, the reaction to power relations now becomes a turning inward, or more precisely a hollowing out or an "unhinging" of an interior that, while always relating to forms of power and knowledge, cannot be reducible to them. Subjectivation is fundamentally a way to *capacitate,* and it allows for a dimension of subjectivity as a *situated freedom,* which also becomes a problem of *truth* (which also opens up a new relation to psychoanalysis, and particularly to Lacan). This unfolding of truth as a process would then be a history of those ways in which man has constituted himself at once as a subject and an object, explicated his relation to himself, and opened up a space of self-reflection in a "truth game". When Foucault speaks of a "hermeneutics of the self", this relates not to that which is "true or false in knowledge, but to an analysis of those 'truth games,' the games with the true and the false in which being is constituted historically as experience, i.e., as something that can and ought to be thought."[28]

Do we return to the idea of an underlying ontology here? Yes, to the extent that the truth game is played on a level that cannot be reduced to empirically given subjects and objects; but also no, at least if we understand ontology as relating to a sphere outside of mundane practices, since the constitution of experience, of that which can and ought to be thought (a direct echo of Heidegger's *das zu-Denkende*), is inseparable from such practices, which always involve our bodies, desires, and affective relations to the world.

It has sometimes been claimed that the turn towards the construction of individuality, an "ethic" or even "aesthetic of existence", as Foucault sometimes called it, even though it is developed mainly on the basis of Greek and Roman texts, in fact is continuous with the earlier work on biopolitics, and would fit rather smoothly into the kind of entrepreneurial image of the self of neoliberalism.[29] But we must also note that towards the end Foucault came to understand his work as an "ontology of actuality" or a "historical ontology", problematizing the question of truth as situated, historical, and finite, as a series of shifting horizons that must include the present of the questioner, not as a given point of reference, but as a tentative starting point that is only assumed in order to be dislodged by historical research.[30] In this sense, what is at stake is the *limit* of the present: a use of the past that inserts a wedge into the present, so that it splits up in multiple directions, some of which will re-actualize other pasts and histories that surround our contemporary moment as so many virtual histories. This return to ontology is also and just as much a return to history and to practice; it takes us back to the self in all its corporeal, affective, intellectual, and ideational capacities, as a site of experimentation, which is also a site of resistance.

1   See Gilles DELEUZE, *Foucault,* Paris: Minuit, 1986.

2   Martin HEIDEGGER, *Was heißt Denken?,* Tübingen: Max Niemeyer, 1954.

3   This too relates Foucault to Heidegger; see for instance the comments on Heraclitus in *Letter in Humanism,* where Heidegger discusses ethos as an abode *(Aufenthalt)*: "If then, in accordance with the basic meaning of the word *ethos,* the name 'ethics' says that it considers the true habitation of human beings, then that thinking which thinks the truth of being as the primary element of human beings, as something which exists, is already an originary ethics. This thinking, then, is not first of all ethics, because it is ontology." Martin HEIDEGGER, *Wegmarken,* Frankfurt am Main: Vittorio Klostermann, 1978, p. 353.

4   See Michel FOUCAULT: "Introduction", in: FOUCAULT, *Dits et écrits,* edited by Daniel DEFERT and François EWALD, 4 VOLS., Paris: Gallimard, 1994, VOL. 1, pp. 65–119.

5   See Michel FOUCAULT: "Préface à l'Histoire de la sexualité", in: FOUCAULT, *Dits et écrits,* VOL. 4, pp. 578–84.

6   For a discussion of the continuity of the theme of "experience" in Foucault, see Timothy O'LEARY, "Foucault, Experience, Literature", in: *Foucault Studies,* no. 5, 2008, pp. 5–25.

7   Perhaps it would be possible to re-apply Michel Serres' description of the logic of Foucault's narrative to the place that the book holds within Foucault's own trajectory: it is a kind of dense overlay of "geometric" figures, whose reciprocal differences and relations will be gradually worked out as he proceeds. See Michel SERRES, *Hermès I: La communication,* Paris: Seuil, 1969, pp. 167–191.

8   See Jacques DERRIDA, "Cogito et histoire de la folie", in: DERRIDA, *L'écriture et la différence,* Paris: Seuil, 1967.

9   To "neutralize" or "suspend" would be operations aligned with Husserlian phenomenology, i. e. a bracketing of earlier philosophies in order to uncover a more profound stratum of reason; by "dismantling" I here understand the development of Husserl's project in Heidegger, who speaks of *Destruktion* and *Abbau,* operations that while criticizing some of the tendencies in Husserl still remain within the horizon of a transcendental foundation, or fundamental ontology. These concepts are still at work in Derrida's essay, which can be read as a defense of philosophy's traditional authority against Foucault's historicist attacks.

10   The text was published as an appendix to the 1972 edition of *Histoire de la folie,* and reprinted in: FOUCAULT, *Dits et écrits,* VOL. 2.

11   See FOUCAULT, "La folie, l'absence d'œuvre" (1964), in: FOUCAULT, *Dits et écrits,* VOL. 1.

12   All of these are reprinted in: FOUCAULT, *Dits et écrits,* VOL. 1. The essays on Hölderlin, Bataille, and Flaubert are translated in Michel FOUCAULT, *Language, Counter-Memory, Practice,* edited by Daniel BOUCHARD, Ithaca: Cornell University Press, 1977.

13   In: FOUCAULT, *Dits et écrits,* VOL. 1. English translation in: Michel FOUCAULT and Maurice BLANCHOT, *The Thought from Outside and Michel Foucault as I Imagine Him,* New York: Zone Books, 1987.

14   The return of language as a historical opacity is what heralds the breakdown of the system of representation that characterized the classical age, although language is now spread out in many functions, from the formalist attempts at finding a pure universal language to the celebration of its

infinity in literary writing. For modernity, Foucault suggests, the problem of language unfolds in the interval between Nietzsche's question "Who speaks" and Mallarmé's answer: the being of the Word itself, to which the intransitivity of literary writing testifies in the highest degree. See *Les mots et les choses*, Paris: Gallimard, 1966, pp. 314–318. For a discussion of this, see Tilottama RAJAN, "The Phenomenological Allegory: From 'Death and the Labyrinth' to 'The Order of Things'", in: *Poetics Today*, VOL. 19, 1998, pp. 439–466.

15 Another crucial reference can be found in the two radio lectures from 1966 on "Heterotopias" and "The Utopian Body". The first would be developed the following year into the lecture on "other spaces", which since its belated publication in 1984 has become a frequent reference in art and architecture theory. The second radio talk is immediately relevant for a discussion of the persistence of phenomenological themes in Foucault, and in addressing the "utopian body" in terms of an inner ego-oriented space it retrieves many of the phenomenological concepts that Foucault was struggling with at the time. Once more in close parallel to Merleau-Ponty, he analyzes how a utopian desire emerges out of the body riveted to an irreducible and ineluctable factuality, by way of a fantasy of an other and glorious body, or a soul that wholly escapes it; from within a certain phenomenology, but also by brushing against its grain, Foucault here provides what we could call a genealogy of transcendence. See Michel FOUCAULT, *Die Heterotopien. Der utopische Körper | Les hétérotopies. Le corps utopique,* Frankfurt am Main: Suhrkamp, 2005. I discuss the relation between utopia and heterotopia in these texts in the chapter "Imagining Otherwise", in my *Architecture, Critique, Ideology: Essays on Architecture and Theory,* Stockholm: Axl Books, forthcoming.

16 Michel FOUCAULT, *Naissance de la clinique. Une archéologie du regard médical,* Paris: Presses universitaires de France, 1963, p. 202.

17 For a discussion of this, see Frédéric GROS, "Quelques remarques de méthode à propos de *Naissance de la clinique*", in: *Michel Foucault et la médecine: Lectures et usages,* edited by Philippe ARTIÈRES and Emmanuel DA SILVA, Paris: Kimé, 2001, pp. 49–59.

18 Gilles DELEUZE, *Spinoza, philosophie pratique,* Paris: Minuit, 1981.

19 Michel FOUCAULT, *Discipline and Punish,* translated by Alan Sheridan, London: Penguin, 1977, p. 308.

20 For Deleuze's comments on these disputes, see DELEUZE, "Désir et plaisir," in: DELEUZE, *Deux régimes de fous,* Paris: Minuit, 2003.

21 Gilles DELEUZE and Félix GUATTARI, *Mille plateaux,* Paris: Minuit 1980.

22 Michel FOUCAULT, *Security, Territory, Population: Lectures at the Collège de France, 1977–1978,* edited by Michel SENELLART, translated by Graham Burchell, Basingstoke: Palgrave Macmillan, 2007 · *The Birth of Biopolitics: Lectures at the Collège de France, 1978–1979,* edited by Michel SENELLART, translated by Graham Burchell, Basingstoke: Palgrave Macmillan, 2008 · *"Society Must Be Defended": Lectures at the Collège de France, 1975–1976,* edited by Mauro BERTANI and Alessandro FONTANA, translated by David Macey, New York: Picador, 2003.

23 Michel FOUCAULT, *The History of Sexuality,* VOL. 1: *An Introduction,* translated by Robert Hurley, New York: Vintage, 1978, p. 143.

24 Foucault's interest in liberalism and its connection to biopolitics has produced a huge debate; for a recent collection of responses, see *Foucault, Biopolitics, and Govermentality,* edited by Jakob NILSSON and Sven-Olov WALLENSTEIN, Huddinge: Södertörn University, 2013.

25 See for instance Michel FOUCAULT, "Questions of Method" (1980), in: *The Foucault Effect,* edited by Graham BURCHELL, Colin GORDON, and Peter MILLER, Chicago: University of Chicago Press, 1991, p.86, where he speaks of "the effect on historical knowledge of a nominalist critique itself arrived at by way of a historical analysis".

26 See Gilles DELEUZE, "Postscript on Control Societies", in: *Negotiations, 1972–1990,* translated by Martin Joughin, New York: Columbia University Press, 1995, pp.177–182. Deleuze's analysis of the societies of control points to many of these problems, although Deleuze was undoubtedly not aware of the particular inflection that Foucault's analysis of biopolitics had taken in the late 1970s.

27 His trajectory in this period is still impossible to reconstruct in its entirety, above all since the lectures from 1979 and 1981, *Du gouvernement des vivants* and *Subjectivité et Vérité,* still remain to be published. A reasonable conjecture would however be that these moves constitute different steps in a gradual slide from discipline to subjectivation, a process in which the problem of biopolitics may be taken to form an intermediary stage that was essential in redirecting the investigation, and yet remained too closely affiliated with a conception of power that tended to preclude or at least downplay processes of self-formation, which is the focus of the "ethical" turn in the last work.

28 Michel FOUCAULT, *L'Usage des plaisirs,* Paris: Gallimard, 1984, pp.12–13. This idea of a hermeneutics of the self is the explicit theme of a series of lectures given at the Collège de France in 1981–82. See Michel FOUCAULT, *The Hermeneutics of the Subject. Lectures at the Collège de France 1981–1982,* edited by Frédéric GROS, translated by Graham Burchell, Basingstoke: Palgrave Macmillan, 2005.

29 See for instance Louis MCNAY, "Self as Enterprise: Dilemmas of Control and Resistance in Foucault's *The Birth of Biopolitics*", in: *Theory Culture Society,* VOL. 26, 2009, no. 6, pp.55–77.

30 For a series of inventive analyses of this theme in Foucault, see Ian HACKING, *Historical Ontology,* Cambridge, MA and London: Harvard University Press, 2002.

PHILIPP OSTEN

Architecture for Patients: Medicine and City Planning in Berlin, 1860–1960

"Berlin — who doesn't know it? — is the ugliest big city in the world. Paris, London,
Rome, New York, Kyoto, Moscow, were gradually built by their own inhabitants;
Berlin was hastily constructed by contractors. With the exception of a few, very few,
buildings, single streets and squares, it is a city wholly lacking in architectural charm,
fascination — an endless heap of stone and mortar, nothing else. Despite this it
possesses, for instance, more bath tubs than Paris, and before the war had the reputation
of being the cleanest capital of the world, a fact not to be underestimated. In short, the
ugliest of the world […], but always meticulously clean."[1]

The above quotation comes from the novel *The Ninth of November* by Bernhard
Kellermann (1871–1951), published at the beginning of 1920. The description of
the recklessly built city repeats a widespread cliché about Berlin, one discussed
more fiercely than ever in the period immediately after World War I. City planners such as Martin Wagner (1885–1957) set about transforming this stone desert
"constructed by contractors". Real estate taxes were supposed to enable the City
of Greater Berlin to highlight social issues. It is no coincidence that in the above
quotation Bernhard Kellermann compares the number of baths with the soul-
lessness of the tenement buildings, since of course already during the German
Empire politics and public authorities were concerned about hygiene and discipline. And indeed, to quote a senior official from 1882, "without giving space to
an overly extensive humanity or even luxury".[2]

Hygiene and health regulations were not primarily the dictates of a human-
itarian nature, but rather of a rational economic one. Indeed, the mandatory
minimum size of an inner courtyard in Berlin was not oriented to the amount

IN / KIRSTEN WAGNER AND JASPER CEPL (EDITORS) /
IMAGES OF THE BODY IN ARCHITECTURE: ANTHROPOLOGY AND BUILT SPACE /
TÜBINGEN · BERLIN / ERNST WASMUTH VERLAG / 2014 / PP. 319–344

of sunlight that was able to reach the window of a ground-floor apartment, but to the turning circle of a fire engine, and that amounted to exactly 5.34 by 5.34 m according to official regulations.[3]

The present essay is concerned with the links between architecture and the body from a medical-historical perspective. "The Birth of the Clinic" was the name Michel Foucault (1926–1984), Professor of the History of Systems of Thought at the Collège de France in Paris, gave to the epoch preceding 1850 in which — initially with autopsy and medical statistics; later with clinical thermometer, stethoscope, and ophthalmoscope — a number of techniques were brought together that have determined the knowledge about the human body up to the present. A new "apparatus in which the technologies that make it possible to see",[4] raised results taken directly from the patient to the decisive criterion of diagnostics. That led to new classifications of illnesses. Soon it was no longer a patient's social status that decided which section of a hospital he would be accommodated in, but the clinical image he presented to his doctors. Accordingly, the dispositif of accommodation and care[5] that had prevailed in the hospitals of the early modern period was gradually replaced by that of order, discipline and the control of epidemics. Due to the strictly regulated daily routine, the clear hierarchies, and the military procedures, the sociologist Erving Goffman classified hospitals — along with prisons, mental hospitals, and barracks — as total institutions.[6] That was especially true in Prussia, where, until the beginning of the 20th century, public (non-denominational) hospitals were subject directly to the police authorities and the running of hospitals was given over almost exclusively to military personnel. A prototype of a municipal hospital in Berlin, the Hospital Am Urban, was built by the architect of barracks, prisons, and schools, Hermann Blankenstein (1829–1910), and was assigned to General (ret.) Adolf Hagemeyer (d. 1896).[7]

But if architecture was geared to subjecting patients as smoothly as possible to a medical organization, what role should real bodies play for architecture? Patients' bodies were determined by the structure of the institutions in which they were interned. Nevertheless, from the beginning of organized workers' councils at the latest, one can no longer speak so straightforwardly of an unconditional self-disciplining, as was still the case when, in order to be admitted to a hospital, the urban and rural poor had to make a formal request to their prince.[8] A departure from this subjugation is illustrated by a report in a Berlin newspaper, *Vorwärts*. The Berlin venereologist Ignaz Zadek (1858–1931) arranged for the publication of the reports of his patients from the notorious hospital, Neue Charité in Berlin, about which, in August 1893, a patient wrote in *Vorwärts*: "On being admitted I had the impression [...] of having ended up in a prison."[9] That culminated in autumn 1893 with the Charité boycott, during which patients, referring doctors, and a number of health insurance organizations called unanimously for "friendlier wards" and an "end to the barracks mentality".[10]

However, those were genuinely political aims, aims that were pushed through using political means — but which did not give rise to a medical debate. In the city planning of the mid-19th century, on the other hand, natural-scientific concepts gained considerably in influence.[11] Long before bacteriology identified microorganisms as the cause of diseases, statistics established the importance of topographical conditions for the formation of diseases. Solely through the meticulous recording of dates of death, daily temperature, and the location of the deceased, it became possible, more than a quarter of a century before Robert Koch (1843–1910), to detect the cause of cholera. Fatalities could be ascribed to water intake. The infectious agent increased with rising temperature.

In London the outbreaks of cholera in the catchment area of the South Water Works led early on to a change in hygiene and building regulations. They "played their part in preserving England from epidemic cholera for the last three decades of the century".[12] In Munich, after the cholera epidemic of 1854, Max von Pettenkofer (1818–1901) matched the death certificates of the 2090 victims with the course of the water supply system.[13] It was not until the Hamburg cholera epidemic of 1892, however, that the municipal building policy in Germany underwent a decisive about-face.[14] Investors were now obliged to connect new buildings to the sewer system. Not without reason, the historian Ulrich Koppitz (b. 1965) argues that the architecture that most clearly represented the medical status of a city and the socio-political drive to reform was the wastewater system.[15]

Records on infant mortality, tuberculosis epidemiology, and life expectancy focused on single streets and blocks. They formed the statistical framework which, in the last third of the 19th century, provided support for both city planners and public health and prevention experts in equal measure. They also influenced the building of hospitals and homeless shelters, and shortly afterwards they would fuel the utopia of healthy residential quarters, whose realization would become the first agenda item of the fragile young Weimar democracy with a potential for consensus.

CONCEPTS OF DIETARY BALANCE

Beginning in the second half of the 19th century, the literature on architecture and the body was determined by empirical findings obtained from the largest possible cohort. Earlier dietary concepts containing detailed statements about the individual and the space immediately surrounding him disappeared. Balance had been the highest goal of dietetics. It closely followed humoral-pathological concepts, which were defining for medicine from antiquity far into the early modern period. If the relation between the most important bodily fluids/ humours (yellow bile, black bile, blood, and phlegm) becomes unbalanced, the organs may be damaged. However, physicians did not only counter this unbalance with bleeding and dietary prescriptions. Beginning in the Middle Ages dietetics encompassed six so-called "non-natural things" (*sex res non naturales*).[16] Here, those conditions are named that a person is able to influence in relation to his own body. These include the food he ingests, the air he breathes, the temperature he exposes himself to, and the rhythm of sleep and wakefulness he imposes on himself. Depending on one's interpretation, clothing and spatial surroundings are either directly or indirectly related to this.[17] These ideas remained current in academic medicine until the beginning of the 19th century, and found their echo in the natural-philosophical concepts of Friedrich Wilhelm Schelling (1775–1854). They propagated both an equilibrium of forces and an analogical thinking in which it was entirely imaginable to create an equilibrium of the soul through the form of a building. In popular belief and among general practitioners, it continued to have an effect for some time afterwards. Essays on architecture had a permanent place in popular household books. In a guide to dietetics, for example, which, beginning in 1847, passed through numerous editions at the Leipzig publisher Otto Wigand (1795–1870), one also finds a chapter on "Habitation and Domesticity".[18]

In public secular buildings, which, during the extended building phase of German industrialization, were expected to orient themselves to economic and purely scientific criteria, these theories were hardly taken into account. Only through a historicizing formal language drawing on elements of the Baroque and classicism did they find their way into architecture in a sublimated form at the turn of the 20th century. Since then they form a continuum that finds its expression above all in the artistic treatment/interpretation of architecture. Reflected in the designs of the Gläserne Kette (Glass Chain), whose utopias strove in crystalline form to bring together individual, soul, and infinity, are natural-philosophical theories of the early 19th century. Bruno Taut's (1880–1838) Glass Pavilion for the Cologne Werkbund Exhibition of 1914, for example, became an icon of this conception, which still plays a role in contemporary art.

Artistic works dealing with archetypes, esotericism, and the sacral via the medium of architecture can be provided with their own category. This category is opposed by a second group of artworks, which do not intend to focus on anthropological categories or 'types'. These works are concerned with individual needs and socio-cultural developments and place the main focus on the interaction between space and individual.

In many cases architects requested doctors to provide them with guidelines for a humane architecture. Although the architects' need in that respect seems to have been great, the guidelines provided by medicine are few and far between. What the doctors offered instead was hygiene-based building regulations. In short, the construction of hospitals was not oriented to the human body, but to dispositifs of bacteriology and the internal differentiations of medicine. Instead, it tended to be artistic concepts that provided architecture much more frequently with ideas for dealing with fundamental anthropological issues. Examples show that it is often philosophy which is at the basis of these issues and not medicine or natural science.

A recent example of utopian architecture tailored directly to the human body are the *Cellules* (**FIG. 1**) of the Israeli artist Meir Eshel (called Absalon) who

died in 1993. The minimal structures already carry a reference to biology in their name. Their walls allow their inhabitants only a few restricted movements; the openings grant only a limited view to the exterior. The artist created them as mirrors of the interior. Niklas Maak has described these buildings as a "minimal armour" ("Minimalpanzerungen") of the self.[19]

HOUSING IN THE EMPIRE

Around 1900 "living spaces that grant the first requirement of health, light, and air in the greatest possible abundance"[20] were the declared aim of city planners and doctors. In practice, however, generous light-filled working class housing remained a utopia. The discovery of the tubercle bacillus in 1882 and the subsequent rise of bacteriology did not mean progress but a setback for the arguments of the housing reformers. From now on not dark and damp courtyard-facing rooms but bacteria were considered the cause of disease. Over the following decades, the state invested less in the construction of tenements than in the isolation of agents of infection. That led to the building of hospitals and sanatoria.

During the German Empire attempts at a fundamental reform of Berlin tenement buildings remained isolated cases. Alfred Messel's (1853–1909) building project in Proskauer Straße was, as the illustrated postcard shows (**FIG. 2**), real-

ized long before the surrounding buildings to function as an example for investors. The generous residential complex contained light, easily ventilated apartments and a small park in the inner courtyard. The park was twice as large as the courtyards of the immediately neighboring tenements which, contrary to the hopes of the director of city planning Ludwig Hoffmann (1852–1932), were put up shortly afterwards.

In the 1860s, city planning had been shaped by the concept of the *Mietskaserne* (literally, tenement barracks). Unlike the less regular apartment buildings, the military order of barracks should prevail. The *Stumme Portier* (silent doorman) in the entrance is a token from this time. Whoever's name was listed on this large wooden board, was also registered in precisely this way in the City's official address book and could be easily traced.

Doctors disagreed with the dispositif of the *Mietskaserne*. In 1882 a German building and health act was launched, a draft of which the Leipzig doctor Otto Kuntze sent as a petition to the Reichstag. He suggested "supporting the people's welfare" with cheap and healthy apartment buildings.[21] The buildings should have a maximum of three floors. The minimum height of the rooms should range between 3.25 m in the first floor and 2.75 m in the third floor. In the case of terrace housing, damp would be prevented by ventilation between the fire walls. The residents reached their apartments via half-open galleries, through which the chimneys and ventilation passed. Kuntze referred directly to Anglo-American models. In his petition Kuntze wrote that the mortality in German cities was "10–20%, and in part 100%, greater than in England and the United States".[22] These figures were still pure estimation. Around 1900, with the

PHILIPP OSTEN

appearance of the first valid statistics comparing international infant mortality, it became clear that Germany had the highest rates: on average 25%, even reaching 40% during the summer months in the northern districts of central Berlin. A similarly devastating situation could only be found in Austro-Hungary and Tsarist Russia.[23]

Beginning in the 1870s Berlin was one of the first cities to have a comprehensive drinking water supply and sewer system. For that the city could be grateful to the persistent warnings of Rudolf Virchow (1821–1902), the founder of modern cellular pathology. With a sharp tongue the doctor and politician pressed for an urban redevelopment founded on the principles of hygiene. Virchow's reasoning, which was oriented to natural-scientific methods, culminated in a dictum coined by Samuel Neumann (1819–1908) in 1848: "Medicine is a social science, and politics is nothing more than medicine writ large."[24] Indeed, natural-scientific arguments were by and large the only instrument with which the state could be pressured into a socio-political engagement of the state.

As a result of a closing of ranks between monarchists and liberals in the so-called *Kulturkampf* (literally "culture struggle", a term coined by Virchow[25]), the socio-political function of the church was diminished. The new task of the state resulting from this situation is made clear in the architecture of public buildings. Elements of sacral architecture could be found on schools, on courts, and on numerous hospital buildings.

BERLIN HOSPITALS

For a long time Berlin's only hospital was the Royal Charité, built in 1710 due to the threat of a smallpox epidemic. It was run by the military and served primarily for the training of military field surgeons. The students of the university founded 100 years later did not initially set foot in this building. In 1835, however, the military hospital became Berlin's first and only municipal hospital. For each year the City accounted for 100,000 boarding days for its poor. Already in 1880, however, approximately 500,000 were needed.

Neither the staff nor the administration, which now came from the higher ranks of the police force, was well respected. A new building was erected besides the old, the so-called Neue Charité. Its patients were basically prisoners, since the Neue Charité admitted patients suffering from venereal diseases, the mad, and sick prison inmates. Charité became the object of a growing discontent among the populace. An alternative to the 'unchristian' Charité was later provided by Berlin's first denominational hospital. At the topping-out ceremony, the highest representative of the Catholic Hedwiggemeinde, Wilhelm Emmanuel Freiherr von Ketteler (1811–1877), summarized what patients could expect of his institution built in 1852 "in coarse Gothic" by the master builder of Cologne Cathedral

Vinzenz Statz (1819–1898) and expanded roughly 50 years later by his son Franz Statz (1848–1930) for the requirements of the 20th century: "We want to accommodate you, we want to care for your sick body and, when you are in mortal danger, for your soul."[26] The hospital as church — the small Catholic community had created an institution that did not only respond to medical needs.

AIR

It was again a smallpox epidemic that led Berlin to the construction of a municipal hospital in Moabit in 1871 — but now according to entirely different principles. The days of the long hospital corridor were numbered; a new concept had come into fashion: the pavilion hospital. The earliest designs for an *architecture civile* go back to the year 1805, when the Parisian architect Jean-Nicolas-Louis Durand (1760–1834) presented his ideal plan for a hospital in Paris. Order, control, and equality were the basic principles of his classical geometrical plans. Durand's plans were blueprints for schools, hospitals, and prisons. His ideal hospital with 14 pavilions, seven on each side of a central axis was never built, however. Nevertheless, just over a half-century later the architect's vision for patients would become a reality — although the order of the ground plan was now no longer justified with political-philosophical arguments, but with the requirements of modern medicine. During the American Civil War military doctors in the USA had compared the mortality in different types of military hospital:

> [T]he high mortality in the existing multi-storey hospitals with their corridors between the wards and, on the other hand, the beneficial experiences during the war in the United States, where the sick and wounded were accommodated in airy huts and tents, taught with unmistakable clarity what form the hospital of the future must have. Increasingly, one felt the necessity to supply the sick and wounded with air in sufficient quantities and the greatest possible purity. The simultaneous rise of hygienics led to the same results: the concentrating of the sick in large barracks-like buildings was abandoned to accommodate them in single separated buildings, pavilions or barracks.[27]

Already from the Crimean War military doctors had reported astonishing figures: in the military hospital in Scutari, 47.7% of the 2500 wounded died, while in the wooden huts that stood in the sea wind near to Balaklava, mortality amounted to only 3%.[28]

Charité ventured an experiment. Four "children's barracks" — one for measles, one for diphtheria, and two for non-infectious diseases — were erected in 1888 in the form of iron-framed buildings without side windows but with skylights above. The formula for the relation between room and patient was: 35 m^3

of air per bed — 45 m³ for patients with infectious diseases. Air became a criterion for the size of the space. During this period it was impossible to publish on
public secular buildings that did without a detailed description of the amount
of air in cubic metres available to the individual patients. Modern ventilation
systems offered an alternative to the high ceilings and larger wards by producing
75 m³ of air per hour per bed.

Considered for many years as the most modern institute vis-à-vis the rational industrial accommodation of people was Blankenstein's municipal homeless
shelter in Berlin (**FIG. 3**). The dormitories in Fröbel Straße, Prenzlauer Berg, held

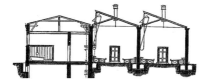

3
HERRMANN
BLANKENSTEIN /
MUNICIPAL
SHELTER /
BERLIN / FRÖBEL
STRASSE /
VIEW FROM
ABOVE · CROSS
SECTION ·
AND PLAN /
1896

4000 people. In 1896 the Journal of the Association of Berlin Architects reported how this building was the first to make use of the insights made in English
factory architecture for the erection of mass accommodation. Like factories and
storehouses the asymmetric roofs of the dormitories contained skylights. It was
thus possible to line up the windowless dormitories in rows and let the air enter
from above. Each of the dormitories held 70 people.

Evening admission began around 6 p.m. Whoever wanted to be sure of getting a place arrived at the gate at least two hours in advance. Here, identification
papers were inspected. Immediately behind the asylum was the municipal disin-
fection establishment. Clothing and belongings were packed into bags and disinfected using steam. The beds had no mattresses, but a steel-spring base. Each
inmate received a blanket, which was disinfected daily. Pillows were formed
from rolled jackets in which the inmates carefully wrapped their belongings.
Men and women were accommodated separately. Collective accommodation for
100 families with children was available at the front of the building.

In 1896 Hoffmann was appointed the director of city planning for Berlin. The architect, who had made a name for himself with the construction of the Supreme Court in Leipzig, was well respected among the conservative middle classes. However, he also had the social-democratic faction behind him, especially the city councillor Paul Singer (1844–1911). Hoffmann saw the chance to liberate hospitals and sanatoria from the "brick uniforms" to which his predecessor Blankenstein had decreed barracks, homeless shelters, schools, and hospitals. Instead, Hoffmann allowed them to appear at least in a few details like palaces. In the year he took office, Berlin residents had given vent to their anger over the relations in the Royal Charité in mass demonstrations. In leaflets the patients demanded: at most 18 patients per room, separate toilets and washrooms, healthy fare and an "end to the barracks mentality".[29] Hoffman wanted to counter such discontent with a complex that would radiate monastic calm.

After a ten-year planning phase Hoffmann's Rudolf Virchow Hospital in Berlin Wedding was opened in September 1906. The patients entered the municipal

4
RUDOLF
VIRCHOW
HOSPITAL /
PORTAL IN
AUGUSTEN-
BURGER
PLATZ

hospital through a generous castle courtyard (**FIG. 4**). Hoffmann took the design for the stairwell from the baroque priory St. Florian in Austria.[30] At the opposite

5
RUDOLF
VIRCHOW
HOSPITAL /
MORTUARY

end of the grounds was the building for the mortuary and pathology designed in the style of a rural chapel (**FIG. 5**). From there a path lined with weeping willows led to the street. Situated between the entry building and the mortuary were numerous hospital buildings to which Hoffmann gave the form of freestanding rural villas, an elongated farmyard recalling royal stables, and 21 patient pavil-

6
RUDOLF
VIRCHOW
HOSPITAL /
PATIENT
PAVILIONS

ions (FIG. 6). 20 patients could be accommodated in each ward under a vaulted ceiling. In the interior above the door portals were murals in a baroque style. Each pavilion possessed two wards, which formed elongated wings on either side of a two-storeyed building at the centre. The planning phase coincided with the rise of X-ray diagnostics. Due to the unproblematic incorporation of new functional buildings, the pavilion system made it possible to react quickly to the new technical development.

Julius Posener (1904–1996) describes Ludwig Hoffmann's architecture as "unorthodox historicist".[31] Unlike many of his contemporaries, Hoffmann did not copy historical models; he preferred to quote single elements from famous buildings that he studied on his extensive research trips. For Hoffmann, sacral buildings, gardens and palaces provided a better source of inspiration than the many European hospitals that he visited only grudgingly. With regard to the latter, the architect confessed his unease in his autobiography: "If the most recent hospitals had hit upon some very interesting solutions as regards hygiene, solutions which were valuable for medical treatment, I now understood the reserve of the populace concerning the accommodation in such an establishment."

Hoffmann calculated that in the first ten years of its existence his hospital would treat 28,000 patients, who would stay an average of a month. His architectural concept to overcome the patient's "reserve" was a "loving architecture, expressed in the building's design, its pleasant setting in friendly gardens, in spaces that put one at one's ease, and in a sensitive and loving treatment of all the details."[32]

He attempted to keep the patients away from unpleasant impressions. He hid the building containing the operating rooms so as not to attract the attention of anxious patients. The relatives' funeral processions to the mortuary were not visible from the grounds. Hoffmann saw the necessity of smooth washable walls and light for patient examinations, but in the hospitals he visited the architect experienced the same discomfort he felt "in a photography studio".[33] "I thought", Hoffmann wrote in his memoirs, "that some patients would be severely aggrieved to discover on waking in the morning that he found himself in a room with numerous fellow sufferers that were perhaps still unknown to him. Therefore, on the wall opposite each bed I had painted a small scene: a child's head, a bird's nest, a bouquet of flowers or some other inoffensive motif. In that way the patient's first impression would be of a sense of attentiveness."[34]

With similar thoroughness Hoffmann prepared himself for the design of a mental hospital in Buch. Situated far away in the northern outskirts of Berlin, more than 2000 people should be accommodated in 40 buildings. From "an outstanding psychiatrist" Hoffmann made himself familiar "with the different types of these diseases". His advisor asked him to keep the mental patients away from bleak and desolate impressions, and "due to the agitation of the patients the number of pieces of furniture should be kept to a minimum", and nothing should be hung on the walls.[35] Accordingly, Hoffmann decided to create variety solely through the building's design, and to avoid ornamental decoration: red brick walls alternated with white architectural elements, gables and towers softened the monotony of the roof areas, and numerous bays enlivened the bare walls. The inmates could walk freely through the extensive gardens without having their attention drawn to the fact that they were actually confined in enclosed grounds.

Seen in a sober light, the history of Berlin hospital architecture during the German Empire — if one ignores the complex calculations of air volume, the experiences of the American Civil War that suggested tents as ideal hospital architecture, and the requests of psychiatrists for quiet forms — is hardly shaped by medical knowledge. Instead, the rational architecture of Blankenstein was replaced by precisely what in the *Kulturkampf* (i. e. the abolition of the privileges of the Catholic Church by the Prussian state) had been lost: the sacral.

ARCHITECTURE SHAPES THE BODY. A CASE STUDY

The close link between architecture and medicine, which entered public awareness with the end of the German Empire, can be illustrated by the story of a three-year-old boy growing up in northeast central Berlin at the beginning of World War I.

Arthur H. lived with his parents and four siblings in a tenement building in Choriner Straße 16. The three-year-old boy had not yet learnt to walk and was unable to stand unaided. Arthur H. suffered from the deficiency disease rickets, which at the time was so widespread that in 1908 Berlin school doctors diagnosed it in a third of first-year pupils. In the case of a small infant who supports itself on its arms while crawling, the wrists begin to widen. When children with rickets begin to walk, the bones of the lower leg cannot support the weight of the body, leading to bowlegs or knock knees. The bone lacks calcium. But however many units of this mineral doctors administered to their patients, the calcium did not find its way to the bones.

Rickets had always been a sign of poverty. But children who grew up in the back courtyards of large tenements seemed especially hard hit. In December 1918, two months after the end of World War I, the father of Arthur H. was at a loss. He brought his son to the Oskar Helene Heim Hospital for disabled children in a southern suburb of Berlin, where he was admitted to the ward of the pediatrician Kurt Huldschinsky (1883–1941). Huldschinsky noticed a further symptom: all children diagnosed with the rickets were conspicuously pale. That gave the pediatrician an idea. Each day he placed his charges for a few minutes beneath the ultraviolet light of a sunlamp. The therapy worked. The bones of the children began to absorb calcium and, despite the insufficient diet in the first winter after the war, the symptoms of rickets disappeared. Arthur H. was the first patient on whom Huldschinsky tested the sunlamp treatment.[36] His case entered medical history. In 1929 Huldschinsky was nominated for the Nobel Prize[37] — which did not, however, prevent the pediatrician from losing his medical licence in 1934 and being forced to leave Germany. He died in exile in Egypt under still unknown circumstances in 1941.

The young boy was made to lie under the ultraviolet lamp once a day until spring. On May 8, 1919, Huldschinsky noted in the patient files: "Beginning of sunny weather!" He terminated the therapy and sent Arthur H., who was now able to walk independently, onto the hospital's sun terrace. A few years later, biochemists discovered the cause of the phenomenon. To supply the bones with calcium the body requires vitamin D, and that is only activated when the skin has contact with ultraviolet light. In all larger towns and cities, municipal health funds installed public light-bath facilities. Children with rickets lacked sunlight.

People who suffer from rickets as children show signs of the disease throughout their lives. In the 1960s the back courtyards of East and West Berlin were enlarged, tenement blocks were knocked down, and open spaces were created. The bodies of their former inhabitants were marked by the architecture of the tenements and back courtyards: architecture forms the body, not the other way round.

LIGHT

Consequently, in the first half of the 20th century light played an important role in the combatting of infectious diseases. In 1903 the Danish-Icelandic doctor Niels Finsen (1860–1904) received the Nobel Prize for the treatment of *lupus vulgaris* with light. With his sanatorium in Leysin, Switzerland, the doctor Auguste Rollier (1874–1954) celebrated a number of successes with the sunlight treatment of tuberculosis. Between 1920 and 1950 every noteworthy newly constructed hospital in Germany was equipped with a sun terrace or *Liegehalle* (a veranda for reclining patients). A pioneering role was assumed by the tuberculosis sanatoria. In spring and summer the patients spent the day lying in semi-open *Liegehallen*.[38]

Sanatoria for well-heeled patients, such as the vegetarian Monte Verità colony in Ascona, were equipped with separate freestanding *Liegehallen*.[39] In 1905 the *Jugendstil* designer Albin Müller (1871–1941) conceived a *Lufthütte* (air hut)

7
ALBIN MÜLLER /
AIR HUT / 1905

(FIG. 7) for the noble Sanatorium Barner in the Harz. The two-storeyed wooden construction was designed for the company Christoph & Unmack in Upper Lusatia, run by a carpenter and an architect, to serve as a prototype for a rural one-room house colony. Only one was produced. The wooden hut was the first building by Albin Müller, the later director of the Mathildenhöhe artists' colony in Darmstadt.[40] By 1914 Müller would combine the three villas making up the sanatorium to form a complex. Three dining rooms, each with their own color scheme, and single rooms with colorful Lincrusta wallpaper (a wall covering made of asbestos and sawdust to create a textured design)[41] were allocated to patients according to their individual needs. The treatment, which made use of light effects, recalls the esoteric experiments in Felix Peipers' (1873–1944) theosophical private sanatorium in Munich where patients were exposed in 20-minute sittings to variously colored light sensations in geometrically designed colored chambers.[42]

In the hospital construction of the 1920s the trend for light and air cannot be ignored. Of course, for reasons of asepsis, recently operated patients could hardly be placed in an open *Liegehalle* in the forest. Gradually, however, sick wards were converted into open-air *Liegehallen*. In professional spheres this development was called the "Dosquet system". The Berlin doctor Wilhelm Dosquet (1859–1938) had set up a private hospital in Berlin Niederschönhausen (**FIG. 8**) whose windows extended from the ceiling to the floor. Behind the mostly open three-part sash windows was a long ward whose depth was a maximum of four

Krankenhaus Nordend
Berlin-Nieder-Schönhausen

8
PRIVATE
HOSPITAL /
NIEDER-
SCHÖNHAUSEN /
BUILT 1905 /
FIELD
POSTCARD /
JUNE 1916

metres in which up to ten beds could be placed next to one another. Privacy was created on request through partition walls.

Previously sunlight had been recognized primarily as a cure for tuberculosis. Sun terraces were considered as the trademark of lung sanatoria. Dosquet now also reported on successes with healing wounds. The disinfecting effect of ultraviolet light was known. Around 1900 it had been verified in laboratory tests as part of research on X-rays. Dosquet's hospital, which was constantly being expanded with new horseshoe-shaped light wards, as made famous by the architect Richard Döcker (1894–1968), became a model (FIG. 9). Döcker quoted Dosquet's window fronts in 1926 in a new hospital construction in Waiblingen

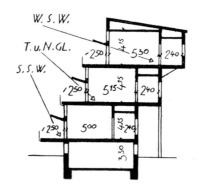

THE ABBREVIATIONS
INDICATE THE
ANGLE OF LIGHT AT
THE TIME OF THE
WINTER SOLSTICE
(WINTERSONNEN-
-WENDE, W.S.W.),
THE EQUINOX
(TAG UND NACHT
GLEICHE, T.U.N.GL.)
AND THE SUMMER
SOLSTICE
(SOMMERSONNEN-
WENDE, S.S.W.)

near Stuttgart (FIG. 10). The role Döcker ascribed to light becomes clear with the title given by the construction manager of the Weißenhofsiedlung to his *Neues Bauen* manifesto. He called the book *Terrassen Typ* (Terrace type).[43]

The Dosquet system became a general model for modern hospital construction. The director of city planning for Leipzig, Hubert Ritter (1886–1967), dedicated a large part of his book *Der Krankenhausbau der Gegenwart* (Contemporary hospital construction) to the discussion on the incidence of sunlight in hospital wards. The book was illustrated with examples taken from the Netherlands, Switzerland, the USA, and Germany. When the Frankfurt architect Walter Schwagenscheidt (1886–1968) suggested fitting the bright white hospital rooms behind the glass façades with movable shades, Döcker protested: "Not shade but sun is important for the healing process."[44] What is striking is the resonance between the new tendencies in hospital architecture and private secular architecture. The most popular socialist health guide of the Weimar Republic was written by the writer, dramatist, and doctor Friedrich Wolf (1888–1953). In the book an important section is made up by the chapter "Wie sollen wir wohnen?" (How should we live?). The double spread illustrated here (**FIG. 11**) presents a

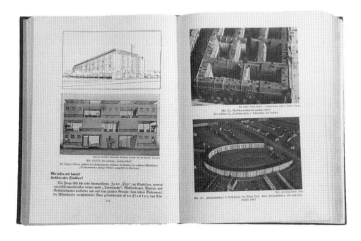

juxtaposition of the old Berlin tenements with Le Corbusier's 120 villas in Bordeaux, "fused together" to form a tower block,[45] and Bruno Taut and Martin Wagner's Hufeisensiedlung in Berlin Britz. Wagner was the first director of city planning for Greater Berlin, which merged in 1920. Already before World War I Wagner had petitioned for funding for social housing through the introduction of a real estate tax, as noted above.

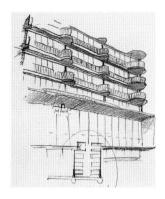

Perhaps one of the last hospitals of the "terrace type" is Erich Mendelsohn's Maimonides Hospital in San Francisco (**FIG. 12**), whose filigree balconies floated in front of a glass façade that is now hidden behind concrete panels.

At the end of the 1960s, a period in which hospital construction in the Federal Republic of Germany reached its peek, the architects Gertrud and Hansgeorg Knoblauch formulated a future model for hospitals that would be oriented to the needs of the patients. Bed and single room should ensure a small intimate personal area: "The mitigation of loneliness, of fear [...] should be the guiding principle of the design. That begins on entering, with the reception into the hos-

13
MEDIZIN UND STÄDTEBAU / COVER OF THE TWO-VOLUME WORK PUBLISHED ON THE OCCASION OF *INTERBAU 1957*

pital, and culminates in the patient's bed, where he is left alone."[46] In the 1920s, with the well-lit Dosquet wards, private space was ensured through partitions and screens. In the 1960s the demand for single rooms, individual visiting hours and — especially in children's hospitals — the possibility of accommodating parents and children in a single room, was only to be heard from patient self-help associations. Economists rejected single rooms; doctors considered visitors as avoidable sources of infection. As a result, in the 1960s patients' rooms resembled primate compounds at the zoo: tiled to the ceiling and easily washable.

In their vision for the future of hospitals Gertrud and Hansgeorg Knoblauch drew a conclusion that recalls long-past humoral-pathological concepts from a time in which measuring, classifying, and counting still carried no signifi-cant weight within medicine. They call for balance: no austere sterility and "no shocks".⁴⁷ Sick rooms should serve to temper the emotions. Thus, in the second half of the 20th century too, dietary concepts are made a part of many discus-sions on medicine and architecture. That becomes clear, for example, with the help of the two-volume work *Medizin und Städtebau* (Medicine and City Plan-ning) edited by Paul Vogler and Erich Kühn in 1957 (**FIG. 13**) on the occasion of the *Interbau* (*International Building Exhibition*).

Two thirds of the 1400-page work are placed under the heading "Die sinn-widrige Gross-Stadt. Möglichkeiten der Abhilfe" ("The Nonsensical City. Pros-pects of Redress"). The "ravages of civilization" in almost all areas of medicine were brought into connection with the city, from eye, skin and respiratory dis-eases resulting from environmental and sound pollution to psychosocial distur-bances. Surprisingly, in both of the lavishly designed *Interbau* volumes, a promi-nent role is played by medical-historical surveys. Historical data serves as the basis for future scenarios.⁴⁸ Decline in birth rate, spectacular successes with the reduction of infant mortality, and the rise in life expectancy held the prospect of a fundamental demographic change.⁴⁹

One detailed medical-historical survey focuses on the ancient world and the continuing relevance of humoral-pathological concepts for the modern period. Werner Leibbrand's (1896–1974) contribution visibly avoids representing medi-cal history as a history of increased rationalization. With regard to the architec-ture of hospitals, however, the Munich professor looked sceptically to the future:

> *The curve-grid medicine* [Kurvenraster-Medizin], *comparable with the diagram and symbol experiments of modern architecture and city plan-ning appears [...] as a necessarily abstract transitional stage. What it is reproached with on the part of the pathosophers is its failure in relation to the human encounter, without which medicine is finally as impracticable as house building. In current hospital construction, the architectural climate for such an encounter has still not been completely found. Here, an architec-tural will to safeguard the intimate zones must first make its demand felt in architecture. That too rests on anthropological foundations. Its basic creed would be something like: intimacy in spite of organization.*⁵⁰

The above remarks have a certain pathos about them; their vocabulary is taken from psychosomatics. The latter discipline, an offshoot of internal medi-cine, marked from the 1930s to the 1950s a shift in medicine to individual, no longer purely biological, explanatory models, without placing natural science fundamentally in doubt. What is striking about the above quotation from to-day's point of view is its sceptical assessment of two developments that were seen as parallels: the formal language of a rational, modern architecture, on the one hand, and, on the other, the technical framework conditions of a medicine that was on the point of installing intensive care units. At the same time, both aspects — redevelopment in the sense of a rational architecture and medical treatment in a technical-instrumental sense — were synonyms of the German economic miracle. 12 years after the end of the war West Germany had the third largest pharmaceutical industry in the world.

Following the introduction and the historical survey, the third medical-theoretical classification of modern hospital construction was undertaken by one of the two editors: Paul Vogler (1899–1965). The Charité professor lived in Zehlendorf in West Berlin. The central theme of his contribution is the integration of body, spirit and soul. Vogler confronts the mistrust in the rational concepts of modern natural science with the promise of healing of a holistic medicine.[51] From a neurophysiological point of view, in the 1950s there were primarily two models to choose from to explain the interaction between man and environment. It is significant that in the book *Medizin und Städtebau* they are described of all people by a professor who crossed the border between East and West Berlin on a daily basis on his journey to and from work.

One of these models was represented by the Heidelberg students of Ludolf von Krehl (1861–1937): Richard Siebeck (1883–1965) and Victor von Weizsäcker (1886–1957). Particularly in the case of Weizsäcker natural-scientific and psychoanalytic approaches were interwoven — in the spirit of the 1930s — with a good measure of mysticism. According to Weizsäcker, buildings, spaces, and forms roused memories of archetypal experiences. Via haptic, visual, and acoustic sensory impressions, these primordial sensations had an influence on the organism and the psyche.

The second model was represented by the Leningrad doctor Konstantin Mikhailovich Bykov (1886–1959), a student of Ivan Pavlov. For the Soviet scientist it was measurable nerve stimuli, with which the internal organs, mediated by the cerebral cortex, enter into relation with their surroundings. For the Soviet doctor architecture is a scientifically recognized mediator between social and bodily processes.

The doctors almost unanimously linked the impending ravages of civilization with the stimuli of the modern city. Besides doctors, prominent architects were also represented in the two volumes. After World War II Döcker was briefly general building director for the City of Stuttgart (the first major city to announce itself free of rubble after 1945).[52] He writes about the hygienic problems of cities in hot zones.[53] Programmatically, the most striking essay comes from Hans Scharoun (1893–1972). He calls for a rethinking in the building of residential quarters during the reconstruction period.

The essential process of finding a design presupposes the building of an organic principle. From such a principle, the technical-scientific, artistic-spiritual conditions are to be reassigned to a whole. From such a principle, geometry in the sense of the law of the work can also once again be integrated into a whole, in the service precisely of the organic principle, and not as a geometric principle."[54]

With Scharoun, what was only vaguely outlined by the psychosomatically oriented doctors, assumes concrete forms. Already in the 1920s demands for individuality, as expressed by Leibbrand, were realized by Scharoun — for example, in his singles hostel in Wrocław (then Breslau). Scharoun's answer to the demands of rationality and efficiency is not historicist, as was the case with Hoffmann, who 60 years earlier answered a similar situation with recourse to the Baroque. To the side of a building or city structure's function, Scharoun wanted to place an "organic principle". The defining role played by the experience of totalitarianism and hardship from the recent past for the development of his formal language, is laid bare by Scharoun in the final paragraphs of his essay:

Today it is the economy that determines the production, indeed even the biological and spiritual existence, of man. The time which enabled institutions regulating aspects of the spiritual as well as of power politics would finally come to an end with the Third Reich. The nature of the structural, in its meaning, and recognized in the meaning of the necessary application, will show us the way to a new and fruitful linking of creative forces.[55]

CONCLUSION

A notable position is assumed by Le Corbusier's Venice hospital project, which takes up Scharoun's call for biomorphic structures. Like a plant that spreads over the ground, the units of the single-storey building lie next to one another. Light falls from above as once into the dormitories of the municipal shelter in Berlin. But here in the interior there is space for many single rooms. They fulfil the demand for individuality and privacy. As Hoffmann 80 years earlier, Le Corbusier bases his call for single rooms on considerations about the patient's period of hospitalization.[56]

Admittedly, the *Modulor,* Le Corbusier's homunculus for the measuring of a space oriented to man,[57] appears against the background of the history of hospital construction as a hybrid being. He embodies the struggle for specific anthropological, but also entirely individual, features. At the same time he professes to be a product of statistics. The measure of his limbs and the degree of freedom of his joints feed on the same principle as clinical medicine, a modern science whose basis is measuring and counting.

NOTES

1   Bernhard KELLERMANN, *The Ninth of November,* New York: Robert M. McBride & Company, 1925, translated by Caroline V. Kerr, pp. 328–329. (First German edition: *Der 9. November. Roman,* Berlin: S. Fischer, 1920)

2   "Geheimer Sanitätsrath" LEWIN and "Sanitätsrath" BAER, "Die Gefängnisse Berlins", in: *Hygienischer Führer durch Berlin. Im Auftrage der städtischen Behörden als Festschrift für die Versammlung des Deutschen Vereins für Gesundheitspflege und des Deutschen Vereins für Gesundheitstechnik, Berlin, 16. bis 20. Mai 1883,* edited by Paul BOERNER, Berlin: Max Pasch, 1882, pp. 282–291, here p. 282: „ohne zu weit gehender Humanität oder gar Luxus Raum zu geben."

3   See Johann Friedrich GEIST and Klaus KÜRVERS, *Das Berliner Mietshaus,* 3 VOLS., Munich: Prestel, 1980–1989, VOL. 2: *Das Berliner Mietshaus 1862–1945,* 1984, p. 231.

4   Michel FOUCAULT, *Discipline and Punish. The Birth of the Prison,* translated by Alan Sheridan, New York: Random House, 1995, p. 171.

5   On the concept of a dispositif see Michel FOUCAULT, *The Will to Knowledge. The History of Sexuality: 1,* translated by Robert Hurley, London: Penguin Books, 1998.

6   See Erving GOFFMAN, *Asylums. Essays on the Social Situation of Mental Patients and Other Inmates,* New York: Anchor Books, 1961.

7   See A. [Adolf] HAGEMEYER, *Das neue Krankenhaus der Stadt Berlin am Urban, seine Einrichtung und Verwaltung,* Berlin: August Hirschwald, 1894.

8   On the attempt to usher Foucault's works on the early modern period seamlessly into the 20th century see Philipp SARASIN, *Reizbare Maschinen. Eine Geschichte des Körpers 1765–1914,* Frankfurt am Main: Suhrkamp, 2001. Giorgio Agamben provides a more attentive consideration of historicity.

9   Anonymous, "Ueber unsere Krankenhäuser", in: *Vorwärts,* August 24, 1893 (no. 198): „Bei meiner Aufnahme glaubte ich [...] in ein Gefängnis geraten zu sein".

10   Forderungen der Berliner Krankenkassen an die Charité vom Herbst 1893 (demands of the Berlin health insurance organizations to Charité from autumn 1893), Geheimes Staatsarchiv Preußischer Kulturbesitz: "Fortfall des Kasernentones", "freundliche Ausstattung der Krankensäle". A facsimile is found in Reinhard FREIBERG, *Der Charité-Boykott im Jahr 1893 in Berlin. Eine medizinhistorische Studie über Auswirkungen der Arbeitersozialreformen der 80er und 90er Jahre des 19. Jahrhunderts,* Ph.D. Thesis, Humboldt University Berlin, 1997.

11   The standard work on the theme of medicine and city planning deals with the example of London. See Anne HARDY, *The Epidemic Streets. Infectious Disease and the Rise of Preventive Medicine 1856–1900,* Oxford: Clarendon Press | New York: Oxford University Press, 1993. From the point of view of administration, see Brian LADD, *Urban Planning and Civic Order in Germany, 1860–1914,* Cambridge, MA and London: Harvard University Press, 1990.

12   Anne HARDY, "Cholera, Quarantine and the English Preventive System, 1850–1895", in: *Medical History,* VOL. 37, 1993, pp. 250–269, here p. 268.

13   See H. BUCHNER, "Assanierung Münchens", in: *Die Entwicklung Münchens unter dem Einflusse der Naturwissenschaften während der letzten Dezennien,* edited by the City of Munich, Munich: [n.p.], [1899], pp. 12–27.

14 On the social geography of the Hamburg epidemic, see Richard J. Evans, *Death in Hamburg. Society and Politics in the Cholera Years, 1830–1910,* Oxford: Clarendon Press, 1987, pp. 416–432.

15 See Ulrich Koppitz, "Constructing Urban Infrastructure for Multiple Resource Management: Sewerage Systems in the Industrialization of the Rhineland, Germany", in: *Resources of the City: Contributions to an Environmental History of Modern Europe,* edited by Dieter Schott, Bill Luckin, and Genevieve Massard-Guilbaud, Aldershot and Burlington, VT: Ashgate, 2005, pp. 168–184.

16 Light and air, food and drink, work and rest of the body, sleep and wakefulness, emptying and filling of the body, movements of the soul.

17 On the temporal attribution and the extension of the objects to which the *sex res non naturales* are related, as well as their erroneous localization in the context of the Galen's writings, see Werner F. Kümmel, *Musik und Medizin. Ihre Wechselbeziehungen in Theorie und Praxis von 800 bis 1800,* Freiburg and Munich: Karl Alber, 1977, pp. 131–137 · On the popular understanding of the dietetics of middle-class apartments, see E. von Russdorf, *Die Diätetik. Bearbeitet für gebildete Frauen,* Berlin: Heinrich Schindler, 1854, pp. 15–17.

18 A. H. [August Heinrich] Röbbelen, *Die wichtigsten Momente der Diätetik für das mittlere und höhere Lebensalter. Mit besonderer Rücksicht auf die betreffenden Tagesfragen kritisch erörtert,* part 2, Leipzig: Otto Wigand, 1852, pp. 66–70.

19 Niklas Maak, "Wie das Wohnen zur Welt kommt", in: *Frankfurter Allgemeine Zeitung,* December 9, 2010 (no. 287), p. 31.

20 Tidemann, "Wohnungswesen, Badewesen", in: *Bremen in hygienischer Beziehung,* edited by [Hermann] Tjaden, Bremen: Gustav Winter, 1907, pp. 165–199, here p. 165: „Wohnräume, die das erste Erfordernis der Gesundheit, Licht und Luft in möglichst reichem Maße gewähren".

21 F. O. Kuhn, "Wohnung", in: *Bericht über die Allgemeine deutsche Ausstellung auf dem Gebiete der Hygiene und des Rettungswesens,* 3 vols., edited by Paul Boerner, Breslau: S. Schottlaender, 1885–1886, vol. 1, p. 483–552, here p. 490: „das Erbauen gesunder billiger Familienhäuser, die das Volkswohl fördern". The quote is from: Otto Kuntze, *Motivierter Entwurf eines deutschen Gesundheits-Baugesetzes. Als Petition an den Bundesrat und Reichstag,* Leipzig: Paul Frohberg, 1882.

22 Ibid., p. 491: „Dr. Kuntze weist darauf hin, dass in deutschen Städten die Kindersterblichkeit eine 10–20%, theilweise 100% grössere sei, als in England und den Vereinigten Staaten."

23 Marie Baum, "Bekämpfung der Säuglingssterblichkeit", in: *Zeitschrift für das Armenwesen,* vol. 7, 1906, pp. 45–52.

24 S [Salomon] Neumann, *Die öffentliche Gesundheitspflege und das Eigenthum. Kritisches und Positives mit Bezug auf die preußische Medizinalverfassungs-Frage,* Berlin: Adolph Rick, 1847, p. 65: „Medizin ist eine sociale Wissenschaft. Und Politik ist nichts anders als Medizin im Großen."

25 See for example Georg Franz, *Kulturkampf. Staat und katholische Kirche in Mitteleuropa von der Säkularisation bis zum Abschluss des preussischen Kulturkampfes,* Munich: Georg D. W. Callwey, 1955.

26 "Hilferuf zur Errichtung eines Kathol. Krankenhauses zu Berlin" (appeal for help for the building of a Catholic hospital in Berlin), in: *Schlesisches Kirchenblatt,* vol. 16, 1850, pp. 282–283, here p. 282: „Wir wollen sie aufnehmen, wir wollen für ihren kranken Körper und, wenn sie in Todesgefahr sind, für ihre Seele sorgen."

27 *Hygienischer Führer durch Berlin,* ed. BOERNER, p. 236: „die hohe Sterblichkeit in den beste-henden vielstöckigen Anstalten mit ihren Corridoren zwischen den Krankensälen und auf der anderen Seite die günstigen Erfahrungen während des Krieges in den Vereinigten Staaten, wo man die Verwundeten und Kranken in luftigen Hütten und Zelten unterbrachte, lehrten mit nicht miß-zuverstehender Deutlichkeit, welche Gestalt das Krankenhaus der Zukunft haben müsse. Immer mehr wurde die Notwendigkeit festgestellt, den Verwundeten und Kranken Luft in genügendem Maße und möglicher Reinheit zuzuführen. Der Aufschwung, den gleichzeitig die Gesundheitsleh-re machte, führte zu den gleichen Resultaten, die Kranken in großen kasernenartigen Gebäuden zu vereinigen, wurde aufgegeben, um sie in einzelnen von einander getrennten Baulichkeiten, Pavillons oder Baracken unterzubringen."

28 See Wilhelm DOSQUET, *Das moderne Krankenhaus in baulicher, sozialer und therapeutischer Beziehung,* Berlin: Richard Schoetz, 1930, p. 27.

29 See FREIBERG, *Der Charité-Boykott im Jahre 1893 in Berlin.*

30 See Dörte DÖHL, *Ludwig Hoffmann. Bauen für Berlin 1896–1924,* Tübingen and Berlin: Ernst Wasmuth, 2004, p. 71.

31 Julius POSENER, "Ludwig Hoffmann", in: *Arch+,* no. 53, 1980, pp. 8–15, here p. 11.

32 Ludwig HOFFMANN, *Lebenserinnerungen eines Architekten,* edited by Wolfgang SCHÄCHE, Berlin: Gebr. Mann, 1983, p. 114: „liebevolle Bauweise, die in der Gestaltung des Baukörpers, in einer angenehmen Einfügung des Gebäudes in freundlichen Gartenanlagen in behaglichen Raum-formen und in einer feinsinnigen und liebevollen Behandlung aller Einzelheiten sich ausdrückt."

33 Ibid., p. 136.

34 Ibid.: „Ich dachte, dass es manchen Kranken arg bedrücke, wenn er des Morgens beim Erwa-chen merkt, dass er sich mit zahlreichen, ihm vielleicht noch fremden Leidensgenossen in einem Raume befindet. Gegenüber jedem Bett ließ ich deshalb an der Wand eine kleine Liebenswürdig-keit, ein Kinderköpfchen, ein Vogelnest, einen Blumenstrauß oder ein anderes ganz harmloses Motiv aufmalen. So empfindet der Kranke schon früh beim ersten Blick eine Aufmerksamkeit."

35 Ibid., p. 146.

36 See Philipp OSTEN, *Die Modellanstalt. Über den Aufbau einer "modernen Krüppelfürsorge" 1908–1933,* Frankfurt am Main: Mabuse, 2004, pp. 247–250.

37 On Huldschinsky see Thomas LENNERT, "Kurt Huldschinsky und das Kaiserin Auguste Vic-toria Haus", in: *Schriftenreihe zur Geschichte der Kinderheilkunde aus dem Archiv des Kaiserin Au-guste Victoria Hauses (KAVH) — Berlin,* edited by Leonore BALLOWITZ, no. 11, Herford: Humana Milchwerke Westfalen, 1993, pp. 5–19.

38 See [Moritz William Theodor BROMME], *Lebensgeschichte eines modernen Fabrikarbeiters,* ed-ited and introduced by Paul GÖHRE, Jena and Leipzig: Eugen Diederichs, 1905, pp. 302–333.

39 See Andreas SCHWAB, *Monte Verità. Sanatorium der Sehnsucht,* Zürich: Orell Fuessli, 2003.

40 See Heinrich WURM, "Albinmüllers 'Einzimmerhaus' in Braunlage", in: *Kunst in Hessen und am Mittelrhein,* VOL. 20, 1981, pp. 79–83.

41 See Ludger FISCHER, "Sanatorium Dr. Barner in Braunlage/Harz", in: *Baumeister,* VOL. 97, 2000, no. 10, pp. 72–79.

42 See Peter SELG, *Anthroposophische Ärzte. Lebens- und Arbeitswege im 20. Jahrhundert. Mit einer Skizze zur Geschichte der anthroposophischen Medizin bis zum Tod Rudolf Steiners (1925),*

Dornach: Verlag am Goetheanum, 2000, p. 100 · Helmut Zander, *Anthroposophie in Deutschland. Theosophische Weltanschauung und gesellschaftliche Praxis 1884–1945,* 2 vols., Göttingen: Vandenhoeck & Ruprecht, 2007, vol. 2, pp. 1474–1481.

43 Richard Döcker, *Terrassentyp. Krankenhaus, Erholungsheim, Hotel, Bürohaus, Einfamilienhaus, Siedlungshaus, Miethaus und die Stadt,* Stuttgart: Akademischer Verlag Dr. Fritz Wedekind, 1929.

44 Hubert Ritter, *Der Krankenhausbau der Gegenwart. Wirtschaft, Organisation und Technik,* Stuttgart: Julius Hoffmann, 1932: „Nicht Schatten, sondern Sonne ist für den Heilprozess wichtig".

45 Friedrich Wolf, *Die Natur als Arzt und Helfer,* Stuttgart, Berlin, and Leipzig: Deutsche Verlags-Anstalt, 1928, p. 234.

46 Gertrud Knoblauch and Hansgeorg Knoblauch, "Modelle zukünftiger Krankenhäuser", in: *Historia Hospitalium,* vol. 11, 1976, pp. 199–226, here p. 212: „Die Entschärfung der Verlassenheit, der Angst […] sollte Leitgedanke des Entwurfs sein. Das fängt an mit dem Betreten, dem Empfang im Krankenhaus, und findet seine höchste Steigerung im Krankenbett, wo er allein gelassen wird."

47 Ibid: „kein Schockieren".

48 See Ernst Haas, "Sozialanthropologische Entwicklungstendenzen", in: *Medizin und Städtebau. Ein Handbuch für gesundheitlichen Städtebau,* 2 vols., edited by Paul Vogler and Erich Kühn, Munich, Berlin, and Vienna: Urban & Schwarzenberg, 1957, vol. 1, pp. 25–45.

49 See Jörg Vögele, *Sozialgeschichte städtischer Gesundheitsverhältnisse während der Urbanisierung,* Berlin: Duncker & Humblot, 2001.

50 Werner Leibbrand, "Medizin und Städtebau. Medizinische Entwicklung" in: *Medizin und Städtebau,* ed. Vogler and Kühn, vol. 1, pp. 131–142, here pp. 141–142: „Die Kurvenraster-Medizin, wohl vergleichbar mit den Diagramm- und Symbolversuchen der modernen Architektur und Städteplanung erscheint […] als notwendiges abstraktes Durchgangsstadium. Was ihr seitens der Pathosophen vorgeworfen wird, ist ihr Versagen vor der menschlichen Begegnung, ohne die nun einmal Medizin so wenig betreibbar wird wie der Hausbau. Das architektonische Klima für solche Begegnung ist im heutigen Krankenhausbau noch nicht völlig gefunden. Hier wird erst ein bauherrlicher Wille zur Sicherung der Intimitätszone seine Forderung bei der Baukunst anmelden müssen. Auch er ruht auf anthropologischem Grunde. Sein Grundbekenntnis wäre etwa: Intimität trotz Organisation".

51 See Paul Vogler, "Denkmodelle und Ordnungen in der Medizin", in: *Medizin und Städtebau,* ed. Vogler and Kühn, vol. 1, pp. 142–179.

52 See "Echt orientalisch", in: *Der Spiegel,* vol. 14, 1960, no. 15, pp. 33–37.

53 See Richard Döcker, "Städte in heißen Zonen", in: *Medizin und Städtebau,* ed. Vogler and Kühn, vol. 2, pp. 155–158.

54 Hans Scharoun, "Ordnungsprinzipien und Begriffe in der Stadtstruktur", in: *Medizin und Städtebau,* ed. Vogler and Kühn, vol. 2, pp. 165–171, here p. 171: „Der Prozess des Gestaltwesens, das Gestaltanliegen setzt Bauen organischen Prinzips voraus. Aus solchem Prinzip heraus sind die technisch-wissenschaftlichen, künstlerisch-geistigen Vorraussetzungen neu einem Ganzen zuzuordnen. Aus solchem Prinzip heraus ist auch die Geometrie im Sinne des Werkgesetzes wieder in ein Ganzes einfügbar, im Dienste eben des organischen Prinzips und nicht als ein geometrisches Prinzip."

55 Ibid: „Heute ist es die Wirtschaft, welche die Produktion, ja die biologische und geistige Existenz des Menschen bestimmt. Die Zeit, welche eindeutige Institutionen auf dem Aspekt des Seelischen oder Machtpolitischen ermöglichte, sollte mit dem Dritten Reich endgültig vorüber sein. Das Wesen des Strukturellen, in seiner Bedeutung und in der Bedeutung der notwendigen Verwendung erkannt, wird uns den Weg zu einer neuen fruchtbaren Bindung der schöpferischen Kräfte weisen.“

56 See Wolfram FUCHS, "Gedanken zur Aktualität des Projektes", in: *H VEN LC. Le Corbusiers Krankenhausprojekt für Venedig,* edited by Robert WISCHER, Berlin: Dietrich Reimer, 1985, pp. 11–20, here p. 13.

57 On Le Corbusier's *Modulor* see the essays by Christoph Schnoor and Frank Zöllner in this volume.

IMAGES

Author's collection: FIGS. 1, 2, 4–6, 8 · Bundesarchiv Berlin: FIG. 3 · Johann Barner, Braunlage: FIG. 7 · Richard DÖCKER, *Terrassentyp. Krankenhaus, Erholungsheim, Hotel, Bürohaus, Einfamilienhaus, Siedlungshaus, Miethaus und die Stadt,* Stuttgart: Akademischer Verlag Dr. Fritz Wedekind, 1929, p. 13: FIG. 9 and p. 62: FIG. 10 · Friedrich WOLF, *Die Natur als Arzt und Helfer,* Stuttgart, Berlin, and Leipzig: Deutsche Verlags-Anstalt, 1928, p. 254–255: FIG. 11 · Susan KING, *The Drawings of Eric Mendelsohn,* Berkeley: The Regents of the University of California, 1969, p. 106: FIG. 12 · *Medizin und Städtebau. Ein Handbuch für gesundheitlichen Städtebau,* 2 VOLS., edited by Paul VOGLER and Erich KÜHN, Munich, Berlin, and Vienna: Urban & Schwarzenberg, 1957, VOL. 1, cover: FIG. 13

IRENE NIERHAUS

Body, Order, and Border

EIN-RICHTUNG[1] AS BIOPOLITICAL PROCEDURE IN RESIDENTIAL BUILDING AFTER
1945, AND ITS CRITIQUE IN THE VISUAL MEDIA OF THE 1960S

RESIDENTIAL BUILDING — BODY — POPULATION

This essay focuses on the relationship between residential architecture and its
inhabitants in the formation of population and social, disciplined bodies in the
historical context of the post-war and reconstruction period.[2] Population will
be understood with Michel Foucault as a biopolitical configuration of the inhabitants, as a global and serializable mass of a biological type.[3] Since 1800, the
biopolitical population principle and its differentiation and homogenization in
birth and death rates, birth control, age, standardization of sexuality, heredity,
etc., has established itself as the basic structure of modern regulative power and
safety technology, and hence of state, society, or city. Foucault has contrasted
and explored the interplay between population ("in which bodies are replaced
by general biological processes") and the earlier disciplinary dressing of the individual body, emerging in the 17th and 18th centuries ("in which the body is
individualized as an organism endowed with capacities").[4] The interconnection
between body/discipline and population/regulation is read in Foucault especially for example in sexuality. Historically, this can be observed in the ruptures
and continuities of German sexual politics during the post-war and reconstruction period. Since with the (re)construction of the state and the (re)building
of the cities — the latter largely a matter of residential architecture — the German notion of *Schutz der Jugend* (youth protection), which can be interpreted
in disciplinary and biopolitical terms, was used to enforce increasingly restric-
tive ideas about sexuality, along with comparable paradigms of family and marriage.[5] These focused on dwelling and residential architecture, the social setting

IN / KIRSTEN WAGNER AND JASPER CEPL (EDITORS) /
IMAGES OF THE BODY IN ARCHITECTURE: ANTHROPOLOGY AND BUILT SPACE /
TÜBINGEN · BERLIN / ERNST WASMUTH VERLAG / 2014 / PP. 345–365

of the social subject, and his/her regulated interaction with society (ideally, in the form of the family). For this, it was necessary to align city and population with the level of the body, whereby the family is a "privileged segment, because whenever information is required concerning the population (sexual behavior, demography, consumption, etc.), it has to be obtained from the family."[6] This also becomes strikingly clear in German films of the 1950s, which are so often concerned with 'natural' social as opposed to 'unnatural' asocial relations. The production of patriarchal familial and sexual orders in the love stories of these films invariably ends with the founding of a family and/or the recognition of hierarchies, such as in films dealing with the restoration of the family unit in which a mum has to be found for dad, or the *Heimat* (homeland) films in which the governing forest ranger, mayor, and parish priest is pitted against poachers

1
COMMUNAL
HOUSING IN
VIENNA / 10TH
DISTRICT /
1950S

and other disruptors.[7] In the amalgam of family, territoriality and order, population formation and body discipline are a dense and complex mesh of articulations and figurations around the reconstruction period. Dwelling and residential architecture are the space or *Raumanordnung* (spatial order) in which body/discipline and population/regulation are interconnected most enduringly in their effects, and are globally and abundantly diffused (birth control, medical and environmental hygiene, physical and sexual education according to gender attribution, etc.). In the 1960s and 70s, this field was examined by the sociopolitical and cultural critique that intervened in the hegemonic discourse, including, not least, Foucault himself, as well as the responses within visual culture that will be discussed in the following.

After 1945, urban construction or planning was largely residential housing organized around a looser urban structure, that is, an ensemble of architectural units interspersed with open spaces (FIG. 1). The expansion of the residential town reintegrated the landscape into the built areas in order to guarantee hygiene, recreation, individual space, and social integration. In socio-political terms, the aim was to spatially order large gatherings of people in a zone of reproduction (procreation, recreation, etc.), including the flow of goods, for which, at least since 1900, rural models were favored, as can be seen in the discussion on small towns internationally, especially since the 1930s.[8] The concept of the neighborly housing complex as a unit within a green area allowed a centering of the in-

2
VIENNA /
PUBLIC
HOUSING / SELF-
PRESENTATION
OF THE
MUNICIPALITY
OF VIENNA /
1950S

habitants without the dreaded risk of an uncontrollable agglomeration, as was still the case in the wildly proliferating 19th-century city, which was thus often described as a "jungle" and, hence, as out of control nature. The housing development is an act of territorialization meant to guarantee surveillance, social cohesion, and control, including self-control, and the commitment to the territory, whereby the terms change according to their ideological orientation: from *Blut und Boden* (blood and soil) or *Scholle* (clod) to *soziales Grün* (social green), or from *Ortszelle* (local cell) to *Nachbarschaft* (neighborhood).

After 1945, housing complexes, decentralized within multipliable "democratic" uniformity should, through enhanced hygiene and the elementary qualities of "light — air — sun — greenery" (FIG. 2), generally co-form the urban structure, not as difference but as an "organic" component.[9] They are the socio-political matrix of the society of the reconstruction period, in which the restoration of regulations and orders is now conducted with all social groups as "organically" integrated. Hence, processes of social naturalization inherent to the project of modernity become explicit parameters of naturalness as a reasonable social force — which converts into biopolitical principles. The transformation from a class society to a *Volksgemeinschaft* (people's community) that had already been carried out by National Socialism was now to be "organically" homogenized "on the basis of natural communities, families, and neighborhoods" through "social and economic decentralization".[10]

The public art programs for housing developments show the various levels of naturalness of the social: the non-competitive but still entirely hierarchical cohabitation of social classes (in scenes of construction showing builders, planners, and politicians); the integration into nature in images of flora and fauna; the natural cycles in images showing the changes of the days and seasons and the stations of life; the reproduction of life with endless mother-and-child

3
SCULPTURE
IN COMMUNAL
HOUSING IN
VIENNA · 10TH
DISTRICT /
WALTER
LACKNER / *ZWEI
PFERDE. MUTTER
UND KIND*
(TWO HORSES.
MOTHER AND
INFANT) /
1955–58

images as well as their analogy in scenes of animal mother and animal infant (**FIG. 3**).[11] After 1945, the most conspicuous sign of naturalization, in the sense of a becoming-landscape, was the green area that spread out 'under' and around all architecture.

In the following I shall focus literally on this ground: on the green area that, after 1945, spread out 'under' and around all architecture and, ideally in combination with the strips of asphalt supporting the streams of traffic, became the foundation of the city. The green areas, which in the 19th century were distributed throughout the city in insular patches such as parks, cemeteries, etc., were to be multiplied and joined together. Historically, the motif of the continuous green space is evoked in the 19th-century saying: "Ganz Deutschland ein großer Garten" (the whole of Germany a great garden).[12] Under National Socialism, "Germans [should] be the first Western nation to create their spiritual environment in the landscape" and to follow "the right path in the healthy and intuitive pursuit of connected green spaces with a view of the landscape".[13] Although after 1945 nature and green spaces in residential architecture are constantly emphasized in commentaries, they still remain curiously opaque as if they were intrinsic and inevitable. Accordingly, Werner Durth has summarily characterized the reconstruction effort as "open, light spaces […], as an attempt at reconciliation with a defiled, burnt, bombed nature beneath the city's plan."[14] The new spaces thus penetrate urban tradition and history to a 'primordial ground' of nature. What and, above all, how, is this primordial nature "beneath the city's plan"? The city becomes a landscape and this is a medium "in which cultural meanings and values are encoded […]. Landscape is a medium in the fullest sense of the word. It is a material 'means' […] like language or paint, embedded in a tradition of cultural signification and communication, a body of symbolic forms capable of being invoked and reshaped to express meanings and values."[15] The green expanse appears as the structural screen of society: a space of projection and production with a capacity for homogenization, which brings together and neutralizes different and heterogeneous images — beyond society and history, but nevertheless grounding society.

In the following, the green area as homogenizing green plan and its potential operations are considered in the context of nature, territory, and the landscape of ruins. This context is conceived as a palimpsest and situation, and adheres to National Socialism in repetitions, de-namings, and differences. Concerning collective memory, Maurice Halbwachs has remarked, "the place a group occupies is not like a black board, where one might write and erase figures at will."[16] The green expanse is a membrane similar to the Freudian *"Wunderblock",* a place of vestiges, and simultaneously such an erased black board, a membrane of decodification — and the devastation of World War II is described among other things as an "Entleerung" (emptying out).

The bombed cities are like the return of the wilderness: "And suddenly we can imagine how it continues to grow, how a primeval forest extends over our cities, prospering slowly, inexorably, despite the absence of people, a hush made of thistles and moss, an unwritten earth, accompanied by the twittering of birds, spring, summer and autumn, the breath of the years that are no longer counted."[17] Already during the war, the erasure of civilization brought about by the destruction suggested the idea of letting the bombed cities revert to nature as a landscapes of ruins, to allow a "state forest" to grow over the rubble in the centre of Hamburg for instance, and to "freely" plan new cities on top of or next to such a "state forest", such as Dresden, Mainz, Kiel, or Nuremberg. Werner Heldt's

4
WERNER HELDT /
BERLIN AM
MEER (BERLIN
ON THE SEE) /
LITHOGRAPH /
1946

lithograph (**FIG. 4**) "Berlin am Meer" from 1946 records the city's transformation back into nature. The collapsed stone sea of Berlin becomes a primordial ground and the colossal rebirth potentially contained in this: "Everywhere beneath the asphalt of Berlin is the sand of our region. And that was once seabed. [...] The city sinks back into nature. Its downfall is the beginning of another age."[18] The relationship between city, landscape, and nature has been part of the modern discourse on the city since the Romantic period, one in which the city is not only described in opposition to nature, or as wilderness, but also as a beautiful or dangerous landscape — as for instance in Adalbert Stifter, William Wordsworth, or later Stefan Zweig. Furthermore, wartime and post-war practices such as seeking protection "beneath the earth" in bunkers — one might think of Henry Moore's shelter drawings — or the temporary vegetable gardens set up in urban parks — disrupted normal distinctions between nature and city. With military camouflage techniques, blackout or taking-cover, the mimetic merging with the ground became part of the common experience of war in the city. And, to a previously unanticipated degree, air raids turned the city into a kind of no-man's-land, a shifting terrain between destruction and preservation, "a constantly shifting line between two sides […] as the most enduring and unsettling idea […] of being situated between the known and the unknown, the familiar and the uncanny".[19] In Roberto Rossellini's 1947 film *Germany Year Zero,* the no-man's-land of a devastated Berlin becomes a space evoking the destruction of the individual, social, and moral fabric; these are the ruins of a body politic. The rubble is both destruction and the sign of destruction; and between the two a margin opens for processes of aestheticization. For example, a resident of Berlin sketching during the air raids reports: "Day and night, the air-raids […] which

5
FRIEDRICH
SEIDENSTÜCKER /
*ZERSTÖRTE
HÄUSERZEILE
AM SPREE-UFER*
(DESTROYED
ROW OF HOUSES
ON THE BANKS
OF THE SPREE) /
BERLIN 1946

continue to grow in force and frequency produce […] ever-new motifs. […] It was here that I made my watercolors, often interrupted by snowstorms and daylight raids […], the view over the burnt-out houses with their mass of chimneys now elongated like the necks of skeletons due to the missing roofs. […] Undamaged and burnt-out wagons and rows of wagons in dark dirty, mostly reddish-brown and olive green tones as well as fresh loam-yellow craters created unusual patches and bands among this mesh of lines; and the completely burnt-out houses extended in a brown sooty horizon. […] I was alive with the 'beauty' of this motif."[20] Despite (or because of?) the extraordinariness of the historical situation, this process of aestheticization allows us to consider such works in the context of occidental traditions in visual culture such as landscape painting and the landscape with ruins. In their contemplative and elementary view of nature, both genres are central media for strategies of subjectivity, and the grounding of bourgeois identity. Through the displayed presence of the pictorial elements, Friedrich Seidenstücker's 1946 photograph *Zerstörte Häuserzeile am Spree-Ufer* (Destroyed row of houses on the banks of the Spree) (FIG. 5) assumes its part in the tradition of the ruin in art and its poetical function, and ascribes the expanse of ruins to the landscape. "The world is out of joint [...]; culture is in ruins, but the rubble has been cleared away, and where ruins have been left standing, they have a venerable appearance", wrote Theodor W. Adorno.[21] The "precarious balance"[22] in such images of ruins corresponded to the shifting state of the no-man's-land, the de- and re-coding of the urban terrain. The city as landscape of ruins harbors a combination of transitoriness and apotheosis — one that has been cultivated in the Occident in scenarios of urban decay and rebirth, such as Rome, Jerusalem, and Babylon. In most German *Trümmerfilmen* (the films set in the ruins of World War II) similar traits of apotheosis and transitoriness were presented on the basis of personalized, 'purely human' portrayals of individual fates. A contemporary film critic writes rather ironically of the excessively determined function of ruins and rubble: "They found a new ingenious and cheap setting: the ruins. [...] Just in time the black marketers are downgraded to villains who fall into the hands of justice [...], while the upright home comer clears away the rubble. [...] Awash with the tones of Beethoven, ruins grin through the backdrops, and souls are made of brown plush. Whether the two get together, or whether one commits suicide — the projector gushes noble mindedness."[23] After 1945, the devastated city is a vacuum populated with vagrant images in which acts of territorialization are contested. Allusions to "nature" are the promise of an extra-social "better" founding of society, as understood in the historical situation, and one that allows a resettlement of exactly this social quality — the so-called zero hour of space as territory.

The zero hour of territory as beginning, origin, primordial ground, or nature appears in a broad range of discourses. The political theorist Carl Schmitt, for example, describes space as a primordial grounding of political action, which constitutes territory. He speaks of the "great primordial acts" of the law as "localizations tied to the earth" listing as examples, "land occupation, the founding of cities and colonies".[24] Territory is a system for organizing the earth's surface and its inhabitants into powerful relations of appropriation, creating an interpretive framework that is extended over a broad range of discourses, from geopolitics, geography, planning, and art, to sexuality. There is "no country [...] that is not tied to something imaginary"; hence, landscape as "dream work".[25] And through this interpretive framework wander images of the pastor, the shepherd, the master, the father, and the authority — a pastoral with a pastor in Foucault's sense. The accumulation of the images of the "pastor" as president, mayor, chief planner, patron[26] in front of the model of an urban-development project in reconstruction, like Theodor Heuss in the exhibition *Mensch und Raum* (Man and Space) in Darmstadt in 1951 (**FIG. 6**), also points to the mythical constitution of planning — and, "planning is the major instrument of reconstruction".[27] Whereby the plan as both a linguistic notion as well as in images was common on the one hand through the war and the concomitant visual experience of plans of attack, conquest, and colonization (territorial maps, strategic maps, plans of architectural visions), while on the other hand it promised order in the shifting and threatening no-man's land and its voids. The green space is a figure for the healed and undamaged ground after the war, and at the same time a metonym for the biopolitical foundation of the population — a literally "natural" biopolitical *Raumgrundierung* (spatial grounding) of post-war society. A green area can be understood as a membrane of an order in which social processes can be presented in a naturalized way. The line of domesticity is horizontal, an earth-bound line of human life; hence, Frank Lloyd Wright described dwelling as "countryside". Dwelling is grounded in the green spaces common to everyone; it is the figure of a kind of homogenized *Seinslandschaft* — as Martin Heidegger in his 1951 Darmstadt lecture put it: "To be a human being means to be on the earth as a mortal. It means to dwell" and "Dwelling [...] is the main feature of being", preceding building.[28] Even if Heidegger, by grounding everything in language, negates the promise of origin, in its thorough cleansing and de-interpretation, and above all in the iconography of his examples — Black Forest farmhouse, childbed, *"Totenbaum"* (literally, "tree of death", the local term for a coffin) — and the linguistic reference to Old-High-German terms, his linguistic performance is fixed in a patriarchal agro-romantic imagery that provides a pre-

6
THEODOR HEUSS
(LEFT) IN THE
EXHIBITION
*MENSCH UND
RAUM* (MAN
AND SPACE) /
DARMSTADT /
1951

carious (because apparently causal) topology for living and dwelling after 1945, especially since the text became a central reference in the field of architecture. With the becoming-landscape of the city of the 1950s, dwelling, which since the beginning of modernity was placed in relation to ideas of nature and naturalness, became widely and comprehensively converted into biopolitical principles. In the green space, the metric order of the biopolitical becomes visible as space; the geometric aspect of the plan is operating between territory and inhabitants, the planning as a biopolitical regulation and corporal disciplining.

The extent to which the biometricizing and disciplining space of the 20th-century city is a prohibitively sealed off or porous space of action depends on the possibilities of intervention by the inhabited and the inhabitants. In the planning of green spaces, since the 1970s, the Kassel School, for example, has very directly and literally dealt with the rights of inhabitants (public paths, etc.) in relation to the regulated use of green spaces (prohibitions against playing and trespassing, planning zones, etc.). Also the 1996 action "Making Off. Rio de Janeiro" by Mario Schifano can be understood as a disruption of urban homogenization. The Italian artist reacted to measures taken by Rio de Janeiro's government to transform the favelas into a landscape by painting them green. In protest, Schifano painted a barrack in the favela Santa Marta with white paint, and thereby perforated the cityscape which had been transcribed as a beautiful view while neutralizing and naturalizing social poverty.

BODY AND IMAGE POLITICS: INTERVENTIONS

In socio-political terms, housing after 1945, pragmatically focusing on building economy, represents the land surveyance of a biopolitical mass, whose translations and discursive formations were produced, in picture and text, in images of home, family, and child, and then continuously repeated in variations. The network of representations of housing and residing woven into a pictorial regime wanders and strays through the reconstruction heads. Such vagrant images of the "nature" of home or of social naturalness formed the social, colonizing, and self-colonizing foundations to be found for example in the discourses around *Heimat* and exoticism. In interior design, this might extend for instance from a naked "negro" girl as a lamp stand or the picture of a female "gypsy" in the bedroom to the small porcelain shepherds on the sideboard in the living room or a painting of a regional landscape. Such images are extended and modified in films, in the *Heimat* and exotic genres for example. In the years after 1945 and in the 1950s, the (re)formulation of the population was supported by an excessive disciplining, which in housing not only affected the spatial organization of the population; it was also aimed directly at the bodies of the inhabitants. It was a comprehensive textual and visual didactics on dwelling (life-style advice or exhibitions, magazines, films, etc.), in which patterns of behavior are inscribed onto bodies.[29] One of these instructional films, *Der schön gedeckte Tisch* (The well set table), shows the ideal arrangement of the elements for breakfast, lunch, and dinner (table, arrangement of the dishes, choice of color for the tablecloth, etc.). Following the directions of a voice-over, a female body, which is only visible in segments, sets the table. The scene is a choreographically orchestrated interaction of objects and bodies, the disciplinary character of which corresponds to the typical visual representations of domesticity in the 1950s. The process of adapting to a middle class lifestyle is clearly complicated, and the presentation of ease and happiness shows — from today's point of view — the effort organization involves. The allegories and didactic elements in public art also have the same authoritative trait of the warning finger. The years from the end of the 1940s to the mid-1950s — that is, the main period of reconstruction — are visibly marked by disciplinary elements which only gradually changed in the 1960s.

Such wanderings and mutations of images follow the progressions and ramifications of discourses, and operate in a *trans-media* fashion, i.e. across different media, that is, they appear converted — as well as fragmented, contingent, paradoxical, and with no clear, general plan — within a range of media and their types and genres. They are generated within the situational collection of attributions, media positioning (architecture, visual culture, fine art, film, etc.) at concrete historical moments in time. Thus, in the debate around correct living, in film, or in images of the female body, from public art to magazine covers, the profile "mother" is represented as domesticity, love and the production of offspring.[30] Accordingly, the *trans-media* trajectories of images pass through a complex structure in which "very diverse acts, not only linguistic, but also perceptive, mimetic, gestural, and cognitive"[31] exist. Which is to say that they do not form any clearly definable areas or totalities, but mutating compendia and heterogeneous combinations of readings and productivities. These are not powerless plays of images, but rather a historically dimensioned and hegemonic look-at-this, a selection of representations in which not everything is equally presented. Intervening in this harmony and hegemony, especially since the 1960s, are, increasingly, social and cultural movements that operate against concrete practices and functions of governing in the land surveyance of bodies and their transformation into a biopolitical corpus of knowledge. That shows yet again that 'body' resides in a system of corporeality, which is distinguished among other things according to corpus, corps, corporation, body, or flesh, no form of which can be understood as the exclusive and proper one. All these formations contain the social and the societal (as well as individual) conventions, whether in the sensory flesh, in the perceiving body, in the corpus as the archive of social corporeality with its attributions to gender, social status, and "ethnic" groups, or in the corps, to that which most clearly names the aspect of disciplining and differentiation according to units, thus also in the 'body', which brings together both the relative wholeness of the individual and the social arrangements of corporeality and subject. Accordingly, the social corpus is not placed in opposition to the subjective body; there is no clear line of division between the body as a social sign system and its representation in visual media for example and an actual body as pure presence or place of retreat from the social. Only within this non-integrity of the body, in which the body "does not exceed language by anything whatsoever" and is "a word like any other" does it form "a minuscule excrescence [which is] never disposed of".[32]

With the social, political, and feminist movements of the 1960s and 70s came a series of interventions in the biopolitical and disciplinary corporeality, and the related *Ein-Richtung* — in the literal and figurative sense — of the inhabitants. From communards to designers, ideas on dwelling were formulated anew. One example was "de-furnishing", in favor of interior elements that were now seen as fundamental, such as mattresses or so-called *Sitzlandschaften* (seating landscapes). This is seen for instance in the cave dwellings of Ferdinand Spindel or the organoid interior designs of Verner Panton. In the following, to convey the *trans media* mode of the *Ein-Richtung* with its wandering images, I shall examine three examples of interventions from the field of visual culture.

The subject of the film *Themroc* by Claude Faraldo (France 1972, **FIG. 7**) is the extracting of an essentialized corporeality opposed to the disciplining of dwelling. The male protagonist tears an enormous hole in the wall of his building, demolishes his apartment, and hurls out furniture and utensils, thereby reducing dwelling to a primordial residing. It is as if the generation of 1968 is yelling:

7
CLAUDE
FARALDO /
THEMROC /
1972

"The private is political; we destroy the total surveyance of our lives by (state) authority and consumerism" from the enormous hole ripped in the wall through which it is possible to make out the surrounding neighborhood and the gathering police operation.

In the act of destruction, the male protagonist attempts to cast off the social corpus in favor of 'an' elementarized body. Language, too, is reduced to a wordless, sentence-less and grammar-less babbling, grunting, and sighing. In fact the real protagonist is the half-naked body of the principal character (literally embodied by Michel Piccoli), structuring the film through the explicit presence of the corporeality and gestures of the acting body. This body is opposed to dwelling as a site of convention and state power in the form of a police corps, which intervenes against the body's attempts at liberation. In the film, dwelling, as a bourgeois site of a doubled *Ein-Richtung,* is analogized through the living space of the mother (in her role as housewife and mother as nurturer, which has been biologically argued for women since the 19th century), who represents convention, and from whom the protagonist separates himself by means

IRENE NIERHAUS

of a raised wall in order to practice a bodily form of dwelling seen as primary. Here, sexualization plays a decisive role: the cause of the separation and the undermining of the domestic order is generated from the viewpoint of the (old and sighing) mother's distracted gaze at the naked breasts of a young woman. Henceforth, the male protagonist copulates happily with woman/women in his cave dwelling. However, this behavior, which is followed with curiosity in the neighborhood, is fought by a growing police operation, and finally submitted to an *Ein-Richtung* within the designated framework. The hole in the wall of the building is eventually closed under police control. The violence of an enforced domestication in architecture is encapsulated at the end of the film when hands desperately poke out from the few openings in the cave dwelling that has been walled-up again, and the pan to a window frame of a housing block makes strikingly clear the analogy to a prison. In the film, the naturalized disciplining of dwelling is ruptured by sexuality, operating as a sign of the actual body liberated by the male protagonist. Sexuality promises the emergence of an — always also

sexually produced — corporeality and carnality. With this, the naturalization of space and discourse is ruptured by a sexuality appearing in the 'wrong' place and decoupled from the duty of reproduction, in which (also sexual) corporeality and carnality is produced, which in the customary image of the city appears sealed, tamed, and controlled by the geometry of the urban plan. The decomposition of dwelling to a rough-hewn cave visualized as a process of renaturalization alludes to the contemporary rediscovery of the cave habitation (Matera, Cappadocia, etc.), which was meant to represent a way out of civilized domestication, as a kind of 'anthropological alternative'. Such a relief from the pressures of culture and civilization together with the desire for an outside is anchored in the occidental display of primitivism and exoticism. *Themroc* intervenes in a social spatial geometry and translates it into a new spatial landscape determined by the de-formed, the presence of the material and the primacy of explicit corporeality and sexuality as bearers of an act of liberation. At this point one might ask: What is uncovered by the order shattering male author, and what position is assigned to the female protagonists? Where do these protagonists become

coveted interstice, where are they 'liberated' spatial ground, and where self regulating inhabitants? The artist Birgit Jürgenssen examines dwelling and the body
in the context of a critique of the gender system. In the *Hausfrauen-Küchen-
schürze* (Housewives-Apron) from 1975 (**FIG. 8**), she shows herself as a female
body that has joined together with a cooker to form a new organism. Since the
19th century, this merging of female body, furniture, and interior can be traced
through different levels of discourse (social attribution of female social functions, physio-psychic gender attribution, interior theory,[33] etc.). The stove-body
allows for the doubled reproduction of the housewife and mother: the baking

8
BIRGIT
JÜRGENSSEN /
*HAUSFRAUEN-
KÜCHENSCHÜRZE*
(HOUSEWIVES-
APRON) /
PHOTOGRAPH /
1975

of the bread and the gestation of offspring. In this way, the biopoliticized female
body committed to birth rates and family and marriage hygiene, and its locating
in reproduction and dwelling is made visible. It is this body that is fought for
by Doctor Antonio, who, in the film *Le Tentazioni del Dottor Antonio* (Federico
Fellini, part of the portmanteau film *Boccaccio '70,* Italy 1962), is placed in the
intellectual context of Catholic conservatism of post-Fascist Italy. The object of
his passionate struggle against sexual permissiveness is a giant bill board put up
in front of his living room window on which a lascivious, busty and exuberant
blond (Anita Ekberg) is reclined on a sofa to advertise more milk consumption
(a fusion of mother's body and body of desire). In a fantasy / nightmare she later
climbs out of the poster and wanders through the nocturnal city as a giant seductive body (**FIG. 9**). This city is EUR, which from 1937 to 1942 was partly built
as Fascist ideal city and exhibition area on the axis Rome–Ostia, and after 1952

was gradually completed. EUR is a strictly symmetrical ensemble of monumental and residential buildings, a white stone city placed in the open countryside. Such strict orthogonality corresponds to the Italian Fascist notion of *disciplina*. *Disciplina* should lead to the general creation of a strict, hierarchically organized social corps. In the film, through the colossal liveliness of the female body, the city becomes a model. The blond woman's body is thus both the Other of the stereometric architecture and, in the geometricizing modelling of the body, an echo of the city's monumental sculpture; it is order come to life, but also the counterpart to order. As such, it is her corporeality that undermines the order,

including that of Doctor Antonio. Therefore, in this instance, too, it is sexuality that produces an irritation in the order, and Fellini treats this along two lines of desire: for the lusted-after body and for the mother's body.

To a great extent in his attempt to pit the resistance of reality to social rhetoric, Pier Paolo Pasolini attempted to portray the body as a "never disposed of excrescence" and as "distance".[34] His film *Mamma Roma* (Italy 1962) set in the periphery of Rome speaks of the body — of the body of the city, the flesh, the bodies of the inhabitants, the corpus of capitalist bourgeois society, dealing with the power relations within these constellations. Pasolini searches for a body aimed towards the outside and what is outer, and hence treats the dramaturgy of the edge and the periphery on many levels. Mamma Roma (the female figure of the city, mother, market woman and prostitute) searches for social advancement for her son Ettore, which ultimately ends in failure: after a theft, he dies as a feverish body strapped down on a board of institutional order — a Foucauldian table, between dissecting table, bier, and altar (**FIG. 10**). The peripheral movements begin in the Roman province, followed by an impoverished suburban estate with an ominous view of the cemetery, followed again by an apartment in the newly built suburb. From here the hopeful view extends to

10
PIER PAOLO
PASOLINI /
MAMMA ROMA /
1962

the next periphery of the city, a white cubic mass, like a giant city wall before a wasteland dominated by a church dome that seems to refer to "Rome", rule and church. The curved form of the dome is a visual-spatial motif running through the whole film forming frame, perimeter or opening. The view onto the white row of houses is repeated with the stony face of Mamma Roma framed in the window after she has learned of the death of her son. "At the edge of this sea-like meadow, in front of the hill is a row of ivory houses. […] Around the meadow, star-shaped tenements stick out like fish bones. [T]his is followed by other meadows with different meandering fake-ivory tenements for the sub-proletariat."[35] The wasteland with wild meadows, antique ruins, underground enclosures, and refuse serves as a counterpoint to the housing development. This is Ettore's primary haunt where he whiles away the time with friends and his first love Bruna, where he hides and reappears among the ruins; running, lying, scuffling, lazing around, and loving. While in this landscape scattered with ruins we hear baroque music, twittering and chirping, the city is accompanied by the noises of sirens and engines. Compared with the unruly meadows, the apartment blocks and asphalt areas are identified as the grids of a (petit-)bourgeois Catholic (family) order — Pasolini spoke of camps. Hence, the petit-bourgeois girls appear on this enclosed surface; they only enter the meadows in groups. The promiscuous Bruna, on the other hand, passes over the edge of the street to the wasteland, sits on a road barrier cutting through space and image at the end of a broad asphalt road behind which the meadows begin — this is followed by a view of her décolleté, the threshold between dress and skin. Waste dumps, meadows, and ruins describe a movement to an outer and other. The long rows of the aqueduct ruins appear in the backgrounds of the images as spatial and temporal edge — in historical visual culture, the area around the aqueducts was a central icon of the

Roman Campagna. Pasolini draws on the images of the Roman pastoral with its crumbling walls, goats among ruins, and roaming shepherds, which in the high culture of Europe were melancholic symbols of the meditation on time and a yearning for a space far from culture and free of rules, populating it with signs of proletarian urban everydayness as a mythical primordial ground of vitality

and resistance to the Catholic bourgeoisie and capitalism. The film's space is a web of spatially and temporally multiplying edges (streets, paths, house rows, arches, street barriers, necklace, tie, straps, etc.) with closed or open areas (asphalt, bare wall, meadow, etc.), in which territorialities and extra-territorialities are produced, and in which the protagonists shrink, wander, and pulse. Pasolini searches for capitalism's edges and gaps, increasingly detaching them from their geographical and temporal coordinates to turn them into something mythical and archaic that would signify the horizon of an outside. The presented time-space does not carry the action, but is incorporated into the city, landscape and into bodies and "fleshy phantasms".[36] The Roman suburb and the protagonists become a sign for territorial games and struggles around the *Ein-Richtung* of the inhabitants, their gender and their bodies as a "minuscule excrescence [which is] never reabsorbed" and as "limit — external border, the fracture and intersection of anything foreign in a continuum of sense, a continuum of matter."[37]

NOTES

1   *Ein-Richtung* (from the German *Einrichtung*) can be thought as "accommodation" or "installation" and, in a more authoritarian sense, "institution".

2   This reading of residential architecture results primarily from developments in Germany and Austria, whereby the basic urbanistic principle is an international one, though modified according to the region and characterized above all by the respective housing policies and the public and/ or private developers (a stronger differentiation is revealed in the inner partition of the housing). See for example the urbanistic concepts of the few publicly built housing developments in Rome; in contrast, the privately built housing is characterized by the extreme density of the buildings.

On public housing in Rome, see *Guida ai quartieri romani INA Casa,* edited by Margherita Guc-
cione, Maria Margarita Segarra Lagunes, and Rosalia Vittorini, Rome: Gangemi, 2002.

3   Michel Foucault, "[Biopolitik: Leben machen und sterben lassen]. Vorlesung vom 17. März
1976", in: Foucault: *Kritik des Regierens. Schriften zur Politik,* edited by Ulrich Bröckling, Berlin: Suhrkamp, 2010, pp.63–88. The text provides a succinct survey of the concept of biopolitics.
For more detailed argument, see Foucault, *Sicherheit, Territorium, Bevölkerung. Geschichte der
Gouvernementalität I. Vorlesung am Collège de France 1977–1978,* edited by Michel Sennelart,
translated by Claudia Brede-Konersmann and Jürgen Schröder, Frankfurt am Main: Suhrkamp,
2004 · Foucault, *Die Geburt der Biopolitik: Geschichte der Gouvernementalität II. Vorlesung am
Collège de France 1978–1979,* edited by Michel Sennelart, translated by Jürgen Schröder, Frankfurt am Main: Suhrkamp, 2006.

4   Foucault, "[Biopolitik: Leben machen und sterben lassen]", p.73.

5   On this, see Dagmar Herzog, *Die Politisierung der Lust. Sexualität in der deutschen Geschichte des 20. Jahrhunderts,* Munich: Siedler, 2005. Particularly insightful is the presentation of the
immediate post-war period in which a diversity of voices is raised for the liberalization of sexual
politics, which are excluded in the later period of reconstruction. The historical argumentation
on the "Schutz der Jugend" (protection of the youth) should be read in relation to the "theory of
degeneration" that Foucault names in connection with the disciplining of the body and biopolitics
(Foucault, "[Biopolitik: Leben machen und sterben lassen]", p.76). Since, in the argument on
security and protection against sexual opening and heterogeneous sexual relations, a role is played
for example by the argument of the sexual degeneration of National Socialism, or else the latter
allows one to distance oneself from National Socialism (as sexual degeneration and perversion).

6   Foucault, "Vorlesung 4. (Sitzung vom 1. Februar 1978)", in: Foucault, *Sicherheit, Territorium, Bevölkerung,* pp.134–172, here p.157 · See also Foucault, "Die 'Gourvernementalität' (Vor-
trag). Vorlesung vom 1.Februar 1978", in: Foucault, *Kritik des Regierens,* pp.91–117, here p.110, for
a description of the family "as an element internal to population, and as a fundamental instrument
in its government".

7   See Irene Nierhaus, "Wie im Film: Heimat als fundamentales Projekt des Wiederaufbaus", in:
Nierhaus, *Arch 6. Raum, Geschlecht, Architektur.* Vienna: Sonderzahl, 1999, pp.59–86.

8   The connection between dwelling and land(scape) has its pre-history in the garden city movements and, since the 1930s, has internationally favored the ideal of the small town over the city as
a place of a potential community.

9   Such an "organic" integration is supported by organicist metaphors in urbanism and architecture. See for example Kathrin Peters, "Vom Leben der Städte um 1960" and Stefanie Hennecke,
"Aus ParZellen keimt die Stadt. Anmerkungen zu einem organischen Leitbild für Berlin", in: *Landschaftlichkeit. Forschungsansätze zwischen Kunst, Architektur und Theorie,* edited by Irene Nierhaus, Josch Hoenes, and Annette Urban, Berlin: Dietrich Reimer, 2010, pp.81–90 and pp.91–101.

10   On this, see Foucault, who in the reading of Röpke's orientation of German economic policy
in 1950 analyzes the development of the neoliberal *homo oeconomicus* during the reconstruction
period. Foucault, *Die Geburt der Biopolitik,* pp.147–148 and on this note 61.

11   Irene Nierhaus, *Kunst-am-Bau im kommunalen Wiener Wohnbau der 50er Jahre,* Vienna,
Cologne, and Weimar: Böhlau, 1993.

12 See the article with the same name by Gert GRÖNING and Joachim WOLSCHKE-BULMAHN, "'Ganz Deutschland ein großer Garten'. Landespflege und Stadtplanung im Nationalsozialismus", in: *Kursbuch,* no.112: *Städte bauen,* 1993, pp.29–46.

13 Erhard MÄDING, quoted ibid., p.32: „die Deutschen [...] als erstes abendländisches Volk in der Landschaft auch ihre seelische Umwelt gestalten" (from: "Die Gestaltung der Landschaft als Hoheitsrecht und Hoheitspflicht", in: *Neues Bauerntum,* VOL.35, 1943, pp.22–24), and Karl HOFF-MANN on the industrial estate Böhler, Kapfenberg (1940), quoted in Helmut LACKNER, *Der soziale Wohnbau in der Steiermark 1938–1945,* Graz: Selbstverlag der Historischen Landeskommission für Steiermark, 1984: „gesundheitlichen und gefühlsmäßigen Streben nach zusammenhängenden Grünflächen mit Ausblick in die Landschaft den rechten Weg".

14 Werner DURTH, "Stadt und Landschaft — Kriegszerstörungen und Zukunftsentwürfe", in: *Architektur_theorie.doc. Texte seit 1960,* edited by Gerd DE BRUYN and Stephan TRÜBY with the collaboration of Henrik MAULER and Ulrich PANTLE, Basel, Boston, and Berlin: Birkhäuser, 2003, pp.326–344, here p.327: „offene, lichte Räume [...], als Versuch der Versöhnung mit der geschändeten, verbrannten, zerbombten Natur unter dem Grundriss der Städte."

15 W.J.T. MITCHELL, *Landscape and Power,* Chicago and London: University of Chicago Press, 2002, p.14.

16 Maurice HALBWACHS, *Das kollektive Gedächtnis,* translated by Holde Lhoest-Offermann, Frankfurt am Main: Fischer, 1991, pp.130–131. (Original French edition: *La mémoire collective,* edited by Jeanne ALEXANDRE. Paris: Presses Universitaires de France, 1950. First German edition: Stuttgart: Ferdinand Enke, 1967).

17 Max Frisch on the occasion of a visit to Frankfurt am Main in 1946, quoted in Hermann GLASER, "So viel Anfang war nie", in: *So viel Anfang war nie. Deutsche Städte 1945–1949,* edited by Hermann GLASER, Lutz VON PUFENDORF, and Michael SCHÖNEICH, Berlin, Siedler, 1989, pp.8–23, here pp.10–11: „Und plötzlich kann man sich vorstellen, wie es weiter wächst, wie sich ein Urwald über unsere Städte zieht, langsam, unaufhaltsam, ein menschenloses Gedeihen, ein Schweigen aus Disteln und Moos, eine geschichtslose Erde, dazu das Zwitschern der Vögel, Frühling, Sommer und Herbst, Atem der Jahre, die niemand mehr zählt."

18 Werner Heldt, quoted in GLASER, "So viel Anfang war nie", p.11: „Unter dem Asphaltpflaster Berlins ist überall der Sand unserer Mark. Und das war früher einmal Meeresboden. [...] Die Stadt sinkt in Natur zurück. Ihr Untergang ist der Beginn eines anderen Erdzeitalters"

19 In relation to World War I, see Stephen KERN, "Der kubistische Krieg", in: *Kultur und Geschichte. Neue Einblicke in eine alte Beziehung,* edited by Christoph CONRAD and Martina KESSEL, Stuttgart: Philipp Reclam jun., 1998, pp.319–361, here pp.340–341.

20 Alfred Mahlau, written down in 1946, drawn in 1944, quoted in Johann Friedrich GEIST and Klaus KÜRVERS, *Das Berliner Mietshaus,* 3 VOLS., Munich: Prestel, 1980–1989, VOL.3: *Das Berliner Mietshaus 1945–1989,* 1989, pp.99–100: „[Die] an Häufigkeit und Stärke stetig zunehmenden Luftangriffe [...] schufen [...] täglich und nächtlich immer noch mehr neue Motive. [...] Hier aquarellierte ich, öfter von Schneestürmen und Tagesangriffen unterbrochen [...] den Blick über die leergebrannten Häuser mit ihrem Massenaufgebot von Schornsteinen, die wegen der weggebrannten Dächer lang geworden waren, wie die Hälse von Skeletten. [...] heile und ausgebrannte Waggons und Waggonreihen in dunklen schmutzigen, vorwiegend braunroten und olivgrünen

Farben sowie frische lehmgelbe Minentrichter brachten außergewöhnliche Flecken und Bänder in dieses Linienfiligran; und völlig ausgebrannte Häuserzeilen leiteten über zu einem braunen rußigen Horizont. [...] Ich war erfüllt von der ‚Schönheit‘ dieses Motivs".

21 Theodor W. ADORNO, quoted in GLASER, "So viel Anfang war nie", p. 22: „Die Welt ist aus den Fugen [...]; die Kultur in Trümmern, aber die Trümmer sind weggeräumt, — wo sie noch stehen, sehen sie aus, als wären sie ehrwürdige Ruinen."

22 Hartmut BÖHME, "Die Ästhetik der Ruinen", in: *Der Schein des Schönen*, edited by Dietmar KAMPER and Christoph WULF, Göttingen: Steidl, 1989, pp. 287–304, here p. 287: Ruins show a "precarious balance between preservation and decay, nature and history, violence and peace, memory and presence, mourning and the desire for redemption that is never achieved by an intact building or artwork". ("prekäre Balance von erhaltener Form und Verfall, Natur und Geschichte, Gewalt und Frieden, Erinnerung und Gegenwart, Trauer und Erlösungssehnsucht, wie sie von keinem intakten Bauwerk oder Kunstobjekt erreicht wird".)

23 Rolf FLÜGEL, "Typologie des Zeitfilms" (in: *Glanz*, no. 1, 1949, pp. 29–31), quoted after Ulfilas MEYER, "Trümmerkino", in: *Soviel Anfang war nie*, ed. GLASER, VON PUFENDORF, and SCHÖNEICH, pp. 258–267, here p. 260 and p. 262: „Sie fanden eine neue raffinierte und preiswerte Kulisse: die Ruinen. [...] Die zeitnahen Schwarzhändler zerfallen dann rechtzeitig in vom Arm der Gerechtigkeit erhaschte Bösewichter [...], während das Beispiel des wackeren Heimkehrers die Trümmer wegräumt." „Durch die Wolkenstores grinsen die Ruinen, von Beethoven umspült, und die Seelen sind aus braunem Plüsch. Ob sich die beiden kriegen, oder ob einer von ihnen ins Wasser geht, — der Edelmut spritzt aus dem Projektionsapparat".

24 Carl SCHMITT, "Das Recht als Einheit von Ordnung und Ortung", in: SCHMITT, *Der Nomos der Erde im Völkerrecht des Jus Publicum Europaeum*, Cologne: Greven, 1950; 4th edition, Berlin: Duncker und Humblot, 1997, pp. 13–19, here p. 15: „Die großen Ur-Akte des Rechts dagegen bleiben erdgebundene Ortungen. Das sind: Landnahmen, Städtegründungen und Gründungen von Kolonien."

25 André CORBOZ, *Die Kunst, Stadt und Land zum Sprechen zu bringen*, Basel, Boston, and Berlin, Birkhäuser, 2001, p. 149: „kein Land [...] ohne ein damit verbundenes Imaginäres". The term "dream work" is used by Mitchell in connection with landscape and imperialism (MITCHELL, *Landscape and Power*, p. 10).

26 The figure of the planner is depicted in the public art of a housing development in Vienna for example as an engineer accompanying the building work, supported by depictions of builders.

27 FOUCAULT, "Vorlesung 3. (Sitzung vom 25. Januar 1978)", in: FOUCAULT, *Sicherheit, Territorium, Bevölkerung*, pp. 87–133, here p. 118.

28 Martin HEIDEGGER, "Building, Dwelling, Thinking", in: HEIDEGGER, *Poetry, Language, Thought*, translated by Albert Hofstadter, New York: Harper and Row, 1971, pp. 143–159, here p. 147 and p. 158.

29 On the didactic enterprises of the Werkbund, see Nicola VON ALBRECHT and Renate FLAGMEIER, "Sich einrichten. Die Wohnberatung des Deutschen Werkbundes", in: *Die Stadt von morgen. Beiträge zu einer Archäologie des Hansaviertels Berlin*, edited by Annette MAECHTEL and Kathrin PETERS, Cologne: Walther König, 2008, pp. 120–125.

30 On living, see Johanna HARTMANN, "Aber wenn die Frau aus ihren Grenzen tritt, ist es für sie noch viel gefährlicher. Geschlechtermodelle für die Stadt von morgen", ibid, pp. 200–207 · On public art, see Irene NIERHAUS, *Kunst-am-Bau* · On magazines, see Marie-Louise ANGERER, Irene NIERHAUS, Judith SCHÖBEL, and Alfred SMUDITS, "Wandel medialer Körperbilder. Am Beispiel von Illustrierten-Titelbildern im Zeitraum von 1955 und 1986", in: *Semiotik der Geschlechter. Akten des 6. Symposiums der Österreichischen Gesellschaft für Semiotik, Salzburg 1987,* edited by Jeff BERNHARD, Theresia KLUGSBERGER, and Gloria WITHALM, Stuttgart and Vienna: Hans-Dieter Heinz, 1989, pp. 121–139.

31 Gilles DELEUZE and Felix GUATTARI, *A Thousand Plateaus. Capitalism and Schizophrenia,* translated by Brian Massumi, Minneapolis and London: University of Minnesota Press, 1987, p. 7. (Original French edition: *Mille Plateaux,* Paris, Les Éditions de Minuit, 1980).

32 Jean-Luc NANCY, *Corpus,* translated by Richard A. Rand, New York: Fordham University Press, 2008, p. 21.

33 See Irene NIERHAUS, "Text und Textil: Zur Geschlechterfigur von Material und Innenraum", in: NIERHAUS, *Arch 6,* pp. 115–139.

34 NANCY, *Corpus,* p. 21.

35 Pier Paolo PASOLINI, "Eine Bauerngeschichte", in: PASOLINI, *Alí mit den blauen Augen. Erzählungen, Gedichte, Fragmente,* translated by Bettina Kienlechner and Hans-Peter Glückler, Munich and Zurich: Piper, 1990, pp. 59–74, here p. 70. (Original Italian edition: *Alí dagli occhi azzurri,* Milan: Aldo Garzanti, 1965).

36 Alessandro CAPPABIANCA, "Pasolini a Roma. Dal Sogno all'incubo", in: *Roma nel cinema,* edited by Americo SBARDELLA, Rome: Semar, 2000, pp. 27–37, here p. 33.

37 NANCY, *Corpus,* p. 21 and p. 17.

IMAGES

Archive of Irene Nierhaus: FIGS. 1, 2, 3, 4 (© VG Bild-Kunst, Bonn 2014), 7, 9, and 10 · *So viel Anfang war nie. Deutsche Städte 1945–1949,* edited by Hermann GLASER, Lutz VON PUFENDORF, and Michael SCHÖNEICH, Berlin, Siedler, 1989, p. 171: FIG. 5 · *Neue Städte aus Ruinen. Deutscher Städtebau der Nachkriegszeit,* edited by Klaus VON BEYME, Werner DURTH, Niels GUTSCHOW, Winfried NERDINGER, and Thomas TOPFSTEDT, Munich: Prestel, 1992, p. 13: FIG. 6 · *Donna: Avanguardia Femminista negli Anni '70 dalla Sammlung Verbund Vienna,* edited by Gabriele SCHOR, Milan: Electa, 2010, p. 202: FIG. 8 (© VG Bild-Kunst, Bonn 2014)

GÜNTHER FEUERSTEIN

My Home is My Body: Human and Animal Forms in Architecture

Curiously, although the era of myth and magic has long since past, we still feel the need to animate 'dead' things, like the cosmos — and architecture. That is not only a psychological phenomenon; it is also a matter of fact that in the last century our attitude to our environment, to nature and art — and thus also to architecture — has undergone a fundamental transformation. We are no longer merely viewers, users, or even tolerators of our environment, we also want to communicate with it, to enter into a dialog, a conversation with questions and answers, a discourse, which can also have a critical character. This communication — that is the thesis — will be successful once we are able to rediscover in architecture characteristics of ourselves. Two joint characteristics can be found very easily and almost always: the *Baukörper* (the building "body") and the *faccia(ta)* (the face/façade). But we search for considerably more.

NUMBER · MEASURE

We want to become integrated into a universal field of reference, to be provided with a premonition of the cosmic universality of which already the ancients dreamed.

Since antiquity, the Middle Ages, at the latest since the Renaissance, we have had at our disposal a wonderful rational and irrational key: number, measure, and geometry — an amazing construct, actually beyond all pragmatics, but one that has provided us with a wonderful common denominator that applies equally to God, man, and architecture. God created the world according to measure and number: "omnia in mensura et numero et pondere disposuisti" — all things are arranged by measure and number and weight.

IN / KIRSTEN WAGNER AND JASPER CEPL (EDITORS) /
IMAGES OF THE BODY IN ARCHITECTURE: ANTHROPOLOGY AND BUILT SPACE /
TÜBINGEN · BERLIN / ERNST WASMUTH VERLAG / 2014 / PP. 367–394

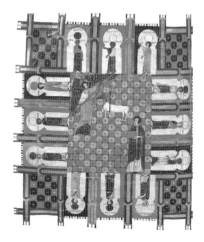

1

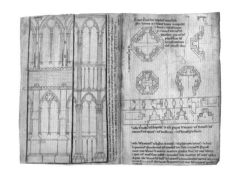

2

3

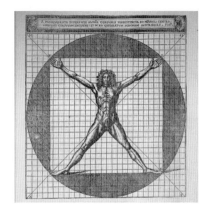

4

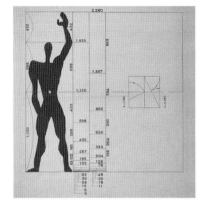

4

6

FIG. 1 New Jerusalem will be measured by an angel with a measuring rod. It is square or round.

FIG. 2 The medieval cathedral, this wonderful anticipation of New Jerusalem, is a marvel of geometry not only in the larger measurements of plan and section, but also in the finest details of its tracery.

FIG. 3 Back in antiquity, the Greek column and the Doric temple require number and measure to achieve harmony. There is no doubt, however, that the column is of an anthropomorphic nature. That becomes literally manifest in the Porch of the Maidens on the Acropolis, for instance.

FIG. 4 Already Vitruvius was able — without metaphysical speculation — to integrate man into the system of number, measure, and geometry. He describes him as "homo ad quadratum" and "homo ad circulum". Later renaissance theoreticians, like Cesare Cesariano, took considerable trouble to visualize the idea.

FIG. 5 The great triumph is the supposedly ultimate mathematization of the beautiful, human, and divine: a : b = b : a + b seems to be the magic formula. And even nature, it has repeatedly been claimed, is constructed according to the golden section. If that were so, a great secret would have been deciphered, and even Le Corbusier (1887–1965) fell prey to this ideology. Almost a cynicism to enlist a larger than average person — a man of course — of 1.83 m as a universal system of measurement: the *Modulor*.

As fascinating as it would be to have found a mathematical and metaphysical codex that could still be applied to architecture today, here too a communicative access to architecture appears extremely problematic. Despite the optimistic pronouncements of more recent aesthetes, we no longer have the sensorium to read the latent classical harmonies. — If we want to communicate with architecture, other pointers would be helpful beyond the abstract analogy of number.

PHYSIOGNOMY · *FACCIA*

For an anthropomorphic and communicative approach we will need features that are clearly visible and perceivable. The greater the number of legible features from our own bodies we find reflected in architecture, the easier our approach will be. Man's main identifying feature is the face and, in turn, the eyes.

FIG. 6 In his treatise on architecture Francesco di Giorgio Martini (1439–1501) shows us that the capital is indeed a *caput* (head).

7

8

9

10

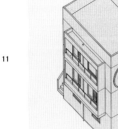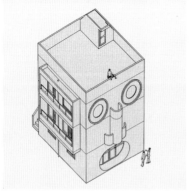

11

12

FIG. 7 In his *Cours d'architecture* Jacques-François Blondel (1705–1774) derives the 'profile' in architecture from the human profile (in 1771).

In the case of a physiognomic architecture — and this applies generally to anthropomorphism — it is necessary to distinguish three aspects:

1. The physiognomy is planned and intended by the designer, and is also easily read as such.

2. The physiognomy is not intended, but read in by the viewer. This is accepted by the designer. If not, he would have to change the arrangement of the design.

3. A formal arrangement is turned into a physiognomy through a supplement or addition, often of a humoristic sort. This is accepted or rejected by the designer.

Now it is important that, in the viewing of architecture, we do not, as is the case in most histories of architecture, exclude the comic, banal, grotesque, naïve, or trivial. Indeed, for the latter, there exist substantial testimonies that go far beyond the 'high art' of architecture. A subject that appears repeatedly is, for instance, the face, the inhabited head — often treated ironically, humorously or grotesquely. Heads 'accommodate' thoughts, ideas, and fantasies. Is it not possible for them to accommodate bodies or people too?

FIG. 8 In the extraordinary Sacro Bosco (Sacred Grove) in Bomarzo near Rome there is a head that can in fact be used and inhabited. At night the eyes of the pavilion, by Vicino Orsini (1523–1585), emit an uncanny glow. The eyes observe us benignly, threateningly, and playfully.

FIG. 9 And do these jaws — in a palazzo by Federico Zuccari (ca. 1542–1609) in Rome (1592) — threaten to devour us?

FIG. 10 Surely Niki de Saint Phalle (1930–2007) with her *Golem* (Jerusalem, 1972) could not be so cruel, since this is a children's playhouse. All uncanniness has been removed from this head-creature: it is a colorful cephalopod.

FIG. 11 In the case of the Kazumasa Yamashita's (b.1937) graphics studio in Kyoto (1974) we are obviously dealing with an intentional architectural joke too.

If the previous faces could be made out without much difficulty, other buildings present more of a problem.

FIG. 12 In the case of the Casa Batlló (1904–06) in Barcelona, it seems fairly certain that Antoni Gaudí (1852–1926) was thinking of the physiognomic, but are we looking at carnival masks or skulls? The interpretation depends on one's personal disposition.

13

14

15

16

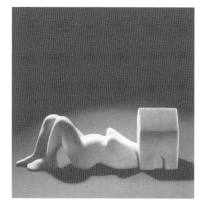

17

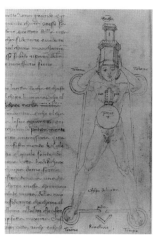

18

FIG. 13 The physiognomy is less clear in the case of an apartment building in Berlin (1986–88) by John Hejduk (1929–2000), but shouldn't we read the half gable as ears?

FIG. 14 Simultaneously symbolic and witty, the Secession in Vienna, by Joseph Maria Olbrich (1867–1908), becomes an enormous spherically crowned countenance with a small mouth. In the intervention realized by Doug Aitken (b. 1968) in 2000, the façade really 'speaks': the eyes are a film projection and wink at you.

BODY · HOUSE

Having reflected on the face, let us now take a look at the whole human body, the complex structure.

FIG. 15 The investigations of psychoanalysis — and here above all the dream symbolism of Sigmund Freud (1856–1939) — can provide important insights into the relation between body and building. In his *Vorlesungen zur Einführung in die Psychoanalyse* (*Introductory Lectures to Psychoanalysis*) Freud explains:

> *The only typical, that is, regular representation of the human person as a whole is in the form of a house [...]. It occurs in dreams that a person, now lustful, now frightened, climbs down the fronts of houses. Those with entirely smooth walls are men; but those which are provided with projections and balconies to which one can hold on, are women.*[1]

And he later claims: "Ladders, ascents, steps in relation to their mounting, are certainly symbols of sexual intercourse."[2] What we are concerned with here is reverse substitution: the building is not interpreted as a person; rather, the person is represented through a building; the building 'body' and the human body are interchangeable.

FIGS. 16, 17 The *Femmes-Maisons* of the French-American artist Louise Bourgeois (1911–2010), in which house and person become identical, could be seen as an illustration to Freud. However, it is not the house that is interpreted as figure, but the figure as house.

Let us now visit a few building 'bodies' that do not require any interpretation since they have been declared as anthropomorphic by their creators.

FIG. 18 In a revealing drawing Francesco di Giorgio Martini attempts to show that the pentagonal fortresses found frequently during the Renaissance can be made to coincide with the human figure.

19

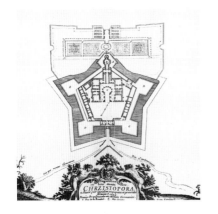

20

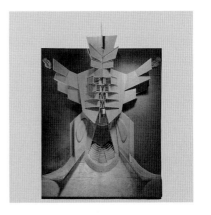

21

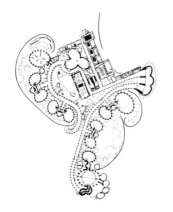

22

23

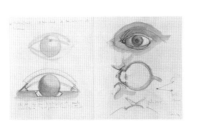

24

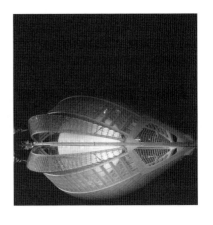

FIG. 19 What is surprising is that such a fortress was actually built. Around 1627 in East Poland the noble Ossolinski family had a fortress built in Krzyżtopór that was doubtless influenced by the ideas of the Italian theorist.[3] With a little interpretive freedom Francesco's anthropomorphic understanding can be read into the building.

FIG. 20 In the architecture of the present no other architect has so openly professed to anthropomorphic readings of his work as Ricardo Porro (b. 1925). The Youth Center, designed for Vaduz, Lichtenstein, in 1972, shows this most clearly. **FIGS. 21, 22** His first significant work, the School of Fine Arts complex in Havana (1961–65) was built in the early years of the Cuban Revolution. Porro has repeatedly acknowledged comparisons with the human body and the explicitly erotic character of his buildings. Furthermore, he is not afraid to make very detailed comparisons between vegetal and human nature.

FIGS. 23, 24 In the case of Santiago Calatrava (b.1951) we need not be hesitant with our interpretations. Less through words than through his many drawings he clearly acknowledges the inspiration of living creatures. Whether this should be seen as a poetic comparison or a real constructive inspiration, however, is not quite clear. With the Planetarium (1995–98) in Valencia, Spain, due to the ingenious reflection in the water, it is impossible to avoid the definition: 'eye'.

CHURCH · WOMAN

In the Pauline epistles the "body is a temple of the Holy Spirit", and in the First Epistle to the Corinthians (3:16) Saint Paul asks: "Know ye not that ye are the Temple of God, and that the Spirit of God dwelleth in you?"

If every Christian is spoken of as the temple of God, how much more could that be said of Christ himself? In the Gospel of John (2:19, 21) we find a clear testimony: "Jesus said unto them, Destroy this temple, and in three days I will raise it up. [...] But he spake of the temple of his body." This thought is an unprecedentedly substantial metaphor linking man and building: man's death and resurrection are compared with the destruction and reconstruction of a building.

The church is the mystical body of Christ, formed primarily through the community of the faithful, the saints, gathered around Christ himself. The parallels with church architecture are patent: this is a body that accommodates the community, but simultaneously represents it in the sense of a *representatio*.

In the symbolic thought of the Middle Ages the identification of the cruciform church plan with Christ's cross has a fixed place. The churches were built "in modum crucis", and just as the church in its entirety represents the "corpus Christi mysticum", the church building itself is the representation of Christ's

25

26

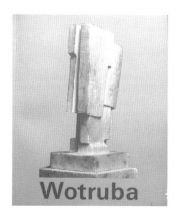

27

28

29

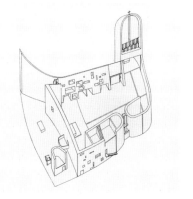

30

cross. Otto von Simson, in his seminal study *The Gothic Cathedral* (1956, **FIG. 25**), claims: "The cathedral […] is an image of the cosmos. But it is also an image of Christ, who had himself compared his death and resurrection to the destruction and rebuilding of the Temple. Consistent with this idea, the Middle Ages perceived in the church edifice an image of Christ crucified"[4]. Besides the numerous verbal references there are only few visual documents of this mystical union between Christ and church, and these have mostly come down to us from the Renaissance.

FIG. 26 In a drawing by Pietro Cataneo (1510?–1569?) from 1567 the human body is convincingly brought in line with the 'body' of the building shown in ground plan. Although it is not a representation of Christ, the outstretched arms recall the crucifixion; at the crossing is the heart, and the figure's head fills the apse, the site of the bishop as Christ's representative.

FIG. 27 Beginning in 1960, the Austrian sculptor Fritz Wotruba (1907–1975) increasingly turned his attention to work on the tectonic "construction" of figures.

FIG. 28 In 1974 Wotruba was charged with the design for a church on the Georgenberg in the outskirts of Vienna. If Wotruba's sculptural works were essentially architecturally interpreted figures, the so-called "Wotruba Church" — actually the Church of the Holy Trinity, with Fritz Gerhard Mayr (b.1931), 1974–76 — is now a figuratively interpretable architecture. Although, admittedly, it is scarcely possible to make out any single figures, the stereometric and figural stratification of the earlier work of the sculptor can still be invoked as an analogy.

The great veneration of the Virgin Mary in the Middle Ages brings a different aspect to the symbolism of the church building: not Christ, but Mary is identified with the church. Saint Ambrose (339–397) sees an analogy between the womb of the Virgin and the bridal chamber[5] — a surprising anticipation of Freudian dream symbolism. When Christ emerges from the gates of heaven, the *porta coeli,* then he also comes out of the body of the Virgin; her birth organs become the portal of heaven and the gate of paradise, as is stated very clearly by Saint Peter Damian (1007–1072): "This virgin will be the door of paradise, who gives God back to the world and opens heaven to us."[6]

FIGS. 29, 30 For Otto Mauer (1907–1973) Le Corbusier's Ronchamp chapel (1950–55) is also the great mother: "Everything is interior and protection. Light penetrates only through the deep shafts of the window niches. But inside is warmth, intimacy, and wellbeing. As in the womb of the Catholic Church, the womb of the Virgin, the child in God's keeping."[7] He adds: "The Ark has reached land and the Lord's house has set itself down besides us: virgin, mother, church."[8]

31

32

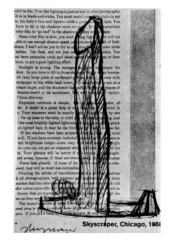

Skyscraper, Chicago, 1958

33

34

35

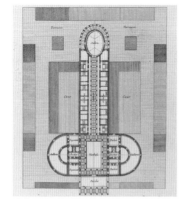

36

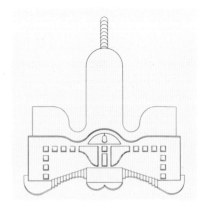

However, Mary is not only regarded as motherly church. In the Psalms one also finds the metaphor of the "Tower of David", and this is also related to the Mother of God. Thus, Mary also acquires a masculine interpretation.

FIG. 31 The notion of a woman that can be entered is, surprisingly, also one that can be encountered in the recent past. *Hon — en katedral* (She — a cathedral) is the suggestive title given by Niki de Saint Phalle to her enormous sculpture of a woman in the Moderna Museet in Stockholm (1966).

TOWER · MAN

The phallic metaphor of the high-rise or skyscraper has certainly been dealt with sufficiently, but cannot go unmentioned here.

FIG. 32 Hans Hollein (1934–2014) states it most clearly in his design for a sky-scraper in Chicago (1958). He spares us the associative interpretation in the iconic and simultaneously provocative representation.

On the other hand, the readings are entirely open in the case of two strikingly similar associations.

FIG. 33 In London Norman Foster (b.1935) designed the tower "30 St Mary Axe" (1997–2004), which is discretely described as "The Gherkin".

FIG. 34 The Torre Agbar (2001) in Barcelona by Jean Nouvel (b.1945) is meant to be considered as a reinterpretation of the 'tower' theme in Antoni Gaudí.

FIG. 35 The phallic is less often to be encountered as a ground plan. However, it is explicit in the case of Claude-Nicolas Ledoux (1736–1806), who gives his "Maison du Plaisir" an unambiguous form.

FIG. 36 Christian W. Thomsen notes on the Daisy House (1978) by Stanley Tiger-man (b.1930): "This plan designates the house as a whole as male genitalia, while in the windows of the living area the male and female principle penetrate one another."[9]

CREATURE · ZOON

Modern urban man's relation to animals is extremely ambivalent: more consumption than admiration. As a result the appearance of animals in architecture

37

38

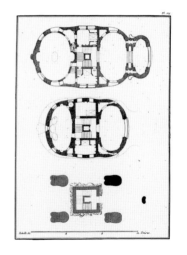

39

40

41

42

comes as a surprise. A zoomorphic — or better theriomorphic — architecture is encountered either overtly or encoded. However, this phenomenon does not shed much light on our real position with regard to animals.

Of course large cumbersome animals are particularly suited to being used as buildings.

FIGS. 37, 38 Charles-François Ribart designed an "Éléphant Triomphal" for the Champs-Élysées in Paris, in 1758. The interior contained elegant salons and a fountain sprayed from its trunk.

FIG. 39 Jean-Jacques Lequeu (1757–1826) made a design for a cowshed in the form of a cow (ca.1800). A typical *architecture parlante* from the time of the French Revolution. Although this may seem a fanciful proposal at first glance, it is a matter of making a building's concrete contents and functions visible on the outside — a concern that found renewed interest after the end of functionalism in the 1970s.

In contemporary architecture too we have no trouble locating zoomorphic buildings. As in the 18th century, elephants are currently still among the favoured animal buildings.

FIG. 40 With a little interpretive freedom we can discover something entirely animalistic in a building by Sir Hugh Casson (1910–1999), Neville Conder (1922–2003), and Partners. The Elephant and Rhinoceros Pavilion in London Zoo (1962–65) is in no way a direct copy of the animal, but the bulky structures surmounted with a 'head' and the surface treatment of the concrete clearly refer to the pachyderms housed within, and the grouping of the individual buildings gives the impression that the enormous animals have gathered into a herd.

FIG. 41 At the garden show in the German city of Hamm, Westphalia, Horst Rellecke (b.1951) transformed a disused coal washing plant into an elephant (1981–84). The closed structure of the silo is used without alteration as the body and supplemented with steel and glass constructions. The backbone forms a sort of loft, the lift moves in the trunk, and the head contains a restaurant with a panoramic view.

FIG. 42 In the USA we have less trouble than in Europe finding a direct and overt animal 'architecture'. Curious animal buildings were built in America long before the 'invention' of Pop Art. James V. Lafferty (1856–1898) erected his elephant in 1881 in the outskirts of Atlantic City. It served as a small hotel and later as an office for an estate agent.

43

 44

45

 46

47

 48

FIG. 43 Clearly animals with massive bodies are predestined to be turned into 'animal architecture', and in that context one should not leave out the dinosaur. The dinosaur craze in the USA also led to the building of such animals. The ones depicted here, by Claude K. Bell (1897–1988), were built in Cabazon, California, between 1964 and 1988. Dinosaurs like these found use as freeway service stations or exhibition pavilions, and a number of design teams specialized in the building of these giant animals.

These examples, which we readily dismiss as trivial or kitsch, can be counterposed with thoroughly serious works of architecture. However, the latter mostly acquired their animal appellation only later — in the vernacular so to speak.

FIG. 44 The auditorium of Delft University of Technology was designed in 1961 by (Van den Broek and) Jacob Berend Bakema (1914–1981) entirely in line with the Brutalism of the 1960s. It very quickly acquired the appellation: "Dinosaur".

FIG. 45 "Friendly Alien" is the name given by the residents of Graz to the art museum that Peter Cook (b. 1936) and Colin Fournier (b. 1944) let land in the city centre in 2002.

FIG. 46 The hall of a convent (1974–77), also in Graz, by Günther Domenig (1934–2012), is a grotto, cave, or womb on the inside, but a vast reptile outside.

FIG. 47 Situated deliberately at the threshold of art, triviality, and irony are the works of Claes Oldenburg (b. 1929), and one of his works could surely be classified as zoomorphic architecture: a colossal monument in the form of a teddy bear he proposed in 1965 for Central Park in New York, perhaps for use as an office building. The children's soft toy enters into competition with Manhattan's phallic skyscrapers.

FIG. 48 The theme of the banal has been continued by Robert Venturi (b. 1925), Denise Scott Brown (b. 1931), and Steven Izenour (1940–2001) who, in their seminal study *Learning from Las Vegas,* explained the considerable importance of the trivial for our living environment. As a result of their philosophy, the "duck" on Long Island — and it is far from being the only example — has acquired a new architectural-philosophical status. To them, "The duck is the special building that is a symbol" [10]. Indeed, dogs, horses, cats, and other animals extend the zoological repertoire of 'inhabitable' creatures in America.

It is not without a deeper meaning that Daedalus, the master architect of mythology, managed to carry out a successful flight with his flying machine, while his hubristic son Icarus was less fortunate. Since then architects have repeatedly

49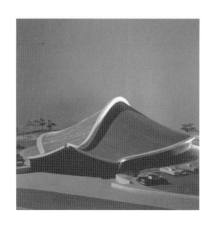

 50

51

52

53

54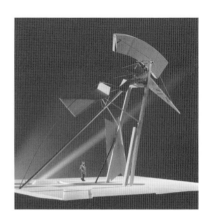

dreamed of flying, or rather that their buildings could take off, that they could become dematerialized and thus weightless. Since that has rarely been the case, the bird has become a favoured metaphor in architecture — that is, the animal that most intensely contradicts the basic principle of weight in building.

FIGS. 49, 50 The notion of flying, of wings, seems to be disconnected from the actual material. The idea of taking off appears in the works of Eero Saarinen (1910–1961) irrespective of the weighty concrete. In the case of the ice hockey stadium at Yale University in New Haven the functional structure, developed by the structural engineer Fred Severud (1899–1990), would initially have had a considerably simpler appearance: a reinforced concrete arch ending at supports in the ground spans the stadium; from this the roof surfaces swing up to peripheral concrete supports. For Saarinen this construction recalled a turtle, and this hulking metaphor was not at all welcome. He therefore extended the construction with a thoroughly non-functional element: the backbone is extended out beyond the supports, bringing the roof surface with it, and the shelled animal is transformed into a soaring bird.

FIGS. 51, 52 The work of Coop Himmelb(l)au (founded by Wolf D. Prix, Helmut Swiczinsky, and Michael Holzer in Vienna, Austria, in 1968) repeatedly alludes to animals, above all the motif of the wing and flying. The light, transparent, open, moving, and transitory are the main concerns of Coop Himmelb(l)au that run like a thread through their entire body of work. The motifs are not always taken solely from zoology, but also from mythology: the wings of angels, gods, spirits, and the flicker and flare of flames still count as viable metaphors. It is not by chance that they called a music bar in Vienna (1980–81) "Roter Engel" (Red Angel): "The angel of tone is the built breath of the singer."

Flying knows no gravity and thus also no above and below, no right angle, no rational geometry. In this way the formal world of the so-called "Deconstructivists", of which Coop Himmelb(l)au are among the main exponents, acquires a new area of motivation. With Himmelb(l)au, Gaudí's crooked reptilian spinal columns become taught springy arcs, the exposed skeletons of fantastical flying animals.

FIG. 53 One of these creatures has just landed on the roof of a 19th-century building in Vienna: probably the most beautiful conference room in contemporary architecture, built for a law firm in 1983–88.

FIG. 54 But birds can also strut around graciously and comically with *The Long Thin Yellow Legs of Architecture* (Rotterdam, 1988), unsure of whether to stalk, fly or rake.

55

56

57

58

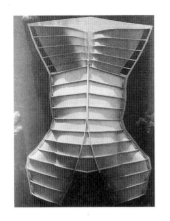

59

60

FIG. 55 If flying is beyond our reach, then at least we might try levitation, the *elevatio* occasionally accomplished by the great saints. The latter may have been achieved by Coop Himmelb(l)au's Musée des Confluences (2001–14) in Lyon, France. The architects want to move their creations in the direction of land, air, and water. That fish are also well suited as human residences, we know from the Bible, from fables and legends.

FIG. 56 But what does a modern architect such as Frank O. Gehry (b. 1929) find so fascinating about the fish motif? At the beginning it only appears in his more modest works; however, it steadily develops increasingly notable proportions. In 1983 he designed a garden folly for an exhibition at the Castelli Gallery in New York: a vast fish formed from a beautiful wood construction, which inevitably also recalls a ship. In 1992 he conceived another "fish" for the urban regeneration area in Barcelona, originally used as the Olympic Village. Although it cannot be entered, its location and the context with the surrounding houses certainly give it the character of a building.

FIG. 57 For the DG Bank (now DZ Bank) in Pariser Platz, Berlin (1995–2000), Gehry created a building characterized by a surprising formal tension: while the exterior is required to conform to Berlin's building regulations, which stipulate a largely conventional formal code for the whole context of the city, for the interior Gehry devised structures of extreme complexity. A second construction that is implanted like a 'house in a house' — or better: a 'creature in a house' — in the building's courtyard has an even more complex appearance. The conference room is accommodated in an entirely 'organic' looking form. It has been described as a "shell sculpture" or horse's head and this terminus alone would speak for a zoomorphic architecture.

FIG. 58 Let us finally cast a glance at smaller creatures: In 1966 Laurids Ortner (b. 1941), later a founder of Haus-Rucker-Co, drew tiny animals and wrote: "The thought gradually took hold of me that it must be wonderful to live inside an insect, to use its insides as stairs and ramps, in short, to create in it a strange but still human surroundings."[11] Insects and bones were the source of inspiration for Ortner's designs while still a student, and with extraordinary meticulousness he pursues the externally invisible morphology of the animals. The visual translation into a concrete building can be illustrated by Ortner's design for a new airport (1965).

FIGS. 59, 60 Also in the case of the design for the Teatro Puccini (1986) in Torre del Lago by Paolo Portoghesi (b. 1931) we do not have to rely on speculation: the architect himself adds a drawing of an animal, perhaps a gigantic insect or shellfish that has settled like a helmsman in a boat.

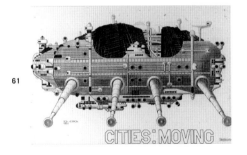

61

62

63

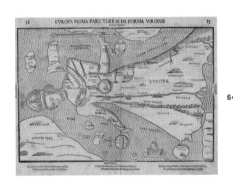

64

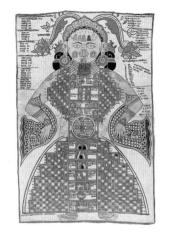

65

66

FIG.61 The extreme magnification of sinister spider- or insect-like creatures, which become roaming buildings, is a common motif in horror and science-fiction films. The intention of the English Archigram group, visualized in a drawing by Ron Herron (b.1930), was certainly not to represent a horror scenario. Rather, their *Walking City* from 1964 should be the extreme model of a flexible urban society. The enormous compact agglomerations are able to travel over sea and temporarily hook up with each other using telescopic pipes.

CITY · WORLD

Let us now set off towards the body's unlimited magnification.

FIG.62 Superimposed over the town plan of Suchindram in South India is the town's female deity. She becomes pregnant with the male Shiva temple in the centre, while four further temples mark the outline of her body.

FIG.63 A closely related theme is the anthropomorphization of the landscape. Our capacity for projection, through popular appellations, has repeatedly anthropomorphized parts of the landscape. Faces or lying figures are read above all from mountains. According to Vitruvius the architect Dinocrates even wanted to transform Mount Athos into a vast sculpture of Alexander the Great.

FIG.64. In Heinrich Bünting's *Itinerarium Sacrae Scripturae,* first published in 1581, a symbolic map shows Europe represented as a maiden.

FIG.65 The Jains in India do not content themselves, like the Europeans, with superimposing female figures over countries or continents. Rather, the "Cosmic Woman" (18th century) represents the whole universe.

DIGITAL? · VIRTUAL?

With the triumphal march of computer-aided design, with the digitalization of building, are the chances for an anthropomorphic or zoomorphic architecture finally over? Not at all. The new tool could not invalidate such an ancient thought; it even supports it. A couple of examples should show the proximity of the protagonists of the new design methods to an architecture of the body.

FIG.66 Take for instance the Freshwater Pavilion (Neeltje Jans Island, The Netherlands, 1994–97), by Lars Spuybroek (b.1959) of NOX Architects. The gleaming silver building seems to writhe like a beached sea monster.

67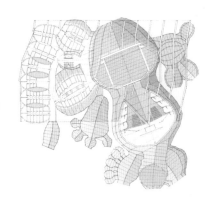

68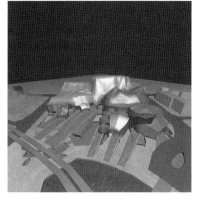

69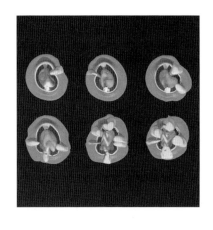

70

71

72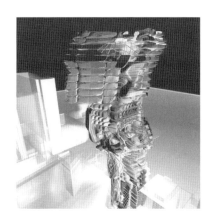

FIGS. 67, 68 With an approach that makes use of endless series of computer animations, Greg Lynn (b.1964) has acquired a leading position in the architecture of "hybrid space", for instance with his 1994 competition design for Cardiff Bay Opera House. The computer-generated figurations make the associations with organic architecture seem compelling.

FIGS. 69, 70 Lynn provides a catchword for an anthropomorphic architecture describing one of his series of house studies as "Embryological House". In a figurative sense the connection with "embryo" suggests the undeveloped, the just developing. In Lynn's terminology we find attractive concepts that are certainly related with the organic. For instance, when he uses ideas such as the "Pliant" or the "Supple", or calls for "anexact yet rigorous" geometries.[12]

FIG. 71 Lynn also seeks inspiration from scienticsts such as the British geneticist William Bateson (1861–1926) to substantiate his argument.

FIG. 72 Surprisingly, mythological creatures can serve as a direct inspiration for computer-generated designs. Sulan Kolatan (b.1956) and William J. MacDonald (b.1958) of KOL/MAC, New York, characterize their spatial productions as a "chimerical hybrids". The chimera, a female monster, is made up of a lion's head, a goat's body, and a dragon's tale.

CONCLUSION

Admittedly, nowadays it is rare to encounter anthropomorphism as directly and openly as it is presented here. However, precisely latent phenomena can signal to a large extent elementary wishes, dreams and desires.

One of anthropomorphism's other virtues is that it represents a clear alternative to functionalism. If, today, we concede to architecture the capacity to deal, far beyond the functional and material, with the existential problems of our lives, an anthropomorphic and zoomorphic architecture could acquire a new status. The rediscovery of the analogies between 'creature' — in the sense of the Greek *zoon* — and architecture, regardless of how openly or symbolically they are presented, could open up new approaches to architecture and new levels of interpretation of our built environment.

Are we beginning to redefine the long problematic set of relations to our own bodies and to those of animals? Are architecture and the object world the appropriate media for that?

If we entrust the built environment with the ability to deal with all being, then an anthropomorphic and zoomorphic architecture would have a new chance in the architecture of the present.

NOTES

1   Sigmund FREUD, *A General Introduction to Psychoanalysis*, translated by G. Stanley Hall, New York: Horace Liveright, 1920, p. 125. (First German edition: *Vorlesungen zur Einführung in die Psychoanalyse*, 3 parts, Leipzig and Vienna: Hugo Heller, 1916–1917). See Sigm. FREUD, *Gesammelte Schriften*, 12 VOLS., Leipzig, Vienna, and Zurich: Internationaler Psychoanalytischer Verlag, 1924–1934, here VOL. 7, 1924, p. 154: „Die einzig typische, d. h. regelmäßige Darstellung der menschlichen Person als Ganzes ist die als Haus [...]. Es kommt im Traume vor, daß man, bald lustvoll, bald ängstlich von Häuserfassaden herabklettert. Die mit ganz glatten Mauern sind Männer; die aber mit Vorsprüngen und Balkonen versehen sind, an welchen man sich anhalten kann, das sind Frauen."

2   Ibid., p. 130 · FREUD, *Gesammelte Schriften*, VOL. 7, p. 159: „Leiter, Stiege, Treppe, respektive das Gehen auf ihnen, sind sichere Symbole des Geschlechtsverkehres."

3   See Nils MEYER, "Krzyżtopór — Der Herrscher als Festung | Krzyżtopór — The Ruler as a Fortress", in: *Daidalos*, no. 45, 1992, pp. 80–83.

4   Otto VON SIMSON, *The Gothic Cathedral. Origins of Gothic Architecture and the Medieval Concept of Order*, New York: Pantheon Books, 1956, p. 36 note 38.

5   See Anselm WAGNER, "Die Jungfrauen und der Bräutigam. Zur Ikonologie der romanischen Wandmalereien von Müstair und Hocheppan", in: *Belvedere: Zeitschrift für bildende Kunst*, VOL. 5, 1999, no. 2, pp. 46–57, here p. 56.

6   Ibid.: „Diese Jungfrau wird die Tür des Paradieses sein, die Gott der Welt zurückgibt und uns den Himmel öffnet." Wagner's source is: Anselm SALZER, *Die Sinnbilder und Beiworte Mariens in der deutschen Literatur und lateinischen Hymnenpoesie des Mittelalters*, Linz: Selbstverlag des K. K. Ober-Gymnasiums [der Benedictiner, Seitenstetten, Lower Austria], 1893, p. 541: "Haec virgo verbo gravida / Fit paradisi iauua, Quae Deum mundo reddidit / Caelum nobis aperuit".

7   Otto MAUER, "Ronchamp" (first published in: *Werk und Wahrheit*, VOL. 10, 1955, pp. 878–880), in: MAUER, *Über Kunst und Künstler*, edited by Günter ROMHOLD, Salzburg and Vienna: Residenz Verlag, 1993, pp. 219–223, here p. 222: „Alles ist Innenraum der Geborgenheit, nur durch Luken bricht das Licht, durch tiefe Schächte. Aber im Innern ist Wärme, Innigkeit, Geborgensein. Wie im Mutterleib der katholischen Kirche, wie im Schoße Marias das Kind in Gotteshut."

8   Ibid., p. 223: „Die Arche ist gestrandet, und Gottes Haus hat sich bei uns niedergelassen, die Jungfrau, die Mutter, die Kirche."

9   Christian W. THOMSEN (with two contributions by Angela KREWANI), *Bauen für die Sinne. Gefühl, Erotik und Sexualität in der Architektur*, Munich and New York: Prestel, 1996, p. 65: „Der Plan weist das Haus insgesamt als männliches Genital aus, wobei sich in den Fenstern des Wohnbereiches männliches und weibliches Prinzip einander durchdringen." (English Edition: *Sensuous Architecture: The Art of Erotic Building*, Munich and New York: Prestel, 1996, p. 65).

10   Robert VENTURI, Denise SCOTT BROWN, and Steven IZENOUR, *Learning From Las Vegas. The Forgotten Symbolism of Architectural Form*, revised edition (first edition 1972), Cambridge, MA and London: The MIT Press, 1977, p. 87.

11   Laurids ORTNER: "Insekten und Knochen" (1965), in: Günther FEUERSTEIN, *Visionäre Architektur. Wien 1958/1988*, Berlin: Ernst & Sohn, 1988, p. 265. „In mir setzte sich der Gedanke fest, daß

es wunderbar sein müßte, in einem Insekt zu leben. Seine Innereien als Stiegen und Rampen zu benützen, kurz in ihm eine eigenartige, aber doch menschliche Umgebung zu schaffen."

12 See Greg LYNN, "Architectural Curvilinearity. The Folded, the Pliant and the Supple", in: *Architectural Design,* VOL. 63, 1993, no.3/4 (March/April), pp.8–15.

IMAGES

Facundus-Beatus, Madrid, Biblioteca Nacional, Ms Vit.14.2, f°253v, 1047: FIG.1 · Villard de Honnecourt, Portfolio, Paris, Bibliothèque nationale de France (MS Fr 19093), fol. 62–63: FIG.2 · Walter HEGE and Gerhart RODENWALDT, *Die Akropolis,* Berlin: Deutscher Kunstverlag, 1930, plate 90: FIG.3 · Cesare CESARIANO, *Di Lucio Vitruvio Pollione de Architectura Libri Dece traducti de latino in Vulgare [...],* Como: Gotardus de Ponte, 1521, fol.50r: FIG.4 · LE CORBUSIER, *Le Modulor,* Boulogne-sur-Seine: Éditions de l'Architecture d'Aujourd'hui, 1950: FIG.5 (© FLC/VG Bild-Kunst, Bonn 2014) · Francesco DI GIORGIO MARTINI, Codex Saluzziano 148, Turin, Biblioteca Reale, fol.14v: FIG.6 and fol.3r: FIG.18 · J. F. [Jacques-François] BLONDEL, *Planches pour le premier volume du Cours D'Architecture, Qui contenient Les Leçons données en 1750, & les années suivantes,* Paris: Desaint, 1771, plate XII: FIG.7 · Ernst GULDAN, "Das Monster-Portal am Palazzo Zuccari in Rom. Wandlungen eines Motivs vom Mittelalter zum Manierismus", in: *Zeitschrift für Kunstgeschichte,* VOL.32, 1969, pp.229–261, here p.251: FIG.8 and p.231: FIG.9 · Archive of Günther Feuerstein, Vienna: FIGS.10, 14, 59, and 60 · "Kyoto Face", in: *Architectural Review,* VOL.158, 1975, p.381: FIG.11 · Günther Feuerstein, Vienna: FIGS.12 and 13 · Sigm. FREUD, *Vorlesungen zur Einführung in die Psychoanalyse,* 4th edition, Leipzig, Vienna, and Zurich: Internationaler Psychoanalytischer Verlag, 1922, pp.II–III: FIG.15 · *Louise Bourgeois,* edited by Marie-Laure BERNADAC, Paris: Editions Du Centre Pompidou, 2008, p.144: FIG.16 and p.143: FIG.17 (© The Easton Foundation / VG Bild-Kunst, Bonn 2014) · Samuel VON PUFENDORF, *Sieben Bücher, Von denen Thaten Carl Gustavs, Königs in Schweden: Mit Vortrefflichen Kupffern ausgezieret und mit nöthigen Registern versehen,* Nuremberg: Christoph Riegel, 1697: FIG.19 · *Ricardo Porro: Architekt,* Klagenfurt: Ritter, 1994, p.85: FIG.20, p.56: FIG.21, and p.57: FIG.22 · Santiago CALATRAVA, *Geheimbuch,* edited by Mirko ZARDINI, Basel: Wiese-Verlag, 1996, p.21: FIG.23 · Günther FEUERSTEIN, *Biomorphic Architecture. Menschen- und Tiergestalten in der Architektur | Human and Animal Forms in Architecture,* Stuttgart and London: Axel Menges, 2002, p.107: FIG.24 and p.115: FIG.40 · Otto VON SIMSON, *The Gothic Cathedral. Origins of Gothic Architecture and the Medieval Concept of Order,* New York: Pantheon Books, 1956, dust jacket: FIG.25 · Pietro CATANEO, *L'architettvra di Pietro Cataneo,* Venice: Aldus [Manutius], 1567, p.76: FIG.26 · Fritz WOTRUBA, *Skulpturen und Zeichnungen,* Salzburg: Galerie Welz, 1967, cover: FIG.27 · F. Basti: FIG.28 · LE CORBUSIER, *Œuvre Complète,* VOL.6: *1952–1957,* edited by Willy BOESIGER, Zurich: Editions Girsberger, 1957, p.27: FIG.29 and p.25: FIG.30 (© FLC / VG Bild-Kunst, Bonn 2014) · Pontus HULTÉN, *Niki de Saint Phalle,* Ostfildern: Gerd Hatje, 1992, p.69: FIG.31 (© VG Bild-Kunst, Bonn 2014) · Archive of Hans Hollein: FIG.32 · Foster + Partners, London: FIG.33 · www.torreagbar.cat: FIG.34 · Claude-Nicolas LEDOUX, *L'architecture considérée sous le rapport de l'art, des moeurs et de la législation,* 2 VOLS., Paris: [chez l'auteur], 1804, VOL.1, plate 104: FIG.35 · Stanley TIGERMAN, *Versus. An American Architect's Alter-*

natives, New York: Rizzoli, 1982, p.114: FIG. 36 · [Charles-François] RIBART, *Architecture Singuliere. L'Éléphant Triomphal. Grand Kiosque a la Gloire du Roi,* Paris: P. [Pierre] Patte, 1758, plate VI: FIG. 37 and plate VII: FIG. 38 · Philippe DUBOY, *Lequeu. An Architectural Enigma,* London: Thames and Hudson, 1986, p.239: FIG. 39 · www.fotocommunity.de (fc-foto: 31936666): FIG. 41 · Library of Congress, Prints & Photographs Division, HABS, HABS NJ,1-MARGCI,1--7 (CT): FIG. 42 · The Center for Land Use Interpretation, Land Use Database (http://clui.org/ludb/site/cabazon): FIG. 43 · Van den Broek und Bakema, "Auditoriengebäude der Technischen Hochschule Delft", in: *Bauen + Wohnen,* VOL. 22, 1968, pp. 175–179, here p.176: FIG. 44 · Universalmuseum Joanneum (Graz, Austria), Nicolas Lackner: FIG. 45 · Günther DOMENIG, *Werkbuch,* Salzburg and Vienna: Residenz Verlag, 1991, p.75: FIG. 46 · *Claes Oldenburg. Coosje van Bruggen,* edited by Germano CELANT, Milan: Skira, 1999, p.20: FIG. 47 · Peter BLAKE, *God's own Junkyard. The Planned Deterioration of America's Landscape,* New and updated edition, New York, Chicago, and San Francisco: Holt, Rinehart and Winston, 1979 (first published 1964), p.120: FIG. 48 · Library of Congress, Prints & Photographs Division, Balthazar Korab Archive at the Library of Congress, LC-DIG-krb-00548: FIG. 49 · Library of Congress, Prints & Photographs Division, photograph by Carol M. Highsmith (LC-DIG-highsm-04251): FIG. 50 · Archive of Coop Himmelb(l)au, Vienna: FIGS. 51–55 · *el croquis,* no. 74/75, 1995, p.20: FIG. 56 · Wolfgang Staudt, 2008 (http://farm4.staticflickr.com/3149/2825932828_ac2f5bb70e_o_d.jpg): FIG. 57 · Günther FEUERSTEIN, *Visionäre Architektur. Wien 1958/1988,* Berlin: Ernst & Sohn, 1988, p. 73: FIG. 58 · *Visionen und Utopien. Architekturzeichnungen aus dem Museum of Modern Art,* edited by Matilda McQUAID, Munich, Berlin, London, and New York: Prestel, 2003, p.151: FIG. 61 · Jan PIEPER, "Häuser des Narziß. Architektur nach des Menschen Bild und Gleichnis | Houses of Narzissus. Architecture According to the Image of Man", in: *Daidalos,* no. 45, 1992, pp.30–47, here p.40: FIG. 62 and p.41: FIG. 65 · Johann Bernhard FISCHER VON ERLACH, *Entwurff Einer Historischen Architectur, In Abbildung unterschiedener berühmten Gebäude des Alterthums und fremder Völcker; umb aus den Geschicht-büchern, Gedächtnüß-münzen, Ruinen, und eingeholten wahrhafften Abrißen, vor Augen zu stellen,* Leipzig: [n. p.], 1725, plate XVIII: FIG. 63 · Heinrich BÜNTING, *Itinerarium Sacrae Scripturae. Intinerarivm Sacrae Scriptvrae. Das ist, Ein Reisebuch, Vber die gantze heilige Schrifft, in zwey Buecher getheilt,* Helmstedt: Jakobus Lucius, 1582 (first edition 1581): FIG. 64 · NOX Architects, Rotterdam: FIG. 66 · Archive of Greg Lynn: FIG. 67, 68 · Lawrence BIRD and Guillaume LaBELLE, "Re-Animating Greg Lynn's Embryological House: A Case Study in Digital Design Preservation", in: *Leonardo,* VOL. 43, 2010, pp.242–249, here p.242: FIGS. 69 and 70 · William BATESON, *Materials for the Study of Variation. Treated with Especial Regard to Discontinuity in the Origin of Species,* London and New York: Macmillan and Co, 1894, p.335: FIG. 71 · Sulan KOLATAN: "Chimaera: Über die Bildung organischer Hybridität", in: *Archithese,* VOL. 32, 2002, no. 2, pp.32–37, here p.33: FIG. 72

THE AUTHORS

Claire BARBILLON is associate professor at the Department of Art History and Archeology of the Université Paris Ouest Nanterre La Défense. From 2003 to 2011 she was director of studies at the École du Louvre. As associate professor she lectured at the Université Bordeaux-Montaigne from 2001 to 2003. Between 1991 and 1998 she held a position at the Musée d'Orsay, where she was responsible for publications. She is a member of the editorial boards of *Histoire de l'art, Studiolo: Revue de l'Académie de France à Rome–Villa Médicis,* and *Perspective: La revue de l'INHA* (Institut national d'histoire de l'art). She is also on the Conseil scientifique du Musée Rodin. Her research focuses on 19th-century sculpture. Recent publications include: *Le relief, au croisement des arts du XIXe siècle,* Paris: Éditions A. et J. Picard, 2014 · *Histoire de l'art du XIXe siècle (1848–1914), bilans et perspectives,* edited by Claire BARBILLON, Catherine CHEVILLOT, and François-René MARTIN, Paris: École du Louvre, 2012 · *Écrire la sculpture,* with Sophie MOUQUIN, Paris: Citadelles & Mazenod, 2011 · *Histoire de l'histoire de l'art en France au XIXe siècle,* edited by Roland RECHT, Philippe SÉNÉCHAL, Claire BARBILLON, and François-René MARTIN, Paris: La Documentation Française, 2008 · *Les canons du corps humain au XIXe siècle. L'art et la règle,* Paris: Odile Jacob, 2004.

Jasper CEPL is visiting professor for architectural theory at the Dessau Institute of Architecture / Hochschule Anhalt. He was an adjunct lecturer for architectural history at the University of Cologne in 2013 and 2014. He has taught architectural theory as assistant professor at the Technische Universität Berlin from 2003 to 2013. His publications include: "Richard Lucae and the Aesthetics of Space in the Age of Iron", in: *The Aesthetics of Iron Architecture: Formations, Exchanges, Transformations,* edited by Paul DOBRASZCZYK and Peter SEALY, Farnham and Burlington, VT: Ashgate, forthcoming in 2015 · "Über Konvention und Satzung in Haus- und Stadtbau", in: *Die Gestalt der Stadt. Satzungen in Geschichte und Gegenwart,* edited by Christoph MÄCKLER and Alexander PELLNITZ, Sulgen: Niggli, forthcoming in 2014 · "Stahlskelette in tönernen Körpern: Terrakotta im frühen amerikanischen Hochhausbau", in: *In Situ. Zeitschrift für Architekturgeschichte,* VOL. 5, 2013, pp. 235–248 · "Townscape in Germany", in: *Journal of Architecture,* VOL. 17, 2012, pp. 777–790 · *Oswald Mathias Ungers. Eine intellektuelle Biographie,* Cologne: Verlag der Buchhandlung Walther König, 2007 · *Kollhoff e Timmermann architetti: Tutte le opere,* edited by Jasper CEPL, Milan: Electa, 2003, English edition 2004.

Tobias CHEUNG is associate professor at the Institute of Cultural Studies of the Humboldt Universität zu Berlin and visiting scholar at the Max-Planck-Institute for the History of Science (Berlin). He is interested in the history of science, philosophy, literature, architecture and East Asian cultural studies. His recent publications include: *Organismen: Agenten zwischen Innen- und Außenwelten, 1780–1860,* Bielefeld: Transcript, 2014 · "Limits of Life and Death: Legallois's Decapitation Experiments", in: *Journal of the History of Biology,* VOL. 46, 2013, pp. 283–313 · *Transitions and Borders between Animals, Humans, and Machines, 1600–1800,* edited by Tobias CHEUNG, Leiden: E. J. Brill, 2010 · "System, Mikrooperator und Transformation: Leibniz' gemeinsames Ordnungsdispoitiv der Monade und des Lebendigen im naturgeschichtlichen Kontext", in: *Der Monadenbegriff zwischen Spätrenaissance und Aufklärung,* edited by Hanns-Peter NEUMANN, Berlin and New York: Walter de Gruyter, 2009, pp. 143–202 · *Res vivens. Agent Models of Organic Order 1600–1800,* Freiburg i. Br., Berlin, and Vienna: Rombach, 2008.

Günther FEUERSTEIN is professor emeritus at the Universität für künstlerische und industrielle Gestaltung Linz, where he taught environmental design (Umraumgestaltung) from 1973 to 1996. He studied architecture at the Technische Universität Wien (until 1951), where he also taught as assistant professor (at the chair of Karl Schwanzer) from 1961 to 1968. His "Klubseminar der Architekturstudenten" became a highly influential incubator for architectural discourse in Vienna, with members of Coop Himmelb(l)au, Haus-Rucker-Co, or Zünd-up among the participants. He has written intensively on images of the body in architecture and on other topics. Between 1970 and 1989 he edited the architecture journal *Transparent*. His publications include: *Visionäre Architektur. Wien 1958/1988*, Berlin: Ernst & Sohn, 1988 · *Androgynos. Das Mann-Weibliche in Kunst und Architektur | The Male-Female in Art and Architecture*, Stuttgart and London: Axel Menges, 1997 · *Biomorphic Architecture*, Stuttgart and London: Axel Menges, 2002, with 2 supplements published as *Zoon. Anthropomorphes Bauen. Architektur als Wesen*, Vienna: Grafisches Zentrum HTU, 2003 and 2004.

Tanja JANKOWIAK was a cultural studies scholar and architect. She studied architecture at Technische Universität Berlin, the Akademie der bildenden Künste in Vienna, and the Architectural Association in London, and cultural studies, philosophy, and art history at Humboldt Universität zu Berlin and Freie Universität Berlin. She was on the academic staff of the Department of Architecture at Bauhaus-Universität Weimar until 2010. Her publications include: *Architektur und Tod. Zum architektonischen Umgang mit Sterben, Tod und Trauer. Eine Kulturgeschichte*, Munich: Wilhelm Fink, 2010 · *Von Freud und Lacan aus: Literatur, Medien, Übersetzen. Zur „Rücksicht auf Darstellbarkeit" in der Psychoanalyse*, edited by Tanja JANKOWIAK, Karl-Josef PAZZINI, and Claus-Dieter RATH, Bielefeld: Transcript, 2006.

Eckhard LEUSCHNER is professor of art history at Julius-Maximilians-Universität Würzburg. He was professor of art history and theory at Universität Erfurt from 2011 to 2014. His research areas are concepts of the body, the canon, and measurements in the arts, and image cultures from the 19th to the 21st century; art in Italy from the 15th century to the present; reproductive methods in the arts; iconography and cultural exchange in the early modern period. His publications include: *Architektur- und Ornamentgraphik der Frühen Neuzeit: Migrationsprozesse in Europa | Gravures d'architecture et d'ornement au début de l'époque moderne: processus de migration en Europe*, edited by Sabine FROMMEL and Eckhard LEUSCHNER, Rom: Campisano Editore, 2014 · *Figura umana: Normkonzepte der Menschendarstellung in der italienischen Kunst 1919-1939*, edited by Eckhard LEUSCHNER, Petersberg: Michael Imhof, 2012 · "Zur graphischen Formung des Menschen in der Frühen Neuzeit", in: *GedankenStriche: Zeichnungen und Druckgraphiken aus der Universitätsbibliothek Salzburg*, edited by Renate PROCHNO and Andrea GOTTDANG, Salzburg: Müry Salzmann, 2012, pp. 22-30 · "Rules and Rulers: Robert Morris, Canonical Measures and the Definition of Art in the 1960s", in: *Münchner Jahrbuch der Bildenden Kunst*, VOL. 60, 2009, pp. 139-160 · "Wie die Faschisten sich Leonardo unter den Nagel rissen: eine architekturgeschichtliche Station des 'Vitruvianischen Menschen' auf dem Weg zum populären Bild", in: *Beständig im Wandel: Innovationen — Verwandlungen — Konkretisierungen. Festschrift für Karl Möseneder zum 60. Geburtstag*, edited by Christian HECHT, Berlin: Matthes & Seitz 2009, pp. 425-440.

Harry Francis MALLGRAVE has enjoyed a career as an architect, scholar, translator, and editor, and is presently a distinguished professor of architectural history and theory at Illinois Institute of Technology. Among his numerous publications are: *Architecture and Embodiment: The Implications of the New Sciences and Humanities for Design,* London and New York: Routledge, 2013 · *The Architect's Brain. Neuroscience, Creativity and Architecture,* Chichester and Malden, MA: Wiley-Blackwell, 2010 · *Modern Architectural Theory: A Historical Survey 1673–1968,* Cambridge and New York: Cambridge University Press, 2009 · *Gottfried Semper: Architect of the Nineteenth Century,* New Haven, CT and London: Yale University Press, 1996 · *Empathy, Form, and Space. Problems in German Aesthetics, 1873–1893,* Introduction and translation by Harry Francis Mallgrave and Eleftherios Ikonomou, Santa Monica: Getty Publications Program, 1994.

Indra Kagis McEWEN is adjunct professor of art history at Concordia University in Montreal since 2003. Indra McEwen has taught at several universities as well as, for more than a decade, at the National Theatre School of Canada. She holds a professional degree in architecture, and a PhD in art history (McGill University, Montreal). Her publications include: "Midsummer Moderns: the Foundation of the Paris Observatory, 21 June 1667", in: *Intersections. Yearbook for Early Modern Studies,* VOL. 25, 2012, pp. 335–362 · "Virtù-vious: Roman Architecture, Renaissance Virtue", in: *Cahiers des études anciennes,* VOL. XLVIII, 2011, pp. 255–282 · *Vitruvius: Writing the Body of Architecture,* Cambridge, MA and London: The MIT Press, 2003 · Claude PERRAULT, *Ordonnance for the Five Kinds of Columns After the Method of the Ancients,* translated by Indra Kagis McEwen, Santa Monica: The Getty Center, 1993 · *Socrates' Ancestor: An Essay on Architectural Beginnings,* Cambridge, MA and London: The MIT Press, 1993.

Irene NIERHAUS is professor for art, sciences and aesthetics at the Universität Bremen. She is director of the research program *wohnen+/–ausstellen* (living+/–exhibiting) of the Mariann-Steegmann-Institute Art & Gender as well as a member of the editorial boards of *Interiors: Design, Architecture, Culture Journal* and *FKW//Zeitschrift für Geschlechterforschung und visuelle Kultur.* Her recent publications include: *Wohnen Zeigen: Modelle und Akteure des Wohnens in Architektur und visueller Kultur,* edited with Andreas NIERHAUS, Bielefeld: Transcript, 2014 · "Verräumlichung von Kultur: wohnen +/– ausstellen. Kontinuitäten und Transformationen eines kulturellen Beziehungsgefüges", with Kathrin HEINZ and Christiane KEIM, in: *Transformationen des Kulturellen. Prozesse des gegenwärtigen Kulturwandels,* edited by Andreas HEPP and Andreas LEHMANN-WERMSER, Wiesbaden: Springer VS, 2013, pp. 117–130 · *Landschaftlichkeit zwischen Kunst, Architektur und Theorie,* edited with Josch HOENES and Annette URBAN, Berlin: Dietrich Reimer, 2010 · "The Modern Interiors. Geography of Images, Spaces and Subjects: Mies van der Rohe's and Lilly Reich's Villa Tugendhat 1928–1931", in: *Designing the Modern Interior: From the Victorians to Today,* edited by Penny SPARKE, Anne MASSEY, Trevor KEEBLE, and Brenda MARTIN, Oxford and New York: Berg Publishers, 2009, pp. 107–118 · *Urbanografien: Stadtforschung in Kunst, Architektur und Theorie,* edited with Elke KRASNY, Berlin: Dietrich Reimer, 2008 · *RÄUMEN: Baupläne zwischen Raum, Geschlecht, Visualität und Architektur,* edited with Felicitas KONECNY, Vienna: Edition selene, 2002.

Philipp Osten teaches history of medicine and medical ethics at Heidelberg University since 2007. He worked at the Institut für Geschichte der Medizin of the Robert Bosch Stiftung in Stuttgart from 2003 to 2008. His recent books are: *Das Tor zur Seele. Schlaf, Somnambulismus und Hellsehen im frühen 19. Jahrhundert*, Paderborn: Ferdinand Schöningh, 2014 (forthcoming) · *Die Modellanstalt. Über den Aufbau einer "modernen Krüppelfürsorge" 1905-1933*, Frankfurt am Main: Mabuse, 2012 · *Schlachtschrecken. Konventionen. Die Gründung des Roten Kreuzes und die Erfindung der Menschlichkeit im Kriege*, edited with Wolfgang U. Eckart, Freiburg i. Br.: Centaurus, 2011 · *Patientendokumente. Krankheit im Selbstzeugnis*, edited by Philipp Osten, Stuttgart: Franz Steiner, 2010.

Heleni Porfyriou is an urban historian and head of the Rome Unit of the Institute for the Conservation and Enhancement of Cultural Heritage of the National Research Council of Italy. Her research regards urban aesthetics and conservation as well as heritage enhancement policies in Europe and China. She is coordinator of the CNR Unit of the FP7 – *Marie Curie Actions* project "Planning, Urban Management and Heritage" (2012-15), and of the *European Culture Programmes* "Water Shapes" (2010-12) and "Preserving Places" (2008-10). Her publications include: "Camillo Sitte und das Primat des Blicks", in: *Kunst des Städtebaus. Neue Perspektiven auf Camillo Sitte*, edited by Klaus Semsroth, Kari Jormakka, and Bernhard Langer, Vienna, Cologne, and Weimar: Böhlau, 2005, pp. 239-256 · with M. Boone, "Markets, Squares, Streets: Urban Space, a Tool for Cultural Exchange", in: *Cultural Exchange in Early Modern Europe*, VOL. II: *Cities and Cultural Exchange in Europe, 1400-1700*, edited by Donatella Calabi and Stephen Turk Christensen, Cambridge, New York, Melbourne, Madrid, Cape Town, Singapore, and São Paulo: Cambridge University Press, 2007, pp. 227-253 · "Greci ortodossi a Venezia e nella Penisola," in: *Il Rinascimento italiano e l'Europa*, VOL. VIII: *Luoghi, spazi, architetture*, edited by Donatella Calabi and Elena Svalduz, Vicenza: Angelo Colla, 2010, pp. 567-585 · "Spazio urbano come luogo. Camillo Sitte e il ruolo della visione nella Modernità", in: *Spazio fisico / Spazio vissuto*, edited by Michele Di Monte and Manrica Rotili, Milan: Mimesis, 2010, pp. 261-278.

Paolo Sanvito is professor of architectural history at the Università degli Studi di Napoli Federico II. In 2013-14 he is fellow at the Studienzentrum Venedig. Before that he was associate researcher in the *Sonderforschungsbereich* "Transformationen der Antike" and lecturer at the Centre Marc Bloch, and the departments of art history and cultural studies of Humboldt-Universität zu Berlin, where he taught seminars on architecture and urban planning of the early modern period. Since 1993 he has been teaching at the universities of Frankfurt, Rome "Sapienza", Leicester, and the University of Notre Dame. His publications include: *Vitruvianismus. Ursprünge und Transformationen*, edited by Paolo Sanvito, forthcoming · *Il Teatro Olimpico di Vicenza. La genesi di un'impresa architettonica e l'Accademia sua fondatrice*, Naples: Paparo, 2012 · *Imitatio. L'amore dell'immagine sacra*, Pescara: ZiP, 2009 · "Artisti transalpini itineranti nell'area adriatica: alcune questioni ancora aperte", in: *Universitates e Baronie. Arte e architettura in Abruzzo e nel regno al tempo dei Durazzo*, 3 VOLS., edited by Pio Francesco Pistilli, Francesca Manzari, and Gaetano Curzi, Pescara: ZiP, 2008, VOL. 1, pp. 191-212 · *Il tardogotico del duomo di Milano*, Münster, Hamburg, and London: LIT, 2002.

Christoph SCHNOOR is associate professor in architecture at Unitec Institute of Technology in Auckland, New Zealand. He received his doctorate on Le Corbusier's early urban design treatise "La Construction des villes" from Technische Universität Berlin in 2002. His research areas are the architecture and perception of urban space, history and theory of modernist architecture, in particular Le Corbusier, and theorizing architectural transfer, such as the German colonial architecture in Samoa or Ernst Plischke's architecture between Vienna and Wellington, New Zealand. His publications include: "Munich to Berlin: The Urban Space of German Cities", in: *Le Corbusier: An Atlas of Modern Landscapes*, edited by Jean-Louis COHEN, New York: Museum of Modern Art, 2013, pp. 84–91 · "Bernhard Hoesli and Colin Rowe: Phenomenal Transparency as Method for Analysis and Design", in: *Fabulation. Proceedings of the 29th Annual Conference of the Society of Architectural Historians, Australia and New Zealand*, edited by Stuart KING and Stephen LOO, published on CD-ROM, 2012 · "Colin Rowe: Space as Well-Composed Illusion", in: *Journal of Art Historiography*, no. 5, 2011 · "The Idea of an Imperceptible Modernism in Ernst Plischke's Work", in: *Audience. Proceedings of the 28th Annual Conference of the Society of Architectural Historians, Australia and New Zealand*, edited by Antony MOULIS and Deborah VAN DER PLAAT, published on CD-ROM, 2011 · *La Construction des Villes. Le Corbusiers erstes städtebauliches Traktat von 1910/11*, translated, edited, and with an essay by Christoph SCHNOOR, Zürich: gta, 2008.

Kirsten WAGNER is professor of cultural studies and director of the research project "Photography and Media" at the University of Applied Sciences in Bielefeld. From 2002 to 2010 she was research assistant at the Institute for Cultural Studies at Humboldt Universität zu Berlin and the *Sonderforschungsbereich* "Cultures of the Performative" at Freie Universität Berlin. Her research areas are anthropology and architecture, theories of space, spatial organization of knowledge, structures in photography. Her publications include: "Architektur mit dem Körper denken. Zu einer kritischen Anthropologie der Architektur", in *Architektur und Philosophie*, edited by Jörg H. GLEITER and Ludger SCHWARTE, Bielefeld: Transcript, 2014 (forthcoming) · "Topologie der Sinne. Experimentelle Raumerzeugung am Körper", in: *Übertragungsräume. Medienarchäologische Perspektiven auf die Raumvorstellungen der Moderne*, edited by Eva JOHACH and Diethard SAWICKI, Wiesbaden: Ludwig Reichert, 2013, pp. 53–72 · "Gehraum, Sehraum, Tastraum: zur Formation des anthropologischen Raumes auf physiologischem Feld", in: *Konfigurationen. Gebrauchsweisen des Raums*, edited by Iris DÄRMANN and Anna ECHTERHÖLTER, Berlin: Diaphanes, 2013, pp. 221–241 · *Museum, Bibliothek, Stadtraum. Räumliche Wissensordnungen 1600–1900*, edited with Robert FELFE, Berlin: LIT, 2010 · *Datenräume, Informationslandschaften, Wissensstädte. Zur Verräumlichung des Wissens und Denkens in der Computermoderne*, Freiburg i. Br. and Berlin: Rombach, 2006.

Sven-Olov WALLENSTEIN is professor of philosophy at Södertörn University, Stockholm, and editor-in-chief of *Site*. He is the translator of works by Baumgarten, Winckelmann, Lessing, Kant, Hegel, Frege, Husserl, Heidegger, Levinas, Derrida, Deleuze, Foucault, Rancière, and Agamben, as well as the author of numerous books on philosophy, contemporary art, and architecture. Recent publications include: *Architecture, Critique, Ideology: Essays on Architecture and Theory* (forthcoming in 2014) · *Foucault, Biopolitics, and Governmentality*, edited with Jakob NILSSON, Huddinge: Södertörn University, 2013 · *Heidegger, språket och poesin,* edited with Ola NILSSON, Stockholm: Drucksache, 2013 · *Aisthesis: Estetikens historia del 1,* edited with Sara DANIUS and Cecilia SJÖHOLM, Stockholm: Thales, 2012 · *Translating Hegel: The Phenomenology of Spirit and Modern Philosophy,* edited with Brian Manning DELANEY, Huddinge: Södertörn University, 2012 · *Edmund Hussserl,* edited with Daniel BIRNBAUM, Stockholm: Axl Books, 2011 · *Nihilism, Art, Technology,* Stockholm: Axl Books, 2011 · *Swedish Modernism: Architecture, Consumption and the Welfare State,* edited with Helena MATTSSON, Stockholm: Black Dog Publishing, 2010 · *Biopolitics and the Emergence of Modern Architecture,* New York: Princeton Architectural Press, 2009 · *Svar på frågan: Vad var det postmoderna?,* Stockholm: Axl Books, 2009.

Frank ZÖLLNER is professor for art history at Universität Leipzig. From 1983 to 1985 he was a fellow at The Warburg Institute in London. In 1987 he received his doctorate at Universität Hamburg with a thesis on "Vitruvs Proportionsfigur". From 1988 to 1992 he was assistant at the Bibliotheca Hertziana, Rome and in 1987/1988 and 1992/1993 he received a fellowship of the Gerda Henkel-Stiftung. Among his numerous publications are: *Bewegung und Ausdruck bei Leonardo da Vinci,* Leipzig: Plöttner, 2010 · *Michelangelo 1475–1564. Complete Works* (with Christof THOENES and Thomas PÖPPER), Cologne: Benedikt Taschen, 2007 (revised edition 2014) · *Sandro Botticelli,* Munich and New York: Prestel, 2005 · "The 'Motions of the Mind' in Renaissance Portraits. The Spiritual Dimension of Portraiture," in: *Zeitschrift für Kunstgeschichte,* VOL. 68, 2005, pp. 23–40 · *Leonardo da Vinci 1451–1519. Paintings and Drawings,* Cologne: Benedikt Taschen, 2003 (revised editions 2007 and 2011).

Beatrix ZUG-ROSENBLATT studied philosophy, sociology, and art history at the Georg-August-Universität Göttingen as well as architecture at the Technische Universität Berlin. In 2007 she received her doctoral degree at the Technische Universität Berlin with a thesis on the philosophy of art of John Dewey and Arnold Gehlen. Her publications include: *Kunst als Handeln,* Tübingen and Berlin: Ernst Wasmuth, 2007 · "Bewegung und Gestaltung als Grundlagen der Architektur", in: *Architektur denken. Paul Schatz und die Organik von Zeit und Raum* (Special issue of *Mensch + Architektur,* no. 59/60), 2007, pp. 28–33 · *Die Anthropologie des Raumes in der Architekturtheorie des frühen 20. Jahrhunderts,* Tübingen and Berlin: Ernst Wasmuth, 2006.

We would like to thank the *Deutsche Forschungsgemeinschaft*
and the *Fritz Thyssen Stiftung für Wissenschaftsförderung*
for their support, which made the present volume possible.

COPY EDITING   Geoffrey Steinherz, Schornsheim
GRAPHIC DESIGN   Jasper Cepl, Cologne
PRINTING AND BINDING   AZ Druck und Datentechnik, Kempten

© 2014 by Ernst Wasmuth Verlag Tübingen · Berlin
www.wasmuth-verlag.de
ISBN 978 3 8030 0731 5
Printed in Germany

COVER ILLUSTRATION   Terra-cotta relief of a girl with a plump bob. Executed by
Friedrich Tieck, after a design by Karl Friedrich Schinkel,
for the façade of the Bauakademie in Berlin.